Scotland! Scotland!

THE AUTHOR

Dean Hayes took up full-time writing after a career in teaching and a spell as a professional cricketer. He has written over 80 sporting books, including *The Ashes: Cricket's Greatest Rivalry*, *Northern Ireland's Greats* and *Living the Dream: Manchester City*.

Scotland! Scotland!

THE COMPLETE **WHO'S WHO** OF **SCOTLAND PLAYERS** SINCE 1946

Dean P. Hayes

MERCAT PRESS

First published in 2006 by Mercat Press Ltd
10 Coates Crescent, Edinburgh EH3 7AL
www.mercatpress.com

ISBN-10: 1-84183-103-4
ISBN-13: 978-1-84183-103-9

Set in Ehrhardt with headings in Gill Sans at Mercat Press

Printed and bound in Great Britain by Bell & Bain Ltd

CONTENTS

INTRODUCTION

Scotland! Scotland! The Complete Who's Who of Scotland Players since 1946 revisits the contrasting post-war experiences of the national side through its lifeblood—the players.

A total of 480 players have appeared for Scotland in the post-war period. They appear here in chronological order—that is, in the order in which they made their international debut. There are, of course, matches where a number of players made their debut at the same time, and in such cases they are listed alphabetically. Should you be unsure of the decade in which a particular favourite played, there is an index at the back of the book for easy reference.

In a number of the entries, reference is made to wartime caps. Though international games continued during the hostilities, the Victory matches of 1946 and the wartime fixtures of 1939–1945 were not recognised as full internationals, and therefore these appearances are not included in the total number of caps won. In the statistics section at the head of each players' entry, match dates are listed according to the year that marked the end of the season in which the game was played. Every post-war game is included in the book up to October 2006.

For each player, I have aimed to provide the following information: full name, recognised position, period as a Scotland player, height and weight, date and place of birth and place of death, career details, breakdown of appearances and goals scored for Scotland, and biography. Weights should only be regarded as approximate figures, since they obviously varied throughout the player's career.

The book is a collection of statistics and biographies. But I hope it is more than that: it is a celebration of the great game. Since international football resumed in 1946, a number of Scotland records have been broken, anniversaries marked and personal bests established. These include Kenny Dalglish becoming the first Scotland player to register 100 caps and Billy Steel gaining the unwanted distinction of becoming the first Scotland player to be sent off in a full international, against Austria in May 1951. Jim Craig scored on his debut before he had kicked the ball. Against Sweden in April 1977 he came on as a substitute for Kenny Burns and scored with his first touch—a header! When John Hewie made his international debut for Scotland against England at Hampden Park in April 1956, it was the first time the South African-born defender had ever been to Scotland!

Every game and every tournament brings a new chapter. The story will continue.

Dean P. Hayes
Pembrokeshire, October 2006

THE 1940s

Scotland's international form deteriorated in the immediate post-1946 period. Of their first eleven peacetime fixtures, just two were won. Several factors accounted for these disappointing results. The selectors had resorted to calling up players who knew little about each other, whilst most opponents seemed to perform at their peak! According to George Young, some referees were biased—when Switzerland scored their winner in the 2-1 defeat in Berne, the official is reputed to have danced with delight and congratulated the scorer! Fans then demanded that the selectors pick Rangers 'Iron Curtain' defence and Hibernian's 'Famous Five' forwards!

In fact, following the end of the hostilities, Scottish teams beat no British opponents until the seventh attempt—Wales, 3-1—but by then it was October 1948 and three months later the qualifying procedures for the 1950 World Cup were announced.

Scottish supporters who were still revelling in their 3-1 victory over England at Wembley in April 1949 paid dearly for the arrogant attitude towards FIFA displayed by their Football Association. FIFA were prepared to give the United Kingdom two places in the 1950 World Cup Finals with the winners and the runners–up in the Home International Championships qualifying. But the proud Scots insisted that they would only go to Brazil if they were actually to win the domestic tournament.

Both Scotland and England easily beat Wales and Northern Ireland, setting up a showdown at Hampden Park. England won 1-0, although Scotland were unlucky when Willie Bauld's shot bounced off the bar and hit the goal-line but did not go in. A draw would have meant that Scotland, the previous year's champions, would have retained the trophy and gone to the World Cup.

JIMMY DELANEY
Outside-right

Born: James Delaney, Cleland, 3 September 1914
Died: 26 September 1989, Cleland
Height: 5ft 9in
Weight: 12st 9lb
Clubs: Stoneyburn Juniors; Glasgow Celtic; Manchester United; Aberdeen; Falkirk; Derry City; Cork Athletic; Elgin City
Scotland Caps: 13
Scotland Goals: 3

1936 v Wales (drew 1-1), v Ireland (won 2-1)
1937 v Germany (won 2-0) 2 goals, v England (won 3-1), v Austria (drew 1-1), v Czechoslovakia (won 3-1)

1938 v Ireland (drew 1-1)
1939 v Ireland (won 2-0) 1 goal, v Wales (won 3-2)
1947 v England (drew 1-1)
1948 v N Ireland (lost 0-2), v Wales (lost 1-2), v England (lost 0-2)

One of the most inspirational footballers the game has ever seen, Jimmy Delaney appeared in 13 internationals for Scotland. He endeared himself to the Scottish fans in the Victory International against England on 13 April 1946. The game was goalless, and with just a minute to go, when Jackie Husband flighted a free-kick out on the left across the face of the goal. Willie Waddell touched it on and Jimmy Delaney crashed it into the net past Frank Swift.

Delaney joined Celtic from Lanarkshire junior club Stoneyburn in 1934, succeeding Bertie Thomson on the right-wing. A year later he scored the opener for Scotland against England at Hampden in the George V Silver Jubilee international. Delaney netted a hat-trick when Celtic beat Rangers 4-2 in the Charity Cup Final at Hampden in May 1936 and was at outside-right when Celtic beat Everton in the final of the Exhibition Trophy in June 1938. Delaney's left arm was stamped on in a goalmouth collision and both bones shattered so badly that the surgeon wanted to amputate!

Though he returned to action during the war years, Delaney left Parkhead in February 1946, joining Manchester United as Matt Busby was team-building. A speedy winger, he delighted the Old Trafford fans with his pace and ability to shoot on the run. By the time he left the Reds to return north of the border to play for Aberdeen, he had won League Championship and FA Cup winners' medals and four Scotland caps to add to the nine he gained with Celtic before the hostilities.

After a year at Pittodrie, he moved to Falkirk and then to Derry City, for a then record Irish fee of £1,500. With Derry he created football history. Playing in the 1954 Irish Cup Final he became the first man to win Cup winners' medals in Scotland, England and Northern Ireland. He won a Scottish medal with Celtic in 1937, was a member of the United side which beat Blackpool in 1948 and his Irish medal came six years later with Derry. He then became player-manager of Cork and played for them in the FA of Ireland Cup Final, but Cork threw away a two-goal lead and lost to Shamrock Rovers, thus denying Delaney what surely would have been an unrepeatable feat.

On returning to Scotland he played Highland League football for Elgin City before retiring in 1957 after 27 years as a player.

WILLIE MILLER
Goalkeeper
Born: William Miller, Glasgow, 20 November 1924
Height: 5ft 11in
Weight: 11st 7lb
Clubs: Maryhill Harp; Glasgow Celtic; Clyde; Stirling Albion; Hibernian
Scotland Caps: 6

1947 v Wales (lost 1-3), v England (drew 1-1), v Belgium (lost 1-2), v Luxembourg (won 6-0)
1948 v N Ireland (lost 0-2)

Unfortunately for Willie Miller, he was at his best when his team, Celtic, were at their worst!

Miller joined the Parkhead club in 1942 and over the next eight years proved himself to be a brilliant keeper, equally adept at high and low shots and superb in anticipation and clean handling.

In the Inter-League match on 12 March 1947, Miller was concussed and had his nose broken in two places trying to prevent Kippax's second goal. He went off, but within a couple of minutes he returned to a tremendous Hampden roar. Thankfully he had recovered to play in his second international match for Scotland against England at Wembley on 12 April 1947. Miller was unlucky in that recognition at this level was delayed because of Bobby Brown in the Scotland goal and that he was denied further caps by the emergence of Jimmy Cowan. In that game against England, Miller suffered a severe head injury, but time after time his blood-bandaged head was thrown back as his body arched backwards to tip over yet another English volley in a 1-1 draw.

Back at Parkhead, Miller held out alone against team after team while the defence in front of him dithered dismally. He knew that whilst playing for Celtic, everything depended on him. Many was the time that he had to dash off his line and make a save at the feet of an on-rushing forward—the number of stitches he had in his scalp being too numerous to count!

Miller, who appeared in 265 games for Celtic, was eventually put on the transfer list, and in 1950 he joined Clyde. He gave four good years to the Bully Wee, and though by 1954 he was waning by his own high standards, he moved to Hibernian before deciding to retire and go on the road as a whisky rep.

JIMMY STEPHEN
Full-back

Born: James Findlay Stephen, Fettercairn, 23 August 1922
Height: 5ft 9in
Weight: 10st 8lb
Clubs: Bradford Park Avenue; Portsmouth; Yeovil Town; Bridgewater; Newport; Waterlooville
Scotland caps: 2
1947 v Wales (lost 1-3)
1948 v Wales (lost 1-2)

Jimmy Stephen won two full Scottish caps, playing twice against Wales—once as captain—in both full-back berths.

Stephen's headmaster was the chairman of the Scottish Schoolboys Association and he recommended him to Bradford Park Avenue. After turning professional he made his League debut against Luton Town and followed this with another home match against Millwall. The day after the Lions' visit to Park Avenue,

Prime Minister Neville Chamberlain declared that Britain was at war with Germany, and this brought suspension to League football.

Too young to be called up, he joined an engineering company but when peace was declared in 1945, the engineering company closed and Stephen, who represented Scotland on five occasions during the hostilities was called up to work down the mines. He then began his National Service with the RAF, returning to Park Avenue for weekends.

Realising that Bradford would never reach the First Division, he asked for a transfer and in 1949 he joined Portsmouth for £15,000, which at the time was a record for a full-back. Once the 1950-51 season got underway, Stephen, who had by now left the RAF, settled down to play League football with no distractions. He was a regular for the south-coast club for the next three seasons, appearing in 103 games before injuries took a hold.

In May 1955, Pompey, not short of accomplished full-backs, released Stephen with nine other players. He joined Yeovil Town and then became player-manager of Bridgewater before playing for Newport, Isle of Wight and Waterlooville.

DAVE SHAW
Left-back
Born: David Shaw, Annathill, 5 May 1917
Died: 20 January 1977
Height: 5ft 9in
Weight: 11st 9lb
Clubs: Grange Rovers; Hibernian; Aberdeen
Scotland caps: 8
1947 v Wales (lost 1-3), v N Ireland (drew 0-0)
1948 v England (lost 0-2), v Belgium (won 2-0), v Switzerland (lost 1-2), v France (lost 0-3)
1949 v Wales (won 3-1), v N Ireland (won 3-2)

Dave Shaw's first senior club was Hibernian, who he joined from Grange Rovers just prior to the outbreak of the Second World War. Once the hostilities had ended he resumed his career with the Easter Road club, turning in such outstanding performances that he was rewarded with an international call-up for the match against Wales at Wrexham.

He skippered Hibs to the 1947 Scottish Cup Final but they were beaten 2-1 by Aberdeen. Little did Dave Shaw know that Hibs' opponents that day would be his second and only other professional club.

Dave Shaw signed for the Dons in the summer of 1950 and was immediately appointed captain. He spent three seasons as a player at Pittodrie, his final outing being the 1-0 defeat by Rangers in the 1953 Scottish Cup Final replay. On hanging up his boots, he became Aberdeen's trainer, though this was not a new role for him, as he had been performing the dual position of player and trainer since Jock Pattillo's departure earlier in the year.

He spent a couple of seasons as the Dons' trainer and his influence helped the Pittodrie club win the League Championship for the first time in their history in 1955. Shortly after this success, manager Dave Halliday left to take charge at Leicester City and Dave Shaw was offered the manager's position at Aberdeen.

In 1955-56, his first season in charge, he guided the Dons to League Cup glory as they beat St Mirren 2-1 in the final. After that, injuries to his star players including Paddy Buckley and Archie Glen didn't help his cause and in November 1959 he decided to return to what he enjoyed doing best, namely being the club's trainer. He remained in this post until 1967 when he left Pittodrie.

HUGH BROWN
Right-half
Born: Hugh Brown, Carmyle, 7 December 1921
Died: 28 July 1994
Height: 5ft 11in
Weight: 12st 4lb
Clubs: Yoker Athletic; Partick Thistle; Torquay United
Scotland caps: 3
1947 v Wales (lost 1-3), v Belgium (lost 1-2), v Luxembourg (won 6-0)

A well-built, tough-tackling right-half, Hugh Brown was the first Partick Thistle player to be capped by Scotland after the Second World War, when he was selected against Wales, Belgium and Luxembourg.

Though the 1944-45 season at Firhill was not a memorable one in terms of League results, it did see the arrival of Brown, a real power-house of a player who would make a big impact on the club in the years ahead. Bringing strength to the half-back line, he helped the Jags win that season's Summer Cup. Though this competition has made a habit of appearing and disappearing over the years, only to surface again in various guises, Thistle have won it only once. After a 4-4 home draw against Dumbarton, Partick won 2-1 at Boghead before facing Hearts in the quarter-final. A 3-0 home win was followed by a 2-1 reversal at Tynecastle but Thistle were through to the semi-final where they met Morton at Hampden. A 1-0 win was secured to send Partick through to the final against Hibernian. Hugh Brown made both Partick's goals, scored by on-loan Jimmy Johnston from Stockport County in a 2-0 win.

When peacetime football resumed in 1946-47, Hugh Brown was an integral member of the Thistle side and, over the next few seasons, hardly missed a game, going on to score 18 goals—usually from long-range—in 149 appearances for the Firhill club.

His departure from Partick to Torquay United, an English Third Division club in December 1951, surprised the football world. He went on to play in 55 League games for the Devon club before leaving the game in 1952.

FRANK BRENNAN

Centre-half

Born: Frank Brennan, Annathill, 23 April 1924
Died: 5 March 1997
Height: 6ft 3in
Weight: 13st 3lb
Clubs: Coatbridge St Patrick's; Airdrieonians; Newcastle United; North Shields
Scotland caps: 7
1947 v Wales (lost 1-3), v N Ireland (drew 0-0)
1953 v Wales (won 2-1), v N Ireland (drew 1-1), v England (drew 2-2)
1954 v N Ireland (won 3-1), v England (lost 2-4)

Seven Scotland caps came Frank Brennan's way over an eight-year period but his popularity back in his native country was never as great as it was in England with Newcastle United.

After signing for Coatbridge St Patrick's, his incisive kicking and tackling brought him to the attention of Scottish League sides and also of English club, Wolves. A move to the Midlands fell through as did a contract with Albion Rovers but in February 1941, he signed for Airdrieonians. He was still a part-timer at the local pit and brick works and appeared for the Broomfield Park club throughout the war years.

Brennan's qualities were noticed by Scotland's selectors and he was chosen for the Victory International against England at Hampden Park in 1946. England centre-forward Tommy Lawton never got a look in and Newcastle United who had failed in a bid to lure Rangers' Willie Woodburn to St James Park, paid £7,500 to take Brennan to Tyneside.

In 1947-48 he was outstanding as the Magpies returned to the First Division—an ever-present, his powerful heading ability and firm tackles gave confidence to the whole side. Built like a colossus, his long legs, at the end of which were size-12 boots, dominated the Newcastle penalty area for ten years. The 1950-51 season ended in Wembley triumph as Brennan kept Stan Mortensen and the Blackpool forwards at bay in a 2-0 win. In the following year's victory over Arsenal, Brennan held together an off-form Newcastle side as they overcame the Gunners to win 1-0. By the time Newcastle reached Wembley for a third time in 1955, Frank Brennan was reaching the end of his playing career. But instead of going out in style, a series of controversial bust-ups with the club's directors ended a marvellous association with a somewhat bitter taste.

In March 1956, Brennan left St James Park to become player-coach of North Shields, this after 347 appearances for the Magpies. After six years with North Shields, he coached in Singapore for the British Council before returning to North Shields and guiding them to an FA Amateur Cup Final victory in 1969. He then managed Darlington before leaving to concentrate on his sports business.

JACKIE HUSBAND
Left-half

Born: John Husband, Dunfermline, 28 May 1918
Died: 30 April 1992
Height: 5ft 10in
Weight: 11st 6lb
Clubs: Yorker Athletic; Partick Thistle
Scotland caps: 1
1947 v Wales (lost 1-3)

One day in March 1939, Jackie Husband turned up to watch his club Partick Thistle play Hibernian in a Scottish League match, only to find himself being pressed into service. He was taken to one side by Peter McKennan who told him: 'Any time you're in trouble son, give the ball to me.' Under these instructions, Husband helped to give McKennan a hat-trick in a 4-1 win.

Husband had signed for Partick Thistle from Yoker Athletic in November 1938 and played his first game for the club at Love Street against St Mirren reserves. He went on to make five first team appearances in his first season with the club, and was then more or less a permanent fixture in the side until the beginning of the 1950-51 season, clocking up 371 League appearances.

He was a member of the Thistle side that won the Summer Cup in 1944-45 and played for Scotland against England in the Victory International of 1946. Scotland won 1-0 with the goal coming from a Jackie Husband free-kick, knocked down by Willie Waddell and scored by Jimmy Delaney. Though the balls in those days could become extremely heavy towards the end of a game on a muddy pitch, Jackie Husband could launch the ball right into the opponents' six-yard box.

Towards the end of his playing career he acted as the reserves trainer and took up physiotherapy. In 1964 he was selected as Scotland's trainer on their tour of Ireland, Norway and Spain.

When he died in 1992, Jackie Husband was still connected to the Firhill Club. With the exception of 18 months spent managing Queen of the South, he had given over 50 years service to Partick Thistle, as player, trainer, coach, masseur and general mentor. It was most fitting when Firhill's new East Stand was opened in 1994 and named the Jackie Husband Stand.

WILLIE WADDELL
Outside-right

Born: William Waddell, Forth, 7 March 1921
Height: 5ft 11in
Weight: 12st 2lb
Clubs: Strathclyde; Glasgow Rangers
Scotland caps: 17
Scotland goals: 6
1947 v Wales (lost 1-3) 1 goal

1949 v Wales (won 3-1) 2 goals, v N Ireland (won 3-2), v England (won 3-1),
      v France (won 2-0)
1950 v N Ireland (won 8-2) 2 goals, v England (lost 0-1)
1951 v England (won 3-2), v Denmark (won 3-1), v France (won 1-0),
      v Belgium (won 5-0) 1 goal, v Austria (lost 0-4)
1952 v N Ireland (won 3-0), v Wales (lost 0-1)
1954 v N Ireland (won 3-1)
1955 v Wales (won 1-0), v N Ireland (drew 2-2)

Exceptionally well-built for a winger, skilful and powerful, there was always the chance of excitement when he had the ball. Well-placed centres brought Willie Thornton many goals, though Waddell himself netted his fair share with 143 in 588 League and Cup matches.

Waddell scored from the penalty-spot on his international debut, though the Scots were beaten 3-1 by Wales at Wrexham's Racecourse Ground. The Rangers' winger, who had made five appearances for Scotland in wartime internationals, netted a double in Scotland's next meeting with Wales as they reversed the scoreline, and then repeated the feat during the 8-2 demolition of Northern Ireland at Windsor Park. Though he scored six goals in his 17 international appearances, he created numerous chances for his team-mates. When Scotland beat England 3-1 at Wembley in April 1949, it was Willie Waddell's inch-perfect cross that allowed Lawrie Reilly to head home his side's third goal.

A fast and fearless winger, Waddell, who joined Rangers in 1938, won four League Championship medals and two Scottish Cup winners' medals prior to playing his last game in 1956.

A year later he was appointed manager of Kilmarnock and in eight years brought surprising success to the Rugby Park club. Killie won the League Championship in 1964-65 and were runners-up four times. They also reached a Scottish Cup Final and two League Cup Finals but were never on the winning side.

In December 1969, Willie Waddell became manager of Rangers, where just over a year later he faced probably the greatest challenge of his public life. On 2 January 1971, Rangers drew 1-1 with Celtic at Ibrox in front of an 80,000 crowd. In a match without any unruly incident, on the field or on the terraces, Jimmy Johnstone had scored for Celtic in the last minute, only for Colin Stein to equalise with just 15 seconds left to play. Rangers fans, spilling down Stairway 13, met disaster and one fan, riding on another's shoulders, toppled forward near the top of the exit staircase. The domino effect sent the huge crowd sprawling down the stairway, with the result that 66 people were crushed to death and 145 injured in one of football's worst disasters.

Waddell took command. Two days later Rangers contributed £50,000 to the Lord Provost's Appeal Fund for the relatives. Waddell also saw to it that the club were represented at each of the 66 funerals. The players and many former players were summoned and ordered to take part.

It was time to make changes at Ibrox and Waddell researched the modern grounds in Germany and elsewhere throughout Europe, and within the decade he had transformed Ibrox into the most sophisticated stadium in Britain. It is without doubt a magnificent monument to the man. Waddell was also a visionary—he brought in Jock Wallace as coach and, in June 1972, made him team manager. It was the beginning of better days for the Light Blues.

NEIL DOUGALL
Inside-right/ Right-half

Born: Corneilius Dougall, Falkirk, 7 November 1921
Height: 5ft 10in
Weight: 12st 0lb
Clubs: Burnley; Birmingham City; Plymouth Argyle
Scotland caps: 1
1947 v Wales (lost 1-3)

Neil Dougall came from distinguished footballing stock; his father William played for Falkirk, Burnley and the Scottish League and his uncle Jimmy represented Preston North End and Scotland.

Dougall joined Burnley and in 1940 signed professional forms. He was in the RAF during the hostilities and 'guested' for Oldham Athletic, Watford, Walsall and Coventry City but in 1945 he signed for Birmingham City. At the end of his first season at St Andrew's, he won a Football League (South) Championship medal, scoring 10 goals in 38 games and helped the club reach the semi-finals of the FA Cup.

A powerful, red-headed inside-forward, he didn't score too many goals thereafter but still remained a vital cog in the Blues' attacking mechanism, helping the club win promotion to the First Division in 1947-48. It was his form during the early part of that season that led to him winning full international honours for Scotland against Wales.

In March 1949 he left St Andrew's, joining Plymouth Argyle for a fee of £13,000. At Home Park, he was at his best at right-half, but while with the Pilgrims he played in every position except goalkeeper. Fast and able to exploit openings with some fine passes, he gained two Third Division Championship medals with Argyle.

From March 1960, Dougall shared the managerial tasks at Home Park with George Taylor but this proved difficult to implement and in the summer of 1961, he took sole charge. However, in November of that year he left the Devon club after the team had conceded five goals in each of three consecutive matches!

WILLIE THORNTON
Centre-forward/ Inside-forward

Born: William Thornton, Winchburgh, 3 March 1920
Height: 5ft 10in
Weight: 12st 3lb

Clubs: Winchburgh Albion; Glasgow Rangers
Scotland caps: 7
Scotland goals: 1
1947 v Wales (lost 1-3), v N Ireland (drew 0-0)
1948 v N Ireland (lost 0-2), v England (lost 0-2)
1950 v France (won 2-0)
1952 v Denmark (won 2-1) 1 goal, v Sweden (lost 1-3)

Though Willie Thornton was a prolific scorer for Rangers, his only goal in seven international appearances for Scotland came in his penultimate game, a 2-1 win against Denmark in Copenhagen in May 1952.

Thornton was only 16 years old when he made his Rangers debut in 1936 and was only 19 when he won the first of four League Championship medals in 1938-39. Though not on the tall side for a centre-forward, his heading ability was lethal and he was the club's leading scorer in that season. During the Second World War, Thornton was awarded the Military Medal but when League football resumed in 1946-47, he was a member of the Rangers side that retained the League Championship and won the Scottish League Cup, beating Aberdeen 4-0 in the final.

His form led to him representing the Scottish League XI and winning his first cap against Wales. Despite not being as successful as Scottish fans would have hoped during his time as a full international, he helped the Ibrox club win further League titles in 1948-49 and 1949-50, along with three Scottish Cup winners' medals and another League Cup winners' medal.

Thornton, who gave Rangers lengthy and loyal service, was voted Scotland's 'Player of the Year' in 1952 and continued to represent the Glasgow giants until 1954.

On finishing playing, he was appointed manager of Dundee, spending five years in charge of the Dens Park club before taking over the reins at Partick Thistle. Thornton was hugely popular at Firhill, but in September 1948, he returned to Ibrox to become Rangers' assistant-manager.

JIMMY BLAIR
Inside-forward
Born: James Alfred Blair, Glasgow, 6 January 1918
Died: 12 July 1983, Llanelli
Height: 5ft 10in
Weight: 11st 1lb
Clubs: Cardiff City; Blackpool; Bournemouth; Leyton Orient; Ramsgate
Scotland caps: 1
1947 v Wales (lost 1-3)

Glasgow-born Jimmy Blair, whose grandfather, father and brother were all professional footballers, represented Wales at schoolboy level! He signed for Blackpool as an amateur from Cardiff City in the summer of 1915, having appeared in a number of Central League games for Birmingham City.

Blair's Football League debut for the Seasiders was against Stoke City in September 1937, just a few months before his 19th birthday His early displays for Blackpool led to those in the know suggesting that he was destined for international honours. Unfortunately, his career with the Bloomfield Road club was up and down, and he scored just eight goals in 51 appearances.

However, he did obtain one Scottish international cap when in October 1946 he played against Wales at the Racecourse Ground.

A year later he joined Bournemouth for a fee of £4,150 and in two seasons with the Dean Court club was a virtual ever-present, scoring eight goals in 80 games. Over Christmas 1949, Blair signed for Leyton Orient and his four seasons at Brisbane Road were the best of his career. In 1950-51 he topped the club's goalscoring charts with 16 goals and netted a superb individual effort in the O's' 3-1 defeat of Dutch side Racing Club of Haarlem in the 1951 Festival of Britain match.

Surprisingly transfer-listed in October 1951, he ended up staying with the O's for a further two years before having a spell as player-manager of Kent League side Ramsgate Athletic.

BILLY LIDDELL

Outside-left

Born: William Beveridge Liddell, Dunfermline, 10 January 1922
Died: 3 July 2001
Height: 5ft 10in
Weight: 12st 11lb
Clubs: Lochgelly Violet; Liverpool
Scotland caps: 28
Scotland goals: 6
1947 v Wales (lost 1-3), v N Ireland (drew 0-0)
1948 v N Ireland (lost 0-2), v Wales (lost 1-2), v England (lost 0-2)
1950 v Wales (won 2-0), v England (lost 0-1), v Portugal (drew 2-2), v France (won 1-0)
1951 v Wales (won 3-1) 1 goal, v N Ireland (won 6-1), v Austria (lost 0-1),
       v England (won 3-2) 1 goal
1952 v N Ireland (won 3-0), v Wales (lost 0-1), v England (lost 1-2),
       v United States (won 6-0), v Denmark (won 2-1), v Sweden (lost 1-3) 1 goal
1953 v Wales (won 2-1) 1 goal, v N Ireland (drew 1-1), v England (drew 2-2)
1954 v Wales (drew 3-3)
1955 v Portugal (won 3-0) 1 goal, v Yugoslavia (drew 2-2), v Austria (won 4-1) 1 goal,
       v Hungary (lost 1-3)
1956 v N Ireland (lost 1-2)

Billy Liddell joined Liverpool as an 18-year-old from the Fifeshire junior club, Lochgelly Violet and began to learn his trade in the Lancashire Midweek League, only to see the first six years of his career lost to the war. Though he served as an RAF navigator, he played almost 150 games for the Reds as football continued on a regional basis, netting a hat-trick in a 7-3 win over Manchester

City. His reputation as a flying winger with a powerful shot in either foot was growing as he made eight appearances for Scotland in wartime internationals.

In 1946-47 he helped Liverpool win the first post-war Championship. Revealing the pace and power that were to be his hallmark for almost 15 years, Liddell also showed the dashing style that was to make him one of Liverpool's most prolific goalscorers. In 1949-50 Liverpool were unbeaten in their opening 19 matches, setting a record in a 42-match season. During that run, Liddell was at his best, creating havoc among opposition defences and scoring goals. Unfortunately he didn't add an FA Cup winners' medal to it, for Arsenal beat Liverpool 2-0 in the final.

A vital member of the Scottish national side, he and Stanley Matthews were the two players to appear in both the Great Britain v Rest of the World and Rest of Europe matches.

When Liverpool were relegated to the Second Division at the end of the 1952-53 season, Liddell's reaction was typical of the man. He showed great determination and in his first four seasons out of the top flight, he scored 101 goals in 156 League games. He was so popular and had such an immense influence on the side that the fans re-christened the club 'Liddellpool' and made Billy Liddell their 'King'.

During Billy Liddell's last season, the attendances at Anfield started to drop. Almost 44,000 had watched the opening match but only 13,000 watched the final home game. Yet the loyalty of the fans towards Billy Liddell remained unchanged—over 38,000 paid tribute to him in a benefit match between Liverpool and an All-Star team.

One of the greatest Anfield heroes of all-time, Billy Liddell set a wonderful example to any young player aspiring to greatness and on his retirement, he became a bursar at Liverpool University after studying accountancy throughout his playing career. He was also appointed a Justice of the Peace and undertook a great amount of work for boys' clubs.

BOBBY BROWN

Goalkeeper

Born: Robert Brown, Dunipace, 19 March 1923
Height: 6ft 0in
Weight: 11st 3lb
Clubs: Queen's Park; Glasgow Rangers; Falkirk
Scotland caps: 3
1947 v N Ireland (drew 0-0)
1949 v N Ireland (won 3-2)
1952 v England (lost 1-2)

Bobby Brown began his career with Queen's Park in 1939, playing his first match for them against Celtic at Parkhead in April 1940. A crowd of 50,000 witnessed a memorable match, which ended all-square at 4-4.

During the Second World War, Brown served in the Fleet Air Arm and 'guested' for a number of Football League clubs including Portsmouth, Plymouth Argyle, Chester and Chelsea.

In 1945 whilst still an amateur, he won international honours when selected to play against England at Villa Park. Facing the likes of Lawton, Matthews and Mortensen, Bobby Brown produced a number of top-class saves though the Scots went down 3-2.

Once the hostilities were over, Brown enrolled at Jordanhill College to train as a PE teacher. In May 1946 Brown turned professional and signed for Rangers, making his debut that same month in a Victory Cup match at Airdrie. Succeeding the popular Jerry Dawson, the Ibrox crowd expected a lot of Brown and were quick to let him know this! Brown, who had negotiated his own signing-on fee and terms was the highest paid player at Ibrox at this time. Yet after qualifying as a PE teacher, he took up a post at Denny High School, remaining a part-time player throughout his ten years with Rangers.

During his first six seasons with the club, he missed just one game and helped them win three League Championships, three Scottish Cups and two League Cups. The last line of Rangers' famous 'Iron Curtain' defence, he won three full caps for Scotland and made 296 appearances for the Ibrox club. After 1952, his first team appearances became more limited, though it was four years later before he moved to Falkirk, who paid £2,200 for his services.

Within a year, Brown had retired from the game and moved into management with St Johnstone, whom he led to promotion to the First Division. In February 1967 he took charge of the national team, a position he held until the summer of 1971. He later had a spell as Plymouth Argyle's Scottish scout.

GEORGE YOUNG
Right-back/Centre-half

Born: George Lewis Young, Grangemouth, 27 October 1922
Died: 10 January 1997
Height: 6ft 1in
Weight: 14st 3lb
Clubs: Kirkintilloch Rob Roy; Glasgow Rangers
Scotland caps: 53

1947 v N Ireland (drew 0-0), v England (drew 1-1), v Belgium (lost 1-2),
v Luxembourg (won 6-0)

1948 v N Ireland (lost 0-2), v England (lost 0-2), v Belgium (won 2-0), v Switzerland (lost 1-2),
v France (lost 0-3)

1949 v Wales (won 3-1), v N Ireland (won 3-2), v England (won 3-1)

1950 v France (won 2-0), v N Ireland (won 8-2), v Wales (won 2-0), v England (lost 0-1),
v Switzerland (won 3-1), v Portugal (drew 2-2), v France (won 1-0)

1951 v Wales (won 3-1), v N Ireland (won 6-1), v Austria (lost 0-1), v England (won 3-2),
v Denmark (won 3-1), v France (won 1-0)

1952 v N Ireland (won 3-0), v Wales (lost 0-1), v England (lost 1-2),
v United States (won 6-0), v Denmark (won 2-1), v Sweden (lost 1-3)

1953 v Wales (won 2-1), v N Ireland (drew 1-1), v England (drew 2-2), v Sweden (lost 1-2)

1954 v N Ireland (won 3-1), v Wales (drew 3-3)
1955 v Wales (won 1-0), v N Ireland (drew 2-2), v Portugal (won 3-0), v Yugoslavia (drew 2-2)
1956 v N Ireland (lost 1-2), v Wales (won 2-0), v England (drew 1-1), v Austria (drew 1-1)
1957 v Wales (drew 2-2), v N Ireland (won 1-0), v Yugoslavia (won 2-0), v England (lost 1-2),
      v Spain (won 4-2), v Switzerland (won 2-1)

After playing in 53 full internationals, George Young was suddenly dropped from the Scottish team before the final qualifying match prior to the 1958 World Cup Finals. There was, according to reports, no word of explanation or sympathy. Young was understandably upset and he retired soon afterwards. He was a fit 35 and could have gone on at club level for at least two more seasons.

Young's introduction to Rangers, the club he was to lead for so long, was a little fortuitous. The Grangemouth-born defender played for a while for a local club whilst a friend, an aspiring boxer as it happened, was training at Falkirk's ground at the time and he found he so liked football that he became a goalkeeper and eventually signed for Rangers' junior club, Kirkintilloch Rob Roy. He told his new club about Young—they had a look, signed him, passed him on to Rangers in 1941, and within 18 months he had been converted from left-back into Scotland's centre-half for a wartime international against England.

George Young was always a versatile player. He scored two penalties in the 1949 Cup Final against Clyde and, in 1953, played in goal to earn a draw and a successful replay against Aberdeen.

Known to all as 'Corky' because he always carried the cork from the champagne bottle with which Rangers celebrated their 1948 Scottish Cup win over Morton, Young rated the highlight of his career, like most Scottish internationals, to be a defeat of England. That was at Wembley in 1949. 'When we came out my eyes caught the scoreboard with just two words on it: England, Scotland. And I remember thinking: What's it going to say at the finish? And I never thought about it again until I looked up in the second-half and saw England 0, Scotland 3. I'd seen Jimmy Mason, Billy Steel and Lawrie Reilly score their goals, but it was only when I saw the figures that it really dawned.' England got one back, but it remains a famous victory.

After a brief spell managing Third Lanark, he retired to take over a hotel, keeping in touch with the game via the odd newspaper piece. No doubt it was a welcome break for a man who had broken his nose three times, his fingers once and had his leg in plaster on six occasions!

WILLIE CAMPBELL
Right-half
Born: William Bowie Campbell, Greenock, 26 July 1920
Height: 5ft 9in
Weight: 11st 12lb

Clubs: Greenock Bluebell; Morton
Scotland caps: 5
1947 v N Ireland (drew 0-0)
1948 v England (lost 0-2), v Belgium (won 2-0), v Switzerland (lost 1-2), v France (lost 0-3)

A player whose career was cut short on health grounds, Willie Campbell was a gifted wing-half, noted for his calculated and perfectly-timed tackles.

The Greenock-born youngster played his early football for Greenock Bluebell prior to joining Morton in the summer of 1942. Energetic and forceful, he soon won a regular place in the Morton side. His form was such during the hostilities that he represented Scotland in a wartime international.

When League football resumed in 1946-47, Campbell's displays led to him representing the Scottish League XI and shortly afterwards, he won the first of five full international caps when he played in the goalless draw against Northern Ireland. Though Scotland were blessed with players of the calibre of Jimmy Cowan, George Young, Gordon Smith and Billy Liddell, results didn't always go their way and Campbell was only on the winning side once in his five appearances—that against Belgium in April 1948 when the Scots won 2-0.

On his return to Cappielow Park, he helped Morton reach the 1948 Scottish Cup Final where their opponents were Rangers. Campbell had an outstanding game as the teams played out a 1-1 draw but then in the replay he picked up an early injury which contributed to Rangers holding out for a 1-0 win.

Campbell was at the peak of his powers when ill-health forced his retirement during the early part of 1949.

HUGH LONG
Left-half
Born: Hugh Long, Glasgow, 2 January 1923
Height: 5ft 8in
Weight: 10st 8lb
Clubs: Maryhill Harp; Glasgow Celtic; Clyde; Worcester City
Scotland caps: 1
1947 v N Ireland (drew 0-0)

Hugh Long joined Celtic from Maryhill Harp in August 1942, a wartime winger who was to later make his name as the classiest left-half ever to wear the famous white shirt of Clyde.

Long left Parkhead in March 1944, snapped up by the Bully Wee manager, Paddy Travers, and though he had played many of his early games for Celtic at outside-left, he was versatile enough to be able to occupy any position in the team. One of his best displays for Clyde came on 23 March 1946 when they beat his former club Celtic 6-3 in a League Cup tie. His form led to him winning full international honours for Scotland in a goalless draw against Northern Ireland at Hampden Park on 27 November 1946.

Long played for Clyde in the Scottish Cup Final on 23 April 1949 against

Rangers before a Hampden Park crowd of 120,162 though the Ibrox club ran out winners 4-1.

A player who always gave 100% effort, he was one of the game's toughest competitors. For Clyde against Hearts on 4 February 1950, Hugh Long refused to leave the pitch and played on with a broken jaw!

The red-haired Long, a human whirlwind, left Shawfield Park in April 1954 and the following summer joined non-League side Worcester City, for whom he played for two years before deciding to retire.

GORDON SMITH
Outside-right

Born: Gordon Smith, Edinburgh, 25 May 1924
Died: 7 August 2004
Height: 5ft 9in
Weight: 11st 10lb
Clubs: Montrose Roselea; Dundee North End; Hibernian; Heart of Midlothian; Dundee; Morton; Drumcondra
Scotland caps: 18
Scotland goals: 4

1947 v N Ireland (drew 0-0), v England (drew 1-1)
1948 v Wales (lost 1-2), v Belgium (won 2-0), v Switzerland (lost 1-2), v France (lost 0-3)
1952 v England (lost 1-2), v United States (won 6-0)
1955 v Portugal (won 3-0), v Yugoslavia (drew 2-2) 1 goal, v Austria (won 4-1) 1 goal, v Hungary (lost 1-3) 1 goal
1956 v N Ireland (lost 1-2), v Wales (won 2-0), v England (drew 1-1)
1957 v Spain (won 4-2), v Switzerland (won 2-1), v Spain (lost 1-4) 1 goal

One of the most revered and famous footballers of Scottish post-war football, Gordon Smith was a goalscoring cavalier of immense grace, elegance and skill, who established football records unlikely to be equalled, let alone surpassed.

The undisputed king of the wing spent 18 years with Hibernian and shorter yet equally magical spells with both Hearts and Dundee. Often compared to the England wizards Stanley Matthews and Tom Finney, he is the proud possessor of five League Championship medals, three won with Hibs and one each with both Hearts and Dundee. That is a unique achievement, and he represented all three teams in the European Cup, twice playing in the semi-finals.

His international career spanned 13 years from a Wembley debut in wartime to his final appearance against Spain in a World Cup qualifying match in which he signed off with Scotland's only goal.

Although born in Edinburgh, he grew up in Montrose. A schoolboy international, he played junior football for Montrose Roselea and Dundee North End, when he was selected to play for a Junior XI against a Hearts-Hibs select, scoring a hat-trick in a 3-2 win. The newspapers the following day claimed he was heading for Hearts, but Hibs manager Willie McCartney had other ideas and travelled to meet the youngster face to face. As it happened, his Hibs debut was against Hearts and he made an immediate impact, scoring a hat-trick in a 5-3 win. During those war years he made 139 'league' appearances, scoring 96 goals; after the war he made a further 314 league appearances, scoring 127 times. In all competitions, he scored 364 goals—a club record. He famously scored five goals in an 8-0 rout of Third Lanark, and was the club's top scorer between 1943 and 1950.

After requiring an ankle operation, Hibs thought he was finished and let him join Hearts on a free transfer. Hearts beat Third Lanark to lift the League Cup and then went on to win the 1959-60 Championship by four points from Kilmarnock. After two seasons at Tynecastle, he moved on to Dundee and helped the club win the title in his first season at Dens Park. In 1962-63 he helped Dundee reach the European Cup semi-final, where they were beaten by the eventual winners AC Milan. He then had a brief alliance with Morton and Dublin club Drumcondra, before it was time for him to rest on those many laurels.

GEORGE HAMILTON
Inside-forward

Born: George Hamilton, Irvine, 7 December 1917
Height: 5ft 10in
Weight: 11st 7lb
Clubs: Irvine Meadow; Queen of the South; Aberdeen; Heart of Midlothian; Hamilton Academicals
Scotland caps: 5
Scotland goals: 4
1947 v N Ireland (drew 0-0)
1951 v Belgium (won 5-0) 3 goals, v Austria (lost 0-4)
1954 v Norway (won 1-0) 1 goal, v Norway (drew 1-1)

George Hamilton played five times for his country and in only his second appearance, he netted a hat-trick in a 5-0 defeat of Belgium.

One of the many stars to have cut his teeth in junior football in Ayrshire, he joined Queen of the South from Irvine Meadow in the summer of 1937, spending a year with the Doonhamers before being sold to Aberdeen for what was then a club record fee of £3,000.

In his first season at Pittodrie, he topped the club's scoring charts with 18 goals, but then his career, like so many others of his generation, was interrupted by the outbreak of the Second World War. At the end of the hostilities he returned to Aberdeen, playing in the 'unofficial' 3-2 League Cup Final win over Rangers in May 1946.

In April 1947, Hamilton was back at Hampden Park, netting Aberdeen's equaliser in the 2-1 defeat of Hibs, that gave the Dons the Scottish Cup for the first time in their history. At the end of the year he was transferred to Hearts as part of the deal that took Archie Kelly to Pittodrie but within six months he was back with the Dons, with whom he was to spend a further seven seasons.

By the time Aberdeen won the League Championship in 1954-55, Hamilton had become a 'squad' player, although he did score twice in the four games he played. It was fitting that Hamilton's final game for the Dons came in the match against Clyde at Shawfield as Archie Glen converted the penalty that gave Aberdeen their first-ever title. George Hamilton's appearance in that match gave him the distinction of being the only player to be present when the Dons celebrated both major domestic 'firsts'—the League Championship and the Scottish Cup.

In the summer of 1955 he signed for Hamilton Academicals, where he spent just six months before hanging up his boots.

JIMMY DUNCANSON
Inside-forward/ Outside-left

Born: James Duncanson, Glasgow, 13 October 1919
Died: 1 January 1996
Height: 5ft 10in
Weight: 11st 2lb
Clubs: Dunoon Milton Rovers; Glasgow Rangers; St Mirren; Stranraer
Scotland caps: 1
1947 v N Ireland (drew 0-0)

Jimmy Duncanson joined Rangers in 1939 but had to wait until after the Second World War to realise his enormous potential as a forward. In fact, he was referred to as '...the suave, scintillating inside-forward', although he was no mean winger either.

Duncanson developed the useful habit of scoring goals when most needed, helping Rangers to win the League Championship in 1946-47, 1948-49 and 1949-50. He was also on the winning side in three successive Scottish Cup Finals and had League Cup success in 1947 and 1949. His form for Rangers, especially in the immediate post-war years was outstanding and led to him winning his one and only full international cap in November 1947 against Northern Ireland at Hampden Park, though he had appeared in a couple of wartime internationals. Though the game was goalless, Duncanson hit the post and laid on goalscoring chances for both Rangers' team-mate Willie Thornton and Liverpool's Billy Liddell.

He went on to score 142 goals in 299 games for the Ibrox club—a terrific ratio for a player who played many of his games on the wing—before, in November 1950, leaving to play for St Mirren. He continued to find the net on a regular basis in three seasons at Love Street before moving to Stranraer, where he ended his playing days after two seasons at Stair Park.

JOCK SHAW
Left-back

Born: John Shaw, Annathill, 29 November 1912
Died: 20 June 2000

Height: 5ft 7in
Weight: 11st 8lb
Clubs: Airdrieonians; Glasgow Rangers
Scotland caps: 4
1947 v England (drew 1-1), v Belgium (lost 1-2), v Luxembourg (won 6-0)
1948 v N Ireland (lost 0-2)

Dubbed 'Tiger' Shaw by the Ibrox faithful, he played in two wartime internationals in 1941 and 1943, both at Hampden and both against England, and in Victory internationals in 1945 and 1946. Indeed, he and his brother David of Hibernian formed the full-back partnership in the 1946 Victory international against England which Scotland won 1-0. He played in four of Scotland's 1947 international matches, but was succeeded over the next couple of years in the national team by his younger brother.

He began his career with Airdrie in 1933 after they had taken him from Glasgow junior club Benburb, and spent five seasons with them until being transferred to Rangers for a fee of £2,000 in the summer of 1938.

After helping the Ibrox club win the League Championship in his first season with the club, the rock solid full-back was a mainstay of Rangers' post-war 'Iron Curtain' defence. He was club captain too and collected four League Championships, three Scottish Cups and two Scottish League Cups—included in that array of honours was the double of 1949-50, achieved in his 38th year.

Jock Shaw was 42 years old when he finally retired. This came about following an extensive Rangers tour in the summer of 1954 to Canada and the United States. In view of his playing style, which was uncompromising, this was a tribute to his fitness, sustained over so many years.

He subsequently had a long and successful association with the Ibrox club as trainer and later groundsman.

ARCHIE MACAULAY
Wing-half
Born: Archibald Renwick Macaulay, Falkirk, 30 July 1915
Died: 20 June 1993
Height: 5ft 10in
Weight: 11st 8lb
Clubs: Camelton Juniors; Glasgow Rangers; West Ham United; Brentford; Arsenal; Fulham; Guildford City
Scotland caps: 7
1947 v England (drew 1-1)
1948 v N Ireland (lost 0-2), v Wales (lost 1-2), v England (lost 0-2); v Belgium (won 2-0), v Switzerland (lost 1-2), v France (lost 0-3)

Archie Macaulay began his football career with Glasgow Rangers, winning Scottish League and Cup winners' medals before being transferred to West Ham United for £6,000 in 1937.

In the two seasons prior to the outbreak of the Second World War, Macaulay was the Hammers' leading scorer, netting a hat-trick in a 6-1 home win over Tranmere Rovers towards the end of the 1938-39 season. In 1940 he played for West Ham in the first wartime FA Cup Final before 'guesting' for Falkirk, Northampton Town, Aldershot and Doncaster Rovers. When peacetime football resumed in 1946-47, he played in just a handful of games for West Ham before being transferred to Brentford.

The Bees were relegated at the end of his first season at Griffin Park and against strong competition, Arsenal signed him for £10,000 in July 1947. In his first season at Highbury, Macaulay won a League Championship medal and was unlucky not to win the only honour to elude him—an FA Cup winners' medal—because after playing in the semi-final against Chelsea, Alex Forbes was preferred for the 1950 FA Cup winning team.

In June 1950 he joined Fulham where he finished his first-class career three years later. He went into management with non-League Guildford City before becoming trainer-coach at Dundee. However, he still hankered for a managerial post in English soccer and in April 1957 came the offer to manage Norwich City.

Macaulay took the Canaries from the re-election zone to the semi-finals of the FA Cup in 1959, and the following season gained promotion to the Second Division as runners-up to Southampton. He had offers to manage at a higher level and took charge at West Bromwich Albion. Eighteen months later he decided to leave the club after complaining of not being given a free hand. He later managed Brighton and Hove Albion to the Fourth Division Championship, but after a few mediocre seasons, decided to resign—a manager who was innovative and a tactician ahead of his time.

WILLIE WOODBURN
Centre-half

Born: William Alexander Woodburn, Edinburgh, 8 August 1919
Died: 2 December 2001
Height: 6ft 0in
Weight: 12st 11b
Clubs: Musselburgh Athletic; Queen's Park Victoria; Glasgow Rangers
Scotland caps: 24
1947 v England (drew 1-1), v Belgium (lost 1-2), v Luxembourg (won 6-0)
1948 v N Ireland (lost 0-2), v Wales (lost 1-2)
1949 v England (won 3-1)
1950 v France (won 2-0), v N Ireland (won 8-2), v Wales (won 2-0), v England (lost 0-1), v Portugal (drew 2-2), v France (won 1-0)
1951 v Wales (won 3-1), v N Ireland (won 6-1), v Austria (lost 0-1), v England (won 3-2), v Denmark (won 3-1), v France (won 1-0), v Belgium (won 5-0), v Austria (lost 0-4)
1952 v N Ireland (won 3-0), v Wales (lost 0-1), v England (lost 1-2), v United States (won 6-0)

One of the all-time greats for Rangers, Willie Woodburn joined the Ibrox club in 1937 and was their centre-half in the team that won the domestic treble in 1948-49.

Prior to that success, he had won the first of 24 Scotland caps when he played in the 1-1 draw against England at Wembley. Though the Scots led 1-0 at the interval, the second-half belonged to the home side and it was only Woodburn's shackling of the great Tommy Lawton plus his goal-line clearance from Raich Carter that saved the day. Over the next few seasons, Woodburn missed very few matches at national level, always seeming to save his best for the Auld Enemy. Two years later at Wembley, he was a member of the Scotland team that had Morton keeper Jimmy Cowan to thank for a 3-1 win.

A strong, dominating centre-half, reputedly one of the most stylish ever to play for the Ibrox club, he won four League Championship medals in 1946-47, 1948-49, 1949-50 and 1952-53, four Scottish Cup winners' medals and two League Cup winners' medals.

Woodburn, who played in over 300 first team games for Rangers had a stormy career, punctuated by much-publicised brushes with authority.

In fact, in 1954, Willie Woodburn, the most gifted of footballers, was barred from football indefinitely by the Scottish FA after a history of disciplinary offences had been taken into account. He left the club the following year but even when the ban was lifted in April 1957, Woodburn, who was then 37, would not resume playing.

ALEX FORBES
Wing-half

Born: Alexander Rooney Forbes, Dundee, 21 January 1925
Height: 5ft 9in
Weight: 11st 11lb
Clubs: Dundee North End; Sheffield United; Arsenal; Leyton Orient; Fulham
Scotland caps: 14
1947 v England (drew 1-1), v Belgium (lost 1-2), v Luxembourg (won 6-0)
1948 v N Ireland (lost 0-2), v Wales (lost 1-2)
1950 v England (lost 0-1), v Portugal (drew 2-2), v France (won 1-0)
1951 v Wales (won 3-1), v N Ireland (won 6-1), v Austria (lost 0-1)
1952 v Wales (lost 0-1), v Denmark (won 2-1), v Sweden (lost 1-3)

Wing-half Alex Forbes was a Scottish hockey international who began his football career with Dundee North End during the war.

He signed for First Division Sheffield United as a centre-forward in 1944 but had made little progress in that position. Lacking nothing in energy and fierce determination, he was tried at left-half and was an immediate and lasting success, being a regular member of the Blades' side during the first two seasons of peacetime football. Forbes' consistency with the Bramall Lane club won him the first of 14 caps when he played against England at Wembley.

After being sidelined by an appendix operation, Forbes was transfer listed. It was his great friend Archie Macaulay, the Arsenal wing-half who persuaded Forbes to join the Gunners in February 1948 for a fee of £16,000.

After helping the North London club to win the League Championship in

1947-48, it was ironic that Forbes was to keep Macaulay out of the club's 1950 FA Cup Final side when Arsenal beat Liverpool 2-0. Forbes was a regular in the Arsenal side for seven seasons following his transfer, helping the side to a second League Championship victory in 1952-53. Forbes had played in 240 League and Cup games for the Gunners when a cartilage operation kept him out of the side during the 1955-56 season. Unable to win back his place, he was transferred to Leyton Orient in the close season.

After one season at Brisbane Road, Forbes joined Fulham where he finished his playing career. He returned to Highbury in the early sixties to coach the club's reserve side, later leaving to coach and manage in South Africa.

ANDY McLAREN
Inside-forward

Born: Andrew McLaren, Larkhall, 24 January 1922
Died: 13 January 1996
Height: 5ft 7in
Weight: 10st 7lb
Clubs: Larkhall Thistle; Preston North End; Burnley; Sheffield United; Barrow; Bradford Park Avenue; Southport; Rochdale
Scotland caps: 4
Scotland goals: 4
1947 v England (drew 1-1) 1 goal, v Belgium (lost 1-2), v Luxembourg (won 6-0) 2 goals
1948 v Wales (lost 1-2) 1 goal

A prolific scorer in wartime football, Andy McLaren returned to Deepdale in December 1946 following his time in the forces, and after just 11 games in Preston North End's colours, won an unexpected place in Scotland's team for the game against England at Wembley. He scored their only goal in a 1-1 draw and went on the Scottish tour of Belgium and Luxembourg. The following season he played against Wales at Hampden Park, scoring four goals in as many appearances at international level.

McLaren joined the groundstaff at Preston just days prior to the start of the Second World War. In 1940-41 North End became champions of the Northern Regional League and added to that honour when they were winners of the second wartime Cup Final. Their opponents, Arsenal, missed a third-minute penalty before the young Scot gave North End the lead, but with time running out, Denis Compton drew the Gunners level. In the replay, two goals from Bobby Beattie gave North End a 2-1 victory. A defeat at Blackpool had left Preston needing to win the last game of the season at Liverpool in order to clinch the title. They did so, with Andy McLaren scoring all six goals in a 6-1 rout of the Anfield club

In 1947-48, his first full season of League football with the Lancashire club, he was North End's leading scorer with 17 goals, two of which came in the latter stages of the club's 7-4 win over top-of-the-table Derby County. After being injured in the early part of the following season, he struggled to find form and was surprisingly exchanged for Burnley's Jack Knight.

However, things didn't work out for McLaren at Turf Moor and he soon moved on to Sheffield United. He stayed at Bramall Lane for two seasons before moving to Barrow where he scored 52 goals in 155 league appearances for the Holker Street club. He later played for Bradford Park Avenue and Southport before ending his League career with Rochdale.

BILLY STEEL
Inside-left

Born: William Steel, Denny, 1 May 1923
Died: Los Angeles 13 May 1982
Height: 5ft 6in
Weight: 11st 0lb
Clubs: Dunipace Thistle; Bo'ness Cadora; Leicester City; St Mirren; Morton; Derby County; Dundee; Los Angeles Danes and Hollywood FC (United States)
Scotland caps: 30
Scotland goals: 12

1947 v England (drew 1-1), v Belgium (lost 1-2) 1 goal, v Luxembourg (won 6-0) 2 goals
1948 v N Ireland (lost 0-2), v Wales (lost 1-2), v England (lost 0-2), v France (lost 0-3)
1949 v Wales (won 3-1), v N Ireland (won 3-2), v England (won 3-1) 1 goal
1950 v France (won 2-0) 2 goals, v N Ireland (won 8-2) 1 goal, v Wales (won 2-0), v England (lost 0-1), v Switzerland (won 3-1), v Portugal (drew 2-2), v France (won 1-0)
1951 v Wales (won 3-1), v N Ireland (won 6-1) 4 goals, v Austria (lost 0-1), v England (won 3-2), v Denmark (won 3-1) 1 goal, v France (won 1-0), v Belgium (won 5-0), v Austria (lost 0-4)
1952 v Wales (lost 0-1)
1953 v Wales (won 2-1), v N Ireland (drew 1-1), v England (drew 2-2), v Sweden (lost 1-2)

Billy Steel, a stocky inside-left, lightning quick at making or taking goals, played so well on his international debut against England in April 1947 that, a few weeks later, he was playing for Great Britain against the Rest of Europe, and soon Derby County were paying Morton a British record fee of £15,000 for the blond-haired forward. He went on to make 30 appearances for Scotland, scoring four goals in a 6-1 defeat of Northern Ireland.

Though he had only played a handful of League games for Morton when he won his first cap for Scotland, Billy Steel fitted in well in a Great Britain forward line that contained Matthews, Mannion, Lawton and Liddell, and he scored the most spectacular of Britain's six goals.

Although he went on to have many fine games for Derby with his terrific left-foot shot and ball control, Steel was difficult to play with and was a law unto himself. Many of his County team-mates felt he reserved his best displays for the national side or for games in London. They also resented his status and the fact that he had other 'jobs' which increased his earnings in the days of maximum wages. His pleasant smile also masked an intolerant side to his character. Many former Rams players of his era still blame Billy Steel for the decline of the 1950s, after several unsettled stars left the club. Having scored 35 goals in 124 League and Cup games for Derby County, he was eventually transferred to Dundee for a Scottish record fee of £23,000.

Steel helped Dundee to two League Cup Final victories—beating Rangers 3-2 in 1951-52 and Kilmarnock 2-0 in 1952-53—and to a Cup Final in 1952 where the Dark Blues were beaten 4-0 by Motherwell.

On hanging up his boots in 1954, Billy Steel, who holds the unenviable distinction of being the first Scottish player to receive his marching orders, left Dens Park to emigrate to the United States, where he took up a position in advertising.

TOMMY PEARSON
Outside-left
Born: Thomas Usher Pearson, Edinburgh, 16 March 1913
Died: 1 March 1999
Height: 5ft 11in
Weight: 10st 7lb
Clubs: Murrayfield Amateurs; Newcastle United; Aberdeen
Scotland caps: 2
1947 v England (drew 1-1), v Belgium (lost 1-2)

Tommy Pearson is the only player to have appeared for both Scotland and England in international football, turning out for the English in an emergency during a wartime fixture on Tyneside when news of a car crash involving England winger Eric Brook was announced. He was on the victorious side against his countrymen, England winning 2-1. After the conclusion of the hostilities, aged 34, he made his debut in his country's blue shirt against England, thus becoming the subject of football quiz nights all over the country!

The Lothian-born winger was transferred from Murrayfield Amateurs to Newcastle United in 1933 and was a loyal servant to the Magpies for over a decade and, but for the Second World War, would probably have become a huge international star.

Serving in the RAF during the war, Tommy Pearson was always guaranteed a match on his travels around the country, playing for Blackburn Rovers, Bolton Wanderers, Tottenham Hotspur, Birmingham, Liverpool, Stoke City, Walsall and Blackpool, whom he helped to the 1944 North Cup Final.

Possessing immaculate ball control, he was especially noted for his touchline runs, which featured body-swerves and foot shuffles as well as crowd-pleasing nutmegs! He was a regular in the Newcastle side for six peacetime seasons until being unfairly treated by the club during the 1947-48 promotion campaign. Branded a troublemaker by some sections of the management, he left Tyneside with a sour taste having scored 52 goals in 228 League and Cup games.

Although he was reaching the veteran stage, his departure to Aberdeen opened another door and he became associated with the Dons for over 30 years as player, coach, manager and local sports journalist. He had made his debut in a 1-0 defeat at the hands of Partick Thistle on Valentine's Day 1948, and though he was playing with the Dons during a particularly unsuccessful spell for the Pittodrie club, it says much for his ability that he still managed to attract his own band of fans who followed him everywhere!

On severing connections with the Dons, he returned to the city of his birth, Edinburgh, where he opened a jewellery business as well as becoming a first-class amateur golfer, good enough to compete in the Open Championship.

BOBBY CAMPBELL
Winger

Born: Robert Inglis Campbell, Glasgow, 28 June 1922
Height: 5ft 9in
Weight: 11st 7lb
Clubs: Falkirk; Chelsea; Reading
Scotland caps: 5
Scotland goals: 1
1947 v Belgium (lost 1-2), v Luxembourg (won 6-0)
1950 v Switzerland (won 3-1) 1 goal, v Portugal (drew 2-2), v France (won 1-0)

Winger Bobby Campbell, who was able to play on either flank, provided chances for his team-mates wherever he played and could capitalise on chances himself.

He began his career with Falkirk just after the outbreak of the Second World War, during which time he 'guested' for Queen's Park Rangers. In fact, his debut for the London club was against Chelsea, the club he was to make his name with after leaving Ochilview Park for Stamford Bridge in May 1947.

Though he lost some of his best playing years to the war, he was an immediate success at Chelsea. A fast, direct wide-man, he later played as an inside-forward, going on to score 40 goals in 213 games for the Blues. Capped five times by Scotland, he got on the scoresheet in the 3-1 win over Switzerland at Hampden in April 1950, and though he created the only goal of the game scored by Allan Brown against France in Paris, it turned out to be his last appearance for the national side.

Appointed player-coach at Reading, he then had a year in charge at Dumbarton before joining Bristol Rovers as coach under Bert Tann in 1962. He stayed with the then Eastville club for 17 years, the last two as manager. When he took over from Don Megson as manager, he was 55 years old but showed the enthusiasm of a much younger man. He bought and sold well on the transfer market but after a poor start to the 1979–80 season, he was sacked. He later worked for the Bristol City Council, arranging soccer matches for the unemployed.

BOBBY FLAVELL
Centre-forward

Born: Robert Flavell, Annathill, 1 September 1921
Died: 18 March 2005
Height: 5ft 6in

Weight: 11st 8lb
Clubs: Kirkintilloch Rob Roy; Airdrieonians; Heart of Midlothian; Millionarios Bogota
(Colombia); Dundee; Kilmarnock; St Mirren
Scotland caps: 2
Scotland goals: 2
1947 v Belgium (lost 1-2), v Luxembourg (won 6-0) 2 goals

An aggressive and dangerous centre-forward whose display in scoring five goals for the Scottish League against the Irish League earned him two full international caps for Scotland.

The much-travelled striker started out with Kirkintilloch Rob Roy before joining Airdrie in January 1938, and though he appeared on a regular basis, he was only 18 when war broke out. He gained valuable experience during the hostilities against seasoned professionals, 'guesting' for Arsenal, Brentford, Crystal Palace and Spurs. In February 1944 he played for Scotland against England in a wartime international, and when peacetime football returned, he remained with Airdrie.

In December 1947 he was transferred to Heart of Midlothian, and his displays for the Tynecastle club led to him being one of several leading British players lured to Colombia by the promise of untold riches. He signed for the Millionarios club of Bogota, and like most of those who tried their luck in South America, he did not enjoy the experience. After just one year he returned to Scotland to play for Dundee.

He appeared for the Dens Park club in the 1952 Scottish Cup Final, before winning his only domestic honour as a member of the team that won the Scottish League Cup in 1952—beating Rangers 3-2 and in 1953, defeating Kilmarnock 2-0. On leaving Dundee he played for Kilmarnock and St Mirren where he finished his playing days and moved onto the coaching staff.

In November 1961 he was appointed manager of Ayr United but the job only lasted 17 days, for the next month he accepted a similar post with St Mirren. Thirteen months later he went back to Ayr and this time stayed until December 1964. In 1965-66 he managed Albion Rovers and served them again in that capacity for a short time from November 1969. He was later a director of Albion Rovers and a scout for Berwick Rangers.

WILLIE MacFARLANE
Outside-right
Born: William MacFarlane, Fallin, 1 October 1923
Height: 5ft 6in
Weight: 9st 11lb
Clubs: Bathgate Thistle; Heart of Midlothian; Stirling Albion; Kilmarnock; Caledonian FC
Scotland caps: 1
1947 v Luxembourg (won 6-0)

Diminutive winger Willie MacFarlane replaced Gordon Smith in the Scotland team that defeated Luxembourg 6-0 in May 1947 and had a hand in most of the goals in a game in which McLaren, Steel and Flavell scored two goals apiece. On that same trip to the continent, he played for an SFA team against the British Army of the Rhine, whilst a month before his international debut he had played for the Scottish League XI in a 7-4 defeat of the Irish League.

The dashing right-winger was spotted by Hearts while playing for Bathgate Thistle Juniors and signed by the Tynecastle club in March 1942. He played mainly for the club's reserve side until 1943-44 when the goalscoring winger established himself in the first team. He was able to play regularly during the Second World War as he was in a reserved occupation, being an electrician at Fallin coal mine. When peacetime football resumed, he helped Hearts to the Scottish League Cup semi-final in 1947.

Over the next few seasons, Willie MacFarlane demonstrated his art as one of the finest wingers of his era, using his great pace and crossing ability to open defences. He remained a regular in the Hearts side until 1950 when following a cartilage operation, he then appeared mainly for the reserves.

Having scored 30 goals in 187 games for Hearts, MacFarlane moved on to play for Stirling Albion before ending his career with a brief spell for Kilmarnock and Caledonian FC.

JIMMY WATSON
Inside-forward

Born: James Watson, Cowie, 16 January 1924
Height: 5ft 10in
Weight: 11st 7lb
Clubs: Armadale Thistle; Motherwell; Huddersfield Town; Dunfermline Athletic
Scotland caps: 2
1948 v N Ireland (lost 0-2)
1954 v N Ireland (won 3-1)

Jimmy Watson graduated through the ranks at Armadale Thistle to become a prolific marksman for Motherwell. He scored their goal in the 1945 Southern League Cup Final when Rangers beat The Well 2-1, and netted twice in the outstanding 4-1 League Cup quarter-final defeat of Celtic. His partnerships with players like Archie Kelly and Jim Forrest helped Motherwell make steady progress in the First Division and caught the selectors' eyes too, winning his first full cap against Northern Ireland in October 1947.

He netted the opening goal—his 66th in 195 games—in Motherwell's 4-0 Scottish Cup Final win over Dundee in 1952, but left the club a few weeks later in controversial circumstances. His departure to Huddersfield Town for a fee of £16,000 owed more to money than any football shortcomings.

The Yorkshire club had just been relegated for the first time in their history and Watson's skills helped them make a swift return to the First Division. Watson possessed superb ball control and his defence-splitting passes were a fine feature of his cultured play. Even when he switched from his regular inside-forward berth to fill in as an emergency left-half, he continued to be an effective schemer. Winning a second cap, he left Leeds Road after scoring 32 goals in 148 games to return north of the border to play for Dunfermline Athletic.

He helped the Pars win promotion to the First Division in his first season at East End Park but the highlight of his stay had to be the 10-1 win over Partick Thistle—a result that ensured Dunfermline's top flight safety. Remarkably, Jimmy Watson failed to score in that goal avalanche!

JOCK GOVAN
Right-back
Born: John Govan, Larkhall, 16 January 1923
Height: 5ft 11in
Weight: 11st 12lb
Clubs: Larkhall Thistle; Hibernian; Ayr United
Scotland caps: 6
1948 v Wales (lost 1-2), v England (lost 0-2), v Belgium (won 2-0)
     v Switzerland (lost 1-2), v France (lost 0-3)
1949 v N Ireland (won 3-2)

The nephew of Tom Miller, who played for Liverpool, Manchester United and Scotland, Jock Govan was often described as the first overlapping full-back.

Playing his early football for Larkhall Thistle, he joined Hibs in the summer of 1942 and during the remaining war years, he established himself as an important member of the Easter Road club's side.

When peacetime football resumed in 1946-47, Jock Govan, who was ideally built, sound and uncompromising, played an important role in the club's early post-war purple patch. He helped Hibs to win three League Championships, the first in 1947-48, when his performances earned him selection for Scotland at full international level. Govan in fact, went on to win six full caps in 1948 and 1949. He also represented the Scottish League on a couple of occasions. With Govan in their side, Hibs went on to win the League Championship in seasons 1950-51 and 1951-52 and as in their first League success in 1947-48, Rangers were the runners-up on each occasion.

Govan, who linked up well down the right with Gordon Smith of the 'Famous Five' fame, liked nothing better than to get forward in support of the attack, but surprisingly he never got on the scoresheet in any of his 163 League games.

In 1954 he left Easter Road to join Ayr United, but after just one season at Somerset Park when the club came very close to winning promotion from the Second Division, he decided to retire.

IAN BLACK
Goalkeeper
Born: Ian Henderson Black, Aberdeen, 27 March 1924
Height: 6ft 0in
Weight: 12st 4lb
Clubs: Aberdeen; Southampton; Fulham; Bath City; Canterbury City

Ian Black had his first taste of professional football during the later stages of the Second World War, playing for Aberdeen in 1944 and 'guesting' for Chelsea in 1945. When he was demobbed, he asked Aberdeen to release him to allow him to join Southampton where he found employment as a mechanic. The Pittodrie club, realising Black's talents, were reluctant to let him go and Saints' manager Bill Dodgin was lucky to be able to recruit such an excellent goalkeeper.

Within a few months of arriving at The Dell, Ian Black had won a Scottish cap against England and, strangely, that was the last time that a Southampton player appeared for Scotland until Neil McCann, who joined the Saints from Rangers in 2003.

In August 1950, after playing in 97 League games for the Saints, Black followed Dodgin to Craven Cottage, where the former Southampton manager had taken over the reins of Fulham.

Black made his debut for the Cottagers in a 1-0 defeat at Manchester United on the opening day of the 1950-51 season. Black was ever-present during that campaign and in eight seasons at Craven Cottage, missed very few games. In the second game of the 1952-53 season, Black became the only goalkeeper ever to score for Fulham in a League game. Replacing an injured player in the match at Leicester City, he was moved to centre-forward and scored the Cottagers' only goal in a 6-1 defeat.

Black had played 277 League and Cup games for Fulham when, after losing his place to Tony Macedo, he left to play Southern League football, first for Bath City and then Canterbury City. When he retired from football in 1957, Black opened a sports shop in London.

BOBBY COMBE
Wing-half/ Inside-left
Born: James Robert Combe, Leith, 29 January 1924
Died: 19 November 1991
Height: 5ft 7in
Weight: 11st 2lb
Clubs: Inveresk Athletic; Hibernian
Scotland caps: 3
Scotland goals: I
1948 v England (lost 0-2), v Belgium (won 2-0) I goal, v Switzerland (lost 1-2)

Capped by Scotland as a schoolboy, he won three full caps in 1948 against England, Belgium and Switzerland, and was in the initial Scotland squad for the 1954 World Cup Finals. However, he did not travel because Scotland decided to limit the pool of players they took to 13.

He began his career in 1941, and in his first year in the Hibernian side, scored four goals in an 8-1 rout of Rangers. After playing in the majority of Hibs' wartime matches, Combe was among the stars of the side that won the League Championship in 1947-48, 1950-51 and 1951-52. Lining up alongside Gordon Smith, Bobby Johnstone, Lawrie Reilly, Eddie Turnbull and Willie Ormond, Combe, who played the majority of his games at inside-forward, was part of the Hibs' forward line considered to be one of the most devastating strike forces of the Scottish game.

Though he was considered the sixth man of the 'Famous Five' line-up, the fact that he could play almost anywhere on the park counted against him. Nevertheless, Bobby Combe enjoyed the consolation of being the Easter Road club's captain and giving 16 years' loyal service. He scored 67 goals in 354 League and Cup games, but on retiring from playing at the end of the 1956-57 season, he became Hibs' assistant-trainer before having a short spell as manager of Dumbarton in the late 1950s.

On ending his involvement with the game he became a shopkeeper in Leith, later employed in the marketing department of the Scottish Gas Board.

JIMMY COWAN
Goalkeeper
Born: James Clews Cowan, Paisley, 16 June 1926
Died: 20 June 1968
Height: 5ft 11in
Weight: 11st 7lb
Clubs: Mossvale Juniors; St Mirren; Morton; Sunderland; Third Lanark
Scotland caps: 25
1948 v Belgium (won 2-0), v Switzerland (lost 1-2), v France (lost 0-3)
1949 v Wales (won 3-1), v England (won 3-1)
1950 v France (won 2-0), v N Ireland (won 8-2), v Wales (won 2-0), v England (lost 0-1), v Switzerland (won 3-1), v Portugal (drew 2-2), v France (won 1-0)
1951 v Wales (won 3-1), v N Ireland (won 6-1), v Austria (lost 0-1), v England (won 3-2), v Denmark (won 3-1), v France (won 1-0), v Belgium (won 5-0), v Austria (lost 0-4)
1952 v N Ireland (won 3-0), v Wales (lost 0-1), v United States (won 6-0), v Denmark (won 2-1), v Sweden (lost 1-3)

In April 1949, not long after recovering from a broken arm, goalkeeper Jimmy Cowan defied England's forwards in a 3-1 win for Scotland. His display gave Scottish football a tremendous boost following an indifferent period immediately after the Second World War. Cowan was carried off the field as a hero, the first time that had happened since a Scottish team carried off Harry McNeil at Hamilton Crescent in 1874!

A centre-forward during his schooldays, Jimmy Cowan was coached as a goalkeeper by the legendary Harry Rennie and blooded in army representative games before making a dramatic entry into Scottish League football.

In January 1947, while on leave from Germany, he went into the Morton team at short notice and saved two penalties, just like Jimmy Brownlie! In fact, Cowan's call-up to the Morton side was so late that some newspaper reports of the game attributed his saves to the club's regular goalkeeper Archie McFeat. Morton had signed Cowan on a free transfer from his home-town club, St Mirren, but his value grew quickly when he made his name in the 1948 Scottish Cup Final, holding the mighty Rangers to a replay. In May 1949, Cowan had to turn down a chance to tour the United States with the Scottish side because of his mother's illness, but after that he made 18 consecutive international appearances for Scotland.

In June 1953 he was transferred to Sunderland for a fee of £8,000, but in November 1955 after making 28 First Division appearances for the Wearsiders, he returned north of the border to play out his career with Third Lanark.

Jimmy Cowan died suddenly aged 42, following a short illness, but he will never be forgotten in Scottish football.

LESLIE JOHNSTON
Inside-forward/ Centre-forward
Born: Leslie Hamilton Johnston, Glasgow, 16 August 1920
Died: 2 October 2001
Height: 5ft 8in
Weight: 10st 8lb
Clubs: Clydebank; Clyde; Hibernian; Glasgow Celtic; Stoke City; Shrewsbury Town; Hinckley Athletic
Scotland caps: 2
Scotland goals: 1
1948 v Belgium (won 2-0), v Switzerland (lost 1-2) 1 goal

Ship's carpenter Leslie Johnston was known as the strolling player of the football world. He started his career with Clydcbank Juniors, helping them win the Scottish Junior Cup in 1942. Shortly afterwards he joined Clyde and was chosen to play for Scotland against England at Hampden Park in April 1945 as a substitute for Hibs' Tommy Bogan, who was injured in a clash with England keeper Frank Swift. Johnston scored Scotland's goal in a 6-1 defeat.

His form with Clyde led to Hibernian paying £10,000 for his services in February 1947—the first five-figure fee paid for a Scot by a Scottish club. However, his stay at Easter Road was brief and after just eight months he rejoined Clyde. On his return to Shawfield, he won full international honours, appearing in two games and scoring in the second, a 2-1 defeat by Switzerland.

When Celtic signed Leslie Johnston in October 1948 for a then Scottish record of £12,000, he became Scotland's first £30,000 footballer in accumulated transfer fees. Though he was a proven goalscorer, he found goals hard to come by at Parkhead and after losing his place to Mike Haughney at the start of the 1949-50 season, he moved to Stoke City for a club record £5,000.

After four seasons at the Victoria Ground in which he scored 22 goals in 88 games, he joined Shrewsbury Town in July 1953. Never having lost his appetite for the game, he later played non-League football for Hinckley Athletic and continued playing and refereeing five-a-side games well into his fifties.

EDDIE TURNBULL

Inside-left/ Right-half

Born: Edward Hunter Turnbull, Falkirk, 12 April 1923
Height: 5ft 9in
Weight: 11st 0lb
Clubs: Forth Rangers; Hibernian
Scotland caps: 8
1948 v Belgium (won 2-0), v Switzerland (lost 1-2)
1951 v Austria (lost 0-1)
1958 v Hungary (drew 1-1), v Poland (won 2-1), v Yugoslavia (drew 1-1), v Paraguay (lost 2-3),
v France (lost 1-2)

Eddie Turnbull won the first of his eight international caps in 1948 and made his last appearance some ten years later in the 1958 World Cup Finals in Sweden.

Though he was probably the unsung hero of the 'Famous Five', he was certainly one of the longest serving. He made his Hibs debut in an 'A' Division game against Third Lanark in November 1946, and at the end of his first season at Easter Road, played in the 1947 Scottish Cup Final against Aberdeen, a match Hibs lost 2-1. The following season he won the first of three League Championship medals with Hibs as they finished two points clear of runners-up Rangers.

Playing in the most potent strike force the club—and arguably the country—has ever seen, Turnbull helped the club win further League Championships in 1950-51 and 1951-52, and appeared in another Scottish Cup Final in 1958 as Hibs lost 1-0 to Clyde.

Turnbull also holds the distinction of being the first British player to score in European competition when, on 14 September 1955, Hibs travelled to Germany to play Rot Weiss Essen. He put the club ahead in the first-half, whilst further goals from Reilly, Ormond and another from Turnbull made the final score 4-0 to Hibs. Turnbull, who made his last appearance in a Hibs shirt against Real Gijon in May 1959 during a four-game tour of Spain, had scored 141 goals in 321 League games when he hung up his boots.

After a spell coaching Queen's Park, he was appointed manager of Aberdeen, helping the Dons to win the Scottish Cup in 1970. On leaving Pittodrie in 1971, he returned to Easter Road to manage Hibs. He was in charge for almost a decade and though his 'Turnbull's Tornadoes' were chasing Celtic—under Jock Stein—for everything, they did win the League Cup in 1972-73, beating Celtic 2-1 in the final. Though Turnbull's tactical genius won admirers throughout the game, and Hibs had their most famous left-wing partnership together again once Willie Ormond had finished with Scotland and Hearts to become No.2 to Turnbull, Hibs slid towards the First Division and Turnbull parted company with the club.

DAVIE DUNCAN

Outside-left

Born: David Millar Duncan, Milton of Balgonie, 21 November 1921

Died: 11 January 1991
Height: 5ft 8in
Weight: 11st 8lb
Clubs: Lochgelly Albert; Raith Rovers; Glasgow Celtic; East Fife; Raith Rovers; Crewe
 Alexandra; Brechin City
Scotland caps: 3
Scotland goals: 1
1948 v Belgium (won 2-0) 1 goal, v Switzerland (lost 1-2), v France (lost 0-3)

At East Fife, Davie Duncan became the first Division 'B' player to win a full Scottish cap when he scored one of the goals in a 2-0 win over Belgium at Hampden Park in April 1948.

Davie Duncan played locally for Woodside Amateurs and Milton of Balgonie before going junior with Lochgelly Albert in 1939. He joined Raith Rovers towards the end of that year, but following a brief loan spell with Heart of Midlothian, he left Stark's Park to join Celtic in December 1942. He wasn't given much of a chance at Parkhead, and in November 1944 after scoring three goals in just 14 appearances, he joined East Fife on loan, later joining the Fifers on a permanent basis.

Expert at penalties and free-kicks, while also possessing a long throw, he made his peacetime debut for East Fife against Dundee in August 1946, and was with the Bayview Club until the 1953-54 season. He was in the team that won the 'B' Division title in 1947-48, and when East Fife won the League Cup for the first time in 1947, he scored a hat-trick in the 4-1 replay win over Falkirk—the first treble in a League Cup Final. Duncan was also in the team that won the League Cup for a second time, scoring in a 3-0 defeat of Dunfermline Athletic.

He lost his place to Andy Matthew towards the end of the 1952-53 season, and though he returned for odd games, he left East Fife to rejoin Raith Rovers in January 1954, having scored 98 goals in 248 games.

Freed in May 1955, he joined Crewe Alexandra but was released midway through the following season. He then saw out his career with Brechin City where he scored 37 goals in 112 games before retiring at the end of the 1958-59 season.

EDDIE RUTHERFORD
Winger
Born: Edward Rutherford, Glasgow, 8 February 1921
Height: 5ft 9in
Weight: 11st 3lb
Clubs: Mossvale Amateurs; Glasgow Rangers; Heart of Midlothian; Raith Rovers; Hamilton
 Academicals
Scotland caps: 1
1948 v France (lost 0-3)

Able to play on either flank, winger Eddie Rutherford joined Rangers from Mossvale Amateurs in the summer of 1941, and in his early years with the club was also employed as a commercial traveller in the Glasgow area for a firm of chemists.

During the Second World War he served in the RAF and 'guested' for Leeds United, Bradford City and Lincoln City, impressing each of his three clubs. When peacetime football resumed in 1946-47, Rutherford was back at Ibrox, and at the end of his first season, won a League Cup winners' medal as Rangers beat Aberdeen 4-0. He spent 10 very successful seasons with Rangers, helping them win two League Championships, three Scottish Cup Finals and to secure another victory in the League Cup Final in 1948-49. That season Rangers completed the treble, and Rutherford was selected to play for Scotland against France in Paris, a match the Scots lost 3-0.

In November 1951 he left Ibrox to join Hearts in an exchange deal involving Colin Liddell moving in the opposite direction. He did well at Tynecastle, helping to bring on some of the club's young attackers. However, knee injuries and a cartilage operation reduced his effectiveness, and early in 1955 he moved on to Raith Rovers, later ending his career with Hamilton Academicals before going to run a newsagency at Rutherglen.

CHARLIE COX
Right-half
Born: Charles John Cox, Glasgow, 19 February 1926
Height: 5ft 8in
Weight: 10st 0lb
Clubs: Yoker Athletic; Heart of Midlothian; Motherwell
Scotland caps: 1
1948 v France (lost 0-3)

Cultured wing-half Charlie Cox, the nephew of Scottish international John Blair, started his football career with Dumbarton Academy and captained the side that won the Dumbarton League Shield. He then left to join Yoker Athletic but such was his outstanding talent that he was soon snapped up by Hearts in the summer of 1944.

Though he was a part-timer at Tynecastle, his form was such that he was capped at full international level for the match against France in Paris, a game that saw Scotland beaten 3-0. Though he didn't score too many goals, he did net a remarkable winner against Rangers while a 'passenger' on the wing, following an injury to his right knee.

He left Tynecastle along with Tommy Sloan, the pair of them joining Motherwell for a fee of £6,500 in December 1951. Within six months of his arrival, he had helped the Steelemen win the Scottish Cup, beating Dundee 4-0 in the final.

Along with Sloan, he settled in quickly at Fir Park, helping the Steelemen continue the offside-trap that had served them well in the previous decade. A meticulous player who linked defence and attack with considerable skill, all his goals for Motherwell were scored in the Scottish Cup—one of them the last gasp equaliser in an unforgettable 5-5 draw against Aberdeen at Pittodrie!

Though he was a member of the Motherwell side that was relegated in 1952-53, his experience was of great importance the following season as the club made an immediate return to the top flight with a 'B' Division title win. Though injuries hampered his progress in his last few years at Fir Park, Cox made 89 appearances before hanging up his boots in 1958.

HUGH HOWIE
Full-back/ Wing-half/ Centre-half
Born: Hugh Howie, Glasgow, 14 February 1924
Died: 14 January 1958
Height: 6ft 0in
Weight: 11st 12lb
Clubs: Hallside Juveniles; Newton Juniors; Hibernian
Scotland caps: 1
Scotland goals: 1
1949 v Wales (won 3-1) 1 goal

Probably Hugh Howie's greatest moment came when he won his first full cap for Scotland against Wales on 23 October 1948, in a 3-1 win in which he scored his side's opening goal. Surprisingly, it was Howie's only cap, just as Hibernian were his only senior club.

A fine utility player able to play at full-back, wing or centre-half, he played his early football for Hallside Juveniles and Newton Juniors in Glasgow before joining Hibs in 1943. Following the end of the Second World War, he established himself as a regular in the Hibs side. Another great moment in the career of Hugh Howie came in one of the longest-ever Scottish Cup matches—Hibernian v Motherwell—a semi-final tie on 29 March 1947. The game took two hours and 22 minutes to complete with Hibs eventually winning 2-1. With the teams locked at 1-1 after ninety minutes and unable to score during the following thirty minutes of extra-time, the game simply continued until a goal was scored. It was Hugh Howie who lobbed the winner from long distance.

Howie helped Hibs to win the League Championship three times—1947-48, 1950-51 and 1951-52—during his time at Easter Road.

Shortly after making his international debut, he suffered a long illness which kept him out of the game for over a season. He came back bravely and went on to make 132 League appearances for the Easter Road club before retiring from playing in 1954.

He then took up journalism, but sadly, four years later, nearing his 34th birthday, he was tragically killed in a car accident.

BOBBY EVANS
Right-half/ Centre-half
Born: Robert Evans, Glasgow, 16 July 1927
Died: 1 September 2001

Height: 5ft 8in
Weight: 12st 0lb
Clubs: Glasgow Celtic; Chelsea; Newport County; Morton; Third Lanark; Raith Rovers
Scotland caps: 48

1949 v Wales (won 3-1), v N Ireland (won 3-2), v England (won 3-1)

1950 v France (won 2-0), v N Ireland (won 8-2), v Wales (won 2-0), v Switzerland (won 3-1),
        v Portugal (drew 2-2)

1951 v Austria (lost 0-1), v England (won 3-2)

1952 v N Ireland (won 3-0)

1953 v Sweden (lost 1-2)

1954 v N Ireland (won 3-1), v Wales (drew 3-3), v England (lost 2-4), v Norway (won 1-0),
        v Finland (won 2-1)

1955 v N Ireland (drew 2-2), v Portugal (won 3-0), v Yugoslavia (drew 2-2),
        v Austria (won 4-1), v Hungary (lost 1-3)

1956 v N Ireland (lost 1-2), v Wales (won 2-0), v England (drew 1-1), v Austria (drew 1-1)

1957 v W Germany (won 3-1), v Spain (lost 1-4)

1958 v N Ireland (drew 1-1), v Switzerland (won 3-2), v Wales (drew 1-1), v England (lost 0-4),
        v Hungary (drew 1-1), v Poland (won 2-1), v Yugoslavia (drew 1-1), v Paraguay (lost 2-3),
        v France (lost 1-2)

1959 v England (lost 0-1), v W Germany (won 3-2), v Holland (won 2-1), v Portugal (lost 0-1)

1960 v N Ireland (won 4-0), v Wales (drew 1-1), v England (drew 1-1), v Poland (lost 2-3),
        v Austria (lost 1-4), v Hungary (drew 3-3), v Turkey (lost 2-4)

The legendary Bobby Evans captained Scotland in all three World Cup matches in Sweden in 1958, but perhaps his most satisfying match was at Wembley in 1959. It had been eight years since he had played in the stadium and he was back for Billy Wright's 100th appearance for England. Then challenging George Young as Scotland's most capped player, his Scotland team later beat West Germany 3-2 as Bobby Evans gave one of his finest-ever performances.

Bobby Evans took some time to establish himself at Celtic after joining them from a Glasgow junior club, St Anthony's, in 1944. He was smallish and had not yet developed the powerful physique that later enabled him to be such a hard-running wing-half. He was then an inside-forward, tenacious and energetic but short in the forward skills. It was not until he dropped back to the half-back line that he developed his full potential. In that position, his tireless running had a great effect on opposing attacks and this was backed with hard, sure tackling.

The hard little red-headed man found the partners he needed when he was joined by Bertie Peacock and Jock Stein to form what was one of Celtic's best-ever half-back lines. Evans was the hard-running tackler, always involved in the play; Stein was the composed static defender, cool and sure in the air; Peacock the subtle player, the creator and an excellent passer of the ball.

Celtic won the League and Cup double in 1954—their first for 40 years—with a team which had, during the previous close season, won the Coronation Cup, the tough competition in which Arsenal, Manchester United, Spurs and Newcastle United had represented England, and Rangers, Hibs, Aberdeen and Celtic had played for Scotland. Evans was a lively inspiration in the middle of the team which beat Arsenal 1-0 and then Manchester United 2-1. By the time the final was played, the strength of the half-back line had encouraged the forwards and Hibs were beaten 1-0. Evans also had an outstanding game when Rangers were thrashed 7-1 in the 1957-58 League Cup Final.

The highest tribute paid to Bobby Evans at that time was that he never played a poor game. He was indeed a player who was never off colour, who always had abundant energy. In 1960, after appearing in 535 League and Cup games for Celtic, he signed for Chelsea, later playing for Newport County and finally Morton. Despite a back injury, he continued to play into his forties, having a brief spell at Third Lanark, and then playing a major part in Raith Rovers' return to the First Division in 1967.

WILLIE REDPATH
Left-half

Born: William Yates Redpath, Stoneyburn, 8 August 1922
Height: 5ft 8in
Weight: 11st 0lb
Clubs: Polkemmet Juniors; Motherwell; Third Lanark
Scotland caps: 9
1949 v Wales (won 3-1), v N Ireland (won 3-2)
1951 v England (won 3-2), v Denmark (won 3-1), v France (won 1-0), v Belgium (won 5-0), v Austria (lost 0-4)
1952 v N Ireland (won 3-0), v England (lost 1-2)

A cultured and creative player, Willie Redpath was looked upon as something of a lucky mascot at international level. Having played his first game for the Scottish League XI against the Football League in 1948, a match that ended all-square at 1-1, he still hadn't been on the losing side eight games later, and starred in an 8-1 defeat of the Irish League. Redpath's full international debut came against Wales in October 1948, and again the Motherwell player enjoyed six of his nine caps without tasting defeat!

Redpath earned himself a big reputation as a wartime footballer and was the youngest member of the Wanderers XI, a wartime side that toured the Middle East for four years. During the hostilities he even appeared on stage with the *Sunday Mail*'s 'Rex' as a ball juggler!

When he arrived at Fir Park from Polkemmet, Redpath quickly supplemented his club wages by betting his team-mates that he could run two laps of the Fir Park ground while playing 'Keepy-up'!

Redpath was a key player in a Motherwell side that won the Scottish Cup in 1952. Though he was an elegant performer who created numerous goalscoring chances for his colleagues, he scored twice during the club's successful run, netting in the 3-1 semi-final second replay win over Hearts and in the final itself as Motherwell beat Dundee 4-0.

In his prime, Willie Redpath was a great attraction at the gate and went on to score 20 goals in 226 games before leaving Motherwell to join Third Lanark in 1956. He had just one season at Cathkin Park before hanging up his boots.

JIMMY MASON

Inside-forward

Born: James Mason, Glasgow, 18 June 1919
Died: 8 December 1971
Height: 5ft 7in
Weight: 9st 5lb
Clubs: Mossvale YMCA; Third Lanark
Scotland caps: 7
Scotland goals: 4
1949 v Wales (won 3-1), v N Ireland (won 3-2) 1 goal, v England (won 3-1) 1 goal
1950 v N Ireland (won 8-2) 1 goal
1951 v N Ireland (won 6-1), v Belgium (won 5-0) 1 goal v Austria (lost 0-4)

Jimmy Mason's was a great natural talent—he had marvellous ball control and a superb subtlety, which, together with a pleasing and unassuming temperament, made him deservedly popular.

He joined Third Lanark in the summer of 1936 and made a handful of first team appearances in the years prior to the outbreak of the Second World War. During the hostilities he turned out for both Portsmouth and Brentford but most of his games during the wartime period were for Charlton Athletic. When peacetime football returned in 1946-47, the Addicks were, not surprisingly, keen to sign Mason, but he returned to Scotland to continue his career with Third Lanark.

His performances at club level led to him winning selection for the Scottish League and in October 1948 it came as no surprise when he made his international debut for Scotland against Wales at Ninian Park, a match the Scots won 3-1. Though he didn't get on the scoresheet, he netted the winner in his next game as Northern Ireland were beaten 3-2 and then scored the opener in Scotland's 3-1 win over England at Wembley, his header going in off the far post. Mason, who appeared seven times for his country, was involved in some big wins, especially over Northern Ireland, who were beaten 8-2 in October 1949 and 6-1 in November 1950. However, the first time he was on the losing side—against Austria in May 1951—it signalled the end of his international career.

Mason continued to be a regular for Third Lanark until April 1953 when injury forced his premature retirement from the game. For many years afterwards, he was a licensee in Bridgton, Glasgow.

LAWRIE REILLY

Centre-forward/ Inside-left

Born: Lawrence Reilly, Edinburgh, 28 October 1928
Height: 5ft 7in
Weight: 10st 6lb
Clubs: Edinburgh Thistle; Hibernian
Scotland caps: 38
Scotland goals: 22

1949 v Wales (won 3-1), v England (won 3-1) 1 goal

1950 v France (won 2-0), v N Ireland (won 8-2) 1 goal, v Wales (won 2-0), v Switzerland (won 3-1), v France (won 1-0)

1951 v Wales (won 3-1) 2 goals, v England (won 3-2) 1 goal, v Denmark (won 3-1) 1 goal, v France (won 1-0) 1 goal, v Belgium (won 5-0), v Austria (lost 0-4)

1952 v N Ireland (won 3-0), v Wales (lost 0-1), v England (lost 1-2) 1 goal, v United States (won 6-0) 3 goals, v Denmark (won 2-1) 1 goal, v Sweden (lost 1-3)

1953 v Wales (won 2-1), v N Ireland (drew 1-1) 1 goal, v England (drew 2-2) 2 goals, v Sweden (lost 1-2)

1954 v Wales (drew 3-3) 1 goal

1955 v Hungary (lost 2-4), v England (lost 2-7) 1 goal, v Portugal (won 3-0) 1 goal, v Yugoslavia (drew 2-2) 1 goal, v Austria (won 4-1) 1 goal, v Hungary (lost 1-3)

1956 v N Ireland (lost 1-2) 1 goal, v Wales (won 2-0), v England (drew 1-1), v Austria (drew 1-1)

1957 v Wales (drew 2-2) 1 goal, v N Ireland (won 1-0), v Yugoslavia (won 2-0), v England (lost 1-2)

For Scotland, Lawrie Reilly's strike-rate eclipsed that of Denis Law and Kenny Dalglish, who share the record for most goals for Scotland. Reilly scored 22 goals in 38 appearances (including a hat-trick against the United States)—a better strike-rate than Law's 30 goals in 55 games and Dalglish's 30 goals in 102 appearances. Throughout his Scotland career, Lawrie Reilly did not go more than four internationals without scoring. He acquired the nickname 'Last Minute Reilly' after twice scoring late in a game against England in 1953 that resulted in a 2-2 draw. He was also something of a lucky charm—Reilly's first 12 games for Scotland each ended in victory!

Lawrie Reilly was a Hibs fan before he was a Hibs player. He made his debut for the Easter Road club in October 1945 in a Southern League fixture against Kilmarnock. He was aged 16, and though youth kept him out of the side that won the League Championship during the 1947-48 season, there was no doubt about his presence when Hibs again became League Champions in 1950-51 and 1951-52. Between seasons 1950-51 and 1956-57, Reilly was Hibs' leading scorer with his best return being 30 in 1952-53.

Reilly, who scored 185 goals in 253 league games for Hibs, scored many with spectacular strikes. One of his best remembered came against Falkirk in his most prolific season, when he headed a cross from Eddie Turnbull with such perfect timing that the ball screamed into the net. Against Motherwell, he collected the Motherwell keeper's clearance on the halfway line, nodded the ball over their centre-half, took the ball for a run past nearly half-a-dozen players before walking it round the Fir Park's bemused goalkeeper for a tap-in!

Sadly injuries and arrogance denied him the World Cup stage he surely deserved. By the time of the 1958 World Cup in Sweden, he had retired from the game, having had to hang up his boots because of cartilage problems on the eve of Hibs' Scottish Cup Final appearance of that year against Clyde.

At one time a painter and decorator, he later became a licensee in the Edinburgh area.

JOHNNY KELLY
Outside-left

Born: John Carmichael Kelly, Paisley, 21 February 1921
Height: 5ft 7in
Weight: 10st 12lb
Clubs: Arthurlie; Glasgow Celtic; Morton; Barnsley; Falkirk; Halifax Town; Portadown
Scotland caps: 2
1949 v Wales (won 3-1), v N Ireland (won 3-2)

A winger who could demoralise the best full-backs in the land, Johnny Kelly is the only one of Barnsley's innumerable Scottish players to win full international honours, which he did against Wales and Northern Ireland in 1949.

After working on a building site and in a bleach factory and playing football for Glasgow junior team Arthurlie, he became a professional with Celtic in 1938. During the course of that year he won junior international honours for Scotland against England and played regularly in the Celtic team during the first two wartime seasons. A hand injury sustained in previous employment disqualified him from military service and throughout the war he worked as a lorry driver.

In 1941 he joined Morton, and for four seasons their left-wing pairing was Kelly and Billy Steel—the man who in 1947 became British football's costliest player on his transfer to Derby County.

In December 1945, Kelly joined Barnsley, his performances for the Oakwell club leading to him being one of the most sought after players in the country, but the maximum wage then in operation meant he would not benefit financially by being transferred. Although the Tykes consistently refused to transfer him, there was an approach made directly to him in the summer of 1950. The offer came from the Millionarios in Bogota, Colombia, and though Kelly had no intention of going to Bogota, the Barnsley directors didn't know that and did all they could to get him to stay! When he signed for the Yorkshire club, his wife stayed at the family home in Barrhead and so the board allowed him a five-day expenses-paid visit to Barrhead each month!

On an icy pitch at Southampton in December 1950, Kelly damaged his knee so badly that he was out of the game for 12 months. When he returned to action it was apparent his best years were behind him, and a season later he joined Falkirk. He later had a second spell with Morton and seasons with Halifax Town and Portadown in the Irish League, before acting as Barnsley's Scottish scout.

BILLY HOULISTON
Centre-forward

Born: William Houliston, Dumfries, 4 April 1921
Died: 10 February 1999
Height: 5ft 10in
Weight: 12st 0lb
Clubs: Crichton Institute; Queen of the South; Berwick Rangers; Third Lanark
Scotland caps: 3

Scotland goals: 2
1949 v N Ireland (won 3-2) 2 goals, v England (won 3-1)
1950 v France (won 2-0)

Billy Houliston remains the only Queen of the South player to have won full international honours, winning his first cap against Northern Ireland in 1949. In this match he inspired his side to a 3-2 victory, scoring twice; one of his goals being among the best-ever scored at Hampden Park. Ireland had gone 2-0 up in the opening five minutes but Houliston pulled one back when ten yards from goal, he met the ball on the turn, firing it high into the net to bring the Scots back into the game. Willie Waddell provided him with a header in the dying seconds.

He made his debut for Queen of the South against Morton in 1945—it was an inauspicious match as the Dumfries side lost 7-1. However, he was to go on and score 67 goals in 154 games for the club.

His dashing and hard style earned him the nickname 'Basher', and this toughness attracted the attention of the Scotland selectors who chose him to wear the dark blue of the Scottish League against the Irish League at Parkhead in 1948. He scored twice in a 3-0 victory for the Scottish side. Shortly after his international debut came the highlight of his career when he was chosen to play against the Auld Enemy at Wembley. The home supporters booed him constantly, while the English press were critical of his performance in their after-match reports of the Scots' 3-1 victory.

In the summer he toured the United States with his Scottish team-mates. Two goals in St Louis against an All Stars XI in a 6-0 win was followed by one against the American Soccer League in New York. Sadly, though, an ankle injury brought a premature end to the tour, and he experienced an early journey home alone on the *Queen Mary*, for an operation.

Released in 1952, Berwick Rangers officials tracked him down in a pub while holidaying in Blackpool and urged him to join the club, which he did, albeit only for a season. A brief spell with Third Lanark followed before he retired. He later renewed his acquaintance with Queens in 1957 as a director, becoming chairman in 1962, and proudly taking the club back into the big time.

SAMMY COX
Left-back/ Left-half
Born: Samuel Richmond Cox, Darvel, 13 April 1924
Height: 5ft 8in
Weight: 10st 5lb
Clubs: Queen's Park; Third Lanark; Dundee; Glasgow Rangers; East Fife
Scotland caps: 24
1949 v England (won 3-1)
1950 v France (won 2-0), v N Ireland (won 8-2), v Wales (won 2-0), v England (lost 0-1), v Switzerland (won 3-1), v Portugal (drew 2-2), v France (won 1-0)
1951 v England (won 3-2), v Denmark (won 3-1), v France (won 1-0), v Belgium (won 5-0), v Austria (lost 0-4)

1952 v N Ireland (won 3-0), v Wales (lost 0-1), v United States (won 6-0),
       v Denmark (won 2-1), v Sweden (lost 1-3)
1953 v Wales (won 2-1), v N Ireland (drew 1-1), v England (drew 2-2)
1954 v N Ireland (won 3-1), v Wales (drew3-3), v England (lost 2-4)

A regular member of the Scotland team from 1949 to 1954, Sammy Cox was essentially a left-sided player, but appeared with distinction in either full-back position and either wing-half position. Indeed, he played an international match against France in Paris in 1950 as an inside-forward. He also captained Scotland against England in the Hampden match of 1954, his last appearance for the national side.

He played as a teenage amateur during the Second World War with Queen's Park, Third Lanark and Dundee before, in May 1946, joining Rangers as a professional. Within a year he had established himself as a vital member of the Rangers team, playing in every League game of the 1947-48 season.

Cox, whose play was characterised by balance, quickness and a supreme confidence based on his exceptional technical ability, helped Rangers win four League Championship titles, a League Cup and three Scottish Cup Finals. He also possessed a sophisticated football brain which, in spite of his slight frame, allowed him to make the most crisp and incisive tackles. His positional and tactical sense led him to base his defensive work on manoeuvring opponents into dead-end situations and he had particular success against greats such as Tom Finney and Stanley Matthews.

Sammy Cox went on to score 18 goals in 310 games during a 10-year career with Rangers, then played a few more seasons with East Fife before emigrating to Canada in 1959.

GEORGE AITKEN
Wing-half
Born: George Graham Aitken, Lochgelly, 28 May 1925
Died: 22 January 2003
Height: 5ft 10in
Weight: 11st 12lb
Clubs: Wolverhampton Wanderers; Lochgelly St Andrew's; East Fife; Third Lanark; Sunderland; Gateshead
Scotland caps: 8
1949 v England (won 3-1), v France (won 2-0)
1950 v N Ireland (won 8-2), v Wales (won 2-0), v Switzerland (won 3-1)
1953 v Wales (won 2-1), v N Ireland (drew 1-1)
1954 v England (lost 2-4)

Capped eight times by Scotland, the first in a 3-1 win over England in April 1949, wing-half George Aitken won his first five caps with East Fife—a club record—and was on the winning side each time. In fact, the only time Aitken was on the losing side was his last appearance at national level, as Scotland went down 4-2 to England at Hampden Park in April 1954.

On leaving school, Aitken joined Wolverhampton Wanderers but was unable to settle in the Midlands and returned home to become a miner at the Jenny Gray Colliery in Lochgelly. Playing for Lochgelly St Andrew's, his performances attracted the attention of a number of Scottish clubs, and in 1943, he signed for East Fife. He wasn't called up for military service as mining was a 'reserved occupation', and so was able to play regularly for the Fifers during the war.

He made his official debut for East Fife against Dundee in August 1946 and became part of the legendary half-back line of which the two other members were Jimmy Philp and Willie McKinlay. He was also a member of the East Fife teams that won the League Cup in 1947 and 1949 and 'B' Division in 1947-48. Having scored seven goals in 136 games for East Fife, he refused to resign for the Bayview Park club at the start of the 1950-51 season and was out of football until his transfer to Third Lanark in February 1951.

His stay with the now defunct Scottish club was brief, and in November of that year he was transferred to Sunderland for a fee of £19,500. A virtual ever-present for the next six seasons, Aitken, who played in the sides that reached the FA Cup semi-finals in 1955 and 1956, took his tally of League and Cup appearances for the Wearsiders to 267 before leaving Roker Park in March 1959 to join Gateshead. He remained with them until they were voted out of the Football League, when he decided to hang up his boots.

THE 1950s

Scotland lost their first-ever match against a foreign team in December 1950 when Austria won 1-0. The return fixture was even worse: Scotland lost 4-0 in Vienna in May 1951 when Billy Steel became the first Scottish international to be sent off.

The possibility of qualifying for the 1954 World Cup in Switzerland looked a strong one and so the SFA decided for the first time ever to appoint an individual to manage the national team. The man selected was Andy Beattie, manager of Huddersfield Town, himself a former Scottish international. Having beaten Northern Ireland and drawn with Wales, it seemed as if the match against England at Hampden Park would determine whether or not the Scots would go to the finals. They were dealt a double blow when Lawrie Reilly and George Young were declared unfit, but following Wales' defeat of Northern Ireland the night before the England game, Scotland were guaranteed second place in the Home International Championship and a place in the World Cup Finals. For the record, England beat Scotland 4-2 —it was a very disappointing display by the home side.

Scotland's opening game in the 1954 finals saw them take on Austria and after having early appeals for a penalty turned down, they fell behind to a 35th minute strike by Probst. Though it turned out to be the only goal of the game, Mochan's last minute effort brought a fine save out of the Austrian keeper Schmied. The Scots nation eagerly awaited the next game against Uruguay, especially as the teams' performance against Austria had been one of the best since the war. As the match began, the Swiss fans, impressed by Scotland's showing against Austria, got firmly behind the Scots, but by the end of the game, which Uruguay won 7-0, they were jeering the Scots' every move.

For the 1958 World Cup, Scotland were placed in a tough European qualifying section—facing Spain and Switzerland in a three-team group with only one country qualifying for the finals. The Spaniards, who reckoned they were the best team in Europe, were beaten 4-2 at Hampden with Jackie Mudie netting a hat-trick. He scored the winner in Scotland's next group game, a 2-1 defeat of Switzerland in Basle, but then a 4-1 defeat by Spain in Madrid left Scotland needing to beat Switzerland at Hampden for a place in the finals. It was a hard fought game but Scotland won 3-2. Matt Busby was named as Scotland's manager for the finals in Sweden but in February of that year, he was severely injured in the Munich air crash and went into a coma. He later received regular blood transfusions and was placed in an oxygen tent.

In his prolonged absence, goalkeeper and captain Tommy Younger gave the team talks, and Scotland, who had a 'goal' disallowed in the final moments, drew their opening game against Yugoslavia 1-1. The second game against Paraguay saw the Scots go down 3-2 to leave them bottom of their group, whilst in their final match against France, they lost 2-1. Towards the end of this match, Collins put Mudie clear on goal, but he stumbled over the ball, and as the chance went missing, the Scottish World Cup effort was ended for the 1950s.

HENRY MORRIS
Centre-forward

Born: Henry Miller Morris, Dundee, 17 December 1919
Died: Kirkcaldy 13 March 1993
Height: 5ft 10in
Weight: 12st 6lb
Clubs: Lochee Central; Dundee Violet; East Fife; Dundee United; Portadown
Scotland caps: 1
Scotland goals: 3
1950 v N Ireland (won 8-2) 3 goals

Henry Morris was the only player to have scored three goals on his international debut for Scotland and never be capped again! The match against Northern Ireland at Windsor Park, Belfast, which the Scots won 8-2, was Scotland's first-ever World Cup qualifying match.

Henry Morris started his career in his native Dundee with Lochee Central and then junior club Dundee Violet before appearing in just one wartime game for Dundee. He was signed by East Fife in June 1946 and made his Scottish League debut against his home-town team the following August. During the course of his first season with the Bayview Park club, he proved himself to be a prolific scorer, finding the net 33 times.

In 1947-48 when East Fife won the 'B' Division and League Cup, beating Falkirk 4-1 after a goalless draw, Morris scored 41 League goals—a total equalling the club record set by Jock Wood in 1926-27. Also that season he netted 13 goals in Scottish Cup and League Cup games, plus eight in the Supplementary Cup which East Fife also won.

In the same month that Morris made his international debut, he was a member of the East Fife team that won the League Cup for a second time, scoring one of the goals in the 3-0 defeat of Dunfermline Athletic. During the 1950-51 season he lost his place in the team, though he spent another couple of seasons playing reserve team football before, in May 1953, after scoring 154 goals in 177 games, he left East Fife to join Dundee United. Six months later he left Tannadice and ended his career with a short spell playing for Portadown.

JOHN McPHAIL
Utility Player

Born: John McPhail, Lambhill, Glasgow, 27 December 1923
Died: 8 November 2000
Height: 5ft 11in
Weight: 12st 0lb

Clubs: St Mungo's Academy; Glasgow Celtic
Scotland caps: 5
Scotland goals: 3
1950 v Wales (won 2-0) 1 goal
1951 v Wales (won 3-1), v N Ireland (won 6-1) 2 goals, v Austria (lost 0-1)
1954 v N Ireland (won 3-1)

Utility player John McPhail won his first cap for Scotland against Wales in November 1949, and scored the opening goal at a fog-bound Hampden Park as Scotland went on to win 2-0. Having played regularly for his country in 1951, he was a shock choice as centre-forward for Scotland against Northern Ireland in Belfast in October 1953, and though the Scots won 3-1, it was the last of his five appearances at international level.

Known as 'Hooky' because of the 'extraordinary way he jab-cutted the ball with his right foot', he broke into the Celtic League team as a versatile player during the war years. By the time the 1946-47 season got underway, he was seriously ill in hospital with tuberculosis, and missed virtually the whole campaign.

On making a full recovery, he was appointed Celtic's captain, and in the Charity Cup Trophy Final in May 1950, he netted a hat-trick against Rangers in the space of just eight minutes. He also scored the only goal of the game as the Scottish League beat the Football League 1-0. In the Scottish Cup Final of 1951, he scored the game's only goal as Celtic beat Motherwell to win their first Scottish Cup since 1937.

After a couple of seasons he began to be troubled by weight problems and he was sent to a health farm in Tring to diet off the excess. Unable to lose the weight, he was reluctant to play in midfield, but did lead the attack in the Scottish Cup Final against Clyde in April 1955, which ended all-square at 1-1. He was dropped for the replay and thereafter his appearances grew fewer. Retiring in May 1956, McPhail, who had scored 87 goals in 204 appearances, went to work as a journalist for the *Daily Record*, and later for the club newspaper.

ALEX LINWOOD
Centre-forward
Born: Alexander Bryce Linwood, Drumsmudden, 13 March 1920
Died: 26 October 2003
Height: 5ft 9in
Weight: 11st 7lb
Clubs: Muirkirk Athletic; St Mirren; Middlesbrough; Hibernian; Clyde; Morton
Scotland caps: 1
Scotland goals: 1
1950 v Wales (won 2-0) 1 goal

Alex Linwood was unlucky enough to play in the wartime international against England at Maine Road when Scotland were beaten 8-0. Even so, he touched the ball more than his team-mates... 9 times... but they were all kick-offs!

On leaving school, he went into the mines near Drongan in Ayrshire. Playing for Muirkirk Juniors, he soon attracted the scouts of Hearts, St Mirren, Ayr and Kilmarnock, and in 1938 he signed for St Mirren. But then war broke out and although he continued to play, he had to go back down the pit as part of the war effort. Linwood was transferred to Middlesbrough in 1946, but failed to settle at Ayresome Park, and so a season later was transferred to Hibs. Again, after just one season at Easter Road, he was on the move again, this time to Clyde for a fee of £8,000.

At the end of his first season, Clyde reached the Scottish Cup Final against Rangers but were beaten 4-1. Despite this, the Bully Wee flirted dangerously with relegation and finished third from bottom, missing the drop by just two points!

Linwood, who played in a 1-0 win over the Irish League in 1949, also scored in his only full international appearance as Wales were beaten 2-0 at Hampden Park in April 1950, with John McPhail getting the other goal. His best season in terms of goals scored for Clyde was 1949-50 when he found the net 30 times.

He spent just over three seasons at Shawfield Park before leaving to see out his career with Morton for whom he played until 1955.

IAN McCOLL
Right-half

Born: John Miller McColl, Alexandria, 7 June 1927
Height: 5ft 10in
Weight: 11st 6lb
Clubs: Vale of Leven; Queen's Park; Glasgow Rangers
Scotland caps: 14
1950 v England (lost 0-1), v France (won 1-0)
1951 v Wales (won 3-1), v N Ireland (won 6-1), v Belgium (won 5-0)
1957 v Wales (drew 2-2), v N Ireland (won 1-0), v Yugoslavia (won 2-0), v England (lost 1-2), v Spain (won 4-2), v Switzerland (won 2-1), v West Germany (won 3-1)
1958 v N Ireland (drew 1-1), v England (lost 0-4)

The grandson of William McColl, the Renton centre-half who represented Scotland in 1895, he developed into one of Scotland's finest right-halves. McColl, who played for the national side on 14 occasions, was only on the losing side three times, all against England!

Having played his early football for the Vale of Leven club, he joined Queen's Park in 1943, before, two years later, signing for Rangers. He soon established himself in the side and his displays for the Ibrox club led to him representing the Scottish League XI prior to him making his full international debut against England at Hampden in April 1950.

McColl ended the first season of peacetime football with a League Championship and League Cup winners' medal, and was to win a host of domestic honours with the Ibrox side—six League Championship medals and success in five Scottish Cup Finals and two League Cup Finals. One of his

Ian McColl

best displays in a Rangers shirt came in the 1960 Scottish Cup Final against Kilmarnock. Recalled to the side following a long absence, he was totally committed and his excellent passing skills set up both his side's goals in a 2-0 win over the Rugby Park club.

McColl, who played in over 400 games for Rangers, was still turning out for the club when he was appointed manager of Scotland. Though he didn't have sole charge of the national side— the SFA picked the teams and also had a great say in tactics—the results were indifferent, the best result being a 6-2 win in Spain in June 1963.

Within a month of leaving his post, he was appointed manager of Sunderland. He spent £340,000 on new players, including Jim Baxter from his former club and Neil Martin from Hibs, but they rarely showed good form. The club just avoided relegation to the Second Division, but disappointing results the following season led to McColl, who was a qualified engineer, having gained his BSc at Edinburgh University, parting company with the Wearsiders.

WILLIE MOIR
Inside-right

Born: William Moir, Bucksburn, 19 April 1922
Died: 9 May 1988
Height: 5ft 8in
Weight: 9st 13lb
Clubs: Bucksburn Juniors; Bolton Wanderers; Stockport County
Scotland caps: 1
1950 v England (lost 0-1)

During the Second World War, Willie Moir joined the RAF and was posted to a camp at Kirkham in Lancashire where he was spotted playing for the station team by Bolton Wanderers' chief scout Bob Jackson in April 1943. Moir signed for Bolton as an amateur, and within a fortnight had signed as professional. During the war he 'guested' for Aberdeen and Dundee and played for Bolton in the North v South Cup Final in 1945.

He went on to play in every position in the forward line for the Wanderers but had most success at inside-right. After the resumption of League football, Moir played mostly at outside-left, although he was a naturally right-footed player. At the beginning of the 1948-49 season, however, he was switched to inside-right and scored four goals in a 4-2 win at Aston Villa. He went on to play in every League game that season and topped the First Division scoring charts with 25 goals.

Moir's only Scottish appearance came against England in Glasgow in April 1950, and, as club captain, he led the Bolton team out at Wembley in the legendary 1953 'Matthews Final'. The fact that Moir scored one of Bolton's goals was of little consolation, as his depleted side lost 4-3 to Blackpool.

Two years later, in September 1955, after scoring 134 goals in 358 League and Cup games, Moir joined Stockport County. Playing alongside the prolific Jack Connor in a County side which scored 90 and 91 goals respectively over the next two seasons, his reputation as a leader saw him elevated to the manager's seat for the start of the 1956-57 season. He continued to play until February 1958 and though his third season in charge saw County 'qualify' for the newly formed Third Division, this was followed by relegation to Division Four.

After losing his job in the summer of 1960, Moir joined Lancashire Combination side Nelson as manager and then scouted for them before becoming a sales representative. He then renewed his links with Bolton, helping out on the commercial side until his death in May 1988.

WILLIE BAULD

Centre-forward

Born: William Russell Logan Baird, Newcraighall, Edinburgh, 24 January 1928
Died: 11 March 1977
Height: 5ft 8in
Weight: 11st 4lb
Clubs: Edinburgh Waverley; Musselburgh Athletic; Heart of Midlothian; Newtongrange Star; Edinburgh City
Scotland caps: 3
Scotland goals: 2
1950 v England (lost 0-1), v Switzerland (won 3-1) 1 goal, v Portugal (drew 2-2) 1 goal

It was in 1950 that Willie Bauld won his three international caps for Scotland— against England, Switzerland and Portugal—and if there were no more to follow in the years ahead, at least Bauld could content himself with a rush of silver at club level for Heart of Midlothian.

The young Bauld had many admirers north and south of the border, and though he put pen to paper on a professional deal with Sunderland, the deal could never be formalised and it was the quick-thinking of the then secretary at Tynecastle, Jimmy Kean, that managed to steer Willie Bauld to the club he had always supported. Yet even Bauld had to serve an apprenticeship, and he was farmed out to Newtongrange Star and Edinburgh City before he made his first team debut for Hearts just three months short of his 21st birthday. He could hardly have marked his arrival in more dramatic style, scoring a hat-trick in a 6-1 defeat of East Fife and then repeating the feat in his next match as Queen of the South were beaten 4-0. Not surprisingly he finished his first season as the club's top scorer with 24 goals.

Under manager Tommy Walker, the Tynecastle club were to win seven trophies in nine years, ending a 48-year famine with a 4-2 defeat of Motherwell in the 1954 League Cup Final, with Bauld netting a hat-trick.

Bauld was often accused of being laid-back in his approach to the game, but it was just that he had the ability to drift through games and then seize the moment when it came! In his 16 years at Tynecastle, Willie Bauld scored 355 goals in 510 appearances, 183 of which came in just 292 league games.

Though he was honoured with a testimonial game against Sheffield United in November 1962, when he received his cheque he found that the price of the match ball and other expenses had been deducted! It was to be over 12 years before Bauld returned to Tynecastle, but, in 1977, the whole of Edinburgh was stunned when he died prematurely after attending a supporters' function.

BOBBY DOUGAN
Centre-half
Born: Robert Dougan, Glasgow, 3 December 1926
Height: 5ft 11in
Weight: 11st 1lb
Clubs: Shawfield Juniors; Heart of Midlothian; Kilmarnock
Scotland caps: 1
1950 v Switzerland (won 3-1)

Though he was signed by Hearts from Shawfield Juniors in September 1946, Bobby Dougan was allowed to play at junior level for a further period and during that time earned international honours and a Scottish Junior Cup winners' medal.

When he arrived at Tynecastle, Dougan was a constructive wing-half and though he impressed the fans, he earned greater acclaim when he moved to centre-half in 1948. He was a cultured player whose positional sense and creative ability set him aside from other defenders of that era. Indeed, only a series of injuries prevented the tall Glaswegian from gaining the highest honours in the game.

By the age of 23, his displays at the heart of the Tynecastle club's defence led to him winning what, surprisingly, turned out to be his only full international cap, when he had a good game in the 3-1 defeat of Switzerland at Hampden Park. He then played twice for the Scottish League XI, but in the second game in September 1951 he suffered a severe ankle injury that saw him sidelined for almost a year. He came back to establish himself again in the Hearts side and was selected for a third time for the Scottish League against the Football League in March 1953. Unfortunately, Bobby Dougan was then hampered by further injuries, and in 1953-54 when the Tynecastle club finished runners-up in the First Division, he was out for a long spell after a cartilage operation.

He never full recovered and in December 1954 after appearing in 212 games for Hearts, he was allowed to join Kilmarnock for a fee of £4,300. He served the Rugby Park club well, helping them to the 1957 Scottish Cup Final, where they lost 2-1 to Falkirk after a 1-1 draw, and to finish runners-up to his former club in the First Division in 1959-60. After this he retired.

ALLAN BROWN
Inside-forward

Born: Allan Duncan Brown, Kennoway, 12 October 1926
Height: 5ft 10in
Weight: 11st 12lb
Clubs: East Fife; Blackpool; Luton Town; Portsmouth; Wigan Athletic
Scotland caps: 14
Scotland goals: 6
1950 v Switzerland (won 3-1) 1 goal, v Portugal (drew 2-2) 1 goal, v France (won 1-0) 1 goal
1952 v United States (won 6-0), v Denmark (won 2-1), v Sweden (lost 1-3)
1953 v Wales (won 2-1) 1 goal
1954 v Wales (drew 3-3) 1 goal, v England (lost 2-4) 1 goal, v Norway (won 1-0),
     v Norway (drew 1-1), v Finland (won 2-1), v Austria (lost 0-1), v Uruguay (lost 0-7)

Allan played for Scotland in the 1954 World Cup Finals, and, but for injuries, would have won more than 14 caps. His first three appearances for the national side came while he was with East Fife, and on each occasion he found the net.

He played several times for East Fife during the war, before making his Scottish League debut against Dunfermline Athletic in January 1947. He was then called up for National Service, and spent much of his time in India before, in 1948-49, he became a regular in the East Fife side. A member of the side that won the League Cup, he scored the opening goal in the 2-1 League Cup semi-final defeat of Rangers—the first time the Fifers had beaten the Glasgow giants in a peacetime match. Brown refused to re-sign for East Fife at the start of the 1950-51 season, and was out of football until the end of the year when Blackpool paid £27,500 for his signature.

Brown was virtually ever-present in the Blackpool side for the next seven seasons, though injuries were to rule him out of both the club's FA Cup Final appearances at Wembley in 1951 and 1953. In 1951 he damaged his right knee in the match at Huddersfield, while two years later he broke his leg when scoring the 88th minute winner in the FA Cup sixth round defeat of Arsenal. Linking up well with Stan Mortensen, Brown scored 14 goals in 37 games in 1951-52 including hat-tricks in away wins at Newcastle United and Stoke City. Brown's best season in terms of goals scored was 1952-53 when his total of 15 in 29 games included another treble in a 5-1 win at Aston Villa.

Allan Brown in his days as a manager

In February 1957, Brown, who had scored 74 goals in 185 games, left the Seasiders to play for Luton Town. Thankfully injuries didn't prevent him from playing for the Hatters in the 1959 FA Cup Final, but they were beaten 2-1 by Nottingham Forest. After ending his first-class playing career with Portsmouth, he went into management with Cheshire League Wigan Athletic. Under his management the Latics won four trophies in a season and went 52 games without defeat!

Luton Town saw his potential and appointed him manager in November 1966. The Hatters were firmly rooted to the foot of the Fourth Division but within two years he had led them to that division's Championship. There followed managerial spells with Torquay United, Bury, Nottingham Forest and Southport before he returned to Bloomfield Road to take over the reins at Blackpool.

The Seasiders were relegated to the Third Division for the first time in their history and Brown was sacked. After a spell coaching in Kuwait he returned to Bloomfield Road for a second spell as the club's manager. Unable to prevent their relegation to the League's basement, he again parted company with the club.

WILLIE McNAUGHT
Left-back
Born: William McNaught, Dumfries, 7 May 1922
Height: 5ft 10in
Weight: 11st 10lb
Clubs: Dumfries Park Rovers; Dundee North End; Raith Rovers; Brechin City
Scotland caps: 5
1951 v Wales (won 3-1), v N Ireland (won 6-1), v Austria (lost 0-1)
1952 v England (lost 1-2)
1955 v N Ireland (drew 2-2)

The father of Ken McNaught, who won numerous honours with Aston Villa and Everton, he played his early football for Dumfries Park Rovers, whilst during the Second World War he had a few games with Dundee North End.

In 1941 he joined Raith Rovers and during his first few years with the club, he showed his versatility by playing in a variety of positions including inside-forward, outside-left and half-back before settling at left-back. When League football resumed in 1946-47, McNaught was Raith's first-choice left-back, his performances earning him selection for the Scottish League XI.

In 1948-49 he helped the club finish the campaign as champions of the Scottish League 'B' Division. It was an exciting season with Rovers winning the title from Stirling Albion on goal difference. Also that season, Raith reached the Scottish Cup Final but lost 2-0 to Rangers.

McNaught's consistency on the left side of the Raith defence led to him winning the first of five full international caps against Wales at Ninian Park in October 1950, a match the Scots won 3-1. He kept his place for the visit of

Northern Ireland and had little to do in a 6-1 rout of the Irish. He lost his place after a defeat by Austria before earning a recall against England in April 1952. Marking the legendary Tom Finney, he gave a good account of himself but two Stan Pearson goals gave the visitors a 2-1 win. McNaught's final appearance in a Scotland shirt came two-and-a-half years later against Northern Ireland.

McNaught, who had a number of games towards the end of his Stark's Park career at centre-half, was named Scotland's 'Player of the Year' for 1956. He remained with Raith until 1962 when he left to end his career with Brechin City. Midway through his first season, when in his 41st year, he retired, and after scouting for Sunderland, he became coach of Ladybank Victoria.

BOBBY COLLINS
Inside-forward

Born: Robert Young Collins, Glasgow, 16 February 1931
Height: 5ft 4in
Weight: 10st 3lb
Clubs: Glasgow Celtic; Everton; Leeds United; Bury; Morton; Ringwood City; Hakoah (Australia); Shamrock Rovers; Oldham Athletic
Scotland caps: 31
Scotland goals: 10

1951 v Wales (won 3-1), v N Ireland (won 6-1), v Austria (lost 0-1)
1955 v Yugoslavia (drew 2-2), v Austria (won 4-1), v Hungary (lost 1-3)
1956 v N Ireland (lost 1-2), v Wales (won 2-0)
1957 v Wales (drew 2-2), v England (lost 1-2), v Spain (won 4-2),
　　　　v Switzerland (won 2-1) 1 goal, v West Germany (won 3-1) 2 goals, v Spain (lost 1-4)
1958 v N Ireland (drew 1-1), v Switzerland (won 3-2), v Wales (drew 1-1) 1 goal,
　　　　v Hungary (drew 1-1), v Poland (won 2-1) 2 goals, v Yugoslavia (drew 1-1),
　　　　v Paraguay (lost 2-3) 1 goal, v France (lost 1-2)
1959 v Wales (won 3-0) 1 goal, v N Ireland (drew 2-2) 1 goal, v England (lost 0-1),
　　　　v West Germany (won 3-2), v Holland (won 2-1) 1 goal, v Portugal (lost 0-1)
1965 v England (drew 2-2), v Spain (drew 0-0), v Poland (drew 1-1)

One of the game's greatest inside-forwards, Bobby Collins began his career with Celtic, making his debut in a 3-2 defeat of Rangers in a Scottish League Cup tie in August 1949. In 10 years at Parkhead, he won a Scottish League Championship medal in 1954, Scottish Cup winners' medals in 1957 and 1958, and appeared for the Scottish League 16 times. He remains one of the few players to score a hat-trick of penalties, which he did against Aberdeen in September 1953. During his final season with Celtic, Collins, who had won his first international cap in 1951, scored heavily to take his tally of goals to 115 in 320 games before, in September 1958, he joined Everton for £23,000.

Nicknamed 'the Little General', he became captain under the Blues' newly appointed manager Johnny Carey, and for two seasons was arguably the major factor in the club retaining their top flight status. Collins' supreme talent was to make Everton play, dictating the pattern of games with his crisp, incisive passes. He loved the ball, using it to pick out his team-mates in dangerous positions with astonishing accuracy. He was quick too, yet, in March 1962, this complete footballer was allowed to join Leeds United for £25,000.

Collins was the platform on which Don Revie launched his great sixties side. He captained Leeds to the Second Division title in 1963-64 and the following season was voted Footballer of the Year as United came close to the League and Cup double. He was also recalled to the Scottish side after an absence of six years.

He left Elland Road on a free transfer to join Bury and then embarked on a journey which took in Morton and Australian clubs Ringwood and Hakoah. He had a spell with Shamrock Rovers, followed by Oldham Athletic, where he was the club's player-coach before stepping up to assistant-manager.

Collins later held a number of coaching and management posts before leaving the game to spend eight years working in the wholesale fashion business. Now retired after two years working as a driver at Leeds University, he still plays in the occasional charity match.

BOBBY JOHNSTONE
Inside-forward
Born: Robert Johnstone, Selkirk, 7 September 1929
Height: 5ft 7in
Weight: 10st 7lb
Clubs: Newtongrange Star; Hibernian; Manchester City; Oldham Athletic; Witton Albion
Scotland caps: 17
Scotland goals: 9
1951 v England (won 3-2) 1 goal, v Denmark (won 3-1), v France (won 1-0)
1952 v N Ireland (won 3-0) 2 goals, v England (lost 1-2)
1953 v England (drew 2-2), v Sweden (lost 1-2)
1954 v Wales (drew 3-3) 1 goal, v England (lost 2-4), v Norway (won 1-0),
        v Finland (won 2-1) 1 goal
1955 v N Ireland (drew 2-2) 1 goal, v Hungary (lost 2-4) 1 goal, v England (lost 2-7)
1956 v N Ireland (lost 1-2), v Wales won 2-0) 2 goals, v England (drew 1-1)

One of Hibernian's 'Famous Five', Bobby Johnstone, the winner of 17 Scottish caps, was the creative cog in the combination, and though he was the main supplier to Gordon Smith, he was so abundantly blessed with skill that he could score goals as well. Though the five only really performed as a unit for six years, the successes achieved by Hibs at the time—three League titles in five years—are synonymous with them. His performances alongside the likes of Smith, Turnbull, Reilly and Ormond brought him to the attention of a host of top clubs south of the Border, and it was Manchester City who secured his services in March 1955.

After making his debut in a 4-2 home win over Bolton Wanderers, he went on to become an important member of the City side. In January 1956 he scored the first of three hat-tricks for the club in a 4-1 defeat of Portsmouth, and at the end of the season, in which he had scored 16 goals in 38 games, he played in the FA Cup Final defeat against Newcastle United. The following season in which he scored further hat-tricks against Chelsea and Cardiff City, Johnstone became the first man to score in successive Wembley Cup Finals when he netted in City's 3-1 win over Birmingham. Whilst with City, Johnstone won a further four Scottish caps and represented Great Britain against the Rest of Europe.

In September 1959, Johnstone returned to play for Hibernian, but within a few months had returned to the north-west to play for Oldham Athletic. The highest Boundary Park crowd for over six years—17,116—saw him score on his debut as the Latics beat Exeter City 5-2. He went on to score 42 goals in 143 games for Oldham before hanging up his boots.

The architect of many wonderful wins for both Hibernian and Manchester City—and the creator of countless magical moments in football—Johnstone can be compared favourably with the likes of Mannion and Doherty as a schemer and ball-artist.

JIMMY SCOULAR
Right-half
Born: James Scoular, Livingston, 11 January 1925
Died: 19 March 1998
Height: 5ft 7in
Weight: 11st 6lb
Clubs: Gosport Borough; Portsmouth; Newcastle United; Bradford Park Avenue
Scotland caps: 9
1951 v Denmark (won 3-1), v France (won 1-0), v Austria (lost 0-4)
1952 v England (lost 1-2), v United States (won 6-0), v Denmark (won 2-1), v Sweden (lost 1-3)
1953 v Wales (won 2-1), v N Ireland (drew 1-1)

One of the biggest characters of the immediate post-war years, Jimmy Scoular was born in Livingston, the son of a miner. On leaving school, he became a steel-foundry worker, though he had always had a keen interest in football. His father Alex had played in the Scottish League for a number of clubs and at 14, Jimmy was following in his footsteps, being capped by his country and reaching Scottish international trials.

He won junior caps before joining the Royal Navy in 1943, when he was posted 500 miles away from his home—to *HMS Dolphin* near Portsmouth. There he played for Gosport Borough and the Navy team. Both Southampton and Portsmouth showed an interest in signing the 17-year-old, but it was Pompey who secured his signature. Though he signed professional forms in December 1945, he could not devote his attention to full-time football until his demobilisation a year later. For almost seven seasons, he was part of a great half-back line of Scoular, Flewin and Dickinson—the backbone of Portsmouth's League Championship victories of 1948-49 and 1949-50. Nicknamed 'Ironman' by the press, Scoular had an unshakable will to win. He was always in the thick of the action and was sent-off a few times, including the first match of the club's South American tour of 1951.

He was capped nine times by Scotland while at Fratton Park, winning the first in a 3-1 win over Denmark in 1951.

After appearing in 264 League and Cup games for Pompey, he moved to Newcastle United for £22,250. Appointed captain in place of Joe Harvey, he skippered the Magpies to Wembley in 1955, and helped bring the FA Cup to Tyneside for the third time in five seasons. He had played in 271 games for Newcastle when he accepted the player-manager's job at Bradford Park Avenue.

He took them to Division Three and then saw the club relegated two years later. Scoular finally hung up his boots in March 1964, and later that year became manager of Cardiff City. In the nine years he was in charge at Ninian Park, Cardiff won the Welsh Cup seven times and reached the semi-finals of the European Cup Winners' Cup in 1967-68. A brief stay with Newport County followed until he left the manager's merry-go round in January 1978.

BOBBY MITCHELL
Outside-left

Born: Robert Carmichael Mitchell, Glasgow, 16 August 1924
Died: Newcastle-upon-Tyne, 8 April 1993
Height: 5ft 11in
Weight: 11st 11lb
Clubs: Third Lanark; Newcastle United; Berwick Rangers; Gateshead
Scotland caps: 2
Scotland goals: 1
1951 v Denmark (won 3-1) 1 goal, v France (won 1-0)

Scotland honoured Bobby Mitchell only twice, for he was to be second choice to Liverpool's Billy Liddell throughout his career.

Soon after signing for Third Lanark he was drafted into the Navy as a telegraphist and posted to destinations as far as Sydney. After the war, Portsmouth wanted to sign him, but he preferred to return home to Scotland and back to Third Lanark, where he made his first team debut. Mitchell quickly climbed to the top, being picked for the Scottish League side in 1946 and becoming Scotland's top League scorer a year later with 22 goals. His lazy, deceptive stride, shooting and crossing ability had the mark of greatness about it, and when Newcastle United signed him for £16,000 in February 1949, it was a record fee for a winger.

For the next decade and over, Newcastle fans witnessed many outstanding performances. In the FA Cup runs of 1951 and 1952, Mitchell was every bit as much a dangerman as Milburn. He figured strongly in both finals and also at Wembley for a third time against Manchester City in 1955. Mitchell scored one of the goals in a 3-1 win, and though he was now at the veteran stage of his career, he remained with the Magpies for a further six years.

Towards the end of the fifties, he found himself in and out of the Newcastle side and agreed terms with Notts County before the deal fell through. He went on to make 408 appearances for United and was almost 37 years old when he played his last game for the club.

He left St James Park in the summer of 1961, joining Berwick Rangers. He later returned to Tyneside as player-manager of Gateshead, but quickly became disillusioned with football and left the scene soon afterwards.

TOMMY ORR
Inside-forward

Born: Thomas Bingham Orr, Greenock, 21 April 1924
Died: 20 June 1972
Height: 5ft 11in
Weight: 12st 4lb
Clubs: Morton
Scotland caps: 2
Scotland goals: 1
1952 v N Ireland (won 3-0) 1 goal, v Wales (lost 0-1)

Morton inside-forward Tommy Orr scored on his international debut in a 3-0 win over Northern Ireland at Windsor Park, Belfast in October 1951, and though he kept his place for Scotland's next match, a 1-0 home defeat at the hands of Wales, it proved to be his final appearance for his country.

Joining the Cappielow Park club in 1942, Tommy Orr went on to give long and distinguished service, playing his last game in 1958.

During the Second World War, he 'guested' for Arsenal, and though the Highbury club wanted to sign him on a permanent basis, he returned to Scotland to continue his career with Morton. In 1948, Orr was a member of the Morton side that upset the odds by reaching the Scottish Cup Final. Though they held the mighty Rangers to a 1-1 draw, they lost 1-0 in the replay, this after Orr had almost won the game for them with a shot that came back off an upright.

In 1949-50, Orr was in outstanding form as Morton won the Second Division Championship, finishing the campaign three points ahead of runners-up Airdrieonians.

In the early fifties, Orr had a number of chances to leave Morton and continue his career with much more fashionable clubs north and south of the border. He opted to stay with The Ton, for whom his son Neil later played, and still holds the club record for the transfer fee received when he joined West Ham United for £350,000.

TOMMY DOCHERTY
Wing-half

Born: Thomas Henderson Docherty, Glasgow, 24 April 1928
Height: 5ft 6in
Weight: 10st 10lb
Clubs: Shettleston Juniors; Glasgow Celtic; Preston North End; Arsenal; Chelsea
Scotland caps: 25

Scotland goals: I

1952 v Wales (lost 0-1)
1953 v England (drew 2-2), v Sweden (lost 1-2)
1954 v Norway (won 1-0), v Norway (drew 1-1), v Austria (lost 0-1), v Uruguay (lost 0-7)
1955 v Wales (won 1-0), v Hungary (lost 2-4), v England (lost 2-7) I goal, v Austria (won 4-1),
       v Hungary (lost 1-3)
1957 v Yugoslavia (won 2-0), v England (lost 1-2), v Spain (won 4-2), v Switzerland (won 2-1),
       v West Germany (won 3-1), v Spain (lost 1-4)
1958 v N Ireland (drew 1-1), v Switzerland (won 3-2), v Wales (drew 1-1),
       v England (lost 0-4)
1959 v Wales (won 3-0), v N Ireland (drew 1-1), v England (lost 0-1)

Tommy Docherty

The irrepressible Tommy Docherty, one of the best-known characters in soccer, has now come to the end of his career in football, but in his day, he was dedicated, dynamic, reckless, ruthless, seldom predictable and always controversial.

Tommy Docherty started life in Glasgow's notorious Gorbals, and after junior football and National Service with the Highland Light Infantry—he played for the regiment in Palestine—he signed for Glasgow Celtic in June 1948. In the shadow of the great Bobby Evans at Parkhead, he soon moved to Preston North End as a replacement for Bill Shankly, who had retired a year earlier to take up coaching duties with North End's reserve team.

The Scottish international selectors were greatly impressed by Docherty's displays at wing-half, and after making his debut against Wales in November 1951, he went on to win a total of 25 caps.

Docherty had been at Deepdale eight seasons when Preston manager Cliff Britton, bowing to the Scotsman's persistent and mystifying requests for a move, transferred him to Arsenal for £28,000 in August 1958. Docherty had appeared in 323 of a possible 356 league games for North End, missing 21 through injury and seven through international calls. Only Shankly with 294 games had a comparable record as a North End wing-half. Tragically ironic for Docherty was his misfortune in breaking a leg when playing for the Gunners against North End!

Stamford Bridge was his next port of call when he was signed as a player-coach in February 1961. Shortly afterwards, manager Ted Drake left and Docherty was put in charge. He could not prevent Chelsea's relegation in his first season but they bounced straight back the following term. The League Cup was won in 1965, and the Doc also took Chelsea to their first Wembley Cup Final. Docherty resigned as Chelsea manager in October 1967, and after taking charge of both Rotherham United and Queen's Park Rangers he was appointed manager of Aston Villa. Though he became a great favourite with the fans and attendances doubled, the bubble burst when midway through the 1969-70 season Villa were bottom of Division Two and he was sacked.

In September 1971 the Doc became Scotland's national team manager. The Scots made a remarkable recovery when he took over the reins and he restored the team's pride. But in December 1972 he accepted an offer to manage Manchester United.

Certainly the United job seemed to suit him and he assembled some exciting sides during his four and a half years at Old Trafford. Although he steered them clear of relegation, they dropped into Division Two in 1974, winning the title at the first attempt the following season. In 1975-76 the Reds finished third in Division One and reached the FA Cup Final only to lose to Second Division Southampton. They won the trophy the following year, beating Liverpool 2-1 but it was Docherty's final achievement at Old Trafford.

He later managed Derby County and Queen's Park Rangers for a second time before moving to Australia to manage Sydney Olympic. On his return to UK shores he took charge of Preston North End before ending his first-class managerial career with Wolverhampton Wanderers. He now earns his money as an after-dinner speaker with engagements all over the world.

IAN McMILLAN
Inside-forward

Born: John Livingstone McMillan, Airdrie, 18 March 1931
Height: 5ft 6in
Weight: 10st 7lb
Clubs: Airdrieonians; Glasgow Rangers; Airdrieonians
Scotland caps: 6
Scotland goals: 2
1952 v England (lost 1-2), v United States (won 6-0) 2 goals
1955 v England (lost 2-7)
1956 v England (drew 1-1)
1961 v Czechoslovakia (lost 0-4)

Dubbed the 'Wee Prime Minister' because of his control of affairs, and in recognition of the then Prime Minister Harold MacMillan, he was an old-style inside-forward and a player of the highest class.

He began his career with his home-town club and during a decade of senior football with them, won international recognition. McMillan won five of his six caps with Airdrie, his last coming following his move to Rangers, nine years after he had made his debut.

Following his transfer to Rangers in October 1958, the Ibrox club went 23 matches with only one defeat and in doing so, won the League Championship by two points from Hearts. With the advent of Jim Baxter in the summer of 1960, one of the great Rangers inside-forward partnerships was in place. These two players were the architects of Rangers success during the first half of the 1960s. McMillan relied on his skills—he was not a physical player but a good, talented old-fashioned dribbler who formed excellent right-wing partnerships with both Alex Scott and Willie Henderson.

He helped Rangers win another League Championship in 1960-61, three Scottish Cup Finals and two League Cup Finals. Playing the last of his 194 games, in which he scored 55 goals, in April 1964, McMillan then returned to his former club and spent another three seasons playing for Airdrie. He then became coach, manager and subsequently director of his home-town club, his first and last love.

HUGH KELLY
Left-half

Born: Hugh Thomas Kelly, Fife, 23 July 1923
Height: 5ft 10in
Weight: 11st 6lb
Clubs: Jeansfield Swifts; Blackpool; Ashton United
Scotland caps: 1
1952   v United States (won 6-0)

Hugh Kelly joined Blackpool from Scottish junior club Jeansfield Swifts in the summer of 1943, though he spent the rest of the Second World War 'guesting' for a number of clubs north of the Border, particularly East Fife.

He appeared in 16 games for Blackpool during the 1945-46 Football League (North) season, and in the third meeting with Middlesbrough at Elland Road in that campaign's FA Cup competition, Kelly made his League debut for the Seasiders in a 1-0 home win over Aston Villa in the seventh game of the 1946-47 season, but it was midway through the following campaign before he won a regular place in the Bloomfield Road club's side.

It was around this time that the club's legendary half-back line of Johnston, Hayward and Kelly was beginning to take shape. Kelly played in the 1948 and 1951 FA Cup Final defeats but when the Seasiders did win the trophy in 1953, he was missing from the side, having earlier damaged an ankle in the 3-1 win over Liverpool. However, the club asked the FA to produce a special winners' medal for his nomination as 12th man.

Following Harry Johnston's retirement in 1955, Kelly was appointed club captain, and in his first season as skipper, led the Seasiders to runners-up spot in the First Division.

Kelly, whose only appearance for Scotland came in the 6-0 defeat of the United States in April 1952, went on to score nine goals in 468 League and Cup games before leaving to become player-manager of non-League Ashton United. He later returned to Bloomfield Road to work as part of the club's backroom staff.

ANDY PATON
Centre-half

Born: Andrew Paton, Dreghorn, 2 January 1923

Height: 5ft 10in
Weight: 12st 0lb
Clubs: Kello Rovers; Motherwell; Hamilton Academicals
Scotland caps: 2
1952 v Denmark (won 2-1), v Sweden (lost 1-3)

Andy Paton hailed from an established footballing family—he had an uncle who had played for Motherwell, another for Newcastle United and yet another for Portsmouth, while his father had played for St Mirren, Derby County, Spurs and Watford.

Joining Motherwell as a 19-year-old from Kello Rovers, his early years at Fir Park were blighted by indiscipline. In one notable incident in 1947, he was head-butted by an irate Partick Thistle player! Once Paton had put his youthful impetuosity behind him, he matured into one of Scotland's outstanding defenders.

He helped Motherwell win the Scottish League Cup in 1951, beating Hibs 3-0 in the final—Paton in fact, was the Steelmen's captain that day, as he was later in the season when they reached the Scottish Cup Final, only to lose 1-0 to Celtic. A year later, he was instrumental in the club reaching another Scottish Cup Final. Playing 10 games, including three against Hearts at the semi-final stage, Motherwell beat Dundee 4-0 in the final.

His performances led to him winning two full international caps for Scotland against Denmark and Sweden.

Andy Paton was the first player to win the Motherwell Supporters' Association's 'Player of the Year' award, but in the summer of 1958, after making 301 appearances for the Fir Park club, he joined Hamilton Academicals. After a year of playing for the Douglas Park side, he became their manager, presiding over one of their most successful spells. In 1965 he steered the club into the top flight but severed his connections with the Accies two years later.

WILSON HUMPHRIES
Forward
Born: Wilson Humphries, Motherwell, 1 July 1928
Height: 5ft 9in
Weight: 12st 0lb
Clubs: Motherwell; St Mirren; Dundee United; Hamilton Academicals
Scotland caps: 1
1952 v Sweden (lost 1-3)

Wilson Humphries joined Motherwell as a 17-year-old just before the end of the Second World War. Well-built and powerful, he was able to play in any of the forward positions and like many of his era, he would have made more appearances for the Fir Park club but for National Service.

As it was, Humphries scored 69 goals in 199 league appearances for Motherwell and was prolific in the Scottish League Cup too, netting 31 goals in just 47 matches. When Motherwell won the Scottish Cup in 1951–52, Humphries netted four goals in the run to the final where he added another in the 4-0 defeat of Dundee. However, the highlight of Humphries' time at Motherwell was when he scored six goals in the club's record 12-1 win over Dundee United on 23 January 1954. Just over two years later, Humphries, who had been capped by both the Scottish League and the national side, moved to St Mirren.

He spent just over a season with the Paisley club before moving to Dundee United and finally Hamilton Academicals, for whom he played his last game in 1962.

He then enjoyed a coaching career that started with a return to Fir Park before spells with St Mirren and later Hibernian. He then became assistant-manager of Airdrieonians, a position he relinquished in March 1982.

It was strange that Humphries should have enjoyed such a prolonged career in the game, for he was a well qualified man to pursue such a precarious occupation! Having graduated from Glasgow University with a BA, he entered teaching and during the course of his career, taught several future Motherwell players at Dalziel High School.

GEORGE FARM
Goalkeeper
Born: George Neil Farm, Slateford, Edinburgh, 13 July 1924
Died: 14 July 2004
Height: 5ft 11in
Weight: 12st 3lb
Clubs: Armadale; Hibernian; Blackpool; Queen of the South
Scotland caps: 10
1953 v Wales (won 2-1), v N Ireland (drew 1-1), v England (drew 2-2), v Sweden (lost 1-2)
1954 v N Ireland (won 3-1), v Wales (drew 3-3), v England (lost 2-4)
1959 v West Germany (won 3-2), v Holland (won 2-1), v Portugal (lost 0-1)

After playing his early football for Armadale, George Farm, who went on to win 10 caps for Scotland, was third-choice keeper for Hibernian when Blackpool manager Joe Smith paid £2,700 to take him to Bloomfield Road in September 1948.

Replacing the out-of-form Joe Robinson, Farm made his Football League debut in a 2-2 draw at Bolton Wanderers, going on to play in 171 consecutive league games for the Seasiders from his debut. Though later in his career he established a new club record when appearing in 202 consecutive league games. Ever-present in seven of his 12 seasons with the club, Farm also appeared in 47 consecutive FA Cup matches!

George Farm was a perfectionist and could often be found practising on the club's training ground long after his team-mates had left. One of the bravest keepers ever to play for the Seasiders, it didn't matter to him how he kept the ball out—even heading it clear in his efforts to keep a clean sheet!

Farm, who was in goal when Blackpool lost 2-0 to Newcastle United in the 1951 FA Cup Final, returned to Wembley two years later. Though the Seasiders came from behind to beat Bolton Wanderers 4-3, Farm, who had already won his first Scottish caps, was criticised after seemingly letting in two soft goals.

During the 6-2 home defeat at the hands of local rivals Preston North End on 29 October 1955, Farm injured a shoulder and replaced fellow Scottish international Jackie Mudie at centre-forward, from where he went on to open the scoring! Farm played in 512 League and Cup games for the Seasiders before Blackpool boss Ron Suart reluctantly let him join Queen of the South for a fee of £3,000 in February 1960.

He was player-manager at Palmerston Park for a couple of years before hanging up his boots and concentrating solely on managing the club. He later had two spells managing Raith Rovers either side of time spent in charge of Dunfermline Athletic. After leaving management he became a lighthouse keeper and a sports commentator with Radio Forth.

TOMMY WRIGHT

Outside-right

Born: Thomas Wright, Blairhall, 20 January 1928
Height: 5ft 9in
Weight: 11st 0lb
Clubs: Blairhall Colliery; Partick Thistle; Sunderland; East Fife; Oldham Athletic
Scotland caps: 3
1953 v Wales (won 2-1), v N Ireland (drew 1-1), v England (drew 2-2)

Uncle of fellow Scottish international Jackie Sinclair, who made his name with Leicester City, and father of Tommy who played for Leeds United, Oldham Athletic and Leicester City, he began his career with Partick Thistle, joining the Jags in 1945.

Though he was primarily a winger, Wright had the capability of playing anywhere in the attack and it was this that persuaded Sunderland manager Bill Murray to pay £9,000 for his services in March 1949. During his first season at Roker Park, Wright struggled to make much of an impression and wasn't helped by a bad leg injury which kept him out of action for a number of months.

He returned to first team action in readiness for the start of the following season, when Sunderland finished third in Division One. Wright was ever-present and scored 13 goals from the wing, including his only hat-trick for the club in a 4-2 home win over Everton. He reached double figures again in 1950-51 before another spate of niggling injuries kept him out of the side. He was back to his best in 1952-53, and at the end of the season won three full caps for Scotland. Wright's best season in terms of goals scored was 1953-54, when he netted 18 in 38 games, but in January 1955 after he had scored 55 goals in 180 League and Cup outings, he returned to Scotland and joined East Fife in part-exchange for Charlie Fleming.

Two years later, after regaining some of his sharpness in front of goal, he returned to the Football League with Oldham Athletic, but decided to retire after just one season with the Boundary Park club.

JIMMY LOGIE

Inside-right

Born: James Tulips Loggia, Edinburgh, 23 November 1919
Died: 16 May 1984
Height: 5ft 5in
Weight: 9st 9lb
Clubs: Lochore Welfare; Arsenal; Graveness and Northfleet
Scotland caps: 1
1953 v N Ireland (drew 1-1)

Jimmy Logie was widely tipped for national recognition after peacetime football returned, but he was nearing 33 when he made his full international debut against Northern Ireland in November 1952. Having to compete against the likes of Bobby Johnstone and Jimmy Mason, it was his only appearance for the full Scotland team.

Logie joined Arsenal in the summer of 1939 from Scottish junior side Lochore Welfare. However, just five weeks after arriving at Highbury, he was called up and joined the Navy, where he spent the following seven war years.

He made his debut for the Gunners on the opening day of the 1946-47 season in the match against Wolverhampton Wanderers. Over the next nine seasons, Logie was a virtual ever-present in the Arsenal side, consistently masterminding the North London club's attack. During his time at Highbury, he guided Arsenal to two League Championships in 1947-48 and 1952-53, when his goal secured the points in the vital clash against Burnley, and was a member of the Arsenal side that beat Liverpool 2-0 in the 1950 FA Cup Final.

In 1951-52, Arsenal's valiant attempt to do the 'double' ended in disappointment, for after finishing the season in third place in Division One, they lost 1-0 to Newcastle United in the FA Cup Final. Arsenal's team was wracked by injuries to three key players on the day, including Jimmy Logie who suffered from internal bleeding in a thigh injury.

Later in his career he captained the Gunners when regular skipper Joe Mercer was not available, and by the time he left Highbury in February 1955, he had scored 76 goals in 326 League and Cup games. On parting company with Arsenal, he became player-manager of non-League Gravesend and Northfleet before later running a newspaper stand in central London for many years.

DOUG COWIE

Wing-half

Born: Douglas Cowie, Aberdeen, 1 May 1926
Height: 5ft 7in
Weight: 10st 3lb
Clubs: Aberdeen St Clement's; Dundee; Morton
Scotland caps: 20
1953 v England (drew 2-2), v Sweden (lost 1-2)
1954 v N Ireland (won 3-1), v Wales (drew 3-3), v Norway (drew 1-1), v Finland (won 2-1),

v Austria (lost 0-1), v Uruguay (lost 0-7)
1955 v Wales (won 1-0), v N Ireland (drew 2-2), v Austria (won 4-1), v Hungary (lost 1-3)
1956 v Wales (won 2-0), v Austria (drew 1-1)
1957 v Wales (drew 2-2), v N Ireland (won 1-0)
1958 v Hungary (drew 1-1), v Poland (won 2-1), v Yugoslavia (drew 1-1), v Paraguay (lost 2-3)

The only Scottish international to play in both the 1954 and 1958 World Cup Finals, Doug Cowie was one of the game's most polished midfield players. He played his early football for Aberdeen St Clement's before joining Dundee in 1945. He spent 16 seasons at Dens Park, during which time he represented Scotland at 'B' and full international level, as well as playing for the Scottish League XI.

In 1951-52, Dundee reached the finals of both the Scottish Cup and League Cup, and though they lost 4-0 to Motherwell in the Scottish Cup Final, they beat Rangers 3-2 to win the League Cup. The following season, the Dark Blues retained the League Cup with a 2-0 win over Kilmarnock, and this led to Cowie winning the first of 20 caps for Scotland when he played in the 2-2 draw against England at Wembley. A member of Scotland's 1954 World Cup party, he was one of just four players who retained their place in the national side following the 7-0 defeat by Uruguay in Basle. Cowie, along with Tommy Docherty, was named in the 1958 World Cup party, but only the Dundee man took to the field.

A player who led by example, inspiring his colleagues at both club and international level, Cowie parted company with the Dens Park club in 1961, joining Morton as their player-coach. After two seasons at Cappielow Park, he was appointed manager of Raith Rovers, but left Stark's Park after just one season in charge. He later returned to Morton as coach, before joining Dundee United in a similar capacity. Though he later left the club, he did eventually return to Tannadice to take up scouting duties.

JOHNNY LITTLE
Left-back
Born: John Little, Calgary, Canada, 7 July 1930
Height: 5ft 8in
Weight: 12st 0lb
Clubs: Queen's Park; Glasgow Rangers; Morton
Scotland caps: 1
1953 v Sweden (lost 1-2)

One of only a handful of Rangers players to have been capped by Scotland who were born outside the country, Johnny Little was born in Calgary in Canada but came to Scotland as a boy. His first school was rugby-playing, but he started to play football when entering Queen's Park Secondary School—a famous football nursery—became a schoolboy international, and, after joining Queen's Park, an amateur international.

In July 1951, Little joined Rangers and soon emerged as the ideal successor to Jock Shaw at left-back. His sheer speed, energy and enthusiasm succeeded with a vengeance and Rangers were secure in the position for a decade after the long years of the immensely durable Jock Shaw. Few wingers ever got past Johnny Little and if they did, he invariably caught them!

He helped Rangers to two League Championship wins in 1952-53 and 1955-56 and to victory in two Scottish Cup Finals as the Ibrox club beat Aberdeen 1-0 in 1953 and Kilmarnock 2-0 in 1960. Little, who had represented the Scottish League, was given his full international debut in place of his team-mate Sammy Cox for the match against Sweden, but the Scots went down 2-1.

One of the best loved players in the game, Johnny Little made 275 appearances for Rangers before moving to end his playing days with Morton in the summer of 1962. He later taught Physical Education in a school in Greenock.

JACKIE HENDERSON
Forward

Born: John Gillespie Henderson, Bishopbriggs, Glasgow, 17 January 1932
Died: 26 January 2005
Height: 5ft 9in
Weight: 11st 4lb
Clubs: Portsmouth; Wolverhampton Wanderers; Arsenal; Fulham; Poole Town
Scotland caps: 7
Scotland goals: 1
1953 v Sweden (lost 1-2)
1954 v N Ireland (won 3-1) 1 goal, v England (lost 2-4), v Norway (drew 1-1)
1956 v Wales (won 2-0)
1959 v Wales (won 3-0), v N Ireland (drew 2-2)

A dynamic raider who could play in any forward position but specialised on the left-wing, he never played football as a schoolboy but joined a youth club side at Kirkintilloch as a teenager.

Portsmouth were quick to spot his potential and signed him in January 1949 when they were one of the most successful sides in Britain. He made his League debut at Sunderland in September 1951, after which he established himself as a first team regular.

He won the first of seven international caps against Sweden in May 1953 and the last against Northern Ireland almost six years later.

He had scored 73 goals in 233 games for Portsmouth when he left Fratton Park to endure a short, unhappy stint with Wolverhampton Wanderers.

Signed by Arsenal for £20,000 in October 1958, he announced his arrival at Highbury by scoring with two flashing headers in a 4-3 defeat of West Bromwich Albion. He went on to net 12 times in 21 league outings that term, his direct, hard-running style and blistering shot in either foot, being seen to maximum advantage. Henderson could also cross the ball at speed, was strong in the air and played a significant part in securing third place in Division

One for the Gunners. His enterprising displays won him a fleeting return to international favour, but while he was usually in Arsenal's line-up during the next two campaigns, the team's form dipped depressingly. A victim of his own versatility, often moved in reshuffles, he was one of the Highbury dressing-room's liveliest characters.

Having scored 29 goals in 111 games for Arsenal, he was signed by Fulham in January 1962, but unfortunately for the Cottagers he proved to be past his best and moved into non-League football to end his career with Poole Town.

TOMMY RING
Outside-left
Born: Thomas Ring, Glasgow, 8 August 1930
Died: 2 October 1997
Height: 5ft 7in
Weight: 10st 8lb
Clubs: Springburn United; Glasgow Ashfield; Clyde; Everton; Barnsley; Aberdeen; Fraserburgh
Scotland caps: 12
Scotland goals: 2
1953 v Sweden (lost 1-2)
1955 v Wales (won 1-0), v N Ireland (drew 2-2), v Hungary (lost 2-4) 1 goal, v England (lost 2-7)
1957 v England (lost 1-2) 1 goal, v Spain (won 4-2), v Switzerland (won 2-1) v West Germany (won 3-1), v Spain (lost 1-4)
1958 v N Ireland (drew 1-1), v Switzerland (won 3-2)

A slick-moving tricky winger, Tommy Ring won 12 caps for Scotland, the first against Sweden in 1953, and scored two goals at international level against the mighty Hungary and England at Wembley in 1957.

He became a Clyde player in 1948, though Blackpool tried to sign him when he was doing his RAF training at Squire's Gate. When Clyde won the Second Division Championship in 1952 and again in 1957, Tommy Ring passed the 20-goal mark on both occasions. He starred on the wing for Clyde in the mid-fifties and played a major role in helping them to win the Scottish Cup in 1955 when they beat Celtic 1-0 after a replay. Ring scored the goal and was a Cup winner again in 1958, with a 1-0 victory over Hibernian.

In January 1960 he was signed by Everton for £12,000, his wife preventing him from moving to Cardiff City because she didn't want him moving too far south! After breaking his leg, he appeared in only 27 games for Everton, but scored six goals from his left-wing. In November 1961 he moved to Barnsley, but only spent one season at Oakwell. Not a great lover of training, he hated the boring regime of just running up and down the terrace steps—no ball-work whatsoever!

Midway through the 1962-63 season he returned to Scotland to play for Aberdeen, before finishing his playing career at Fraserburgh in the Highland League.

CHARLIE FLEMING

Forward

Born: Charles Fleming, Blairhall, 12 July 1927
Died: 14 August 1997
Height: 5ft 11in
Weight: 11st 10lb
Clubs: Blairhall Colliery; East Fife; Sunderland; Bath City; Trowbridge Town
Scotland caps: 1
Scotland goals: 2
1954 v N Ireland (won 3-1) 2 goals

In December 1951, Charlie Fleming played for the Rest of the UK against Wales in the Welsh FA's 75th Anniversary match—he was the only uncapped player, and though he scored, the Rest lost 3-2. Fleming also scored twice on his international debut as Scotland beat Northern Ireland 3-1, but it was to be his only appearance for the national side!

Signed by East Fife from junior club Blairhall Colliery in June 1947, Charlie Fleming scored two goals on his Scottish League debut against Stenhousemuir in April 1948 as East Fife were winning the 'B' Division Championship. Charlie Fleming soon established himself in the East Fife first team in the 'A' Division in 1948-49. Popularly known as 'Legs' or 'Cannonball' because of his strength of shot, he was a member of the side that won the League Cup in 1949. In the semi-final he scored the winner in a 2-1 defeat of Rangers that took East Fife to the final. The excitement was too much for club chairman John McArthur, who died in the grandstand from a heart attack. Fleming also netted in the final as East Fife beat Dunfermline Athletic 2-1. Also that season, East Fife reached the Scottish Cup Final but lost 3-0 to Rangers.

In 1952-53, Charlie Fleming was the joint-top scorer in Scotland with Hibernian's Lawrie Reilly with 32 League and Cup goals. The following season he was a member of the East Fife team that won the League Cup for a third time, beating Partick Thistle 3-2 in the final in October 1953. Though he had to go in goal when the East Fife keeper went off for treatment to a dislocated finger, he returned to the forward line and promptly scored his side's second goal. That season, Fleming netted 38 goals to take his career total to 167 in 239 games for East Fife.

In January 1955 he was transferred to Sunderland for £7,000 plus Tommy Wright, who moved to the Bayview Park club after scoring 55 goals in 180 games for the Wearsiders. Fleming stayed with the then Roker Park club until they were relegated in 1958, appearing in the FA Cup semi-finals of 1955 and 1956. In 1955-56 he was Sunderland's top scorer with 32 goals, but didn't always have his shooting boots on, because one of his efforts in the game against Aston Villa went wide of the upright and removed a nearby policeman's helmet! Having scored 71 goals in 122 games, Fleming was transfer-listed and left the north-east club to become player-manager of first Bath City and then Trowbridge Town.

Hanging up his boots in 1966, he coached in the United States, Canada and Australia before returning to Scotland, where he coached at schoolboy level.

WILLIE TELFER
Centre-half
Born: William Douglas Telfer, Larkhall, 26 October 1925
Height: 6ft 0in
Weight: 11st 10lb
Clubs: Burnbank Athletic; St Mirren; Glasgow Rangers; Queen of the South
Scotland caps: 1
1954 v Wales (drew 3-3)

Willie Telfer was a gentleman and a player of honesty with a respect for the game. On his international debut for Scotland against Wales at Hampden Park in November 1953, John Charles, Wales' magnificent centre-forward, got past Telfer and made for goal. Telfer, half a yard behind him, could easily have brought the giant Welshman down with a 'professional foul', but chose not to. Charles went on and scored. Telfer was much criticised and was never selected again for Scotland. The match was drawn 3-3.

Powerfully built, Willie Telfer began his career with St Mirren, where prior to him making his international debut, he had represented the Scottish League XI. A bustling, vigorous central defender, he helped St Mirren reach the 1956 League Cup Final, where they lost 2-1 to Aberdeen in a close-fought match.

Rangers had just lost 7-1 to Celtic in the League Cup Final when they decided to pay £10,000 for the 32-year-old Telfer's services in November 1957. Though the signing was said to be a knee-jerk reaction to this resounding defeat and he was only a stop-gap replacement for Woodburn, the move was a resounding success—one of the Ibrox club's most profitable purchases.

It was Telfer's experience that held the Rangers team together and allowed the club to assemble their outstanding team of the early sixties. In 1958-59, he was part of the Rangers side that won the League Championship, finishing two points clear of runners-up Hearts. He had made 97 appearances in the blue shirt of Rangers, when in November 1960 he was allowed to leave Ibrox and join Queen of the South, where he ended his playing career.

Telfer later moved into management and spent three seasons in charge of Albion Rovers.

JOHNNY McKENZIE
Outside-right
Born: John Archie McKenzie, Glasgow, 4 September 1925
Height: 5ft 10in
Weight: 11st 10lb
Clubs: Petershill; Partick Thistle; Bournemouth; Fulham; Dumbarton; Derry City
Scotland caps: 9
Scotland goals: 1
1954 v Wales (drew 3-3), v England (lost 2-4), v Norway (drew 1-1) 1 goal,
    v Finland (won 2-1), v Austria (lost 0-1), v Uruguay (lost 0-7)

1955 v Hungary (lost 2-4), v England (lost 2-7)
1956 v Austria (drew 1-1)

The pinnacle of winger Johnny McKenzie's international career came on a very murky December afternoon in 1954 at Hampden Park, as the magnificent footballers of Hungary beat Scotland 4-2. Despite this defeat, Johnny McKenzie was simply outstanding, and no less a football master than the great Ferenc Puskas himself declared that he had never before seen wing play of such a high standard. McKenzie's total of nine caps earns him the honour of being Partick Thistle's second most-capped player after Alan Rough. Also, there is little doubt that his haul would have been much higher had he not been a contemporary of Hibs' Gordon Smith or Rangers' Willie Waddell, both top-class right-wingers.

Unusually big for a winger, which made him even more dangerous as a supplier of goalscoring opportunities, McKenzie played his early football for Petershill Juniors before joining Partick Thistle in 1944. He had only appeared in a handful of games when he was called up for military service. Stationed on the south coast, he joined Bournemouth on loan for the 1947-48 season before returning to Firhill for the start of the following season.

Known as the 'Firhill Flyer', Johnny McKenzie had everything—speed, artistry and power, and was an immaculate crosser of the ball. He went on to give Thistle a decade and a half of splendid service, helping them to two Scottish League Cup Finals in 1954 (when they lost 3-2 to East Fife) and 1957 (when they went down 1-0 to Celtic after a goalless draw). McKenzie went on to score 53 goals in 396 games for Thistle before leaving Firhill in March 1958 to play for Fulham.

His stay at Craven Cottage was brief, and after rejoining Thistle for a second spell, he moved to Dumbarton before ending his career with Derry City when he was in his 40th year.

MIKE HAUGHNEY
Right-back
Born: Michael Haughney, Paisley, 10 December 1926
Died: Peoria, Illinois, United States, 23 February 2002
Height: 5ft 11in
Weight: 12st 0lb
Clubs: Newtongrange Star; Glasgow Celtic
Scotland caps: 1
1954 v England (lost 2-4)

Mike Haughney's only cap for Scotland was against England at Hampden Park on a bleak Saturday in April 1954, when the Celtic defender found himself on the end of a 4-2 drubbing as West Brom's Ronnie Allen and Johnny Nicholls got amongst the goals.

After playing his early football for Dalkeith St David's and Newtongrange Star, Haughney joined Celtic. On his debut against Rangers, he started at outside-left, but with the scores level at 2-2 and time running out, he was switched to centre-forward. Shortly afterwards, his powerful shot beat Bobby Brown to give the Bhoys a 3-2 win. At this time, Mike Haughney was a part-time footballer and eventually lost his first team place. In his first game for the reserves against Raith Rovers at Parkhead, he scored a hat-trick in the opening four minutes of the game!

Yet despite this he was moved to right-back, playing his first game in this position in another 3-2 defeat of Rangers in the 1950 Danny Kaye Charity Cup Final. He was also at right-back in the Celtic sides that won the St Mungo Cup in 1951 and the Coronation Cup in 1953.

In 1953-54, Haughney was virtually ever-present in the Celtic side that won the 'double' under skipper Jock Stein.

Haughney later reverted to the forward-line, and though he scored in the 1956 Scottish Cup Final against Hearts, it was to no avail as the Tynecastle club won 2-1. Haughney played the last of his 233 games for Celtic, in which he scored 44 goals against Rangers in May 1957.

An ex-Commando and captain in the Seaforth Highlanders, he then emigrated to Indiana in the United States.

WILLIE ORMOND
Outside-left
Born: William Esplin Ormond, Falkirk, 23 February 1927
Died: 4 May 1984
Height: 5ft 8in
Weight: 10st 10lb
Clubs: Gairdoch Juveniles; Stenhousemuir; Hibernian; Falkirk
Scotland caps: 6
Scotland goals: 1
1954 v England (lost 2-4), v Norway (won 1-0), v Finland (won 2-1) 1 goal, v Austria (lost 0-1), v Uruguay (lost 0-7)
1959 v England (lost 0-1)

As part of the Hibernian 'Famous Five', Willie Ormond won three Scottish League Championships and six Scottish caps. He was awarded the OBE in 1975, partly in recognition for managing Scotland during the 1974 World Cup Finals, held in West Germany. Though Scotland did not get beyond the first round, they returned with their heads held high, undefeated in their three games.

Willie Ormond's name is also commemorated at three Scottish League grounds—the Ormond Stand at St Johnstone's McDiarmid Park, the hospitality lounge at Stenhousemuir's Ochilview Park, and of course the Famous Five Stand at Hibs' Easter Road Stadium.

After playing his early football with Stenhousemuir, Ormond joined Hibernian, where his trademark was to push the ball down the wing and chase after it, before cutting inside to unleash a shot. Not afraid of physical contact, he often had his legs taken from under him by frustrated defenders, with the result that he suffered three broken legs during his playing career.

On leaving Easter Road, he had a season with his home-town team Falkirk, later becoming their assistant-trainer. He then became manager of St Johnstone, leading the club to a famous UEFA Cup victory over SV Hamburg in the 1971-72 season.

In January 1973 he was appointed manager of Scotland, later making way for Ally MacLeod. He then briefly managed Hearts before taking the short journey back to Easter Road, initially as assistant to Eddie Turnbull, and then, in April 1980, taking over the reins when Turnbull and Hibs finally parted company. However, there was never enough time to stave off the relegation that had been threatening since long before he arrived. After a good start to the following season, Willie Ormond gave up the post due to ill-health and to concentrate on running his public house in Musselburgh.

FRED MARTIN
Goalkeeper
Born: Fred Martin, Carnoustie, 13 May 1929
Height: 6ft 2in
Weight: 13st 5lb
Clubs: Carnoustie Panmure; Aberdeen
Scotland caps: 6
1954 v Norway (won 1-0), v Norway (drew 1-1), v Austria (lost 0-1), v Uruguay (lost 0-7)
1955 v Hungary (lost 2-4), v England (lost 2-7)

Fred Martin was Scotland's keeper in their first appearance in the World Cup Finals in 1954. Though he was probably the most surprised goalkeeper to find himself in the World Cup Finals, he was assuredly gaining confidence and had a good game in Scotland's opening fixture, a 1-0 defeat at the hands of Austria. Sadly Scotland lost their second group game 7-0 to Uruguay. Martin's last appearance for his country came in 1955, when Scotland played England at Wembley. The big keeper froze with nerves as 40-year-old Stanley Matthews gave Harry Haddock the run around of his life, setting up four goals for Dennis Wilshaw in a then Wembley record win for England, 7-2.

Fred Martin joined Aberdeen from Carnoustie Panmure in October 1946 as an inside-forward, before being converted to goalkeeper when on National Service, during which time he played for the British Army.

When he returned to Pittodrie in 1949, Martin continued in his new position as the last line of defence. He made his Scottish League debut for the Dons in a 3-1 defeat at East Fife in the penultimate game of the 1949-50 season, keeping his place for the final game of the campaign in which Aberdeen beat Stirling Albion 6-2.

As a goalkeeper, Martin's anticipation, judgement and burly presence gained him higher honours, for in 1952 he represented the Scottish League and two years later kept a clean sheet on his international debut as Scotland beat Norway 1-0.

Throughout the 1950s, Fred Martin was a familiar and popular figure between the posts at Pittodrie, helping the Dons win the Scottish First Division

Championship in 1954-55 and finish runners-up the following season. He also played in three losing Aberdeen sides in the 1953, 1954 and 1959 Scottish Cup Finals. He had appeared in 291 League and Cup games for Aberdeen, though for most of his last three seasons at Pittodrie he struggled with injury, eventually retiring in 1960.

WILLIE CUNNINGHAM
Full-back

Born: William Carruthers Cunningham, Cowdenbeath, 22 February 1925
Died: 15 November 2000
Height: 5ft 9in
Weight: 12st 0lb
Clubs: Crossgates Primrose; Dunfermline Athletic; Airdrieonians; Preston; North End; Southport
Scotland caps: 8
1954 v Norway (won 1-0), v Norway (drew 1-1), v Finland (won 2-1), v Austria (lost 0-1), v Uruguay (lost 0-7)
1955 v Wales (won 2-0), v Hungary (lost 2-4), v England (lost 2-7)

Willie Cunningham was Scotland's captain during the 1954 World Cup Finals in Switzerland, but unfortunately they found themselves in probably the toughest section of the competition. Their opponents in their first match were Austria, who had qualified by beating Portugal 9-1 in Vienna. There was an embarrassing moment for Cunningham as he shook hands with Austrian captain Ocwirk in the centre-circle. Ocwirk presented Cunningham with a commemorative pennant—Cunningham found himself with nothing to give in return. Cunningham damaged a shoulder in the 1-0 defeat but an X-ray showed no break and he took his place in an unchanged team to face World Cup holders Uruguay. He probably wished he hadn't, as the Scots lost 7-0 to the South American side!

Cunningham joined Dunfermline Athletic as a part-timer. He was then 18-years-old, but had been working down the pit for almost four years. He continued to combine soccer with mining for a further six years, but by now he had moved to Airdrie, where he made a name for himself as a resourceful and skilful defender.

In July 1949, a £5,000 bid took him to Preston North End and he remained a fixture in the Deepdale club's side until 1963. Though injuries forced him to miss a number of games in his first two seasons with the club, he helped North End win the Second Division Championship in 1950-51. Shortly afterwards he was appointed club captain and led the side to the 1954 FA Cup Final, where they were beaten 3-2 by West Bromwich Albion.

A stocky, menacing figure who introduced fear to the football pitch, he went on to appear in 487 League and Cup games for North End before leaving Deepdale for a short spell as player-manager of Southport. The lure of Deepdale though was much too strong, and he had no hesitation in returning to North End when asked to take the job of reserve team trainer soon afterwards.

JOCK AIRD
Full-back

Born: John Rae Aird, Glencraig, 18 February 1926
Height: 5ft 8in
Weight: 11st 12lb
Clubs: Jeanfield Swifts; Burnley; Eastern Union (New Zealand); Hakoah
    (Australia)
Scotland caps: 4
1954 v Norway (won 1-0), v Norway (drew 1-1), v Austria (lost 0-1), v Uruguay (lost 0-7)

Jock Aird was a latecomer into English League football, arriving at Turf Moor, the home of Burnley, in the summer of 1948 from the Scottish junior club Jeanfield Swifts. He was 22 and it was as a centre-forward that he attracted the attention of the Clarets' scouts!

By 1950, Aird had been converted into a full-back and his pace and stamina eventually brought him into contention for a first team place. He replaced Arthur Woodruff at right-back for the match against Liverpool, and though he had a daunting task opposing the legendary Liverpool and Scotland international Billy Liddell, he acquitted himself well and kept his place in the Burnley side.

When Woodruff later left to play for Workington in 1952, Aird was seen as his natural successor, and so accomplished did he become that he caught the eye of the national selectors. He first pulled on the blue shirt of Scotland for the match against Norway in May 1954, a match the Scots won 1-0. Strangely enough, all but a handful of his games for Burnley were at right-back, yet for his country, he demonstrated his versatility by playing at left-back, partnering Preston North End's Willie Cunningham.

By the summer of 1955, Jock Aird had lost his first team place at Burnley to Harold Rudman, and with John Angus waiting in the wings, Aird decided to seek pastures new.

In September 1955 he set sail for New Zealand, having been contracted to play for Eastern Union FC of Gisborne. He later played for Hakoah in Australia, and when his playing days were over, continued to coach for a number of years in New South Wales, where he still lives.

JIMMY DAVIDSON
Wing-half/ Centre-half

Born: James Anderson Davidson, Douglas Water, 8 November 1925
Height: 5ft 10in
Weight: 11st 7lb
Clubs: Muirkirk; Partick Thistle; Inverness Caledonian
Scotland caps: 8
1954 v Norway (won 1-0), v Norway (drew 1-1), v Austria (lost 0-1), v Uruguay (lost 0-7)
1955 v Wales (won 1-0), v N Ireland (drew 2-2), v Hungary (lost 2-4), v England (lost 2-7)

Jimmy Davidson began his career as a wing-half, making his Partick Thistle debut in a Victory Cup match at Inverness Clachnacuddin in 1946. The result was a 2-2 draw, though the Jags were somewhat fortunate in bringing the Highland League team back to Firhill. The replay saw Thistle win 7-1, with Willie Sharp netting four of the goals.

A cousin of Hull City's long-serving Andy Davidson, he went on to have a wonderful career at Firhill, and after playing for the Scottish League side on a number of occasions, made his international debut in a 1-0 win over Norway at Hampden Park in May 1954. Davidson, who won eight caps for Scotland, represented his country in that summer's World Cup in Switzerland.

Affectionately known by his adoring fans as 'JD', he appeared in three Scottish League Cup Finals for Thistle, but on each occasion was on the losing side—1954 (East Fife 2-3), 1957 (Celtic 0-3 after a goalless draw) and 1959 (Hearts 1-5). In 1957 Thistle had reached the final thanks to a Jimmy Davidson free-kick. The first game in the semi-final against Dundee had ended all-square, and the scores in the replay stood at 2-2 when Thistle were awarded a free-kick 25 yards out. The man with dynamite in his boots stepped up to deceive Bill Brown in goal and surprise the crowd with a delicate, beautifully-judged chip into the top corner. In the final he played with a nasty cut above the eye, but was forced to miss the replay.

Davidson, who switched from wing-half to centre-half midway through his career after a good number of seasons shrewdly directing midfield operations, went on to score 46 goals in 411 first team games for Partick Thistle. After making the last of these appearances in 1960, he joined Inverness Caledonian and gave them three seasons' service before retiring. He then returned to his beloved Firhill as Thistle's groundsman.

PADDY BUCKLEY
Centre-forward

Born: Patrick McCabe Buckley, Leith, 31 January 1925
Height: 5ft 6in
Weight: 11st 12lb
Clubs: Bo'ness United; St Johnstone; Aberdeen; Inverness Caledonian
Scotland caps: 3
Scotland goals: 1
1954 v Norway (won 1-0)
1955 v Wales (won 1-0) 1 goal, v N Ireland (drew 2-2)

Capped three times by Scotland and scoring the only goal of the game against Wales in October 1954, Paddy Buckley began his career with St Johnstone before Aberdeen paid £7,500 for his services at the conclusion of the 1951-52 season. He had in fact joined St Johnstone following a dispute that he had also signed for Celtic!

It took him just 18 minutes to open his account for the Dons, but they went down 5-2 at Motherwell. Though he was on the small side for a centre-forward, standing just 5ft 6in, he certainly won his fair share of high balls, and many of the 92 goals scored for Aberdeen in 252 games were from headers.

One of the games that endeared him to the hearts of all Aberdeen followers was the 1954 Scottish Cup semi-final against the holders Rangers. Though the Ibrox side were in the middle of a crisis of confidence, few of the Pittodrie club's most ardent fans could have expected that the Glasgow giants were to be given their biggest ever defeat in the competition. Joe O'Neil netted a hat-trick, whilst Aberdeen's other scorers in a 6-0 win, that shocked the 111,000 in Hampden Park, were Graham Leggatt, Jack Allister and a diving header in the final minute from Paddy Buckley. However, in the final, the Dons lost 2-1 to Celtic despite another Buckley goal just after half-time.

In 1954-55, Paddy Buckley was Aberdeen's leading scorer with 28 goals, as the Dons won the League Championship for the first time in their history. Sadly, injury forced him to sit out the 1-0 win at Clyde that clinched the title. That was particularly hard on the diminutive striker, as he had netted a hat-trick the previous week in a 4-0 defeat of Rangers.

He continued to play for Aberdeen for another couple of seasons, and then had a brief spell with Inverness Caledonian before a bad knee injury forced his premature retirement.

NEIL MOCHAN
Outside-left
Born: Neil Mochan, Larbert, 6 April 1927
Died: Falkirk, 28 August 1994
Height: 5ft 7in
Weight: 12st 0lb
Clubs: Dunipace Thistle; Morton; Middlesbrough; Glasgow Celtic; Dundee United; Raith Rovers
Scotland caps: 3
1954 v Norway (drew 1-1), v Austria (lost 0-1), v Uruguay (lost 0-7)

Neil Mochan won the first of his three Scottish caps against Norway on 19 May 1954, and went with Scotland to the World Cup in Switzerland. He was in the side beaten 7-0 in suffocating heat by Uruguay in Basle. Ever the optimist, he sat down at the end of the game and said 'We could have beaten them!'

After playing his early football for Dunipace Thistle, he joined Morton in April 1944. His performances for the Cappielow Park club led to a number of top clubs showing an interest in his future, and in the summer of 1951 Middlesbrough paid £14,000 to take him to Ayresome Park. Mochan, who played his first game for the club in the Festival of Britain against Partizan Belgrade, went on to score 14 goals in 39 games during 1951-52, but after just one more season on Teeside, he returned to Scotland to play for Celtic.

Mochan was the inspiration behind the Celtic team that did the League and Cup double in 1953-54. In the game against Hibs at Easter Road, Celtic needed two points for the title and came away with a 2-0 win, courtesy of two Mochan goals, the first after only three minutes. He won his first League Cup medal against Partick Thistle in October 1956, and his second a year later as Celtic beat

Rangers 7-1. He went on to score 111 goals in 268 games for the Parkhead club, before leaving to join Dundee United in November 1960. He later had a spell with Raith Rovers before returning to Celtic as Jock Stein's trainer.

He prepared the Celtic teams that contested the European Cup Finals of 1967 and 1970, but sadly this most popular of players took ill during the summer of 1994 and died of leukaemia within a week of the death of the former England captain, Billy Wright.

JOHN ANDERSON
Goalkeeper
Born: John Anderson, Barrhead, 8 December 1929
Height: 5ft 9in
Weight: 11st 6lb
Clubs: Arthurlie; Leicester City; Peterborough United; Nuneaton Borough; Bedworth Town
Scotland caps: 1
1954 v Finland (won 2-1)

During his days with Arthurlie, where he began his career, John Anderson was capped in the only junior international match ever to be staged at Hampden Park, when Scotland entertained the Republic of Ireland in May 1948.

Though he was on the short side for a goalkeeper, Anderson nonetheless possessed sharp reflexes and a good sense of anticipatory position.

After a series of impressive performances for Arthurlie, Leicester City manager John Duncan paid a nominal fee to take him to Filbert Street. Intermittent first team appearances marked his early years with the Foxes, but he became a regular between the sticks in 1951-52. During his military service, Anderson represented the British Army before regaining his first team spot on his return to Filbert Street.

He was ever-present in Leicester City's Division Two Championship-winning season of 1953-54, keeping 14 clean sheets in his 42 games. At the close of that season, he won a Scotland 'B' cap, and then made his single full international appearance in a 2-1 win against Finland.

Sadly injury sidelined Anderson for the run-in to the 1956-57 Championship, and he subsequently had to battle with Dave MacLaren for the senior jersey. Anderson had made 277 League and Cup appearances for Leicester City when in the summer of 1960 he was allowed to join Peterborough United. He suffered even worse luck whilst with the Posh when he found himself permanent reserve during their record-breaking initial season in the Football League, and played in only a single League Cup defeat.

After playing non-League football for Nuneaton Borough and Bedworth Town, Anderson set up in business as a painter and decorator in Leicester.

ALEX WILSON
Full-back
Born: Alexander Wilson, Buckie, 29 October 1933
Height: 5ft 9in

Weight: 11st 6lb
Clubs: Buckie Rovers; Portsmouth; Chelmsford City
Scotland caps: 1
1954 v Finland (won 2-1)

Able to play in either full-back position, Alex Wilson played his early football with his home-town club Buckie Rovers before joining Portsmouth on amateur forms in 1949.

Though he turned professional in November 1950, he had to wait almost a year before making his Football League debut. Wearing the No.6 shirt as a replacement for the injured Pompey legend Jimmy Dickinson, he was a member of the Portsmouth side beaten 5-0 by West Bromwich Albion at the Hawthorns. Over the next few seasons, Wilson made just spasmodic appearances, and in fact had only appeared 25 times in the Portsmouth side when he was awarded his one and only full international cap against Finland in May 1954.

There is no doubt that Wilson experienced the highs and lows of football with the south coast club. He played in the opening 15 games of the 1954-5 season when Pompey finished third in Division One, before the club suffered relegation to Division Two four seasons later. In 1960-61 Wilson saw his club relegated for the second time as Portsmouth entered the Third Division. Missing very few games, he won a Third Division Championship medal as the club returned to Division Two at the first time of asking.

He made the last of his 381 League and Cup appearances for the club in a goalless draw at Derby County in April 1967, after which, on leaving Fratton Park, he went to play non-League football for Chelmsford City.

DAVE MATHERS
Left-half
Born: David Cochrane Mathers, Glasgow, 23 October 1931
Height: 5ft 9in
Weight: 11st 2lb
Clubs: Partick Thistle; Headington United; Partick Thistle; East Stirlingshire
Scotland caps: 1
1954 v Finland (won 2-1)

Dave Mathers, a Scottish schoolboy international, joined Partick Thistle straight from school and after some impressive displays for the club's reserve side, made his first team debut in 1950. His silky skills thrilled many a Thistle crowd as he adopted what used to be known as 'the scientific approach'. That is, he fed his forwards with passes they could make full use of and defended intelligently.

His early performances for Thistle led to him winning his one and only full international cap when he played for Scotland against Finland in Helsinki in May 1954, a match the Scots won 2-1. Despite a confident display, his through ball leading to Bobby Johnstone's winner, he was omitted from the party of 13 to play in that summer's World Cup in Switzerland, although he was one of eight players whose names were submitted to FIFA on a stand-by basis.

He received another honour at the start of the 1956-57 season when he was chosen to play for the Scottish League against the Irish League in Belfast.

Mathers stayed at Firhill until September 1959 when he left to play non-League football for Headington United (later Oxford United) but a year later he was back with the Jags, taking his total of first team appearances to 272 before leaving Firhill a second time to play for East Stirling. He spent a year with 'the Shire' before deciding to retire.

WILLIE FERNIE
Inside-forward

Born: William Fernie, Kinglassie, 22 November 1928
Height: 5ft 9in
Weight: 10st 10lb
Clubs: Leslie Hearts; Kinglassie Colliery; Glasgow Celtic; Middlesbrough; Glasgow Celtic; St Mirren; Alloa Athletic; Fraserburgh; Coleraine; Bangor
Scotland caps: 12
Scotland goals: 1
1954 v Finland (won 2-1), v Austria (lost 0-1), v Uruguay (lost 0-7)
1955 v Wales (won 1-0), v N Ireland (drew 2-2)
1957 v Wales (drew 2-2) 1 goal, v N Ireland (won 1-0), v Yugoslavia (won 2-0), v England (lost 1-2)
1958 v Switzerland (won 3-2), v Wales (drew 1-1), v Paraguay (lost 2-3)

Willie Fernie's 12 caps spanned four years, starting with a World Cup qualifier against Finland in 1954, and included appearances in the 1954 and 1958 World Cup Finals in Switzerland and Sweden. In the 1954 competition he played in one of Scotland's heaviest defeats—7-0 to Uruguay. His last international against Paraguay was in the 1958 finals, six months before he left Celtic for Middlesbrough.

Having made his Celtic debut in a 1-0 win at St Mirren in March 1950, Fernie soon established himself as a first team regular at Parkhead. The club's journey through the fifties was an erratic one—they beat Motherwell 1-0 to win the 1951 Scottish Cup, yet were eliminated in the first round stage the following year. The double won in 1954 was the club's first for 40 years, Fernie's dribble and cross for Sean Fallon to score having brought the Scottish Cup back to Parkhead in the process. The decade though did contain the result that had acted as a source of provocation to Rangers' supporters since Celtic won the League Cup at Hampden—Fernie netting a last minute penalty in a 7-1 win for Celtic!

In December 1958, Fernie left Celtic to join Middlesbrough for a fee of £18,000. The fee matched the Teeside club's record transfer paid to take Bill Harris from Hull City four years earlier. Though he was a regular in his 22-month Boro career, his return of just three goals in 68 games was disappointing.

Three games into the 1960-61 season, Boro manager Bob Dennison allowed Fernie to leave. He was transferred back to Celtic, taking his tally of goals to 74 in 317 appearances before leaving to play for St Mirren. He helped the Saints to the 1962 Scottish Cup Final before later trying his hand at management with a spell in charge of Kilmarnock.

WILLIE FRASER
Goalkeeper

Born: William Alexander Fraser, Australia, 24 February 1929
Died: 20 June 1996
Height: 6ft 0in
Weight: 11st 13lb
Clubs: Cowie; Third Lanark; Airdrieonians; Sunderland; Nottingham Forest; South Shields
Scotland caps: 2
1955 v Wales (won 1-0), v N Ireland (drew 2-2)

Though he was born in Australia, goalkeeper Willie Fraser was of Scottish descent and thus qualified to play for Scotland. He made two full appearances for the national side in the 1954-55 season, keeping a clean sheet in a 1-0 win over Wales on his debut and making a number of fine saves against Northern Ireland in a 2-2 draw.

Ideally built for the custodian's job, he began his career with junior club Cowie before joining Third Lanark as peacetime football resumed. Though his first team opportunities were limited, when he did get the nod, he impressed enough for Airdrieonians to guarantee him first team football. Signed just before the start of the 1949-50 season, Fraser was in fine form and instrumental in the Diamonds winning promotion to the First Division as runners-up to Morton. Fraser remained at Broomfield Park for another four seasons, hardly missing a game before, following the club's relegation in 1953-54, he joined Sunderland for a fee of £5,000.

Fraser kept a clean sheet on his Football League debut as the Wearsiders recorded a 3-0 win against Tottenham Hotspur at White Hart Lane. Even so, Scottish international keeper Jimmy Cowan returned for the next game. However, the following week, Sunderland were beaten 4-3 at Liverpool and Cowan was deemed responsible for all of the goals. Fraser was back in the side for the next game and held his place until the end of the season. In 1954-55, the Wearsiders finished fourth in Division One, thanks in the main to the outstanding form of Willie Fraser. Also that season, Sunderland reached the FA Cup semi-finals where despite heroics from Fraser they lost 1-0 to Manchester City at Villa Park.

After four seasons at Roker Park, Fraser, who had made 143 League and Cup appearances, thrilling the fans with a number of sensational saves, was transferred to Nottingham Forest. He had made just two appearances for Forest when injuries and a loss of form forced him to leave the City Ground and move into non-League football back in the north-east with South Shields.

HARRY YORSTON
Inside-right
Born: Henry Yorston, Aberdeen, 9 June 1929
Height: 5ft 7in
Weight: 11st 0lb
Clubs: Aberdeen St Clement's; Aberdeen
Scotland caps: 1
1955 v Wales (won 1-0)

An inside-forward who spent his entire career with Aberdeen, Harry Yorston was the nephew of Ben Yorston, the former Dons' centre-forward, who despite being among the smallest forwards around, scored 38 goals in 38 league outings in 1929-30.

Harry Yorston was a wholehearted, dashing, free-scoring forward, who was not only able to score his fair share of spectacular goals but was also renowned for missing the most open of goals! This part of his game annoyed a section of the Aberdeen fans, but the Pittodrie crowd underrated a potential match-winner.

Having represented Scotland at 'B' international level and appeared for the Scottish League XI, he played for Aberdeen in the Scottish Cup Final of 1953 but the Dons lost 1-0 to Rangers after the sides had played out a 1-1 draw.

In October 1954, Yorston was capped at full international level when he replaced Blackpool's Allan Brown for the match against Wales at Ninian Park. Despite giving a good account of himself in a 1-0 win, it was his only appearance at this level.

The 1954-5 season saw Aberdeen win the League Championship, finishing three points ahead of runners-up Celtic. The following year he was a member of the Aberdeen side that won the League Cup, beating St Mirren 2-1 in the final. In 1957, Yorston, aged only 28, decided to retire to follow in his father's occupation as a fish porter. A big pools win enabled him to leave this job, though he later became a van driver! In the late seventies, Yorston returned to the game to coach Aberdeen schoolboys.

HARRY HADDOCK
Left-back/ Left-half
Born: Harry Haddock, Glasgow, 25 July 1925
Died: 18 December 1998
Height: 5ft 7in
Weight: 10st 6lb
Clubs: Renfrew Juniors; Clyde
Scotland caps: 6
1955 v Hungary (lost 2-4), v England (lost 2-7), v Portugal (won 3-0), v Yugoslavia (drew 2-2), v Hungary (lost 1-3)
1958 v England (lost 0-4)

Harry Haddock made his international debut for Scotland in December 1954 against Hungary with Puskas in their ranks at Hampden. He then played a further four times that season in the left-back position, before waiting over three years to make his sixth and final international appearance.

During his service with the RAF, Haddock played for Exeter City for a couple of years, but when the war was finished, a large number of aircrews were made redundant and he had to take a new trade. After training he became a PT Instructor, later joining GTC as a bus driver. He was then reinstated to junior football and signed for Renfrew Juniors. Within four or five months his performances had attracted a number of top Scottish clubs, and in 1947 he signed for Clyde.

Shortly after putting pen to paper for the Bully Wee, he received a bad injury which almost finished his career before it had started. He was out of action for over 18 months before returning to first team action.

A cultured full-back, he enjoyed great success with the Bully Wee, particularly in the mid-fifties when Clyde won the Scottish Cup in 1955, beating Celtic 1-0 after the first game had been drawn 1-1 and in 1958 when Haddock captained Clyde to a 1-0 win over Hibernian. Haddock also skippered the then Shawfield club to the Second Division Championship in 1956-57, when they finished 13 points clear of runners-up Third Lanark.

Despite being of slight build, Haddock, who was Scottish 'Player of the Year' in 1959, was reputed to have the longest throw in Scottish football during the fifties. He continued to play for Clyde until 1963, but then joined Celtic's backroom staff, where he remained until the early seventies.

JOHN CUMMING
Left-half

Born: John Cumming, Carluke, 17 March 1930
Height: 5ft 8in
Weight: 10st 8lb
Clubs: Castlehill Colliery; Carluke Rovers; Heart of Midlothian
Scotland caps: 9
1955 v Hungary (lost 2-4), v England (lost 2-7), v Portugal (won 3-0), v Yugoslavia (drew 2-2)
1960 v England (drew 1-1), v Poland (lost 2-3), v Austria (lost 1-4), v Hungary (drew 3-3), v Turkey (lost 2-4)

John Cumming, who won nine international caps for Scotland, making his debut in a 4-2 reversal at the hands of Hungary in 1955, spent so much time playing the game in Carluke that he didn't actually see a professional match until he was 19. Shortly after that, he joined Hearts and made his debut for the Tynecastle club in December 1950 in a 2-2 draw with Celtic.

Though he arrived at Tynecastle as a left-winger, Cumming made his name as a rugged left-half, good in the air and courageous in the tackle. In his early days with the club, he played in a Hearts forward line which was made up of Tommy Sloan, Alfie Conn, Willie Bauld, Jimmy Wardhaugh and himself. A member of the Hearts side that won the League Championship in 1957-58, he had been appointed captain when the club won the title again in 1959-60.

Cumming, who collected more winners' medals in a Hearts shirt than any other player, played in the four League Cup winning teams of the fifties and sixties and in the 1956 Scottish Cup triumph. His last medal at Hearts came in the 1962 League Cup as Kilmarnock were beaten 1-0, but by this time he was combining playing with coaching.

He went on to score 58 goals in 612 first team games, and though he had a reputation as a hard player, he was never booked once.

As well as coaching at Tynecastle, he was involved with the Scottish international squad under Bobby Brown, but later gave this up to devote his full attention to his beloved Hearts. Working under John Harvey, Bobby Seith and John Hagart and as a player and coach, he spent just under 27 years at Tynecastle. On leaving football he worked in the steel industry.

JIMMY WARDHAUGH
Inside-left
Born: James Wardhaugh, Marshall Meadows, Berwick-on-Tweed, 21 March 1929
Died: 2 January 1978
Height: 5ft 9in
Weight: 10st 6lb
Clubs: Shaftesbury Park; Heart of Midlothian; Dunfermline Athletic
Scotland caps: 2
1955 v Hungary (lost 2-4)
1957 v N Ireland (won 1-0)

Although John Robertson eclipsed Jimmy Wardhaugh's league scoring record for Hearts, he will go down as the most consistent goalscorer in the club's history with 376 goals in 519 games. Yet, unbelievably, he only made two full international appearances for Scotland—scant reward for his goalscoring exploits, though he did represent the Scottish League on nine occasions.

Though he was born in Marshall Meadows near Berwick-on-Tweed, he was brought up in Edinburgh, where he had a reputation as a good rugby player and cricketer. He joined Hearts from Shaftesbury Park as a 17-year-old in 1946, and Davie McLean, the then Hearts manager, used the young forward sparingly in his early days with the club.

Wardhaugh had played a few matches alongside Alfie Conn, but when McLean brought in a young Willie Bauld to play centre-forward in October 1948, no-one could have predicted what a rich vein of goals the Tynecastle club would strike. With Conn at inside-right and Bauld at centre-forward, Wardhaugh ended the 1948-49 season with 10 goals, including a hat-trick against Albion Rovers. In 1949-50 he found the net 24 times, and in one match against Clyde he helped himself to four in a 6-2 win. But it was not until 1954-55 that he managed to finish as the club's top scorer and top scorer in the First Division, when he amassed 34 as Hearts finished runners-up to Celtic.

Finally there was something tangible for Hearts to show for all his goals when in 1954 they won the League Cup, beating Motherwell 4-2 in the final.

Wardhaugh led the First Division scoring charts again in 1955-56 with 34 goals, and also claimed a Scottish Cup winners' medal as Hearts beat Celtic 3-1. Twice during that season he scored four goals in wins against Clyde and Motherwell as well as a hat-trick of hat-tricks. He netted 29 goals the following season as Hearts finished runners-up to Rangers, but it was 1957-58 that he really shone, scoring 37 goals in all competitions. That season Hearts won the Scottish League Championship and Wardhaugh was Scotland's top-scorer as the Tynecastle club set a new record with 132 goals. His last full season saw him win a League Cup winners' medal.

He later ended his career with Dunfermline Athletic before becoming a full-time sports journalist and later publicity officer with the BBC.

TOMMY YOUNGER
Goalkeeper

Born: Thomas Younger, Edinburgh, 10 April 1930
Died: 13 January 1984
Height: 5ft 10in
Weight: 11st 13lb
Clubs: Hutchison Vale; Hibernian; Liverpool; Falkirk; Stoke City; Leeds United
Scotland caps: 24
1955 v Portugal (won 3-0), v Yugoslavia (drew 2-2), v Austria (won 4-1); v Hungary lost 1-3)
1956 v N Ireland (lost 1-2), v Wales (won 2-0), v England (drew 1-1), v Austria (drew 1-1)
1957 v Wales (drew 2-2), v N Ireland (won 1-0), v Yugoslavia (won 2-0), v England (lost 1-2),
      v Spain (won 4-2), v Switzerland (won 2-1), v West Germany (won 3-1),
      v Spain (lost 1-4)
1958 v N Ireland (drew 1-1), v Switzerland (won 3-2), v Wales (drew 1-1),
      v England (lost 0-4), v Hungary (drew 1-1), v Poland (won 2-1), v Yugoslavia (drew 1-1),
      v Paraguay (lost 2-3)

Tommy Younger was a player of considerable renown, winning 24 caps for Scotland and, unusually for a goalkeeper, captaining his country during the 1958 World Cup Finals staged in Sweden. He was also the man, who, having played for Hibs, Liverpool, Falkirk, Stoke City and Leeds United, came through the ranks of the Scottish Football Association to reach the very top of the game, as SFA president and able football administrator.

He began his career with Scottish junior club Hutchison Vale before joining Hibernian in the summer of 1948. He did his National Service with the BAOR and flew home from Germany each weekend to play for the Easter Road club. Once in an Army game he bet one of his team-mates that he could score a hat-trick if he played at centre-forward. He was taken on—and he did!

It was during his first season with Hibs that he must have thought he was due his first piece of silverware. Hibs had reached the final of the League Cup and were to play Motherwell, whom they had comfortably defeated at Fir Park a fortnight previously, scoring six goals in the process. It looked like it would be a formality, but Motherwell won 3-0, with Younger responsible for the third goal following a poor clearance. However, he did win two League Championship medals with Hibs in 1951 and 1952 before, in June 1956, a £9,000 move took him to Liverpool.

There was little to cheer about in the Liverpool side of the late 1950s, yet the one player who always looked convincing was Tommy Younger. He was a majestic heir to the tradition of Liverpool goalkeepers. He was safe, agile and consistent, though he added little else to his collection at Anfield, other than 16 more well-deserved international caps.

In the summer of 1959 he was appointed player-manager of Falkirk, but quit because of back trouble in February 1960. However, the following month he made a dramatic comeback with Stoke City before later playing for Leeds United. A year after his arrival at Elland Road he became a scout for the club before coaching Toronto City in Canada. He then returned to Scotland as public relations officer at Hibernian, where he also became a director, having built up a tidy business supplying vending machines. From his position on the board he built up influence at the Scottish FA, his step from vice-president to presidency involving a hectic schedule of representing the Association throughout the world.

ALEX PARKER
Right-back
Born: Alexander Hershaw Parker, Irvine, 2 August 1935
Height: 5ft 8in
Weight: 11st 2lb
Clubs: Kello Rovers; Falkirk; Everton; Southport; Ballymena United
Scotland caps: 15
1955 v Portugal (won 3-0), v Yugoslavia (drew 2-2), v Austria (won 4-1)
1956 v N Ireland (lost 1-2), v Wales (won 2-0), v England (drew 1-1), v Austria (drew 1-1)
1957 v Wales (drew 2-2), v N Ireland (won 1-0), v Yugoslavia (won 2-0)
1958 v N Ireland (drew 1-1), v Switzerland (won 3-2), v Wales (drew 1-1),
      v England (lost 0-4), v Paraguay (lost 2-3)

Alex Parker began his career as a centre-forward, but was switched to wing-half shortly after joining Kello Rovers. After moving to Falkirk, he began to play full-back and in May 1955 he won the first of 15 Scottish caps when selected to play against Portugal. In fact, Parker won all but one of those caps while with the Bairns, and it was something of a mystery that, after his move to Everton in the summer of 1958, he was picked just once more for his country. However, there was no shortage of pundits on Merseyside who blamed the fact on his 'Anglo' status!

Signed with Eddie O'Hara, a year after the

Alex Parker

two of them had helped Falkirk win the Scottish Cup, Parker was prevented by National Service from making an early Blues debut, his duties for the Royal Scots Fusiliers taking him to Cyprus until November. It wasn't long before he made up for lost time though, displaying consistently immaculate form.

The man who elevated the sliding tackle into an art form, Parker was a virtual ever-present in the Everton side for the next five seasons, appearing in 219 games for the Goodison club, but after losing his place to the up-and-coming Tommy Wright he joined Southport, where he ended his league career.

He later became player-manager of Irish League side Ballymena United, before returning to Haig Avenue in 1970 as manager of Southport.

ARCHIE ROBERTSON
Inside-forward
Born: Archibald Clark Robertson, Busby, 15 September 1929
Died: 28 January 1978
Height: 5ft 11in
Weight: 12st 0lb
Clubs: Rutherglen Glencairn; Clyde; Morton
Scotland caps: 5
Scotland goals: 2
1955 v Portugal (won 3-0), v Austria (won 4-1) 1 goal, v Hungary (lost 1-3)
1958 v Switzerland (won 3-2) 1 goal, v Paraguay (lost 2-3)

Inside-forward Archie Robertson, who joined Clyde straight from Eastwood Academy, played his early football for Rutherglen Glencairn. A fine ball player, he could control a ball from one end of the Shawfield ground to the other without letting it touch the floor!

He enjoyed a good career with Clyde, helping them win the Scottish League 'B' Division Championship in 1951-52, when they pipped Falkirk for the title by a point. An intelligent two-footed player, able to put dead-ball situations to good use, he was a member of the Clyde sides that won the Scottish Cup Finals in 1955 and 1958 as Celtic and Hibernian were beaten respectively. Shortly after the first success against the Bhoys, Robertson won the first of five full caps for Scotland as Portugal were beaten 3-0. He helped the Bully Wee to another Second Division title in 1957, the season that they finished the campaign 13 points clear of second-placed Third Lanark.

Robertson played for Clyde until 1961, when he left to end his career with Morton, where, after two years at Cappielow Park, he hung up his boots.

He was an industrial chemist and worked for the National Coal Board as well as managing Cowdenbeath on a part-time basis. After three years in charge, he resigned for health reasons, but later became manager of Clyde midway through the 1967-68 season. He led the club to the Second Division Championship in 1972-73, but early the following season he parted company with the club prior to spending a short time acting as a scout for Tottenham Hotspur.

TOMMY GEMMELL
Inside-left
Born: Thomas Gemmell, Tarbolton, 2 July 1930
Died: 8 January 2004
Height: 5ft 7in
Weight: 10st 7lb
Clubs: Irvine Meadow; St Mirren
Scotland caps: 2
Scotland goals: 1
1955 v N Ireland (won 3-0) 1 goal, v Yugoslavia (drew 2-2)

Tommy Gemmell played all his first-class football for St Mirren, after joining the Love Street club Irvine Meadow in 1951. The scheming inside-forward, whose main features of play were his ball control and agility to prise open the opposition back four with defence-splitting passes, won a regular place in the Buddies line-up shortly after joining the club.

During the course of his career, he also scored his fair share of goals—many of his strikes netting St Mirren vital points. It was this kind of form that led to Gemmell winning representative honours, playing for the Scottish League XI and for Scotland at 'B' international level. Eventually he got his chance for the senior national side, and made a goalscoring debut in a 3-0 win over Portugal at Hampden Park in May 1955. Later that month he was in the side that drew 2-2 against Yugoslavia in Belgrade.

On the domestic scene, Gemmell was instrumental in St Mirren reaching the League Cup Final in 1956, but the Buddies lost 2-1 to Aberdeen. He was still a member of the side that gained revenge three years later, beating the Dons 3-1 in the Scottish Cup Final.

Gemmell, who gave 11 years loyal service to St Mirren, hung up his boots at the end of the 1961-62 season.

ANDY KERR
Utility player
Born: Andrew Kerr, Ayr, 29 June 1931
Height: 5ft 10in
Weight: 11st 2lb
Clubs: Lugar Boswell Thistle; Partick Thistle; Manchester City; Kilmarnock; Sunderland; Aberdeen; Glentoran; Inverness Caledonian
Scotland caps: 2
1955 v Austria (won 4-1), v Hungary (lost 1-3)

Beginning his career with Partick Thistle, utility player Andy Kerr was signed from another Thistle, the Lugar Boswell variety, as a centre-half in the summer of 1952. As he was perhaps just an inch or two short in height for that position, the Jags converted him initially into a full-back, where he starred for several seasons.

Having played for the Scottish League and Scotland at 'B' international level, he made his full international debut as a full-back in a 4-1 win over Austria in Vienna, and held his place for the game against Hungary ten days later, a match the Scots lost 3-1.

In December 1957 in Jimmy McGowan's benefit match, Thistle experimented with Andy Kerr as a centre-forward, and he went from strength to strength after that. His form for the Firhill club prompted Manchester City to pay £11,000 for his services in May 1959, but he failed to settle at Maine Road, and just over six months later he returned to Scotland to play for Kilmarnock.

He was a prolific scorer for the Rugby Park club—netting 113 goals in 134 games including a club record 34 in 1960-61. It was a mystery to most Scottish supporters of that time why Kerr wasn't called up to add to his total of international appearances. His displays again attracted clubs from south of the Border, and in April 1963 he joined Sunderland for a fee of £22,500.

Though he only spent one season at Roker Park, scoring just five goals in 19 games, much of his time was spent on the treatment table. He joined Aberdeen and spent a year at Pittodrie, before having brief spells with Glentoran and Inverness Caledonian.

During his time in Scottish football, Andy Kerr was on the losing side in all five of his major Cup Final appearances!

JOE McDONALD
Left-back
Born: Joseph McDonald, Blantyre, 10 February 1929
Died: 8 September 2003
Height: 5ft 8in
Weight: 10st 9lb
Clubs: Belshill Athletic; Falkirk; Sunderland; Nottingham Forest; Wisbech Town; Ramsgate
Scotland caps: 2
1956 v N Ireland (lost 1-2), v Wales (won 2-0)

Joe McDonald played in goal for his school, St Joseph's in Blantyre, and at right-back for both Belshill Athletic and Falkirk, with whom he began his first-class career. He had an early taste of representative football when picked for the Lanarkshire Youth team against Glasgow Catholic Youth in 1946. Another minor honour later came his way when he played for Scotland 'B' against the Army.

He spent three seasons with Falkirk, before leaving the Bairns to join Sunderland. He represented Great Britain against the Rest of Europe and helped the Wearsiders reach two FA Cup semi-finals in 1955 and 1956. Shortly before his second appearance at this stage of the competition, he was capped twice by Scotland. He went on to appear in 155 League and Cup games for Sunderland, his only goal coming in the 3-3 home draw against Portsmouth in October 1956.

Incisive in the tackle and showing good positional sense, he joined Nottingham Forest in the summer of 1958. By the end of his first season at the City Ground, he had helped Forest win the FA Cup, defeating Luton Town 2-1 in the 1959 Final. He went on to make 124 senior appearances for Forest, before leaving to play non-League football for Wisbech Town.

In July 1963 he was appointed player-manager of Ramsgate, before later spending two years as manager of Yeovil Town. Known as 'The Gentleman of Soccer', Joe McDonald spent his last years in Adelaide, Australia.

ARCHIE GLEN
Left-half

Born: Archie Glen, Coalburn, 16 April 1929
Died: 30 August 1998
Height: 5ft 11in
Weight: 11st 8lb
Clubs: Cumnock Academy; Ballochmyle Thistle; Annbank United; Aberdeen
Scotland caps: 2
1956 v N Ireland (lost 1-2), v England (drew 1-1)

Archie Glen, club captain of Aberdeen, was an inspirational figure for the Dons as they went through a difficult period during the second half of the 1950s. In 1956 he was selected to play for Scotland twice, picking up caps in the games against Northern Ireland and England. In addition he also represented the Scottish League on six occasions.

The young inside-forward, as he was then, was spotted playing for Ayrshire junior outfit Annbank United by a future Aberdeen team-mate, George Hamilton, and made his first team debut for the Dons in a 2-1 win at Falkirk in February 1949. However, because of National Service, Glen's appearances in the Pittodrie club's first team were limited, and it wasn't until 1953-54 that he really established himself in the Dons' side.

Along with Allister and Young, he helped form one of the Dons' best-ever half-back lines and was ever-present during the club's League Championship winning campaign of 1954-55. In fact, it was Archie Glen's successful spot-kick at Clyde on 9 April 1955 that secured the club's inaugural title.

Archie Glen was something of a superstitious player—always liking to be the last out of the dressing-room. He played his last game for Aberdeen in a 3-1 win at Arbroath in April 1960, a victory that ensured the club's safety on the penultimate Saturday of another disappointing season.

Having spent 13 seasons at Pittodrie, Archie Glen, who was only in his early thirties, decided to leave the game at the top and, in the close season, announced his retirement.

JOHN HEWIE
Utility player

Born: John Davidson Hewie, Pretoria, South Africa, 12 December 1928
Height: 6ft 2in
Weight: 11st 9lb

Clubs: Arcadia FC (South Africa); Charlton Athletic; Arcadia Shepherds (South Africa); Bexley United

Scotland caps: 19

Scotland goals: 2

1956 v England (drew 1-1), v Austria (drew 1-1)

1957 v Wales (drew 2-2), v N Ireland (won 1-0), v Yugoslavia (won 2-0), v England (lost 1-2), v Spain (won 4-2) 1 goal, v Switzerland (won 2-1), v West Germany (won 3-1), v Spain (lost 1-4)

1958 v Hungary (drew 1-1), v Poland (won 2-1), v Yugoslavia (drew 1-1), v France (lost 1-2)

1959 v Holland (won 2-1), v Portugal (lost 0-1)

1960 v N Ireland (won 4-0) 1 goal, v Wales (drew 1-1), v Poland (lost 2-3)

Though he was one of the most versatile players ever to wear the shirt of Charlton Athletic, South African-born 'Long' John Hewie's best position was probably as an uncompromising defender with his long clearances and aerial power.

It was in this position that he won his 19 full Scottish international caps between 1956 and 1960. Hewie also won a Scottish 'B' international cap in 1953 and an Under-23 cap in 1957 as an over-age player. Hewie made his full international debut against England at Hampden with Graham Leggatt scoring Scotland's goal in a 1-1 draw. The first of his two goals at international level came from the penalty spot in a 4-2 defeat of Spain, while his second was the result of a back post header in a 4-0 win over Northern Ireland in Belfast. At club level, John Hewie started games in every position for the Addicks, apart from the two wings. He even had a four-game spell as the club's goalkeeper during the 1961-62 season, when both Charlton's keepers were injured. In those games, the Addicks were undefeated, winning two and drawing two. Having made his Football League debut against Portsmouth in August 1951, Hewie remained at The Valley until July 1960 when he left to return to South Africa.

But within five months he was back with the Addicks, playing on for another six seasons. By the time he left Charlton a second time in 1966, John Hewie had scored 38 goals in 530 games.

After spending two years playing for Arcadia Shepherds in his native South Africa, he returned to become player-manager of non-League Bexley United, but a year later he returned once more to South Africa, this time for good.

GRAHAM LEGGATT
Outside-right

Born: Graham Leggatt, Aberdeen, 20 June 1934

Height: 5ft 8in

Weight: 10st 3lb

Clubs: Aberdeen; Fulham; Birmingham City; Rotherham United; Bromsgrove Rovers

Scotland caps: 18

Scotland goals: 8

1956 v England (drew 1-1) 1 goal

1957 v Wales (drew 2-2)

1958 v N Ireland (drew 1-1) 1 goal, v Hungary (drew 1-1), v Poland (won 2-1),
v Yugoslavia (drew 1-1), v Paraguay (lost 2-3)

1959 v Wales (won 3-0) 1 goal, v N Ireland (drew 2-2), v England (lost 0-1),
v West Germany (won 3-2) 1 goal, v Holland (won 2-1) 1 goal

1960 v N Ireland (won 4-0) 1 goal, v Wales (drew 1-1) 1 goal, v England (drew 1-1) 1 goal,
v Poland (lost 2-3), v Austria (lost 1-4), v Hungary (drew 3-3)

One of the most talented stars to grace Pittodrie, Graham Leggatt began his career with Aberdeen, joining the Dons from local side Banks O'Dee in the summer of 1953. A versatile forward, his 11 goals helped the Dons win the League title in 1954-55, and the following year he won the first of 18 international caps, scoring on his debut in a 1-1 draw against England. The 1957-58 season was one that Graham Leggatt would remember for a variety of reasons. He scored an incredible five times in a 6-2 league victory at Airdrie, but then a fortnight later he suffered a broken leg in the clash with Partick Thistle.

On making a full recovery, he was sold to Fulham for a fee of £16,000. He scored on his Cottagers' debut as Stoke City were beaten 6-1 on the opening day of the 1958-59 season. He ended his first campaign in English football with 21 goals, including a hat-trick in a 3-2 win at Middlesbrough as the club won promotion to the First Division. In Fulham's first season in the top flight, Leggatt was the club's top scorer with 18 goals in 28 games, including four in a 5-0 defeat of Leeds United and a hat-trick in a 3-3 draw with Manchester United. He topped Fulham's scoring charts again in 1960-61 with the best return of his career, 23 goals in 36 games. Included in this total were hat-tricks against Bolton Wanderers and Leicester City. When Fulham beat Ipswich Town 10-1 on Boxing Day 1963, Graham Leggatt netted a three-minute hat-trick, a First Division record!

He topped the scoring charts again that season, and in 1965-66 when his total of 15 goals included another treble in a 6-3 home defeat of Aston Villa. The last of Leggatt's eight hat-tricks, a post-war record, came in the 4-2 home win over Leicester City in December 1966.

Surprisingly, Vic Buckingham sold Leggatt, who had scored 134 goals in 280 games, to Birmingham City for £15,000. By now he had lost most of his speed and looked out of condition, and in the summer of 1968, he joined Rotherham United where he ended his league career. After spells as Aston Villa's assistant-coach and player with Bromsgrove Rovers, he emigrated to Canada, where after managing Toronto Star, he hosted his own soccer show for a Toronto-based television station.

ALFIE CONN senior

Inside-right

Born: Alfred Conn, Prestonpans, 2 October 1926
Height: 5ft 8in
Weight: 11st 6lb
Clubs: Inveresk Athletic; Heart of Midlothian; Raith Rovers; Johannesburg Ramblers (South Africa)

Scotland caps: I
Scotland goals: I
1956 v Austria (drew 1-1) I goal

Alfie Conn was the first of the 'Terrible Trio' to sign for Hearts as a 17-year-old in 1944 from Inveresk Athletic. Though he made his debut within four months of putting pen to paper, it wasn't until he was joined by Jimmy Wardhaugh and Willie Bauld that his value to the Tynecastle club was appreciated.

He soon started to make a name for himself, and though the goals flowed for him and his two colleagues, given the fact that he played alongside such prolific scorers, only once did he finish as top-scorer—in 1950-51 when he scored 25 goals. He played in the Hearts team that won the League Cup in 1955, beating Motherwell 4-2, and in 1956 scored the clinching goal when Hearts won the Scottish Cup by beating Celtic 3-1. He was also a member of the team that won the League Championship in 1958, although an ankle injury restricted him to just five games in which he scored four goals.

Conn, who scored against Austria in his only international match, also had the distinction of scoring Hearts' 100th league goal of the campaign in a 4-0 win at Motherwell—as Hearts went on to score 132 goals in the League. A most remarkable fact was that Conn, Wardhaugh and Bauld did not play a single match together!

Having scored 221 goals in 408 games, Conn left Hearts in September 1958, joining Raith Rovers for a fee of £2,250.

The father of Alfie Conn junior, who won two caps while with Spurs, he later had a spell as player-manager of Johannesburg Ramblers. On leaving football, he became a sales director with an international paint company.

HUGH BAIRD
Centre-forward
Born: Hugh Baird, Calderbank, 14 March 1930
Died: 19 June 2006
Height: 6ft 0in
Weight: 11st 7lb
Clubs: Dalry Thistle; Airdrieonians; Leeds United; Aberdeen; Brechin City; Deverondale; Rothes
Scotland caps: I
1956 v Austria (drew 1-1)

Hugh Baird first displayed his goalscoring talent with Dalry Thistle, his performances week in and week out attracting the attention of a number of Scottish League clubs.

In March 1951, Baird joined Airdrieonians, helping the then Broomfield Park club challenge for promotion to the 'A' Division season after season, until in 1954-55 they won the 'B' Division Championship. That campaign saw Hugh Baird score 37 goals in the League and 53 in all competitions as Airdrie dominated the game outside the top flight. Not surprisingly, after continuing to find the net regularly in the 'A' Division, he deservedly earned international recognition, winning what transpired to be his only cap against Austria in May 1956, a match Scotland drew 1-1. .

After six seasons with the Diamonds in which he netted 165 goals, Baird joined Leeds United for a fee of £12,000.

Seen as a successor to the mighty John Charles, he netted 20 league goals in 1957-58—the next highest scorer being Bobby Forrest with seven goals. However, he couldn't settle in Yorkshire, and early the following season he returned to Scotland to play for Aberdeen.

He netted for the Dons in the 1959 Scottish Cup Final when St Mirren beat them 3-1, and continued to score regularly for the Pittodrie club until 1962, when he moved to Brechin City. Baird later played Highland League football for Deverondale and Rothes before hanging up his boots.

MIKE CULLEN
Winger/ Inside-forward

Born: Michael Joseph Cullen, Glasgow, 3 July 1931
Height: 5ft 8in
Weight: 10st 6lb
Clubs: Douglasdale Juniors; Luton Town; Grimsby Town; Derby County; Wellington Town; Burton Albion
Scotland caps: 1
1956 v Austria (drew 1-1)

After representing Scotland at 'B' international level against England in February 1956, Mike Cullen was called into the full Scotland side for the game against Austria at Hampden Park three months later. It was his only international cap and a surprise selection at that, as he was languishing in Luton Town's reserve side at the time!

Mike Cullen was playing Scottish junior football for Douglasdale when Luton Town manager Dally Duncan signed him in August 1949. A Scottish youth international, he arrived at Kenilworth Road as a centre-forward, but because of his size, he was moved out to the wing. He made his Football League debut for the Hatters in a 3-1 defeat at Birmingham City in the penultimate game of the 1951-52 season.

Though never an automatic choice in his time at Kenilworth Road, he was a member of Luton's first team squad for over six seasons, playing in 16 games during the club's promotion-winning season of 1954-55, when they finished runners-up to Birmingham City. Both teams, and for that matter third-placed Rotherham United, all finished on 54 points!

On his day Cullen was a most tricky winger, who liked nothing better than to cut in onto his right foot and have a shot on goal. He scored 20 goals in 125 appearances for the Hatters before leaving Kenilworth Road in April 1958 to join Grimsby Town.

Cullen spent four seasons at Blundell Park, helping the Mariners win promotion to the Second Division in 1961-62 before leaving to end his first-class career with Derby County. He later had a spell playing non-League football for Wellington Town and Burton Albion, before ending his involvement with the game.

JACKIE MUDIE
Inside-forward

Born: John Knight Mudie, Dundee, 10 April 1930
Died: 2 March 1992
Height: 5ft 7in
Weight: 11st 2lb
Clubs: Dunkeld Amateurs; Dundee; Blackpool; Stoke City; Port Vale; Oswestry Town
Scotland caps: 17
Scotland goals: 9

1957 v Wales (drew 2-2), v N Ireland (won 1-0), v Yugoslavia (won 2-0) 1 goal,
v England (lost 1-2), v Spain (won 4-2) 3 goals, v Switzerland (won 2-1) 1 goal,
v West Germany (won 3-1) 1 goal, v Spain (lost 1-4)

1958 v N Ireland (drew 1-1), v Switzerland (won 3-2) 1 goal, v Wales (drew 1-1),
v England (lost 0-4), v Hungary (drew 1-1) 1 goal, v Poland (won 2-1),
v Yugoslavia (drew 1-1), v Paraguay (lost 2-3) 1 goal, v France (lost 1-2)

Jackie Mudie gained his first international cap for Scotland against Wales in October 1956, going on to make 17 full appearances. His best performance for the national side came when he netted a hat-trick against Spain to secure Scotland's place in the 1958 World Cup Finals.

The youngest of six brothers, Dundee-born Jackie Mudie worked as an apprentice decorator and, at one time, was engaged on painting the Romford Hotel owned by Stanley Matthews! At the same time he was playing part-time for Blackpool and sometimes found himself playing alongside seven internationals in the Central League side.

On his league debut in March 1950, he scored the only goal of the game against Liverpool. A year later, after scoring 20 goals, the second-highest scorer to Stan Mortensen, he played in the FA Cup Final against Newcastle United, but after the 2-0 defeat, the Seasiders signed Ernie Taylor and Mudie lost his place. He eventually regained his place in the first team, and the following season scored the last minute winner in the FA Cup semi-final against Spurs before going on to gain a winners' medal. In 1955-56, Mudie took over at centre-forward from Mortensen and scored 22 goals, including hat-tricks against Charlton Athletic and Everton. The following season Mudie established a new club First Division scoring record with 32 goals, plus another six in the FA Cup. His total included four goals in an FA Cup fourth-round defeat of Fulham.

One of football's sportsmen and gentlemen, Mudie had scored 155 goals in 356 League and Cup games for Blackpool when in March 1961 he moved to Stoke City, his six goals in the last few games of the season saving the Potters from relegation to the Third Division. In his second season at the Victoria Ground, he scored 20 goals, but in November 1963 he moved on to Port Vale where he ended his first-class career, prior to a spell playing non-League football for Oswestry Town.

ALEX SCOTT
Outside-right

Born: Alexander Silcock Scott, Falkirk, 22 November 1936
Died: 23 September 2001
Height: 5ft 10in
Weight: 12st 0lb
Clubs: Camelon Thistle; Bo'ness United; Glasgow Rangers; Everton; Hibernian; Falkirk
Scotland caps: 16
Scotland goals: 5
1957 v N Ireland (won 1-0) 1 goal, v Yugoslavia (won 2-0), v West Germany (won 3-1)
1958 v Switzerland (won 3-2) 1 goal, v Wales (drew 1-1)
1959 v Portugal (lost 0-1)
1962 v Czechoslovakia (won 3-2), v N Ireland (won 6-1) 3 goals, v Wales (won 2-0),
         v England (won 2-0), v Uruguay (lost 2-3)
1964 v Norway (won 6-1), v Wales (won 2-1)
1965 v Finland (won 3-1)
1966 v Portugal (lost 0-1), v Brazil (drew 1-1)

Alex Scott, who made his name as a goalscoring winger with Rangers in the 1950s and 1960s, scored the only goal of the game on his international debut against Northern Ireland in November 1956 and then netted a hat-trick against the same opposition five years later.

A member of four Scottish League Championship-winning sides, he also appeared in the final of the European Cup Winners Cup in 1961, as well as helping Rangers beat Kilmarnock 2-0 in the 1960 Scottish Cup Final. Scott, who scored 68 goals in 216 games for Rangers, also won two Scottish League Cup winners' medals before joining Everton for £40,000 in February 1963. It was one of the fiercest transfer battles of the decade. He was pursued by a number of leading English clubs when it became known that he was keen to move south of the Border. Everton and Spurs led the way with a long series of bids, offers and pledges, before the Goodison club won the race for his signature.

Alex Scott

By the end of his first season, 'Chico' as he was popularly known to the fans because of his swarthy skin, had picked up a Championship medal and was an integral part of the set-up. A model of consistency as a goalmaker—he was never as prolific a scorer as in his Rangers days—he was outstanding in the club's run to the FA Cup Final in 1966, where they beat Sheffield Wednesday 3-2. His peak was passing, however, and in September 1967 he joined Hibernian for £15,000.

He spent a couple of seasons at Easter Road, later ending his career with his home-town club Falkirk, before going into business with his younger brother Jim, the former Hibernian and Newcastle player.

SAMMY BAIRD
Wing-half/ Inside-forward

Born: Samuel Baird, Denny, 13 May 1930
Height: 5ft 11in
Weight: 12st 8lb
Clubs: Rutherglen Glencairn; Clyde; Preston North End; Glasgow Rangers; Hibernian; Third Lanark; Stirling Albion
Scotland caps: 7
Scotland goals: 2
1957 v Yugoslavia (won 2-0) 1 goal, v Spain (won 4-2), v Switzerland (won 2-1), v West Germany (won 3-1), v Spain (lost 1-4)
1958 v N Ireland (drew 1-1), v France (lost 1-2) 1 goal

Sammy Baird, who scored on his international debut in a 2-0 defeat of Yugoslavia in November 1956, was a graduate of the famous junior football academy of Rutherglen Glencairn.

A powerful left-sided player, he turned professional with Clyde, helping the Bully Wee win the 'B' Division Championship in 1951-52 as they finished a point ahead of runners-up Falkirk. His impressive form, which had earned him selection for the Scottish League XI, attracted the attention of some of England's leading clubs, and in June 1954, Preston North End manager Scott Symon paid £12,000 to take him to Deepdale.

He found it hard to settle into the English First Division, and when Symon returned to Ibrox as manager, he quickly bought Baird once more, in June 1955, for £10,000. Using his physique to good effect, Baird soon made a name for himself in the Rangers side as an intimidating player—it was certainly not a wise move to foul him! His upright running style earned him the tag 'Straight-backed SB', and this plus his shock of blond hair made it difficult to ignore him on the field.

Very much a type of inside-forward long identified with Rangers—big, industrious and strong in finishing—he helped the Ibrox club win two League Championships, and the 1960 Scottish Cup Final when they beat Kilmarnock 2-0. He had scored 52 goals in 179 games when leaving to have spells with Hibernian and later Third Lanark. He then ended his involvement with the game following a period as player-manager of Stirling Albion.

ERIC CALDOW

Full-back

Born: Eric Caldow, Cumnock, 14 May 1934
Height: 5ft 8in
Weight: 10st 5lb
Clubs: Muirkirk Juniors; Glasgow Rangers; Stirling Albion; Corby Town
Scotland caps: 40
Scotland goals: 4

1957 v England (lost 0-2), v Spain (won 4-2), v Switzerland (won 2-1),
v West Germany (won 3-1), v Spain (lost 1-4)

1958 v N Ireland (drew 1-1), v Switzerland (won 3-2), v Wales (drew 1-1),
v Hungary (drew 1-1), v Poland (won 2-1), v Yugoslavia (drew 1-1), v Paraguay (lost 2-3),
v France (lost 1-2)

1959 v Wales (won 3-0), v N Ireland (drew 2-2), v England (lost 0-1),
v West Germany (won 3-2), v Holland (won 2-1), v Portugal (lost 0-1)

1960 v N Ireland (won 4-0), v Wales (drew 1-1), v England (drew 1-1), v Austria (lost 1-4),
v Hungary (drew 3-3), v Turkey (lost 2-4) 1 goal

1961 v Wales (lost 0-2), v N Ireland (won 5-2) 1 goal, v England (lost 3-9),
v Republic of Ireland (won 4-1), v Republic of Ireland (won 3-0),
v Czechoslovakia (lost 0-4)

1962 v Czechoslovakia (won 3-2), v N Ireland (won 6-1), v Wales (won 2-0),
v Czechoslovakia (lost 2-4), v England (won 2-0) 1 goal, v Uruguay (lost 2-3)

1963 v Wales (won 3-2) 1 goal, v N Ireland (won 5-1), v England (won 2-1)

Eric Caldow had an outstanding career in which he captained both Rangers and Scotland. He played 40 times for Scotland, an international tally that would have been greatly increased but for a vicious tackle he suffered from Bobby Smith, the Tottenham Hotspur centre-forward, after only six minutes of the England v Scotland match at Wembley in 1963. Caldow's left leg was broken in three places. Captain of Scotland for three years, his international career was over—if he had been able to continue, then George Young's Rangers record of 53 caps would surely have been broken.

Caldow was recommended to Rangers director George Brown by Alex Sloan, a schoolteacher friend, and on his arrival at Ibrox, was farmed out to Muirkirk Juniors for a couple of seasons before being recalled in 1952. Within twelve months he was a valuable member of the Rangers side. In fact, he was a member of two of Rangers' greatest teams—the immediate post-war team of the late 1940s and early 1950s and the team of the early 1960s.

Having played in the earliest European matches, he captained Rangers in its first European final, the Cup Winners' Cup of 1961 against Fiorentina. He also led the club to five League Championships and to success in two Cup Finals and three League Cup Finals.

Eric Caldow

His strength at full-back lay in his pace—he was very quick, and if wingers did get past him, they could never get away from him. Never booked once in a long career of 407 matches for Rangers, he did manage to spend a further season playing for the Ibrox club after his broken leg, before being given a free transfer and joining Stirling Albion.

He had a year at Annfield before becoming player-manager of Corby Town, prior to a stint as manager of Stranraer. He was not a success, and after scouting for Queen's Park Rangers, returned to Ibrox to host the new executive facilities with Alec Willoughby.

DAVE MACKAY
Wing-half

Born: David Craig Mackay, Edinburgh, 14 November 1934
Height: 5ft 8in
Weight: 11st 6lb
Clubs: Newtongrange Star; Heart of Midlothian; Tottenham Hotspur; Derby County; Swindon Town
Scotland caps: 22
Scotland goals: 4
1957 v Spain (lost 1-4)
1958 v France (lost 1-2)
1959 v Wales (won 3-0), v N Ireland (drew 2-2), v England (lost 0-1), v West Germany (won 3-2)
1960 v N Ireland (won 4-0), v Wales (drew 1-1), v Poland (lost 2-3), v Austria (lost 1-4) 1 goal, v Hungary (drew 3-3), v Turkey (lost 2-4)
1961 v Wales (lost 0-2), v N Ireland (won 5-2), v England (lost 3-9) 1 goal
1963 v England (won 2-1), v Austria (won 4-1), v Norway (lost 3-4)
1964 v N Ireland (lost 1-2), v Norway (won 6-1) 2 goals, v Wales (won 2-1)
1966 v N Ireland (lost 2-3)

Though he won 22 caps for Scotland between 1957 and 1966, Dave Mackay was less successful on the international stage than in club football.

Dave Mackay served his footballing apprenticeship with the romantically named Newtongrange Star before joining Hearts as a part-time professional in April 1952. He signed up for full-time football after completing his National Service and helped Hearts win the Scottish League Cup Final the following year. Success with Hearts soon brought representative honours, and after playing for Scotland Under-23s against England, and for the Scottish League against the Football League, he made his full international debut against Spain in 1957. Although he helped Hearts win the Scottish League the following year, it was not until June 1958, after he had been voted Scotland's 'Player of the Year', that he won his next full cap. Two more caps and a 1959 Scottish League Cup winners' medal had been added to his collection before his move to Tottenham Hotspur in March 1959.

Spurs' manager Bill Nicholson later described Mackay's signing as his best day's work ever. One of the most colourful and charismatic characters the game has ever

Dave Mackay

seen, he helped Spurs to three FA Cup wins, a League Championship (including the coveted 'double' in 1961) and a European Cup Winners' Cup triumph in nine unforgettable years at White Hart Lane. In March 1960 he became the first Scotsman to represent the Football League and was runner-up to the legendary Stanley Matthews as Footballer of the Year in 1963, which was some consolation for missing out through injury on his club's sensational victory over Atletico Madrid.

A twice-fractured leg sidelined him for the best part of two years, but the real tragedy was that by the time he had returned to full fitness, the great Tottenham side of the early 1960s was no more. Taking over as skipper, Mackay led Spurs to victory in the 1967 FA Cup Final against Chelsea.

In 1968, when a young Brian Clough was looking for an on-field general to lead his promising Derby County out of the Second Division, it was to Mackay that he turned. Twelve months later the title was won, and Mackay, now playing as a sweeper, was named Footballer of the Year for 1969 alongside fellow veteran Tony Book of Manchester City.

After a spell as player-manager of Swindon Town, he took charge of Nottingham Forest before replacing Clough as manager of Derby County. He steered the Rams to the 1974-75 League Championship before leaving in 1976 to manage Walsall. After managing in Kuwait and coaching in Saudi Arabia, he returned to League management with Doncaster Rovers before becoming general manager of Birmingham City. He then had a spell in Qatar before ending his involvement with the game.

IAN GARDINER
Forward

Born: James Ian Gardiner, Balbeggie, 18 September 1928
Height: 5ft 11in
Weight: 11st 8lb
Clubs: Balbeggie Amateurs; East Fife; Motherwell; Raith Rovers; East Fife; St Johnstone; Montrose
Scotland caps: 1
1958 v Wales (drew 1-1)

Hailing from Balbeggie, Ian Gardiner began his career with East Fife, making his Bayview bow during the 1949-50 season. At East Fife he struck up a good understanding with Charlie 'Legs' Fleming, and the two of them scored some important goals as the Fifers won the 1950 League Cup, beating Dunfermline Athletic 3-0 in the final. His form for East Fife was such that midway through the 1954-55 season, he was selected to represent the Scottish League against the Irish League.

Gardiner was Motherwell manager Bobby Ancell's first signing when he was recruited to the Fir Park side in the summer of 1955. He joined the elite band of players who have scored on their Motherwell debut when he netted in a 2-2 draw with Celtic. Standing just under 6ft, he was the tallest member of the Motherwell forward line and his physical build made him stand out from the other forwards. Ancell quickly developed a preference for small, thoughtful players, whereas Gardiner was all about strength and work-rate. Nevertheless, he went on to give Motherwell three-and-a-half seasons invaluable service. He netted 47 goals in 95 appearances, including two hat-tricks in the early part of the 1956-57 season against Queen of the South.

His form was such that, in November 1957, he won full international honours when he played against Wales at Hampden Park.

Despite scoring a goal every other game, the ascendancy of the Ancell 'Babes' signalled the end for Gardiner, and in January 1959 he joined Raith Rovers. He later had a second spell with East Fife before playing for St Johnstone prior to winding down his career with Montrose.

TOMMY EWING
Outside-left
Born: Thomas Ewing, Swinhill, 2 May 1937
Height: 5ft 6in
Weight: 10st 8lb
Clubs: Larkhall Thistle; Partick Thistle; Aston Villa; Partick Thistle; Morton; Hamilton Academicals
Scotland caps: 2
1958 v Wales (drew 1-1), v England (lost 0-4)

Partick Thistle winger Tommy Ewing, who began his career as a left-back, was deservedly capped for Scotland against Wales and England in 1958, but his hopes of participating in that summer's World Cup Finals in Sweden were dashed by National Service.

Though he was small of stature, standing just 5ft 6in, he had the heart of a lion. The Thistle fans took to him straight away, especially after he had scored their goal in a 1-1 draw at mighty Newcastle United prior to the 1955-56 season getting underway. Ewing, who had two spells with Thistle, was unfortunate in the number of injuries he suffered throughout his career.

He was, however, a member of the Thistle side beaten by Celtic and Hearts in the 1957 and 1959 League Cup Finals, but his form for the Jags led to him being selected for the national side. He had also represented the Scottish League when he appeared for much of the game on the other flank.

In February 1962, Ewing left Firhill to join Aston Villa, whose manager Joe Mercer paid £20,000 for his services. Though he suffered more than his fair share of injuries whilst at Villa Park, he created numerous goalscoring chances for his colleagues in his time with the club, while, in 39 games, he found the net on four occasions.

Returning to Firhill, Ewing spent another couple of seasons in the Thistle side, taking his total of goals to 84 in 254 games—a good return for a winger—before later playing for both Morton and Hamilton Academicals. On hanging up his boots, he then spent a year managing the Accies before leaving the game for good.

GEORGE HERD
Outside-right/ Inside-right
Born: George Herd, Lanark, 6 May 1936
Height: 5ft 7in
Weight: 10st 2lb
Clubs: Inverness Thistle; Queen's Park; Clyde; Sunderland; Hartlepool United

Scotland caps: 5
Scotland goals: I
1958 v England (lost 0-4)
1960 v Hungary (drew 3-3) I goal, v Turkey (lost 2-4)
1961 v Wales (lost 0-2), v N Ireland (won 5-2)

While stationed with the army where he was a PT instructor, George Herd played for Inverness Thistle, helping them to win the Highland Cup. On leaving the army he joined Queen's Park, but his stay with the Spiders was brief, and in the summer of 1957 he joined Johnny Haddow's Clyde side.

He had an incredible first season at Shawfield, helping Clyde beat Hibernian 1-0 to win the Scottish Cup, and winning his first full international cap against England in front of a Hampden crowd of 134,000. Devastated to have lost that game 4-0, he must have been relieved to have been injured for the game in April 1961 when England beat Scotland 9-3!

George Herd

Herd, who was capped five times while with Clyde, also represented the Scottish League on four occasions, and though not a prolific scorer, celebrated each of his goals by performing a somersault!

In April 1961, Herd was transferred to Sunderland for a fee of £42,500 and made his debut against Liverpool in the final game of that season. Over the next eight seasons he was a virtual ever-present in the Sunderland side, creating a great number of chances for Brian Clough as well as netting his fair share himself. His best season in terms of goals scored was 1963-64, when the club won promotion to the First Division, Herd netting 13 goals in 39 games. On 7 January 1967 Herd became the first Sunderland substitute to score when he netted against Blackpool at Bloomfield Road. He had scored 55 goals in 326 League and Cup games for the Wearsiders when he decided to retire.

A year later he made a return to Football League action with Hartlepool United, before having a brief spell as manager of Queen of the South. He then coached Darlington before more recently having spells coaching in Kuwait.

JIMMY MURRAY

Inside-right

Born: James Murray, Edinburgh, 4 February 1933
Height: 5ft 8in
Weight: 11st 4lb
Clubs: Merchiston Thistle; Heart of Midlothian; Falkirk; Clyde
Scotland caps: 5

Scotland goals: I
1958 v England (lost 0-4), v Hungary (drew 1-1), v Poland (won 2-1),
   v Yugoslavia (drew 1-1) I goal, v France (lost 1-2)

Jimmy Murray

Jimmy Murray earned the distinction of being the first Scotsman to score a goal in the final stages of the World Cup. Scotland had qualified for the finals in 1954, but had not managed a single goal until Murray broke the deadlock in Scotland's opening match of the 1958 Championship against Yugoslavia in Vasteras in a 1-1 draw. He went on to play in five internationals, after making an impressive debut against England at Hampden Park.

A regular goalscorer, he joined Hearts from Merchiston Thistle in September 1950, scoring on his debut in March 1952 as Stirling Albion were beaten 5-2. During his early days at Tynecastle, he was called up for National Service with the RAF, where he played representative football and 'guested' for Reading.

In the Hearts' Championship-winning side of 1957-58—the first time they had won the title in 61 years—Murray scored 27 goals in 33 games, as he and Alex Young were responsible for netting 51 goals between them. From mid-December to the end of March, Murray scored 17 goals in 15 games, including a hat-trick in a 4-0 defeat of Airdrie. His scoring streak continued in 1958-59 when he scored 19 goals, including two in the Scottish League Cup Final as Hearts beat Partick Thistle 5-1. Hearts finished two points behind Rangers in the Championship race, but Murray contributed a valuable 11 goals in 18 league games the following season as Hearts regained the title.

Murray had scored 103 goals in 191 games for Hearts when he left Tynecastle in 1961 to join Falkirk, for whom he continued to score on a regular basis before moving to Clyde, where he ended his playing career.

He later had a spell as Falkirk's assistant-manager, before deciding to end his involvement with the game.

JIM FORREST
Inside-forward
Born: James Forrest, Bothwell, 31 March 1927
Height: 6ft 0in
Weight: 11st 7lb
Clubs: Newarthill Hearts; Motherwell; Stenhousemuir
Scotland caps: I
1958 v England (lost 0-4)

Not to be confused with Rangers' free-scoring centre-forward of the same name,

Jim Forrest played for most of his career with Motherwell, whom he joined from Newarthill Hearts in the summer of 1949.

A tall inside-forward with an eye for goals, he made his Motherwell debut towards the tail end of the 1949-50 season, and though he didn't score on his debut, he netted a brace on his next appearance against Stirling Albion. In 1950-51 he ended the season as the club's leading scorer, as he and his strike partner Archie Kelly didn't miss a game, League or Cup. Over the next few seasons, Forrest formed an even more formidable strike partnership with Jackie Hunter, and in 1953-54, the two of them netted 52 of Motherwell's 109 goals as they won the Scottish 'B' Division. The club's biggest win that season was a 12-1 demolition of Dundee United. Quite remarkably, Jim Forrest failed to score!

Eventually his goalscoring feats for the Fir Park club were recognised at international level when he was given his full debut for the visit of England to Hampden Park in April 1958. Unfortunately, Jim Forrest had a nightmare game and he never appeared for the national side again.

There is no doubt his confidence was dented, and though he also played full-back and wing-half for the Fir Park club, the goals began to dry up. In 1960, after scoring 58 goals in 215 games, he was given a free transfer and joined Stenhousemuir, where he later ended his playing days.

STEWART IMLACH
Outside-left

Born: James John Stewart Imlach, Lossiemouth, 6 January 1932
Died: Formby 3 October 2001
Height: 5ft 5in
Weight: 10st 8lb
Clubs: Lossiemouth; Bury; Derby County; Nottingham Forest; Luton Town; Coventry City; Crystal Palace; Dover; Chelmsford City
Scotland caps: 4
1958 v Hungary (drew 1-1), v Poland (won 2-1), v Yugoslavia (drew 1-1), v France (lost 1-2)

The first player to be capped by Scotland while on Nottingham Forest's books, Stewart Imlach was introduced into English football by Bury after they signed him from his local club Lossiemouth in May 1952.

Proving a handful to opponents in the lower divisions with a blend of pace and trickery, Imlach went on to score 14 goals from the wing in 71 games for the Shakers, before joining Derby County some two years after arriving at Gigg Lane. But within twelve months, the Rams had been relegated to the Third Division (North), and he joined Nottingham Forest for a fee of £5,000.

There is no doubt that Imlach played the best football of his career with Forest, going on after making his debut against Liverpool on the opening day of the 1955-56 season to become a great favourite with the Forest crowd. Possessing good ball control and a fierce shot with either foot, he not only appeared for Scotland in the 1958 World Cup Finals in Sweden but won an FA Cup winners' medal in 1959 as Forest beat Luton Town 2-1.

After scoring 48 goals in 204 League and Cup games, he left the City Ground to join the Hatters, Forest's opponents in that final. After making just eight appearances, he left Kenilworth Road to continue his career with Coventry City. He later ended his first-class playing days with Crystal Palace before moving into non–League football with Dover and Chelmsford City. He later held coaching positions with Notts County, Everton, Blackpool and Bury.

BILL BROWN
Goalkeeper
Born: William Dallas Fyfe Brown, Arbroath, 8 October 1931
Died: 30 November 2004
Height: 6ft 1in
Weight: 10st 2lb
Clubs: Arbroath; Cliffburn; Carnoustie Juveniles; Carnoustie Panmure; Dundee; Tottenham Hotspur; Northampton Town; Toronto Falcons (Canada)
Scotland caps: 28
1958 v France (lost 1-2)
1959 v Wales (won 3-0), v N Ireland (drew 2-2), v England (lost 0-1)
1960 v N Ireland (won 4-0), v Wales (drew 1-1), v Poland (lost 2-3), v Austria (lost 1-4), v Hungary (drew 3-3), v Turkey (lost 2-4)
1962 v Czechoslovakia (won 3-2), v N Ireland (won 6-1), v Wales (won 2-0), v England (won 2-0)
1963 v Wales (won 3-2), v N Ireland (won 5-1), v England (won 2-1), v Austria (won 4-1)
1964 v N Ireland (lost 1-2), v Norway (won 6-1), v Wales (won 2-1)
1965 v England (drew 2-2), v Spain (drew 0-0), v Poland (drew 1-1), v Finland (won 2-1)
1966 v N Ireland (lost 2-3), v Poland (lost 1-2), v Italy (won 1-0)

Bill Brown missed just one game during Spurs' double-winning season of 1960-61, and helped them win the FA Cup in 1962 and the European Cup Winners' Cup in 1963. On the way to the final of the latter competition, he gave one brilliant performance in Bratislava. With Spurs he won 24 caps to add to the four he won with Dundee—his last international game being a 1-0 victory over Italy in November 1965, beating Jimmy Cowan's record of caps for a goalkeeper. In fact, he would have won more caps but for Spurs refusing to release him to tour with Scotland in Europe!

He helped Dundee beat Rangers 3-2 in the Scottish League Cup Final of 1952, and won a first senior representative honour in February 1956, playing for Scotland 'B' against England 'B' and for the Scottish League eight times. However, he had to stand by as reserve on no less than 24 occasions before winning a first full cap against France in the summer of 1958, Scotland's last match of the World Cup competition.

In the summer of 1959, Brown joined Tottenham Hotspur for £16,500 as part of Bill Nicholson's rebuilding plans, and soon established himself as a worthy successor to England international Ted Ditchburn.

Bill Brown was tall and lean with a safe pair of hands, good positional sense and a very accurate kick or throw that could quickly turn defence into attack. A solid and reliable keeper, his great strength was his consistency, and despite an occasional weakness on gathering crosses, he was basically an unflappable character who instilled confidence in those around him.

It was only injuries and the emergence of Pat Jennings that led to his absence from the Spurs side, and in October 1966 he moved to Northampton Town for a nominal fee, having played his last game for Spurs in a friendly at Dundee earlier that month. He remained with Northampton until the end of the season, and then played for Toronto Falcons in the 'rebel' American National Professional Soccer League before settling in Toronto, where he went into the real estate business.

JOHN GRANT
Utility player
Born: John Grant, Edinburgh, 16 June 1931
Height: 5ft 8in
Weight: 11st 0lb
Clubs: Merchiston Thistle; Hibernian; Raith Rovers
Scotland caps: 2
1959 v Wales (won 3-0), v N Ireland (drew 2-2)

Nicknamed 'The Duke', John Grant made two full international appearances for Scotland against Wales and Northern Ireland and six appearances for the Scottish League.

A rugged and dependable tackler, he was a most versatile player. He eventually ended up as a right-back after successful stints at inside-forward, centre-half and wing-half. Grant joined Hibernian from Merchiston Thistle in the summer of 1949 and soon established himself in the Easter Road club's side. However, he then suffered a series of injuries and a loss of form, and it was the mid-fifties before he won back a regular spot.

When Joe Baker netted all four of Hibs' goals in the 4–3 Scottish Cup quarter-final victory over Hearts, Grant played in midfield, his defence-splitting passes setting up three of the England international's goals. That season, Hibs reached the final, only to lose 1–0 to Clyde. When Hibs' greatest rivals Hearts won the 1959-60 League Championship, the Easter Road club actually scored more goals—106 against Hearts 102. Though it was a Hibs' side of attacking flair and defensive weakness, John Grant was the exception to prove the rule.

Grant, whose two goals for Hibs both came from spectacular long-range efforts, went on to appear in 242 League games for the Edinburgh club before in September 1964 he left to join Raith Rovers. After just one season at Stark's Park, Grant decided it was time to retire, having spent 15 years with his first club.

WILLIE TONER
Centre-half
Born: William Toner, Glasgow, 18 December 1929

Died: 4 March 1999
Height: 5ft 11in
Weight: 12st 0lb
Clubs: Queen's Park; Glasgow Celtic; Sheffield United; Guildford Town; Kilmarnock; Hibernian; Ayr United
Scotland caps: 2
1959 v Wales (won 3-0), v N Ireland (drew 2-2)

Willie Toner signed for Celtic from Queen's Park before National Service, and what chance he had at Parkhead was further spoiled by cartilage trouble. After just a couple of starts, he was invited to join Sheffield United and was outstanding at centre-half at Bramall Lane, winning a Second Division Championship medal in 1952-53.

He left the Blades following a dispute over terms, and took a job driving a van in Glasgow as well as being prepared to travel south to play non-League football for Guildford Town each weekend.

Kilmarnock manager Malky MacDonald took him to Rugby Park in November 1954, and he made his debut as a centre-forward in a 6-0 defeat at Rangers. He continued to play up front for the rest of that season, but during the early part of the 1955-56 campaign he was played at centre-half due to an injury crisis. This soon became his regular position, and Toner, like his partner at the heart of the Killie defence—former Hearts' player Bobby Dougan—was a ball-playing centre-half. Both defenders were capable of passing the ball well and were good readers of the game. Over the next few seasons, Willie Toner was to build a reputation as one of the best uncapped centre-halves in the game. However, in season 1958-59, this changed, for after captaining the Scottish League on a number of occasions, he was capped twice against Wales and Northern Ireland.

Toner then suffered an injury and was replaced by Bobby Dougan, who also had just come back into contention for a first team place. He played so well that when Toner had regained full fitness, he could only get back into the side at right-back. He eventually returned to the centre-half spot and in 1960 was voted Scottish Footballer of the Year by the *Sunday Mail*'s top journalist 'Rex'. This was then a coveted award in the Scottish game, prior to the introduction in 1965 of the Football Writers' award. During his playing days, Willie Toner, who appeared in 248 games for Killie, was chairman of the Scottish Players Union for a spell.

Following the emergence of Jack McGrory, Toner was sold to Hibs in April 1963, but later that year moved to Ayr United as player-coach. He went on to manage Dumbarton for three years, and after a spell out of the game became a prominent member of the Shettleston Junior Committee.

DAVID HERD
Forward
Born: David George Herd, Hamilton, 15 April 1934
Height: 6ft 0in
Weight: 13st 0lb

Clubs: Stockport County; Arsenal; Manchester United; Stoke City; Waterford
Scotland caps: 5
Scotland goals: 3
1959 v Wales (won 3-0), v N Ireland (drew 2-2) 1 goal, v England (lost 0-1)
1961 v Republic of Ireland (won 4-1) 2 goals, v Czechoslovakia (lost 0-4)

David Herd is the son of Alex Herd, the Scottish international who won the FA Cup with Manchester City in 1934. David Herd signed for Stockport County in April 1951 and played in the same forward line as his father.

During his time at Edgeley Park, he played little first-team football due to being called up for two years' National Service. On the day he was demobbed from the RAF, he was transferred to Arsenal for £10,000.

Herd was slowly introduced into the Gunners' first team, and though he didn't gain any club honours at Highbury, he did win the first of five Scottish international caps against Wales in 1959. He scored 107 goals in 180 games for Arsenal, with his best season being 1960-61 when he netted 29 league goals, including four hat-tricks. This was the best total by an Arsenal player since Ronnie Rookes' 33 in 1947-48. He eventually became disillusioned by Arsenal's poor form, and in July 1961 he was transferred to Manchester United for a fee of £35,000.

It was with United that he enjoyed his greatest achievements. He scored twice in United's FA Cup Final victory against Leicester City and this was followed by two First Division Championship wins in 1964-65 and 1966-67. The latter was spoiled by Herd suffering a broken leg in March, an injury from which he never quite recovered. In November 1956 he hit an unusual hat-trick against Sunderland, striking three goals past three different goalkeepers in a 5-0 win! He played irregularly after United's 1966-67 League Championship success, missing United's European Cup victory over Benfica at Wembley in 1968.

Two months later, having scored 144 goals in 263 appearances for the Reds, he was transferred to Stoke City. Torn ligaments restricted his appearances and he joined Waterford. However, his comeback attempt failed and he retired from playing, shortly being offered the manager's job at Lincoln City. After a successful first season in which promotion was nearly achieved, he lost his job to Graham Taylor and left the game to concentrate on running a garage business he bought in Urmston in 1964.

DENIS LAW
Inside-forward
Born: Denis Law, Aberdeen, 24 February 1940
Height: 5ft 9in
Weight: 10st 11lb
Clubs: Huddersfield Town; Manchester City; Torino (Italy); Manchester United; Manchester City
Scotland caps: 55
Scotland goals: 30

1959   v Wales (won 3-0) 1 goal, v N Ireland (drew 2-2), v Holland (won 2-1),
       v Portugal (lost 0-1)
1960   v N Ireland (won 4-0), v Wales (drew 1-1), v England (drew 1-1),
       v Poland (lost 2-3) 1 goal, v Austria (lost 1-4)
1961   v N Ireland (won 5-2) 1 goal, v England (lost 3-9)
1962   v Czechoslovakia (won 3-2) 2 goals, v Czechoslovakia (lost 2-4), v England (won 2-0)
1963   v Wales (won 3-2) 1 goal, v N Ireland (won 5-1) 4 goals, v England (won 2-1),
       v Austria (won 4-1) 2 goals, v Norway (lost 3-4) 3 goals, v Republic of Ireland (lost 0-1),
       v Spain (won 6-2) 1 goal
1964   v Norway (won 6-1) 4 goals, v Wales (won 2-1) 1 goal, v England (won 1-0),
       v West Germany (drew 2-2)
1965   v Wales (lost 2-3), v Finland (won 3-1) 1 goal, v N Ireland (won 3-2),
       v England (drew 2-2) 1 goal, v Spain (drew 0-0), v Poland (drew 1-1) 1 goal,
       v Finland (won 2-1)
1966   v N Ireland (lost 2-3), v Poland (lost 1-2), v England (lost 3-4) 1 goal
1967   v Wales (drew 1-1) 1 goal, v England (won 3-2) 1 goal, v USSR (lost 0-2)
1968   v N Ireland (lost 0-1)
1969   v Austria (won 2-1) 1 goal, v West Germany (drew 1-1), v N Ireland (drew 1-1)
1972   v Peru (won 2-0) 1 goal, v N Ireland (won 2-0) 1 goal, v Wales (won 1-0),
       v England (lost 0-1), v Yugoslavia (drew 2-2), v Czechoslovakia (drew 0-0),
       v Brazil (lost 0-1)
1974   v Czechoslovakia (won 2-1), v Czechoslovakia (lost 0-1), v West Germany (drew 1-1),
       v West Germany (lost 1-2), v N Ireland (lost 0-1), v Zaire (won 2-0)

Denis Law shares the Scotland scoring record with Kenny Dalglish, 30 goals, but in 55 appearances against Dalglish's 102. He is also the only Scottish player to have scored four goals for his country on two occasions—against Northern Ireland in 1962 and Norway in 1963.

Denis Law was one the greatest strikers and characters in the modern game, yet when he arrived at Huddersfield Town from Aberdeen in 1956 he was a thin, bespectacled 16-year-old who looked nothing like a footballer. A year after joining Huddersfield, Law became the youngest player at 18 years and 236 days to represent Scotland in modern times when he made his debut against Wales. He stayed with the Yorkshire club until March 1960, when Manchester City paid Huddersfield £55,000 for his services. It was a League record, surpassing the previous record by £10,000.

On 28 January 1961, Law produced a display of a lifetime to score six goals in a fourth round FA Cup tie, only for the referee to abandon the game with 21 minutes to play! His six goals against Luton Town at Kenilworth Road came within the space of 48 minutes, but the conditions were worsening so the referee abandoned the game.

On 13 July 1961, Italian giants Torino paid £100,000 for Law's skills. It was the first time that a British club had been involved in a six-figure transfer. A year later he joined Manchester United when they became the first British club to pay over £100,000 for a player. He could score goals from impossible situations, and his blond hair and one arm raised to salute a goal helped establish the Law legend. On 3 November 1962 he scored four goals for United against Ipswich,

Denis Law

and rounded off a superb first season by scoring at Wembley in United's 3-1 FA Cup Final victory over Leicester City.

Denis Law holds the record for the most hat-tricks scored in European Cup competitions by anyone playing for a Football League club. Soon his goals were inspiring United to two League Championships, but unfortunately he had to watch United's 4-1 win over Benfica in the 1968 European Cup Final from his hospital bed after a knee operation. Though his disciplinary record prevented him from being voted 'Footballer of the Year', the English writers' counterparts on the continent voted him 'European Footballer of the Year' in 1964.

He later enjoyed an Indian summer with Manchester City after returning to Maine Road in July 1973. Ironically his last goal was a cheeky back-heel, which consigned United to the Second Division—never had he taken less pleasure from a goal.

DUNKY MacKAY
Right-back/ Right-half

Born: Duncan MacKay, Springburn, 14 July 1937
Height: 5ft 9in
Weight: 11st 10lb
Clubs: Maryhill Harp; Glasgow Celtic; Third Lanark; Croatia (Australia); Azzurri (Australia); Essendon (Australia)
Scotland caps: 14
1959 v England (lost 0-1), v West Germany (won 3-2), v Holland (won 2-1), v Portugal (lost 0-1)
1960 v England (drew 1-1), v Poland (lost 2-3), v Austria (lost 1-4), v Hungary (drew 3-3), v Turkey (lost 2-4)
1961 v Wales (lost 0-2), v N Ireland (won 5-2)
1962 v Czechoslovakia (won 3-2), v N Ireland (won 6-1), v Uruguay (lost 2-3)

Dunky MacKay made his Celtic debut in place of the injured Sean Fallon at right-back for the match against Clyde in August 1958. Within weeks, he was being hailed as the discovery of the season, and towards the end of his first full campaign and only just out of part-time football, he stepped out at Wembley behind skipper Bobby Evans for his Scotland debut. Though England won 1-0, Bolton winger Doug Holden barely got a look in as MacKay had a commanding game.

Within 18 months, MacKay had been appointed Celtic's captain and led them in the two Cup Finals against Dunfermline Athletic. Shortly after this he decided he wanted to cash in on his speed and skill and join the exodus of Scottish talent to England. However, though Johnny Carey came to watch him, no English club made an offer for his services and he remained at Parkhead.

Dunky MacKay was the most stylish of full-backs, and, attack-minded by nature, he practised the overlap long before Jim Craig. He lost the captaincy to Billy McNeill in August 1963, and then, a couple of months later, his right-back spot to Ian Young. Having scored seven goals in 236 games, he left Celtic to join Bobby Evans at Third Lanark just months before Stein took over the reins at Parkhead.

He later became player-coach of Australian side Croatia FC, before returning to Scotland where he worked as a manager of a Glasgow manufacturing firm. He subsequently returned to Australia to become player-coach at Azzurri FC in Perth and Essendon Lions in Melbourne.

JOHN DICK
Inside-left
Born: John Dick, Glasgow, 19 March 1930
Died: 23 September 2000
Height: 5ft 11in
Weight: 12st 6lb
Clubs: Maryhill Harp; Crittall's Athletic; West Ham United; Brentford; Gravesend and
Northfleet
Scotland caps: 1
1959 v England (lost 0-1)

Fourth in West Ham United's all-time highest league scorers' list behind Vic
Watson, Geoff Hurst and Jimmy Ruffell, the tall Scot joined the Hammers from
Crittall's Athletic when he was on National Service at Colchester.

In 1953-54, his first season at Upton Park, he netted the first of six hat-
tricks in a 5-0 home win over Bury, while in his second season with the club he
equalled Bill Robinson's post-war record of 26 league goals in a season, including
three in a 4-2 win at Bristol Rovers. In 1955-56 he scored a superb hat-trick at
White Hart Lane when the Hammers drew 3-3 with Tottenham Hotspur in the
sixth round of the FA Cup. He won a Second Division Championship medal in
1957-58, and scored four of the goals in the Hammers' 8-0 win over Rotherham
United.

His best season in terms of goals scored was 1958-59, when he netted 27
goals in 41 league games, including a hat-trick in a 3-1 win over West Bromwich
Albion at Upton Park. It was this kind of form that led to him winning his one
full international cap, when he played for Scotland against England at Wembley
in April 1959.

The following season he hit all three goals in a 3-2 home defeat of
Wolverhampton Wanderers, but in September 1962, after scoring 166 goals in
351 first team games, he was transferred to Brentford for £17,500. His 23 goals
for the Bees that season brought him a Fourth Division Championship medal.

In 1965 he left Griffin Park to join Southern League Gravesend and Northfleet,
later returning to Upton Park to take charge of West Ham's juniors.

BERT McCANN
Left-half
Born: Robert Johnston McCann, Dundee, 15 October 1932
Height: 5ft 9in
Weight: 10st 4lb
Clubs: Dundee Violet; Dundee North End; Dundee United; Queen's Park; Motherwell;
Hamilton Academicals
Scotland caps: 5
1959 v West Germany (won 3-2)
1960 v N Ireland (won 4-0), v Wales (drew 1-1), v England (drew 1-1)
1961 v England (lost 3-9)

Bert McCann began his Scottish League career with Dundee United, having played junior football for both Dundee Violet and Dundee North End, and was a member of the United side that lost 12-1 to Motherwell at Fir Park in January 1954. Not only is it United's record defeat and Motherwell's record win, but he was to join the Steelmen after leaving the Tannadice club for Queen's Park.

McCann spent two seasons at Hampden Park before his career really took off following his move to Motherwell in the summer of 1956.

A clever, gifted player who had both drive and elegance, Bert McCann was a member of the half-back line of Aitken, Martis and McCann—one of the best in the club's history. While with Motherwell, McCann was capped five times by Scotland, making his last appearance in the 9-3 defeat by England in April 1961. In addition he played for Motherwell in three losing Scottish Cup semi-finals. In the last of these in 1964, McCann's career was effectively ended by a crude tackle. The Motherwell club doctor at the time said it was the worst injury he had ever seen, inflicted by studs which had gouged right across the wing-half's thigh muscle!

McCann had scored 21 goals in 246 league games for Motherwell, when in 1965 he left Fir Park to join Hamilton Academicals where he later ended his playing career.

In his early days at Motherwell, McCann was a part-time player while studying Modern Languages at Edinburgh University. Before graduating in 1960, he frequently only met his team-mates on a Saturday—even when he was captaining the side!

JOHN WHITE
Inside-forward

Born: John Anderson White, Musselburgh, 28 April 1937
Died: Crews Hill, Middlesex 21 July 1964
Height: 5ft 8in
Weight: 10st 8lb
Clubs: Bonnyrigg Rose Athletic; Alloa Athletic; Falkirk; Tottenham Hotspur
Scotland caps: 22
Scotland goals: 3
1959 v West Germany (won 3-2) 1 goal, v Holland (won 2-1), v Portugal (lost 0-1)
1960 v N Ireland (won 4-0) 1 goal, v Wales (drew 1-1), v Poland (lost 2-3), v Austria (lost 1-4), v Turkey (lost 2-4)
1961 v Wales (lost 0-2)
1962 v Czechoslovakia (won 3-2), v N Ireland (won 6-1), v Wales (won 2-0), v Czechoslovakia (lost 2-4), v England (won 2-0)
1963 v Wales (won 3-2), v N Ireland (won 5-1), v England (won 2-1)
1964 v N Ireland (lost 1-2), v Norway (won 6-1), v Wales (won 2-1) 1 goal, v England (won 1-0), v West Germany (drew 2-2)

After playing in junior football for Bonnyrigg Rose Athletic, John White had two years with Alloa Athletic before joining Falkirk for £3,000, and within a year of the move was in the Scotland team, scoring on his debut in a 3-2 defeat of West Germany in May 1959. A few months later he played for the Scottish League against the League of Ireland, and his £20,000 move to Tottenham Hotspur was delayed to allow him to play against the Irish League the following month.

When he arrived at White Hart Lane, John White, who had already won four full caps, scored on his debut in a 2-1 defeat at Sheffield Wednesday. From then on, he was an automatic choice, taking over from Tommy Harmer.

John White was blessed with exceptional balance, he was fast and direct and an extremely difficult man to mark, as he had an uncanny ability to slip into goalscoring positions unnoticed to finish with a perfectly placed shot. Spurs fans soon christened him 'The Ghost', as he continually popped up from nowhere to receive or make an incisive or telling pass. An invaluable ever-present cog in the 1961 double-winning team, he helped Spurs retain the FA Cup in 1962 and win the European Cup Winners' Cup in 1963. His supreme talents continued to be displayed on the international stage, as he won a further 18 full caps in his time with Spurs to give him a final tally of 22. White also represented the Football League against the Irish League in 1960, and for Scotland against the Scottish League twice.

After football, golf was the passion in John White's life, and it was while he was sheltering from a thunderstorm on Crews Hill Golf Course at Enfield in July 1964 that his life was tragically ended when the tree he stood under was struck by lightning. It was the bitterest of blows, for at the age of only 27, John White was at the peak of his career.

IAN ST JOHN
Centre-forward

Born: Ian St John, Motherwell, 7 June 1938
Height: 5ft 7in
Weight: 11st 6lb
Clubs: Douglas Water Thistle; Motherwell; Liverpool; Coventry City; Tranmere Rovers
Scotland caps: 21
Scotland goals: 9
1959 v West Germany (won 3-2)
1960 v N Ireland (won 4-0), v Wales (drew 1-1), v England (drew 1-1),
       v Poland (lost 2-3) 1 goal, v Austria (lost 1-4)
1961 v England (lost 3-9)
1962 v Czechoslovakia (won 3-2) 1 goal, v N Ireland (won 6-1), v Wales (won 2-0) 2 goals,
       v Czechoslovakia (lost 2-4) 2 goals, v England (won 2-0), v Uruguay (lost 2-3)
1963 v Wales (won 3-2), v N Ireland (won 5-1), v England (won 2-1), v Norway (lost 3-4),
       v Republic of Ireland (lost 0-1), v Spain (won 6-2) 1 goal
1964 v N Ireland (lost 1-2) 1 goal
1965 v England (drew 2-2) 1 goal

After paying Motherwell £37,500 for the Saint, Bill Shankly described him as the man the Reds couldn't afford not to buy, the most urgently needed component of his new team. In 1959, while playing for the Fir Park club, he set a new record for the fastest hat-trick in Scottish football, netting three goals in the space of two-and-a-half minutes in a match against Hibernian at Easter Road!

His first appearance in a red shirt was in a Liverpool Senior Cup Final against Everton at Goodison Park in August 1961—he was an instant hit with the fans as he scored a hat-trick.

His delicate flicks did much to promote a fine understanding with Roger Hunt—he scored 18 goals that first season as the Reds won promotion to the First Division. St John's first season in the top flight saw him score 19 goals and then 21 in 1963-64 as Liverpool went on to win the Championship. During that successful campaign, Shanks withdrew

Ian St John

St John into a deep-lying role. He showed his true potential and became the mastermind of the Reds' attack. He gave his team-mates plenty of possession and created space for them with his intelligent running. It certainly wasn't the end of his goals, his jack-knife header against Leeds United at Wembley in 1965 winning the FA Cup.

As his fitness began to decline, St John was used a little more sparingly. On the substitute's bench for the Fairs Cup tie against Dynamo Bucharest, he was brought into the game with Liverpool holding a precarious 1-0 lead. With his touch and close passing skills, he laid on two goals near the end of the match to leave the Reds comfortable winners at 3-0.

On leaving Anfield he had short spells with Coventry City and Tranmere Rovers before trying coaching and then management. He didn't succeed as many people thought he might, and he eventually became a TV personality, sharing the screen with another great goalscorer from the 1960s, Jimmy Greaves.

ANDY WEIR
Outside-left
Born: Andrew Best Weir, Paisley, 15 November 1937
Height: 5ft 7in
Weight: 10st 12lb
Clubs: Arthurlie Juniors; Motherwell
Scotland caps: 6
Scotland goals: 1
1959 v West Germany (won 3-2) 1 goal

1960 v England (drew 1-1), v Poland (lost 2-3), v Austria (lost 1-4), v Hungary (drew 3-3),
v Turkey (lost 2-4)

Motherwell's Andy Weir won the first of his six Scotland caps in 1959 when the side that beat West Germany 3-2 contained three players from the Fir Park club—Weir, who scored on his debut, Ian St John and Bert McCann.

Weir joined Motherwell from Arthurlie in 1957 as an orthodox left-winger, and though his speed and trickery made him a feared opponent, his career was hampered by a spate of appalling injuries. The worst of these by far was picked up in Motherwell's match against Third Lanark at Cathkin Park in 1961. Weir sustained his injury in a clash of heads with Third Lanark's right-back Jim Lewis which developed into a near-fatal case of meningitis. Weir was critically ill—the Motherwell player lay in a coma for several days and was out of football for almost a year. Though Weir's injury cast a huge cloud over Fir Park, it actually brought the club together with Ian St John who was anxious to obtain a transfer, who then asked for his request to be withdrawn.

Weir, who scored 45 goals in 202 games for Motherwell, had the ability to score direct from corners and did this on a number of occasions.

Though he was a gentleman on and off the field, there is one rather hilarious incident worth recalling. It came during Motherwell's visit to play Rangers at Ibrox in the early sixties when, in a moment of rashness, he clashed with Bobby Shearer. Completely out of character, Weir threw a left hook that caught Shearer. The Rangers' right-back, who was one of the game's hard men, chased the Motherwell player up the wing before officials intervened!

One of Motherwell's most popular players, he possessed the rare combination of skill, pace and bravery.

ERIC SMITH

Utility player

Born: John Eric Smith, Glasgow, 29 July 1934
Died: Dubai 12 June 1991
Height: 5ft 5in
Weight: 11st 5lb
Clubs: Glasgow Benburb; Glasgow Celtic; Leeds United; Morton
Scotland caps: 2
1959 v Holland (won 2-1), v Portugal (lost 0-1)

Eric Smith began his career with Celtic, who exploited his versatility by playing him at half-back, inside-forward and on both wings. His no-nonsense, all-action style made him very popular with Celtic fans, and though he made his debut in October 1954 and won a Scottish Cup winners' medal in 1956, it was 1957-58 before he became a first team regular.

He won his two caps for Scotland at right-half on the 1959 tour of Holland and Portugal, but for much of his career at Parkhead, fellow international full-back Dunky MacKay wore the No.4 shirt and Smith played inside-right.

Smith had scored 20 goals in 130 games for Celtic when in June 1960 he signed for Leeds United. It was anticipated that his experience and grit would stiffen the Yorkshire club's defence, but that idea was scrapped when he broke a leg in his first season at Elland Road.

In June 1964 he went to Morton, retiring two years later for a spell as coach with the Greenock club. He was manager for a short time in 1972 after spending some time in Cyprus as coach to Pezoporikos of Larnaca. He later managed Hamilton Academicals and held that job for six years until April 1978, when he took over the reins at Sharjah FC in the United Arab Emirates.

In the summer of 1982 he became assistant-manager to Don Revie at Al Nasr, becoming manager in 1984. He later returned to Cyprus to coach Pezoporikos again, but died on holiday while still the Cypriot club's coach.

BERTIE AULD
Outside-left
Born: Robert Auld, Maryhill, 23 March 1938
Height: 5ft 7in
Weight: 10st 6lb
Clubs: Panmure Thistle; Maryhill Harp; Glasgow Celtic; Dumbarton; Birmingham City; Glasgow Celtic; Hibernian
Scotland caps: 3
1959 v Holland (won 2-1), v Portugal (lost 0-1)
1960 v Wales (drew 1-1)

A player of undoubted talent, Bertie Auld also possessed a temper, and on his international outing against Holland in May 1959, he was ordered off in the last minute 'for pushing a Dutch player with a foot in the face.'

After playing his early football for Panmure Thistle, he joined Maryhill Harp and had only appeared in six games at that level when he was invited to Parkhead for signing talks. Before he made his Celtic debut, Auld spent much of the 1956-57 season on loan at Dumbarton. On his return to Parkhead, he made his debut against Rangers in a Glasgow Cup tie, but his early years with the club showed that he had an unfailing capacity for allowing himself to be goaded into misbehaviour, and in April 1961 he was allowed to join Birmingham City for a fee of £15,000.

He made his debut for the Midlands club in an Inter Cities Fairs Cup tie against Inter Milan, and over the next three-and-a-half seasons was a regular member of the Birmingham side. In 1962-63 he scored some vital goals in the club's run to the League Cup Final where they beat Aston Villa over two legs. The following season he was the club's top scorer with 10 goals, but early in 1965 after netting 31 goals in 145 games, he rejoined Celtic for £12,000.

Jock Stein converted him from a winger to a thoughtful, intelligent midfielder—the transformation was quite staggering, and saw him become part of the great Celtic side that won the European Cup in 1967, when arguably he was the club's best player. He won five League Championship medals from 1966 to 1970, three Scottish Cup medals in 1965, 1967 and 1969 and four Scottish League Cup medals in 1966, 1967, 1968 and 1969. His release in April 1971 after scoring 85 goals in 279 games came as a shock.

He played briefly for Hibernian before becoming a coach at Easter Road. He later managed Partick Thistle (twice), Hibernian, Hamilton Academicals and Dumbarton, but there is little doubt that the years he spent with Celtic remain the most cherished of his memories, and affectionate recollection of them overcomes any bitterness he might feel about what happened anywhere else.

THE 1960s

Scotland could not have made a worse start to the decade, beaten 9-3 by England at Wembley—a day of humiliation. Injuries to Bill Brown and Lawrie Leslie had pushed Frank Haffey into Scotland's first-choice keeper, but it was not a weak Scottish team as the line-up included Denis Law, Dave Mackay, Billy McNeill and Ian St John. In England, the match so captured the popular imagination that an LP of the match commentary was released and played to taunt the hapless Scots!

However, Scotland avenged this thrashing the following season with a 2-0 win over England—it was England's first defeat at Hampden Park in 25 years!

The Scots failed to qualify for the 1962 World Cup Finals in Chile, being knocked out in a play-off match with Czechoslovakia.

Scotland's determination to reach the 1966 World Cup Finals in England had been demonstrated at the end of the previous season, when the SFA had begged Celtic to allow Jock Stein to act as caretaker manager of the national side. Their faith in the big man had been borne out in May, when Scotland drew 1-1 with Poland in Chorzow and then four days later beat Finland 2-1. However, Scotland's hopes received a serious setback in October 1965 at Hampden when, without the brilliant Jim Baxter but leading 1-0 with a goal by Billy McNeill, they were beaten by Poland's two late goals. Scotland now had to beat Italy home and away. They achieved their first objective with a John Greig goal in November, but before the return in Naples the following month, Stein lost almost half his squad. Some were injured and some because their English clubs refused to release them, and some were not picked by the SFA. The list of the absent included Baxter, Pat Crerand, Alan Gilzean, Denis Law and Dave Mackay. Stein aimed for a draw, gambling on a replay, but this failed miserably, Italy hammering Scotland 3-0, and Stein's reign ended with him bitterly complaining of the lamentable national set-up.

For Scotland though, the 'real' World Cup Final was played at Wembley on 15 April 1967 and they won it. England's victory the summer before rankled north of the border, so to take on the world champions on their very own pitch and beat them was pure heaven. Although Scotland's margin of victory was a slender 3-2, it was the style that enraptured Scottish fans. Jim Baxter was at his mercurial best, waltzing through an England team which, apart for Jimmy Greaves for Roger Hunt, was the same one that had beaten West Germany. Baxter's dazzling cheek of taunting the England players and defying them to win possession of the ball was emulated by team-mates Denis Law, Billy Bremner and Tommy Gemmell. It was sweet revenge as Scotland embarrassed the Auld Enemy, and completely wiped out the bitter memory of their 9-3 humiliation six years ago to the day.

Scotland failed to reach the 1970 World Cup Finals but they had a good excuse. They had been drawn in the same group as beaten finalists in 1966 West Germany and Austria. Scotland's faint hopes disappeared when they drew 1-1 with West Germany at Hampden, lost 3-2 in Germany and 2-0 in Vienna. They did finish runners-up, edging out Austria by a point.

GEORGE MULHALL
Outside-left

Born: George Mulhall, Falkirk, 8 May 1936
Height: 5ft 8in
Weight: 10st 9lb
Clubs: Kilsyth Rangers; Aberdeen; Sunderland; Cape Town City (South Africa); Halifax Town
Scotland Caps: 3
Scotland Goals: 1
1960 v N Ireland (won 4-0) 1 goal
1963 v N Ireland (won 5-1)
1964 v N Ireland (lost 1-2)

An exciting left-winger with an eye for goal, George Mulhall won all of his three full caps for Scotland against Northern Ireland, scoring on his debut in a 4-0 win in Belfast.

Mulhall came from a footballing family, his two brothers playing for Falkirk and Albion Rovers. After playing his early football for Kilsyth Rangers, he joined Aberdeen in 1953. He served a long apprenticeship at Pittodrie before taking over from the long-serving Jackie Mather, making infrequent appearances until season 1959-60. He had, though, won a 1956 Scottish Cup winners' medal as the Dons beat St Mirren 2-0. He had been at Pittodrie for almost a decade when, after scoring 42 goals in 150 games, he left to join Sunderland.

On his arrival at Roker Park, his form was so good that he was recalled to the national side, while in 1963-64 when the club won promotion to the First Division, he was ever-present. His assertive wing play and good scoring rate was apparent throughout the following seasons as he scored 66 goals in 291 League and Cup outings. On leaving Roker Park he went to play for Cape Town in South Africa, where he won League and Cup medals.

In October 1971 he joined Halifax Town as player-coach before being appointed manager eight months later. He then joined Bolton Wanderers as assistant to Ian Greaves before leaving to become manager of Bradford City in 1978. He returned to Burnden Park for a second spell in the summer of 1981. Though he saved the Trotters from relegation, there was conflict between Mulhall and the Board over the sale of highly rated Paul Jones, and in June 1982 he left the club.

Mulhall then worked as assistant to Frank Worthington at Tranmere before becoming chief scout, youth development officer and assistant-manager of Huddersfield Town before rejoining Halifax for a second spell as manager.

FRANK HAFFEY

Goalkeeper

Born: Frank Haffey, Glasgow, 28 November 1938
Height: 6ft 0in
Weight: 13st 0lb
Clubs: Maryhill Harp; Glasgow Celtic; Swindon Town; St George Budapest; Hakoah, Sutherland (Australia)
Scotland Caps: 2
1960 v England (1-1)
1961 v England (lost 3-9)

Forever saddled with the fact of being Scotland's keeper in the 1961 Wembley debacle when England crushed the Scots 9-3, Frank Haffey began his first-class career with Celtic, whom he joined from Maryhill Harp in 1958.

After many sound displays for Celtic to his credit, Haffey made his full international debut against England at Hampden Park in April 1960. The wicked Hampden wind played havoc with the spectacle and the game was littered with both free-kicks and throw-ins. England had two penalties and Bobby Charlton scored one and missed the other. In fact, Charlton missed it twice, Haffey moving before the ball was kicked to save his first effort. The major controversy of the game came when Joe Baker charged Haffey into the net—the referee ruling 'no goal'. Scotland's goal in the 1-1 draw came courtesy of Graham Leggat.

In the 1961 international against England at Wembley, Frank Haffey appeared to be in a state of shock, and the most charitable estimates blamed the Celtic keeper for three of the goals, though, to be fair, it has to be said that he received little support. The scoreline gave rise to the joke at the goalkeeper's expense: 'What's the time?' asked one fan, 'Nine past Haffey' smirked another!

So affected by the result was Haffey that John Fallon expected to be in the Celtic side in the Cup Final against Dunfermline Athletic the following Saturday. Though he carried on, he was on the losing side as Dunfermline won 2-0 after a goalless draw, and though he later reached another Scottish Cup Final with Celtic two years later, he again had to be satisfied with a runners-up medal as Rangers won 3-0 after a 1-1 draw. The remainder of Haffey's Celtic career was littered with a number of moments of high comedy—an own goal when he attempted to steer a free-kick to Dunky MacKay, slicing the ball into his own net; and then, with Celtic beating Airdrie 9-0, hitting a last minute penalty to Roddie McKenzie's left, only to see the Airdrie keeper bring off a marvellous save!

After breaking his ankle against Partick Thistle in November 1963, Haffey moved on to Swindon Town, but after a handful of games he went to Australia where he assisted St George, Budapest and Sydney clubs Hakoah and Sutherland.

On hanging up his boots, he commenced a new career as a cabaret performer in Australia, and took a vivid interest in Australian Rules football.

ALEX YOUNG
Centre-forward

Born: Alexander Young, Loanhead, 3 February 1937
Height 5ft 11in
Weight: 11st 8lb
Clubs: Newtongrange Star; Heart of Midlothian; Everton; Glentoran; Stockport County
Scotland Caps: 8
Scotland Goals: 5
1960 v England (1-1), v Austria (lost 1-4), v Hungary (3-3) 1 goal, v Turkey (lost 2-4) 1 goal
1961 v Wales (lost 0-2), v N Ireland (won 5-2) 1 goal, v Republic of Ireland (won 3-0) 2 goals
1966 v Portugal (lost 0-1)

Alex Young

Alex Young was a gifted, elegant striker, yet despite his subtlety, skill and natural ability, he only played for Scotland on eight occasions, making his debut in a 1-1 draw against England in 1960—he surely should have played many more times. Like many players with flair and genius, he set himself very high standards and was often very critical of his own game.

He signed for Heart of Midlothian from Newtongrange Star and made his Scottish League debut as an 18-year-old. He made quite an impact as Hearts won their League Cup section, netting a hat-trick in a 4-0 win over East Fife. Young went on to score 23 goals in that first season and was part of the team that won the Scottish Cup with a 3-1 win over Celtic. He was prominent in the club's title success of 1958 with 24 league goals and netted many crucial goals the following campaign as Hearts retained the title.

In November 1960, Young joined Everton in a £55,000 deal that also took team-mate and full-back George Thomson to Goodison. Young didn't make his Everton debut until the following season, because he arrived on Merseyside carrying a nasty knee injury sustained in playing for the British Army.

In Everton's League Championship-winning season of 1962-63, Young ended the season with 22 goals, including the only goal of the game against Tottenham Hotspur that took Everton to the top of the League—a position from which they were never dislodged. Arguably the greatest Scottish player to sign for Everton, he was a major influence on the side that beat Sheffield Wednesday 3-2 in the 1966 FA Cup Final.

In attacking situations, Young always seemed to have plenty of time. He knew where to play the ball instinctively—he didn't have to look where he was passing and was aware of all the options open to him without looking up. For all his flair and grace, he possessed a vicious shot and had good heading ability.

His blond hair made him quite a distinctive figure on the field and the fans called him the 'Golden Vision'. When he was replaced by 16-year-old Joe Royle for a game at Blackpool in 1966, there was a public outcry. Manager Harry Catterick was assaulted by outraged Everton fans, such was Young's popularity.

In August 1968, Young became player-manager of Glentoran, but two months later he returned to league action with Stockport County, where he ended his playing days.

Alex Young was one of the classiest players in post-war football, and Everton fans worshipped him, to them he was the greatest!

WILLIE HUNTER
Inside-forward

Born: William Hunter, Edinburgh, 14 February 1940
Height: 5ft 8in
Weight: 10st 5lb
Clubs: Edinburgh Norton; Motherwell; Detroit Cougars (United States); Hibernian
Scotland Caps: 3
Scotland Goals: 1
1960 v Hungary (3-3) 1 goal, v Turkey (lost 2-4)
1961 v Wales (lost 0-2)

Motherwell manager Bobby Ancell signed Willie Hunter from his local side Edinburgh Norton in the summer of 1957. Within months of his arrival at Fir Park, it was clear that Ancell had snapped up a footballer who was both a brilliant ball player and a most determined performer. While later Ancell would say that Hunter was the most skilful of the 'Ancell Babes', some judges rated the inside-forward's body swerve better than the legendary Gordon Smith's!

During his time with Motherwell, Willie Hunter was always amongst the goals—scoring 40 in 229 games—though he laid on far more than he scored. He had made four appearances for the Scottish League side when in June 1960 he was selected to make his international debut for Scotland against Hungary at Nepstadion, Budapest. Hunter scored his side's first goal in a 3-3 draw. He kept his place in the side for Scotland's next two games, but after defeats to both Turkey and Wales, he made way for a young Denis Law.

Throughout his Fir Park career, Hunter was troubled by a string of injuries and this restricted his first team appearances. He left Motherwell in 1967 and had a brief spell in the United States with Detroit Cougars before returning to Scotland to play for Hibernian. While with the Easter Road club, whom he had supported as a boy, he made an appearance as a substitute in the League Cup Final but was on the losing side as Hibs went down 6-2 to Celtic.

When his playing days ended, he coached in South Africa before spending three years as Portsmouth's assistant-manager. He later managed Queen of the South and Inverness Caledonian before revealing himself to be as comfortable with the pen as the football, being the author of several books.

LAWRIE LESLIE
Goalkeeper

Born: Lawrence Grant Leslie, Edinburgh, 17 March 1935
Height: 5ft 11in
Weight: 12st 0lb
Clubs: Newtongrange Star; Hibernian; Airdrieonians; West Ham United; Stoke City; Millwall; Southend United
Scotland Caps: 5
1961 v Wales (lost 0-2), v N Ireland (won 5-2), v Republic of Ireland (won 4-1), v Republic of Ireland (won 3-0), v Czechoslovakia (lost 0-4)

One of the game's bravest goalkeepers, Lawrie Leslie was actually run over by a truck as a small boy and was told by doctors that he would be lucky if he ever walked again. Needless to say he did, but in a long football career, he broke almost every bone in his body!

He started playing football with Newtongrange Star where his impressive displays between the posts led to him joining Hibernian in the summer of 1956. He was a member of the Easter Road club's side that lost to Clyde in the Scottish Cup Final of 1958, and seemed on the verge of international honours when in November 1959 he was surprisingly allowed to join Airdrieonians.

A popular character who ruled his goal area vociferously, he was appointed captain at Broomfield Road. While with Airdrie, he made three appearances for the Scottish League and was capped five times by Scotland, making his debut against Wales in October 1960.

In June 1961, the crew-cut keeper went south of the border to play for West Ham United, making his debut in a 1-1 draw against Manchester United on the opening day of the 1961-62 season. In November 1962 he broke his leg in the 2-1 home defeat by Bolton Wanderers, and though he made a quite remarkable recovery to play in the last four games of the season, he was overlooked for the start of the 1963-64 campaign. After asking for a transfer, he was signed by Stoke City who paid £14,000 for his services in October 1963, as the Potters sought to consolidate their position in the top flight.

After almost three seasons at the Victoria Ground in which he appeared in Stoke's Football League Cup side of 1964, he returned to London to play for Millwall before ending his career with Southend United. He later became that club's trainer before subsequently coaching in schools.

Ray Wilson of Everton heads clear in a game against Preston North End. Jimmy Gabriel of Everton is close by and Alex Young is at far left of the picture.

JIMMY GABRIEL

Right-half

Born: James Gabriel, Dundee, 16 October 1940

Height: 5ft 10in

Weight: 11st 12lb

Clubs: Dundee North End; Dundee; Everton; Southampton; Bournemouth; Swindon Town; Brentford; Seattle Sounders (United States)

Scotland Caps: 2

1961 v Wales (lost 0-2)

1964 v Norway (won 6-1)

A powerhouse of a right-half, Jimmy Gabriel became one of the most expensive teenagers in British football when he left Dundee for Everton for £30,000 in March 1960. Understandably, the young Gabriel needed time to settle, and in only his third senior outing he was given a fearful run-around by West Bromwich Albion's England international Derek Kevan, who scored five times as Everton were beaten 6-2 at the Hawthorns.

Gabriel, though, went on to build a fine career for himself. His strong, forceful style, particularly effective in defence, made him a near perfect foil for the more adventurous wanderings of Brian Harris on the opposite flank. When Harris lost his place to Tony Kay midway through the 1962-63 season, Gabriel continued to complement his midfield partner, helping the Blues win the League Championship. He was also a leading light in the Merseyside club's 1966 FA Cup Final victory over Sheffield Wednesday. By now he had won two caps for Scotland, and few will forget the Scottish international's gap-toothed grin and sweat-soaked shirt at the end of the Blues' 3-2 win.

In the summer of 1967, Gabriel was surprisingly sold to Southampton where he contributed five years' yeoman service. He was just the sort of player the Saints needed at that time, and when he left to play for Bournemouth in July 1972 he was sorely missed. After just over a year with the Dean Court club, he moved to North America where he played for Seattle Sounders.

In the summer of 1990, Gabriel returned to Goodison Park to help Blues' manager Colin Harvey look after the first team, later taking over as caretaker manager at the end of Howard Kendall's second reign. Despite all the managerial changes at Goodison, Gabriel remained part of the coaching set up until 1997 when he left the club and headed for the United States.

JOHN MARTIS
Centre-half
Born: John Martis, Motherwell, 30 March 1940
Height: 5ft 11in
Weight: 11st 11b
Clubs: Royal Albert; Motherwell; Hellenic (South Africa); East Fife
Scotland Caps: 1
1961 v Wales (lost 0-2)

Signed from Royal Albert—the Larkhall based junior side—John Martis was to prove to be an admirable replacement at Motherwell for the long-serving Andy Paton.

Martis, an out-and-out centre-half, joined Motherwell in 1957 and in his very first game for the Steelmen, came up against Hibernian's prolific scoring centre-forward Joe Baker. There is little doubt that Martis benefited from his baptism of fire, being one of the heroes of Motherwell's 5-2 Scottish Cup win at Ibrox Park. Though the diminutive forward line, known as the 'Ancell Babes', frequently made the headlines, it was often the unsung Martis at the heart of the Motherwell defence that won the day. He was outstanding during the 1959-60 season when Motherwell recorded four victories over the mighty Rangers.

His performances for Motherwell led to him winning caps for Scotland at Under-23 level, before in October 1960 he won his one and only full international cap when he played in the 2-0 defeat by Wales at Cardiff City's Ninian Park ground.

Martis had appeared in 297 league games for Motherwell when in January 1969 he left Fir Park to play with Cape Town-based Hellenic in South Africa.

Towards the end of the year, he returned to Scotland to resume his career with East Fife. This proved to be a huge success, and he was a first team regular at Bayview for six years, before he was eventually appointed manager of the Methil club. When he left his post, he then concentrated on his plumbing business.

DAVIE WILSON
Outside-left
Born: David Wilson, Glasgow, 10 January 1939
Height: 5ft 6in
Weight: 10st 9lb
Clubs: Baillieston Juniors; Glasgow Rangers; Dundee United; Dumbarton
Scotland Caps: 22
Scotland Goals: 9
1961 v Wales (lost 0-2), v N Ireland (won 5-2), v England (lost 3-9) 1 goal, v Republic of Ireland (won 4-1), v Republic of Ireland (won 3-0), v Czechoslovakia (lost 0-4)
1962 v Czechoslovakia (won 3-2), v N Ireland (won 6-1) 1 goal, v Wales (won 2-0), v England (won 2-0) 1 goal, v Uruguay (lost 2-3)
1963 v Wales (won 3-2), v England (won 2-1), v Austria (won 4-1) 2 goals, v Norway (lost 3-4), v Republic of Ireland (lost 0-1), v Spain (won 6-2) 1 goal
1964 v England (won 1-0), v West Germany (2-2)
1965 v N Ireland (won 3-2) 2 goals, v England (2-2), v Finland (won 2-1) 1 goal

Winger Davie Wilson had an outstanding career with both Rangers and Scotland, one of his most famous internationals being against England at Wembley in 1963 when he moved to left-back and played with great distinction after Eric Caldow had broken a leg. Perhaps the most important of Wilson's nine goals for his country was Scotland's first in a 2-0 win over England at Hampden in 1962.

Wilson was arguably Rangers' finest outside-left since the mercurial Alan Morton. He was fast, direct and opportunistic, with a particular talent for being in the right place at the right time when the crosses from outside-rights Alex Scott and Willie Henderson were pouring in. Occasionally playing at inside-left, Wilson scored 155 goals in 373 first team outings for Rangers with his greatest performance coming in March 1962 when he scored six of Rangers' goals in a 7-1 demolition of Falkirk. With Rangers he won two League Championship medals, five Scottish Cup winners' medals and two League Cup winners' medals.

In August 1967, when aged only 28, he and Wilson Wood went to Dundee United in exchange for Orjan Persson. Many people felt that Rangers had released him too soon, and so it proved, as he went on to a number of good seasons with the Tannadice club. He then had a brief spell with Dumbarton before in 1977 they appointed him manager. He spent three years in charge before becoming assistant-manager at Kilmarnock. While at Rugby Park, the club suffered a major injury crisis and Wilson, who was in his 44th year, pulled on his boots again. He later had a second spell managing Dumbarton before leaving to concentrate on his work in the whisky industry.

JACKIE PLENDEREITH
Centre-half

Born: John Boyd Plendereith, Bellshill, 6 October 1937
Height: 5ft 11in
Weight: 12st 1lb
Clubs: Armadale Thistle; Hibernian; Manchester City; Queen of the South; Cape Town City
and Hellenic FC (South Africa)
Scotland Caps: 1
1961 v N Ireland (won 5-2)

Jackie Plendereith followed in a long line of centre-halves at Hibernian, whom he joined from Armadale Thistle in 1954. He made his debut for the Easter Road club just 24 days after his 17th birthday and was a regular at the heart of the Hibs' defence for six seasons. During this time, Hibs reached the 1958 Scottish Cup Final but, in a hard-fought match, lost 1-0 to Clyde.

In July 1960, Plendereith left Easter Road, joining Manchester City for a fee of £17,500. During his first season at Maine Road, Plendereith was capped by Scotland, making his international debut in a 5-2 defeat of Northern Ireland at Hampden Park. Despite having a good game, it was his only appearance at full international level, though he had previously played five times for the Under-23 side.

During that first season with City, he played in the FA Cup fourth round game against Luton Town at Kenilworth Road, which—with City leading 6-2 and Denis Law having scored all six goals—was abandoned! Law was on the scoresheet again in the re-arranged game, but Plendereith and his fellow defenders were under constant pressure as the Hatters ran out 3-1 winners. At the end of the 1962-63 season, City were relegated to Division Two and Plendereith returned to Scotland to play for Queen of the South.

After one season at Palmerston Park, he went to South Africa and played for both Cape Town City and Hellenic FC before later returning to work in Scotland.

JIM BAXTER
Left-half

Born: James Curran Baxter, Hill o' Beath, 29 September 1939
Died: 14 April 2001
Height: 5ft 10in
Weight: 10st 6lb
Clubs: Crossgates Primrose; Raith Rovers; Glasgow Rangers; Sunderland; Nottingham Forest
Scotland Caps: 34
Scotland Goals: 3
1961 v N Ireland (won 5-2), v Republic of Ireland (won 4-1), v Republic of Ireland (won 3-0),
v Czechoslovakia (lost 0-4)
1962 v Czechoslovakia (won 3-2), v N Ireland (won 6-1), v Wales (won 2-0),
v Czechoslovakia (lost 2-4), v England (won 2-0), v Uruguay (lost 2-3) 1 goal

1963   v Wales (won 3-2), v N Ireland (won 5-1), v England (won 2-1) 2 goals,
       v Austria (won 4-1), v Norway (lost 3-4), v Republic of Ireland (lost 0-1),
       v Spain (won 6-2)
1964   v Norway (won 6-1), v Wales (won 2-1), v England (won 1-0), v West Germany (2-2)
1965   v Wales (lost 2-3), v Finland (won 3-1), v N Ireland (won 3-2)
1966   v N Ireland (lost 2-3), v Italy (won 1-0), v Wales (won 4-1), v England (lost 3-4),
       v Portugal (lost 0-1), v Brazil (1-1)
1967   v Wales (1-1), v England (won 3-2), v USSR (lost 0-2)
1968   v Wales (won 3-2)

If ever there has been a player whose career mirrors the outrageous fortunes of
Scotland in the international arena, then it is Jim Baxter.

Jim Baxter won the first of his 34 caps for Scotland against Northern Ireland
in 1961 and was in the 1963 Scottish side which overcame the handicap of losing
Eric Caldow with a broken leg to beat England 2-1. Baxter scored both Scottish
goals that day. In 1967 he was to perform similar heroics, inspiring Scotland
to a 3-2 victory over the reigning world champions—black and white television
footage of Baxter teasing the England defence with an astonishing display of ball
control is still played to this day.

Born in the Fife village of Hill o' Beath, the young Baxter served a brief
apprenticeship as a cabinet maker in nearby Dunfermline before succumbing
to the fate of most working men in a small Fife coal mining community—he
went down the pit. He played his early football with Crossgates Primrose, where
inevitably his performances caught the eye of Raith Rovers. Baxter initially
played part-time at Starks Park and kept on his job at the colliery, but it was
soon evident that Raith would be unable to hold on to such precocious talent
for long.

In the summer of 1960 and with a number of clubs expressing an interest,
Rangers manager Scot Symon gave Rovers a cheque for £27,000 and Baxter was
on his way to Ibrox.

Baxter's talent and not a little cockiness would soon see him establishing as
big a name as any player to have adorned the famous light blue shirt. His liking
for alcohol, however, was becoming almost as legendary as his skills on the
football field. Baxter would often skip training if he had been out on the town
the night before, and such scenarios would exasperate manager Scott Symon.
But Symon knew if he dropped him the Rangers fans would be on his back.

In 1963 Jim Baxter was, perhaps, at the peak of his powers. In October of
that year, to celebrate the centenary of the Football Association, England played
a Rest of the World side at Wembley. There was a glittering array of talent from
across the globe, including such stars as Yashin, Eusebio and Puskas, and in
midfield displaying as much skill as any of the famous names was Jim Baxter.

As the 1960s progressed, Baxter felt he was worth more money than Rangers
were prepared to offer him. He was particularly angered when a deal with
Spurs fell through, and it was clear his unrest could not be allowed to continue.
Eventually, in the close season of 1965, Baxter signed for Sunderland for a fee
of £80,000. The Wearsiders were hardly setting the First Division alight, and

Jim Baxter playing for Rangers (www.snspix.com)

in 1968, after a less than happy time at Roker Park, Baxter joined Nottingham Forest for £100,000.

Despite his previous achievements in a dark blue jersey, he was no longer being picked for Scotland, and it was no surprise that his spell at the City Ground lasted less than two years. Given a free transfer, the great man unexpectedly received an offer to return to Ibrox and play once again in the blue of Rangers. The move back to Glasgow was a big mistake, for the years of drinking and gambling had taken their toll—he was now a pale imitation of the player who set Scottish football alight less than a decade before. Though his glittering career was at an end, Jim Baxter was, at his very best, one of the greatest Scottish players ever.

RALPH BRAND
Inside-left

Born: Ralph Laidlaw Brand, Edinburgh, 8 December 1936
Height: 5ft 7in
Weight: 10st 0lb
Clubs: Broxburn Athletic; Glasgow Rangers; Manchester City; Sunderland; Raith Rovers
Scotland Caps: 8
Scotland Goals: 8

1961 v N Ireland (won 5-2) 2 goals, v Republic of Ireland (won 4-1) 2 goals,
        v Republic of Ireland (won 3-0) 1 goal, v Czechoslovakia (lost 0-4)
1962 v N Ireland (won 6-1) 2 goals, v Wales (won 2-0), v Czechoslovakia (lost 2-4),
        v Uruguay (lost 2-3) 1 goal

In eight international matches, Ralph Brand scored eight goals, including two on his debut in a 5-2 defeat of Northern Ireland. He was perhaps unfortunate in that the great Denis Law was a contemporary.

Brand was seen by Rangers manager, Bill Struth, on television when he played in the England v Scotland schoolboy international at Wembley in 1952. After a spell with Broxburn Athletic, he returned to Ibrox and made his Rangers debut against Kilmarnock, aged just 17. Rangers won 6-0 and the young Brand scored twice—it was an omen of things to come, for Ralph Brand became one of Rangers' greatest-ever goalscorers. After spending 1955 and 1956 doing National Service he returned to Ibrox, and in 1958-59 won his first League Championship medal as Rangers finished two points ahead of runners-up Hearts.

By 1960-61 he had formed a formidable strike partnership with Jimmy Millar, and over the next few seasons, they helped Rangers to three further League Championships and success in three Cup Finals and four League Cup Finals, during which he scored six goals. Ralph Brand put so much into a match that he'd often be found sitting in the dressing-room a full hour after the match, still anxious to talk about it! He was a deep thinker on the game, wanting to talk tactics and eager to do extra skills training. Surprisingly, for someone who scored 206 goals in 317 games for Rangers, he was never over-popular with the Ibrox crowd, who dismissed him as a poacher! With the Rangers team beginning to break up, he was allowed to join Manchester City for £30,000 in the summer of 1965. He ended his first season at Maine Road with a Second Division Championship winners' medal, but after a season in the top flight he moved to Sunderland. Whilst at Roker Park, he qualified as an FA Coach, later returning to Scotland to see out his career with Raith Rovers.

He was briefly in charge at Darlington, who under his management in 1972-73 experienced one of their worst-ever campaigns. He resigned after they had just beaten Yeovil Town in the re-election poll to manage Albion Rovers, later coaching Dunfermline Athletic before working as a taxi-driver.

BOBBY SHEARER

Right-back

Born: Robert Shearer, Hamilton, 29 December 1931
Height: 5ft 7in
Weight: 11st 0lb
Clubs: Burnbank Athletic; Hamilton Academicals; Glasgow Rangers; Queen of the South
Scotland Caps: 4
1961 v England (lost 3-9), v Republic of Ireland (won 4-1), v Republic of Ireland (won 3-0),
v Czechoslovakia (lost 0-4)

Though his lack of pace occasionally left him exposed at higher levels of the game and on his international debut he was part of the Scotland team beaten 9-3 by England at Wembley in April 1961, few Rangers players have collected more trophies than Bobby Shearer.

He played his early football for Hamilton Academicals, where his father was head groundsman. During his time with the Accies he proved his versatility, playing in every position except goal, but in December 1955 he joined Rangers, who paid £2,000 for his services.

For the best part of the next decade, Bobby Shearer was a good, if unpolished full-back who tackled with all the fierce intensity of a Jock Shaw! A red-haired firebrand of a right-back,. Shearer was soon appointed Rangers' captain, and never knowing when he was beaten, led the Ibrox club to six League Championship titles, three Scottish Cup Final victories and success in four League Cup Finals. Known as 'Captain Cutlass', Shearer was a death-or-glory, take no prisoners defender who formed a formidable full-back partnership with Eric Caldow. He also played for Rangers in the 1961 European Cup Winners' Cup Final when the Ibrox club lost 4-1 on aggregate to Fiorentina.

Shearer, who played in 407 games for Rangers, including a run of 165 consecutive matches, later joined Queen of the South as player-coach before in January 1967 becoming manager of Third Lanark. After the club folded the following season, Shearer took charge of Hamilton Academicals before leaving to concentrate on his business interests, which included bus-hiring and building firms.

PAT CRERAND

Right-half

Born: Patrick Timothy Crerand, Glasgow, 19 February 1939
Height: 5ft 11in
Weight: 11st 0lb
Clubs: Duntocher Hibernian; Glasgow Celtic; Manchester United
Scotland Caps: 16
1961 v Republic of Ireland (won 4-1), v Republic of Ireland (won 3-0),
v Czechoslovakia (lost 0-4)
1962 v Czechoslovakia (won 3-2), v N Ireland (won 6-1), v Wales (won 2-0),
v Czechoslovakia (lost 2-4), v England (won 2-0), v Uruguay (lost 2-3)

1963 v Wales (won 3-2), v N Ireland (won 5-1)
1964 v N Ireland (lost 1-2)
1965 v England (2-2), v Poland (1-1), v Finland (won 2-1)
1966 v Poland (lost 1-2)

An utter gentleman off the park, Pat Crerand often had a formidable temper in the heat of the battle. He was ordered off playing for Scotland against Czechoslovakia in Bratislava in May 1961 for an alleged head-butt, and was involved in the fracas against Uruguay at Hampden a year later, when an unidentified Scotland player punched the referee in a melee!

Having joined Celtic from Duntocher Hibs in 1957, he soon won a place in the Parkhead club's side, and during his time with the club, won 11 of his 16 full caps. He also represented the Scottish League and appeared in the 1961 Scottish Cup Final which Celtic lost 2-0 to Dunfermline Athletic after a replay.

In February 1963 he was transferred to Manchester United for £56,000—at the time a record transfer fee for a wing-half. After only a few months with the Reds, he won an FA Cup winners' medal following the 3-1 defeat of Leicester City.

Crerand was a thoughtful player with a firm belief in attacking, constructive football; he initiated numerous attacks with long, shrewd passes. His strong, compact build gave him scope to tackle swiftly and firmly—and began to give United a much more balanced look. Any lack of pace was more than compensated for by his superb distribution skills. 'Paddy' Crerand was an architect, sweeping out accurate crossfield passes of 40 and 50 yards to his forwards.

Along with Bobby Charlton and Nobby Stiles, he formed the midfield that drove Manchester United to victory in the European Cup. He also went on to collect two Championship medals in 1965 and 1967, his creative skills being a big factor behind United's success throughout the 1960s. After United's 4-3 win at Maine Road in the final game of the 1970-71 season, he decided to retire. He had played in 392 first team games for the Reds and though he only scored 15 goals, he made many more.

He then joined United's coaching staff before, in January 1973, becoming the club's assistant-manager. He left Old Trafford in July 1976 to become manager at Northampton Town, where he stayed for six months before leaving the game to run a public house in Altrincham.

BILLY McNEILL
Centre-half
Born: William McNeill, Bellshill, 2 March 1940
Height: 6ft 1in
Weight: 12st 0lb
Clubs: Blantyre Victoria; Glasgow Celtic
Scotland caps: 29
Scotland goals: 3
1961 v England (lost 3-9), v Republic of Ireland (won 4-1), v Republic of Ireland (won 3-0),

v Czechoslovakia (lost 0-4)

1962 v Czechoslovakia (won 3-2), v N Ireland (won 6-1), v England (won 2-0),
v Uruguay (lost 2-3)

1963 v Republic of Ireland (lost 0-1), v Spain (won 6-2)

1964 v Wales (won 2-1), v England (won 1-0), v West Germany (drew 2-2)

1965 v England (drew 2-2), v Spain (drew 0-0), v Poland (drew 1-1), v Finland (won 2-1)

1966 v N Ireland (lost 2-3), v Poland (lost 1-2) 1 goal

1967 v USSR (lost 0-2)

1968 v England (drew 1-1)

1969 v Cyprus (won 5-0), v Wales (won 5-3) 1 goal, v England (lost 1-4),
v Cyprus (won 8-0) 1 goal

1970 v West Germany (lost 2-3)

1972 v N Ireland (won 2-0), v Wales (won 1-0), v England (lost 0-1)

One of Celtic's greatest players of all time, Billy McNeill could do no wrong in Scottish football as his honours list shows—nine League Championship medals, seven Scottish Cup winners' medals and six League Cup winners' medals. He is also the Celtic skipper who raised the European Cup over his head at Lisbon on 25 May 1967 after Celtic had beaten Inter Milan 2-1.

Billy McNeill (www.snspix.com)

He also appeared 29 times for Scotland, though to be fair it should have been more. Even in defeat he showed magnificence—on his international debut he was the one Scottish success in the 9-3 thrashing by England at Wembley on 15 April 1961.

McNeill played the first of 831 competitive games for Celtic in a 2-0 home win over Clyde in August 1958, replacing the injured Bobby Evans. By the start of the 1963-64 season he had replaced Dunky MacKay as the Celtic skipper, and though his performances during that campaign prompted Spurs to make an offer for his services, he decided to remain at Parkhead. Jock Stein was appointed as manager and the corner was turned. McNeill headed home the winner in the 3-2 Scottish Cup Final defeat of Dunfermline to bring Celtic a major trophy after a long barren spell. Another important header came against Vojvodina in the European Cup quarter-final to send the Bhoys into the competition's last four, but probably his best performance in a Celtic shirt came in the semi-final second leg against Dukla Prague, when he nullified the threat of the big Czech Novak in an atmosphere that was fraught with tension for the entire 90 minutes.

McNeill, who was the Scottish 'Player of the Year' in 1965, was awarded the MBE in 1974.

In June 1977 this all-time Celtic great entered management with Clyde before taking over the reins at Aberdeen. The Dons narrowly missed out on the League title and the Scottish Cup, but after a year at Pittodrie he moved back to manage at Parkhead. In five seasons with the club, he won three League Championships and the Scottish Cup and League Cup once apiece. In the summer of 1983 he took charge of Manchester City, leading the Maine Road club to promotion to the First Division in 1984-85 and to the final of the Full Members' Cup where they lost 5-4 to Chelsea. He then had a terrible season with Aston Villa who, after finishing bottom of the First Division, were relegated. He then had a second spell as manager of Celtic, helping them win the Scottish League and Cup double in 1987-88 and to a further Scottish Cup success the following season, before handing over to Liam Brady.

JOHNNY MacLEOD
Winger
Born: John Murdoch MacLeod, Edinburgh, 23 November 1938
Height: 5ft 6in
Weight: 10st 4lb
Clubs: Armadale Thistle; Hibernian; Arsenal; Aston Villa; Mechelen (Belgium); Raith Rovers
Scotland caps: 4
1961 v England (lost 3-9), v Republic of Ireland (won 4-1), v Republic of Ireland (won 3-0), v Czechoslovakia (lost 0-4)

Johnny MacLeod won four Scottish caps, making his international debut in the infamous 9-3 defeat by England in 1961. He also played for Scotland in three World Cup qualifiers in the unsuccessful campaign to qualify for the 1962 World Cup Finals in Chile. In a side dripping with talent—Law, Crerand and St John—they failed to reach the finals after losing 4-0 to Czechoslovakia in what was MacLeod's last appearance for the national side.

He joined Hibernian from Armadale Thistle in 1957 and spent four years at Easter Road. During that time, he was a member of the Hibs' side that lost 1-0 to Clyde in the 1958 Scottish Cup Final, but on a happier note he netted a hat-trick the following year as Hibs beat Partick Thistle 10-2!

Great things were expected of Johnny MacLeod when he crossed the Border to join Arsenal in the summer of 1961 for a fee of £40,000—at the time, the highest fee ever paid for a winger. Many pundits predicted a long and illustrious international career, but he failed to achieve the desired effect for his new employers, and his club form never earned him a further call to his country's colours.

Though he was more adept at crossing the ball accurately than many First Division flankmen and could switch wings when necessary, he was rarely a match-winner. Never a prolific marksman, he can claim the honour of scoring Arsenal's first goal in European competition in the Inter Cities Fairs Cup encounter with Staevnet of Denmark at Highbury in September 1963.

With the younger George Armstrong pushing for a first team place, he was transferred to Aston Villa for £35,000. An instant hit with the fans, he was a first team regular at Villa Park for four seasons before losing his place to Willie Anderson. He later sampled Belgian football with KV Mechelen before ending his career back in Scotland with Raith Rovers.

PAT QUINN

Inside-forward
Born: Patrick Quinn, Glasgow, 26 April 1936
Height: 5ft 6in
Weight: 10st 3lb
Clubs: Bridgeton Waverley; Motherwell; Blackpool; Hibernian; East Fife
Scotland caps: 4
Scotland goals: 1
1961   v England (lost 3-9) 1 goal, v Republic of Ireland (won 4-1),
        v Republic of Ireland (won 3-0)
1962   v Uruguay (lost 2-3)

Pat Quinn made his international debut for Scotland in the 9-3 debacle against England at Wembley in 1961, going on to make four full appearances and play six times for the Scottish League.

He played his early football for Bridgeton Waverley before joining Motherwell in December 1955. He made his debut in rather unusual circumstances, being a substitute for a friendly against Preston North End to mark the opening of Motherwell's floodlights.

Pat Quinn was without doubt a gifted player—his vision and pin-point passing soon enabled him to become a valuable link in the 'Ancell Babes' team. There were many highs in the Fir Park career of a player who relied on an astute football brain as opposed to either speed or strength. In the match against Falkirk in 1962, Quinn scored four times in a 9-1 demolition of the Bairns—it could have been much worse because Motherwell led 9-0 at half-time! He also netted a hat-trick in the 7-0 defeat of Leeds United in a friendly, and he was an integral member of the Motherwell side that beat Rangers 5-2 in a Scottish Cup tie played at Ibrox. Having scored 83 goals in 196 games, Quinn left Fir Park to join Blackpool.

Though he scored on his debut in a 3-1 win for the Seasiders over local rivals Bolton Wanderers, he only remained at Bloomfield Road for a year. He then joined Walter Galbraith's Hibernian side and later became player/assistant-manager of East Fife before taking up coaching roles with Partick Thistle, Hibs, Motherwell and Hamilton Academicals.

ALEX HAMILTON

Right-back

Born: Alexander William Hamilton, Bo'ness, 31 January 1939
Died: 28 July 1993
Height: 5ft 7in
Weight: 11st 0lb
Clubs: Westrigg Bluebell; Dundee; Durban United (South Africa); East London United (South Africa)
Scotland caps: 24

1962 v Wales (won 2-0), v Czechoslovakia (lost 2-4), v England (won 2-0),
v Uruguay (lost 2-3)

1963 v Wales (won 3-2), v N Ireland (won 5-1), v England (won 2-1), v Austria (won 4-1),
v Norway (lost 3-4), v Republic of Ireland (lost 0-1)

1964 v N Ireland (lost 1-2), v Norway (won 6-1), v Wales (won 2-1), v England (won 1-0),
v West Germany (drew 2-2)

1965 v Wales (lost 2-3), v Finland (won 3-1), v N Ireland (won 3-2), v England (drew 2-2),
v Spain (drew 0-0), v Poland (drew 1-1), v Finland (won 2-1)

1966 v N Ireland (lost 2-3), v Poland (lost 1-2)

Still Dundee's most capped player, full-back Alex Hamilton won the first of his 24 caps against Wales in November 1961, a match that ended in a 2-0 win for the Scots. He was a regular in the national side for four years, making the last of his international appearances against Poland. Though he never got on the scoresheet, it wasn't for the want of trying, as his long-range shots hit the woodwork and forced opposition keepers into making tremendous saves.

Hamilton, who also appeared for the Scottish League XI, was a fine defender, short and stocky and seldom outwitted. He joined Dundee from Westrigg Bluebell in March 1957 and missed very few games in 10 years at Dens Park. An important member of the Dundee side that won the League Championship in 1961-62, finishing three points ahead of runners-up Rangers, he was, a year later, outstanding as the Dark Blues reached the semi-final of the European Cup, only to lose 5-2 on aggregate to AC Milan. Hamilton also played in the 1964 Scottish Cup Final when the Dark Blues lost 3-1 to Rangers.

Playing his last match for Dundee in February 1967, Hamilton headed for South Africa where he played for both Durban United and East London United. He then had a spell coaching Dundee Violet, before returning to South Africa to manage East London. Ending his involvement with the game in 1988, he returned to Dundee to take up an administration post.

IAN URE

Centre-half

Born: John Francombe 'Ian' Ure, Ayr, 7 December 1939
Height: 6ft 1in
Weight: 12st 8lb
Clubs: Dalry Thistle; Dundee; Arsenal; Manchester United; St Mirren
Scotland caps: 11

1962 v Wales (won 2-0), v Czechoslovakia (lost 2-4)

1963 v Wales (won 3-2), v N Ireland (won 4-1), v England (won 2-1), v Austria (won 4-1), v Norway (lost 3-4), v Spain (won 6-2)

1964 v N Ireland (lost 1-2), v Norway (won 6-1)

1968 v N Ireland (lost 0-1)

Ian Ure began his first-class career with Dundee, and during his five years at Dens Park, he became one of the leading centre-halves in Europe.

He helped Dundee to their first and only Scottish League Championship in 1961-62, and the same season saw him win the first of 11 international caps. Ure played in the European Cup semi-finals the following season before signing for Arsenal in August 1963 for £62,500—then a world record fee for a centre-half.

Ure established himself in the Gunners' League side in 1963-64, missing only one game. However, during seasons 1964-65 and 1965-66, he played in only half the club's league matches due to poor form and a succession of niggling injuries. He regained his place and fitness in 1966-67 when playing in 37 league games as well as winning back his place in the national side. He appeared in the League Cup Finals of 1968 and 1969 when Arsenal played Leeds United and Swindon Town respectively, but after playing in 202 League and Cup games he was allowed to leave Highbury.

Transferred to Manchester United for £80,000, the solidly-built central defender's blond hair stood out in the Reds' back division. Manager Wilf McGuinness' only signing, he remained at Old Trafford for two seasons before returning to play and manage in Scottish League football with St Mirren and East Stirling.

He then coached in Iceland before returning to Scotland in 1977 to become a social worker based in Kilmarnock.

EDDIE CONNACHAN
Goalkeeper
Born: Edward Devlin Connachan, Prestonpans, 27 August 1935
Height: 5ft 9in
Weight: 12st 13lb
Clubs: Dalkeith Thistle; Dunfermline Athletic; Middlesbrough; Falkirk
Scotland caps: 2
1962 v Czechoslovakia (lost 2-4), v Uruguay (lost 2-3)

Eddie Connachan's daring as a goalkeeper was soundly based on confidence in his own abilities of judgement and assured clean handling.

He began his career with Dalkeith Thistle, where his displays between the posts attracted the attention of a number of Scotland's top clubs. In the summer of 1958, Connachan joined Dunfermline Athletic, and within twelve months of his arrival at East End Park, he made the first of four appearances for the Scottish League.

When Dunfermline won the Scottish Cup in 1960-61, Connachan was in outstanding form. The Pars set out on the Cup trail by beating Berwick Rangers 4-1 and then Stranraer 3-1 before being drawn away to Aberdeen. The whole of Scottish football sat up as Athletic came away from Pittodrie with a 6-3 victory, before booking a place in the semi-final with a 4-3 thrashing of Alloa. Their opponents at Tynecastle were St Mirren, and though Dunfermline dominated the proceedings, the game remained goalless. Dunfermline won the replay to win through to the final, where their opponents were Celtic. Everyone expected the Bhoys to win the Cup, but despite losing Williamson with a leg injury, the 10 men of Dunfermline, thanks in the main to Eddie Connachan, held on for a goalless draw. In the replay, Connachan's goal was under constant siege on an awful wet night, but his handling of the greasy ball was magnificent as Dunfermline won the Cup for the first time in their history.

After winning two full caps for Scotland, Connachan left East End Park to join Middlesbrough for a fee of £5,000.

Though he was the Ayresome Park club's first-choice keeper for three seasons, he was unable to help the Teeside club win promotion to he First Division, and in November 1966 he returned to Scotland to see out his career with Falkirk.

HUGH ROBERTSON
Outside-left
Born: Hugh Robertson, Auchinleck, 29 November 1939
Height: 5ft 5in
Weight: 10st 9lb
Clubs: Auchinleck Talbot; Dundee; Dunfermline Athletic; Arbroath
Scotland caps: 1
1962 v Czechoslovakia (lost 2-4)

Outside-left Hugh Robertson's only Scottish cap came during Dundee's League Championship-winning season of 1961-62 when he played against Czechoslovakia in the World Cup qualifier play-off at the Heysel Stadium in Brussels. It was Robertson who made Scotland's goals in the 4-2 extra-time defeat, both converted by Liverpool's Ian St John. Despite his impressive debut he did not retain his place in the side for Scotland's next game five months later against England at Hampden Park.

He was spotted playing junior football for Auchinleck Talbot prior to joining the Dens Park club in 1957. He gave fine service to the Dark Blues and was particularly outstanding in that League Championship-winning campaign, both scoring and creating numerous goalscoring chances. He was also on the wing in 1964 when Dundee reached the Scottish Cup Final only to lose 3-1 to Rangers. After another season at Dundee, Robertson left to play for Dunfermline Athletic, who paid £10,000 for his services.

The flying winger, who was a good reader of the game, reached another Scottish Cup Final in 1968, but this time was on the winning side as the Pars beat Hearts 3-1. He continued to give good service to the East End Park club for a further three seasons before in 1971 leaving to play for Arbroath.

He was hugely popular at Gayfield Park, but in his only season there he was hampered by a spate of niggling injuries, and in the summer of 1972, he was forced to retire on medical grounds. On leaving the playing side, he stayed with Arbroath as the club's trainer before two years later returning to Dundee, where he built up a considerable reputation as the Dens Park club's chief coach.

BILLY RITCHIE
Goalkeeper
Born: William Ritchie, Newtongrange, 1 September 1936
Height: 5ft 11in
Weight: 13st 0lb
Clubs: Bathgate Thistle; Glasgow Rangers; Partick Thistle; Motherwell
Scotland caps: 1
1962 v Uruguay (lost 2-3)

A series of consistent displays between the posts for Bathgate Thistle led to Billy Ritchie joining Rangers in the summer of 1954. With George Niven ensconced as Rangers' first-choice keeper, Ritchie had to bide his time in the club's reserve side. He made his debut in a Charity Cup game at home to Third Lanark in May 1957 but it was the second-half of the 1957-58 season before he won a regular place in the Rangers' side.

Just before the start of the following campaign, Ritchie's National Service took him to Cyprus, and he missed the whole of the 1958-59 season. When he returned to Ibrox, Niven's form was so good that he found himself back in the club's reserve side.

Following Niven's transfer to Partick Thistle, Ritchie returned to first team action and was a virtual ever-present for the next five seasons. In 1961-62 he helped Rangers win both the Scottish Cup and the League Cup, and was rewarded with an international cap in Scotland's match against Uruguay at Hampden Park, when he came on as a substitute for Dunfermline's Eddie Connachan. Unfortunate to be a contemporary of Spurs' Bill Brown, he helped Rangers win two League Championship titles, four Scottish Cups and three League Cups.

Billy Ritchie was an unassuming and modest character, known as 'The Quiet Man' at Ibrox, but he was also a solidly reliable keeper who kept a clean sheet in every third game he played for Rangers. The last of his 340 games for the Ibrox club came against Aberdeen in a League Cup semi-final at Hampden in October 1966. A year later he moved to Partick Thistle before joining Motherwell as the Fir Park club's player-coach.

Ritchie later coached West Calder before ending his involvement with the game.

WILLIE HENDERSON
Outside-right
Born: William Henderson, Baillieston, 24 January 1944
Height: 5ft 4in
Weight: 10st 3lb

Clubs: Edinburgh Athletic; Glasgow Rangers; Sheffield Wednesday; Hong Kong Rangers; Airdrieonians

Scotland caps: 29

Scotland goals: 5

1963 v Wales (won 3-2) I goal, v N Ireland (won 5-1) I goal, v England (won 2-1), v Austria (won 4-1), v Norway (lost 3-4), v Republic of Ireland (lost 0-1), v Spain (won 6-2) I goal

1964 v N Ireland (lost 1-2), v Norway (won 6-1), v Wales (won 2-1), v England (won 1-0), v West Germany (drew 2-2)

1965 v England (drew 2-2), v Spain (drew 0-0), v Poland (drew 1-1), v Finland (won 2-1)

1966 v N Ireland (lost 2-3), v Poland (lost 1-2), v Italy (won 1-0)

1967 v Wales (drew 1-1), v N Ireland (won 2-1)

1968 v Holland (drew 0-0)

1969 v N Ireland (drew 1-1), v England (lost 1-4), v Cyprus (won 8-0) I goal

1970 v Republic of Ireland (drew 1-1)

1971 v Portugal (lost 0-2)

Willie Henderson was capped by Scotland at the age of 18 years 269 days—only Denis Law in the modern era played for the national side at a younger age. He scored on his debut in a 3-2 defeat of Wales and went on to win 29 caps over an eight-year period.

He was something of a boy prodigy—a schoolboy international with Airdrie Schools, he was one of the few who made the transition to full international status. He won a place in the Rangers team at 18 and stayed there, hastening the departure of Alex Scott to Everton. By the age of 19, he had won every domestic honour the Scottish game could offer, his speed, dribbling skills and ball control being the main features of his game. However, he did have his fair share of injuries, and in 1964-65 a bunion operation caused him several months of inaction. Also Henderson had some eyesight difficulties and he wore contact lenses. The story goes that towards the end of an Old Firm match he rushed over to the bench and asked 'How long to go, how long to go?' Jock Stein replied 'Go and ask at the other dugout you bloody fool—this is the Celtic bench!'

As popular with Ibrox fans as any player in the club's recent history, Henderson had scored 62 goals in 426 games when he left Rangers to join Sheffield Wednesday in the summer of 1972. Though his stay at Hillsborough was only short, he played with all the enthusiasm of a much younger player, helping to inspire the up-and-coming Eric Potts. His skills were evident for all to see and it seemed surprising that manager Dooley had secured his services on a free transfer.

He left Wednesday in May 1974 to join Hong Kong Rangers, his performances leading to him captaining the Hong Kong national side in 1975. He later returned to Scotland to appear in a handful of games for Airdrie.

DAVIE GIBSON

Inside-forward

Born: David Wedderburn Gibson, Winchburgh, 23 September 1938

Height: 5ft 7in

Weight: 10st 10lb
Clubs: Livingston United; Hibernian; Leicester City; Aston Villa; Exeter City
Scotland caps: 7
Scotland goals: 3
1963   v Austria (won 4-1), v Norway (lost 3-4), v Republic of Ireland (lost 0-1),
          v Spain (won 6-2) 1 goal
1964   v N Ireland (lost 1-2)
1965   v Wales (lost 2-3) 1 goal, v Finland (won 3-1) 1 goal

Davie Gibson won seven Scotland caps whilst with Leicester City, playing in the Scotland side that—in front of 94,596 at Hampden Park—was involved in an infamous match against Austria on 8 May 1963. With Scotland 4-1 up, the game was abandoned with just 11 minutes remaining, because of on-field violence by the visitors.

Hailing from the same West Lothian village of Winchburgh—which has produced more famous footballers than seems appropriate for its size—as Willie Harper (Hibs' goalkeeper of the 1920s), Willie Thornton (Rangers and Scotland international) and Bobby Murray (who found fame with West Bromwich Albion in the 1950s), Gibson made his Hibs debut in 1958. A classy inside-forward who had tremendous vision, he was a virtual ever-present in the four seasons that followed. He left Easter Road to join Leicester City in January 1962. However, he still had to complete his National Service when Matt Gillies paid £25,000 to take him to Filbert Street.

As soon as he turned full-time, he forged an unforgettable partnership with Mike Stringfellow, and his elegant control and passing skills were a major prompt to City's Wembley visits in 1963 and 1969. Davie Gibson found the net himself with pleasing regularity, scoring in both legs of the 1964 League Cup Final victory over Stoke City and knocking in three goals in his seven Scottish international appearances.

His artistry was barely on the wane when, after scoring 53 goals in 339 games, he left Leicester to give a veteran's course in midfield style at Aston Villa and Exeter City. While with the former club he returned to Wembley as substitute for the 1971 League Cup Final.

After bowing out of the playing ranks, he worked in the postal service and helped run a residential home for the elderly.

DAVIE HOLT
Left-back
Born: David Duff Holt, Glasgow, 3 January 1936
Height: 5ft 8in
Weight: 11st 9lb
Clubs: Queen's Park; Heart of Midlothian; Partick Thistle
Scotland caps: 5
1963   v Austria (won 4-1), v Norway (lost 3-4), v Republic of Ireland (lost 0-1),
          v Spain (won 6-2)
1964   v West Germany (drew 2-2)

Davie Holt's Scotland debut against Austria at Hampden Park in 1963 was marred by controversy. With Scotland leading 4-1, the match had to be abandoned after 79 minutes due to the rough play of the visitors. Holt, who went on to win five full caps, would surely have won more but for having the misfortune to be competing with Rangers' Eric Caldow for the left-back spot.

He was a late starter to the professional game after playing amateur for several seasons, and he even had a spell with Stockton Amateurs when he was in the RAF. He joined Queen's Park in 1957 and played for Scotland at Under-23 level and Great Britain in the 1960 Rome Olympics.

Joining Hearts in 1960, he soon established himself as the club's first-choice left-back and played in the two League Cup Final matches of 1962 with Rangers, a 1-1 draw and a 3-1 replay defeat. Indeed, Holt was the only player who appeared in all 51 matches for Hearts that season. He did win a League Cup winners' medal in 1963 as Hearts beat Kilmarnock 1-0 and went on to play in 350 games for the club, Rarely venturing across his own halfway line, he did not score a single competitive goal in his time at Tynecastle.

He eventually lost his place to Arthur Mann, but when he was sold to Manchester City for £65,000, Holt returned to first team action, playing his last game for the club against Arbroath in 1969.

Aged 33, Holt then left Hearts to sign for Partick Thistle, but his stay at Firhill was brief.

JIMMY MILLAR
Centre-forward
Born: James Millar, Edinburgh, 20 November 1934
Height: 5ft 6in
Weight: 10st 11lb
Clubs: Merchiston Thistle; Dunfermline Athletic; Glasgow Rangers; Dundee United
Scotland caps: 2
1963 v Austria (won 4-1), v Republic of Ireland (lost 0-1)

Jimmy Millar was an outstanding half-back for Dunfermline when Rangers signed him for £5,000 in January 1955, and at times he played half-back at Ibrox. But above all else he was a dashing centre-forward, a never-say-die player, as courageous as any player Rangers have had on their books.

The move to centre-forward came in May 1959 when Rangers were touring Scandinavia. In a match in Denmark, the score at half-time was 0-0, but with Max Murray injured, Millar was moved up to centre-forward and responded by scoring all Rangers goals in a 4-0 win!

As a centre-forward, Millar led his line well, and although he stood only 5ft 6in, he was quite marvellous in the air and would knock balls down for Ralph Brand, who with him formed a fearsome strike force. The 'M and B Tablets' as they were dubbed, were part of one of Rangers' greatest-ever teams, helping the club win three League Championships, five Scottish Cups and three League Cups.

He made his international debut in the abandoned game against Austria, but sadly his career at this level was compromised by injury. Millar had scored 160 goals in 317 games for Rangers when, in the summer of 1967, he was given a free transfer and joined Dundee United.

He spent two seasons at Tannadice, but much of his time there was spent on the treatment table, and in 1969 he left to become manager of Raith Rovers.

ADAM BLACKLAW
Goalkeeper
Born: Adam Smith Blacklaw, Aberdeen, 2 September 1937
Height: 6ft 0in
Weight: 15st 0lb
Clubs: Burnley; Blackburn Rovers; Blackpool; Great Harwood
Scotland caps: 3
1963 v Norway (lost 3-4), v Spain (won 6-2)
1966 v Italy (lost 0-3)

The son of a ship's carpenter, Adam Blacklaw played his school football in the forward line and represented Aberdeen Schools as a centre-forward. Like many top goalkeepers, his career between the posts began only when he was persuaded to don the green jersey by a teacher. Also, like so many top keepers, he was a natural from the start and was soon selected to represent Scotland schoolboys against England at Filbert Street.

His outstanding display had the scouts drooling, and though the hosts Leicester City wanted to sign him, Burnley were the quickest off the mark and he was recruited to the Turf Moor groundstaff in 1954. After two years as understudy to Colin McDonald, Blacklaw became the club's first-choice keeper following an injury that curtailed the England international's career. Blacklaw's consistency and ability to avoid injury—he missed just three games over the next five seasons—was remarkable.

After playing a key role in the Clarets' League Championship success of 1959-60, the European Cup campaign and the near miss in the League and Cup in 1962 when the club finished runners-up in both competitions, Blacklaw's form brought him the first of three Scotland caps against Norway in Bergen. Unfortunately a Denis Law hat-trick was not enough to prevent a 4-3 victory for the Norwegians.

Dropped by Burnley after a heavy defeat at Leeds United in March 1965, Blacklaw appeared in just a handful of games over the next two seasons before, having appeared in 383 games, he joined Blackburn Rovers. After three seasons at Ewood Park he moved to Blackpool before ending his playing days with non-League Great Harwood.

FRANK McLINTOCK

Wing-half/ Centre-half

Born: Francis McLintock, Glasgow, 28 December 1939
Height: 5ft 10in
Weight: 11st 4lb
Clubs: Shawfield Juniors; Leicester City; Arsenal; Queen's Park Rangers
Scotland caps: 9
Scotland goals: 1
1963 v Norway (lost 3-4), v Republic of Ireland (lost 0-1), v Spain (won 6-2) 1 goal
1965 v N Ireland (won 3-2)
1967 v USSR (lost 0-2)
1970 v N Ireland (won 1-0)
1971 v Wales (drew 0-0), v N Ireland (lost 0-1), v England (lost 1-3)

Frank McLintock possessed the rare combination of toughness and elegance, and soon became an important member of the Leicester City side. Oozing footballing class, it came as no surprise when he graduated to full Scottish honours or when Billy Wright's Arsenal eventually paid the Foxes their then record outgoing fee of £80,000 for his services. While at Filbert Street, McLintock had played in two FA Cup Finals in 1961 and 1963, and both times was on the losing side.

During his first three seasons at Highbury, Frank McLintock was probably the most consistent of all the Arsenal players, in a side that was probably the poorest for many years. In 1967-68 he became team captain and

Frank McLintock

guided Arsenal to the League Cup Final against Leeds. In 1968-69 Arsenal finished fourth in the League, the club's highest position for 15 seasons, and McLintock played in the League Cup Final against Swindon Town. At the beginning of the following season he asked for a transfer owing to the lack of success at Highbury.

Fortunately for both him and the club he was persuaded to stay. In that season, Arsenal gained their first major honour for 17 years, winning the Inter Cities Fairs Cup. In 1970-71, McLintock became only the second player that century to captain a 'double'-winning side and was voted Footballer of the Year. In 1971-72 he captained Arsenal to the FA Cup Final against Leeds, returning to Wembley for his sixth major final. In 1972-73 he led Arsenal to the runners-up spot in the First Division, but at the end of that campaign he was surprisingly allowed to leave Highbury to join Queen's Park Rangers for £20,000.

It looked like a case of him being written off too early, as he assisted Rangers to a near-miss title bid in 1975-76. After four years at Loftus Road, he entered management with Leicester City, but too many of his dealings in the transfer market bore the stamp of desperation, and the club were already certainties for relegation when he resigned in April 1978. After a spell as youth coach at Queen's Park Rangers, he managed Brentford and was assistant at Millwall before becoming a part-time players' agent.

TOMMY LAWRENCE
Goalkeeper

Born: Thomas Lawrence, Dailly, 14 May 1940
Height: 5ft 11in
Weight: 13st 12lb
Clubs: Liverpool; Tranmere Rovers; Chorley
Scotland caps: 3
1963 v Republic of Ireland (lost 0-1)
1969 v West Germany (drew 1-1), v Wales (won 5-3)

When Bill Shankly arrived at Anfield in the summer of 1959, he found Tommy Lawrence languishing in Liverpool's reserve side. Shankly soon promoted him and he went on to play in 387 games for the club.

Affectionately known as 'The Flying Pig', Lawrence was never a spectacular goalkeeper, but was always dependable. What he lacked in height, he made up for with his acute positional sense, and he also had an athleticism that belied his bulk. Defenders liked him, they knew where they were and could trust in his reliability. He operated behind a Liverpool back-four which usually played square and which pushed upfield whenever possible. When it was breached by an opponent's runs from midfield or a penetrating pass, Lawrence was then capable of reacting instantly to danger.

After just one season in the Liverpool side, Lawrence won the first of three full caps for Scotland when he played in the 1-0 defeat at the hands of the Republic of Ireland. The following season of 1963-64 brought a League Championship medal and Lawrence climaxed an accomplished campaign by brilliantly saving a George Eastham penalty, the turning point in a 5-0 demolition of Arsenal, which clinched the title. His consistency in the Liverpool goal over the next few seasons was remarkable, it being a complete mystery that his international recall should have been delayed for six years. Even then, it was limited to two matches, in both of which he found himself unfairly blamed for some of the goals.

He remained Liverpool's first-choice keeper until February 1970—missing only five league games in eight seasons—before finally giving way to Ray Clemence.

He then moved across the Mersey to play for Tranmere Rovers, but after two-and-a-half seasons as the Prenton Park club's first-choice goalkeeper, he left to play non-League football for Chorley before working night shift at a Warrington wire factory.

DAVID PROVAN
Full-back
Born: David Provan, Falkirk, 11 March 1941
Height: 6ft 2in
Weight: 12st 1lb
Clubs: Bonnyvale Star; Glasgow Rangers; Crystal Palace; Plymouth Argyle; St Mirren
Scotland caps: 5
1964 v N Ireland (lost 1-2), v Norway (won 6-1)
1966 v Italy (won 1-0), v Italy (lost 0-3), v Holland (lost 0-3)

Signed by Rangers from Bonnyvale Star as a centre-half—not surprising considering his height and consequent aerial command—he was kept out of that position by the form of Paterson and McKinnon. Converted into a more than useful full-back, he got his chance in the Rangers side when Eric Caldow suffered a broken leg in the Wembley international of 1963.

By the mid-1960s, David Provan had developed from a solid club craftsman into an international class defender, and in October 1963 he won the first of five full caps in the game against Northern Ireland. Provan, who had also represented Scotland at Under-23 level and played for the Scottish League XI, helped Rangers win the League Championship in 1962-63 and 1963-64, the Scottish Cup in 1963, 1964 and 1966 and the League Cup in 1964 and 1965. For much of his time with Rangers, he partnered Caldow, Bobby Shearer and Kai Johansen, and played in the European Cup Winners' Cup Final of 1967 when Rangers lost 1-0 to Bayern Munich.

Having appeared in 262 games for the Ibrox club, he was released by manager Willie Waddell in 1970 and appeared in one game for Crystal Palace before joining Plymouth Argyle. He stayed at Home Park for four seasons, appearing in 128 games for the Pilgrims before returning to Scotland to see out his career with St Mirren.

On hanging up his boots, he remained at Love Street as assistant-manager to Alex Ferguson before leaving to manage Albion Rovers. He later ended his involvement with the game as chief scout for Rangers under the management of John Greig.

ALAN GILZEAN
Forward
Born: Alan John Gilzean, Coupar-Angus, 22 October 1938
Height: 6ft 0in
Weight: 12st 4lb
Clubs: Dundee Violet; Dundee; Aldershot; Tottenham Hotspur; Highland Park (South Africa)
Scotland caps: 22
Scotland goals: 12

1964 v Norway (won 6-1), v Wales (won 2-1), v England (won 1-0) 1 goal,
v West Germany (drew 2-2) 2 goals

1965 v N Ireland (won 3-2) 1 goal, v Spain (drew 0-0)

1966 v N Ireland (lost 2-3) 2 goals, v Poland (lost 1-2), v Italy (won 1-0), v Wales (won 4-1)

1968 v Wales (won 3-2) 2 goals

1969 v Austria (won 2-1), v Cyprus (won 5-0) 2 goals, v West Germany (drew 1-1),
v Wales (won 5-3) 1 goal, v England (lost 1-4), v Cyprus (won 8-0)

1970 v West Germany (lost 2-3) 1 goal, v Austria (lost 0-2), v N Ireland (won 1-0),
v England (drew 0-0)

1971 v Portugal (lost 0-2)

Alan Gilzean, who scored over 100 league goals for Dundee, was a key figure in the Dens Park club's team that won the Scottish League title in 1961-62, reached the semi-final of the European Champions Cup the following season and the 1964 Scottish Cup Final. He won three Under-23 caps, played three times for the Scottish League and won five full international caps, the first in November 1963 against Norway, before a £72,500 move to Tottenham Hotspur.

In November 1964, a month before his move to Spurs, he had scored twice on his White Hart Lane debut for a Scotland XI against Spurs in a memorial match for John White. Though he had been an out-and-out centre-forward with Dundee, Gilzean had Jimmy Greaves alongside him at White Hart Lane and had to adapt his playing style to suit the club's principal goalscorer. A member of the 1967 FA Cup-winning team, his place appeared under threat following the signing of Martin Chivers in January 1968, but Gilzean showed his adaptability and it was Greaves who left White Hart Lane. With Gilzean now partnering Chivers, Spurs won the League Cup in 1971 and 1973 and the UEFA Cup in 1972. He won a further 17 caps for Scotland before finishing his Spurs career on the 1974 tour to Mauritius.

Gilzean, who scored 173 goals in 506 first team games in his 10 years with the North London club, always seemed able to find space and dangerous positions, but without doubt his greatest asset was his exceptional heading ability. It wasn't just powerful, his touch more often than not was deft and delicate.

On leaving Spurs he went to South Africa, but only stayed three months, and for a spell during 1975 was manager of Stevenage Athletic until they folded. After that he worked as a manager of a transport company in Enfield.

JIM KENNEDY
Left-back/ Left-half

Born: James Kennedy, Johnstone, 31 January 1934
Died: 2 December 2003
Height: 5ft 10in
Weight: 11st 11lb
Clubs: Duntocher Hibernian; Glasgow Celtic; Morton
Scotland caps: 6

1964 v Wales (won 2-1), v England (won 1-0), v West Germany (drew 2-2)

1965 v Wales (lost 2-3), v Finland (won 3-1), v N Ireland (won 3-2)

On leaving school, Jim Kennedy joined a Celtic Supporters' Club. He had no desire whatsoever to play football and, in fact, made no attempt to take the game seriously until he undertook National Service in Belgium.

Even then, on his return to Scotland, he only joined his local club Johnstone Glencairn, and that a full six months after leaving the Army. He then had a spell with Duntocher Hibernian before joining Celtic. He made his debut against Partick Thistle in April 1956 facing Johnny McKenzie, Thistle's flying Scottish international winger. Despite the Jags winning 2-0, Kennedy had an outstanding game and was a first team regular at Parkhead for the next few seasons.

Kennedy's display against Rangers in September 1960 led to talk of a Scottish cap, but it wasn't to be, and having given up his job in an Elderslie carpet factory to go full-time, he was forced to miss the Cup Final replay against Dunfermline Athletic with appendicitis.

Dropped in favour of Tommy Gemmell at the start of the 1963-64 season, it wasn't long into the campaign that he received a new lease of life. He was switched to left-half, but when international honours did come his way against Wales in November 1963 he reverted to left-back. He played against England at Hampden Park in the 1-0 win of April 1964 and continued to hold down a first team place with Celtic until the arrival of Jock Stein, who preferred John Clark.

Having appeared in 241 League and Cup games, he left to play for Morton, and in his first full season at Cappielow Park, led the club to promotion. On hanging up his boots, he returned to his beloved Parkhead, where he was appointed liaison officer between Celtic and the Supporters' Club.

CAMPBELL FORSYTH
Goalkeeper
Born: Robert Campbell Forsyth, Plean, 5 May 1939
Height: 6ft 1in
Weight: 13st 5lb
Clubs: Shettleston; St Mirren; Kilmarnock; Southampton
Scotland caps: 4
1964 v England (won 1-0)
1965 v Wales (lost 2-3), v Finland (won 3-1), v N Ireland (won 3-2)

Campbell Forsyth played his early football for Shettleston Juniors before joining St Mirren in 1955. His displays between the posts for the Love Street club led to him winning Under-23 honours for Scotland. In November 1960, Forsyth moved to Kilmarnock, along with £2,000, for Jimmy Brown who joined the Saints.

After making his debut in January 1962 in a 2-2 draw with Celtic, Forsyth shared the goalkeeping duties with Sandy McLaughlan, before in 1963 he made the No.1 jersey his own. Forsyth's career took off at Kilmarnock, for after two appearances for the Scottish League, he won the first of four full caps for Scotland when he was chosen to play against England at Hampden Park in April

1964. Forsyth had an outstanding game, keeping a clean sheet against the likes of Bobby Charlton and Roger Hunt in a 1-0 win for the Scots.

A big man with a commanding presence aided by fine anticipation, he helped Killie win the Scottish League Championship in 1964-65 when he played in 26 of the 34 games. In December 1965 having played in 101 first team games for Kilmarnock, Forsyth left Rugby Park to join Southampton, whose manager Ted Bates paid £10,000 for his services.

He played his part in the Saints' 1965-66 promotion push, and then had the cruel misfortune to break a leg against Liverpool after only eight First Division matches. Although he returned to play in another 26 games for the south coast club, he never really recovered from that injury.

For many years after, he served the Saints as a scout in Scotland and he recommended Jim Steele, among others, to the club.

JOHN GREIG
Wing-half/ Inside-forward

Born: John Greig, Edinburgh, 11 September 1942
Height: 5ft 10in
Weight: 11st 2lb
Clubs: Edina Hearts; Whitburn; Glasgow Rangers
Scotland caps: 44
Scotland goals: 3

1964 v England (won 1-0), v West Germany (drew 2-2)
1965 v Wales (lost 2-3), v Finland (won 3-1), v N Ireland (won 3-2), v England (drew 2-2),
v Spain (drew 0-0), v Poland (drew 1-1), v Finland (won 2-1) 1 goal
1966 v N Ireland (lost 2-3), v Poland (lost 1-2), v Italy (won 1-0) 1 goal,
v Wales (won 4-1) 1 goal, v Italy (lost 0-3), v England (lost 3-4), v Holland (drew 0-0),
v Portugal (lost 0-1), v Brazil (drew 1-1)
1967 v Wales (drew 1-1), v N Ireland (won 2-1), v England (won 3-2)
1968 v N Ireland (lost 0-1), v Wales (won 3-2), v England (drew 1-1), v Holland (drew 0-0)
1969 v Denmark (won 1-0), v Austria (won 2-1), v Cyprus (won 5-0),
v West Germany (drew 1-1), v Wales (won 5-3), v N Ireland (drew 1-1),
v England (lost 1-4), v Cyprus (won 8-0)
1970 v Republic of Ireland (drew 1-1), v West Germany (lost 2-3), v Austria (lost 0-2),
v Wales (drew 0-0), v England (drew 0-0)
1971 v Denmark (won 1-0), v Belgium (lost 0-3), v Wales (drew 0-0), v N Ireland (lost 0-1),
v England (lost 1-3)
1976 v Denmark (won 3-1)

Considered by many to have been the greatest of all Rangers players, John Greig played for Scotland 44 times, 21 matches in succession, and captained his country.

Greig made 857 first team appearances for Rangers, second only to the total of Dougie Gray, the full-back who played in 879 games for the Ibrox club between 1925 and 1945. In fact, but for becoming manager of the club in 1978 when he was still an active player, he would have passed Gray's total. Three times in his

John Greig (www.snspix.com)

Rangers career he was part of a treble-winning team—League, Scottish Cup and League Cup in 1963-64, 1975-76 and 1977-78. Twice he played in a European Cup Winners' Cup Final—in 1967 when Rangers lost 1-0 to Bayern Munich after extra-time, and in 1972 when they beat Moscow Dynamo 3-2 in Barcelona. In his 16 seasons with the club, he averaged close to one domestic honour per season—winning five League Championships, six Scottish Cup Finals and four League Cup Finals. Not surprisingly, for his services to football, John Greig was awarded the MBE in the 1977 Jubilee Honours List.

Though he wasn't the most skilful of players, he was above all a leader of men, a great club servant and captain for whom the Rangers club was life and who carried the team for many years when Jock Stein's Celtic was sweeping all before it. As a player, John Greig will never be forgotten by Rangers fans for his resolution, his leadership and dedication. For his 1978 testimonial match, no fewer than 65,000 crammed into Ibrox.

In May 1978, Greig was appointed Rangers manager, and his first season in charge was a rip-roaring success—both Cups, the best European run since victory in 1972 and the League lost only in a titanic meeting with Celtic in the third-to-last game. But flaws soon began to appear in the team, and though the club kept reaching and winning Cup Finals, it wasn't enough.

He had to cope with one of the greatest periods of transition in the club's history, including the end of a number of long careers, the stadium building and declining crowds. Despite four trophies in five seasons, Greig had had enough of the incessant pressure brought by the lack of a League title, and handed over to his former manager Jock Wallace. He later returned to Ibrox as PR manager and press officer.

JIM CRUICKSHANK
Goalkeeper
Born: James Fergus Cruickshank, Glasgow, 13 April 1941
Height: 5ft 11in
Weight: 11st 6lb
Clubs: Drumchapel Amateurs; Queen's Park; Heart of Midlothian; Dumbarton
Scotland caps: 6
1964   v West Germany (drew 2-2)
1970   v Wales (drew 0-0), v England (drew 0-0)
1971   v Denmark (won 1-0), v Belgium (lost 0-3)
1976   v Romania (drew 1-1)

One of the game's bravest goalkeepers, Jim Cruickshank won his first full cap in 1964 against West Germany. It was to be another six years before he was capped again—against Wales—and his Scotland career was to span 12 years, as his final international appearance was against Romania in 1976.

Cruickshank joined Hearts from his first senior club Queen's Park in May 1960 and by the age of 17, had played for the Tynecastle club's first team. He made his debut in October of that year at Somerset Park, when Hearts went down narrowly 1-0 to Ayr United, and though he made four further appearances that season, it wasn't until the start of the 1963-64 season that he became a regular first team choice. In fact, he did not miss a match for four years, by which time Kenny Garland was challenging him for the No.1 jersey, but Cruickshank was to hold his team-mate at bay, and when Cruickshank left Tynecastle in 1977, Garland had already given up the game, frustrated by his lack of opportunities.

He played in all 34 of Hearts' league matches in 1964-65, when the team was just a goal shy of winning the title, and he also kept goal in the 1968 Scottish Cup Final against Dunfermline and the 1976 Final when Rangers beat Hearts 3-1. He played in the League Cup Final replay in 1961, deputising for Gordon Marshall, but was again on the losing side against Rangers.

Regarded by many as Hearts' finest goalkeeper, Jim Cruickshank had nothing tangible to show for his long years at the club, as Hearts did not enjoy the best of times during that period. Cruickshank, who had a remarkable 102 clean sheets in 394 league appearances for Hearts, was noted for his consistency and went on to play in over 600 games for the club before ending his career with Dumbarton.

Despite the lack of silverware, there were plenty of memories, not least of which was a triple penalty save from Hibs' Joe Davis in an Edinburgh derby in 1967.

RON YEATS
Centre-half
Born: Ronald Yeats, Aberdeen, 15 November 1937
Height: 6ft 2in
Weight: 14st 5lb
Clubs: Dundee United; Liverpool; Tranmere Rovers; Stalybridge Celtic; Barrow
Scotland caps: 2
1965 v Wales (lost 2-3)
1966 v Italy (lost 0-3)

Liverpool manager Bill Shankly's admiration for Ron Yeats dated back to when he was manager of Huddersfield Town. He had attempted to sign Yeats from Dundee United, but the Yorkshire club could not afford the asking price. When installed at Anfield, Shankly failed in an attempt to bring Jack Charlton from Leeds United, so went to Tannadice and paid £30,000 for the man he knew would be the backbone of his first great side.

Shanks called him 'a colossus in defence', and the description was an apt one. Within five months of his arrival in the summer of 1961, Yeats had been made skipper. In his first season the Reds won promotion to the First Division. In the top flight, Yeats proved to be most dominant in the air, while on the ground his tremendous tackling and sensible distribution went to prove what a great capture he had been. He was an inspiring captain, leading the club to two Championships, the FA Cup and a succession of superb European matches.

Throughout the sixties, Yeats was still essentially a rugged centre-half, but as the decade wore on he grew more accomplished. Off the field he was a great influence on the younger players in the Anfield team, and though quietly spoken, his imposing personality made him the ideal choice for dealing with the Liverpool management.

After losing his place to Larry Lloyd, 'Rowdy', nicknamed after Clint Eastwood's TV cowboy of that era, made the short trip to Prenton Park to become Tranmere Rovers' player-manager and later manager.

He then had spells with Stalybridge Celtic and Barrow before he went into the haulage business and then the catering trade. A player who will go down in Liverpool folklore, Ron Yeats is now the chief scout for the Reds.

STEVE CHALMERS
Forward

Born: Stephen Chalmers, Glasgow, 26 December 1936
Height: 5ft 9in
Weight: 10st 12lb
Clubs: Kirkintilloch Rob Roy; Glasgow Ashfield; Glasgow Celtic; Morton; Partick Thistle
Scotland caps: 5
Scotland goals: 3
1965 v Wales (lost 2-3) 1 goal, v Finland (won 3-1) 1 goal
1966 v Portugal (lost 0-1), v Brazil (drew 1-1) 1 goal
1967 v N Ireland (won 2-1)

Celtic legend Steve Chalmers is nowadays immortalised as a Lisbon Lion and scorer of the most important goal in the Parkhead club's history, five minutes from time on 25 May 1967, as the Bhoys beat Inter Milan 2-1 to bring the European Cup to Britain for the first time.

Following criticism from Jimmy Delaney during his early days with the club—he had called him a head-down player with little idea of how to pace a game—Jock Stein took Steve Chalmer's pace and harnessed it to a plan. The transformed Chalmers responded with a second-half hat-trick in a 5-1 defeat of Rangers in January 1966.

He scored many memorable goals, another of which came in the Scottish Cup Final against Rangers in April 1969. A solo run down the left-wing and a shot at the near post made it 4-0 for Celtic—it was Chalmers' third Scottish Cup medal to go with the ones he won in 1965 and 1967. He also won League Championship medals for the five seasons from 1964-65 to 1968-69 and League Cup winners' medals for the same period.

Chalmers, who won five full caps for Scotland, also netted a goal for the national side in the opening minute of the game against mighty Brazil at Hampden Park in June 1966.

Steve Chalmer's career virtually ended after he broke his leg in the League Cup Final against St Johnstone in October 1969. He remained with the Bhoys until September 1971, when he became player-coach of Morton, and later played for Partick Thistle before returning to Parkhead as Celtic coach.

An utter professional, totally dedicated to the game, his total of 241 goals in 405 games in all competitions was a post-war club record, until surpassed by Bobby Lennox in November 1973.

JIMMY JOHNSTONE
Outside-right

Born: James Johnstone, Viewpark, 30 September 1944
Died: 13 March 2006
Height: 5ft 4in
Weight: 9st 8lb
Clubs: Viewpark; Glasgow Celtic; San Jose Earthquakes (United States); Sheffield United; Dundee; Shelbourne; Elgin City; Blantyre Celtic
Scotland caps: 23
Scotland goals: 4

1965 v Wales (lost 2-3), v Finland (won 3-1)
1966 v England (lost 3-4) 2 goals
1967 v Wales (drew 1-1), v USSR (lost 0-2)
1968 v Wales (won 3-2)
1969 v Austria (won 2-1), v West Germany (drew 1-1)
1970 v West Germany (lost 2-3) 1 goal, v England (drew 0-0), v Denmark (won 1-0)
1971 v England (lost 1-3)
1972 v Portugal (won 2-1), v Belgium (won 1-0), v Holland (lost 1-2), v N Ireland (won 2-0), v England (lost 0-1)
1974 v Wales (won 2-0), v England (won 2-0), v Belgium (lost 1-2) 1 goal, v Norway (won 2-1)
1975 v East Germany (won 3-0), v Spain (lost 1-2)

Few players have encapsulated the dual nature of Scottish footballers so well as Jimmy Johnstone, who combined a prodigious talent with a fiery temper.

He must have realised early on that football was going to be special for him. He was a ball boy at Parkhead when he was 13 years old, and three years later, after a brief spell of being 'farmed out' to junior club Blantyre Celtic, he made his first team debut against the touring Icelandic side. That night in 1961 saw Celtic win 10-1, and though he failed to score, his speed, ball control and ability to waltz round defenders was only too evident.

Johnstone had a capacity for getting into scrapes on and off the pitch. In his early days at Parkhead, he was suspended by manager Jock Stein for lunging at an opponent; in 1974 as Scotland's preparations for the World Cup were undermined by constant stories of indiscipline, Johnstone was found drifting in a rowing boat without a paddle in the small hours of the morning!

Yet no-one doubted his ability. His contribution to Celtic's European Cup triumph in 1967 was immense, particularly in the final. Helenio Herrera, the Italians' astute manager, put his top defender Burgnich on Johnstone. The seasoned international endured a 90-minute nightmare as the Scot twisted, turned and tantalised throughout the game. Defenders watched and took note.

Subsequently, Johnstone was to be tested by the hard men of two continents.

Jimmy Johnstone (www.snspix.com)

A year later in the World Club Championship against the disgraceful Argentinian team Racing Club, Johnstone retaliated to the most horrendous of tackles and was sent off, the first of three Celtic players to go in a farcical third match. In the notorious 1974 European Cup semi-final against Atletico Madrid, Johnstone was continually tripped and hacked, and as he left the field, he was kicked in the stomach. In the second leg in Madrid he was given two black eyes by Spanish elbows, yet still kept his head when retaliation would have been only too human.

Johnstone retired from football with a host of domestic honours as well as 23 full international caps. But more than that, 'Jinky' Johnstone left football fans the world over with many wonderful memories of a player whose ball control once persuaded a Scotland manager to abandon a training session early. 'Nobody had a kick. They couldn't get the ball off Johnstone,' he explained!

JIMMY ROBERTSON
Winger

Born: James Gillen Robertson, Glasgow, 17 December 1944
Height: 5ft 8in
Weight: 9st 7lb
Clubs: Cowdenbeath; St Mirren; Tottenham Hotspur; Arsenal; Ipswich Town; Stoke City; Walsall; Crewe Alexandra
Scotland caps: 1
1965 v Wales (lost 2-3)

Jimmy Robertson was a Middlesbrough junior and a part-timer with Celtic before joining Cowdenbeath. He played in the Cowdenbeath side as a 16-year-old amateur, representing Scotland at youth level, and won an amateur cap against Northern Ireland before joining St Mirren. Three months after winning his first Under-23 cap for Scotland against Wales, he was transferred to Tottenham Hotspur for £25,000.

A fast, well-balanced winger who loved to cut inside and try a shot on goal, Jimmy Robertson was able to play on either flank, but he is best remembered at White Hart Lane as a right-winger, a player who supplied the ammunition for the likes of Jimmy

Jimmy Robertson

Greaves and Alan Gilzean. After his move to White Hart Lane, Robertson won three more caps for Scotland at Under-23 level before winning his one and only cap at full international level against Wales in October 1964.

Blessed with great pace and an accurate crosser of the ball, Robertson also varied his play by cleverly holding up the ball and creating chances with perceptive passes through the defence. He was a popular player with the Tottenham faithful, and his finest performance for the North London club probably came in the 1967 FA Cup Final against Chelsea, when he scored the opening goal to launch Spurs on their way to their fifth FA Cup victory.

With wingers seemingly drifting out of fashion, Robertson was allowed to leave White Hart Lane in October 1968, moving to rivals Arsenal in a £55,000 deal which saw David Jenkins travel in the opposite direction. It was not one of manager Bill Nicholson's better decisions, as Robertson had plenty of good football left in him.

Due mainly to the presence of George Armstrong, Jimmy Robertson never really settled at Highbury, and it was no surprise that, after less than two years, he joined Ipswich Town. After useful service at Portman Road, he joined Stoke City before winding down his career with Walsall and Crewe Alexandra.

JACK McGRORY
Centre-half

Born: John McGrory, Glasgow, 15 November 1941
Died: 11 October 2004
Height: 5ft 1in
Weight: 12st 3lb
Clubs: Kilmarnock Amateurs; Kilmarnock
Scotland caps: 3
1965 v Finland (won 3-1), v N Ireland (won 3-2)
1966 v Portugal (lost 0-1)

There are many of the opinion that Jack McGrory was a far better centre-half than Celtic's Billy McNeill or Rangers' Ronnie McKinnon, who were the most capped individuals in his era, but it was their presence that limited the Kilmarnock man to just three international appearances.

Signed from Kilmarnock Amateurs, he was 'farmed out' to Dreghorn Juniors to gain experience before returning to Rugby Park to make his first team debut against Airdrieonians in November 1960, a game that ended all-square at 1-1.

Jack McGrory only ever played for one senior club, though he did go on the transfer list after refusing to re-sign in 1965. He did not make the summer trip to the New York Tournament, nor did he play in the sectional qualifying ties in the League Cup or the few opening league fixtures of the 1965-66 season. He eventually did re-sign, but it cost him the opportunity to play in the European Cup fixtures with Nandori of Albania and Spain's Real Madrid, because he was not a registered player at the club by the time UEFA had decreed.

Having won three caps at Under-23 level, he won his first full international cap against Finland in October 1964 and went on a Far East/World Tour with the SFA side in 1967, although no caps were awarded for games against Australia, New Zealand, Israel and the like.

Jack McGrory, who played the last of his 463 games for Killie against Celtic in September 1972 at Hampden because the Celtic Park Stand was being rebuilt, scored just one goal for the club at first team level. It came in the Fairs Cup tie at home to FC Zurich of Switzerland in the first round second leg. Killie trailed 3-2 from the away leg, but it was Jack McGrory who opened the scoring in the leg at Rugby Park, when he dribbled forward from his own half and sent a low shot speeding into the net from well outside the area. Killie went on to win 3-1 for a 5-4 aggregate success!

WILLIE WALLACE
Forward

Born: William Semple Brown Wallace, Kirkintilloch, 23 June 1940
Height: 5ft 9in
Weight: 12st 7lb
Clubs: Kilsyth Rangers; Stenhousemuir; Raith Rovers; Heart of Midlothian; Glasgow Celtic; Crystal Palace; Dumbarton; Apia (Australia); Ross County
Scotland caps: 7
1965 v N Ireland (won 3-2)
1966 v England (lost 3-4), v Holland (lost 0-3)
1967 v England (won 3-2), v USSR (lost 0-2)
1968 v N Ireland (lost 0-1)
1969 v England (lost 1-4)

From his very early days with Stenhousemuir, to a rich seam of goals at Tynecastle, Willie Wallace had a happy knack of finding the net. It was a talent that was to win him a European Cup winners' medal as part of the Celtic side that became the first British side to win the trophy in 1967. Yet he failed to hit the target in seven full international appearances!

On leaving Stenhousemuir, Wallace spent two years with Raith Rovers before Hearts paid a record fee of £15,000 to take him to Tynecastle. In each of his five seasons with Hearts, he was the club's top scorer, a natural successor to Willie Bauld. His best season in terms of goals scored was 1963-64 when he netted 30 goals. He played in the Hearts side that lost the League Cup Final to Rangers in 1961, but a year later after netting a hat-trick in a 4-0 semi-final defeat of St Johnstone, he collected a winners' medal in the 1-0 win over Kilmarnock. Wallace went on to score 158 goals in 277 games for Hearts before Celtic paid £30,000 for his services.

The most expensive member of Jock Stein's 'Lisbon Lions', he also won a League Championship medal, Scottish Cup and League Cup medal in his first season with the club as Celtic swept the boards. He also played for Scotland in the 3-2 win over then world champions England at Wembley. During his time with Celtic, Wallace scored 135 goals in 234 games, with his most famous coming against Dukla Prague in the European Cup semi-final that sent Celtic to the Czech capital for the second leg, 3-1 up. Also, a week later, he scored both Celtic's goals in a 2-0 defeat of Aberdeen in the Scottish Cup Final.

On leaving Parkhead he joined Crystal Palace, but after just one season at Selhurst Park he was back in Scotland with Dumbarton. He later played in Australia before being appointed player-coach of Ross County, ending his involvement with the game coaching 'Down Under'.

EDDIE McCREADIE
Left-back

Born: Edward Graham McCreadie, Glasgow, 15 April 1940
Height: 5ft 9in
Weight: 11st 3lb
Clubs: Drumchapel Amateurs; Clydebank Juniors; East Stirling; Chelsea
Scotland caps: 23

1965 v England (drew 2-2), v Spain (drew 0-0), v Poland (drew 1-1), v Finland (won 2-1)
1966 v N Ireland (lost 2-3), v Poland (lost 1-2), v Wales (won 4-1), v Italy (lost 0-3),
    v Portugal (lost 0-1)
1967 v England (won 3-2), v USSR (lost 0-2)
1968 v N Ireland (lost 0-1), v Wales (won 3-2), v England (drew 1-1), v Holland (drew 0-0)
1969 v Denmark (won 1-0), v Austria (won 2-1), v Cyprus (won 5-0),
    v West Germany (drew 1-1), v Wales (won 5-3), v N Ireland (drew 1-1),
    v England (lost 1-4), v Cyprus (won 8-0)

Chelsea manager Tommy Docherty described Eddie McCreadie as the best left-back in Europe. McCreadie joined the Blues from East Stirling in April 1962 for a fee of £6,000—a rugged defender whose trademark was a ferocious sliding tackle. Successfully making the transition from part-time footballer in Scotland to the heat of the Second Division promotion battle with Chelsea, McCreadie, who was blessed with tremendous pace and exceptional powers of recovery, took delight in getting forward at every opportunity. In the first leg of the 1965 League Cup Final against Leicester City, McCreadie played centre-forward in the absence of Barry Bridges and scored the winning goal after an epic solo run that carried him the length of the pitch. An emotional man, he was inevitably involved in a number of clashes with Docherty, and his role in the ill-starred Blackpool Affair in April 1965 did nothing to improve matters. The following year, McCreadie put in five transfer requests, but they were all turned down.

McCreadie won the first of his 23 Scotland caps against England two weeks before the dramatic events at Blackpool and regularly represented his country for the next four years.

Sadly, the later stages of McCreadie's career were plagued by a cruel series of injuries. He did play in the 1970 FA Cup Final, but only after he had courageously decided to postpone abdominal surgery. In March 1972 he was appointed club captain in succession to Ron Harris, but his playing days were nearing their end and his appointment as reserve team coach in 1974 was quickly followed by his appointment as Chelsea manager.

He had just three games to stave off the threat of relegation, and though he dropped a number of his former team-mates and appointed 18-year-old

Ray Wilkins captain, the Blues still went down. The following season they raced to promotion—McCreadie had achieved the mission impossible. However, before the new season got underway, he became outraged by the board's lack of appreciation for his efforts and walked out to a new life in America.

BILLY BREMNER
Right-half

Born: William John Bremner, Stirling, 9 December 1942
Died: 7 December 1997
Height: 5ft 6in
Weight: 9st 13lb
Clubs: Leeds United; Hull City; Doncaster Rovers
Scotland caps: 54
Scotland goals: 3

1965 v Spain (drew 0-0)
1966 v Poland (lost 1-2), v Italy (lost 0-1), v Italy (lost 0-3), v England (lost 3-4),
v Portugal (lost 0-1), v Brazil (drew 1-1)
1967 v Wales (drew 1-1), v N Ireland (won 2-1), v England (won 3-2)
1968 v Wales (won 3-2), v England (drew 1-1)
1969 v Denmark (won 1-0), v Austria (won 2-1) 1 goal, v Cyprus (won 5-0),
v West Germany (drew 1-1), v Wales (won 5-3) 1 goal, v N Ireland (drew 1-1),
v England (lost 1-4), v Cyprus (won 8-0)
1970 v Republic of Ireland (drew 1-1), v West Germany (lost 2-3), v Austria (lost 0-2)
1971 v Wales (drew 0-0), v England (lost 1-3)
1972 v Portugal (won 2-1), v Belgium (won 1-0), v Holland (lost 1-2), v N Ireland (won 2-0),
v Wales (won 1-0), v England (lost 0-1), v Yugoslavia (drew 2-2),
v Czechoslovakia (drew 0-0), v Brazil (lost 0-1)
1973 v Denmark (won 4-1), v Denmark (won 2-0), v England (lost 0-5), v N Ireland (lost 1-2),
v England (lost 0-1), v Switzerland (lost 0-1), v Brazil (lost 0-1)
1974 v Czechoslovakia (won 2-1), v West Germany (drew 1-1), v N Ireland (lost 0-1),
v Wales (won 2-0), v England (won 2-0), v Belgium (lost 1-2), v Norway (won 2-1),
v Zaire (won 2-0), v Brazil (drew 0-0), v Yugoslavia (drew 1-1)
1975 v Spain (lost 1-2) 1 goal, v Spain (drew 1-1)
1976 v Denmark (won 1-0)

The summer of 1974 was an eventful time for Billy Bremner, for he had captained Scotland in the World Cup, the highlight of his career, but had nearly missed the tournament after breaking curfew along with Jimmy Johnstone in Brussels. Fortunately the Scottish FA decided not to send the players home. His play in the World Cup, when he was one of Scotland's successes, was perhaps his best for his country, for whom he gained 54 caps.

Billy Bremner, a combative midfield dynamo, was the driving force behind the success story of Leeds United in the 1960s and 1970s. A truly inspirational figure, he gave wonderful service to the club he joined as a 17-year-old in December 1959, after being rejected by both Arsenal and Chelsea.

In his early days at Elland Road he often brushed with football's authorities but gradually matured and collected many honours. Later, as captain, he was the

Billy Bremner

man who ensured that the manager's instructions were carried out on the field. In many ways he epitomised the Leeds spirit of that time. He hated losing and between the club winning the Second Division Championship in 1963-64 and 1974-75, he rarely finished on the losing side. His collection of honours included two League Championship medals (1968-69 and 1973-74) an FA Cup winners' medal (1972) and two UEFA Cup winners' medals (1967-68 and 1970-71).

Because of Leeds' mean streak and Bremner's own aggression, he was never high on the popularity list among many opposing supporters, but everyone in the game recognised the contribution he made to Leeds United's success. He was voted Footballer of the Year in 1970 when Leeds were runners-up in both the League Championship and FA Cup. A fiery competitor, Bremner was sent off along with Kevin Keegan during the 1974 Charity Shield at Wembley. Both players removed their shirts, and as a result both were fined £500 and their suspensions meant that each missed one match.

Bremner moved to Hull City in September 1976 and ended his playing career after joining Doncaster Rovers as player-manager in November 1978. After winning two promotions with the Belle Vue club, he was offered the ultimate post as manager of his beloved Leeds United. After a good first season, the Yorkshire club seemed to go backwards and Bremner was sacked. He had another spell in charge of Doncaster, but parted company in 1992. He was then in great demand as an after-dinner speaker, until his death at the age of 54 in December 1997.

JOHN HUGHES
Outside-left
Born: John Hughes, Coatbridge, 3 April 1943
Height: 6ft 2in
Weight: 13st 7lb
Clubs: Shotts Bon Accord; Glasgow Celtic; Crystal Palace; Sunderland
Scotland caps: 8
Scotland goals: 1
1965 v Spain (drew 0-0), v Poland (drew 1-1)
1966 v N Ireland (lost 2-3), v Italy (won 1-0), v Italy (lost 0-3)

1968 v England (drew 1-1) 1 goal
1969 v Austria (won 2-1)
1970 v Republic of Ireland (drew 1-1)

John Hughes' burly frame earned him the nickname 'Yogi' after the famous TV cartoon character Yogi Bear!

Having had a great game for the Scottish League against the Football League at Hampden Park on St Patrick's Day 1965, when he scored two and gave Jack Charlton a torrid time, he was selected for his first full international against Spain the following May. It was a bruising encounter, but Hughes, playing at outside-left, gave as good as he got and went on to win eight caps for his country.

John Hughes was just 17 years of age when he made his Celtic debut in August 1960, scoring one of the goals in a 2-0 defeat of Third Lanark. The game typified his early days with the club, as he missed the easiest of chances after just 30 seconds before netting with an unstoppable header that Jocky Robertson never even saw! This mixture of brilliance and ineptitude continued until Jock Stein took over as manager, when his strength became allied to intelligence. Having said that, two months before Stein took over, Hughes did net five goals against Aberdeen!

Under Jock Stein he developed into an invaluable team man, whose speciality was to beat man after man with the ball seemingly tied to his boot, before switching it to his right and firing powerfully home. Though there were still times when he had an off day and was the subject of savage barracking, he went on to score 189 goals in 416 League and Cup games for Celtic, before in October 1971 joining Crystal Palace.

In a little over a year at Selhurst Park, Hughes became hugely popular, one of his goals in the game against Sheffield United in December 1971 being featured over and over again as one of the goals of the season. He later joined his brother Billy at Sunderland, but he had made just one appearance for the Wearsiders when injury forced his retirement.

After coaching at Baillieston FC he became manager of Stranraer, later becoming the Scottish Junior FA's first international team manager. Then he took over as licensee of a hostelry in Coatbridge, appropriately named 'The Great Bear'.

NEIL MARTIN
Forward

Born: Neil Martin, Alloa, 20 October 1940
Height: 6ft 0in
Weight: 12st 3lb
Clubs: Alloa Athletic; Queen of the South; Hibernian; Sunderland; Coventry City; Nottingham Forest; Brighton and Hove Albion; Crystal Palace; St Patrick's Athletic
Scotland caps: 3
1965 v Poland (drew 1-1), v Finland (won 2-1)
1966 v Italy (won 1-0)

One of the select band of players to have scored at least 100 goals in both the Scottish and English Leagues, Neil Martin served an apprenticeship as a mining engineer while at Alloa Athletic, where in 1960-61 he scored 32 goals. He later joined Queen of the South, and though he had scored 30 goals for the Doonhamers in 1962-63, he was on the verge of giving up the game to become a lorry driver!

Hibs' manager Walter Galbraith paid £6,000 to take him to Easter Road, and in 1963-64, his first full season with the club, he netted 38 goals in all competitions. That was nothing compared to the following season when he hit the 50 mark, with half of his goals coming in the league. In 1965-66 he netted four goals against his former club Alloa, and another four three days later against Falkirk. Hat-tricks were something of a Neil Martin speciality, and in the space of three seasons with Hibs, he scored ten!

In October 1965, Sunderland manager Ian McColl paid £50,000 for his services, and though he took a little time to settle into his new surroundings, he netted 26 goals in 1966-67, including hat-tricks against Blackpool and Peterborough United. Having scored 46 goals in 100 games for the Wearsiders, he left to play for Coventry City in February 1968.

Though he only played in the last 15 games of the season, he was the club's joint-top scorer with eight goals, including another treble against Sheffield Wednesday which helped the Sky Blues avoid the drop into Division Two. His form earned him a recall to the national squad, but after four seasons at Highfield Road in which he scored 45 goals in 122 games, he was surprisingly allowed to join Nottingham Forest. Injuries hampered his progress at the City Ground, and he moved on to have spells with both Brighton and Crystal Palace.

His playing days over, he enjoyed a spell in Kuwait as assistant-manager to Arabic Sporting Club. In 1981 he became co-manager at Walsall before taking over the reins the following year, but in his only season in charge, the Saddlers just missed relegation by one place on goal difference.

WILLIE HAMILTON
Inside-forward

Born: William Murdoch Hamilton, Airdrie, 16 February 1938
Died: Calgary, Canada, 22 October 1976
Height: 5ft 9in
Weight: 10st 7lb
Clubs: Drumchapel Amateurs; Sheffield United; Middlesbrough; Heart of Midlothian; Hibernian; Aston Villa; Heart of Midlothian; Ross County
Scotland caps: 1
1965 v Finland (won 2-1)

Hibernian, like many clubs, has had its fair share of players who have won one cap, and, by the same token, its fair share of players who deserved more. Yet Willie Hamilton, who won his single Scottish cap against Finland in May 1965, may have been lucky to have scaled that particular height.

Hamilton was that classic mix of frustrating genius, a player of great skill who appeared to know only how to squander it.

Having played his early football for Drumchapel Amateurs prior to spells in the Football League with Sheffield United and Middlesbrough, he first played Scottish League football for Hearts. He joined Hibs in October 1963, signed for just £6,000 by Walter Galbraith. But it was Galbraith's successor, Jock Stein, who tempered Hamilton's tendency to self-destruct, so much so that it was under Stein that he received his Scotland call-up.

Hamilton, who drank pints of milk to ease the discomfort of a stomach ulcer, was also reputed to drink too much of other types of beverage. However, he began to shine on the field, helping Hibs beat Real Madrid in a friendly and then scoring the winner against Rangers in the Scottish Cup, the first time the Ibrox club had been beaten in the competition for over four years. On a tour to Canada and the United States, Hamilton was presented with a silver salver for scoring seven goals in one game in Ottawa. However, it wasn't long before he was back in English football with Aston Villa, sold by Stein's successor Bob Shankly, probably—so one journalist said—that he could sleep soundly at nights!

Hamilton later returned for a second spell with Hearts and subsequently played in South Africa before joining Ross County in 1970.

Following a career marred by injury and illness, he died a few years later from a heart seizure—his family had by then settled in Canada.

WILLIE JOHNSTON
Outside-left

Born: William Johnston, Glasgow, 19 December 1946
Height: 5ft 7in
Weight: 11st 0lb
Clubs: Lochore Welfare; Glasgow Rangers; West Bromwich Albion; Vancouver Whitecaps (Canada); Birmingham City; Glasgow Rangers; Heart of Midlothian; Falkirk
Scotland caps: 22

1966 v Poland (lost 1-2), v Wales (won 4-1), v England (lost 3-4), v Holland (lost 0-3)
1968 v Wales (won 3-2), v England (drew 1-1)
1969 v N Ireland (drew 1-1)
1970 v N Ireland (won 1-0)
1971 v Denmark (won 1-0)
1977 v Sweden (won 3-1), v Wales (drew 0-0), v N Ireland (won 3-0), v England (won 2-1), v Chile (won 4-2), v Argentina (drew 1-1), v Brazil (lost 0-2)
1978 v East Germany (lost 0-1), v Czechoslovakia (won 3-1), v Wales (won 2-0), v Wales (drew 1-1), v England (lost 0-1), v Peru (lost 1-3)

One of the most controversial footballers of the modern game, Willie Johnston was an outside-left of blistering pace and dazzling dribbling skills, yet he may be better remembered for an appalling disciplinary record and for being banned from the international game following a drugs test at the 1978 World Cup Finals in Argentina.

Johnston was just 17 when he made his Rangers debut against St Johnstone in August 1964, and a couple of months later, he was a member of the Rangers side that beat Celtic 2-1 to win the League Cup. So skilled was Johnston, that he progressed from Scottish youth international to full international status in the space of six months, and was first capped at 18 in a World Cup qualifying match against Poland.

He was an entertainer—his speed, strength and skill with the ball gave him a rapport with the Ibrox fans. He could also be argumentative and was, clearly too often, with referees. Rangers began to tire of his lack of discipline, and a nine-week suspension after being sent off against Partick Thistle was the final straw and he was transferred to West Bromwich Albion for £135,000. Just six months earlier, he had been a European Cup Winners' Cup medal winner, scoring two of Rangers' three goals in the final against Moscow Dynamo in Barcelona. In fact, Johnston's goals had been instrumental in taking Rangers to that final—his four strikes included valuable away goals at Rennes and Turin.

Johnston played well at West Bromwich, though he was sent off in the League Cup tie against Brighton for kicking the referee up the backside! His form led to him being brought into the Scotland squad for the World Cup Finals in Argentina. Following the match against Peru which the Scots lost 3-1, Johnston was routinely tested and found to have taken a banned substance. He was withdrawn from the tournament, sent home and banned from playing for Scotland ever again.

Although Johnston's arrival at the Hawthorns was too late to prevent the club's relegation in 1973, he was a vital part of Johnny Giles' promotion-winning side three years later and went on to see Albion established as a top flight side before leaving to play for Vancouver Whitecaps. He later had a loan spell at Birmingham City before rejoining Rangers for two years under manager John Greig. Sent off in a League Cup match at Aberdeen, he later played briefly for Hearts and Falkirk before becoming a licensee in Kirkcaldy.

BOBBY MURDOCH
Midfield

Born: Robert Murdoch, Bothwell, 17 August 1944
Died: 15 May 2001
Height: 5ft 10in
Weight: 12st 8lb
Clubs: Motherwell; Cambuslang Rangers; Glasgow Celtic; Middlesbrough
Scotland caps: 12
Scotland goals: 5
1966 v Italy (won 1-0), v Wales (won 4-1) 2 goals, v Italy (lost 0-3), v England (lost 3-4)
1967 v N Ireland (won 2-1) 1 goal
1968 v N Ireland (lost 0-1)
1969 v Cyprus (won 5-0) 1 goal, v West Germany (drew 1-1) 1 goal, v Wales (won 5-3), v N Ireland (drew 1-1), v England (lost 1-4)
1970 v Austria (lost 0-2)

A legendary midfielder and mainstay of Jock Stein's successful Celtic side of the 1960s and 70s, Bobby Murdoch started out with non-League Cambuslang Rangers before joining the Bhoys on a trial basis in 1959 and then as a full-timer two years later. It was a wise decision by the Parkhead club, and in 14 years with them, he went on to score 61 goals in 291 league games. As Murdoch was amassing those impressive statistics, Celtic dominated the Scottish scene and spread their wings over Europe. The midfielder, whose supreme pass-making abilities were used to maximum effect, collected no less than eight consecutive Scottish League title medals between 1966 and 1973. He also gained four Scottish Cup winners' medals and was prominent as Celtic took the Scottish League Cup from 1966 to 1970. He was a

Bobby Murdoch

member of the Celtic team that lifted the European Cup in Lisbon in 1967 when Celtic beat Inter Milan 2-1, and he was in the side when they lost to Feyenoord after extra-time in the 1970 European Cup Final in Milan.

At international level, he won the first of 12 Scottish caps in which he scored five goals, in a 1-0 victory over Italy in November 1965. Two of his goals came on his next appearance for the national side as Wales were beaten 4-1 at Hampden Park.

In September 1973 he left Parkhead to join Middlesbrough on a free transfer, proving to be an inspirational buy, playing a crucial role in steering the north-east club into the First Division. He was thought to have his best days behind him, but he helped Boro cement their place in the top flight before ending his playing days. He stayed at Ayresome Park to coach the club's juniors, but after six years in the backroom staff, Murdoch took over the managerial reins on the departure of John Neal in 1978.

His only season in charge saw the club relegated to the Second Division, and after a poor start to the following campaign, it signalled the end of his reign and culmination of a nine-year association with the Teeside club. Prior to his untimely death, he spent his Saturdays as a matchday host at Parkhead.

RON McKINNON
Centre-half
Born: Ronald McKinnon, Glasgow, 20 August 1940

Height: 5ft 11in
Weight: 10st 10lb
Clubs: Benburb, Dunipace Juniors; Glasgow Rangers
Scotland caps: 28
Scotland goals: 1
1966 v Italy (won 1-0), v Wales (won 4-1), v Italy (lost 0-3), v England (lost 3-4),
 v Holland (lost 0-3), v Brazil (drew 1-1)
1967 v Wales (drew 1-1), v N Ireland (won 2-1), v England (won 3-2)
1968 v N Ireland (lost 0-1), v Wales (won 3-2) 1 goal, v England (drew 1-1),
 v Holland (drew 0-0)
1969 v Denmark (won 1-0), v Austria (won 2-1), v Cyprus (won 5-0),
 v West Germany (drew 1-1)
1970 v Republic of Ireland (drew 1-1), v West Germany (lost 2-3), v Austria (lost 0-2),
 v N Ireland (won 1-0), v Wales (drew 0-0), v England (drew 0-0)
1971 v Denmark (won 1-0), v Belgium (lost 0-3), v Portugal (lost 0-2), v Denmark (lost 0-1),
 v USSR (lost 0-1)

A member of the Scotland side that beat world champions England 3-2 at Wembley in 1967, Ron McKinnon was without doubt the best centre-half Rangers had had since Willie Woodburn.

He was a product of Benburb, the local Govan team, and of Dunipace Juniors before signing for Rangers in the summer of 1959. Though he signed for the Ibrox club as a wing-half, he was converted into a centre-half and developed in the reserves. When he made his first team debut for Rangers midway through the 1961-62 season, he was considered a stop-gap, as both Baillie and Paterson were out with short-term injuries. However, he stayed and developed into an international class defender, sharing the centre-half duties in the Scotland side with Celtic captain, Billy McNeill.

Ron McKinnon was a well-rounded footballer—composed, stylish and authoritative, he had a calming effect on the Rangers defence. Comfortable on the ball, he never seemed under pressure, and the half-back line of Greig, McKinnon and Baxter was one of the finest at both club and international level.

In November 1971 he broke a leg in the away European match against Sporting Lisbon, and so missed a chance of playing in Rangers' European Cup Winners Cup Final triumph the following May. He stayed at Ibrox until the end of the 1972-73 season, when, after appearing in 473 games, he played for a year in South Africa and then moved onto Australia.

CHARLIE COOKE
Winger/ Inside-forward
Born: Charles Cooke, St Monance, 14 October 1942
Height: 5ft 8in
Weight: 12st 6lb
Clubs: Port Glasgow; Renfrew Juniors; Aberdeen; Dundee; Chelsea; Crystal Palace; Chelsea;
 Memphis Rogues (United States)

Scotland caps: 16

1966 v Wales (won 4-1), v Italy (lost 0-3), v Portugal (lost 0-1), v Brazil (drew 1-1)

1968 v England (drew 1-1), v Holland (drew 0-0)

1969 v Austria (won 2-1), v Cyprus (won 5-0), v West Germany (drew 1-1),
v Wales (won 5-3), v N Ireland (drew 1-1), v Cyprus (won 8-0)

1970 v Austria (lost 0-2)

1971 v Belgium (lost 0-3)

1975 v Spain (drew 1-1), v Portugal (won 1-0)

Charlie Cooke playing for Chelsea

Charlie Cooke, a Scottish winger in the traditional mould, had the ability to beat defences on his own. He began his career with Aberdeen before moving to Dundee where he won full international honours.

He joined Chelsea in April 1966 for a club record fee of £72,000, as a direct replacement for Terry Venables. In his early days at Stamford Bridge, he found it impossible to adapt to the team's established style. He was moved out to the wing to provide pin-point crosses for Tony Hateley, but he never seemed to produce his best form on the flanks.

Always needing to be at the heart of the action, his ball-juggling skills made him hugely popular with the Stamford Bridge crowd, and in 1967-68 he was voted the Blues' 'Player of the Year'. When Dave Sexton took over the reins at Stamford Bridge, he was unconvinced about Charlie Cooke's contribution, and the Fife-born player soon realised he would have to harness his individualism to the collective effort of the team. In 1969-70 he seemed a more rounded performer and was still very effective when given a chance in the middle of the park. Few will forget his performance in the FA Cup Final replay when he outshone Billy Bremner and created Peter Osgood's goal with an exquisite chip. Charlie Cooke was a player who could be relied upon to produce his best on the big occasions, and in the matches against Real Madrid in Athens he was outstanding. Yet in spite of these performances, he couldn't find the consistency to earn a regular place in the Blues' midfield and in September 1972 he joined Crystal Palace.

He spent 15 unhappy months at Selhurst Park before rejoining Chelsea for a bargain price of £17,000. Playing wide on the left, his displays were inspired, but sadly, despite having rediscovered his old passion for the game, he began to suffer a series of niggling injuries. Nevertheless he was able to help guide Eddie McCreadie's young team to promotion in 1976-77 before leaving to play in the United States with Memphis Rogues.

BOBBY FERGUSON
Goalkeeper

Born: Robert Ferguson, Ardrossan, 1 March 1945
Height: 5ft 11in
Weight: 11st 1lb
Clubs: Kilmarnock Amateurs; Kilmarnock; West Ham United; Sheffield Wednesday (loan); Leicester City (Loan); Port Elizabeth (Australia)
Scotland caps: 7
1966 v Wales (won 4-1), v England (lost 3-4), v Holland (lost 0-3), v Portugal (lost 0-1), v Brazil (drew 1-1)
1967 v Wales (drew 1-1), v N Ireland (won 2-1)

Bobby Ferguson attended a rugby-playing school and only took to playing the association code on leaving. After impressing with Kilmarnock Amateurs, he joined Kilmarnock in 1963 and made his debut in a 2-0 away win over Hibernian in October 1964, when Killie's first-choice keeper Campbell Forsyth was playing for Scotland that day against Wales in a Home International.

With seven games remaining in that 1964-65 season, Ferguson replaced Forsyth, his outstanding performances helping the club to win the title. In the match against Hearts, he made a breathtaking save in the last minute to ensure Killie won 2-0, to take the title on goal average by 0.042 of a goal. If Hearts had scored and Killie had won 2-1, then Hearts would have been champions! With the Rugby Park club, Ferguson was ever-present in 1965-66 when they finished third in the Scottish League First Division, and in 1966-67 he kept goal during the Killies run to the semi-finals of the Inter Cities Fairs Cup.

During his time with Kilmarnock, Ferguson made two appearances for

Bobby Ferguson

the Scottish League and won seven full caps for Scotland, his first against Wales in 1966.

In May 1967, Ferguson was sold to West Ham United for a then British record fee for a goalkeeper of £65,000. The Hammers had been wanting to sign Ferguson for a while, but had to wait until the Scottish club were eliminated from the Inter Cities Fairs Cup.

Though he had one or two erratic spells at Upton Park, losing his place to both Peter Grotier and Mervyn Day, he was, at his best, a superb performer with 'miracle' saves a-plenty! He went on to play in 276 League and Cup games in 13 seasons with the Hammers, but failed to add to the seven full caps he won while with Kilmarnock. He had brief loan spells with Sheffield Wednesday and Leicester City, but when Phil Parkes arrived at Upton Park in February 1975, it signalled the end of Ferguson's career with the Hammers.

Later he emigrated to Australia, where after playing for Port Elizabeth, he became a partner in a Sports Complex and Marina Business in the early 1990s.

JIM FORREST
Centre-forward/ Winger

Born: James Forrest, Glasgow, 22 September 1944
Height: 5ft 8in
Weight: 11st 0lb
Clubs: Drumchapel Amateurs; Glasgow Rangers; Preston North End; Aberdeen; Hong Kong Rangers
Scotland caps: 5

1966 v Wales (won 4-1), v Italy (lost 0-3)
1971 v Belgium (lost 0-3), v Denmark (lost 0-1), v USSR (lost 0-1)

One of the game's greatest goalscorers, as his goals-to-game ratio for Rangers (145 in 164 games) testifies, Jim Forrest was capped five times by Scotland but failed to find the net!

He joined Rangers as a schoolboy, but was sent briefly to Drumchapel Amateurs to aid his development before lining up in a Rangers side. Forrest could combine unselfishly with other players and hold the forward line together well. One of only a handful of players to have scored a hundred league goals in the post-war years, his tally of 57 in all competitions in 1964-65 remains a record to this day. He had helped Rangers win the 1963-64 League Championship and that season's League Cup when he scored a record four goals in the 5-0 final win over Morton. For the record, Rangers' other goal was scored by his cousin Alex Willoughby. In fact, Willoughby was a colleague at Drumchapel Amateurs, Aberdeen and Hong Kong—a remarkable instance of family loyalty! Jim Forrest scored four goals more than once, and in October 1965 scored five in a 7-1 win over Hamilton Academicals at Douglas Park.

Forrest's Ibrox career ended under the cloud of the infamous Scottish Cup defeat by Berwick Rangers in January 1967. Unbelievably blamed for this surprise reversal, he was transfer-listed and within weeks had joined Preston North End.

After a year at Deepdale, he returned north of the Border to play for Aberdeen, helping the Pittodrie club win the 1970 Scottish Cup Final. He left the Dons in 1973 to see out his career with Hong Kong Rangers.

TOMMY GEMMELL
Full-back

Born: Thomas Gemmell, Glasgow, 18 October 1943
Height: 6ft 1in
Weight: 12st 2lb
Clubs: Coltness United; Glasgow Celtic; Nottingham Forest; Dundee
Scotland caps: 18
Scotland goals: 1
1966 v England (lost 3-4)
1967 v Wales (drew 1-1), v N Ireland (won 2-1), v England (won 3-2), v USSR (lost 0-2)
1968 v N Ireland (lost 0-1), v England (drew 1-1)
1969 v Denmark (won 1-0), v Austria (won 2-1), v West Germany (drew 1-1),
          v Wales (won 5-3), v N Ireland (drew 1-1), v England (lost 1-4),
          v Cyprus (won 8-0) 1 goal
1970 v Republic of Ireland (drew 1-1), v West Germany (lost 2-3), v England (drew 0-0)
1971 v Belgium (lost 0-3)

People will always remember full-back Tommy Gemmell's unstoppable drive that guided Celtic to victory in the European Cup Final of 1967. He repeated the feat three years later in another European Cup Final against Feyenoord of Holland in the San Siro Stadium. There was to be no happy ending this time though. The Dutchmen came back to equalise through Rinus Israel, and snatched the trophy in extra-time with a goal from Ove Kindval. Gemmell was also on target in the final of the World Club Championship in 1968 against the notorious Racing Club of Buenos Aires, when he netted with a penalty-kick. You could say that he was a man for the big occasion!

Jock Stein once tried Gemmell at centre-forward in 1966 in a tour game in America. Gemmell promptly rattled in a hat-trick and Stein said: 'You're wasted at centre-forward... you would have got at least four at left-back.'

Gemmell, who made his Celtic debut in a 5-1 win at Aberdeen in January 1963 must rate as the best full-back ever to pull on the green and white of the Parkhead club.

Capped 18 times by Scotland, he holds a couple of unwanted distinctions—an own goal that sailed over the head of Ronnie Simpson to put the USSR into the lead in May 1967, and then playing against Germany in Hamburg in May 1969, he took a flying kick at Haller in retaliation near the end of the game and was sent off.

Gemmell was known as 'Danny Kaye' to his colleagues, bearing an uncanny resemblance to the American comedian. He also enjoyed a good joke when he was playing. His tussles with Rangers winger Willie Henderson were legendary—a game within a game.

Following his dismissal against Germany, Celtic disciplined him by giving Davie Hay the left-back spot for the League Cup Final against St Johnstone three days later. After that, relations between the club and the player, who won six League Championship medals, three Scottish Cup winners' medals and four League Cup winners' medals, were never the same.

In December 1971, Gemmell, who had scored 64 goals in 418 games for Celtic, left Parkhead to join Nottingham Forest. Though he skippered the City Ground club in 1972-73, a lawn-mower accident seemed to have damaged his prospects in the Football League, but he bounced back with Dundee, helping them beat his old club Celtic in the League Cup Final of 1973!

ANDY PENMAN
Inside-right
Born: Andrew Penman, Rosyth, 20 February 1943
Died: 20 July 1994
Height: 5ft 11in
Weight: 11st 7lb
Clubs: Everton; Dundee; Glasgow Rangers; Arbroath; Inverness Caledonian
Scotland caps: 1
1966 v Holland (lost 0-3)

Andy Penman was a brilliant boy prodigy, and at the age of only 15 made his senior debut for Everton in the Liverpool Senior Cup. Feeling that his chances of success at Goodison Park were limited, he returned to Scotland to play as an amateur for Dundee in January 1959. Penman was still not quite 16 when he made his debut for the Dark Blues, and was without doubt one of the youngest amateur internationals.

Capped at youth level, Penman also played for the Scotland Under-23 side prior to making his only full international appearance against a very strong Dutch side in May 1966—a match the Scots lost 3-0.

Prior to this, Penman had helped Dundee win the League Championship in 1961-62—a master in precision distribution, especially the lofted pass over opposing defenders, he created numerous openings for his team-mates as well as scoring his fair share of goals. He helped Dundee reach the Cup Final in 1964 where they lost 3-1 to Rangers. In fact, the Ibrox side were Penman's next club as he and George McLean left Dens Park in April 1967.

A wonderfully gifted inside-forward, Penman spent five years with Rangers, helping them reach two Cup Finals in 1969 and 1971, but as on his first appearance in such a match, he was on the losing side on both occasions. Penman later completed his first-class career with Arbroath, before leaving Gayfield Park to end his playing days with Inverness Caledonian.

Penman, who was a diabetic throughout his playing career and was a motor mechanic by trade, died aged just 51 in the summer of 1994.

JIM SCOTT
Outside-right
Born: James Scott, Falkirk, 21 August 1940
Height: 5ft 9in
Weight: 10st 12lb
Clubs: Denny Rovers; Falkirk; Bo'ness United; Hibernian; Newcastle United; Crystal Palace; Hamilton Academicals
Scotland caps: 1
1966 v Holland (lost 0-3)

Jim Scott came from a noted footballing family. His father turned out for Falkirk and Burnley, while his brother Alex appeared for Rangers and Everton, and like Jim was capped by Scotland.

Jim Scott was a player with a delicate touch, able to operate on the flank or in midfield, and arrived at Easter Road in season 1958-59. He spent eight seasons with Hibs, his loyalty to the club being rewarded with 76 goals. Scott was a member of the Hibs side that won the Summer Cup against Aberdeen in 1964, while his one Scottish cap was against Holland in 1966, in the same match that Hibs' team-mate Pat Stanton made his international debut.

His finest goal came in the Edinburgh version of the English Charity Shield, which was played as a curtain-raiser during the 1950s and 1960s, when a Hibs-Hearts Select XI took on a top English team. In this particular game played at Easter Road, Newcastle United were the opponents. Scott gathered the ball on the halfway line before embarking on a mazy run upfield, and finished in style by walking the ball around the bemused Magpies' keeper.

Scott then joined Newcastle and gave the Magpies two very good seasons, as the Tyneside club qualified for Europe in 1967-68 and the following term when the Inter Cities Fairs Cup was secured. He is credited with netting the club's first-ever goal in European competition against Feyenoord, and during that memorable season, Scott linked with 'Pop' Robson and Wyn Davies to good effect. He often struck important goals, one in the Fairs Cup semi-final against Ujpesti Dozsa.

After a spell with Crystal Palace, he ended his career back in Scotland, playing for Falkirk and Hamilton Academicals before teaming up with his brother to run a long-established public house with a footballing theme in Falkirk.

DAVE SMITH
Left-half

Born: David Bruce Smith, Aberdeen, 14 November 1943
Height: 5ft 10in
Weight: 10st 9lb
Clubs: Aberdeen; Glasgow Rangers; Arbroath; Los Angeles Aztecs (United States); Berwick Rangers; Peterhead
Scotland caps: 2
1966 v Holland (lost 0-3)
1968 v Holland (drew 0-0)

Dave Smith's two full international appearances for Scotland were both against Holland, matches that were two years apart and in which Scotland failed to score.

The brother of Dundee United's Doug Smith, he began his career with his home-town club Aberdeen, where his performances for the Pittodrie club led to him winning selection for the Under-23 and Scottish League sides prior to him winning the first of his two caps. He was an elegant player, a beautiful stylist whose cool positional sense and anticipation, as well as his precise passing of the ball, made his one of the most sought-after signatures in the game.

In August 1966, Smith left Aberdeen to join Rangers for a fee of £50,000. A superb cultured left-half, he succeeded Jim Baxter but never quite had the acclaim he should have had. Smith, who should have played more often for Scotland, was at centre-half in the 1972 European Cup Winners Cup Final when Rangers beat Moscow Dynamos 3-2 to lift the trophy. It was his only domestic honour in eight years with the Ibrox club, as they had been beaten finalists in the 1967 League Cup Final and 1969 Cup Final, both times to Celtic. Dave Smith had scored 13 goals in 300 games for Rangers, when in November 1974 he was allowed to join Arbroath for £12,000.

He hadn't been at Gayfield Park long when he was made player-coach, but just over a season later he was on the move again, this time to Berwick Rangers as the club's player-manager. He spent four years with the Borderers, leading them to the 1978-79 Second Division Championship and to the following season's Scottish Cup quarter-final, before joining Peterhead in a similar capacity.

PAT STANTON

Right-half

Born: Patrick Gordon Stanton, Edinburgh, 13 September 1944
Height: 5ft 9in
Weight: 11st 0lb
Clubs: Edina Hearts; Bonnyrigg Rose Athletic; Hibernian; Glasgow Celtic
Scotland caps: 16
1966 v Holland (lost 0-3)
1969 v N Ireland (drew 1-1)
1970 v Republic of Ireland (drew 1-1), v Austria (lost 0-2)
1971 v Denmark (won 1-0), v Belgium (lost 0-3), v Portugal (lost 0-2), v Denmark (lost 0-1), v USSR (lost 0-1)
1972 v Portugal (won 2-1), v Belgium (won 1-0), v Holland (lost 1-2), v Wales (won 1-0)
1973 v Wales (won 2-0), v N Ireland (lost 1-2)
1974 v West Germany (lost 1-2)

Pat Stanton's total of 16 full international caps spread over eight years is without doubt an inadequate reflection of his true worth.

Signed by Hibs' manager Walter Galbraith, he made his league debut as a 19-year-old against Motherwell in October 1963, when he scored in a 4–3 defeat. Over the next 13 years, Pat Stanton played in 399 league games for the Easter Road club, scoring 50 goals. Perhaps his most famous goal was an injury-time equaliser in an Edinburgh derby at Tynecastle, when he towered above the Hearts defence to head home powerfully. He was also on target in the 5–0 defeat of Napoli in the 1967-68 Fairs Cup to reverse a 4–1 first leg deficit. Perhaps one of his most unhappy moments in a Hibs shirt came in the 1973-74 UEFA Cup, when he missed during a penalty shoot-out, his effort rebounding agonisingly off the post.

During the early 1970s, Hibs failed to convert their talent into trophies; their only success other than a couple of Dryborough Cup wins was the League Cup triumph of 1972, when Pat Stanton, as Hibs skipper, scored one of the goals in a 2–1 defeat of Celtic.

He left Easter Road in 1976, and at Parkhead won the League Championship and Scottish Cup winners' medal that eluded him during his time with Hibs. He had become an important member of the Celtic side, when in August 1977 in the match against Dundee United at Tannadice, he was stretchered off with an injury that finished his playing career. His standing in the game was such that over 20,000 fans turned up to pay tribute at a testimonial game between Hibs and Celtic at Easter Road.

He later assisted Alex Ferguson, manager of Aberdeen, and managed himself at Cowdenbeath and Dunfermline Athletic before returning to take charge at Easter Road. Not the most demonstrative of managers—nicknamed 'The Quiet Man'—he later took charge of Musselburgh Athletic before finishing with the game.

WILLIE BELL
Left-back

Born: William John Bell, Johnstone, 3 September 1937
Height: 5ft 10in
Weight: 11st 2lb
Clubs: Neilston Juniors; Queen's Park; Leeds United; Leicester City; Brighton and Hove Albion
Scotland caps: 2
1966 v Portugal (lost 0-1), v Brazil (drew 1-1)

Having joined Queen's Park from Neilston Juniors in 1957, Willie Bell rejected an offer from Stoke City, completed an engineering apprenticeship and won two Scottish Amateur caps before taking his chance with Leeds United.

When he arrived at Elland Road in the summer of 1960, he was a run-of-the-mill left-back, but was soon successfully converted into one of the best full-backs the Yorkshire club ever had. Succeeding Grenville Hair, he became an important part of the Leeds' defence in the early 1960s.

Bell won a Second Division Championship medal in 1963-64 and appeared for Leeds in the 1965 FA Cup Final when they lost 2-1 to Liverpool after extra-time. He also played for United in the 1967 Fairs Cup Final when Leeds were beaten 2-0 on aggregate by Dinamo Zagreb. Whilst with Leeds, Bell was capped twice by Scotland, playing against Portugal and Brazil in 1966.

Having to make way for Terry Cooper, Bell left Elland Road in September 1967, joining Leicester City for a fee of £45,000. Replacing Richie Norman, the hefty defender brought solidity rather than flair to his rearguard duties, but failed to survive manager Matt Gillies' departure, despite being named as temporary first team coach. Bell headed for the south coast and Brighton and Hove Albion, after Frank O'Farrell had taken City to the 1969 FA Cup Final without him.

After a spell coaching at St Andrew's—the Blues were fined for employing Bell in this capacity while he was still a registered player with Brighton—he was appointed manager of Birmingham City. He then became manager of Lincoln City but resigned in October 1978 to join an evangelical religious movement—the Campus Crusade for Christ—in the United States.

JACKIE SINCLAIR
Winger

Born: John Evens Wright Sinclair, Culross, 21 July 1943
Height: 5ft 6in
Weight: 9st 9lb
Clubs: Blairhill Colliery; Dunfermline Athletic; Leicester City; Newcastle United; Sheffield Wednesday; Chesterfield; Durban (South Africa); Stenhousemuir
Scotland caps: 1
1966 v Portugal (lost 0-1)

A Jock Stein signing for Dunfermline Athletic, Jackie Sinclair was a nippy goalscoring winger who came close to glory in both European competition and the 1965 Scottish Cup Final, when Leicester City manager Matt Gillies paid £25,000 to take him to Filbert Street to forge an instantly successful strike partnership with Derek Dougan.

Able to play on either flank, it was no surprise that he won a full Scotland cap at the end of his first season with the Foxes, making up for the earlier disappointment of being chosen for a postponed Scottish League representative game. After two years in the First Division with Leicester, Sinclair was still bettering the classic striker's average of a goal-every-other-game, and though the 1967-68 season was a little disappointing for him, he was, in the eyes of many Leicester fans, sold to Newcastle United for £67,500 too soon.

Sinclair, who had scored 53 goals in 113 games for Leicester, never quite reached the heights expected of him on Tyneside. However, he did have a good spell in the black and white shirts of Newcastle as the Fairs Cup was secured in 1968-69, netting a crucial goal in the semi-final battle with Rangers.

He was exchanged by Newcastle manager Joe Harvey for Sheffield Wednesday's David Ford, and Sinclair did well at Hillsborough before returning to his roots at East End Park with a second spell for Dunfermline Athletic. He later ended his career with Stenhousemuir before working for the National Coal Board.

Jackie Sinclair is a nephew of Sunderland's Tommy Wright, also a Scottish international, while his brother Willie turned out for Falkirk and Huddersfield, and his cousin, another Tommy Wright, also appeared for Leicester. Sinclair's son Chris was on Dunfermline's books and took part in the 1991 Scottish League Cup Final.

JOHN CLARK
Left-half
Born: John Clark, Bellshill, 13 March 1941
Height: 5ft 8in
Weight: 11st 5lb
Clubs: Larkhall Thistle; Glasgow Celtic; Morton
Scotland caps: 4
1966 v Brazil (drew 1-1)
1967 v Wales (drew 1-1), v N Ireland (won 2-1), v USSR (lost 0-2)

Though he only won four full caps for Scotland, John Clark's display on his debut against Brazil in June 1966 proved so effective, that the great Pele recognised him at once when their paths crossed years later in the lobby of a New York hotel!

After Larkhall Thistle had refused the deal offered by Birmingham City, Clark joined Celtic and played his first game for the Parkhead club's reserve side in a half-back line reading Crerand, McNeill and Clark. His career began to flourish once Jock Stein had arrived at Parkhead as Celtic's new manager. He decided to play with a sweeper system and chose John Clark.

Clark won League Championship medals in 1965-66, 1966-67 and 1967-68 and three Scottish Cup winners' medals in 1965 as Dunfermline were beaten 3-2, 1967 as Aberdeen were defeated 2-0 and 1969, when he was on the bench for the 4-0 rout of Rangers. Clark also won four League Cup winners' medals in 1966, 1967, 1968 and 1969 when again he was a substitute. He was also a member of the Celtic side that won the European Cup in 1967. Though he was often played at right-half, it was patently obvious to the Celtic faithful that he was far more comfortable and instinctive at left-half.

He had appeared in 318 games for Celtic when in the summer of 1971 he left Parkhead to join Morton. After two years at Cappielow Park, he had spells as assistant-manager with Aberdeen and Celtic—both with Billy McNeill as his boss—before taking over the reins at Cowdenbeath. He later took charge at both Stranraer and Clyde before managing Shotts Bon Accord.

PETER CORMACK
Midfield

Born: Peter Barr Cormack, Granton, 17 July 1946
Height: 5ft 8in
Weight: 10st 12lb
Clubs: Heart of Midlothian; Hibernian; Nottingham Forest; Liverpool; Bristol City; Hibernian
Scotland caps: 9
1966 v Brazil (drew 1-1)
1969 v Denmark (won 1-0)
1970 v Republic of Ireland (drew 1-1), v West Germany (lost 2-3)
1971 v Denmark (won 1-0), v Portugal (lost 0-2), v Wales (drew 0-0), v England (lost 1-3)
1972 v Holland (lost 1-2)

Beginning his first-class career with Hibernian, Peter Cormack, who had actually been on the groundstaff of rivals Hearts, was just 19-years-old when he starred for Scotland against a Brazil side that included the peerless Pele. Cormack went on to win nine caps for his country—under five different managers!

As a youngster at Hibs, he scored with a left-foot volley against Real Madrid in a friendly organised by the then Hibs manager Jock Stein—a game Hibs won 2-0.

In March 1970, Cormack left Easter Road to join Nottingham Forest for a fee of £80,000, but after a little over two seasons at the City Ground, Bill Shankly paid £110,000 to take him to Anfield.

Replacing Brian Hall, he soon showed his mettle with incisive displays at the heart of the Liverpool midfield. Never one to shirk a tackle, he was also good in the air, and in October 1972 ghosted in at the near post to head the only goal of the Merseyside derby against Everton. Cormack went on to win two League Championship medals and tasted UEFA Cup glory before a combination of cartilage trouble and the advance of other midfielders precipitated a November 1976 move to Bristol City.

He spent three years at Bristol City, and in an Anglo-Scottish Cup game against his first club Hibs, he was sent off!

Returning to Easter Road for a second spell in February 1980, he took his tally of league goals to 71 in 203 games, but his hopes of being installed as successor to managers Eddie Turnbull and Willie Ormond were dashed by the appointment of Bertie Auld. He then spent three years as manager of Partick Thistle and a couple of years as assistant at St Mirren. He then rejoined Hibs as assistant to Alex Miller, but there was an acrimonious split between the two, with Cormack being the one to go. He later managed in Cyprus and was briefly in charge of the Botswana national side.

JOE McBRIDE
Forward
Born: Joseph McBride, Govan, 10 June 1938
Height: 5ft 9in
Weight: 11st 8lb
Clubs: Shettleston Town; Kirkintilloch Rob Roy; Kilmarnock; Wolverhampton Wanderers; Luton Town; Partick Thistle; Motherwell; Glasgow Celtic; Hibernian; Dunfermline Athletic; Clyde
Scotland caps: 2
1967 v Wales (drew 1-1), v N Ireland (won 2-1)

A man of many clubs, Joe McBride was a tremendous header of the ball and could take a half chance on the ground.

In 1957 he went from Rob Roy Juniors to Kilmarnock, and after two years at Rugby Park, moved to Wolves for £12,000. After less than a season at Molineux, he swapped the gold of Wolves for the white of Luton Town, but returned to Scotland and Partick Thistle in the same year in exchange for Jim Fleming.

McBride joined Motherwell in November 1962, and in his first full season at Fir Park, scored 34 League and Cup goals. Included in that total were hat-tricks against Dumbarton, Falkirk, Hearts and Hibs, while in 1964-65 he netted 30 goals before leaving for Celtic for just £22,000.

He was Jock Stein's first signing for Celtic and was a member of the sides that beat Rangers in the League Cup Finals of 1965 and 1966. He won League Championship medals for 1965-66 and 1966-67, and won the first of two Scottish caps against Wales in Cardiff in October 1966, and the other against Northern Ireland the following month at Hampden. During the latter of those two Championship-winning seasons, his knee broke down against Aberdeen on Christmas Eve, and though he didn't play again that season, he was the Division One top scorer with 33 goals!

After that his first team appearances were restricted, as Stein opted to partner Wallace and Lennox up front, and in November 1968 he joined Hibs as a replacement for Colin Stein. Despite regaining some of his old form, he was transferred to Dunfermline Athletic on Christmas Day 1970, later ending his playing career with Clyde.

BOBBY LENNOX
Outside-left/ Inside-left
Born: Robert Lennox, Saltcoats, 30 August 1943
Height: 5ft 7in

Weight: 11st 4lb
Clubs: Ardeer Recreation; Glasgow Celtic; Houston Hurricanes (United States)
Scotland caps: 10
Scotland goals: 3
1967 v N Ireland (won 2-1) 1 goal, v England (won 3-2) 1 goal, v USSR (lost 0-2)
1968 v Wales (won 3-2), v England (drew 1-1)
1969 v Denmark (won 1-0) 1 goal, v Austria (won 2-1), v Cyprus (won 5-0),
v West Germany (drew 1-1)
1970 v Wales (drew 0-0)

Bobby Lennox, who scored on his international debut against Northern Ireland, also netted the second of Scotland's goals in the famous 3-2 victory over world champions England at Wembley on 15 April 1967.

Having made his Celtic debut in a 2-1 home win over Dundee in March 1962, Bobby Lennox developed into the fastest man in Scottish football. His goals total for Celtic—273 in 571 League and Cup games—is second only to Jack McGrory, and might even have been much higher but for flag-happy linesmen down the years, unable to believe that anyone could be so quick! Perhaps the most notorious of these disallowed goals came against Liverpool at Anfield in the European Cup Winners' Cup semi-final in April 1966, which would have seen the Bhoys through on the away goals rule.

He was preferred to John Hughes for the 1967 European Cup Final triumph over Inter Milan, and gave the Italians' defence a torrid time. However, in the World Club Championship play-off in Montevideo in November 1967, he was sent off, but later exonerated by the SFA as a case of mistaken identity.

Unbelievably, for a player who was supposedly on his way out of Parkhead at the time of Jock Stein's appointment, Bobby Lennox won 11 League Championship medals, eight Scottish Cup medals and four League Cup medals.

He later had a brief spell playing for Houston Hurricanes in North America before returning to Parkhead as the club's coach. Recognised by the Queen with an MBE for his services to Celtic FC, Bobby Lennox, who later ran 'Bobby's Bar' in his home-town of Saltcoats, is one of the club's greatest-ever players.

JIM McCALLIOG
Inside-forward
Born: James McCalliog, Glasgow, 23 September 1946
Height: 5ft 9in
Weight: 10st 5lb
Clubs: Leeds United; Chelsea; Sheffield Wednesday; Wolverhampton Wanderers; Manchester
United; Southampton; Chicago Stings (United States); Lincoln City; Runcorn
Scotland caps: 5
Scotland goals: 1
1967 v England (won 3-2) 1 goal, v USSR (lost 0-2)
1968 v N Ireland (lost 0-1)
1969 v Denmark (won 1-0)
1971 v Portugal (lost 0-2)

Jim McCalliog

Jim McCalliog scored Scotland's third goal on his international debut as they beat world champions England 3-2 at Wembley. The Scots' passionate performance gave them the Home International Championship, and kept them in the lead for a place in the 1968 European Nations final.

Beginning his first-class career with Chelsea, Jim McCalliog was a potentially outstanding player who might well have enjoyed great success at Stamford Bridge had he been prepared to wait a little longer for first team football. As it was, he spent most of his time with the Blues as Terry Venables' understudy, and after firing off a volley of transfer requests, he left Chelsea in October 1965 to join Sheffield Wednesday in a £37,500 deal, and in doing so at 19, became the country's costliest teenager.

At the end of his first season at Hillsborough, he helped the Owls reach the FA Cup Final and scored the first goal in the 3-2 defeat by Everton. He went on to score 27 goals in 174 appearances for Wednesday, but he became unsettled and joined Wolverhampton Wanderers for a fee of £70,000.

One of only two ever-presents in his first season at Molineux, he went on to appear in 77 consecutive league games from his debut, and in five seasons with the club missed very few matches. He captained the team to the 1971-72 UEFA Cup Final, where he scored Wolves' goal in the 2-1 home leg defeat by Spurs. He had scored 48 goals in 210 games when, after a short spell with Manchester United, he joined Southampton.

This gifted ball-player scored two vital goals in the club's run to the 1976 FA Cup Final, and was the architect of the goal that helped beat Manchester United to give the Saints the Cup. After leaving The Dell, he played in the United States for Chicago Stings before returning to the Football League as player-manager of Lincoln City. He later held a similar position with non-League Runcorn before managing Halifax Town.

RONNIE SIMPSON

Goalkeeper

Born: Ronald Campbell Simpson, Glasgow, 11 October 1930
Died: 19 April 2004
Height: 5ft 1in
Weight: 11st 13lb

Clubs: Queen's Park; Third Lanark; Newcastle United; Hibernian; Glasgow Celtic
Scotland caps: 5
1967 v England (won 3-2), v USSR (lost 0-2)
1968 v N Ireland (lost 0-1), v England (drew 1-1)
1969 v Austria (won 2-1)

When Ronnie Simpson stepped out for his Scottish international debut against England at Wembley in April 1967, he possibly thought he had reached the pinnacle of a remarkable career that stretched back over 22 years to the day when he made his senior debut for Queen's Park in 1945, when he was only 14 years old! At the age of 36, Simpson was now the oldest footballer ever to have made his full international debut for Scotland. Yet there were to be more successes, and just a few weeks later, Simpson was a member of the Celtic team which became the first British side to win the European Cup.

By the time he retired in 1970, this remarkable goalkeeper had clocked up 750 senior appearances in a career which spanned a quarter of a century. In England he played in two FA Cup-winning teams for Newcastle United in 1952 and 1955, and in Scotland he won Scotland League Championship medals for 1966 to 1969 inclusive, and played in two Scottish Cup Finals. Add to that his European Cup winners' medal and five Scottish caps, and you have one of the most successful career records of any player in the history of the British game.

After a distinguished amateur career which saw him play for Great Britain, including two appearances in the 1948 Olympic Games, Simpson, who had signed professional forms for Third Lanark, joined Newcastle United in February 1951 for a fee of £8,750. After appearing in 295 games for the Magpies, he was badly injured on a tour of Romania and was out of the game for two years. He eventually returned to action with Hibernian, but four years later, at a time when most players are contemplating retirement, he joined Celtic.

Under Jock Stein's management, Celtic won honours galore, and Simpson had a major hand in their triumphs before injury forced his retirement. After a spell coaching for the Parkhead club, he managed Hamilton Academicals before leaving the game to embark on a career which took in many occupations. A fine golfer and a past winner of the 'Footballers Championship', Ronnie Simpson was one of those rare footballers who enjoyed two long and successful careers either side of the Border.

WILLIE MORGAN
Winger
Born: William Morgan, Sauchie, 2 October 1944
Height: 5ft 9in
Weight: 10st 11lb
Clubs: Fishcross; Burnley; Manchester United; Burnley; Bolton Wanderers; Chicago Stings and Minnesota Kicks (United States); Vancouver Whitecaps (Canada); Blackpool
Scotland caps: 21
Scotland goals: 1

1968 v N Ireland (lost 0-1)

1972 v Peru (won 2-0), v Yugoslavia (drew 2-2), v Czechoslovakia (drew 0-0),
v Brazil (lost 0-1)

1973 v Denmark (won 4-1) 1 goal, v Denmark (won 2-0), v England (lost 0-5),
v Wales (won 2-0), v N Ireland (lost 1-2), v England (lost 0-1), v Switzerland (lost 0-1),
v Brazil (lost 0-1)

1974 v Czechoslovakia (won 2-1), v Czechoslovakia (lost 0-1), v West Germany (drew 1-1),
v West Germany (lost 1-2), v N Ireland (lost 0-1), v Belgium (lost 1-2),
v Brazil (drew 0-0), v Yugoslavia (drew 1-1)

Willie Morgan

In 1974, following Manchester United's relegation to Division Two, Willie Morgan was off to West Germany with Scotland's World Cup party. He played in the goalless draw with Brazil in Frankfurt and made the last of his 21 international appearances in a 1-1 draw with Yugoslavia, also in Frankfurt, as the unbeaten Scots failed by a goal to qualify for the group stages.

One of the finest wingers in British football, Willie Morgan began his first-class career with Burnley where he was reckoned to be the first player in England to have his own fan club! Brilliant on the ball and able to beat opponents at will, Willie Morgan quickly became one of the most feared wingers in the game. His crosses were delivered with pinpoint accuracy and he supplied them regularly during 1965-66 for Andy Lochhead and Willie Irvine. The pair scored 60 goals between them, steering the Clarets to a third place finish and a place in Europe. The summer after he won his first international cap, European champions Manchester United moved in with an offer of £117,000, too much for the Clarets to refuse.

Slotting in on the right-wing with inside-forwards Brian Kidd and Denis Law, Bobby Charlton in the middle and an up-and-coming youngster on the other flank called George Best, his first goals came in an 8-1 drubbing of Queen's Park Rangers when he netted a hat-trick. There were a few lean years ahead for the Old Trafford club, certainly in the League, although Willie Morgan enjoyed some stirring campaigns in various cup competitions without landing any of the top prizes. He did win a Second Division Championship medal as United bounced back to the top flight following their relegation, but following the emergence of Steve Coppell, he returned to Burnley in the summer of 1975. The move was not a success, and in March 1976 he joined Bolton Wanderers on a free transfer.

He was instrumental in the Wanderers' success in the Second Division over the next few seasons, fourth in both 1975-76 and 1976-77, a League Cup semi-final place in 1977 and the Second Division Championship in 1977-78. Also while at Burnden Park he spent his summers playing in the NASL. He later ended his career with Blackpool, but now runs a successful marketing and promotions company in Manchester.

BOBBY CLARK
Goalkeeper

Born: Robert Brown Clark, Glasgow, 26 September 1945
Height: 6ft 1in
Weight: 12st 4lb
Clubs: Glasgow YMCA; Queen's Park; Aberdeen; Clyde
Scotland caps: 17
1968 v Wales (won 3-2), v Holland (drew 0-0)
1970 v N Ireland (won 1-0)
1971 v Portugal (lost 0-2), v Wales (drew 0-0), v N Ireland (lost 0-1), v England (lost 1-3), v Denmark (lost 0-1), v USSR (lost 0-1)
1972 v Belgium (won 1-0), v N Ireland (won 2-0), v Wales (won 1-0), v England (lost 0-1), v Czechoslovakia (drew 0-0), v Brazil (lost 0-1), v Denmark (won 4-1)
1973 v England (lost 0-5)

In his first 16 international appearances for Scotland, Bobby Clark only conceded 13 goals. However, on 14 February 1973, Clark was in goal when England were invited to Hampden Park to launch the Scottish Football Association's Centenary celebrations. The visitors produced their best display for a good number of years, beating Scotland 5-0. The heavy defeat signalled Clark's last appearance for his country.

The son of a Clyde director who became treasurer of the Scottish FA, Bobby Clark began his career with Queen's Park before becoming Eddie Turnbull's first signing when the former Hampden Park boss became manager of Aberdeen. Following the departure of John Ogston to Liverpool, Clark became the Don's first-choice

Bobby Clark

keeper, making his Scottish League debut in a 2-2 draw at St Johnstone in September 1965. Over the years, Clark established a reputation as an extremely competent and confident goalkeeper, though the latter did not reveal itself with any hint of showiness.

After making his international debut, a loss of form led to Clark losing both his Aberdeen and Scottish spots to his understudy Ernie McGarr. During that time, Clark turned to outfield play and even made an appearance at centre-half in a 3-1 defeat at St Johnstone in September 1969. By the start of the 1969-70 season, Clark was back between the posts and was instrumental in the Dons winning the Scottish Cup Final against Celtic 3-1.

Throughout the seventies, Clark became an almost permanent fixture in the Aberdeen goal, limiting such deputies as Andy Geoghegan to just a handful of appearances. His performances led to a number of Football League clubs making inquiries about his availability, and though he almost joined Stoke City in 1972, the deal fell through. Remaining at Pittodrie, Clark set new appearance records for the club. He won a League Cup winners' medal in 1976, before, in a fitting climax to a long career with the Dons, he won a League Championship medal in 1979-80. Clark, who had made 593 first team appearances for the Dons, left Pittodrie to end his career with Clyde.

After turning his attention to coaching, Clark became actively involved in the emerging African soccer scene, before becoming New Zealand's national coach. He then returned to America with Stanford University, where he has become one of the most respected figures in the game in his adopted country.

JIM CRAIG
Right-back
Born: James Philip Craig, Glasgow, 7 May 1943
Height: 6ft 2in
Weight: 11st 5lb
Clubs: Glasgow University; Glasgow Celtic; Hellenic (South Africa); Sheffield Wednesday
Scotland caps: 1
1968 v Wales (won 3-2)

When Jim Craig was capped for Scotland against Wales in November 1967, it was a significant honour because it gave Celtic 14 internationals on the staff, thus exceeding Rangers' 13 of 1932-33, a record for a Scottish club.

Jim Craig took over at right-back for Celtic from the injured Ian Young at Muirton in November 1965, and held his place and made his European debut in the Cup Winners' Cup against Dynamo Kiev in Tbilisi, where 'inexperience' saw him receive his marching orders in the 66th minute after a scuffle! Though he lost his place to Young for that season's Scottish Cup Final against Rangers which ended all-square, he returned to the side for the replay which Celtic lost 1-0. After helping the Bhoys win that season's League title, he returned to University to do his finals before rejoining Celtic for the start of the Grand Slam season of 1966-67.

It was midway through this campaign that Craig became Celtic's right-back in partnership with Tommy Gemmell. In the European Cup Final of 1967 against Inter Milan in Lisbon, it was Craig who cut the ball back for Gemmell to thunder home Celtic's equaliser. However, throughout all this time, Craig was only a part-time footballer, being first and foremost a dentist!

Because of dentistry, Jim Craig's career with Celtic ended prematurely and he played the last of his 231 games in the Scottish Cup Final of 1972, when Hibernian were beaten 6-1. He intended making his future as a dentist in South Africa, but before long he was back on these shores, seeing out his career with Sheffield Wednesday.

On hanging up his boots, he had a spell as manager of Waterford before making a successful side career as a broadcaster and journalist. Nowadays he is a dentist at a Glasgow Health Centre.

DOUG FRASER
Right-back/ Wing-half
Born: Douglas Michael Fraser, Eaglesham, 8 December 1941
Height: 5ft 9in
Weight: 11st 4lb
Clubs: Blantyre Celtic; Aberdeen; West Bromwich Albion; Nottingham Forest; Walsall
Scotland caps: 2
1968 v Holland (drew 0-0)
1969 v Cyprus (won 5-0)

Doug Fraser was a fearsome tough-tackling player who, after being rejected after trials with Celtic and Leeds United in the 1950s, made his name with some excellent performances for Aberdeen in the Scottish First Division.

In September 1963, Fraser was one of West Bromwich Albion manager Jimmy Hagan's first signings for the Hawthorns club, when he paid £23,000 for his services. After making his debut in the local derby against Birmingham City, a match Albion won 3-1, Fraser kept his place in the side for the next seven seasons. Appointed the club's captain, he led the Baggies out at Wembley in the 1970 League Cup Final against Manchester City, but Albion went down 2-1.

Playing most of his games at wing-half, but with occasional games at right or left-back, the versatile defender recorded over 300 games for the club, and along with fellow defenders John Kaye and Graham Williams, made up one of the toughest defensive line-ups ever fielded by the Hawthorns club. He had appeared in all of the club's Cup Final appearances during this period—1966, 1967, 1968 and 1970—before, in November 1970, he played his last game against Chelsea.

Two months later, Albion manager Alan Ashman sold him to Nottingham Forest for £35,000. In March 1972 he returned to the Hawthorns as Forest's captain in a relegation decider that Albion won 1-0.

In the summer of 1973, Fraser returned to the West Midlands with Walsall, and shortly after making his debut for the Saddlers, hit the headlines for being sent off for fighting in a match against Bristol Rovers—with his former Albion team-mate Kenny Stephens! At the start of the 1974-75 season, Fraser was appointed Walsall's manager, but after two years at the helm, he retired to take up a career as a prison warder in Nottingham.

BOBBY HOPE
Inside-left

Born: Robert Hope, Bridge of Allan, 28 September 1943
Height: 5ft 7in
Weight: 11st 3lb
Clubs: Drumchapel Amateurs; West Bromwich Albion; Birmingham City; Sheffield Wednesday
Scotland caps: 2
1968 v Holland (drew 0-0)
1969 v Denmark (won 1-0)

Bobby Hope, who, for most of the 1960s, controlled West Bromwich Albion's midfield, was often homesick during his early days with the club, and came close to signing for his boyhood heroes, Glasgow Rangers—had he indeed returned to Scotland, he would undoubtedly have won more than the two Scottish caps that he was awarded.

Hope made his Albion debut against Arsenal in 1960 as a 16-year-old—the last amateur player to turn out for the club. Within two years, he was a fixture in the Baggies' side, creating many of the goals scored by Tony Brown, John Kaye and Jeff Astle. Legendary Liverpool manager Bill Shankly said of him: 'Stop Bobby Hope and you stop Albion' during the epic sixth round FA Cup tie between Liverpool and the Baggies in 1968, and it was certainly true. If Hope had a bad game, then so did Albion. That season, Hope was outstanding as Albion lifted the FA Cup, beating Everton 1-0 in the final.

Hope made over 400 appearances for Albion, scoring 40 goals, the most memorable of which, perhaps, came in the run to the final of the 1970 League Cup, when he chipped an 11-man wall on the Ipswich Town goal-line from an indirect free-kick! Though Albion lost that season's final 2-1 to Manchester City, Hope did pick up a League Cup winners' medal in 1965, when, entering the competition for the first time, they beat West Ham United 5-3 in the two-legged final.

Hope was eventually sold by Albion manager Don Howe—a former team-mate—to Birmingham City in May 1972, later playing for Sheffield Wednesday before taking over as manager of Bromsgrove Rovers. After taking them to their highest-ever placing near the top of the Vauxhall Conference, he later resigned to concentrate on his business interests.

GEORGE McLEAN
Wing-half/ Inside-forward

Born: George Tomlinson McLean, Paisley, 26 May 1943
Height: 6ft 1in
Weight: 12st 12lb
Clubs: Drumchapel Amateurs; St Mirren; Glasgow Rangers; Dundee; Dunfermline Athletic; Ayr United; Hamilton Academicals

Scotland caps: I
1968 v Holland (drew 0-0)

One of the game's most enigmatic and controversial figures, 'Dandy' McLean, originally a wing-half, began his career with St Mirren. He forced himself on the attention of Rangers when he had an outstanding game against them for the Love Street club in the 1962 Scottish Cup Final, which Rangers won 2-0. McLean joined Rangers in January 1963 for a then record fee between Scottish clubs of £26,500.

George McLean was indeed a 'Dandy'—a driver of quality cars, a sharp dresser and one who away from the game enjoyed the good life. Though Rangers manager Scot Symon had the occasional problem in trying to control him, there was nothing malicious in it all.

McLean, who could play equally well at inside-forward as well as wing-half, was not a physical player, and there were times when he could look a little cumbersome. Yet when he was moved and played as a striker, he was a prolific scorer alongside Jim Forrest. Having helped Rangers win the League Championship and Scottish Cup in 1963-64, it was his goal against Aberdeen that put Rangers into the Scottish Cup Final of 1965-66. After missing the final against Celtic, which ended all-square, he was back for the replay, helping the Ibrox club to a 1-0 win. That season he scored no fewer than 41 goals in all competitions, but after Rangers lost to lowly Berwick Rangers in one of the most infamous of Scottish Cup defeats, he left Ibrox shortly afterwards to join Dundee in exchange for Andy Penman.

McLean, who had scored 82 goals in 116 games for Rangers, helped Dundee reach the 1968 League Cup Final, but in one of the competition's most exciting finals they lost 5-3 to Celtic. He later played for Dunfermline Athletic, Ayr United and Hamilton Academicals, before going to work for a double glazing company.

BOBBY MONCUR
Central defender

Born: Robert Moncur, Perth, 19 January 1945
Height: 5ft 10in
Weight: 10st 9lb
Clubs: Newcastle United; Sunderland; Carlisle United
Scotland caps: 16
1968 v Holland (drew 0-0)
1970 v Republic of Ireland (drew 1-1), v N Ireland (won 1-0), v Wales (drew 0-0),
      v England (drew 0-0)
1971 v Denmark (won 1-0), v Belgium lost 0-3), v Portugal (lost 0-2), v Wales (drew 0-0),
      v N Ireland (lost 0-1), v England (lost 1-3), v Denmark (lost 0-1)
1972 v Peru (won 2-0), v N Ireland (won 2-0), v Wales (won 1-0), v England (lost 0-1)

Bobby Moncur, who was one of Newcastle United's finest captains and a superb central defender, won full international honours for Scotland in May 1968 when he

Bobby Moncur

played against Holland in Amsterdam. After only six appearances for his country, he was given the captaincy ahead of John Greig and went on to play in 16 internationals.

A centre-back with the ability to read the game well and an aggressive, strong tackler, he was commanding in the air and a great marshal of the side. But he will always be remembered primarily for the hat-trick of goals he netted in the Inter Cities Fairs Cup Final of 1969 against Ujpesti Dosza.

Captain of the Scottish Schoolboys and a youth international, Moncur was soon being tipped for the professional game. A number of top clubs showed an interest, but Moncur opted for the Magpies. He played in various positions during his early days, with his first taste of success coming in the FA Youth Cup of 1962, when he scored United's winner in the final against Wolves.

Moncur played a handful of games during Newcastle's Second Division Championship-winning season of 1964-65, but was something of a slow developer, and manager Joe Harvey almost sold him to Norwich City. The deal fell through and Moncur worked hard at his game, gradually establishing himself in the No.6 shirt. Forming a fine central defensive partnership with John McNamee, he led Newcastle to the 1974 FA Cup Final at Wembley, but the Magpies were outplayed by Liverpool. He never kicked another ball for United, and on being released after 346 appearances, he joined Sunderland.

In 1975-76 he helped the Wearsiders win the Second Division Championship, but in November 1976 he joined Carlisle United as player-manager. Resigning after the Cumbrian club slipped into Division Three, he then moved to take over the reins at Heart of Midlothian, leading the Tynecastle side to the Scottish First Division Championship. Shortly afterwards he was appointed manager of Plymouth Argyle, but he left Home Park after a difference of opinion with the directors and then quit football altogether.

JIMMY SMITH
Midfield
Born: James Smith, Glasgow, 20 January 1947
Height: 5ft 11in
Weight: 11st 8lb
Clubs: Benburb Juniors; Aberdeen; Newcastle United; Glasgow Celtic (loan); Whitley Bay

Scotland caps: 4

1968   v Holland (drew 0-0)

1974   v West Germany (drew 1-1), v N Ireland (lost 0-1), v Wales (won 2-0)

A master craftsman, 'Jinky' Smith had a languid, lazy style, but also possessed a tantalising right foot with which he mesmerised opponents.

He made a name for himself with Aberdeen, for whom he helped reach the 1967 Scottish Cup Final where they went down 2-0 to Celtic. Also that year, he represented Scotland at Under-23 level before the following season making his full international debut against Holland. In four seasons at Pittodrie, Smith scored 37 goals in 140 games, before moving to Newcastle United for what was reported as a £100,000 deal—the first six-figure fee paid by the Tyneside club. However, details indicate the transfer fee was much less, with only add-ons increasing the overall amount.

Smith took time to adapt to the different English game, but by season 1971-72 had settled and become the darling of the Newcastle fans, able to hit a match-winning pass with the most delicate of through balls and chips. One record he does hold is the club's fastest dismissal—it came in the Texaco Cup match of December 1973 against Birmingham City, when he was sent off after just 53 seconds! Missing a season with cartilage injury, he returned to enjoy two-and-a-half seasons of top class performances, before another knee complaint put him on the sidelines.

New manager Gordon Lee sent him on loan to Celtic, but his knee failed again and Smith was forced to halt his career. Following a testimonial he went into a trophy business in Newcastle, but it failed controversially; he also went through a disturbing period with a betting addiction, but thankfully that is now all behind him.

JIM HERRIOTT
Goalkeeper

Born: James Herriott, Chapelhall, 20 December 1939

Height: 6ft 0in

Weight: 11st 6lb

Clubs: Douglasdale; Dunfermline Athletic; Birmingham City; Mansfield Town (loan); Aston Villa (loan); Hibernian; St Mirren; Partick Thistle; Dunfermline Athletic; Morton

Scotland caps: 8

1969   v Denmark (won 1-0), v Cyprus (won 5-0), v Wales (won 5-3), v N Ireland (drew 1-1), v England (lost 1-4), v Cyprus (won 8-0)

1970   v Republic of Ireland (drew 1-1), v West Germany (lost 2-3)

When Jim Herriott replaced the injured Tommy Lawrence for Scotland against Wales at the Racecourse Ground in May 1969, he became only the second goalkeeping substitute to appear in an international match at Wrexham's ground. The first was 61 years earlier, when Bev Davies took over from Leigh Roose in the Welsh side against England.

A bricklayer by trade, Jim Herriott signed amateur forms for Dunfermline

Athletic in 1957, before turning professional the following year. He spent seven years at East End Park, first as deputy to Scottish international keeper Eddie Connachan, but when Connachan was sold to Middlesbrough in the summer of 1963, Herriott took over as the club's first-choice keeper. His performances led to him winning Scottish 'B' and Under-23 honours, and it wasn't long before clubs south of the Border began to take an interest in him.

In May 1965, shortly after playing in the Scottish Cup Final, Herriott joined Birmingham City for a fee of £17,000. The Blues had just lost their First Division status, but were hoping to bounce back into the top flight after just one season. Over the next four seasons, Herriott missed very few games and appeared in the 1967 League Cup and 1968 FA Cup semi-finals, and was at this time the best keeper in the Football League outside of the First Division.

An unspectacular but safe keeper, Herriott had loan spells with Mansfield Town and Aston Villa, and after appearing in 212 games for the Blues, was transferred to Hibernian in August 1971. At the end of his first season at Easter Road, he was again on a losing side in the Scottish Cup Final, but in 1973 he won a League Cup winners' medal as Hibs beat Celtic 2-1.

He later had brief spells with St Mirren, Partick Thistle, Dunfermline Athletic and Morton, before leaving the first-class game.

TOMMY McLEAN
Outside-right
Born: Thomas McLean, Ashgill, 2 June 1947
Height: 5ft 4in
Weight: 10st 6lb
Clubs: Birkenshaw Amateurs; Kilmarnock; Glasgow Rangers
Scotland caps: 6
Scotland goals: 1
1969 v Denmark (won 1-0), v Cyprus (won 5-0), v Wales (won 5-3) 1 goal
1970 v N Ireland (won 1-0), v Wales (drew 0-0)
1971 v Denmark (lost 0-1)

Tommy McLean began his first-class footballing career with Kilmarnock, signing for Willie Waddell and playing mostly as a winger. Tommy's father had persuaded him to sign for Killie, turning down an approach from Scot Symon of Rangers. He did later join Rangers, by that time managed by the same Willie Waddell!

McLean made his first team debut for Kilmarnock in the Summer Cup semi-final first leg against Hibernian in May 1964, when Killie won 4-3, though three days later they lost the second-leg 3-0. His next first team game was in one of the club's greatest-ever results, a 5-1 home win over Eintracht Frankfurt in the Fairs Cup. Killie had lost 3-0 in Germany in the first leg, and then fell further behind in the opening minutes at Rugby Park before coming back to win 5-4 on aggregate—Tommy McLean was hailed as Man-of-the-Match. He actually made his league debut against Dunfermline four days after the defeat of Eintracht.

Having been honoured by selection for the Scottish League, McLean won his first full cap against Denmark in October 1968, but by the time he had made his sixth and last international appearance against the same opposition, he had signed for Rangers.

During his time with Killie, Tommy Docherty had tried to sign him for Chelsea, but McLean, who went on to score 71 goals in 300 games, didn't feel he was ready for English football.

With Rangers, McLean won three League Championship medals in 1974–75, 1975–76 and 1977–78, five Scottish Cup winners' medals and two League Cup winners' medals. He was also a member of the Rangers side that won the European Cup Winners' Cup in 1972, beating Moscow Dynamo 3-2 in Barcelona. McLean's first step on the managerial ladder was when he became first team coach and then assistant-manager at Ibrox.

In November 1983 he joined Morton as manager, leading them to a First Division Championship. He repeated this success with Motherwell, winning the First Division Championship in 1984–85 and a Scottish Cup win in 1991. He left Motherwell after a disagreement, and after a short time joined Hearts as manager in June 1994. On leaving Tynecastle he had a very brief spell with Raith Rovers before taking over the reins at Dundee United. He led the Tannadice club to the Coca Cola Cup Final in November 1997, but the Terrors lost 3-0 to Celtic. He left United by mutual consent in September 1998 after a series of poor results.

COLIN STEIN

Centre-forward

Born: Colin Stein, Linlithgow, 10 May 1947
Height: 5ft 11in
Weight: 12st 8lb
Clubs: Broxburn Strollers; Armadale Thistle; Hibernian; Glasgow Rangers; Coventry City; Glasgow Rangers; Kilmarnock (loan)
Scotland caps: 21
Scotland goals: 10

1969 v Denmark (won 1-0), v Cyprus (won 5-0) 2 goals, v Wales (won 5-3) 1 goal, v N Ireland (drew 1-1) 1 goal, v England (lost 1-4) 1 goal, v Cyprus (won 8-0) 4 goals

1970 v Republic of Ireland (drew 1-1) 1 goal, v West Germany (lost 2-3), v Austria (lost 0-2), v N Ireland (won 1-0), v Wales (drew 0-0), v England (drew 0-0)

1971 v Denmark (won 1-0), v Belgium (lost 0-3), v Denmark (lost 0-1), v USSR (lost 0-1)

1972 v Czechoslovakia (drew 0-0)

1973 v England (lost 0-5), v Wales (won 2-0), v N Ireland (lost 1-2), v England (lost 0-1)

Despite scoring four goals in a World Cup qualifying match against Cyprus in May 1969, Colin Stein's main claim to fame was that he was the first player to be transferred between two Scottish clubs for a six-figure fee, his £100,000 move from Hibs to Rangers taking place in October 1968, three years after he joined the Easter Road club from Armadale Thistle.

Colin Stein playing for Coventry City

Stein could score goals. He famously scored Hibs' fifth goal in their 5-0 rout of Napoli in the 1967-68 Fairs Cup. In fact, season 1967-68 was full of rich pickings for Stein, who finished as Hibs' top scorer for the season with 29 goals—not bad for a player who started out as a left-back!

On joining Rangers, Stein, who had scored 41 goals in 75 games for Hibs, made an instant impact. He scored hat-tricks in his opening games at Arbroath and at home to his former club Hibs, and that meant instant popularity with the

Ibrox crowd. Stein was almost an old-fashioned centre-forward, strong, bustling and with a rather short fuse, resulting in him being sent off several times in his career. Stein, who scored in Rangers' 1972 European Cup Winners' Cup Final success over Moscow Dynamo, was transferred in October of that year to Coventry City for £90,000 plus Quinton Young, a former Ayr United winger.

He had some initial success at Highfield Road, scoring 12 goals in 35 games, and though he struggled to find the net as often in 1973-74, he did score a hat-trick in a 5-1 League Cup defeat of Darlington. His form for the Sky Blues led to him adding another four Scottish caps to his collection. However, in February 1975, when it appeared that Coventry could no longer maintain the transfer instalments, Stein rejoined Rangers.

Though his appearances were restricted by the form of Derek Johnstone and Derek Parlane, he did net the equaliser against Hibs, the draw giving Rangers their first League Championship win in eleven years. During the 1977-78 season, he had a spell on loan with Kilmarnock, but at the end of the campaign, he decided to hang up his boots.

EDDIE GRAY
Outside-left

Born: Edwin Gray, Bellshill, 17 January 1948
Height: 5ft 10in
Weight: 11st 5lb
Clubs: Leeds United; Whitby Town
Scotland caps: 12
Scotland goals: 3
1969 v England (lost 1-4), v Cyprus (won 8-0) 1 goal
1970 v West Germany (lost 2-3), v Austria (lost 0-2)
1971 v Wales (drew 0-0), v N Ireland (lost 0-1)
1972 v Belgium (won 1-0), v Holland (lost 1-2)
1976 v Wales (won 3-1) 1 goal, v England (won 2-1)
1977 v Finland (won 6-0) 1 goal, v Wales (won 1-0)

Eddie Gray was a most gifted and graceful player, but his career was plagued by a succession of injuries which would have prompted a lesser man to quit the game long before he did. Eddie Gray could confuse a full-back simply by dropping one of his hunched shoulders and feinting one way before dribbling off in the other direction!

Eddie Gray's early performances for Leeds United led to him winning two Under-23 caps for Scotland, before he gained his full international spurs against England at Wembley. That came at the end of a season in which Leeds won the League Championship. The following year, Eddie Gray gave a virtuoso performance in the FA Cup Final against Chelsea. However, after establishing himself as one of Scotland's most exciting post-war players, he ran into injury problems that threatened to end his career. He was written off by a number of people connected with the club, but manager Jimmy Armfield was full

Eddie Gray

of encouragement. Gray fought his way back to full fitness, and during his rehabilitation coached the Leeds' juniors.

Gray was still playing when he was appointed the Yorkshire club's player-manager in July 1982. Though he had no managerial experience, he had impressed when coaching the juniors. He ended his playing days at left-back while at the same time bringing back Peter Lorimer as captain. Gray, who received an MBE for his services to football, was unable to win back Leeds' First Division place, although they were promotion candidates for three successive seasons. In October 1985, Gray was sacked, thus ending a 22-year association with the club.

He later joined former team-mate David Harvey as player for non-League Whitby Town, before working as Middlesbrough's reserve and youth team coach. In December 1986 he was appointed Rochdale's manager before leaving to take charge of Hull City in the summer of 1988. After just one season at Boothferry Park, he was sacked, and after concentrating on outside business interests, returned to Leeds as junior coach when Howard Wilkinson was their manager. Appointed assistant-manager when David O'Leary took over the reins, Eddie Gray then replaced Peter Reid as boss, but lost his job after Leeds lost their Premiership status.

THE 1970s

The two previous wins Scotland secured against Denmark under the stewardship of Tommy Docherty virtually clinched Scotland's place in the 1974 World Cup Finals in West Germany. By September, all Willie Ormond's team had to do was beat Czechoslovakia once, either home or away. But in the first match at Hampden, the Czechs drew first blood when, in the 33rd minute, Nehoda broke clear on the right and his spectacular cross skated under the goalkeeper. Within seven minutes, Jim Holton had equalised, heading home Tommy Hutchison's corner. In the second half Scotland threw everything into attack. In the 70th minute, with the Czech defence under fearful pressure, a Billy Bremner free-kick struck the post, and it seemed the Czechs had survived another onslaught. But the ball broke to Willie Morgan, and Joe Jordan, brought on to replace Kenny Dalglish six minutes earlier, became Scotland's hero as he met Morgan's centre to head home the winner. The return match in Bratislava was irrelevant, although any disappointment the team may have had by going down to a Nehoda penalty was tempered by the news that England had been eliminated by Poland!

Scotland's pride in being the only British representatives in the tournament was ultimately dented by their own naivety. Their first match, when they beat Zaire 2-0, was their downfall. A brave goalless draw with Brazil followed. Billy Bremner was inspirational and was unlucky not to score, as were Joe Jordan and Peter Lorimer. In the meantime, though, Yugoslavia had demolished Zaire 9-0, a scoreline that hardly reflected their total domination of the match.

With the Yugoslavs holding such a huge goals advantage, Scotland had to beat them. But Scotland slipped behind eight minutes from time, and a late equaliser from Jordan was not enough to save them as Brazil beat Zaire 3-0 to edge Scotland out by a single goal, the first time the World Cup Finals had used goal difference to separate teams. Strangely, Scotland were the only team in the tournament not to have lost a match, as West Germany lost to East Germany 1-0 in their first meeting since the countries had been divided after the Second World War.

In June 1977, the biennial visit to Wembley by Scotland's travelling army of fans was truly an invasion. After the 2-1 defeat of England, hordes of drunken Scottish fans, bedecked in tartan scarves and caps, charged across the pitch to fete their victorious players. They then turned their attentions to the goal posts—tearing them down and ripping out the nets—and the Wembley turf, carving pieces out to take home as souvenirs. The result meant that Scotland had retained the Home International Championship, but aside from large amounts of alcohol, it was hard to understand what excited the Scottish fans!

Scotland were the only country from the British Isles to qualify for the 1978 World Cup Finals in Argentina, and they booked their tickets to South America at the expense of Wales. Although Czechoslovakia were the other team in the Scotland-Wales group, it always looked as if qualification was between the British pair after both had beaten the Czechs at home. The deciding match against Wales was played at Anfield, because none of the Welsh stadiums met the requisite safety standards.

There were just 12 minutes remaining when the French referee awarded Scotland a penalty for disputed handball. Don Masson converted and Scottish fans in the capacity crowd went delirious. Television replays, however, showed that the referee had got it wrong. Three minutes from time, a scintillating header from Kenny Dalglish put the result beyond doubt.

Ally MacLeod's team arrived in South America on the wave of Tartan sentiment and expectation. It was hailed as the greatest team to compete in the World Cup, and with Kenny Dalglish, Alan Gilzean, Joe Jordan, Lou Macari, Dave Mackay and Bruce Rioch in their squad, Scotland seemed to have good grounds for optimism. With the exception of Holland, their group looked easy enough, with Iran playing in their first-ever World Cup and unfancied Peru in their third.

In the match against Peru, Jordan gave Scotland the lead, but then they went to pieces and Teofilo Cubillas ran riot to help the South American side to a 3-1 win. If that wasn't bad enough, Willie Johnston was sent home and banned for a year from international football for failing a random drugs test after the match. Scotland's nightmare was only beginning, as they produced a totally inept performance to draw 1-1 with Iran. They now needed to beat Holland by three goals or get on the plane home. Scotland rose to the challenge—Dalglish equalised an early Dutch goal before Gemmill's penalty put them ahead, and with Scottish tails up, Gemmill scored the goal of the tournament. Starting his run outside the penalty area, he beat three Dutch defenders before chipping the keeper. Holland pulled a goal back but, once again, Scotland had their World Cup glory!

Towards the end of the decade, the SFA, desperate to recover lost pride, turned to their greatest-ever club manager in Jock Stein to take over the national side—he had much to do.

WILLIE CALLAGHAN
Right-back
Born: William Thomas Callaghan, Cowdenbeath, 12 February 1943
Height: 5ft 9in
Weight: 11st 2lb
Clubs: Crossgates Primrose; Dunfermline Athletic; Berwick Rangers; Cowdenbeath
Scotland caps: 2
1970 v Republic of Ireland (drew 1-1), v Wales (drew 0-0)

Willie Callaghan was a skilful defender and excellent club man, being associated with Dunfermline Athletic for a decade and a half. He joined the East End Park club from Crossgates Primrose in 1957, turning professional three years later.

He soon established himself in the Pars' side, and both he and his brother Tommy, a Dunfermline team-mate, were honoured by selection for the Scottish League. Willie Callaghan was a member of the Dunfermline side beaten 3-2 by Celtic in the 1965 Scottish Cup Final, but was on the winning side three years later when the Pars beat Hearts 3-1. Shortly after this success, Willie Callaghan scored one of Scottish football's quickest two own goals, when after less than 90 seconds he knocked the ball past keeper Duff in the game against Dundee United in December 1969. He made amends a week later with an outstanding display against crack Belgian side Anderlecht, with a couple of goal-line clearances and last-ditch tackles.

Callaghan, who holds the Dunfermline club record for the most appearances in European competitions with 34 games, won his first full cap when he came on as a substitute for Celtic's Tommy Gemmell in the match against the Republic of Ireland in September 1969. He then started the game against Wales, giving a sound display in a goalless draw.

On leaving East End Park, Callaghan had a couple of seasons playing for Berwick Rangers before winding down his career with his home-town club, Cowdenbeath.

ERNIE McGARR
Goalkeeper
Born: Ernest McGarr, Glasgow, 9 March 1944
Height: 6ft 0in
Weight: 11st 4lb
Clubs: Kilbirnie Ladeside; Aberdeen; Dunfermline Athletic; East Fife; Cowdenbeath; Airdrieonians; Berwick Rangers
Scotland caps: 2
1970 v Republic of Ireland (drew 1-1), v Austria (lost 0-2)

Ernie McGarr won his first cap for Scotland against the Republic of Ireland, starring in a 1-1 draw. His second and last appearance for his country came in the World Cup qualifying match against Austria in Vienna in November 1969. As they were already out of the World Cup, the Scots' visit was meaningless, an aggravation which they could well have done without! McGarr was the fourth keeper Scotland had called upon in six World Cup matches, and though he gave a solid display, the Austrians won 2-0.

Ernie McGarr joined Aberdeen from Kilbirnie Ladeside in 1965 as understudy to Bobby Clark. Following an injury to Scotland's No.1 keeper, McGarr made his Aberdeen debut in a 2-1 defeat at Hearts in October 1967. Though he began the following season in the Dons' reserve side, it wasn't long before his performances led to him replacing Clark in the Aberdeen side. An acrobatic keeper who had the ability to make the impossible save, McGarr played in the last 20 games of the 1968-69 season and helped the Dons reach the semi-finals of the Scottish Cup.

McGarr was still Aberdeen's first-choice keeper when the 1969-70 season got under way, but in a remarkable turnaround at the midway stage of the campaign, Clark regained the No.1 jersey. The last of McGarr's 58 first team appearances for the Dons was in a 2-0 win over Motherwell on the final day of that season, after which he spent half a season in the reserves before joining Dunfermline Athletic in January 1971.

A tall and commanding goalkeeper, he was unable to settle at East End Park and the following year joined East Fife. He enjoyed five good seasons at Bayview before moving on to Cowdenbeath. In 1978 he joined Airdrie before two years later moving to Berwick Rangers, with whom he ended his Scottish League career.

FRANCIS BURNS
Left-back/ Wing-half

Born: Francis Burns, Glenboig, 17 October 1948
Height: 5ft 8in
Weight: 10st 10lb
Clubs: Manchester United; Southampton; Preston North End; Shamrock Rovers
Scotland caps: 1
1970 v Austria (lost 0-2)

Another in the long line of Manchester United players who came to maturity through the club's junior ranks. This Lanarkshire-born player came to Old Trafford as a 15-year-old in 1964, and three years later, he was lining up at left-back as the Reds took on West Ham United. He went on to enjoy 45 outings that season, playing in most of the European Cup games but missing out at the end of United's great run, through injury.

Injuries, particularly cartilage trouble, dogged his career, and over the next five seasons, his first team appearances were dictated by his fitness.

Burns, who was capped at every level by Scotland, won just one cap as a full international, when he played in the 2-0 defeat against Austria in November 1969.

He eventually left Old Trafford in June 1972, having appeared in 155 League and Cup games for the Reds, to join Southampton for a fee of £60,000. Burns never really settled on the south coast, and after just 14 months at The Dell, he jumped at the chance to return to the north-west with Preston North End.

At Deepdale he teamed up with his old Manchester United colleague, Bobby Charlton, who was manager at the time. Persistent injury problems again prevented Burns from regularly displaying his enormous talent at the club, but nevertheless, he still managed to clock up 273 games for North End before moving to Shamrock Rovers during the twilight of his career.

HUGH CURRAN
Forward

Born: Hugh Patrick Curran, Glasgow, 25 September 1943
Height: 5ft 9in
Weight: 11st 8lb
Clubs: Shamrock Rovers; Third Lanark; Corby Town; Millwall; Norwich City; Wolverhampton
    Wanderers; Oxford United; Bolton Wanderers; Oxford United
Scotland caps: 5
Scotland goals: 1
1970 v Austria (lost 0-2)
1971 v N Ireland (lost 0-1), v England (lost 1-3) 1 goal, v Denmark (lost 0-1),
    v USSR (lost 0-1)

Hugh Curran, who won five caps for Scotland, was an amateur at Old Trafford in 1958-59 but was not offered terms, and he left United to sign for Shamrock Rovers, moving back across the Irish Sea to join Third Lanark in 1962.

Unsuccessful trials then followed with a number of clubs before he teamed up with non-League Corby Town in the summer of 1963. In March 1964 he finally made it into the 'big arena' when he joined Millwall. Curran never looked back after that, going on to score 27 goals in 57 league games for the Lions before joining Norwich City for a fee of £10,000 in January 1966.

In his first two seasons at Carrow Road, he was hampered by injuries, but in 1967-68 he was the club's only

Hugh Curran

ever-present player and top scorer with 16 goals, including a hat-trick in a 4-2 home win over Birmingham City. The following season he was still the club's leading scorer, having netted 22 goals in 31 games, including a treble in the League Cup tie against local rivals Ipswich Town, before being transferred to Wolverhampton Wanderers.

Curran continued to find the net following his move to Molineux, topping the club's scoring charts in 1969-70 with 23 goals. It was this kind of form that led to him winning his first full cap against Austria in November 1969. Curran, whose only piece of silverware was a runners–up medal presented to him after Wolves had lost the 1972 UEFA Cup Final to Spurs, had scored 47 goals in 98 games prior to joining Oxford United.

After a couple of seasons at the Manor Ground, he joined Bolton Wanderers, and in his only full season at Burnden Park, he was the Lancashire club's leading scorer. He later had a second spell with Oxford United, before in March 1979, being forced to retire through injury.

PETER LORIMER
Forward

Born: Peter Patrick Lorimer, Dundee, 14 December 1946
Height: 5ft 10in
Weight: 11st 2lb
Clubs: Leeds United; Toronto Blizzard (Canada); York City; Vancouver Whitecaps (Canada); Leeds United; Whitby Town; Hapoel Haifa (Israel)
Scotland caps: 21
Scotland goals: 4

1970 v Austria (lost 0-2)
1971 v Wales (drew 0-0), v N Ireland (lost 0-1)
1972 v N Ireland (won 2-0) 1 goal, v Wales (won 1-0) 1 goal, v England (lost 0-1)
1973 v Denmark (won 4-1), v Denmark (won 2-0) 1 goal, v England (lost 0-5), v England (lost 0-1)
1974 v West Germany (drew 1-1), v England (won 2-0), v Belgium (lost 1-2), v Norway (won 2-1), v Zaire (won 2-0) 1 goal, v Brazil (drew 0-0), v Yugoslavia (drew 1-1)
1975 v Spain (lost 1-2)
1976 v Denmark (won 1-0), v Denmark (won 3-1), v Romania (drew 1-1)

Peter Lorimer, who was a key figure in Scotland's 1974 World Cup campaign, boasted one of the hardest shots in football.

He was Leeds United's youngest debutant, making his Football League debut in a 1-1 draw against Southampton in September 1962 when aged just 15 years and 289 days. Lorimer once scored 176 goals in a season during his time at Stobswell School, Dundee, and had attracted the attention of a host of top clubs. Indeed, Leeds' manager Don Revie was in such a hurry to sign him that he was stopped for speeding on his way up north!

Lorimer joined the Yorkshire club in May 1962, and won Scottish amateur caps on a tour of Kenya before turning professional in December 1963. In his early days at Elland Road he broke his leg, but recovered to establish himself as an important member of the Leeds side. It was 1965-66 before he won back his regular place, helping Leeds to finish as runners-up in the First Division—they would finish in that spot another four times in Lorimer's career there. He won a League Championship medal in 1968-69, and the following season won the first of 21 international caps when he played against Austria.

Lorimer's thunderous shooting helped Leeds reap a rich harvest of honours, but 1972-73 was the only season when he headed the club's scoring charts—his total of 15 league goals included a last day hat-trick in a 6-1 defeat of Arsenal. In March 1979, Lorimer left Leeds to play for Toronto Blizzard, but six months later he returned to England to sparkle in York City's ranks. In March 1980, he

Peter Lorimer of Leeds

returned to Canada as player-coach with Vancouver Whitecaps. In December 1983, at the age of 37, Lorimer rejoined Leeds United—where he was older than manager Eddie Gray! In his second spell he overhauled John Charles' league aggregate of 153 goals before moving to non-League Whitby Town in December 1985.

On leaving Whitby, Lorimer had a brief spell in Israel as player-coach of Hapoel Haifa, before returning to Leeds where he appears on the local radio station and sometimes on Radio Five as a summariser.

WILLIE CARR
Midfield

Born: William McInanny Carr, Glasgow, 6 January 1950
Height: 5ft 8in
Weight: 10st 4lb
Clubs: Coventry City; Wolverhampton Wanderers; Millwall; Worcester City; Willenhall; Stourbridge
Scotland caps: 6
1970 v N Ireland (won 1-0), v Wales (drew 0-0), v England (drew 0-0)
1971 v Denmark (won 1-0)
1972 v Peru (won 2-0)
1973 v Denmark (won 2-0)

Willie Carr

Willie Carr's performances in midfield led to him winning the first of six full caps for Scotland when he played in a 1-0 win over Northern Ireland in April 1970—in fact, the opposition failed to score in each of his appearances for the national side. He seemed certain to be chosen for Scotland's 1974 World Cup squad, but, unfortunately, he badly injured his knee in a clash with Liverpool's Phil Boersma at Highfield Road.

A slightly built but highly effective midfield grafter, who worked tirelessly behind his strikers, red-haired Willie Carr's excellent touch and foresight and capacity for hard work, made him a player who simply couldn't be left out of the team.

Though born in Glasgow, Carr moved to Cambridge with his parents at the age of 13, and was actually chosen for an England schoolboy trial!

After joining Coventry City he graduated through the ranks, first featuring in a star-studded Sky Blues youth side before eventually winning a first team place against Arsenal in September 1967. By the start of the 1968-69 season, Carr was an established member of the Coventry City side and although not a prolific scorer, he netted a hat-trick in a 3-0 home win over West Bromwich Albion in August 1969. Although goals were not Willie Carr's forte, he was famous for his part in the 'donkey-kick' free-kick that was introduced to Match of the Day viewers in the autumn of 1970. Carr had scored 37 goals in 298 games for the Sky Blues when he was allowed to join Wolverhampton Wanderers for the knock-down price of £80,000.

At the end of his first season at Molineux, Wolves were relegated—but after winning the Second Division Championship in 1976-77, they entered a purple patch in the club's history, reaching the FA Cup semi-final twice and winning the League Cup in the next three years. Carr had made 289 appearances for Wolves when, in August 1982, he joined Millwall. His stay at the Den was brief, and he moved into non-League football with Worcester City, later playing for Willenhall and Stourbridge.

BILLY DICKSON
Full-back

Born: William Dickson, Larkhall, 8 April 1945
Height: 5ft 8in
Weight: 10st 8lb
Clubs: Larkhall Academy; Birkenshaw Amateurs; Kilmarnock; Motherwell
Scotland caps: 5
1970 v N Ireland (won 1-0), v Wales (drew 0-0), v England (drew 0-0)
1971 v Denmark (lost 0-1), v USSR (lost 0-1)

Full-back Billy Dickson, who played his early football for Larkhall Academy and Birkenshaw Amateurs, joined Kilmarnock as an amateur in October 1962. A former Scottish amateur and youth international, he made his first team debut for Killie in a Scottish Summer Cup game at left-back in the club's Championship-winning season of 1964-65 as Killie beat Hibs 4-3. At the end of that campaign, he represented the club in the New York International soccer tournament.

Over the next three seasons, Billy Dickson found himself in and out of the Kilmarnock side, until in the club's centenary season of 1968-69, he established himself as the club's first-choice left-back. Missing just one game, he was a virtual ever-present for the next five seasons, during which time he won five full caps for Scotland, the first in a 1-0 defeat of Northern Ireland. In fact, Scotland's opposition failed to register a single goal in Dickson's first three appearances, and even though he was on the losing side against Denmark and the USSR, each team only scored one goal. He also represented the Scottish League, but, in 1973-74, he struggled to get into the Kilmarnock side, and in the close season, he left to play for Motherwell.

Unfortunately his move to Fir Park didn't work out, and he made only 12 appearances for the Steelmen.

He did coach Ayr United for a brief spell before going into the bookmaking business with another former Kilmarnock player, Robert Connor—who won caps with Dundee and Aberdeen—and then later as a player's agent.

DAVID HAY
Midfield
Born: David Hay, Paisley, 29 January 1948
Height: 5ft 11in
Weight: 11st 7lb
Clubs: Glasgow Celtic; Chelsea
Scotland Caps: 27
1970 v N Ireland (won 1-0), v Wales (drew 0-0), v England (drew 0-0)
1971 v Denmark (won 1-0), v Belgium (lost 0-3), v Portugal (lost 0-2), v Wales (drew 0-0),
v N Ireland (lost 0-1)
1972 v Portugal (won 2-1), v Belgium (won 1-0), v Holland (lost 1-2)
1973 v Wales (won 2-0), v N Ireland (lost 1-2), v England (lost 0-1), v Switzerland (lost 0-1),
v Brazil (lost 0-1)
1974 v Czechoslovakia (won 2-1), v Czechoslovakia (lost 0-1), v West Germany (lost 1-2),
v N Ireland (lost 0-1), v Wales (won 2-0), v England (won 2-0), v Belgium (lost 1-2),
v Norway (won 2-1), v Zaire (won 2-0), v Brazil (drew 0-0), v Yugoslavia (drew 1-1)

Scotland's most outstanding player in the 1974 World Cup Finals, David Hay, who won all of his 27 caps whilst with Celtic, was taken off by manager Bobby Brown in the match against Denmark in November 1970 to placate the chants of Rangers' fans, who were shouting for substitute Jardine to replace the Celtic utility player.

He won his first medal in the 1969-70 League Cup when the Bhoys beat St Johnstone 1-0 in the final, and though he appeared in the next four finals, he was never on the winning side. He won two Scottish Cup winners' medals in 1971 and 1974 as Rangers and Dundee United were beaten respectively, and was a member of the Celtic side that won the League Championship for five consecutive seasons from 1970. He suffered a bad injury in a Scottish Cup replay against Hearts at Tynecastle in March 1973, and was out of the game for a lengthy period. On his return to the side he pleaded for a better deal for injured players, and when this fell on deaf ears, he put in his first transfer request. He even refused to train, but eventually the differences were patched up and he saw out the season prior to the World Cup Finals with a series of unforgettable performances.

In July 1974, immediately after the World Cup Finals, Hay joined Chelsea for a fee of £225,000, making him London's most expensive footballer. It took him some time to settle in his new surroundings, and after undergoing surgery for the removal of a cataract, he found he was still not sure of a place in the Chelsea side. Eventually, though, he was paired with Steve Wicks at the heart of the Chelsea defence, and they proved to be the cornerstone of the club's ultimately successful challenge for promotion to the First Division in 1976-77. Further problems with the same eye then curtailed his season and threatened his career, but after no fewer than three operations to repair a detached retina, the courageous player made a comeback. However, the fates hadn't yet finished with him, and he suffered a knee injury that forced his premature retirement a year later.

He remained at Stamford Bridge as the Blues coach before joining Motherwell as manager. He later returned to Parkhead as Celtic boss, leading the club to success in the 1985 Scottish Cup Final and to the League Championship in 1985-86. On parting company with the club he managed Norwegian club Lillestroem and St Mirren before becoming Celtic's chief scout. Following a spell as manager of Dunfermline Athletic, Hay is now General Manager of Livingston.

JOHN O'HARE
Forward

Born: John O'Hare, Dumbarton, 24 September 1946
Height: 5ft 9in
Weight: 11st 7lb
Clubs: Drumchapel Amateurs; Sunderland; Derby County; Leeds United; Nottingham Forest; Dallas Tornado (United States); Belper Town
Scotland caps: 13
Scotland goals: 5
1970 v N Ireland (won 1-0), v Wales (drew 0-0), v England (drew 0-0)
1971 v Denmark (won 1-0) 1 goal v Belgium (lost 0-3), v Wales (drew 0-0), v N Ireland (lost 0-1)
1972 v Portugal (won 2-1) 1 goal, v Belgium (won 1-0) 1 goal, v Holland (lost 1-2), v Peru (won 2-0) 1 goal, v N Ireland (won 2-0), v Wales (won 1-0)

During his time with Derby County, John O'Hare made such a great impression that he played in all three of the Home Internationals for the full Scotland team in April 1970, netting the only goal of the game against Northern Ireland on his debut and remaining in the side for the next couple of seasons.

John O'Hare played his early football for Drumchapel Amateurs before signing amateur forms for Sunderland in 1962. He turned professional in October 1963, and was helped by Brian Clough, who was Sunderland's youth coach. O'Hare was Clough's first signing for Derby County in August 1967, the striker costing the Rams £22,000. In his second season at the Baseball Ground, O'Hare, who netted 10 goals in 41 games, helped Derby win the Second Division Championship.

John O'Hare

During the course of that 1968-69 season, he was chosen to represent Scotland at Under-23 level for the match against England, but the game was cancelled because of bad weather. He finally made it in January 1970 when he played for the Scottish Under-23s against Wales, and scored two goals in a 4-0 victory.

O'Hare was Derby's leading scorer on a number of occasions, and won a League Championship medal in 1971-72. But after seven years at the Baseball ground, he joined Leeds United in a deal involving John McGovern. Under the brief but turbulent reign of Brian Clough, O'Hare played in just six games for Leeds before following Clough to Nottingham Forest with McGovern in February 1975. That move opened up another chapter of glory, as O'Hare won another League Championship medal in 1977-78 along with a League Cup winners' medal and European Cup winners' medal in 1980.

He was loaned to Dallas Tornado in the NASL in 1977, and then left the professional game in the summer of 1981. He later played non-League football for Belper Town, and after working for International Combustion, he became a stock controller at Toyota's European plant on the outskirts of Derby.

SANDY JARDINE
Right-back/Midfield

Born: William Pullar Jardine, Edinburgh, 31 December 1948
Height: 5ft 10in
Weight: 10st 8lb
Clubs: Edinburgh Athletic; Glasgow Rangers; Heart of Midlothian
Scotland caps: 38

1971 v Denmark (won 1-0)
1972 v Portugal (won 2-1), v Belgium (won 1-0), v Holland (lost 1-2)
1973 v England (lost 0-1), v Switzerland (lost 0-1), v Brazil (lost 0-1)
1974 v Czechoslovakia (won 2-1), v Czechoslovakia (lost 0-1), v West Germany (drew 1-1),
    v West Germany (lost 1-2), v N Ireland (lost 0-1), v Wales (won 2-0),
    v England (won 2-0), v Belgium (lost 1-2), v Norway (won 2-1), v Zaire (won 2-0),
    v Brazil (drew 0-0), v Yugoslavia (drew 1-1)
1975 v East Germany (won 3-0), v Spain (lost 1-2), v Spain (drew 1-1), v Sweden (drew 1-1),
    v Portugal (won 1-0), v Wales (drew 2-2), v N Ireland (won 3-0), v England (lost 1-5)
1977 v Sweden (won 3-1), v Chile (won 4-2), v Brazil (lost 0-2)
1978 v Czechoslovakia (won 3-1), v Wales (won 2-0), v N Ireland (drew 1-1),
    v Iran (drew 1-1)
1980 v Peru (drew 1-1), v Austria (drew 1-1), v Belgium (lost 0-2), v Belgium (lost 1-3)

William Pullar Jardine, nicknamed 'Sandy' because of the colour of his hair, was, at his best, a world-class player. He and Celtic's Danny McGrain formed a first-class partnership for Scotland as the full-back pairing on 19 occasions, and Jardine played in the World Cup Finals in Germany in 1974 and Argentina in 1978.

Sandy Jardine was a cultured, elegant footballer, strong, very fast and scrupulously fair. Originally a wing-half, he played there at midfield, as a sweeper and full-back, and even had a spell at centre-forward when Davie White was Rangers' manager. It was Willie Waddell who converted him to full-back, where he was able to play comfortably on either side. Jardine had arrived at Ibrox from Edinburgh junior football—he lived very close to the Hearts' ground, and was just 18 when he made his Rangers debut against Hearts, of all teams— Rangers winning 5-1. A member of the Rangers side that won the European Cup Winners' Cup in Barcelona in 1972, Jardine was also one of the few players to be twice voted the sports writers' Player of the Year. With Rangers, he won three League Championships, and was on the winning side in five Scottish Cup and five League Cup finals. Jardine had scored 76 goals in 671 games for Rangers when, after the Scottish Cup Final of 1982, he was released by manager John Greig.

Aged 33, he joined Hearts, where he had a marvellous Indian summer to his career, writing his name in the record books as the only Scottish player to play in 1,000 games. As sweeper, he was a mainstay of the Hearts 1985-86 teams which came so close to doing a Scottish 'double', but finished runners-up in both League and Scottish Cup. Jardine later became assistant-manager to Alex Macdonald, before leaving Hearts to work as a marketing manager for the Scottish Breweries.

ARCHIE GEMMILL
Midfield

Born: Archibald Gemmill, Paisley, 24 March 1947
Height: 5ft 5in
Weight: 11st 2lb
Clubs: Drumchapel Amateurs; St Mirren; Preston North End; Derby County; Nottingham Forest; Birmingham City; Jacksonville Teamen (United States); Wigan Athletic
Scotland caps: 43
Scotland goals: 8

1971 v Belgium (lost 0-3)
1972 v Portugal (won 2-1) 1 goal, v Holland (lost 1-2), v Peru (lost 0-2), v N Ireland (won 2-0), v Wales (won 1-0), v England (lost 0-1)
1976 v Denmark (won 3-1), v Romania (drew 1-1), v Wales (won 3-1), v N Ireland (won 3-0) 1 goal, v England (won 2-1)
1977 v Finland (won 6-0), v Czechoslovakia (lost 0-2), v Wales (won 1-0), v Wales (drew 0-0), v N Ireland (won 3-0), v England (won 2-1), v Chile (won 4-2), v Argentina (drew 1-1), v Brazil (lost 0-2)
1978 v East Germany (lost 0-1), v Bulgaria (won 2-1) 1 goal, v N Ireland (drew 1-1), v Wales (drew 1-1), v England (lost 0-1), v Peru (lost 1-3), v Iran (drew 1-1), v Holland (won 3-2) 2 goals
1979 v Austria (lost 2-3), v Norway (won 3-2) 1 goal, v Portugal (lost 0-1), v Norway (won 4-0)
1980 v Austria (drew 1-1) 1 goal, v Portugal (won 4-1) 1 goal, v N Ireland (lost 0-1), v Wales (won 1-0), v England (lost 0-2), v Hungary (lost 1-3)
1981 v Sweden (won 1-0), v Portugal (drew 0-0), v Israel (won 1-0), v N Ireland (drew 1-1)

A valued member of the Scotland squad, Gemmill played 43 times for his country—and no one who saw his goal against Holland in the 1978 World Cup will ever forget it. He had already scored from the penalty-spot to give the Scots a 2-1 lead when, in the 68th minute of this vital match, he picked up the ball wide on the right. He threaded his way through the Dutch defence, evading three strong challenges before shooting home past the diving Jongblood.

Archie Gemmill played his early football for St Mirren before first arriving in England in June 1967, when he signed for Preston North End for a fee of £16,000. After three years at Deepdale, he moved to Derby County for £60,000, and it was under Brian Clough's management that his career really began to take off. He played a highly significant part in proceedings when the Rams won the League Championship in 1971-72, even though Archie and his team-mates were lying on a Spanish beach at the time it was settled—having already completed their fixtures as rivals Arsenal and Liverpool fought in vain to snatch the title from their clutches. Gemmill won a second League Championship medal in 1974-75, before moving across the East Midlands to Nottingham Forest in October 1977.

The manager of Nottingham Forest was Brian Clough, his former boss at the Baseball Ground. Gemmill was a non-stop 90-minute competitor; he was at his best when running with the ball, and this industrious side to Gemmill's talents obviously appealed to Clough. He went straight into the Forest side, and in the 34 games he played, he was only on the losing side twice. At the end of the campaign, Gemmill picked up his third League Championship medal. Then, in 1978-79, he was instrumental in helping Forest reach the European Cup Final. However, he didn't play on the big day, being on the substitute's bench as Forest beat Malmo 1-0 in Munich.

In August 1979 he was allowed to leave Forest to join Birmingham City. He later played for Wigan Athletic before returning to the Baseball Ground for a second spell. Gemmill joined Forest's coaching staff in August 1985, and was re-registered as a player early the following year. He later shared the managerial duties at Rotherham United with former Forest colleague John McGovern, but is now involved in a talent-spotting role for the Scottish FA.

TONY GREEN
Midfield

Born: Anthony Green, Kinning Park, Glasgow, 30 October 1946
Height: 5ft 7in
Weight: 10st 13lb
Clubs: Drumchapel Amateurs; Kirkintilloch Rob Roy; Albion Rovers; Blackpool; Newcastle United
Scotland caps: 6
1971 v Belgium (lost 0-3), v Portugal (lost 0-2), v N Ireland (lost 0-1), v England (lost 1-3)
1972 v Wales (won 1-0), v England (lost 0-1)

Tony Green began his all too brief career with Albion Rovers before Blackpool manager Stan Mortensen paid £15,000 for his services in the summer of 1967. Despite Blackpool losing 3-1 at home to West Bromwich Albion on his debut, Green was cheered from the field. Seasiders' fans in the 9,986 crowd had no doubt that they had seen a star in the making.

Archie Gemmill

In 1967-68, his midfield partnership with Alan Suddick helped Blackpool almost win promotion to the top flight, the Seasiders finishing third in Division Two. Though he wasn't often on the scoresheet, he laid on most of Gerry Ingram and Alan Skirton's goals, both strikers netting 17 goals each. After another impressive season, it seemed only a matter of time before he won full international honours for Scotland, but he suffered a serious ankle injury in training and was forced to miss the entire promotion-winning season of 1969-70.

Though the Seasiders were relegated in 1970-71, Green, who had returned to first team action against Everton in September, had a good season and won the first of six international caps when he came on as a substitute against Belgium.

After refusing new terms at the beginning of the 1971-72 season, Green, who had scored 19 goals in 137 games, moved to Newcastle United for a fee of £150,000.

He transformed the Magpies as he combined with Hibbitt in midfield and Macdonald in attack. Possessing splendid ball control, a thundering shot and a stunning change of pace, Green was sadly hampered by injury after a heavy challenge against Crystal Palace saw him stretchered off with a knee ligament complaint. Months of surgery followed, but he was forced to quit the game at an age when he should have been at his peak. After leaving Tyneside, Green returned to the Fylde coast where he became a schoolteacher.

JIM BROGAN
Left-back/ Left-half
Born: James Brogan, Glasgow, 5 June 1944
Height: 5ft 10in
Weight: 11st 8lb
Clubs: St Roch's; Glasgow Celtic; Coventry City; Ayr United
Scotland caps: 4
1971 v Portugal (lost 0-2), v Wales (drew 0-0), v N Ireland (lost 0-1), v England (lost 1-3)

Without doubt, the best year of Jim Brogan's career was 1971, when he was named runner-up to Martin Buchan as Scottish Player of the Year, had an outstanding game against the Football League, and won four full Scottish caps, culminating in him nursing a hairline fracture of the leg in the match against England at Wembley.

Succeeding John Clark as runner and grafter in the Celtic team, he made his Scottish League debut at Falkirk in September 1963, and though he struggled to hold down a regular place in his early days with the club, all that changed following the appointment of Jock Stein as manager.

He won seven League Championship medals with Celtic for the seasons 1967-68 to 1973-74, and Scottish Cup medals in 1969 (beating Rangers 4-0), 1971 (beating Rangers 2-1 after a 1-1 draw), 1972 (beating Hibernian 6-1) and 1974 (beating Dundee United 3-0).

Though he didn't score too many goals from his left-back or left-half slot, he did pop up in the penalty area to head a last-gasp winner for Celtic against

Rangers in January 1972. In 1975, with his place at Parkhead under threat from the emerging talents of Pat McCluskey and Andy Lynch, Jim Brogan, who had appeared in 339 games for the Bhoys, was granted a free transfer. After skippering Celtic on his last appearance against Rangers in a match to celebrate Glasgow's 800th birthday, he moved south of the border to join Coventry City.

He spent just one season at Highfield Road, making 28 League appearances for the Sky Blues before returning to Scotland to end his career with Ayr United.

Brogan, who became a millionaire businessman, might well have made the Parkhead club an excellent Chief Executive in the early nineties.

DREW JARVIE
Forward

Born: Andrew Jarvie, Annathill, 5 October 1948
Height: 5ft 9in
Weight: 11st 7lb
Clubs: Kilsyth Rangers; Airdrieonians; Aberdeen; Airdrieonians; St Mirren
Scotland caps: 3
1972 v Portugal (lost 0-2), v N Ireland (lost 0-1), v England (lost 1-3)

Drew Jarvie, who made three substitute appearances for Scotland, first came to prominence with Airdrieonians, whom he joined from Kilsyth Rangers in November 1966. He soon formed a prolific strike partnership with Drew Busby, and his goalscoring feats led to Aberdeen paying £76,000 for his services in the summer of 1972.

He scored on his Dons' debut in a 4-0 League Cup success at Queen of the South, and went on to net six goals in his first four games. He ended that 1972-73 season as the club's leading scorer with 28 goals, a feat he repeated in each of the following two campaigns. After a disappointing first season of Premier League football, Jarvie was partnered with Joe Harper, his former striking partner who had left Hibs, for whom he had played after joining Everton, to return to Pittodrie. That season, it was Harper's flicked header to Jarvie that allowed him to net the equaliser in the eventual 2-1 defeat of Celtic in the League Cup Final.

The Jarvie-Harper strike force continued to destroy opposition defences over the next couple of seasons, although Jarvie was on his own for much of the League Championship-winning season of 1979-80 as Harper was injured for much of the campaign. Jarvie netted 14 goals, many of his strikes netting vital points.

With his best years now behind him, Drew Jarvie found his first team opportunities limited, though he did an excellent job in bringing on the Pittodrie club's youngsters in the reserves. His last first team game for the Dons was against his former club Airdrieonians in April 1982, and the following October he rejoined the Broomfield Road club.

He then had a short spell as player-coach at St Mirren, and was later part of the Dundee management team before returning to Pittodrie, where he became responsible for youth development.

DAVE ROBB
Forward

Born: David Thomson Robb, Broughty Ferry, 15 December 1947
Height: 5ft 11in
Weight: 12st 4lb
Clubs: Chelsea; Newburgh Juniors; Aberdeen; Tampa Bay Rowdies (United States); Norwich City; Philadelphia Fury (United States); Vancouver Whitecaps (Canada)
Scotland caps: 5
1971 v Portugal (lost 0-2), v Wales (drew 0-0), v England (lost 1-3), v Denmark (lost 0-1), v USSR (lost 0-1)

Aberdeen's Dave Robb's robust, not to mention successful, approach brought him to the attention of the international selectors, and in 1971, he won five full caps for Scotland.

He signed for the Dons in 1965, following a short spell down south with Chelsea, though it was January 1967 before he made his first team debut for them—starring in a 5-0 Scottish Cup win at Dundee. It was 1968-69 before he won a regular pace in the Dons' side, while the following season he played in all the club's 34 league games. He was also a member of the Aberdeen side that won that season's Scottish Cup, beating Celtic 2-1 in the final.

In 1972 the bustling forward picked up a cartilage injury, which was to continue causing problems for him for the remainder of his career. Even so, he still continued to turn out for the majority of the games, season after season.

One of Dave Robb's most memorable games came in the League Cup Final meeting with Celtic in November 1976. The Bhoys took an early lead through a Kenny Dalglish penalty, but a Drew Jarvie goal took the game into extra-time. Robb, who was on the bench that day, replaced the goalscorer Jarvie. Only three minutes of the additional time had been played when he crashed home what proved to be the winning goal, to give the Dons the trophy for the first time in 21 years.

After playing the last of his 345 games—in which he scored 98 goals—against Celtic in January 1978, he spent a while involved in the United States soccer scene before returning to end his career with a brief spell at Norwich City.

FRANK MUNRO
Central defender

Born: Francis Michael Munro, Dundee, 25 October 1947
Height: 6ft 0in
Weight: 13st 11lb
Clubs: Chelsea; Dundee United; Aberdeen; Wolverhampton Wanderers; Glasgow Celtic; Hellas (Australia)
Scotland caps: 9
1971 v N Ireland (lost 0-1), v England (lost 1-3), v Denmark (lost 0-1), v USSR (lost 0-1)
1975 v Sweden (drew 1-1), v Wales (drew 2-2), v N Ireland (won 3-0), v England (lost 1-5), v Romania (drew 1-1)

Frank Munro playing for Wolverhampton Wanderers

Frank Munro, who won nine full caps for Scotland, was once an amateur centre-forward with Chelsea, but he was released by the London club. He was transformed into a strongly built, physical and unflagging central defender who went on to give Wolves terrific service for eight years.

On leaving school he went south to try his luck with Chelsea, but soon returned to Scotland to sign for Dundee United. While at Tannadice, he won four youth caps for Scotland, but in October 1966 he was, perhaps surprisingly, transferred to Aberdeen for a fee of £10,000. A year later he collected a runners-up medal as the Dons were beaten 2-0 by Celtic in the Scottish Cup Final.

His move to Molineux came in January 1968, a few months after he had played so well for Aberdeen against Wolves in a tournament in America. Wolves' boss Ronnie Allen was so impressed with the way Munro performed in that final, when he netted a hat-trick, that he had no hesitation in paying £55,000 for his services.

He soon became a big favourite with everyone associated with the club, after taking up his position at the heart of the Wolves defence. He partnered the like of John Holsgrove and John McAlle, and appeared in the 1972 UEFA Cup Final and the League Cup Final victory over Manchester City two years later. He also helped Wolves regain their top flight status in 1976-77, but five months after that Second Division triumph, Munro, who had made 371 appearances for Wolves, returned to his native Scotland to join his boyhood heroes, Celtic.

Made captain for the day on his debut, he put through his own goal in a 2-1 defeat at St Mirren, and though he played in the 1978 League Cup Final, which Celtic lost 2-1 to Rangers, he then opted to try his luck in Australia where he played initially for Hellas, before becoming coach in turn of Albion Rovers, Hamlyn Rangers and Keilor Austria.

TOM FORSYTH
Midfield/ Defender
Born: Thomas Forsyth, Glasgow, 23 January 1949
Height: 5ft 9in
Weight: 10st 9lb
Clubs: Stonehouse Thistle; Motherwell; Glasgow Rangers
Scotland caps: 22
1971 v Denmark (lost 0-1)
1974 v Czechoslovakia (lost 0-1)
1976 v Switzerland (won 1-0), v Wales (won 3-1), v N Ireland (won 3-0), v England (won 2-1), v Finland (won 6-0)
1977 v Sweden (won 3-1), v Wales (drew 0-0), v N Ireland (won 3-0), v England (won 2-1), v Chile (won 4-2), v Argentina (drew 1-1), v Brazil (lost 0-2)
1978 v Czechoslovakia (won 3-1), v Wales (won 2-0), v N Ireland (drew 1-1), v Wales (drew 1-1), v England (lost 0-1), v Peru (lost 1-3), v Iran (drew 1-1), v Holland (won 3-2)

Tom Forsyth captained Scotland in only his third international appearance, a 1-0 defeat of Switzerland in 1976, and was a prominent member of the national squad in the 1978 World Cup Finals in Argentina.

After signing for Motherwell from Stonehouse Thistle in 1967, he spent five years at Fir Park, playing mainly as an inside-forward or wing-half, his displays leading to him winning the first of his 22 caps against Denmark in 1971. He went on to appear in 150 games for Motherwell before a £40,000 transfer in October 1972 took him to Rangers.

He became something of a legend at Ibrox. Originally a midfielder, Jock Wallace converted him into the complete defender. Though he rarely ventured forward, in the 100th Scottish Cup Final, a meeting with Celtic, he scored the winning goal, forcing the ball home after Derek Johnstone's header had struck a post and rolled along the line. Forming a formidable partnership at the heart of the Rangers defence with Colin Jackson, Forsyth was part of the Rangers treble-winning side of 1976.

Nicknamed 'Jaws' due to his uncompromising style of play and fearsome tackling, he helped the club to three League Championship titles, four Scottish Cup victories and two League Cup wins. He had played in 324 games for Rangers when, in March 1982, he was forced to retire because of injury.

In the autumn of that year, Forsyth was appointed manager of Dunfermline Athletic, but having formed a close affinity and friendship with Tom McLean whilst at Ibrox, he joined him as his assistant at Motherwell. When McLean moved to Hearts, Tom Forsyth went with him, but it proved to be his last post in senior Scottish football.

JOCKY SCOTT
Inside-forward
Born: John Scott, Aberdeen, 14 January 1948
Height: 5ft 8in
Weight: 11st 5lb
Clubs: Chelsea; Dundee; Aberdeen; Dundee
Scotland caps: 2
1971   v Denmark (lost 0-1), v USSR (lost 0-1)

A member of the Chelsea groundstaff, Jocky Scott was just 16 when he left Stamford Bridge to return to Scotland to sign for Dundee in the summer of 1964.

The talented inside-forward, who was instinctively attack-minded, soon settled into the Dark Blues side. Missing very few games, he helped Dundee reach the 1968 League Cup Final, but in a high-scoring final, the Dens Park club lost 5-3 to Celtic. Six years later, Scott and Dundee were in another League Cup Final, but this time, they ran out 1-0 winners against Celtic.

In between these two League Cup Final appearances, Scott won selection for the national side, making his debut from the bench as a replacement for Jim Forrest in a 1-0 defeat against Denmark in Copenhagen. Five days later, he made his first full start in the match against the USSR in Moscow, but again the Scots lost 1-0.

In August 1975, Scott left Dundee to join his home-town team of Aberdeen for a fee of £15,000 plus another player. In his second and final season at

Pittodrie, Scott made his third appearance in a League Cup Final, and again finished up with a winners' medal as the Dons beat Celtic 2-1.

Scott then rejoined Dundee, later being appointed that club's coach. It was at Dens Park that he started his managerial career in June 1986, by succeeding Archie Knox, who had left to become assistant-manager at Aberdeen. In the summer of 1988, Scott resigned as Dundee boss to take over the reins at Aberdeen from Ian Porterfield. In September 1991, he went to manage Dunfermline Athletic, later taking charge of Arbroath before resigning after just four months. He then managed Hibs, before in 1997 joining the coaching staff of Dundee United. The following year he returned to his beloved Dundee as manager. On losing his job to Ivano Bonetti, he then had a brief spell in charge of Raith Rovers.

JOHN BROWNLIE
Right-back

Born: John Brownlie, Caldercruix, 11 March 1952
Height: 5t 10in
Weight: 11st 13lb
Clubs: Hibernian; Newcastle United; Middlesbrough; Valaudus (Sweden); Hartlepool United; Berwick Rangers; Blyth Spartans
Scotland caps: 7
1971 v USSR (lost 0-1)
1972 v Peru (won 2-0), v N Ireland (won 2-0), v England (lost 0-1)
1973 v Denmark (won 4-1), v Denmark (won 2-0)
1976 v Romania (drew 1-1)

John Brownlie won the first of his seven Scottish caps at the tender age of 19 years and 95 days when he played against the USSR in June 1971.

He began his career with Hibs in the role of sweeper, but he was soon to make the right-back position his own after coming on as a substitute for the injured Chris Shevlane against St Johnstone in August 1969. Though he joined Hibs under manager Bob Shankly, it was under Eddie Turnbull that he made his name. One of his most memorable moments came in the 1973 League Cup semi-final against Rangers when he scored the goal that took the club through to the final against Celtic. One of the low points of his time with Hibs was a missed penalty in the 1975-76 UEFA Cup against Liverpool. Joe Harper had given Hibs the lead but Brownlie missed the opportunity of extending their lead and Liverpool won the second leg 3-1 to send Hibs crashing out on a 3-2 aggregate.

Towards the end of the decade, Brownlie was out of action for over a season with a badly broken leg, and never quite regained the impressive form that had made him the target of nearly every top English club. By the time he left Easter Road to join Newcastle United, Brownlie, who was attempting to resurrect a career that had stagnated, had appeared in 341 games for Hibs.

He quickly became a favourite of the Magpies' fans, showing glimpses of a quality player in a very ordinary United side. Always willing to surge forward in support of the attack, he packed a powerful shot. An injury saw him out of the reckoning for a long period, then a dispute with the club over terms saw him leave St James Park as the Magpies were becoming a force again.

Brownlie remained in the north-east with Middlesbrough, and later Hartlepool United, but at each club he was hampered by injuries. He then returned to play in Scotland with Berwick Rangers, and after going into hotel management on the north-east coast, ended his playing career in non-League football with Blyth Spartans. Brownlie later had a spell as manager of Arbroath.

BOBBY WATSON

Right-half/ Inside-right

Born: Robert Watson; Airdrie; 16 May 1946
Height: 5ft 9in
Weight: 10st 8lb
Clubs: Glasgow Rangers; Motherwell
Scotland caps: 1
1971 v USSR (lost 0-1)

Bobby Watson, who won a Scottish cap against the USSR in 1971, was signed by Rangers in 1963, and, while at Ibrox, won a Scottish Cup winners' medals as the Blues beat Celtic 1-0 after a goalless draw in 1966. However, Watson was never an automatic choice at Rangers, and in 1970 he left to join Motherwell.

His transfer to Fir Park involved a three-player deal that saw Watson and Brian Heron come to Motherwell and goalkeeper Peter McCloy move to Ibrox. Shortly after putting pen to paper, Motherwell manager Bobby Howitt made Watson captain, and he responded by netting a memorable first goal for the club in an outstanding Texaco Cup win over the mighty Tottenham Hotspur. It was even more memorable when one considers that he netted only two goals in a Motherwell career of 182 appearances over six years.

Watson, who began his career as an old-fashioned wing-half, was a powerhouse of a player who could combine effective tackling and enthusiasm with good distribution. Yet, when he retired prematurely from playing in 1976, he was an orthodox defender. On hanging up his boots he concentrated on his steel stockholding business, but he was unable to keep away from football.

Watson was a frequent visitor to Airdrie matches, and was soon installed as the Broomfield Park club's manager. In 1983 he returned to Motherwell as their manager; however the Steelmen were going through a bad period in the club's history, and when they were relegated in May 1984, he parted company with the Fir Park club.

MARTIN BUCHAN

Left-half

Born: Martin McLean Buchan, Aberdeen, 6 March 1949
Height: 5ft 10in
Weight: 11st 11lb

Clubs: Aberdeen; Manchester United; Oldham Athletic
Scotland caps: 34

1972 v Portugal (won 2-1), v Belgium (won 1-0), v Wales (won 1-0), v Yugoslavia (drew 2-2),
v Czechoslovakia (drew 0-0), v Brazil (lost 0-1)
1973 v Denmark (won 4-1), v Denmark (won 2-0), v England (lost 0-5)
1974 v West Germany (lost 1-2), v N Ireland (lost 0-1), v Wales (won 2-0),
v Norway (won 2-1), v Brazil (drew 0-0), v Yugoslavia (drew1-1)
1975 v East Germany (won 3-0), v Spain (drew 1-1), v Portugal (won 1-0)
1976 v Denmark (won 1-0), v Romania (drew 1-1)
1977 v Finland (won 6-0), v Czechoslovakia (lost 0-2), v Chile (won 4-2),
v Argentina (drew 1-1), v Brazil (lost 0-2)
1978 v East Germany (lost 0-1), v Wales (won 2-0), v N Ireland (drew 1-1), v Peru (lost 1-3),
v Iran (drew 1-1), v Holland (won 3-2)
1979 v Austria (lost 2-3), v Norway (won 3-2), v Portugal (lost 0-1)

There was no doubting Martin Buchan's immense talent, and he was to gain 34 international caps for Scotland, the highlights of which were appearances at both the 1974 World Cup Finals in Germany and the ill-fated 1978 Finals in Argentina. Ironically, the opposition for the last of his 34 caps in 1979 was Portugal, against whom he had made his international debut almost eight years ago.

In his early days with Aberdeen, Buchan found himself dropped from the side on numerous occasions, but by the age of 20, he had been appointed captain of the Dons—one of the youngest club captains in the country. Eddie Turnbull's team provided one of the biggest shocks in Scottish Cup history by beating Celtic 3-1 to win the 1967 Final, and Buchan, who had come of age just weeks before the game, became the youngest-ever captain, at 21, to lift the Scottish Cup at Hampden.

It was hardly surprising that a talent such as Buchan would have a host of top clubs throughout the country chasing his signature. But with the Dons determined to hang on to Buchan and the English giants equally determined to win the chase for the starlet, there ensued months of transfer speculation. Eventually, Jimmy Bonthrone accepted Manchester United's offer of £125,000 and Buchan was on his way south.

This was a dream move for Buchan, but it was soon to turn sour. After a season of near-relegation, United lost their First Division status in 1974 and a year in the Second Division did little for Buchan's self-confidence. He remained an integral part of the United side which stormed back into the big time in 1975-76, finishing third in the First Division, four points behind champions Liverpool. Buchan was now playing as well as ever, and in 1977 led out Manchester United at Wembley for the FA Cup Final against Liverpool. United won 2-1, and enabled Buchan to enter the history books as the only player to have captained winning Cup Final sides in both Scotland and England.

When Martin Buchan left Old Trafford in 1983, he was bitterly disappointed not to have won more domestic honours with United. With his playing career over after a brief spell with Oldham Athletic, he was appointed manager of

Burnley. However, for a player who displayed such style and elegance on the park, the cut-throat world of football management was not for him.

EDDIE COLQUHOUN
Centre-half
Born: Edmund Peter Skiruing Colquhoun, Prestonpans, 29 March 1945
Height: 6ft 0in
Weight: 12st 2lb
Clubs: Edinburgh Norton; Bury; West Bromwich Albion; Sheffield United
Scotland caps: 9
1972 v Portugal (won 2-1), v Holland (lost 1-2), v Peru (won 2-0), v Yugoslavia (drew 2-2), v Czechoslovakia (drew 0-0), v Brazil (lost 0-1)
1973 v Denmark (won 4-1), v Denmark (won 2-0), v England (lost 0-5)

Eddie Colquhoun was a centre-half adaptable enough to adequately perform at full-back and wing-half too. He began his career with Bury, where his impressive displays at the heart of the Shakers defence led a number of the First Division scouts to Gigg Lane. He had appeared in 81 league games for Bury, when in February 1967, he joined First Division West Bromwich Albion.

He had spent a little over a season at the Hawthorns when a broken leg kept him out of the first team. On his return to fitness, Colquhoun left the Baggies to join Second Division Sheffield United, who paid £27,500 for his services. On his arrival at Bramall Lane, Colquhoun was immediately appointed captain. After two fairly successful seasons, he led the Blades to promotion to the top flight in 1970-71 as runners-up to Leicester City. Their best performance in the First Division came in 1974-75 when they finished sixth but the following season they won just six games, and in doing so ended the campaign at the foot of Division One.

Colquhoun was a first team regular at Sheffield United for 10 seasons, going on to score 21 goals in 363 league appearances before injury forced his retirement. Granted a testimonial in March 1980, he went on to run a Post Office in South Yorkshire.

ALEX CROPLEY
Midfield
Born: Alexander James Cropley, Aldershot, 16 January 1951
Height: 5ft 8in
Weight: 10st 4lb
Clubs: Edina Hearts; Hibernian; Arsenal; Aston Villa; Newcastle United (loan); Portsmouth
Scotland caps: 2
1972 v Portugal (won 2-1), v Belgium (won 1-0)

If Alex Cropley hadn't suffered serious leg breaks, he would surely have found the consistency to build on the two caps he won for Scotland. Despite his birthplace, and because of his parentage, his country was Scotland.

Nicknamed 'Sodjer'—he was born in the military town of Aldershot—the son of a former Shotts' player, Alex Cropley was a classy left-sided midfielder and the key to the success of the 1970s Hibernian side managed by Eddie Turnbull.

While with Hibs he helped them win the Scottish League Cup in 1973, beating Celtic 2-1 in the final. There were also some memorable European ties, not least against Leeds United at Elland Road. He was allowed to leave Easter Road and join Arsenal for £100,000 in December 1974.

His 20-month stay at Highbury was littered with niggling and serious injuries, including a broken leg, which was first diagnosed a day after playing at Middlesbrough! Unfortunately, within a few weeks of his comeback, he broke the leg again. Despite his lack of opportunities due to these injuries, he had become a great favourite of the Arsenal fans because of his tough tackling and never-say-die attitude.

In September 1976 he was transferred to Aston Villa for £125,000, and ended his first season with a League Cup Winners' tankard after Everton had been beaten at the third attempt. In December 1977, he broke his leg for a third time against West Bromwich Albion, and though on his return from injury he had a loan spell at Newcastle United, he left Villa Park in September 1981 to join Portsmouth where his injuries finished his career at the age of 30.

Cropley then opened a public house close to Hibs' Easter Road ground.

GEORGE GRAHAM
Inside-forward
Born: George Graham, Coatbridge, 30 November 1944
Height: 5ft 11in
Weight: 12st 3lb
Clubs: Aston Villa; Chelsea; Arsenal; Manchester United; Portsmouth; Crystal Palace
Scotland caps: 12
Scotland goals: 3
1972 v Portugal (won 2-1), v Holland (lost 1-2) 1 goal, v N Ireland (won 2-0),
v Yugoslavia (drew 2-2), v Czechoslovakia (drew 0-0), v Brazil (lost 0-1)
1973 v Denmark (won 4-1), v Denmark (won 2-0), v England (lost 0-5),
v Wales (won 2-0) 2 goals, v N Ireland (lost 1-2), v Brazil (lost 0-1)

George Graham was a Scottish schoolboy and youth international when he joined Aston Villa in December 1961. Although he spent three seasons at Villa Park, he failed to establish a regular place in the club's first team, and, in July 1964, Tommy Docherty signed him for Chelsea for a bargain £8,000.

Although he was no great runner and lacked pace, he proved to be a prolific marksman, finding the net 17 times in 30 league games in 1964-65. The following season his total of 23 goals in all competitions was not bettered, but the team that had brought Chelsea within touching distance of glory was breaking up amid mounting dressing-room disharmony.

Allowed to join Arsenal in part-exchange for Tommy Baldwin, he helped

George Graham

the club to League Cup Finals in 1968 and 1969, but Arsenal's backroom staff realised that George Graham's skills were being wasted as a centre-forward, so he was switched to a deeper position at inside-forward. This turned out to be a master-stroke; not only did Arsenal win the Inter Cities Fairs Cup in 1970 but did the 'double' the following season. Graham won the first of his 12 Scottish caps in 1971-72 as well as helping Arsenal reach Wembley again. However, after the arrival of Alan Ball, Graham's position in the Arsenal side was not certain, and, in December 1972, he was transferred to Manchester United for £120,000. He spent two years at Old Trafford before finishing his playing career with Portsmouth and Crystal Palace.

After coaching Crystal Palace and Queen's Park Rangers, he was appointed manager of Millwall in December 1982. After helping the Lions win promotion to the Second Division in 1984-85, he was appointed manager of Arsenal, and in his first season back at Highbury, he guided the Gunners to a League Cup Final victory over Liverpool. In 1988-89, Graham achieved his greatest success with Arsenal, winning the League Championship in the last minute of the final game at Anfield. Arsenal repeated the feat with Championship title wins in 1991 and 1992, when they became the first team ever to win the FA Cup and League Cup 'double'. In 1994, Arsenal beat Parma to lift the European Cup Winners' Cup—Graham writing himself into the record books as the first person to play and manage European Cup winning sides.

After leaving Arsenal following speculation about transfer irregularities, Graham took charge of Leeds United before leaving to manage Tottenham Hotspur. Replaced by Glenn Hoddle in April 2001, he is still out of the game, though his name is mentioned for nearly every vacant managerial position!

BOB WILSON
Goalkeeper
Born: Robert Primrose Wilson, Chesterfield, 30 October 1941
Height: 6ft 1in
Weight: 12st 12lb
Clubs: Wolverhampton Wanderers; Arsenal
Scotland caps: 2
1972 v Portugal (won 2-1), v Holland (lost 1-2)

Bob Wilson was training to become a Physical Education teacher at Loughborough College, while playing as an amateur with Wolverhampton Wanderers.

During the summer of 1963, he joined Arsenal as an amateur, turning professional in March 1964 after the Gunners had paid Wolves £5,500. In his first season at Highbury, Wilson played regular reserve team football, though he did appear in five league games, making his debut against Nottingham Forest in October 1963. However, following the signing of Jim Furnell from Liverpool, Wilson found himself back in the reserves for the next three seasons.

After Furnell had made a costly mistake in the FA Cup fifth-round game against Birmingham City in March 1968, Wilson took over and played in the last 13 matches of the season. In 1968-69, Wilson was the club's first-choice keeper and was instrumental in the Gunners' seasonal defensive record at that time, conceding only 27 goals in 40 matches. The following season, despite breaking an arm, Wilson still appeared in 28 matches and helped Arsenal win the Inter Cities Fairs Cup.

Wilson figured prominently in the Gunners' League and FA Cup double-winning side of 1970-71, playing in all of the club's 64 first team games. In 1971-72 he missed just five games, his form leading to him winning two full caps for Scotland, for whom he qualified due to having Scottish parents. He made an outstanding debut at international level as the Scots beat Portugal 2-1 in a European Championship qualifier. Though he was plagued by injuries the following season, he returned to miss just one league game in 1973-74, yet, by the end of the season, he shocked the football world by announcing his retirement from the first-class game at the age of 32!

Bob Wilson later became a leading sports broadcaster and returned to his beloved Highbury as the club's goalkeeping coach. He later signed a lucrative contract with Carlton TV and switched channels, after over 20 years with the BBC.

Bob Wilson

KENNY DALGLISH
Forward

Born: Kenneth Mathieson Dalglish, Glasgow, 4 March 1951
Height: 5ft 8in
Weight: 11st1 3lb
Clubs: Drumchapel Amateurs; Glasgow United; Glasgow Celtic; Liverpool
Scotland caps: 102
Scotland goals: 30

1972 v Belgium (won 1-0), v Holland (lost 1-2)

1973 v Denmark (won 4-1), v Denmark (won 2-0) 1 goal, v England (lost 0-5),
      v Wales (won 2-0), v N Ireland (lost 1-2) 1 goal, v England (lost 0-1),
      v Switzerland (lost 0-1), v Brazil (lost 0-1)

1974 v Czechoslovakia (won 2-1), v Czechoslovakia (lost 0-1), v West Germany (drew 1-1),
      v West Germany (lost 1-2) 1 goal, v N Ireland (lost 0-1), v Wales (won 2-0) 1 goal,
      v England (won 2-0), v Belgium (lost 1-2), v Norway (won 2-1) 1 goal, v Zaire (won 2-0),
      v Brazil (drew 0-0), v Yugoslavia (drew 1-1)

1975 v East Germany (won 3-0) 1 goal, v Spain (lost 1-2), v Spain (drew 1-1),
      v Sweden (drew 1-1), v Portugal (won 1-0), v Wales (drew 2-2),
      v N Ireland (won 3-0) 1 goal, v England (lost 1-5), v Romania (drew 1-1)

1976 v Denmark (won 1-0), v Denmark (won 3-1) 1 goal, v Romania (drew 1-1),
      v Switzerland (won 1-0), v N Ireland (won 3-0) 1 goal, v England (won 2-1) 1 goal

1977 v Finland (won 6-0) 1 goal, v Czechoslovakia (lost 0-2), v Wales (won 1-0),
      v Sweden (won 3-1) 1 goal, v Wales (drew 0-0), v N Ireland (won 3-0) 2 goals,
      v England (won 2-1) 1 goal, v Chile (won 4-2) 1 goal, v Argentina (drew 1-1),
      v Brazil (lost 0-2)

1978 v East Germany (lost 0-1), v Czechoslovakia (won 3-1) 1 goal, v Wales (won 2-0) 1 goal,

v Bulgaria (won 2-1), v N Ireland (drew 1-1), v Wales (drew 1-1), v England (lost 0-1),
v Peru (lost 1-3), v Iran (drew 1-1), v Holland (won 3-2) 1 goal

1979   v Austria (lost 2-3), v Norway (won 3-2) 2 goals, v Portugal (lost 0-1), v Wales (lost 0-3),
v N Ireland (won 1-0), v England (lost 1-3), v Argentina (lost 1-3),
v Norway (won 4-0) 1 goal

1980   v Peru (drew 1-1), v Austria (drew 1-1), v Belgium (lost 0-2), v Belgium (lost 1-3),
v Portugal (won 4-1) 1 goal, v N Ireland (lost 0-1), v Wales (won 1-0),
v England (lost 0-2), v Poland (lost 0-1), v Hungary (lost 1-3)

1981   v Sweden (won 1-0), v Portugal (drew 0-0), v Israel (won 1-0) 1 goal

1982   v Sweden (won 2-0), v N Ireland (drew 0-0), v Portugal (lost 1-2), v Spain (lost 0-3),
v Holland (won 2-1) 1 goal, v N Ireland (drew 1-1), v Wales (won 1-0),
v England (lost 0-1), v New Zealand (won 5-2) 1 goal, v Brazil (lost 1-4)

1983   v Belgium (lost 2-3) 2 goals, v Switzerland (drew 2-2)

1984   v Uruguay (won 2-0), v Belgium (drew 1-1), v East Germany (lost 1-2)

1985   v Yugoslavia (won 6-1) 1 goal, v Iceland (won 3-0), v Spain (won 3-1) 1 goal,
v Wales (lost 0-1)

1986   v East Germany (drew 0-0), v Australia won 2-0), v Romania (won 3-0)

1987   v Bulgaria (drew 0-0), v Luxembourg (won 3-0)

A central figure in the Scottish sides which went to the 1974 and 1978 World
Cup Finals, Scotland's most capped player Kenny Dalglish was a sound enough
finisher to share the Scottish international scoring record of 30 with Denis
Law.

Brought up in the shadow of Ibrox, Kenny Dalglish was always expected
to play in the blue of Rangers and not the green and white hoops. But it was
Celtic who signed him, and in his first season at Parkhead, he scored 17 goals,
and made his international debut as a substitute in a 1-0 defeat of Belgium.
In eight years with Celtic, Dalglish won five League titles, four Scottish Cups
and a Scottish League Cup winners' medal. In his final season at Parkhead, he
led Celtic to yet another League and Cup double, this time as captain. Celtic
manager Jock Stein recognised Dalglish's all-round skills and assigned him to
midfield where he still continued to score memorable goals. But at the age of
26, Dalglish wanted to prove himself in England, and in 1977 Liverpool signed
him for £440,000.

He ended his first season at Anfield as top scorer as Liverpool stormed to the
League title again, and Dalglish was voted 'Footballer of the Year'. After joining
Liverpool he made 177 consecutive League and Cup appearances, before missing
his first game in 1980. That was the year he picked up another European Cup
winners' medal and Liverpool retained their League title.

He had been instrumental in Liverpool winning the 1978 European Cup
Final against Bruges, scoring the only goal of the game. Liverpool continued
to dominate British football and Dalglish remained the key figure. In 1983 he
scored his 100th goal for the Reds, to become only the third player ever to
score a century of goals in both Scottish and English football. He was voted
'Footballer of the Year' again and picked up the players' 'Player of the Year'
award as Liverpool won their 14th Championship.

Following the Heysel Stadium tragedy in 1985, Dalglish was appointed

Kenny Dalglish playing for Liverpool

successor to Joe Fagan as Liverpool's player-manager. His first season in charge could not have been more successful. Liverpool became only the third club in the 20th century to complete the League and FA Cup double. Not only did Dalglish win the 'Manager of the Year' award, but he also collected his 100th cap. In February 1991, Dalglish rocked the football world by resigning, citing the pressures of the job.

He later managed Blackburn Rovers, and after leading the club to the Premiership via the play-offs, helped Rovers win the 1994-95 Premier League title. He then stepped down to become Director of Football, but later announced his departure from Ewood Park. After a spell in charge of Newcastle United, he returned to Parkhead as Director of Football Operations, but left the club following the appointment of Martin O'Neill.

JOHN HANSEN
Right-back
Born: John Angus McDonald Hansen, Sauchie, 3 February 1950
Height: 5ft 11in
Weight: 11st 10lb
Clubs: Sauchie BC; Partick Thistle
Scotland caps: 2
1972 v Belgium (won 1-0), v Yugoslavia (drew 2-2)

The older brother of former Liverpool and Scotland star Alan Hansen, he was spotted playing football for Sauchie Boys Club by Partick Thistle and joined the Firhill club in 1967.

Over the next 11 seasons, he became a good servant to Thistle, an excellent example of the quiet, efficient professional—no frills, ever-reliable and always playing within his strengths. The tough-tackling right-back made his international debut as a substitute for Celtic's Jimmy Johnstone in a 1-0 win over Belgium in November 1971, and then the following summer replaced his Thistle team-mate Alex Forsyth in the game against Yugoslavia in Belo Horizonte which ended all-square at 2-2.

Sandwiched in-between these two appearances for the national side, Hansen was a member of the Thistle team that won the Scottish League Cup, beating Celtic 4-1 in the final. It was a remarkable achievement by the Jags, as the Parkhead club had won the previous six League Championships and were to win that season's title as well!

Hansen continued to be a regular member of the Thistle side for the next six seasons, helping the club win the First Division Championship in 1975-76 when they ended the campaign six points ahead of runners-up Kilmarnock.

He went on to score 14, often spectacular, goals in 317 first team appearances for Thistle before hanging up his boots. He then remained at Firhill as the club's Commercial Manager, later working as a branch manager of a building society.

STEVE MURRAY
Right-half
Born: Stephen Murray, Dumbarton, 9 October 1944
Height: 5ft 9in

Weight: 11st 3lb
Clubs: Dundee; Aberdeen; Glasgow Celtic; Dundee United
Scotland caps: 1
1972 v Belgium (won 1-0)

Having begun his career with Dundee, for whom he made his debut in a 3-2 local derby defeat against Dundee United at Dens Park in August 1964, Steve Murray missed very few games during his time with the Dark Blues. He helped them to the 1968 Scottish League Cup Final, but Dundee went down 5-3 to Celtic in a most entertaining game. In March 1970 he joined Aberdeen, and it was while he was with the Pittodrie club that he won his one and only full international cap when he played in the 1-0 defeat of Belgium.

In May 1973 he signed for Celtic, and ended his first season at Parkhead with a League Championship medal and a Scottish Cup winners' medal after the Bhoys had beaten Dundee United 3-0. In October 1974, during the 6-3 Scottish League Cup Final victory over Hibernian, Murray damaged his right ankle, and the following week against Aberdeen at Parkhead he damaged his right big toe! He battled on to win another Scottish Cup winners' medal against Airdrie but training had become difficult and he decided to retire. He then made a brief comeback before cracking a bone in the same right foot during training in January 1976.

After scouting for Dundee United, Murray ended up having treatment to the injury and found that he could play again. He was a member of United's League Cup winning side in 1979, having received a medal after coming on as a substitute in the first game at Hampden.

He later had a spell of just three days as manager of Forfar Athletic before managing Montrose. Later he returned to Tannadice as Jim McLean's assistant-manager, but after months in the post, he walked out on the club, thus ending his involvement with the game.

WILLIE DONACHIE
Full-back

Born: William Donachie, Glasgow, 5 October 1951
Height: 5ft 9in
Weight: 11st 5lb
Clubs: Glasgow United; Manchester City; Portland Timbers (United States); Norwich City; Burnley; Oldham Athletic
Scotland caps: 35
1972 v Peru (won 2-0), v N Ireland (won 2-0), v England (lost 0-1), v Yugoslavia (drew 2-2), v Czechoslovakia (drew 0-0), v Brazil (lost 0-1)
1973 v Denmark (won 2-0), v England (lost 0-5), v Wales (won 2-0), v N Ireland (lost 1-2)
1974 v N Ireland (lost 0-1)
1976 v Romania (drew 1-1), v Wales (won 3-1), v N Ireland (won 3-0), v England (won 2-1)
1977 v Finland (won 6-0), v Czechoslovakia (lost 0-2), v Wales (won 1-0), v Sweden (won 3-1), v Wales (drew 0-0), v N Ireland (won 3-0), v England (won 2-1),

v Chile (won 4-2), v Argentina (drew 1-1), v Brazil (lost 0-2)
1978 v East Germany (lost 0-1), v Wales (won 2-0), v Bulgaria (won 2-1), v Wales (drew 1-1),
v England (lost 0-1), v Iran (drew 1-1), v Holland (won 3-2)
1979 v Austria (lost 2-3), v Norway (won 3-2), v Portugal (lost 0-1)

Manchester City were the reigning League Champions when Willie Donachie arrived at Maine Road in 1968. He was a midfield player in those days, but with the Blues going on to win the FA Cup in 1969 and the League Cup in 1970, he found it difficult to break into the first team. After replacing broken leg victim Glyn Pardoe, his skill and class were noticed by the international selectors, and he was still only 20 when he won the first of 35 full Scottish caps against Peru in April 1972.

Donachie was a virtual ever-present during his time at Maine Road, all of which was spent in the First Division. He played in two League Cup Finals, City going down to Wolves in 1974, but he collected a winner's medal in 1976 as Newcastle United were defeated at Wembley. He also played in every single game during the 1976-7 season when City were beaten to the League Championship by a single point by Liverpool. With his position eventually coming under threat, City accepted a fee of £200,000 from Portland Timbers in March 1980 and so Donachie took his skills across the Atlantic.

After a brief return to help Norwich City win promotion from the Second Division, he joined Burnley, but was unable to prevent the Clarets' relegation to Division Three at the end of his first season. After another season with Burnley, Donachie joined Oldham Athletic, and, though well into his thirties, became a first team regular. He was later appointed player-coach, and only hung up his boots in 1991 after the Latics had won the Second Division title and so returned to the top flight for the first time since 1923. When he played his last league game, Willie Donachie was three months past his 39th birthday!

After being appointed assistant-manager to Joe Royle at Oldham, he followed the former England international to Everton. The pair began the major task of rebuilding the Merseyside giants by guiding them to victory against Manchester United in the FA Cup Final of 1995. Appointed manager of Manchester City, Royle again wanted Donachie, so he returned to Maine Road as City's head coach. After a spell as first team coach at Sheffield Wednesday, Donachie has teamed up with Royle again, this time at Ipswich Town.

ASA HARTFORD
Midfield
Born: Richard Asa Hartford, Clydebank, 24 October 1950
Height: 5ft 7in
Weight: 10st 6lb
Clubs: Drumchapel Amateurs; West Bromwich Albion; Manchester City; Nottingham Forest; Everton; Manchester City; Fort Lauderdale Sun (United States); Norwich City; Bolton Wanderers; Stockport County; Oldham Athletic; Shrewsbury Town
Scotland caps: 50
Scotland goals: 4

Asa Hartford

1972 v Peru (won 2-0), v Wales (won 1-0), v England (lost 0-1), v Yugoslavia (drew 2-2),
      v Czechoslovakia (drew 0-0), v Brazil (lost 0-1)
1976 v Denmark (won 3-1), v Romania (drew 1-1), v N Ireland (won 3-0)
1977 v Czechoslovakia (lost 0-2), v Wales (won 1-0), v Sweden won 3-1) 1 goal,
      v Wales (drew 0-0), v N Ireland (won 3-0), v England (won 2-1),
      v Chile (won 4-2) 1 goal, v Argentina (drew 1-1), v Brazil (lost 0-2)
1978 v East Germany (lost 0-1), v Czechoslovakia (won 3-1) 1 goal, v Wales (won 2-0),
      v Bulgaria (won 2-1), v Wales (drew 1-1), v England (lost 0-1), v Peru (lost 1-3),
      v Iran (drew 1-1), v Holland (won 3-2)
1979 v Austria (lost 2-3), v Norway (won 3-2), v Portugal (lost 0-1), v Wales (lost 0-3),
      v N Ireland (won 1-0), v England (lost 1-3), v Argentina (lost 1-3) v Norway (won 4-0)
1980 v Peru (drew 1-1), v Belgium (lost 0-2)
1981 v N Ireland (drew 1-1), v Israel (won 3-1), v Wales (lost 0-2), v N Ireland (won 2-0),
      v England (won 1-0)
1982 v Sweden (won 2-0), v N Ireland (drew 0-0), v Portugal (lost 1-2), v Spain (lost 0-3),
      v N Ireland (drew 1-1), v Wales (won 1-0) 1 goal, v England (lost 0-1), v Brazil (lost 1-4)

Named after the American singing star of the first 'talkie' Al (Asa) Jolson, Asa Hartford was one of the best-known, most tenacious and most creative midfield players of the 1970s.

He began his career with West Bromwich Albion, signing professional forms in 1967 and playing in the League Cup Final some three years later. Thrilling the crowds with his skill and vision, it was only a matter of time before the inevitable big money offer arrived to tempt Albion. Hartford gained considerable media attention in November 1971, when a proposed £170,000 move to Don Revie's Leeds United fell through after a routine medical examination revealed a hole-in-the-heart condition. In the event the medical prognosis that raised doubts about his long-term footballing future proved unfounded, and five months later, he won the first of his 50 Scottish caps in a 2-0 win over Peru at Hampden Park.

In August 1974, Hartford joined Manchester City for a fee of £225,000. Making his debut in a 4-0 defeat of West Ham United, he swept away all doubts about his fitness with his stamina and urgent play in midfield. He went on to play a major role in City's glorious era of the late 1970s, picking up a League Cup winners' medal with them in 1976, and helping them finish runners-up in the First Division in 1976-77, just a single point behind champions Liverpool.

In June 1979 he signed for Nottingham Forest under the management of Brian Clough for £500,000, but after only 63 days and three league games, he was on his way back to the north-west with Everton. Then, after two seasons and 98 appearances for the Merseysiders, Hartford moved back for a second spell at Manchester City for £350,000. Having taken his total of first team games for City to 317, he said farewell to Maine Road in May 1984, to join Fort Lauderdale Sun in the NASL.

He later returned to First Division action with Norwich City and helped the Canaries win the 1985 League Cup when his shot was deflected by Sunderland's Chisholm for the only goal of the final. In July 1985 he joined Bolton Wanderers, and in his first season he captained the club to a Wembley appearance in the

Freight Rover Trophy Final. He then went on to join Stockport County as player-manager, before a spell at Oldham and appointment as manager of Shrewsbury Town. He then coached at Blackburn and Stoke before becoming Manchester City's reserve team coach.

ALLY HUNTER
Goalkeeper
Born: Alistair Robert Hunter, Glasgow, 4 October 1949
Height: 5ft 11in
Weight: 11st 7lb
Clubs: Johnstone Burgh; Kilmarnock; Glasgow Celtic; Motherwell; St Mirren; Clydebank
Scotland caps: 4
1972 v Peru (won 2-0), v Yugoslavia (drew 2-2)
1973 v England (lost 0-1)
1974 v Czechoslovakia (won 2-1)

Ally Hunter began his career with Kilmarnock, where his displays between the posts led to him winning Under-23 honours for Scotland before, in April 1972, he won the first of four full caps, keeping a clean sheet in a 2-0 defeat of Peru. Earlier that month he had kept goal for Kilmarnock in the Scottish Cup semi-final, and though 'Dixie' Deans scored both Celtic's goals in a 2-0 win, Hunter had a marvellous game, and following Lou Macari's transfer to Manchester United in January 1973, the Parkhead club used £40,000 of that fee to bring Hunter to the club.

On his arrival at Parkhead, Hunter began to turn in one near-miracle performance after another, culminating in Celtic winning the Scottish League Championship in

Ally Hunter

1972-73. He also helped the Bhoys reach that season's Scottish Cup Final, but despite making a number of fine saves, he couldn't prevent Hibernian from winning 2-1. His displays led to him winning his third international cap, but his first while playing with Celtic, when he kept goal in the match against England at Wembley. Determined to exact revenge for their humiliating 5-0 defeat three months earlier, the Scots almost took the lead after two minutes, but Lorimer's shot was well saved by Shilton. On the half-hour mark, Hunter made two stupendous saves from Clarke and Chivers, the latter resulting in serious injury.

Though he played on, he could do little about Martin Peters' goal which gave England a 1-0 victory.

His outstanding form continued the following season when Celtic retained the League Championship. He hadn't missed a game from his debut until injuring his back in the match against Hibernian, an injury which let in Evan Williams. He came back for the match against Hearts, and despite damaging a leg so that he could not use it, he played the full 90 minutes. This time he was replaced by Denis Connaghan, who went on to win a Scottish Cup medal as Celtic beat Dundee United in the final. Hunter returned to action in 1974-75, and won a Scottish League Cup Final winners' medal as Celtic beat Hibs 6-3.

Following the signing of Peter Latchford, Hunter lost his place and moved to Motherwell in April 1976 for a fee of £20,000. After a season at Fir Park, he moved on to St Mirren where, after a handful of games, he decided at the age of 28 to retire to become a grocer. However, he came out of retirement in October 1978 to play two games for Clydebank.

LOU MACARI
Forward

Born: Luigi Macari, Edinburgh, 7 June 1949
Height: 5ft 5in
Weight: 10st 9lb
Clubs: Kilmarnock Amateurs; Kilwinning Rangers; Glasgow Celtic; Manchester United; Swindon Town
Scotland caps: 24
Scotland goals: 5

1972 v Wales (won 1-0), v England (lost 0-1), v Yugoslavia (drew 2-2) 2 goals, v Czechoslovakia (drew 0-0), v Brazil (lost 0-1)

1973 v Denmark (won 4-1) 1 goal, v England (lost 0-5), v Wales (won 2-0), v N Ireland (lost 1-2), v England (lost 0-1)

1975 v Sweden (drew 1-1), v Portugal (won 1-0), v Wales (drew 2-2), v England (lost 1-5), v Romania (drew 1-1)

1977 v N Ireland (won 3-0), v England (won 2-1), v Chile (won 4-2) 2 goals, v Argentina (drew 1-1)

1978 v East Germany (lost 0-1)

1979 v Wales (won 2-0), v Bulgaria (won 2-1), v Peru (lost 1-3), v Iran (drew 1-1)

Born in Edinburgh of Italian parents, Lou Macari won 24 Scottish caps and scored five goals for his country, but had a poor 1978 World Cup in Argentina, and the SFA responded to an outburst in the press that he never wanted to play for Scotland again by imposing a life ban.

Beginning his career with Celtic, he won League Championship medals in 1970 and 1972, was a Scottish Cup winner in 1971 and 1972 and a League Cup finalist in 1971, 1972 and 1973. Having scored 57 goals in 102 games, and shortly after signing a five-year contract, he asked for a transfer, and in January 1973 he became one of the many Scottish players recruited for Manchester United by Tommy Docherty. The £200,000 paid by United was a record fee for a Scottish player at the time.

A player of great flair, Macari was part of United's attractive side of the mid-1970s. However, at the end of his first full season at Old Trafford, United were relegated for the first time in 37 years. Macari scored the only goal of the victory over Southampton which secured the club's promotion back to the top flight at the first attempt. Then, after playing in the 1976 FA Cup Final defeat, he had a hand in the victory over Liverpool in the 1977 Final, when his shot was deflected over the line by Jimmy Greenhoff for the winning goal. Two years later he was back at Wembley when United lost 3-2 to Arsenal, but by the mid-1980s he had made way for younger men.

In June 1984, Macari left Old Trafford to join Swindon Town as player-manager. Towards the end of his first season at the County Ground, he was sacked after a row with his assistant Harry Gregg. Six days later he was reinstated and went on to steer the club from the Fourth to the Second Division in two seasons. In July 1989, Macari took over the reins at West Ham United, but lasted only seven months, as the FA charged him, along with Swindon chairman Brian Hillier, with unauthorised betting on a Robins match.

Macari later returned to management, taking Birmingham to a Leyland Daf Final and then Stoke City to the Autoglass Trophy Final and the Second Division Championship. In November 1993 he left the Victoria Ground to manage Celtic, but within four months he was back at Stoke. Remaining with the Potters until 1997, he later managed Huddersfield Town, but is now involved in work with the media.

JIMMY BONE
Forward

Born: James Bone, Bridge of Allan, 22 September 1949
Height: 5ft 9in
Weight: 11st 8lb
Clubs: Airth Castle Rovers; Partick Thistle; Norwich City; Sheffield United; Glasgow Celtic; Arbroath; St Mirren; Hong Kong Rangers; Heart of Midlothian
Scotland caps: 2
Scotland goals: 1
1972 v Yugoslavia (drew 2-2)
1973 v Denmark (won 4-1) 1 goal

An electrician by trade, Jimmy Bone began his career with Partick Thistle, for whom his goalscoring feats earned him recognition at international level when he won three Scottish Under-23 caps. His form for the Jags alerted clubs south of the Border, and, in February 1972, Norwich City paid £30,000 to take him to Carrow Road.

After making his debut in a disastrous 4-0 defeat at Birmingham City, he went on to score four goals in the last 13 games of the season to help the Canaries pip the St Andrew's club by one point to win the Second Division Championship. It was Jimmy Bone who netted the East Anglian club's opening goal of their first-ever Division One campaign in a 1-1 home draw against Everton. Though

Jimmy Bone playing for Norwich City

his stay at Carrow Road was short, just a year, his bustling style endeared him to the Norwich faithful and brought him two full caps for Scotland.

The club recouped the £30,000 they had paid for Bone, and gained the services of Trevor Hockey, as the popular forward moved to Sheffield United. He scored some vital goals in the remaining games of the 1972-73 season, helping the Blades finish at mid-table in the First Division. However, a year later and Bone was on the move again, this time to Celtic.

Unable to make much progress at Parkhead, he joined Arbroath where he rediscovered all his deadliness in front of goal. He later played for St Mirren and Hearts, for whom he netted their 6000th goal in league encounters. The scorer of over 100 goals in Scottish League football, Bone then entered management with Airdrie and later St Mirren, before taking charge of East Fife.

ALEX FORSYTH
Full-back

Born: Alexander Forsyth, Swinton, 5 February 1952
Height: 5ft 9in
Weight: 11st 1lb
Clubs: Partick Thistle; Manchester United; Glasgow Rangers; Motherwell; Hamilton Academicals
Scotland caps: 10
1972 v Yugoslavia (drew 2-2), v Czechoslovakia (drew 0-0), v Brazil (lost 0-1)
1973 v Denmark (won 4-1), v England (lost 0-5)
1975 v East Germany (won 3-0), v Spain (lost 1-2), v N Ireland (won 3-0), v Romania (drew 1-1)
1976 v Denmark (won 1-0)

After spending a year on the Highbury ground-staff, Arsenal released Alex Forsyth and he returned home to Scotland to sign for Partick Thistle.

In his time at Firhill, Forsyth made his mark as a tough-tackling full-back, helping the Jags win the 1972 Scottish League Cup Final with a 4-1 defeat of Celtic. Also while with Thistle, he won the first of 10 full Scottish caps against Yugoslavia in June 1972. He had scored nine goals in 110 games for Partick, when he became Manchester United manager Tommy Docherty's first signing in December 1972 for a fee of £85,000.

Able to play in both full-back positions, Forsyth went on to win another six caps for Scotland during his time at Old Trafford, and though he possessed sound all-round defensive work, he also enjoyed going forward and was regularly seen having a shot at goal.

Nicknamed 'Bruce', for obvious reasons, he won a Second Division Championship medal with United in 1974-75, and was a member of the FA Cup Final team of 1976 that surprisingly lost 1-0 to Southampton, for whom Bobby Stokes scored the all-important goal. He had appeared in 119 League and Cup games for the Reds, when, after losing his place to Jimmy Nicholl, he returned to Scotland with Rangers.

He spent four seasons at Ibrox, but found it difficult to hold down a first team place, and in the summer of 1982 he joined Motherwell. By the time of his arrival at Fir Park, Forsyth's pace and strength were on the wane, and after making just a handful of first team outings, he moved to Hamilton Academicals where he ended his first-class career.

JOE HARPER

Centre-forward

Born: Joseph Montgomery Harper, Greenock, 11 January 1948
Height: 5ft 4in
Weight: 9st 6lb
Clubs: Morton; Huddersfield Town; Aberdeen; Everton; Hibernian; Aberdeen; Peterhead
Scotland caps: 4
Scotland goals: 2
1973 v Denmark (won 4-1) 1 goal, v Denmark (won 2-0)
1976 v Denmark (won 1-0) 1 goal
1978 v Iran (drew 1-1)

Joe Harper hit the headlines in 1975 when he was one of five Scotland stars banned from international football for a spell after an incident in Copenhagen.

Following brief spells with Morton and Huddersfield Town, Joe Harper joined Aberdeen in October 1969. A penalty in the 1970 Scottish Cup Final assured his place in the hearts of Dons' fans for all time, and over the next two seasons, he ended both campaigns as Aberdeen's top scorer, including an incredible 42 goals in 47 games in 1971-72. That feat earned him the European 'Bronze Boot' for that particular season. By December 1972, Harper had already scored 27 goals when Everton manager Harry Catterick paid £180,000 to take him to Goodison Park.

Although he missed a penalty on his debut at Spurs, Harper's potential was clear for all to see. However, after 14 months on Merseyside, he was homesick and signed for Hibernian for £120,000.

It was obvious from his first few matches at Easter Road that he was not match-fit, but he soon buckled down and won over the fans. His most memorable moments included a hat-trick against Celtic in the 1975 League Cup Final and five goals in a friendly against Dutch side Nijmegan in August 1974.

In the summer of 1976, Harper returned to Pittodrie, and his second spell with the Dons was an unqualified success. He was top scorer for the next three seasons with tallies of 28, 27 and 32! An injury in a League Cup tie at Parkhead in November 1979 all but ended his playing career, though he remained at the club until the end of the 1980-81 season, taking his total of Aberdeen goals to 191.

He was later involved in Highland League football as player-manager of Peterhead, before becoming Morton's Commercial Manager.

DAVID HARVEY

Goalkeeper

Born: David Harvey, Leeds, 7 February 1948
Height: 5ft 11in
Weight: 11st 10lb
Clubs: Leeds United; Vancouver Whitecaps (Canada); Drogheda; Leeds United; Partick Thistle (loan); Bradford City; Whitby Town; Harrogate Town; Carlisle United
Scotland caps: 16

1973 v Denmark (won 2-0)

1974 v Czechoslovakia (lost 0-1), v West Germany (drew 1-1), v N Ireland (lost 0-1), v Wales (won 2-0), v England (won 2-0), v Belgium (lost 1-2), v Zaire (won 2-0), v Brazil (drew 0-0), v Yugoslavia (drew 1-1)

1975 v East Germany (won 3-0), v Spain (lost 1-2), v Spain (drew 1-1)

1976 v Denmark (won 1-0), v Denmark (won 3-1)

1977 v Finland (won 6-0)

In November 1972, David Harvey won his first cap for Scotland, qualifying because his father was Scottish. Playing in a World Cup qualifier at Hampden Park, Harvey kept a clean sheet as Scotland beat Denmark 2-0. During the 1974 World Cup Finals, David Harvey was rated the best keeper in the competition, keeping another clean sheet in a goalless draw against reigning world champions, Brazil.

David Harvey worked at a shoe factory before signing professional forms for his home-town club Leeds United in February 1965, after a couple of years as an apprentice at Elland Road. Though he made his Leeds debut in October of that year, it was 1971-72 before he won a regular

David Harvey

place in the Yorkshire club's side. The years in between his debut and winning a regular spot were spent as understudy to Welsh international Gary Sprake.

Harvey had appeared in over 200 Central League games when he won a regular place in the Leeds side. That season of 1971-72 saw Leeds finish runners-up to Derby County in the First Division Championship and win the FA Cup, Harvey keeping a clean sheet in the 1-0 defeat of Arsenal. Harvey seemed set for a long run in the Leeds United goal, but a bad car accident in February 1975 saw him temporarily lose his place to David Stewart. Although he won back his place, he later left Elland Road to play for Vancouver Whitecaps. He returned to Leeds United before going back to Vancouver, via the League of Ireland side Drogheda, midway through the 1980-81 season.

He left Canada for Elland Road again in March 1982, and remained a first team regular until going on loan to Partick Thistle in February 1985. Harvey had appeared in 447 League and Cup games—a remarkable achievement when it is considered how many games he also played for Leeds' reserves. Harvey appeared in a few games for Bradford City before going to Whitby Town as player-manager. In 1987 he played for Harrogate Town before joining Carlisle United on a non-contract basis for the following season.

On leaving football he had a variety of occupations, including running a pub, delivering fruit and vegetables to hotels in Harrogate and being a postman in Knaresborough. He later moved to a farmhouse and smallholding on the island of Sanday in the Orkneys.

JIM HOLTON
Centre-half

Born: James Allan Holton, Lesmahagow, 11 April 1951
Died: 4 October 1993
Height: 6ft 2in
Weight: 13st 5lb
Clubs: West Bromwich Albion; Shrewsbury Town; Manchester United; Sunderland; Coventry City; Sheffield Wednesday
Scotland caps: 15
Scotland goals: 2
1973   v Wales (won 2-0), v N Ireland (lost 1-2), v England (lost 0-1), v Switzerland (lost 0-1), v Brazil (lost 0-1)
1974   v Czechoslovakia (won 2-1) 1 goal, v West Germany (drew 1-1) 1 goal, v N Ireland (lost 0-1), v Wales (won 2-0), v England (won 2-0), v Norway (won 2-1), v Zaire (won 2-0), v Brazil (drew 0-0), v Yugoslavia (drew 0-0)
1975   v East Germany (won 3-0)

'Six foot two, eyes of blue, Big Jim Holton's after you!' sang the Stretford End. Holton, who was capped 15 times by Scotland, was a great favourite at Manchester United as they stormed to the Second Division Championship in 1974-75.

Unable to make the grade with West Bromwich Albion, though he had appeared as a substitute for the Baggies without actually playing, Holton joined Shrewsbury Town in the summer of 1971. His performances for the Gay Meadow side led to six clubs, including four from the First Division, making offers for his services. Manchester United's Tommy Docherty won the auction with a bid of £90,000.

Holton was a giant of a centre-half, who towered over many of his colleagues at Old Trafford and must have frightened the wits out of many a striker. But against Sheffield Wednesday in early December 1975, he broke a leg and never played first team football for the Reds again. In a pre-season friendly eight months later, he was all set for a return, but in the pre-match kick-in, he twisted his knee and had to limp off before the game had even begun. Holton recovered fairly quickly, but a few weeks later, playing for the reserves, he tragically broke his leg again.

It marked the end of his United days, and later that year he was transferred to Sunderland. Holton was a determined character, and despite the injuries he clawed his way back to fitness with the Wearsiders. After just six months at Roker Park, he joined Coventry City and stayed with the Sky Blues until 1982, when, after making 100 League and Cup appearances, he moved to Sheffield Wednesday.

On his retirement he ran the Old Stag public house in Coventry until his sudden death in October 1993.

DEREK JOHNSTONE
Centre-half/ Centre-forward

Born: Derek Johnstone, Dundee, 4 November 1953
Height: 6ft 0in
Weight: 13st 2lb
Clubs: Glasgow Rangers; Chelsea; Dundee United (loan); Glasgow Rangers
Scotland caps: 14
Scotland goals: 2

1973 v Wales (won 2-0), v N Ireland (lost 1-2), v England (lost 0-1), v Switzerland (lost 0-1), v Brazil (lost 0-1)
1975 v East Germany (won 3-0), v Sweden (drew 1-1)
1976 v Switzerland (won 1-0), v N Ireland (won 3-0), v England (won 2-1)
1978 v Bulgaria (won 2-1), v N Ireland (drew 1-1) 1 goal, v Wales (drew 1-1) 1 goal
1980 v Belgium (lost 1-3)

Derek Johnstone was just 16 years and 355 days old, the youngest footballer ever to have scored the winning goal in a national cup final, when Rangers beat Celtic 1-0 in October 1970 to lift the League Cup.

He played for Scotland at schoolboy, youth, amateur, Under-23 and senior international level. His first love was Dundee United, and he trained with them for a spell but opted to join Rangers. After making his debut in a 5-0 defeat of Cowdenbeath a month before his League Cup Final heroics, Johnstone was seldom out of the team. One of the most versatile players the Ibrox club has ever had, he won three Scottish Cup medals in three different positions, and scored goals in Scottish Cup Finals from both centre-half and centre-forward positions. Often compared to the great John Charles in his physical power, his exceptional heading abilities, nimbleness over the ground for such a big man and goalscoring ability made him quite an exceptional player.

Johnstone won 14 caps for Scotland and was a member of the national squad for the 1978 World Cup Finals in Argentina, but was not selected to play in any of the matches, an omission that rankled Rangers' fans, especially as he had scored in two of the three preceding international matches!

Rangers boss John Greig made Johnstone, who was Scotland's 'Player of the Year' in 1978, club captain, but for some reason, Johnstone wasn't happy with the post and three years later asked to be relieved of it. He went on to win three League Championships, five Scottish Cup and five League Cup winners' medals, before, in 1983, leaving to play for Chelsea for a fee of £30,000.

After appearing in only one league game for the London club, he went on loan to Dundee United before new Rangers manager Jock Wallace re-signed him for the Ibrox club. Struggling with weight problems, his second spell with the club was not a success, and after scoring 209 goals in 547 games, he was released by Graeme Souness. After a brief spell as manager of Partick Thistle, he went to work for Radio Clyde.

PETER McCLOY
Goalkeeper
Born: Peter McCloy, Girvan, 16 November 1946
Height: 6ft 4in
Weight: 14st 3lb
Clubs: Crosshill Thistle; Motherwell; Glasgow Rangers
Scotland caps: 4
1973 v Wales (won 2-0), v N Ireland (lost 1-2), v Switzerland (lost 0-1), v Brazil (lost 0-1)

The son of a St Mirren goalkeeper, Peter McCloy, who was dubbed the 'Girvan Lighthouse', was certainly the tallest goalkeeper in British football in his time. Standing 6ft 4in, he began his senior career with Motherwell whom he joined from Crosshill Thistle in 1963 as a 17-year-old. He won a Summer Cup medal in 1965, and his displays en route to the final success over Dundee United were excellent given his youth. McCloy was actually in Motherwell's reserves when Rangers swooped in a deal which brought both Brian Heron and Bobby Wilson to Fir Park.

Though he was on the losing side on his debut as Rangers were beaten 2-1 by Dunfermline Athletic, he went on to be a virtual ever-present for the next four seasons, helping the club to numerous honours.

McCloy's height was a great advantage with high crosses and lobs, though there were occasions when he would flap at balls rather than catch or punch. One of the mightiest of kickers, his downfield clearances became an attacking option for Rangers, especially when Derek Johnstone was in the side. McCloy, who won four full caps for Scotland, helped Rangers win the European Cup Winners' Cup Final in 1972, as they beat Moscow Dynamo 3-2 at the Nou Camp.

When Stewart Kennedy joined Rangers the following year, McCloy was forced to share the goalkeeping duties with the former Stenhousemuir keeper before reverting to becoming first choice again in 1978. He held his place in the Rangers' side until the arrival of Jim Stewart in March 1981, though his durability again won the day. McCloy, who helped Rangers win the League Championship in 1975-76 along with five Scottish Cup and five League Cup successes, set a record number of games for an Ibrox keeper, 644 in all, thus passing the 545 which Jerry Dawson had set between 1929 and 1945.

Following the arrival of Graeme Souness and Chris Woods in 1986, McCloy became a coach at Ibrox and subsequently became a freelance coach, working with Hearts and a number of other clubs.

DANNY McGRAIN
Right-back
Born: Daniel Fergus McGrain, Finnieston, 1 May 1950
Height: 5ft 9in
Weight: 12st 1lb

Clubs: Glasgow Celtic; Blackpool; Rochdale Rovers (Australia); Hamilton Academicals

Scotland caps: 62

1973 v Wales (won 2-0), v N Ireland (lost 1-2), v England (lost 0-1), v Switzerland (lost 0-1),
       v Brazil (lost 0-1)

1974 v Czechoslovakia (won 2-1), v Czechoslovakia (lost 0-1), v West Germany (drew 1-1),
       v Wales (won 2-0), v England (won 2-0), v Belgium (lost 1-2), v Norway (won 2-1),
       v Zaire (won 2-0), v Brazil (drew 0-0), v Yugoslavia (drew 1-1)

1975 v Spain (drew 1-1), v Sweden (drew 1-1), v Portugal (won 1-0), v Wales (drew2-2),
       v N Ireland (won 3-0), v England (lost 1-5), v Romania (drew 1-1)

1976 v Denmark (won 1-0), v Denmark (won 3-1), v Switzerland (won 1-0),
       v Wales (won 3-1), v N Ireland (won 3-0), v England (won 2-1)

1977 v Finland (won 6-0), v Czechoslovakia (lost 0-2), v Wales (won 1-0),
       v Sweden (won 3-1), v Wales (drew 0-0), v N Ireland (won 3-0), v England (won 2-1),
       v Chile (won 4-2), v Argentina (drew 1-1), v Brazil (lost 0-2)

1978 v East Germany (lost 0-1), v Czechoslovakia (won 3-1)

1980 v Belgium (lost 1-3), v Portugal (won 4-1), v N Ireland (lost 0-1), v Wales (won 1-0),
       v England (lost 0-2), v Poland (lost 0-1), v Hungary (lost 1-3)

1981 v Sweden (won 1-0), v Portugal (drew 0-0), v Israel (won 1-0), v N Ireland (drew 1-1),
       v Israel (won 3-1), v Wales (lost 0-2), v N Ireland (won 2-0), v England (won 1-0)

1982 v Sweden (won 2-0), v Spain (lost 0-3), v Holland (won 2-1), v N Ireland (drew 1-1),
       v England (lost 0-1), v New Zealand (won 5-2), v USSR (drew 2-2)

One of the best full-backs ever to play for Celtic or Scotland, for whom he won 62 caps, Danny McGrain's story is as much a tribute to his character as his ability.

He grew up supporting Rangers as he learned his football in the Glasgow back streets, the home of so many great Scottish players of earlier eras, and hoped to play for that club. The scout who ran the rule over him, however, decided, misguidedly, that Danny McGrain could only be a Catholic, and so Rangers did not approach him. It was their loss. McGrain, a Protestant, went to Celtic instead, devoting his career to the Parkhead club and developing into a strong leader.

McGrain's courage was beyond comprehension. He fractured his skull in a duel with Falkirk's Doug Somner, but upon his return, there was no hesitation when he was asked to show his worth in packed penalty areas with the ball bobbing around.

Diabetes could also have grounded him as well, but McGrain coped with that too. Then another bad injury—after a collision with John Blackley of Hibs— ruled him out for a year. There were grave doubts about a return, but his remarkable resilience, fortitude and courage saw him through to take his place in the Celtic line-up and encourage those around him.

McGrain's career was embroidered with glittering successes. With Celtic he won every domestic honour, including five League Championships and six Scottish Cup medals, and became the club's most capped player. Jock Stein, with typical wry humour, always insisted, 'He's a brilliant full-back with one weakness—he doesn't score enough goals!'

Though he will not be remembered as a Tommy Gemmell type of full-back, it would be an impossible task to try and work out how many goals he had contributed to during his career—as it was he scored just eight in 657 League and Cup appearances for the Bhoys.

In the 1974 World Cup Finals, he played a heroic part in Scotland's goalless draw against Brazil. He was one of the members who could take great credit for making Scotland a force to be reckoned with again after those finals. It was the first time Scotland had reached that stage in 16 years, and McGrain and company failed only by goal difference. A serious foot injury ruled him out of the 1978 trip to Argentina, but once again he showed his resilience, bouncing back to reclaim his place in the 1982 World Cup with distinction. Fittingly, he ended his international career on the grand stage, making his last appearance in this tournament as a substitute against the USSR.

Awarded the MBE by the Queen in February 1983, Danny McGrain was one of the Celtic reserve team called 'The Quality Street Kids'—all eager to make the big-time. McGrain did so and he never lost that special quality.

DEREK PARLANE
Midfield/ Forward

Born: Derek James Parlane, Helensburgh, 5 May 1953
Height: 6ft 0in
Weight: 12st 2lb
Clubs: Queen's Park; Glasgow Rangers; Leeds United; Bulova (Hong Kong); Manchester City; Swansea City (loan); Racing Jet (Belgium); Rochdale; Airdrieonians; Macclesfield Town
Scotland caps: 12
Scotland goals: 1

1973 v Wales (won 2-0), v Switzerland (lost 0-1), v Brazil (lost 0-1)
1975 v Spain (drew 1-1), v Sweden (drew 1-1), v Portugal (won 1-0), v Wales (drew 2-2), v N Ireland (won 3-0) 1 goal, v England (lost 1-5), v Romania (drew 1-1)
1976 v Denmark (won 3-1)
1977 v Wales (drew 0-0)

The son of former Rangers inside-forward Jimmy Parlane, he began his career as a midfield player with Queen's Park before leaving in 1970 to join the Ibrox club. He made a dramatic debut for Rangers, for, after replacing the injured John Greig in the European Cup Winners' Cup home semi-final, he volleyed home Willie Johnston's corner kick for Rangers second goal.

Tall, strong and energetic, Parlane won a clutch of international and domestic honours whilst with Rangers. In four seasons out of five with Rangers, he was the club's leading scorer, despite being a contemporary of Derek Johnstone for much of the time. He won a dozen full Scottish caps, five at Under-23 level, one at Under-21, and made two Scottish League XI appearances, while at club level he won three League Championship medals, two Cup winners medals and three League Cup winners medals.

In the game against Hearts at Tynecastle in January 1974, Parlane scored all Rangers goals in a 4-2 win, including the clubs 6000th league goal. He had scored 111 goals in 296 games for Rangers, when, in March 1980, he was transferred to Leeds United for £160,000.

Although he scored on his debut, goals did not come easy, and he spent nine months on loan to Hong Kong club Bulova. It was only when he joined Manchester City in the summer of 1983 that he recaptured his scoring form. In January 1985 he started a four-month loan spell with Swansea City before trying his luck with Racing Jet of Belgium. On his return to these shores he joined Rochdale, but a financial crisis at Spotland saw boss Eddie Gray release Parlane. He joined another Leeds old boy, Gordon McQueen, at Airdrie before playing non-League football for Macclesfield Town, for whom he later became a director.

JOE JORDAN
Centre-forward

Born: Joseph Jordan, Carluke, 15 December 1951
Height: 6ft 0in
Weight: 11st 12lb
Clubs: Blantyre Victoria; Morton; Leeds United; Manchester United; AC Milan and Verona (Italy); Southampton; Bristol City
Scotland caps: 52
Scotland goals: 11

1973   v England (lost 0-1), v Switzerland (lost 0-1), v Brazil (lost 0-1)
1974   v Czechoslovakia (won 2-1) 1 goal, v Czechoslovakia (lost 0-1),
v West Germany (drew 1-1), v N Ireland (lost 0-1), v Wales (won 2-0),
v England (won 2-0) 1 goal, v Belgium (lost 1-2), v Norway (won 2-1) 1 goal,
v Zaire (won 2-0) 1 goal, v Brazil (drew 0-0), v Yugoslavia (drew 1-1) 1 goal
1975   v East Germany (won 3-0), v Spain (lost 1-2), v Spain (drew 1-1) 1 goal
1976   v Wales (won 3-1), v N Ireland (won 3-0), v England (won 2-1)
1977   v Czechoslovakia (lost 0-2), v Wales (won 1-0), v N Ireland (won 3-0),
v England (won 2-1)
1978   v East Germany (lost 0-1), v Czechoslovakia (won 3-1) 1 goal, v Wales (won 2-0),
v Bulgaria (won 2-1), v N Ireland (drew 1-1), v England (lost 0-1),
v Peru (lost 1-3) 1 goal, v Iran (drew 1-1), v Holland (won 3-2)
1979   v Austria (lost 2-3), v Portugal (lost 0-1), v Wales (lost 0-3), v N Ireland (won 1-0),
v England (lost 1-3), v Norway (won 4-0) 1 goal
1980   v Belgium (lost 0-2), v N Ireland (lost 0-1), v Wales (won 1-0), v England (lost 0-1),
v Poland (lost 0-1)
1981   v Israel (won 3-1), v Wales (lost 0-2), v England (won 1-0)
1982   v Sweden (won 2-0) 1 goal, v Holland (won 2-1), v Wales (won 1-0), v England (lost 0-1),
v USSR (drew 2-2) 1 goal

Scorer of the goal that took Scotland to the 1974 World Cup Finals, and indeed the only Scot to have scored in three World Cup Finals, volatile Joe Jordan's toothless grin became a regular feature of the Football League circuit—usually after the muscular centre-forward had forced the ball into the back of the net!

Jordan originally worked in an architect's office and was rejected after a trial with West Bromwich Albion. He played for junior side Blantyre Victoria before being picked up by Morton in October 1968. After just a handful of games

Joe Jordan

for the Greenock club, Jordan was recommended to Leeds United by Bobby Collins, and in October 1970 the Yorkshire club signed the 18-year-old for a bargain £15,000.

Although he endured long spells as a substitute, Leeds transformed him into an unselfish and inspirational leader, winning a League Championship medal in 1973-74. Jordan, who won 52 caps for Scotland, also played for Leeds in the two losing European Cup Final teams of 1973 and 1975.

In January 1978, Jordan joined Manchester United for a then-record fee of £350,000. A great favourite with the Old Trafford crowd, he had three good seasons with the Reds before he joined the exodus of British players to Italy, signing for AC Milan in the summer of 1981 for £175,000. He also played for Verona before Southampton brought him back to England in the 1984 close season for around £100,000.

Although he was the Saints' leading scorer in his first season on the south coast, he suffered a series of niggling injuries, and in February 1987 was allowed to join Bristol City as player-coach, eventually becoming their manager. He steered the Robins to the 1988-89 Littlewoods Cup semi-final, and the following season led the Ashton Gate club to promotion from the Third Division.

In September 1990 he was appointed manager of Hearts, who in 1991-92 were runners-up to Rangers. Unable to capitalise on that platform, he had a spell as assistant-manager at Celtic before taking charge at Stoke City. He endured a torrid time there, and embarked on a second spell with Bristol City before later becoming assistant to Northern Ireland manager Lawrie McMenemy. Jordan then joined Portsmouth, and after a brief spell as caretaker boss, he remains at Fratton Park as the south coast club's first team coach.

JOHN CONNOLLY
Winger
Born: John Connolly, Barrhead, 13 June 1950
Height: 5ft 9in
Weight: 10st 7lb
Clubs: Glasgow United; St Johnstone; Everton; Birmingham City; Newcastle United; Hibernian; Gateshead; Blyth Spartans
Scotland caps: 1
1973 v Switzerland (lost 0-1)

A talented though inconsistent winger, John Connolly twice fought his way back from a broken leg. A direct sort of player, more than willing to take on a full-back, he made his name with St Johnstone before Everton manager Harry Catterick paid £75,000 for his services in March 1972.

After some good early displays when he was capped by Scotland against Switzerland, he never really hit it off with Catterick's successor, Billy Bingham, and was placed on the transfer list at his own request. He finally won his battle to leave Goodison before the start of the 1976-77 season, joining up with former Everton team-mates Howard Kendall and Gary Jones at Birmingham City.

He didn't last long at St Andrew's and joined Newcastle United as part of Bill McGarry's rebuilding plans. He was prominent as the Magpies reached the top of Division Two, and looked as though they would regain their First Division status. But the team's good form disappeared, and with it went John Connolly's hopes of a sustained period at St James Park.

He returned to Scotland to play for Hibernian, helping the Easter Road club win the Scottish First Division Championship in 1980-81. He spent another season with Hibs before having a spell playing on the north-east non-League circuit with Gateshead and Blyth Spartans before managing Whitley Bay.

Later he worked for Vaux Brewery before returning to Scotland, where he was employed as an advertising manager for *Golf Monthly* magazine and worked as a part-time coach for Ayr United—his sons Stuart and Graeme both later joined the Honest Men.

GEORGE CONNOLLY
Left-half/ Inside-forward
Born: George Connolly, Fife, 1 March 1949
Height: 6ft 1in
Weight: 12st 0lb
Clubs: Glasgow Celtic; Falkirk; Sauchie FC
Scotland caps: 2
1974 v Czechoslovakia (won 2-1), v West Germany (drew 1-1)

Despite walking out on the Scottish party boarding the plane for Berne at Glasgow Airport in June 1973 because he was allegedly worried over his wife, who was expecting their first baby, George Connolly went on to win a couple of caps. He had an outstanding first game against Czechoslovakia at Hampden Park in September 1973 'with searching passes to both wings' in a 2-1 win for the home side.

Though his early displays for Celtic were disappointing, manager Jock Stein had utter faith in him, and, with Jimmy Johnstone suspended, gave him his place against Rangers in the Scottish Cup Final of April 1969. Connolly rewarded his manager's decision with a superb display in a 4-0 win for the Bhoys.

Initially a ball-playing defender destined for greatness while maturing in the shadow of Billy McNeill, he netted a goal after just 58 seconds of the 1970 European Cup semi-final against Leeds United at Elland Road.

Connolly, who was the Scottish Football Writers' 'Player of the Year' for 1973, was a complex character. In November of that year, he went missing from club training for the first time. His professional behaviour deteriorated rapidly after a clean break of an ankle against Basle put paid to him playing in the 1974 World Cup Finals in West Germany.

He left Parkhead in September 1975, and was given the chance to make a new start with Falkirk. Eager to show his skills away from the Premier League, he appeared in a handful of games before his lack of fitness forced a parting of the ways. He took labouring jobs, but then made a surprise return to the game where it had all begun at Tulliallan. He later joined Sauchie, where SJFA manager John Hughes considered him as a Scottish junior cap prospect!

TOMMY HUTCHISON
Winger
Born: Thomas Hutchinson, Cardenden, Glasgow, 22 September 1947
Height: 6ft 0in
Weight: 11st 2lb

Clubs: Dundonald Bluebell; Alloa Athletic; Blackpool; Coventry City; Manchester City; Bulova (Hong Kong); Burnley; Swansea City

Scotland caps: 17

Scotland goals: 1

1974 v Czechoslovakia (won 2-1), v Czechoslovakia (lost 0-1), v West Germany (drew 1-1), v West Germany (lost 1-2), v N Ireland (lost 0-1), v Wales (won 2-0), v Belgium (lost 1-2), v Norway (won 2-1), v Zaire (won 2-0), v Yugoslavia (drew 1-1)

1975 v East Germany (won 3-0) 1 goal, v Spain (lost 1-2), v Spain (drew 1-1), v Portugal (won 1-0), v England (lost 1-5), v Romania (drew 1-1)

1976 v Denmark (won 1-0)

Tommy Hutchison was an old-fashioned winger, who, though he played for a number of clubs, won all of his 17 full international caps whilst with Coventry City.

Probably one of the most naturally gifted players of the post-war era, Blackpool brought him into League football from Alloa Athletic in 1968. Although Hutchison didn't score many goals himself, he laid on countless for his team-mates, notably Fred Pickering, Alan Suddick and John Craven, and in 1969-70, helped the Seasiders win promotion to the First Division. Success was short-lived, and twelve months later, Blackpool were relegated.

In October 1972, Hutchison was transferred to Coventry City, the Sky Blues offering £140,000 and Billy

Tommy Hutchison playing for Coventry City

Rafferty in exchange. Over the next eight seasons, Hutchison scored 30 goals in 355 League and Cup games, helping to transform the Highfield Road club into one of the most attractive outfits in the top flight.

In 1980 he joined Manchester City to become one of manager John Bond's most influential signings, and from the bottom of the First Division, City progressed to a respectable mid-table finish in the League, the semi-final of the League Cup and the epic FA Cup Final against Tottenham Hotspur in 1981. That final proved to be a bittersweet affair for Hutchison, who headed the Blues into a first-half lead only to have the misfortune of scoring a late equaliser for Spurs, deflecting a shot from Glenn Hoddle past Joe Corrigan and setting up a replay which City lost.

He left Maine Road in the summer of 1982 to spend a season in Hong Kong, before re-appearing on the English scene again in 1983 with Burnley. After two seasons at Turf Moor in which he was ever-present, he joined Swansea as the Welsh club's player-coach. The Swans competed in the 1989-90 European Cup Winners' Cup, and, at 42, Tommy Hutchison became the oldest player ever to play in a European tie. After making more than 800 league appearances, Hutchison decided to retire and received a PFA Merit Award for his services to football.

JOHN BLACKLEY
Central defender

Born: John Henderson Blackley, Westquarter near Falkirk, 12 May 1948
Height: 5ft 10in
Weight: 13st 1lb
Clubs: Gairdoch United; Hibernian; Newcastle United; Preston North End; Hamilton Academicals
Scotland caps: 7
1974 v Czechoslovakia (lost 0-1), v England (won 2-0), v Belgium (lost 1-2), v Zaire (won 2-0)
1976 v Switzerland (won 1-0)
1977 v Wales (won 1-0), v Sweden (won 3-1)

Sufficiently skilled to win seven caps for Scotland and represent his country in the first of Scotland's three games in the 1974 World Cup Finals in West Germany, John Blackley was one of Scotland's most accomplished players. Cool and assured, he was a skilled central defender who liked to play alongside a big partner in the middle of the back four. He had the ability to set attacks moving with accurate distribution and the vision of a midfield player.

He played in the Hibs side that won the Scottish League Cup in 1972, beating Celtic 2-1, but lost the League Cup Finals of 1969 and 1974 as well as the 1972 Scottish Cup Final. Blackey was well known for his superstitious insistence on being the last to appear on the pitch, and kicking the ball into the Hibs net before kick-off.

When he joined Newcastle United in October 1977 for a fee of £100,000, he was reaching the end of his career, but he still displayed his almost casual, arrogant approach to the game. Voted 'Player of the Year', his undoubted talent was unable to halt a United slide which saw the club drop into Division Two, and thereafter John Blackley was more often than not found in the treatment room.

On leaving St James Park, Blackley joined Preston North End, but most of his two-and-a-half seasons at Deepdale were also spent on the treatment table. In 1981 he rejoined Hibs, going on to appear in 276 league games in his two spells with the club.

After a spell as player-manager with Hamilton Academicals, he became assistant-manager to Pat Stanton at Easter Road. In October 1984 he succeeded Stanton, but after two indifferent seasons he resigned. He then managed Cowdenbeath and was coach at Dundee, before becoming Paul Sturrock's coach at Dundee United.

DONALD FORD

Centre-forward

Born: Donald Ford, Linlithgow, 25 October 1944
Height: 5ft 8in
Weight: 9st 6lb
Clubs: Vale of Avon; Bo'ness United; Heart of Midlothian; Falkirk
Scotland caps: 3
1974 v Czechoslovakia (lost 0-1), v West Germany (lost 1-2), v Wales (won 2-0)

Donald Ford made his international debut against Czechoslovakia in a World Cup qualifier in October 1973 in Prague, and earned two further caps against West Germany and Wales. He travelled to the World Cup Finals in West Germany in 1974, but did not play in any of the three matches.

He was 19 years old when he made his debut for Hearts in a 4-2 win over Celtic in September 1964, but had to watch from the stands as Kilmarnock pipped the Tynecastle club for the title on the final day of that season. In the close season Hearts beat Killie 8-3 in an experimental match without 'offside', a game in which Ford scored five of his side's goals.

However, Ford had to wait until the departure of Willie Wallace before making a real impact in the Hearts' side. In 1967-68 he scored 16 goals as Hearts reached the Scottish Cup Final, only to lose 3-1 to Dunfermline Athletic. In the club's run to that final, Ford scored the winner in the quarter-final replay against Rangers. He was a member of the Hearts side that reached the Texaco Cup Final in 1971, and in November of that year, he netted hat-tricks in a 6-1 win over Morton and in a 3-2 defeat of Aberdeen. He also achieved the rare distinction of netting a hat-trick of penalties in a 3-2 victory over Morton in 1973.

During the course of the 1973-74 season, Ford scored 29 goals, including a hat-trick in a 4-1 win over Partick Thistle in the Scottish Cup. This game was being watched by Scotland manager Willie Ormond, and shortly afterwards, Ford received a call-up for the national side.

Ford continued to represent Hearts up until May 1976, when, after scoring 188 goals in 436 matches, he left Tynecastle for a spell with Falkirk.

On hanging up his boots he went to work as a radio commentator, and being a keen photographer, presides over the Donald Ford Gallery in South Queensferry.

THOMSON ALLAN

Goalkeeper

Born: Thomson Sandlands Allan, Longridge, 5 October 1946
Height: 5ft 10in
Weight: 11st 7lb
Clubs: Edina Hearts; Hibernian; Dundee; Meadowbank Thistle
Heart of Midlothian

Scotland caps: 2
1974   v West Germany (lost 1-2), v Norway (won 2-1)

As a schoolboy, Thomson Allan played at left-half before going between the posts. After joining the Hibernian groundstaff, he had a brief spell with Edina Hearts in an attempt to aid his development as a goalkeeper. Allan signed professional forms for the Easter Road club in October 1963, and over the next eight seasons, missed very few games.

Whilst with Hibs he was selected to represent the Scottish League, and helped them finish third in the Scottish First Division in seasons 1967-68 and 1969-70. Allan was also between the posts in the 1969 Scottish League Cup Final when Hibs were the underdogs against Celtic—and though he made a number of fine saves, the mighty Bhoys won 6-2!

In the summer of 1971, Allan, who had earned a big reputation for consistency and reliability in his time at Easter Road, left to play for Dundee. After a couple of seasons of outstanding goalkeeping, Allan had his best-ever campaign in 1973-74. He was in inspirational form as Dundee won the Scottish League Cup beating Celtic 1-0 in the final. That season, his performances for the Dens Park club led to him winning two caps for Scotland against West Germany and Norway.

After that, the goalkeeping of Thomson Allan was the main reason Dundee were constantly challenging for promotion to the Premier Division as they finished third in seasons 1976-77 and 1977-78. When the club won the First Division Championship in 1978-79, Allan received an injury setback midway through the campaign, and after a loan spell with Meadowbank Thistle, he moved to Hearts.

After just one season in which the Tynecastle club won the First Division title, he decided to retire.

BOBBY ROBINSON
Midfield

Born: Robert Sharp Robinson, Edinburgh, 10 November 1950
Died: 24 December 1996
Height: 5ft 11in
Weight: 11st 1lb
Clubs: Newtongrange; Falkirk; Dundee; Dundee United; Heart of Midlothian; Raith Rovers; Forfar Albion; Coupar Angus
Scotland caps: 4
1974   v West Germany (lost 1-2)
1975   v Sweden (drew 1-1), v N Ireland (won 3-0), v Romania (drew 1-1)

After beginning his career as a centre-half with Falkirk, Bobby Robinson, who could also play at full-back, joined Dundee in 1972, and was soon converted into a strong-running midfield player.

Known as 'Trigger', he spent five successful years with the Dens Park club, helping them win the League Cup in 1974 after beating Celtic 1-0 in the final. Having represented Scotland at Under-23 level, he won four full caps for Scotland in the mid-seventies against West Germany, Sweden, Northern Ireland and Romania. Unlucky not to add to his tally of caps, he moved to Dundee United in 1977 for £20,000, but failed to settle at Tannadice, and two years later he returned to his home city and joined Hearts for a similar fee.

Though he only spent two seasons with the Tynecastle club, he was a member of the side that won the First Division Championship in 1979-80, when Hearts finished two points ahead of runners-up Airdrieonians. He parted company with Hearts in the summer of 1983, leaving to play for Raith Rovers, where he saw out his league career. He later played non-League football for Forfar Albion and Coupar Angus before returning to Tannadice to work alongside Jim McLean in helping bring on the club's youngsters.

Bobby Robinson died on Christmas Eve 1996 after a long illness, aged just 46.

KENNY BURNS
Central defender/ Forward

Born: Kenneth Burns, Glasgow, 23 September 1953
Height: 5ft 11in
Weight: 11st 0lb
Clubs: Glasgow Rangers; Birmingham City; Nottingham Forest; Leeds United; Derby County; Notts County; Barnsley; Sutton Town; Stafford Rangers; Gainsborough Trinity; Grantham
Scotland caps: 20
Scotland goals: 1

1974 v West Germany (lost 1-2)
1975 v East Germany (won 3-0) 1 goal, v Spain (lost 1-2), v Spain (drew 1-1)
1977 v Czechoslovakia (lost 0-2), v Wales (won 1-0), v Sweden (won 3-1), v Wales (drew 0-0)
1978 v N Ireland (drew 1-1), v Wales (drew 1-1), v England (lost 0-1), v Peru (lost 1-3), v Iran (drew 1-1)
1979 v Norway (won 4-0)
1980 v Peru (drew 1-1), v Austria (drew 1-1), v Belgium (lost 1-3)
1981 v Israel (won 1-0), v N Ireland (drew 1-1), v Wales (lost 0-2)

Though he began his career with Glasgow Rangers, it was with Birmingham City that Kenny Burns first came to prominence. He joined the St Andrew's club as an apprentice in the summer of 1970 and signed professional forms the following year. Though he made his league debut against Hull City in September 1971, it was 1973-74 before he established himself as a first team regular. During that season, Burns, who had won Scotland youth and Under-23 honours, won the first of his 20 full caps when he played against West Germany.

Also during that 1973-74 season, Burns netted his first hat-trick in League football as the Blues drew 3-3 at Leicester City. In 1976-77, his last season with Birmingham, he formed a formidable striking partnership with Trevor Francis, and scored 19 goals in 36 games, including four in a 5-1 home win over Derby County. Though he had more than his fair share of disciplinary problems, he

Kenny Burns

had scored 53 goals in 204 games for the Blues when Brian Clough signed him for Nottingham Forest for a fee of £150,000 in the summer of 1977.

Switched to the centre of defence, Burns was outstanding as Forest won the League Championship and League Cup in his first season at the City Ground. He was selected as the Football Writers' Association 'Player of the Year', and went to Argentina with the Scotland World Cup squad. The popular Burns went on to win two European Cup winners' medals with Forest, but in October 1981 a lucrative contract lured him to Leeds United.

At Elland Road, Burns was also used in midfield, but he couldn't stop United sliding into Division Two. He was loaned to Derby County in March 1983, and signed permanently for the Rams in February 1984. A year later he went on loan to Notts County before moving to Barnsley in August 1985. On leaving the first-class scene, he joined former Forest colleague John Robertson at Sutton Town, and in the summer of 1986 had trials with Swedish club IF Elsborg. After a period as manager of Sutton Town he joined Stafford Rangers, before having spells with Gainsborough Trinity and Grantham.

ERICH SCHAEDLER
Left-back
Born: Erich Peter Schaedler, Biggar, 6 August 1949
Died: 24 December 1985
Height: 5ft 9in
Weight: 11st 5lb
Clubs: Melbourne Thistle; Stirling Albion; Hibernian; Dundee; Hibernian; Dumbarton
Scotland caps: 1
1974 v West Germany (lost 1-2)

Being the son of a German father who once played for Borussia Moenchengladbach, it was a nice coincidence that Erich Schaedler should win his only full international cap for Scotland against West Germany at Frankfurt in March 1974, a match that the Scots lost 2-1. Schaedler was also a member of the Scotland squad that travelled to West Germany under the management of Willie Ormond for the 1974 World Cup, but he didn't feature in the tournament. There is no doubt, though, if he hadn't been a contemporary of one of the world's best full-backs in Danny McGrain, he would have won many more international caps.

Erich Schaedler began his career with Stirling Albion, but after just nine months at Annfield, he joined Hibernian. He made his debut for the Easter Road club in a friendly against Polish side Gornik Zabrze in December 1969. The story goes that the full-back's first touch was a poor one, leading to his Hibs' team-mate Peter Cormack being badly injured!

He was a tenacious tackler and possessed one of the longest throws in Scottish football. Also, he liked nothing better than to push forward in support of the attack. Despite not being the most skilful member of the Hibs side, he was one of the most committed, and won a Scottish League Cup winners' medal in 1973 as Hibs beat Celtic 2-1.

Allowed to leave Easter Road in November 1977, he joined Dundee, and during a four-year stay at Dens Park, helped the club win the Scottish League Division One Championship in 1978-79, and reach the Scottish League Cup Final in 1981 where they lost 3-0 to Dundee United.

Towards the end of 1981, Schaedler returned to Easter Road, and took his total of league appearances for Hibs in his two spells with the club to 292, before joining Dumbarton. Sadly, problems then led to his untimely death on Christmas Eve 1985.

GORDON McQUEEN
Centre-half

Born: Gordon McQueen, Kilwinning, 26 June 1952
Height: 6ft 3in
Weight: 13st 0lb
Clubs: Largs Thistle; St Mirren; Leeds United; Manchester United; Seiko (Hong Kong)
Scotland caps: 30
Scotland goals: 5

1974 v Belgium (lost 1-2)
1975 v Spain (lost 1-2), v Spain (drew 1-1), v Portugal (won 1-0), v Wales (drew 2-2), v N Ireland (won 3-0), v England (lost1-5), v Romania (drew 1-1) 1 goal
1976 v Denmark (won 1-0)
1977 v Czechoslovakia (lost 0-2), v Wales (won 1-0), v Wales (drew 0-0), v N Ireland (won 3-0) 1 goal, v England (won 2-1) 1 goal
1978 v East Germany (lost 0-1), v Czechoslovakia (won 3-1), v Wales (won 2-0), v Bulgaria (won 2-1), v N Ireland (drew 1-1), v Wales (drew 1-1)
1979 v Austria (lost 2-3) 1 goal, v Norway (won 3-2), v Portugal (lost 0-1), v N Ireland (won 1-0), v England (lost 1-3), v Norway (won 4-0) 1 goal
1980 v Peru (drew 1-1), v Austria (drew 1-1), v Belgium (lost 1-3)
1981 v Wales (lost 0-2)

During the course of his career, Gordon McQueen suffered his fair share of injuries, and one of these, at Anfield in early 1984, not only kept him out of action for the remainder of the season but forced him to miss Scotland's appearance in the 1984 World Cup Finals. Though his last international appearance had been

Gordon McQueen

three years ago, he had recently been touted for a return to the national side.

At school, Gordon McQueen was a goalkeeper, following in the footsteps of his father Tom, who kept goal for Hibernian, Berwick Rangers, East Fife and Accrington Stanley. He switched to playing on the wing before settling at centre-half, where his aerial power made him a formidable opponent, and after unsuccessful trials with both Rangers and Liverpool, he joined St Mirren from Largs Thistle in 1970.

Not long afterwards, Leeds United were looking for a long-term successor to Jack Charlton, and in September 1972 they paid £30,000 to secure his services.

During his time at Elland Road, he developed into an outstanding defender who was first choice during the Yorkshire club's 1973-74 League Championship-winning season. At the end of that campaign, he won the first of his 30 Scottish caps in a 2-1 defeat by Belgium in Brussels.

In February 1978 it cost a then British record fee of £495,000 to take him to Manchester United. A month earlier, United manager Dave Sexton had bought McQueen's great friend and Elland Road team-mate Joe Jordan. McQueen went on to appear with the Reds in three Wembley finals; the 1979 FA Cup defeat by Arsenal, the 1983 Milk Cup defeat by Liverpool and United's two matches against Brighton and Hove Albion which brought them the FA Cup in 1983.

In August 1985 he was appointed coach at Seiko FC in Hong Kong, but after one season he was bedridden and on the danger list with a combination of typhoid fever and septicemia. After making a full recovery, he took over as manager of Airdrieonians, but, in May 1989, he resigned his post because the majority of the Broomfield Park club's players would not play full-time on the contracts offered.

After a spell coaching St Mirren, he was a match analyser for Scottish TV, before entering the English game as reserve-team coach at Middlesbrough.

'DIXIE' DEANS

Centre-forward

Born: John Kelly Deans, Linwood, 30 July 1946
Height: 5ft 7in
Weight: 10st 8lb
Clubs: Neilston Victoria; Motherwell; Glasgow Celtic; Luton Town; Carlisle United; Partick

Deans' exploits in junior football had earned him the nickname 'Dixie' after the great Everton and England centre-forward.

He came to prominence as a prolific goalscorer with Neilston, and when he amassed a staggering 60 goals in one season, Motherwell moved in to pip Newcastle United for his signature. Although only 5ft 7in, he was excellent in the air and powerful on the ground. He made his league debut against Kilmarnock in March 1966 and then the following season broke the club's post-war goalscoring record by netting 30 league goals—his exploits paving the way for promotion. However, during his time at Fir Park, controversy continually clouded his career. Not long after scoring a hat-trick against Dunfermline Athletic, he was sent off against Celtic in December 1966. There followed sendings-off in matches against Aberdeen, Clyde, Hamilton and Stoke City!

In October 1971, after scoring 78 goals in 152 games, he was sold to Celtic for a meagre £17,500, although Deans was serving a six-week suspension at the time!

Deans enjoyed a prolific career with the Parkhead club, especially when the opposition were Hibernian—netting a hat-trick in the 6-1 mauling of the Easter Road club in the 1972 Scottish Cup Final, and another treble in the 6-3 League Cup Final triumph over Hibs in 1974. Deans, who went on to score 124 goals in 184 games, also scored six goals in a game against Partick Thistle which Celtic won 7-0. Whilst with Celtic, he won every domestic honour in the game, and was twice capped by Scotland against East Germany and Spain. Unfortunately Deans is remembered as the Celt who ballooned the very first spot-kick over the bar in the penalty shoot-out against Inter Milan in the semi-final of the European Cup at Parkhead, when the Italians went through to the final 5-4.

Though he scored twice on his debut for Luton Town, his stay at Kenilworth Road was brief, and after a loan spell with Carlisle United, he returned to Scotland to play for Partick Thistle. Immensely popular wherever he played, he had a spell playing in Australia before winding down his career in the League of Ireland with Shelbourne.

GRAEME SOUNESS
Midfield
Born: Graeme James Souness, Edinburgh, 6 May 1953
Height: 5ft 11in
Weight: 12st 13lb
Clubs: Tottenham Hotspur; Montreal Olympic (Canada); Middlesbrough
   Liverpool; Sampdoria (Italy); Glasgow Rangers
Scotland caps: 54
Scotland goals: 4
1975 v East Germany (won 3-0), v Spain (lost 1-2), v Spain (drew 1-1)
1978 v Bulgaria (won 2-1), v Wales (drew 1-1), v England (lost 0-1), v Holland (won 3-2)

1979 v Austria (lost 2-3), v Norway (won 3-2), v Wales (lost 0-3), v N Ireland (won 1-0),
v England (lost 1-3)

1980 v Peru (drew 1-1), v Austria (drew 1-1), v Belgium (lost 0-2), v Portugal (won 4-1),
v N Ireland (lost 0-1)

1981 v Portugal (drew 0-0), v Israel (won 1-0), v Israel (won 3-1)

1982 v N Ireland (drew 0-0), v Portugal (lost 1-2), v Spain (lost 0-3), v Wales (won 1-0),
v England (lost 0-1), v New Zealand (won 5-2), v Brazil (lost 1-4),
v USSR (drew 2-2) 1 goal

1983 v East Germany (won 2-0), v Switzerland (lost 0-2), v Belgium (lost 2-3),
v Switzerland (drew 2-2), v Wales (won 2-0), v England (lost 0-2), v Canada (won 2-0),
v Canada (won 3-0) 1 goal, v Canada (won 2-0)

1984 v Uruguay (won 2-0), v N Ireland (lost 0-2), v Wales (won 2-1)

1985 v Yugoslavia (won 6-1) 1 goal, v Iceland (won 3-0), v Spain (won 3-1), v Spain (lost 0-1),
v Wales (lost 0-1), v England (won 1-0), v Iceland (won 1-0)

1986 v East Germany (drew 0-0), v Australia (won 2-0), v Australia (drew 0-0),
v Romania (won 3-0), v England (lost 1-2) 1 goal, v Denmark (lost 0-1),
v West Germany (lost 1-2)

The dominant personality in the Scotland team in the 1982 World Cup, Graeme Souness has, throughout his career, exhibited a fierce desire to succeed, but with established midfielders of the quality of Mullery, Peters and Perryman at White Hart Lane, the young Souness grew frustrated. After playing for Montreal Olympic in the NASL in the summer of 1972, he walked out on the club before Spurs allowed him to move to Middlesbrough for £32,000.

At the end of his first season at Ayresome Park, Middlesbrough were promoted to Division One, and during his stay in the north-east, Souness developed into one of the game's most influential performers of modern times.

It was Bob Paisley who brought Souness to Anfield in January 1978 for £352,000—then a record deal between Football League clubs. His move to Liverpool to team up with Kenny Dalglish was the foundation stone of the club's success over the next decade. His displays in the European Cup campaign of 1980-81 were particularly eye-catching, with his sense of awareness and ability to rip open the hearts of defences with long, telling passes. He also hit two hat-tricks in the early stages of the competition as Liverpool beat Oulu Palloseura of Finland 10-1 and CSKA Sofia of Bulgaria 5-1 in the Anfield legs. He scored some valuable goals for Liverpool, none more so, perhaps, than the one that beat Everton in the 1984 Milk Cup Final replay. Replacing Phil Thompson as captain, he led the Reds to three successive titles and League Cups and one European Cup, becoming the most successful skipper in the club's history.

In June 1984 he moved to Sampdoria in Italy for £650,000. Two quiet seasons were followed by his surprise appointment as player-manager at Ibrox in 1986. In his first game for Rangers he was sent off! However, by the end of his first season, the club had won the Scottish League and the Skol Cup and reached the final of the Scottish Cup, while in 1989-90 they won the Scottish League title again and, in 1990-91, the Skol Cup. A part-owner of Rangers, Souness was still striving for the European Champions Cup when he left in April 1991 to replace Kenny Dalglish as manager of Liverpool.

Graeme Souness as a Liverpool player

After the shock of undergoing major heart surgery, he led the Reds to the one trophy he had failed to capture as a player, the FA Cup. In January 1994 he left to spend a season in Turkey as manager of Galatasaray, but was sacked after winning the Championship! He later managed Southampton and Torino before taking over the reins at Blackburn Rovers. Having led the Ewood Park club to promotion to the Premiership, he then saw his side win the League Cup, beating Spurs at the Millennium Stadium. He later left Blackburn to manage Newcastle United, but a turbulent reign at St James Park ended in January 2006 when he was sacked.

PAUL WILSON
Forward

Born: Paul Wilson, Milngavie, 23 November 1950
Height: 5ft 7in
Weight: 11st 0lb
Clubs: Maryhill Juniors; Glasgow Celtic; Motherwell; Partick Thistle; Blantyre Celtic
Scotland caps: 1
1975 v Spain (drew 1-1)

Son of a Scottish father and Indian mother, Paul Wilson was a spectacular raider with speed, control and a powerful shot, yet he was unable consistently to command a regular place in the Celtic team.

His first few seasons at Parkhead were disappointing, and it was 1974–75 before he established himself in the left-wing berth. That season was the first that he hadn't started in the reserves and his form throughout—especially against Rangers when he scored with a brilliant header in the Dryborough Cup—saw him win full international honours for Scotland against Spain in Valencia. Coming off the bench to replace Kenny Burns, he was instrumental in the making of Scotland's goal scored by Joe Jordan. Towards the end of that season, he scored Celtic's first two goals in the 3-1 defeat of Airdrie in the Scottish Cup Final. A week after this triumph, he gave a magnificent display of running, shooting and control against Rangers in the Glasgow Cup Final to celebrate the city's 800th birthday—scoring both Celtic's goals in a 2-2 draw.

Though he made way when Alfie Conn arrived at Parkhead in Mach 1977, he was still Jock Stein's first choice for the club's assault on Europe the following season. However, on the domestic scene, Celtic had a disastrous campaign, and Wilson, who had scored 52 goals in 214 games, was allowed to leave Parkhead, and in September 1978 joined Motherwell for £50,000.

His stay at Fir Park was brief, and the following summer he moved to Partick Thistle. He eventually went into junior football, playing for Blantyre Celtic from where John Hughes capped him for Junior Scotland against the Republic of Ireland at Irvine Meadow in October 1980.

BILLY HUGHES
Forward

Born: William Hughes, Coatbridge, 30 December 1948
Height: 5ft 9in
Weight: 10st 2lb
Clubs: Coatbridge Juniors; Sunderland; Derby County; Leicester City; Carlisle United; San Jose Earthquakes (United States); Corby Town
Scotland caps: 1
1975 v Sweden (drew 1-1)

Brother of fellow Scottish international John Hughes, who was forced to quit the game through injury, Billy began his career with Sunderland, joining the

Wearsiders from Coatbridge Juniors in December 1965.

After some impressive displays for the club's reserve side, he made his first team debut in a 2-2 draw at home to Liverpool in February 1967, but in his first few seasons with the club, he was limited to making just a handful of appearances. It was 1968-69 when he established himself as a regular member of the Sunderland side, and for the next nine seasons he missed very few games, being ever-present in 1974-75.

Hughes' best season as a goalscorer was 1972-73, when he scored 19 goals in 43 League and Cup games. His total included a hat-trick in a 3-0 home win over Huddersfield Town, and a goal in the 2-1 FA Cup semi-final win over Arsenal at Hillsborough

Billy Hughes

that helped the Wearsiders into the final, where they beat Leeds United. Hughes' other hat-trick for the club came in a 5-1 defeat of Bristol Rovers in September 1974, as he netted 15 goals in the 1974-75 campaign in which he was ever-present.

It was that kind of form that won him his sole international cap when he came on as a substitute for Scotland against Sweden in 1975. After helping his club win promotion to the First Division in 1975-76, Hughes was hampered by injuries and a loss of form, and in September 1977, after scoring 82 goals in 344 games, he was transferred to Derby County.

After a disappointing start at the Baseball Ground, he was just hitting his goalscoring stride when Leicester City manager Frank McLintock tempted him to join Leicester City in their struggle against relegation. Though he failed to prevent their drop into Division Two, he remained at the club for a further season before drifting off for a brief taste of Stateside football.

COLIN JACKSON
Centre-half

Born: Colin MacDonald Jackson, London, 8 October 1946
Height: 6ft 1in
Weight: 12st 5lb
Clubs: Sunnybank Athletic; Glasgow Rangers; Morton; Partick Thistle
Scotland caps: 8
Scotland goals: 1
1975 v Sweden (drew 1-1), v Portugal (won 1-0), v Wales (drew 2-2) 1 goal

1976 v Denmark (won 3-1), v Romania (drew 1-1), v Wales (won 3-1), v N Ireland (won 3-0),
v England (won 2-1)

Never on the losing side in any of his eight internationals, Colin Jackson joined
Rangers from Sunnybank Athletic in Aberdeen, from under the noses of Pittodrie
scouting staff.

The popular centre-half was to give the Ibrox club 20 seasons of sterling
service. Tall, slender and of no great physique, he was an excellent stopper and
a perceptive penalty-area player, who could deny the opposition strikers space
to move and manoeuvre. Outstanding in the air, he was one of the club's most
dependable players. Though he spent some of his time at Ibrox understudying
both Ronnie McKinnon and Derek Johnstone, he was very patient and eventually
became the club's first-choice centre-half.

Without doubt the greatest disappointment of his playing career was failing
a fitness test on the eve of the 1972 European Cup Winners' Cup Final against
Moscow Dynamo in Barcelona, a match Rangers won 3-2. In contrast, probably
the highlight of his long career came in the dying moments of the 1978-79
League Cup Final against Aberdeen, when, with the referee about to blow for
full-time, he headed the winning goal from a corner-kick.

Jackson went on to win three League Championships with Rangers and was
on the winning side in three Scottish Cup Finals and four League Cup Finals.
One of the game's most effective central defenders, he had scored 40 goals in
506 games for Rangers, when in September 1982 he left to play for Morton. A
year later he joined Partick Thistle, but after one season at Firhill, he left the
game to become a partner in an East Kilbride printing firm.

STEWART KENNEDY
Goalkeeper
Born: Stewart James Kennedy, Stirling, 31 August 1949
Height: 6ft 1in
Weight: 11st 5lb
Clubs: Camelon Juniors; Dunfermline Athletic; Linlithgow Rose; Stenhousemuir; Glasgow
Rangers; Forfar Athletic
Scotland caps: 5
1975 v Sweden (drew 1-1), v Portugal (won 1-0), v Wales (drew 2-2), v N Ireland (won 3-0),
v England (lost 1-5)

After making his full international debut against Sweden in Gothenburg in
April 1975, Stewart Kennedy seemed set for a long run in the national side.
Unfortunately he was part of the Scottish defence that was completely overrun
at Wembley as England ran out 5-1 winners, and was never capped again. Many
people involved with the game thought he had been unjustly treated by the
Scottish selectors, and there is no doubt that their decision affected his form,
and he was never quite the same goalkeeper again.

Stewart Kennedy began his Scottish League career with Dunfermline Athletic,
whom he joined from his local club Camelon Juniors in 1967. However, he was

reinstated to junior football with Linlithgow Rose two years later, but then in April 1971 decided to try the senior game again, joining Stenhousemuir.

His displays for the Warriors led to him joining Rangers in the summer of 1973, and he made his debut in a 5-1 win over Falkirk at Brockville. The following season of 1974-75 saw Kennedy play in every game, as Rangers won their first League Championship since 1963-64. However, after that Kennedy shared the goalkeeping duties with Peter McCloy, helping Rangers win the League Cup in 1975-76 and again in 1977-78, when they also won the Championship.

In April 1980, Kennedy, who had appeared in 131 games for Rangers, moved to Forfar Athletic on a free transfer. He continued his career there, still playing for the Loons at the age of 40.

TED MacDOUGALL
Forward

Born: Edward John MacDougall, Inverness, 8 January 1947
Height: 5ft 10in
Weight: 11st 11lb
Clubs: Liverpool; York City; Bournemouth; Manchester United; West Ham United; Norwich City; Southampton; Bournemouth; Blackpool; Salisbury; Poole Town; Gosport Borough
Scotland caps: 7
Scotland goals: 3
1975 v Sweden (drew 1-1) 1 goal, v Portugal (won 1-0), v Wales (drew 2-2),
 v N Ireland (won 3-0) 1 goal, v England (lost 1-5)
1976 v Denmark (won 3-1) 1 goal, v Romania (drew 1-1)

One of the game's most prolific goalscorers, Ted MacDougall netted for Scotland on his full international debut against Sweden in April 1975, and was only on the losing side once in his seven appearances for the national side.

He began his League career with York City, where he first teamed up successfully with Phil Boyer. Then, in the summer of 1969, he left Bootham Crescent to join Third Division Bournemouth. Here, on 24 November 1970 in the FA Cup tie against Oxford, he scored six goals, and a year later he netted nine in an 11-1 win over Margate—still the all-time record. Therefore it is not surprising that all the top flight clubs in England sought his talents.

Accordingly, in September 1972, amid much publicity, MacDougall signed for Manchester United for a fee of £200,000. Although he had scored 103 goals in 146 first team outings for the Dean Court club, paying so much money for a Third Division striker was a big gamble for United manager Frank O'Farrell. In his first few games for United, MacDougall looked out of place in the top flight, although to be fair to him, he was never given much opportunity afterwards to find his feet. He had played in just 18 games for the Old Trafford club when he was transferred to West Ham United—but he was just as unfortunate there.

So, in December 1973, MacDougall moved again, this time to Norwich City, where he top-scored for three seasons in a row. MacDougall's best season for the Canaries in terms of goals scored was 1975-76, when his total of 23

Ted MacDougall playing for Norwich City

goals included hat-tricks in two successive home games against Aston Villa and Everton. In August 1976, having scored 66 goals in 138 games, MacDougall returned to the south coast with Southampton.

He ended his first season at The Dell as the Saints' top scorer with 23 league goals, and in 1977-78 netted 14 as the club won promotion to the First Division. He had scored 47 goals in 101 games for Southampton, when, in November 1978, he returned to Bournemouth before ending his long career with Blackpool.

Later MacDougall, who was the Seasiders' player-coach, came out of retirement to play non-League football for Salisbury, Poole Town and Gosport Borough.

ARTHUR DUNCAN
Outside-left
Born: Arthur Duncan, Falkirk, 5 December 1947
Height: 5ft 9in
Weight: 11st 1lb
Clubs: Gairdoch United; Partick Thistle; Hibernian; Meadowbank Thistle; Livingston
Scotland caps: 6
1975 v Portugal (won 1-0), v Wales (drew 2-2), v N Ireland (won 3-0), v England (lost 1-5),
    v Romania (drew 1-1)
1976 v Denmark (won 1-0)

Arthur Duncan, who won six caps for his country, began his first-class career with Partick Thistle before joining Hibs for a fee of £35,000 in January 1970.

Duncan's pace down the flanks was a trademark of the famous Hibs sides of the early 1970s, and, in a team dubbed 'Turnbull's Tornadoes', his commitment to the Hibs cause saw him make a staggering club record 446 League appearances for the Edinburgh side. Though he was more of a winger than a striker, Duncan scored 112 goals in his time at Easter Road, and in 1975-76 was the club's leading scorer with 16 goals.

On 23 October 1971 he netted four goals against Falkirk, and in the Ne'erday game against Edinburgh rivals Hearts in 1973, he scored twice in a 7-0 rout. As well as scoring a number of vital and spectacular goals, Arthur Duncan did manage to score one of the most infamous own goals. During the second replay of the 1979 Scottish Cup Final, Rangers beat Hibs 3-2 after extra-time, and the Glasgow side's third goal came off the head of the hapless Duncan following a Rangers corner.

Duncan's days at Easter Road finally came to an end during the summer of 1984, though he didn't have too far to travel to continue playing first-class football, joining nearby Meadowbank Thistle.

Though he later qualified as a chiropodist, he continued to maintain his involvement with football, playing on a part-time basis for Livingston.

BRUCE RIOCH
Wing-half
Born: Bruce David Rioch, Aldershot, 6 September 1947
Height: 5ft 11in
Weight: 12st 5lb
Clubs: Luton Town; Aston Villa; Derby County; Everton; Derby County; Birmingham City;
    Sheffield United; Seattle Sounders (United States); Torquay United
Scotland caps: 24
Scotland goals: 6
1975 v Portugal (won 1-0), v Wales (drew 2-2) 1 goal, v N Ireland (won 3-0),

v England (lost 1-5) 1 goal, v Romania (drew 1-1)

1976 v Denmark (won 1-0), v Denmark (won 3-1) 1 goal, v Romania (drew 1-1) 1 goal,
v Wales (won 3-1) 1 goal, v N Ireland (won 3-0), v England (won 2-1)

1977 v Finland (won 6-0) 1 goal, v Czechoslovakia (lost 0-2), v Wales (won 1-0),
v Wales (drew 0-0), v N Ireland (won 3-0), v England (won 2-1), v Chile (won 4-2),
v Brazil (lost 0-2)

1978 v Czechoslovakia (won 3-1), v N Ireland (drew 1-1), v England (lost 0-1),
v Peru (lost 1-3), v Holland (won 3-2)

Bruce Rioch

The only English-born player to captain Scotland in a full international, Bruce Rioch began his career with Luton Town as an out-and-out attacker before switching to inside-forward. When the Hatters won the Fourth Division Championship in 1967-68, Rioch made his mark as the club's leading scorer with 24 goals, as they finished five points clear of runners-up Barnsley.

In 1969, Tommy Docherty brought Bruce and his brother Neil to Aston Villa in a combined £100,000 deal. In 1971 Bruce collected a runners-up award in the League Cup Final, and in 1972 he won a Third Division Championship medal. In February 1974, a £200,000 offer took him to Derby County, and in his first full season with the Rams, he won a League Championship medal. Shortly afterwards he joined Everton, but his stay at Goodison was brief, and within a year he was back at Derby.

In March 1980 he was released by Derby and joined Seattle Sounders in the NASL, alternating this with the position of player-coach at Torquay United.

Appointed manager of Middlesbrough in February 1986, he guided the club out of a dire financial position, lifting them from the Third to the First Division within two seasons. In 1986-87 he helped the club win promotion to the Second Division, and in 1987-88 he took the club into the top flight via the play-offs. But Boro were relegated in 1988-89, and in March 1990, with the club languishing near the foot of the Second Division, Rioch left Ayresome Park.

In less than a month he was in charge of Millwall, and in 1990-91 he took the London club to the Second Division play-offs. After their form slumped the following season, he resigned to manage Bolton Wanderers. He achieved promotion in his first season as the Wanderers finished runners-up in Division Two. In 1994-95 he took the club to the League Cup Final and promotion to the Premiership via the play-offs.

In June 1995 Rioch left Bolton to manage Arsenal, but was sacked after 15 months and joined Queen's Park Rangers. After this he managed Norwich City and Wigan Athletic, parting company with the Latics in 2001.

ALFIE CONN junior
Inside-forward
Born: Alfred James Conn, Kirkcaldy, 5 April 1952
Height: 5ft 10in
Weight: 11st 5lb
Clubs: Musselburgh Windsor; Glasgow Rangers; Tottenham Hotspur; Glasgow Celtic; Pittsburgh Spirit and San Jose Earthquakes (United States); Heart of Midlothian; Blackpool (loan); Motherwell
Scotland caps: 2
1975 v N Ireland (won 3-0), v England (lost 1-5)

Appearing in the Rangers first team when only 16, Alfie Conn won Scottish amateur youth honours before signing professional forms. A member of Rangers' winning teams in the 1971 Scottish League Cup Final and 1973 Scottish Cup Final, he also helped the Ibrox club win the European Cup Winners' Cup in 1972.

In June 1974, Alfie Conn was Bill Nicholson's last signing for Tottenham Hotspur, but the £140,000 capture made just one appearance for the White Hart Lane club before the arrival of new manager Terry Neill. After making his debut as a substitute, Conn scored a hat-trick in a 5-2 win at Newcastle United on what was his full debut.

A natural showman with magical dribbling talents, Conn was always prepared to take a man on and beat him with pure trickery and skill. With his distinctive long curly locks flowing as defenders were left trailing in his wake, Conn quickly gained cult hero status. Though he wasn't helped by a number of injuries that were a direct result of his tantalising style of play, he did win two full caps for Scotland in May 1975, before finding himself languishing in the club's reserve side.

In March 1977 he joined Celtic on loan, with the £60,000 move made permanent after he had satisfied queries about his long-term fitness. He played for the Bhoys in their 1977 Scottish Cup Final success and helped them win the League Championship in both 1977 and 1978.

During the following season he joined Pittsburgh Spirit, and after a year moved to San Jose Earthquakes.

He then returned to Scotland to sign for Hearts. After a loan spell with Blackpool in March 1981, he joined Motherwell, whom he helped win the Scottish First Division title in 1981-82. During the early part of the 1983-84 season he suffered a bad injury that forced his retirement at 32. He then entered management and led the Coatbridge side which won the 1985-86 Scottish Amateur Cup.

JIM BROWN
Goalkeeper
Born: James Grady Brown; Coatbridge; 11 May 1952
Height: 5ft 11in

Weight: 12st 4lb
Clubs: Bargeddie Amateurs; Albion Rovers; Chesterfield; Sheffield United; Detroit Express; Washington Diplomats, Chicago Sting (United States); Cardiff City; Kettering Town; Chesterfield
Scotland caps: 1
1975 v Romania (drew 1-1)

Jim Brown was a precocious talent, making his Scottish League debut for Albion Rovers as a 16-year-old in 1968 after joining the Cliftonhill club from Bargeddie Amateurs. His displays between the posts led to a number of clubs in both Scotland and England showing an interest in him, and in December 1972, Third Division Chesterfield paid £4,000 for his services. In his second season at Saltergate, he helped the Spireites to finish fifth in Division Three, but in the close season, he moved to First Division Sheffield United for a fee of £60,000.

After an impressive first season at Bramall Lane, in which the Blades finished sixth in the top flight, Brown was capped at full international level for Scotland as they drew 1-1 with Romania. He had already made four appearances for Scotland at Under-23 level, all as substitute goalkeeper.

In 1975-76, Sheffield United finished bottom of the First Division, and Brown spent the next three seasons playing Second Division football, until in March 1979, he left to play in the NASL with Detroit Express. He subsequently assisted two other American clubs, Washington Diplomats and Chicago Sting. It was while playing for Washington Diplomats in April 1981 that he became the first goalkeeper to score in the 14-year life of the NASL!

In December 1982 he returned to these shores to play for Cardiff City, but having failed to win a regular place in the Bluebirds' side, he left to play non-League football for Kettering Town.

In the summer of 1983 he rejoined Chesterfield, and, in 1984-85, he was in goal when they won the Fourth Division Championship. During his second spell at Saltergate, Brown became one of the few keepers to score in a Football League match. He is now back at Chesterfield as the club's Commercial Manager.

WILLIE MILLER
Central defender
Born: William Ferguson Miller, Glasgow, 2 May 1955
Height: 5ft 11in
Weight: 11st 8lb
Clubs: Eastercraigs FC; Aberdeen
Scotland caps: 65
Scotland goals: 1
1975 v Romania (drew 1-1)
1978 v Bulgaria (won 2-1)
1980 v Belgium (lost 0-2), v Wales (won 1-0) 1 goal, v England (lost 0-2), v Poland (lost 0-1), v Hungary (lost 1-3)
1981 v Sweden (won 1-0), v Portugal (drew 0-0), v Israel (won 1-0), v N Ireland (drew 1-1),

v Wales (lost 0-2), v N Ireland (won 2-0), v England (won 1-0)

1982 v N Ireland (drew 0-0), v Portugal (lost 1-2), v Holland (won 2-1), v Brazil (lost 1-4),
v USSR (drew 2-2)

1983 v East Germany (won 2-0), v Switzerland (lost 0-2), v Switzerland (drew 2-2),
v Wales (won 2-0), v England (lost 0-2), v Canada (won 2-0), v Canada (won 3-0),
v Canada (won 2-0)

1984 v Uruguay (won 2-0), v Belgium (drew 1-1), v East Germany (lost 1-2),
v Wales (won 2-1), v England (drew 1-1), v France (lost 0-2)

1985 v Yugoslavia (won 6-1), v Iceland (won 3-0), v Spain (won 3-1), v Spain (lost 0-1),
v Wales (lost 0-1), v England (won 1-0), v Iceland (won 1-0)

1986 v Wales (drew 1-1), v East Germany (drew 0-0), v Australia (won 2-0),
v Australia (drew 0-0), v Israel (won 1-0), v Romania (won 3-0), v England (lost 1-2),
v Holland (drew 0-0), v Denmark (lost 0-1), v West Germany (lost 1-2),
v Uruguay (drew 0-0)

1987 v Bulgaria (drew 0-0), v England (drew 0-0), v Brazil (lost 0-2)

1988 v Hungary (won 2-0), v Luxembourg (drew 0-0), v Saudi Arabia (drew 2-2),
v Malta (drew 1-1), v Spain (drew 0-0), v Colombia (drew 0-0), v England (lost 0-1)

1989 v Norway (won 2-1), v Yugoslavia (drew 1-1)

1990 v Yugoslavia (lost 1-3), v Norway (drew 1-1)

In November 1989, tragedy struck when Willie Miller, in his 65th international, a World Cup qualifier against Norway, sustained an injury that effectively was to end his playing career.

When Willie Miller first arrived at Pittodrie, he was signed as a striker, having been spotted playing for Glasgow side, Eastercraigs. In his first season with the Dons, he was farmed out to Peterhead and continued to find the net on a regular basis before being recalled to Aberdeen. After making his debut in a 2-1 win at Morton in April 1973, Miller was converted to a sweeper and from the beginning of the 1973-74 season, became a first team regular.

Appointed the Dons' skipper in December 1975, he lifted his first domestic trophy less than a year later as Aberdeen beat Celtic 2-1 to win the League Cup. Over the next 14 years or so, Willie Miller was to pick up just about every honour the game has to offer.

The greatest highlight of his long and distinguished career came in 1982-83, when he skippered the Dons to European Cup Winners' Cup glory in Gothenburg, but on top of that, there is the European Super Cup, the full set of domestic trophies, numerous Dons' appearance records including 56 League appearances and the winning of the Scottish 'Player of the Year' award.

When his playing days were over, he remained on the Pittodrie coaching staff, but in February 1992, when Alex Smith became the first Aberdeen manager to be formally sacked by the club, Willie Miller stepped into the breach. In his first season in charge, he led the Dons to two domestic Cup Finals, but in each one they were beaten by Rangers 2-1. The Ibrox club also pipped Aberdeen to the League Championship, the Dons finishing as runners-up nine points adrift of Rangers. Aberdeen were runners-up again in 1993-94, but the following season a disastrous run cost him his posts. Nowadays he remains heavily involved in Scottish football through his work in the media.

STEWART HOUSTON

Left-back

Born: Stewart Mackie Houston, Dunoon, 28 August 1949
Height: 5ft 11in
Weight: 11st 8lb
Clubs: Port Glasgow Rangers; Chelsea; Brentford; Manchester United; Sheffield United; Colchester United
Scotland caps: 1
1976 v Denmark (won 3-1)

Stewart Houston's first Football League club was Chelsea, whom he joined in the summer of 1967 when fellow Scot Tommy Docherty was in charge. Docherty left Stamford Bridge two months after Houston had put pen to paper, and the Dunoon-born defender only appeared in a handful of games for the Blues.

In June 1972 he moved to Brentford for a fee of £17,000, and it was his outstanding performances for the Bees which persuaded Docherty, who by now was manager of Manchester United, to buy him for the Old Trafford club for £55,000.

One of several Scots recruited by Docherty in his early days with the club, Houston went straight into the United League side, making his debut against Queen's Park Rangers in what was George Best's last game for the Reds—for the record, United lost 3-0. A regular in the United side for over six seasons, he was a member of the team beaten 1-0 by Southampton in the 1976 FA Cup Final but missed the Final the following year—which United won 2-1 against Liverpool—when he broke an ankle at Ashton Gate only two weeks before the Wembley date.

Houston, who won his only cap for Scotland in a 3-1 win over Denmark in October 1975, went on to score 16 goals in 250 League and Cup games before leaving Old Trafford to join Sheffield United on a free transfer.

A virtual ever-present in his three seasons at Bramall Lane, he later wound down his League career at Colchester United before joining the Arsenal coaching staff in 1990. Houston was at Highbury for six years, helping the Gunners win the League Championship, FA Cup, League Cup and European Cup Winners' Cup before later having a spell as manager of Queen's Park Rangers.

JOHN DOYLE

Outside-right

Born: John Doyle, Uddingston, 1 May 1951
Died: 19 October 1981
Height: 5ft 8in
Weight: 10st 10lb
Clubs: Viewpark FC; Ayr United; Glasgow Celtic
Scotland caps: 1
1976 v Romania (drew 1-1)

Winger John Doyle began his career with Ayr United, whom he joined from Viewpark FC in the summer of 1970. Able to play on either flank, Doyle's form earned him selection for the Scotland Under-23 side, and it wasn't long before he was capped at full international level. It was Doyle's cross that was converted by the unmarked Bruce Rioch to earn Scotland a 1-1 draw against Romania. Soon scouts from the country's leading sides were regular visitors to Somerset Park.

Noted for his exceptional speed, John Doyle also had a temper, and was under suspension when Celtic paid a club record £90,000 to secure his services at Glasgow Airport on the way to East Germany to play Sachsenring.

He soon became a great favourite with the Celtic faithful, though when the Bhoys won the League Championship against Rangers at Parkhead in May 1979, he received his marching orders. Celtic won the title with 10 men, because in a moment of madness early in the second-half, John Doyle kicked Alex Macdonald as he was lying prone with Rangers leading 1-0. Stunned with remorse, he could barely be persuaded to join in the after-match celebrations. He was a virtual ever-present in the Celtic side until the arrival of Dave Provan, but having scored 36 goals in 180 games, he was electrocuted in a domestic accident, aged just 30.

Celtic played Ipswich Town at Portman Road the following month, and the fans staged a spontaneous two minutes silence for John Doyle in the centre of the Suffolk town.

ANDY GRAY
Forward

Born: Andrew Mullen Gray, Glasgow, 30 November 1955
Height: 5ft 11in
Weight: 11st 13lb
Clubs: Clydebank Strollers; Dundee United; Aston Villa; Wolverhampton Wanderers; Everton; Aston Villa; Notts County; West Bromwich Albion
Scotland caps: 20
Scotland goals: 7

1976 v Romania (drew 1-1), v Switzerland (won 1-0)
1977 v Finland (won 6-0) 2 goals, v Czechoslovakia (lost 0-2)
1979 v Austria (lost 2-3) 1 goal, v Norway (won 3-2)
1980 v Portugal (won 4-1) 1 goal, v England (lost 0-2)
1981 v Sweden (won 1-0), v Portugal (drew 0-0), v Israel (won 1-0), v N Ireland (drew 1-1)
1982 v Sweden (won 2-0), v N Ireland (drew 0-0)
1983 v N Ireland (drew 0-0), v Wales (won 2-0) 1 goal, v England (lost 0-2), v Canada (won 3-0), v Canada (won 2-0) 2 goals
1985 v Iceland (won 1-0)

One of the bravest strikers of his generation, Andy Gray began his career with Dundee United, scoring 44 goals in 76 games for the Tannadice club before moving to Aston Villa for £110,000 in September 1975.

In 1976-77, when Villa finished fourth in Division One and beat Everton in the League Cup Final, Gray was the club's leading scorer with 29 goals. He

Andy Gray in his Everton days

became the first man in the history of the game to receive both the 'Player of the Year' and the 'Young Player of the Year' awards in the same season from the PFA.

After four years at Villa Park, he moved to Wolverhampton Wanderers for a British record fee of £1.5 million. However, his career seemed to be going nowhere at Molineux, and Everton manager Howard Kendall was able to secure his services for just £250,000 in November 1983.

Gray was prone to injury, and many considered him too old when he arrived at Goodison Park. He soon went on to display a new zest for the game, proving to be an important and exciting capture. A very special relationship was forged between Andy Gray and the Everton fans, as he became one of the inspirational figures behind the Blues' great eighties revival.

In the 1984 FA Cup Final against Watford, he scored one of the goals in Everton's 2-0 triumph. Many people thought he had fouled Hornets' keeper Steve Sherwood when he jumped for the ball in front of the posts, but as the video shows, Gray never touched him. After playing his part in the League Championship success of 1984-85 and the European Cup Winners' Cup victory over Rapid Vienna in Rotterdam, where he scored the first goal in a 3-1 defeat of the Austrian side, Gray was dramatically recalled into the Scotland side, eventually ending with 20 full caps to his name.

In July 1985 he was allowed to return to Aston Villa. Though his stay at Goodsion was comparatively short, he scored some crucial goals and inspired all those around him.

After a loan spell at Notts County, Gray joined West Bromwich Albion, but retired shortly after his arrival at the Hawthorns. He returned to Villa Park for a third time in 1991 as assistant-manager to Ron Atkinson, but resigned a year later to pursue a career in television with Sky Sports.

DES BREMNER
Midfield

Born: Desmond George Bremner, Aberchirder, 7 September 1952
Height: 5ft 10in
Weight: 11st 11lb
Clubs: Deverondale; Hibernian; Aston Villa; Birmingham City; Fulham; Walsall; Stafford Rangers
Scotland caps: 1
1976 v Switzerland (won 1-0)

Des Bremner played his early football for Deverondale, joining Hibernian from the Highland League club in November 1972. Slotting into the right-back role after John Brownlie suffered a broken leg, he moved into midfield and helped Hibs reach the Scottish League Cup Final of 1974, where they lost 6-3 to Celtic. Sandwiched in between this and the 1979 Scottish Cup Final when Hibs lost to Rangers 3-2 after two goalless draws—part of the triple header—he won his only Scottish cap against Switzerland in 1976 when he came on as a substitute for Kenny Dalglish.

Des Bremner

Joining Aston Villa in September 1979, Des Bremner went on to appear in 107 consecutive league games after making his Villa debut in a goalless draw with Arsenal. During the course of that run, Villa won the League Championship, and with Bremner's tireless play a great feature of their game, went on to win the European Cup and European Super Cup.

In October 1984, after appearing in 226 first team games for Villa, he moved to Birmingham City. His first season at St Andrew's saw the Blues win promotion to the First Division as runners-up to champions Oxford United. Over the next five seasons, Bremner was a first team regular at St Andrew's, playing in 195 games for the club. He later had spells with Fulham and Walsall, before ending his playing career with non-League Stafford Rangers.

TOMMY CRAIG
Midfield

Born: Thomas Brooks Craig, Penilee, Glasgow, 21 November 1950
Height: 5ft 7in
Weight: 11st 7lb
Clubs: Drumchapel Amateurs; Aberdeen; Sheffield Wednesday; Newcastle United; Aston Villa; Swansea City; Carlisle United; Hibernian
Scotland caps: 1
1976 v Switzerland (won 1-0)

Spotted playing for Drumchapel Amateurs, it looked at one time as if the talented left-footed Tommy Craig would be joining Celtic, but Aberdeen boss Bobby Calder kept chipping and eventually he signed for the Pittodrie club.

After making his debut against Stirling Albion in December 1967, he played for a season and half for the Dons before, still a teenager, he became the first Scottish player to be transferred to an English club for a six-figure fee.

Joining Sheffield Wednesday in May 1969, he was somewhat unlucky to arrive at Hillsborough when the Owls were struggling. Yet Craig's educated left foot both created and scored some vital goals. Made captain of the Scotland Under-23 side, he went on to make 233 appearances over the next six seasons, before he was transferred to Newcastle United at the tail end of 1974.

He was capped by Scotland when at St James Park, as he became an influential United player. Replacing the popular but injured Terry Hibbitt in Newcastle's midfield, he also displaced Geoff Nulty as skipper of the Magpies' Wembley eleven in 1976. Craig also captained his national side at Under-21 and Under-23 level.

Craig left Newcastle in January 1978, joining Aston Villa for a fee of £270,000. A year later he moved to Swansea City, but after three seasons at the Vetch, he found himself at Carlisle United, where he also enjoyed his first taste of football management.

John Blackley, then Hibs boss, persuaded him to return to Scotland as his assistant in 1984, and three years later he took up a similar post with Celtic. His career then went full circle, when in 1995 he rejoined Aberdeen as Roy Aitken's assistant. Following his dismissal along with Aitken in November 1997, Tommy Craig joined another of his former clubs, Newcastle United, as their youth team coach.

Tommy Craig

FRANK GRAY

Left-back

Born: Francis Tierney Gray, Castlemilk, Glasgow, 27 October 1954
Height: 5ft 10in
Weight: 11st 10lb
Clubs: Leeds United; Nottingham Forest; Leeds United; Sunderland; Darlington
Scotland caps: 32
Scotland goals: 1

1976 v Switzerland (won 1-0)
1979 v Norway (won 3-2), v Portugal (lost 0-1), v Wales (lost 0-3), v N Ireland (won 1-0),
  v England (lost 1-3), v Argentina (lost 1-3)
1980 v Belgium (lost 0-2)
1981 v Sweden (won 1-0), v Portugal (drew 0-0), v Israel (won 1-0), v N Ireland (drew 1-1),
  v Israel (won 3-1), v Wales (lost 0-2), v N Ireland (won 2-0), v England (won 1-0)
1982 v Sweden (won 2-0), v N Ireland (drew 0-0), v Portugal (lost 1-2), v Spain (lost 0-3),
  v Holland (won 2-1) 1 goal, v Wales (won 1-0), v New Zealand (won 5-2),
  v Brazil (lost 1-4), v USSR (drew 2-2)
1983 v East Germany (won 2-0), v Switzerland (lost 0-2), v Belgium (lost 2-3),
  v Switzerland (drew 2-2), v Wales (won 2-0), v England (lost 0-2), v Canada (won 3-0)

Although not as gifted as his elder brother Eddie, Frank Gray won 32 caps for Scotland and was their left-back in the 1982 World Cup Finals in Spain.

Frank Gray

A former Parkhead ball-boy, Frank Gray joined Leeds United in the summer of 1970, after the Yorkshire club signed him in the face of stiff competition from a number of other clubs. He turned professional in 1971, and scored on his full debut as Leeds beat Crystal Palace 4-0—in doing so, he emulated another feat of Eddie's. At Elland Road he won five Scottish Under-23 caps before switching from a deep midfield role to left-back. He often played in the same Leeds side as his brother, providing United with a very solid left side.

In July 1979, Leeds banked a then club record £500,000 when he moved to

Nottingham Forest. Under Brian Clough, Gray enjoyed the best years of his career. After making his Forest debut in a 1-0 win at Ipswich Town on the opening day of the 1979-80 season, he went on to play in 118 League and Cup games in two seasons at the City Ground. Also with Forest, in 1980 he won a European Cup winners' medal to go with the loser's one he got with Leeds in 1975.

Returning to Leeds in 1981, Gray was a regular in the United side for a further four seasons, taking his total of first team appearances to 401, before being transferred by his brother Eddie, who was then Leeds manager, to Sunderland for £100,000.

He helped the Wearsiders win promotion from Division Three before being appointed player/assistant-manager at Darlington. He helped steer the Quakers back to the Fourth Division as champions of the GM Vauxhall Conference in 1990. He remained at the Feethams for a further two years, later scouting for Blackburn and Sheffield Wednesday before managing Harrogate Town. He later resigned to take charge of Al Manamah in Bahrain. His son Andy, who now plays for Sheffield United, became the latest of the Gray clan to play for Leeds United.

ALEX MacDONALD
Wing-half/ Inside-forward
Born: Alexander MacDonald, Glasgow, 17 March 1948
Height: 5ft 6in
Weight: 10st 10lb
Clubs: Glasgow United; St Johnstone; Glasgow Rangers; Heart of Midlothian
Scotland caps: 1
1976 v Switzerland (won 1-0)

Alex MacDonald started out with St Johnstone before signing for Rangers in November 1968. A widely respected wing-half, he was a member of the Rangers team that won the European Cup Winners' Cup in 1972, beating Moscow Dynamo 3-2 in the final. The winner of three League Championship medals in 1974-75, 1975-76 and 1977-78, he was also on the winning side in four Scottish Cup Finals and three League Cup Finals. His form for Rangers during that period was such that he won full international honours, playing in the 1-0 defeat of Switzerland at Hampden in April 1976.

In 1980 he left Ibrox to join Hearts for a fee of £30,000. A player of total commitment, he was tigerish in the tackle and could pass the ball with great accuracy. Also able to chip in with the odd goal, he took over the captaincy of Hearts on his arrival at Tynecastle, but even he couldn't stem the tide—Hearts finished bottom of the Premier League and were relegated.

In January 1982, Alex MacDonald was given the role of player-manager. Hearts missed out on promotion by just one point but he was slowly turning things round at Tynecastle and they secured promotion the following season. MacDonald had played in 181 games for Hearts when he decided to hang up his boots and concentrate on management. He took the Tynecastle club into Europe in 1984, and two years later to the verge of the Premiership title. After taking Hearts to runners-up in 1987-88, and to third the season after, he was surprisingly sacked in 1990.

He later went on to success with Airdrie, taking them to two Scottish Cup Finals in 1992 and 1995 and to the runners-up spot in the First Division in 1996-97.

BOBBY McKEAN
Outside-right / Midfield

Born: Robert Munro McKean, East Kilbride, 8 December 1952
Died: Barrhead 15 March 1978
Height: 5ft 10in
Weight: 11st 4lb
Clubs: Blantyre Victoria; St Mirren; Glasgow Rangers
Scotland caps: 1
1976 v Switzerland (won 1-0)

Bobby McKean's only international appearance was as a substitute for goalscorer Willie Pettigrew, in a 1-0 defeat of Switzerland at Hampden Park in April 1976.

A product of the junior club Blantyre Victoria, he then joined St Mirren, and played for the Love Street club as an outside-right. His consistent displays led to a number of Scotland's top clubs showing an interest, and, in September 1974, Rangers paid £60,000 for his services.

Converted into a midfielder, he could play on either side of the team and became one of the most competent players on the Rangers staff. A skilful player who could go off on mazy dribbles, he was also a purposeful, strong all-rounder who could score goals. Forming a particularly effective right-wing partnership with Tommy McLean, he was a huge success in the club's League Championship winning season of 1974-75.

His form led to him being selected for the Scottish League XI prior to him making his full international debut. He was a key player again the following season as Rangers retained the title, but then inconsistency crept in and cost him his first team place.

Although he remained a useful squad member, he began to get distracted by problems off the field, and on 15 March 1978, Bobby McKean was found dead in his car, beside his home in Barrhead. He had committed suicide.

WILLIE PETTIGREW
Centre-forward

Born: William Pettigrew, Motherwell, 29 September 1953
Height: 5ft 11in
Weight: 11st 0lb
Clubs: East Kilbride Thistle; Motherwell; Dundee United; Heart of Midlothian; Morton; Hamilton Academicals

Scotland caps: 5
Scotland goals: 2
1976 v Switzerland (won 1-0) 1 goal, v Wales (won 3-1) 1 goal, v N Ireland (won 3-0)
1977 v Wales (won 1-0), v Sweden (won 3-1)

Willie Pettigrew was a gifted striker, who, following a brief spell in the Scottish Under-21 side, made a scoring debut for the full national side in a 1-0 win over Switzerland. He scored on his next outing too, as Scotland beat Wales 3-1, and can consider himself most unlucky to win just five Scotland caps.

As a youngster he was rejected by Hibernian, and so played his early football for East Kilbride Thistle, before joining Motherwell in 1973. He made his first-team debut in October 1974 as a substitute against St Johnstone, but it was towards the end of that 1973-74 season that he made his breakthrough, netting in the games against Morton, Dumbarton and Falkirk.

He then formed a prolific goalscoring partnership with former Liverpool ace Bobby Graham, and in 1974-75 scored 20 goals, including four in a 5-1 defeat of Ayr United. The following season he was second only to Kenny Dalglish in the Premier League scoring charts, while in 1976-77 he led the way with 21 goals.

Pettigrew was a member of Motherwell sides that reached semi-finals in both the Scottish and Texaco Cups, and in April 1978 he played for the Scottish League against Italy 'B' in Verona. Six months later he represented the Scottish League against the Irish League at Fir Park, and scored Scotland's goal in a 1-1 draw.

In May 1979, after having scored 80 goals in 166 games, he left Motherwell to join Dundee United for £100,000. In his first season at Tannadice he scored 14 goals, including four in a dramatic Scottish Cup derby win over Dundee! He also scored twice in the final as United beat Aberdeen 3-0 after a goalless draw, to pick up their first piece of silverware. The following season he collected another League Cup winners' medal as Dundee were beaten 3-0.

Pettigrew, who later had spells with Hearts, Morton and Hamilton, was a natural goalscorer, who relied on pace and speed of thought for the majority of his goals.

ALAN ROUGH
Goalkeeper

Born: Alan Roderick Rough, Glasgow, 25 November 1951
Height: 6ft 1in
Weight: 13st 5lb
Clubs: Lincoln Amateurs; Partick Thistle; Hibernian; Glasgow Celtic; Hamilton Academicals; Ayr United
Scotland caps: 53
1976 v Switzerland (won 1-0), v Wales (won 3-1), v N Ireland (won 3-0), v England (won 2-1)
1977 v Finland (won 6-0), v Czechoslovakia (lost 0-2), v Wales (won 1-0),
     v Sweden (won 3-1), v Wales (drew 0-0), v N Ireland (won 3-0), v England (won 2-1),
     v Chile (won 4-2), v Argentina (drew 1-1), v Brazil (lost 0-2)
1978 v Czechoslovakia (won 3-1), v Wales (won 2-0), v N Ireland (drew 1-1),

v England (lost 0-1), v Peru (lost 1-3), v Iran (drew 1-1), v Holland (won 3-2)

1979 v Austria (lost 2-3), v Portugal (lost 0-1), v Wales (lost 0-3), v Argentina (lost 1-3),
      v Norway (won 4-0)

1980 v Peru (drew 1-1), v Austria (drew 1-1), v Belgium (lost 0-2), v Belgium (lost 1-3),
      v Portugal (won 4-1), v Wales (won 1-0), v England (lost 0-2), v Poland (lost 0-1),
      v Hungary (lost 1-3)

1981 v Sweden (won 1-0), v Portugal (drew 0-0), v Israel (won 1-0), v N Ireland (drew 1-1),
      v Israel (won 3-1), v Wales (lost 0-2), v England (won 1-0)

1982 v Sweden (won 2-0), v N Ireland (drew 0-0), v Spain (lost 0-3), v Holland (won 2-1),
      v Wales (won 1-0), v England (lost 0-1), v New Zealand (won 5-2), v Brazil (lost 1-4),
      v USSR (drew 2-2)

1986 v Wales (drew 1-1), v England (lost 1-2)

Alan Rough made the first of his 53 international appearances for Scotland against Switzerland at Hampden Park in April 1976. Though he was only the fifth-choice keeper named to face the Swiss, he had an outstanding game in a 1-0 win. He then went on to miss only ten games in the next six years and established himself as a goalkeeper of the highest quality. When he went to Mexico in 1986, it meant he had been in three successive World Cup Finals' squads.

A model of reliability, and an answer to those who claimed that the Scots could not produce a top-class goalkeeper, Alan Rough began his first-class career with Partick Thistle, whom he joined from Glasgow side Lincoln Amateurs in the summer of 1968.

In his early days at Firhill, he helped the Jags win promotion to the First Division, finishing champions of the Second Division in 1970-71, five points clear of East Fife. The following season, Rough was in fine form as Thistle won the Scottish League Cup beating Celtic 4-1. In 1975-76, Rough had an outstanding season, helping Partick Thistle win the First Division Championship. Rough, who appeared in 410 league games for Thistle, had that essential quality required in all the great goalkeepers, flair combined with reliability and confident unflappability.

The left-handed Rough was a cool performer and not averse to using his feet—he even took on Kevin Keegan in one Hampden dribble. When Scotland reached the 1978 World Cup Finals in Argentina, Rough was the only part-timer in the Scottish squad, yet he was one of the key performers and his save from John Toshack at Anfield was crucial to Scotland's progression to those finals.

In 1980-81 Rough was voted the Scottish 'Footballer of the Year' and his save in the 1-0 win over Israel went a long way in helping Scotland reach the 1982 World Cup Finals in Spain.

On his return to Scotland, Rough left Firhill to join Hibernian. It was an inspired signing, and during his five seasons with the club he showed he was still in contention for more international caps as the most experienced deputy for Jim Leighton. In Cardiff, on the night Jock Stein died, he played the second-half in another crucial World Cup game.

In April 1988, at the age of 36, Rough joined Celtic as emergency cover. Spells thereafter at Hamilton Academicals and Ayr United were followed by a move into management with Ayrshire junior club, Glenafton.

Alan Rough

DON MASSON
Wing-half/ Inside-forward

Born: Donald Sandison Masson, Banchory, 26 August 1946
Height: 5ft 8in
Weight: 10st 12lb
Clubs: Middlesbrough; Notts County; Queen's Park Rangers; Derby County; Notts County; Minnesota Kicks (United States); Bulova (Hong Kong); Kettering Town

Scotland caps: 17
Scotland goals: 5
1976 v Wales (won 3-1), v N Ireland (won 3-0) 1 goal, v England (won 2-1) 1 goal
1977 v Finland (won 6-0) 1 goal, v Czechoslovakia (lost 0-2), v Wales (drew 0-0),
       v N Ireland (won 3-0), v England (won 2-1), v Chile (won 4-2),
       v Argentina (drew 1-1) 1 goal, v Brazil (lost 0-2)
1978 v East Germany (lost 0-1), v Czechoslovakia (won 3-1), v Wales (won 2-0) 1 goal,
       v N Ireland (drew 1-1), v England (lost 0-1), v Peru (lost 1-3)

Don Masson

Don Masson, who scored three goals in his first four internationals, was approaching 30 when he made his debut against Wales in May 1976. He was a regular in the Scotland side for the next couple of years, making his last appearance against Peru in the 1978 World Cup Finals.

A dour, strong-tackling but highly creative midfield player, he began his career with Middlesbrough before leaving Ayresome Park in September 1968 to join Notts County for just £6,000. He helped the Meadow Lane side climb from the Fourth to the Second Division during his time with the club, his performances persuading Queens Park Rangers to pay £100,000 for his services in December 1974.

Another signing who underlined the quality of Dave Sexton's judgement, he had four good years with Rangers, winning the first of his 17 international caps two years after arriving at Loftus Road. He played an important role in Rangers finishing the 1975-76 season as runners-up to Liverpool, just one point adrift of the Reds. He went on to score 24 goals in 144 games for Rangers before, in October 1977, he moved to Derby County in exchange for Leighton James.

It was a bad deal for Derby. James was valued at £300,000, and after a disappointing season at the Baseball Ground, he rejoined Notts County on a free transfer. With the Magpies he took part in a third promotion to the First Division in 1980-81, and before leaving to try his luck in North American football with Minnesota Kicks, had taken his tally of League appearances, in which he scored 92 goals, to 403.

After a spell as player-manager of Kettering Town, he managed the sports complex at Notts County, before remaining in Nottingham as owner of the Gallery Hotel.

JOE CRAIG
Forward

Born: Joseph Craig, Bridge of Allan, 14 May 1954
Height: 6ft 0in
Weight: 12st 7lb
Clubs: Sauchie FC; Partick Thistle; Glasgow Celtic; Blackburn Rovers; Hamilton Academicals
Scotland caps: 1
Scotland goals: 1
1977 v Sweden (won 3-1) 1 goal

Joe Craig's only international appearance for Scotland was as a substitute for Kenny Burns in the match against Sweden in April 1977. He is the only Scottish player to score before he'd even kicked the ball—his first touch was a header as Scotland beat the Swedes 3-1.

He was a motor mechanic in Bathgate, and though he was much admired for his football skills by the Football League's leading managers of the day—Bill Shankly at Liverpool and Bill Nicholson at Spurs—it was Partick Thistle manager Bertie Auld who secured his signature, telling the young Craig he would be better off at Firhill. His impressive displays for the Jags, which led to him representing the Scottish League, persuaded Celtic manager Jock Stein to sign him as a replacement for Dixie Deans.

An old-fashioned type of centre-forward, his first season at Parkhead was his best. He helped Celtic to win the League and Cup double, netting 34 goals during the campaign when the Bhoys finished nine points ahead of Rangers, whom they also beat in the Scottish Cup Final. He then seemed to go off the boil, and in September 1978, after scoring 37 goals in 72 games, he went south of the border to play for Blackburn Rovers.

Though he wasn't as prolific at Ewood Park, netting just eight goals in 48 games, he did help Rovers win promotion to the Second Division before returning to Scotland to continue his career with Hamilton Academicals. Unfortunately most of his time with the Accies saw him on the treatment table, and in 1983 he was forced to retire.

He was later a very popular manager with Cowdenbeath, losing his job at Central Park as a result of a boardroom coup. In consequence, the majority of his 18-strong playing staff voted to boycott pre-season training!

RONNIE GLAVIN
Midfield

Born: Ronald Michael Glavin, Glasgow, 27 March 1951
Height: 5ft 10in
Weight: 11st 6lb
Clubs: Lochend Rovers; Partick Thistle; Glasgow Celtic; Barnsley; Beleneuses (Portugal); Stockport County; Cowdenbeath; St Louis Steamers (United States)
Scotland caps: 1
1977 v Sweden (won 3-1)

Ronnie Glavin's only full cap for the national side came against Sweden in April 1977, but an injury in only the third minute when he was replaced by Sandy Jardine forced him to miss the Scottish Cup Final against Rangers a fortnight later, a match Celtic won 1-0.

He began his career with Partick Thistle, and after netting a hat-trick for the Jags' reserve side against Celtic, forced his way into the club's first team. He was an important member of the Thistle side for almost six seasons, going on to win a League Cup winners' medal in October 1971 as the Jags beat the mighty Celtic 4-1. Though Rangers' manager Willie Wallace was interested in taking him to Ibrox, Glavin was Roman Catholic, and so it was to Celtic that he moved in November 1974.

He scored on his debut in a 6-0 demolition of Airdrie, though, until the arrival of Pat Stanton, much of his early time at Parkhead required him to do his fair share of marking. In 1976-7, in a free-running role as successor to Tommy Callaghan, he fed off the chances created by Joe Craig and Kenny Dalglish, and his goals went a long way to helping Celtic win the double. Glavin went on to score 48 goals in 149 games before joining Barnsley for a fee of £50,000 in the summer of 1979.

Glavin spent five seasons as a player at Oakwell. Enjoying more of an attacking role, he scored 73 goals in 176 games, with many of his strikes being spectacular long-range goals. His consistency in the middle of the park was a major factor in the Tykes winning promotion to the Second Division in 1980-81. On leaving Oakwell he went on to play for Portuguese side Beleneuses, before returning to Barnsley as coach.

He later had a spell as player-coach of Stockport County, and appeared for Cowdenbeath on a match-to-match contract before playing indoor football for his brother Tony's team in the United States.

DAVID NAREY

Central defender
Born: David Narey, Dundee, 12 June 1956
Height: 6ft 0in
Weight: 12st 6lb
Clubs: Dundee United; Raith Rovers
Scotland caps: 35
Scotland goals: 1
1977 v Sweden (won 3-1)
1979 v Portugal (lost 0-1), v N Ireland (won 1-0), v Argentina (lost 1-3)
1980 v Portugal (won 4-1), v N Ireland (lost 0-1), v Poland (lost 0-1), v Hungary (lost 1-3)
1981 v Wales (lost 0-2), v England (won 1-0)
1982 v Holland (won 2-1), v Wales (won 1-0), v England (lost 0-1), v New Zealand (won 5-2), v Brazil (lost 1-4) 1 goal, v USSR (drew 2-2)
1983 v East Germany (won 2-0), v Switzerland (lost 0-2), v Belgium (lost 2-3), v N Ireland (drew 0-0), v Wales (won 2-0), v England (lost 0-2), v Canada (won 2-0), v Canada (won 3-0), v Canada (won 2-0)

1986 v Israel (won 1-0), v Romania (won 3-0), v Holland (drew 0-0),
v West Germany (lost 1-2), v Uruguay (drew 0-0)
1987 v Bulgaria (drew 0-0), v Republic of Ireland (drew 0-0), v Belgium (lost 1-4)
1989 v Italy (lost 0-2), v Cyprus (won 3-2)

David Narey, who was Dundee United's first-ever Scottish international, winning the first of his 35 caps against Sweden in April 1977, was a regular in the national side for almost ten years.

He made the first of his 612 Scottish League appearances for the Tannadice club against Falkirk in November 1973, a match United won 2-1. After that, Narey was a virtual ever-present in the United side for the next 18 seasons, missing very few games in the process. He was part of the League Championship-winning side of 1982-83, and shared in two League Cup victories against Aberdeen in 1979-80, and against local rivals Dundee in 1980-81.

Narey, who scored a most spectacular goal to give Scotland the lead in the World Cup match against Brazil in Seville in June 1982, also netted some vital goals at club level, and had his best season in 1975-76 when he found the net six times.

Narey, who, with the exception of the 1990-91 season, stayed remarkably free from injury, appeared in a total of 856 League and Cup games for the Tannadice club, and this included 76 matches in Europe, a record for a Scottish player. In November 1992, Narey was, quite rightly, awarded the MBE for his services to Dundee United and Scottish football in general.

In May 1994 he was given a free transfer and joined Raith Rovers, helping manager Jimmy Nicholl win the Coca-Cola Cup with a penalty shoot-out victory over Celtic after the game had ended all-square at 2-2, and promotion to the Premier League as First Division Champions.

In February 1998, Narey returned to his beloved Tannadice as Dundee United's first team coach, before later parting company with the club.

JIM STEWART
Goalkeeper
Born: James Garven Stewart, Kilwinning, 9 March 1954
Height: 6ft 2in
Weight: 13st 4lb
Clubs: Troon Juniors; Kilmarnock; Middlesbrough; Glasgow Rangers; Dumbarton; St Mirren; Partick Thistle
Scotland caps: 2
1977 v Chile (won 4-2)
1979 v Norway (won 3-2)

Jim Stewart became Kilmarnock's first-choice goalkeeper when he was only 18 years old, making his debut in a 2-1 home win over Rangers in September 1972. During his time at Rugby Park, he was capped by Scotland at youth, Under-21 and Under-23 level, before winning his first full cap as a substitute for Alan Rough in the match against Chile in Santiago in June 1977.

The following summer, having appeared in 226 games for Killie, Stewart joined Middlesbrough who paid £110,000 to take him to Ayresome Park. Yet this brave and agile keeper had to spend much of his time on Teeside as understudy to the club's Northern Ireland international keeper Jim Platt.

In March 1981, Rangers manager John Greig splashed out £115,000 to bring Stewart to Ibrox Park. Three days after putting pen to paper, he made his Rangers debut in a 4-1 home defeat at the hands of Dundee United. However, at the end of the season, Stewart was a member of the Rangers side that reversed the scoreline as they beat Dundee United in the Scottish Cup Final. When Stewart and Rangers won a League Cup medal the following season, the Tannadice club were again Rangers' opponents.

Facing stiff opposition from Peter McCloy, Stewart was blamed for the loss of 'away' goals to Dukla Prague at Ibrox in September 1981 and to Cologne at Ibrox the following year. In fact, the goal scored by the German side should never have been allowed, as it came from a free-kick by Allofs who actually played the ball twice!

Stewart's form began to suffer after this, and midway through the 1983-84 season, he went on loan to Dumbarton. However, in June 1984 after being given a free transfer by Rangers, he joined St Mirren as understudy to Campbell Money. Stewart was in goal on the final day of the 1985-86 season when Celtic beat St Mirren 5-0 at Love Street, a result that allowed them to win the Championship!

After a spell with Partick Thistle, he joined the M.O.D Police and coached on a part-time basis before giving up the police to coach full-time for Kilmarnock, while occasionally turning out for the Rugby Park club's reserves. After then coaching with several other clubs, he returned to Killie as the club's goalkeeping coach, a position he later held in the Scottish international set-up.

ARTHUR GRAHAM
Outside-left
Born: Arthur Graham, Castlemilk, Glasgow, 26 October 1952
Height: 5ft 8in
Weight: 11st 3lb
Clubs: Cambuslang Rangers; Aberdeen; Leeds United; Manchester United; Bradford City
Scotland caps: 10
Scotland goals: 2
1978 v East Germany (lost 0-1)
1979 v Austria (lost 2-3), v Norway (won 3-2), v Wales (lost 0-3),
      v N Ireland (won 1-0) 1 goal, v England (lost 1-3), v Argentina (lost 1-3) 1 goal,
      v Norway (won 4-0)
1980 v Peru (drew 1-1), v Austria (drew 1-1)

Discovered playing for Cambuslang Rangers, the 17-year-old winger found himself thrown in at the deep end by Aberdeen manager Eddie Turnbull when he came on as a substitute for Derek McKay, in a 2-0 win over Dunfermline

Athletic in March 1970. Three weeks later he helped Aberdeen beat Celtic 3-1 to lift the Scottish Cup!

Graham was a virtual ever-present in the Aberdeen side for the next seven seasons, picking up a League Cup winners' medal in 1976 after the Dons had defeated Celtic 2-1 in the final. He went on to score 46 goals in over 300 League and Cup appearances, with two of his strikes in European competitions worthy of special note. In September 1970 he fired the opener in the 3-1 Pittodrie win over Honved in the first round of the European Cup Winners' Cup, while three years later, in the UEFA Cup, he scored a superb individual goal over Irish outfit Finn Harps.

Recognised at Under-23 and Scottish League level while at Pittodrie, he was transferred to Leeds United for £125,000 in the summer of 1977.

Arthur Graham

The direct winger netted three hat-tricks for Leeds, including a quickfire effort at Birmingham in January 1978. After United slumped, he spent just one more season at Elland Road, going on to score 47 goals in 280 games before a surprise £50,000 transfer to Manchester United.

Graham revitalised his career there, and after winning 10 caps while with Leeds, found that there was speculation about a Scotland recall, until he lost his place to Danish international Jesper Olsen.

He then joined Bradford City, and took over as reserve and junior coach when he retired in February 1987. In 1990 he was promoted to assistant-manager and first team coach when Terry Yorath was sacked. On leaving Valley Parade, he became a physiotherapist.

DAVID STEWART
Goalkeeper
Born: David Steel Stewart, Glasgow, 11 March 1947
Height: 6ft 1in
Weight: 12st 10lb
Clubs: Wellshot; Shettleston Violet; Kilsyth Rangers; Ayr United; Leeds United; West Bromwich Albion; Swansea City; Ryoden FC (Hong Kong)
Scotland caps: 1
1978 v East Germany (lost 0-1)

David Stewart

While with Leeds United, David Stewart was good enough to win a full Scottish cap against East Germany, giving the Yorkshire club two Scottish international keepers on their books. Though the East Germans won 1-0, Stewart marked his full international debut with a penalty save!

Stewart played his early football for local Glasgow sides Wellshot, Shettleston Violet and Kilsyth Rangers, winning a Scottish Junior Cup medal with the latter club in 1967. On leaving school, Stewart worked as an upholsterer and carpet fitter, joining Ayr United on a part-time basis. Some excellent displays for the Somerset Park club led to him being capped by Scotland at Under-23 level.

A number of top English clubs showed an interest in the Ayr keeper, but it was Leeds United who won the race for his signature, paying £30,000 to secure his services in October 1973. Although he had to play second fiddle to David Harvey for most of his time at Elland Road, Stewart played in the Leeds side that met Bayern Munich in the European Cup Final of 1975. The game was played in Paris, but it was a match in which United's luck deserted them. They had two penalty appeals rejected, and when Peter Lorimer thundered a 66th minute volley past Maier, only to have it disallowed because skipper Billy Bremner had strayed offside, they knew it wasn't going to be their night. Stewart had a fine game, but could do little to prevent the Germans scoring twice through Roth and Muller.

When Harvey won back his Leeds place, Stewart was sold to West Bromwich Albion for a fee of £70,000. Unable to settle at the Hawthorns, he joined Swansea City in February 1980, helping the Vetch Field club win the Welsh

Cup in 1981. At the end of the following season he went to play for Ryoden FC in Hong Kong, later working as a goldsmith in Swansea.

JIM BLYTH
Goalkeeper

Jim Blyth

Born: James Anton Blyth, Perth, 2 February 1955
Height: 6ft 2in
Weight: 13st 3lb
Clubs: Perth Roselea; Preston North End; Coventry City; Hereford United; Birmingham City; Nuneaton Borough
Scotland caps: 2
1978 v Bulgaria (won 2-1), v Wales (drew 1-1)

On his second full appearance for Scotland against Wales, Jim Blyth was involved in a misunderstanding with Willie Donachie which led to the full-back putting through his own goal. Sadly, this incident probably cost Blyth his place in Scotland's 1978 World Cup squad!

Jim Blyth was on Preston North End's books when Coventry City paid £20,000 for his services in October 1972. The Perth-born keeper had made just one league appearance for the Lilywhites when he arrived at Highfield Road, but soon went on to be rated one of the best custodians in the country. The Sky Blues also had to pay an extra £10,000 when Blyth played in Coventry's first team and won international honours for Scotland.

Blyth's first team debut for Coventry was three years in coming, as he understudied first Bill Glazier and then Bryan King. He eventually played his first game in the senior side in December 1975 as City lost 2-1 at home to Everton. He then appeared in 50 consecutive league games for the Sky Blues, before damaging a knee in a 1-1 draw at home to West Ham United in April 1977.

An expensive transfer to Manchester United fell through when he failed a medical on his back, and from then on he was constantly troubled by the injury. However, he returned to first team action the following season and helped the club to finish in seventh place in the First Division, while his consistent displays earned his full international debut against Bulgaria.

Over the next four seasons, Blyth shared the goalkeeping duties with Les Sealey, but, after a loan spell with Hereford United and appearing in 174 League and Cup games for the Sky Blues, he left to join Birmingham City on a free transfer. At St Andrew's, Blyth was prone to make a number of errors, and so found himself understudying both Tony Coton and David Seaman. After three years with the club, he left to play non-League football for Nuneaton Borough.

STUART KENNEDY
Right-back
Born: Stuart Robert Kennedy, Grangemouth, 31 May 1953
Height: 5ft 9in
Weight: 10st 5lb
Clubs: Bothkennor YM; Falkirk; Aberdeen
Scotland caps: 8
1978 v Bulgaria (won 2-1), v Wales (drew 1-1), v England (lost 0-1), v Peru (lost 1-3), v Holland (won 3-2)
1979 v Austria (lost 2-3), v Portugal (lost 0-1)
1982 v Portugal (lost 1-2)

One of the original breed of overlapping full-backs, Stuart Kennedy began his first-class career with Falkirk before joining Aberdeen for a fee of £40,000 in the summer of 1976.

Though not renowned as a goalscorer, he did manage a vital strike in his first season with the club as Aberdeen beat Kilmarnock 2-1 at Rugby Park. By that time he had already picked up his first medal, having starred in the League Cup Final defeat of Celtic two weeks previously. Two seasons later, Aberdeen reached the final of the Scottish League Cup, and Stuart Kennedy scored three goals as the Dons beat Meadowbank Thistle 5-0, Hamilton Academicals 7-1, and then the extra-time semi-final winner against Hibs. In 1979-80 he picked up a League Championship medal having played in all but one of the title-winning games. He continued to give sterling service to the Dons, winning the first of his eight international caps when he played against Bulgaria in February 1978, a match the Scots won 2-1.

In 1981-82 the domestic collection was completed when the Dons won the Scottish Cup with a 4-1 extra-time win over Rangers. The following season, a Scottish Cup Final berth had already been secured and Kennedy had scored his first goal in Europe as Swiss side Sion were beaten 7-1 in a European Cup Winners' Cup preliminary round first leg tie, and, unless a major disaster occurred, the final of this competition was beckoning. After the semi-final first leg had produced a 5-1 win for Aberdeen over Waterschei, the Dons travelled to Belgium for the second leg. For Stuart Kennedy the game was a personal tragedy. He sustained a serious knee injury, which not only cruelly robbed him of the chance to play in a European Final, but also ended his career.

On being forced to retire, he returned to Falkirk to run his own public house.

IAN WALLACE
Forward

Born: Ian Andrew Wallace, Glasgow, 23 May 1956
Height: 5ft 8in
Weight: 10st 9lb
Clubs: Yoker Athletic; Dumbarton; Coventry City; Nottingham Forest; FC Brest (France); Sunderland; CS Martino (Madeira)
Scotland caps: 3
Scotland goals: 1
1978 v Bulgaria (won 2-1) 1 goal
1979 v Portugal (lost 0-1), v Wales (lost 0-3)

Ian Wallace began his first-class career with Dumbarton, where his goalscoring feats led to Coventry City paying £40,000 for his services in the summer of 1976.

He made his Football League debut for the Sky Blues as a substitute in a 2-1 home defeat at the hands of Sunderland in October 1976, ending the season with nine goals in 26 games, including a hat-trick in a 5-2 win over Stoke City. Yet

Ian Wallace playing for Nottingham Forest

just before Christmas in Wallace's first season at Highfield Road, he was hurled through the windscreen of a car in a road accident, and forced to miss over two months of the season.

In 1977-78 he formed a prolific goalscoring partnership with Mick Ferguson, and was the club's leading scorer with 21 goals in 41 league games, including six in the opening four games of the campaign. His performances this season led to him winning the first of three full caps for Scotland, when he came off the bench to score the winner in a 2-1 defeat of Bulgaria. Wallace went on to score 60 goals in 140 League and Cup games for Coventry, before, in July 1980, he joined Nottingham Forest for a club record fee of £1.25 million.

Though he was hampered by injuries during his early days at the City Ground, he went on to spend four seasons with Forest, scoring 36 goals in 134 league games. On leaving the City Ground, he had a spell in France with FC Brest, before returning to see out his Football League career with Sunderland. He later had a spell with CS Martino of Madeira before moving to play in Australia.

JOHN ROBERTSON
Outside-left

Born: John Neilson Robertson, Uddingston, 20 January 1953
Height: 5ft 8in
Weight: 10st 9lb
Clubs: Drumchapel Amateurs; Nottingham Forest; Derby County; Nottingham Forest; Corby Town; Stamford; Grantham
Scotland caps: 28
Scotland goals: 9

1978　v N Ireland (drew 1-1), v Wales (drew 1-1), v Iran (drew 1-1) 1 goal
1979　v Portugal (lost 0-1), v Norway (won 4-0) 1 goal, v Peru (drew 1-1)
1980　v Austria (drew 1-1), v Belgium (lost 0-2), v Belgium (lost 1-3) 1 goal,
　　　v Portugal (won 4-1)
1981　v Sweden (won 1-0), v Portugal (drew 0-0), v Israel (won 1-0), v N Ireland (drew 1-1),
　　　v Israel (won 3-1) 2 goals, v N Ireland (won 2-0), v England (won 1-0) 1 goal
1982　v Sweden (won 2-0) 1 goal, v N Ireland (drew 0-0), v N Ireland (drew 1-1),
　　　v England (lost 0-1), v New Zealand (won 5-2) 1 goal, v Brazil (lost 1-4),
　　　v USSR (drew 2-2)

1983 v East Germany (won 2-0), v Switzerland (lost 0-2)
1984 v Uruguay (won 2-0) I goal, v Belgium (drew 1-1)

John Robertson's career had its roots in a nursery team by the name of Drumchapel Amateurs, which also had a claim to fame in producing other famous internationals, including John Wark and Asa Hartford. Robertson, who had gained Scottish schoolboy and youth honours, went south of the border to join Nottingham Forest in May 1970.

However, it wasn't until the arrival of managerial duo Brian Clough and Peter Taylor that Robertson's talent began to be harnessed to its best advantage. The pair encouraged him to do his own thing, be individualistic, hug the touchline, demand the ball at his feet—and waited for him to do the rest.

He gained the first of 28 Scottish caps against Northern Ireland in 1978, and won several honours during Forest's glory years. In particular, he played a prominent part in the club's two remarkable European Cup successes in consecutive years. In the first final against Swedish champions Malmo in

John Robertson

Munich, it was his long cross that winged its way over the goal to the far post for Trevor Francis to head home the game's only goal. And twelve months later in Madrid, it was John Robertson's incursion into Hamburg's penalty area, on his right foot, that produced the only goal and kept the top European trophy at the City Ground.

He continued to serve Forest until the summer of 1983, when he left to join Peter Taylor at the Baseball Ground for £135,000, a fee set by an independent tribunal. Unfortunately the winger had to undergo a cartilage operation in his first season at Derby, and two years later he returned to the City Ground. However, his old magic had deserted him, and he moved into non-League football with Corby Town, then Stamford and Grantham.

Most full-backs who figured they knew how to handle the mercurial attacker went into the game assured that Robertson would invariably be at his most dangerous when he cut inside. What they didn't know was exactly when he was going to do it—and that is what made John Robertson lethal.

He later worked as a chief scout for former Forest team-mate Martin O'Neill at Wycombe Wanderers, later continuing to work alongside him as Celtic's assistant-manager.

GEORGE BURLEY
Right-back

Born: George Elder Burley, Cumnock, 3 June 1956
Height: 5ft 8in
Weight: 10st 5lb
Clubs: Ipswich Town; Sunderland; Gillingham; Colchester United
Scotland caps: 11
1979 v Wales (lost 0-3), v N Ireland (won 1-0), v England (lost 1-3), v Argentina (lost 1-3), v Norway (won 4-0)
1980 v Portugal (won 4-1), v N Ireland (lost 0-1), v England (lost 0-2), v Poland (lost 0-1)
1982 v Wales (won 1-0), v England (lost 0-1)

An adventurous defender, George Burley joined Ipswich Town straight from school, and made a memorable debut for the Suffolk club at the age of 17 years and 209 days, when he completely marked George Best out of the game in a 2-0 defeat against Manchester United at Old Trafford in December 1973.

Over the next 12 seasons, Burley missed very few games, and in 1975-76 when the club finished sixth in Division One, he was ever-present. The following season he was voted the club's 'Player of the Year', and in 1978 he won an FA Cup winners' medal when a Roger Osborne goal was enough to beat Arsenal in the Wembley final. Burley, who had won international honours for Scotland at schoolboy and Under-21 level, won the first of 11 full caps for his country in 1979 when he played against Wales.

Sadly he was not a member of the Ipswich side that beat AZ67 Alkmaar to win the UEFA Cup in 1980-81, having severely damaged his knee ligaments in an FA Cup tie at Shrewsbury. Burley went on to appear in exactly 500 first team

George Burley

Scotland! Scotland!—The 1970s   **295**

games for Ipswich Town, before leaving Portman Road in September 1985 to join Sunderland. He played in 54 league games for the Wearsiders before ending his playing career—or so he thought—with Gillingham.

After spells as manager of Ayr United and coach of Motherwell, he took charge as player-manager at Colchester United, but in December 1994 his career came full circle when he returned to Ipswich as manager. At the time of his appointment, the club were firmly rooted at the foot of the Premiership, and though they beat Leicester City 4-1 and won at Anfield for the very first time, the Blues were relegated. After leading the club to seventh place in Division One in 1995-96, Burley took the Blues to the play-offs for the next four seasons, eventually winning promotion in 1999-2000.

In their first season back, Ipswich under Burley finished fifth and so qualified for the following season's UEFA Cup. However, the club were then relegated, and after a poor start to the 2002-03 season, Burley was replaced by Joe Royle. After his name had been mentioned with every vacancy north and south of the border, he eventually took charge of strife-torn Derby County. When he left Pride Park, he returned to Scotland to manage Hearts, and in 2005-06, took them to the top of the Scottish Premier League, before a fall out with the club chairman led to a parting of the ways. Burley is now back in the Football League with Championship club, Southampton.

ALAN HANSEN
Central defender
Born: Alan David Hansen, Alloa, 13 June 1955
Height: 6ft 1in
Weight: 13st 0lb
Clubs: Partick Thistle; Liverpool
Scotland caps: 26
1979 v Wales (lost 0-3), v Argentina (lost 1-3)
1980 v Belgium (lost 0-2), v Portugal (won 4-1)
1981 v Sweden (won 1-0), v Portugal (drew 0-0), v Israel (won 3-1)
1982 v Sweden (won 2-0), v N Ireland (drew 0-0), v Portugal (lost 1-2), v Spain (lost 0-3),
v N Ireland (drew 1-1), v Wales (won 1-0), v England (lost 0-1),
v New Zealand (won 5-2), v Brazil (lost 1-4), v USSR (drew 2-2)
1983 v East Germany (won 2-0), v Switzerland (lost 0-2), v Belgium (lost 2-3),
v Switzerland (drew 2-2)
1985 v Wales (lost 0-1)
1986 v Romania (won 3-0)
1987 v Republic of Ireland (drew 0-0), v Luxembourg (won 3-0),
v Republic of Ireland (lost 0-1)

Making his international debut in 1979 and playing in the 1982 World Cup tournament, Alan Hansen's failure to win more than 26 Scottish caps was a great mystery. He was even omitted from the 1986 World Cup party by Alex Ferguson. His constant rejection by his country's national team selectors may well go down as one of the greatest blunders in Scottish football. He surely

Alan Hansen playing for Liverpool

would have been a permanent fixture in any other national side of the modern era.

A multi-talented sportsman, Alan Hansen was also an above-average scholar, leaving Lornshill Academy with four 'A' levels. He had represented Scotland at golf, squash and volleyball, but it was at football that he excelled. He'd actually had a trial with Liverpool when he was 15, but had been turned down. However, six years later, the Reds changed their minds and Bob Paisley paid Partick Thistle £100,000 for him in April 1977, by which time he had played 100 games for the Firhill club.

Hansen's ability on the ball marked him out as a player of the highest class. His runs forward from defence as he accelerated past people as smoothly as a Rolls-Royce gave Liverpool's attacks an extra dimension. As an orthodox centre-half, he had few peers; his excellent reading of the game was supported by firm tackling and more than adequate ability in the air.

Hansen replaced Phil Neal as captain in October 1985, and it was his leadership that played a vital part in the Reds' League and Cup double that season. It was probably the greatest moment in his illustrious career, for he became one of only five captains in the history of the game to lift the Championship trophy and the FA Cup in the same season. No matter whom he partnered in the centre of the Reds' defence—Thompson, Lawrenson, Gillespie or Hysen—he thrived. However, he realised during the 1988-89 season, during a lengthy lay-off, that the knee trouble he had suffered throughout his career was going to limit his appearances. So it came as no surprise to learn during the following season that he was retiring from the game.

One of TV's top soccer pundits, Alan Hansen displayed a record of consistency and quality that established him as one of the most outstanding post-war defenders.

PAUL HEGARTY
Central defender

Born: Paul Anthony Hegarty, Edinburgh, 25 July 1954
Height: 5ft 11in
Weight: 10st 13lb
Clubs: Hamilton Academicals; Dundee United; St Johnstone; Forfar Athletic
Scotland caps: 8
1979   v Wales (lost 0-3), v N Ireland (won 1-0), v England (lost 1-3), v Argentina (lost 1-3), v Norway (won 4-0)
1980   v Wales (won 1-0), v England (lost 0-2)
1983   v N Ireland (drew 0-0)

Paul Hegarty was originally a forward when he began his career with Hamilton Academicals before being converted into a central defender. He joined the Accies in 1972 when then manager, former Celtic keeper Ronnie Simpson, signed him from Tynecastle Boys Club, but it was a successor to Simpson, Eric Smith, who is credited with transforming Hegarty into a much-in-demand forward. He had scored 30 goals in 104 games when, in November 1974, he was transferred to Dundee United for a fee of £27,500.

Making his United debut as a substitute in a 5-0 home win over Partick Thistle, he teamed up with David Narey at the heart of the Tannadice club's defence. He was the first Dundee United captain to receive a national trophy when the Bell's League Cup was captured in December 1979, and during his team captaincy from 1978 to 1986, he skippered United to the club's first three major honours, including the League Championship in 1982-83. He also appeared in four League Cup Finals and led the club in some memorable nights with Europe's finest.

In May 1979, Paul Hegarty became only the second United player to play for Scotland when he lined up against Wales at Ninian Park, partnering Alan Hansen in defence. Scotland lost 3-0, but the game in Cardiff was the first of five consecutive caps for Hegarty in a two-month period, and the sequence also included a match against England at Wembley. Paul Hegarty was also the first-ever Dundee United player to captain Scotland when he led out the national team in a match against Northern Ireland at Hampden in 1983.

In April 1979, the Scottish Professional Footballers Association voted Hegarty their 'Player of the Year', while in 1987 he played in the UEFA Cup Final against Gothenburg.

In all he made 707 appearances for United and scored 83 goals—quite remarkable for a player who, apart from his first thirty months at Tannadice, was a defender.

In December 1989, the board announced that he was free to leave Tannadice. In fact, they wanted him to stay on in a coaching capacity, but he wanted to carry on playing and joined St Johnstone. While with the Saints he won a First Division Championship medal, but left soon after to play for Forfar Athletic, where, in the summer of 1990, he became player-manager. He parted company with Forfar in April 1992, and a few months later returned to Tannadice as coach, before joining the coaching staff at Hearts in 1995.

Then in 1997 he joined Alex Miller as assistant-manager of Aberdeen, before later taking over the reins. He parted company with the Dons after a brief spell in charge at Pittodrie.

JOHN WARK
Midfield

Born: John Wark, Glasgow, 4 August 1957
Height: 5ft 10in
Weight: 11st 7lb
Clubs: Drumchapel Amateurs; Ipswich Town; Liverpool; Ipswich Town; Middlesbrough; Ipswich Town
Scotland caps: 29
Scotland goals: 7
1979 v Wales (lost 0-3), v N Ireland (won 1-0), v England (lost 1-3) 1 goal, v Argentina (lost 1-3), v Norway (won 4-0)

1980 v Peru (drew 1-1), v Austria (drew 1-1), v Belgium (lost 0-2), v Belgium (lost 1-3)

1981 v Israel (won 1-0), v N Ireland (drew 1-1) 1 goal

1982 v Sweden (won 2-0), v Spain (lost 0-3), v Holland (won 2-1),
　　　v N Ireland (drew 1-1) 1 goal, v New Zealand (won 5-2) 2 goals, v Brazil (lost 1-4),
　　　v USSR (drew 2-2)

1983 v East Germany (won 2-0) 1 goal, v Switzerland (lost 0-2),
　　　v Switzerland (drew 2-2) 1 goal, v N Ireland (drew 0-0), v England (lost 0-2)

1984 v Uruguay (won 2-0), v Belgium (drew 1-1), v East Germany (lost 1-2),
　　　v England (drew 1-1), v France (lost 0-2)

1985 v Yugoslavia (won 6-1)

John Wark

John Wark made his international debut for Scotland against Wales in May 1979 and remained a regular selection until 1984. Having scored seven goals, he played the last of his 29 internationals in a 6-1 rout of Yugoslavia.

Having established himself with Ipswich Town, Wark helped the Portman Road club to the 1978 FA Cup Final, where they beat Arsenal 1-0. Ipswich totally outplayed the Gunners, and Wark, who had an outstanding game, crashed two tremendous shots against the woodwork. In three consecutive seasons from 1979 to 1982, Ipswich came close to winning the League Championship without actually clinching it, and Wark's goals were instrumental in keeping the club at or near the top. Consolation for those near misses was found in the club's UEFA Cup victory of 1980-81, in which Wark's contribution was outstanding. He scored four goals against Aris Salonika in the first round, a hat-trick against Widzew Lodz in the third round, goals in both legs of the fourth round against St Etienne, a goal in the semi-final against Cologne and goals in each leg of the final against AZ67 Alkmaar, which Ipswich won 5-4 on aggregate. In total he scored 14 goals from midfield in 12 games.

It brought him the accolade of his fellow professionals—the PFA senior award as 'Player of the Year'. The added honour he received, and one which must have been totally unexpected, was that of European 'Young Footballer of the Year', an award he travelled specially to Italy to collect. He even made an appearance in a film, having a small part in 'Escape to Victory' alongside Pele and Bobby Moore.

In March 1984 he joined Liverpool for a fee of £450,000, just in time to share in their League Championship triumph. In 1984-85 he top-scored with 18 league goals, including a hat-trick against West Bromwich Albion. Injuries then plagued the rest of his time at Anfield, and caused him to miss out on a League Championship medal in 1985-86.

In January 1988 he moved back to Ipswich, soon proving that he hadn't lost his goalscoring touch. Surprisingly, though, he joined Middlesbrough before the start of the following campaign, but never really settled, and in September 1991 rejoined the Tractor Boys for a third time, apparently to help on the coaching side rather than as a first team player. Remarkably, he returned to the team a month after rejoining the club, and helped them win the Second Division Championship. In 1992-93 he proved he was still good enough to play at the highest level as the Blues embarked on the first season of Premiership football.

Always an inspiration to those around him, John Wark scored 182 goals in 681 first team games in his three spells at Portman Road.

FRANK McGARVEY
Forward

Born: Francis Peter McGarvey, Kilsyth, 17 March 1956
Height: 5ft 10in
Weight: 11st 0lb
Clubs: Kilsyth Rangers; St Mirren; Liverpool; Glasgow Celtic; St Mirren; Clyde; Shotts Bon Accord
Scotland caps: 7
1979 v N Ireland (won 1-0), v Argentina (lost 1-3)
1984 v Uruguay (won 2-0), v Belgium (drew 1-1), v East Germany (lost 1-2),
      v N Ireland (lost 0-2), v Wales (won 2-1)

By the time Frank McGarvey joined Liverpool from St Mirren in 1979 for a huge fee of £250,000, he was a proven marksman, having scored 80 goals in 180 games for the Buddies. Much was expected of him. He was hot property, with Arsenal, Aston Villa and even Ajax all chasing the young man's signature.

He won two Scottish caps while at Anfield, adding to the glut of Under-21 honours he had already won. But success at international level meant little to Liverpool, and with Dalglish, Johnson, McDermott and Case around, McGarvey never even managed a first team outing. Eventually he returned to Scotland, joining Celtic for £325,000.

He was a member of the Celtic team that threw the 1980 League title away, but which beat Rangers 1-0 in that season's Scottish Cup Final. He spearheaded the Celtic teams in the Championship-winning seasons of 1980-81 and 1981-82, his partnerships with Charlie Nicholas and George McCluskey proving prolific. One of McGarvey's goals is still talked about today. In the game against his former club St Mirren in March 1981, McGarvey beat defender after defender before crashing the ball past Billy Thomson—an individual goal of the highest quality. After four seasons with Celtic, he lost his place to Jim Melrose, but was offered a one-year contract. He accepted, and in 1984-85 became the first player to reach 100 Premier League goals (30 for St Mirren). In May 1985, after

Celtic had trailed 1-0 to Dundee United in the Scottish Cup Final, it was his perfect header from Roy Aitken's cross that won the Cup for Celtic with just five minutes to go. On the Monday following, manager Davie Hay offered him a new contract, but after describing it as an insult, he left Parkhead and rejoined St Mirren.

He later became the Love Street club's player/assistant-manager before leaving to take charge of Queen of the South. Dismissed after just one season at Palmerston Park, he returned to playing with Clyde before winding down his career with Shotts Bon Accord.

GEORGE WOOD
Goalkeeper
Born: George Wood, Douglas, 26 September 1952
Height: 6ft 3in
Weight: 14st 0lb
Clubs: Balmoral Hydraulics; East Stirling; Blackpool; Everton; Arsenal; Crystal Palace; Cardiff City; Hereford United; Merthyr Tydfil; Inter Cardiff
Scotland caps: 4
1979 v N Ireland (won 1-0), v England (lost 1-3), v Argentina (lost 1-3)
1982 v N Ireland (drew 1-1)

Though he kept a clean sheet on his international debut against Northern Ireland, George Wood had a dismal time at Wembley against England. John Wark's 21st minute goal for Scotland looked like the first of many, but just before the interval, Barnes' shot crept through the defence and past an unsighted Wood. Just after the hour, Wilkins' shot-cum-centre bounced off Wood's chest and Coppell knocked in the loose ball. Keegan scored a third, but that was of a much higher class.

A giant of a man, George Wood began his career with East Stirling before signing for Blackpool in January 1972. Signed primarily as cover for the tremendously popular John Burridge, Wood eventually made his debut for the Seasiders in April 1972 in a 2-0 win over Oxford United. He then spent the next four years vying with Burridge for the No.1 spot before establishing himself in 1975-76. Wood was never a spectacular keeper, but a safer pair of hands you were not likely to see, reminding many of the club's older fans of George Farm.

In the summer of 1977, Wood joined Everton for a fee of £150,000, and his displays in his first two seasons at Goodison Park, in which he was ever-present, won him three full caps for Scotland. The inconsistency which had dogged his early days gradually returned and he lost his place at Everton to Martin Hodge.

Signed by Arsenal as the possible successor to Pat Jennings, Wood added a fourth full cap to his collection and was selected for Scotland's 1982 World Cup squad. Surprisingly granted a free transfer by the Gunners, he then had five years with Crystal Palace before joining Cardiff City, whom he helped win

George Wood

promotion from the Fourth Division. After a spell with Hereford United, he played non–League football for Merthyr Tydfil and Inter Cardiff, but is now an ornithologist with Glamorgan Wildlife Trust.

IAIN MUNRO
Left–back / Midfield

Born: Alexander Iain Fordyce Munro, Uddingston, 24 August 1951
Height: 5ft 8in
Weight: 11st 8lb
Clubs: Drumchapel Amateurs; St Mirren; Hibernian; Glasgow Rangers; St Mirren; Stoke City; Sunderland; Dundee United; Hibernian
Scotland caps: 7
1979 v Argentina (lost 1-3), v Norway (won 4-0)
1980 v Peru (drew 1-1), v Austria (drew 1-1), v Belgium (lost 0-2), v Wales (won 1-0), v England (lost 0-2)

Iain Munro had a remarkable playing career. It began with Drumchapel Amateurs and took him in turn to St Mirren, Hibs, Rangers, St Mirren again, Stoke City, Sunderland, Dundee United and back to Hibs.

A left-sided midfield player, he was stylish and cultured, and soon forced his way into the St Mirren side in late 1968, prior to joining Hibs five years later. His performances for the Easter Road club, whom he helped to the 1975 League Cup Final where they lost 6-3 to Celtic, led to Rangers parting with Graham

Fyfe and Ally Scot for Munro's services. At Ibrox he was converted into a left-back, and though in terms of his general career this was beneficial to the player, he played little in his short stay with Rangers.

He rejoined St Mirren for a fee of £25,000, and in his second spell at Love Street, he was capped seven times by Scotland, winning his first cap in a 3-1 defeat by Argentina in June 1979.

After impressing on international duty, he joined Stoke City for £150,000, six times what St Mirren paid for him, then he moved for the same fee to Sunderland in July 1981. After three good seasons at Roker Park, he moved to Dundee United, but, after only a year at Tannadice, he was back at Hibs.

His polished skills, with single defence-splitting passes a speciality, and a high work-rate sustained his long and varied playing career, which ended at Easter Road following a second appearance in a League Cup Final in 1986 and another defeat, this time 3-0 by Aberdeen.

After a spell as assistant-manager to Jimmy Nicholl at Raith Rovers, he managed Dundee and Dunfermline Athletic. After his appointment as Pars' boss, a bitter disagreement erupted between the fans and the board at East End Park, the fans being angry at the departure of Jim Leishman. Munro was sacked soon after, later taking charge of Dundee (again), Hamilton Academicals and Raith Rovers.

THE 1980s

As an international tournament, the Home Championships had been in the doldrums for years, but by the 1980s, the international fixture list for both club and country was extremely crowded. With European competitions, European Championships and World Cup qualifying tournaments, only the fixtures between Scotland and England attracted sizeable crowds. For the last of these fixtures, the FA announced that there would be no tickets available for Scotland for the 1981 match at Wembley. The Scottish Supporters' Club unsuccessfully challenged this in the courts, citing the Race Relations Act. With England and Wales refusing to play in Belfast because of the riots during the Maze hunger strike, the Championship was abandoned, despite Scotland having fulfilled all their fixtures. In the end the Championship was finally killed off in 1984, its centenary year.

Along with Northern Ireland, Scotland eased their way past Sweden, Portugal and Israel to win a place in the 1982 World Cup Finals in Spain. Drawn in a difficult group with Brazil and the Soviet Union, the Scots put on a brave show, drawing with the Soviet Union and briefly leading against Brazil before being beaten 4-1. Scotland went out on goal difference and maintained their unenviable record of never having gone beyond the first round of a World Cup Finals despite having qualified five times.

Scotland were never in the hunt for qualification for the finals of the 1984 European Championships, but did qualify for the 1986 World Cup Finals in Mexico. In the final group match, Wales had to beat Scotland at Ninian Park to qualify for a play-off against Australia or New Zealand, both minnows. Wales were 1-0 ahead at half-time and the Scots were despondent. As the second-half wore on, Jock Stein, Scotland's manager, sensed the Welsh had settled for preserving their slender lead, and Davie Cooper was sent on for Gordon Strachan. The Scots were immediately revitalised. However, the goal that levelled the scores and eliminated the Welsh should never have happened. With 10 minutes to go, a dubious handball in the Welsh penalty area was adjudged by the French referee to be a penalty to Scotland. Cooper scored from the spot. Stein, the maestro, had pulled a masterstroke. Sadly, the match will be remembered for the death of the 62-year-old Stein, the most successful manager in Scottish history. Seconds before the final whistle, he collapsed in the tunnel and died of a heart attack. Alex Ferguson, then manager of Aberdeen, stepped in as caretaker-manager for the two-legged play-offs against Australia (which Scotland won) and the finals in Mexico.

Scotland were in a powerful group, nicknamed the Group of Death! Scotland had inadvertently reshaped their team before the tournament started, dropping Alan Hansen. Kenny Dalglish, his Liverpool team-mate, miffed at Hansen's omission, then realised he was carrying an injury.

Scotland lost their first match 1-0 to Denmark and then enjoyed their best game against West Germany, where, shades of 1982 against Brazil, they briefly led courtesy of a goal from Gordon Strachan. In their final match they could only draw 0-0 with a violent Uruguayan team who had a player sent off in the first minute. Had Scotland beaten the 10 men, they would have reached the second round as one of the third-placed teams.

ROY AITKEN
Midfield

Born: Robert Sime Aitken, Irvine, 24 November 1958
Height: 6ft 0in
Weight: 12st 2lb
Clubs: Glasgow Celtic; Newcastle United; St Mirren; Aberdeen
Scotland caps: 57
Scotland goals: 1

1980 v Peru (drew 1-1), v Belgium (lost 1-3), v Wales (won 1-0), v England (lost 0-2),
      v Poland (lost 0-1)
1983 v Belgium (lost 2-3), v Canada (won 3-0), v Canada (won 2-0)
1984 v Belgium (drew 1-1), v N Ireland (lost 0-2), v Wales (won 2-1)
1985 v England (won 1-0), v Iceland (won 1-0)
1986 v Wales (drew 1-1), v East Germany (drew 0-0), v Australia (won 2-0),
      v Australia (drew 0-0), v Israel (won 1-0), v Romania (won 3-0) 1 goal,
      v England (lost 1-2), v Denmark (lost 0-1), v West Germany (lost 1-2),
      v Uruguay (drew 0-0)
1987 v Bulgaria (drew 0-0), v Republic of Ireland (drew 0-0), v Luxembourg (won 3-0),
      v Republic of Ireland (lost 0-1), v Belgium (lost 1-4), v England (drew 0-0),
      v Brazil (lost 0-2)
1988 v Hungary (won 2-0), v Belgium (won 2-0), v Bulgaria (won 1-0),
      v Luxembourg (drew 0-0), v Saudi Arabia (drew 2-2), v Malta (drew 1-1),
      v Spain (drew 0-0), v Colombia (drew 0-0), v England (lost 0-1)
1989 v Norway (won 2-1), v Yugoslavia (drew 1-1), v Italy (lost 0-2), v Cyprus (won 3-2),
      v France (won 2-0), v Cyprus (won 2-1), v England (lost 0-2), v Chile (won 2-0)
1990 v Yugoslavia (lost 1-3), v France (lost 0-3), v Norway (drew 1-1), v Argentina (won 1-0),
      v Poland (drew 1-1), v Malta (won 2-1), v Costa Rica (lost 0-1), v Sweden (won 2-1),
      v Brazil (lost 0-1)
1992 v Romania (lost 0-1)

A regular for Scotland, Aitken led his country in the 1986 World Cup Finals and was indispensable to Celtic, lifting trophy after trophy at Parkhead.

Making his Celtic debut in a 2-0 win at Stenhousemuir in September 1975, he soon settled into the side, and whether he was playing full-back, sweeper, centre-back or in midfield, his commitment to the club was always 100%—he was unable ever to give less than his best on the park. He played a vital role in Celtic winning the 'double' in 1976-77 and in the League Championship-winning sides of 1978-79, 1980-81, 1981-82 and 1985-86. He won a second Scottish Cup medal against Rangers in May 1980, and in the 1985 Final against Dundee United, it was his surge and cross that enabled Frank McGarvey to head home the winner. In 1988, he made his name for ever as the player who captained Celtic to the Centenary Year Double.

At international level, he was made the scapegoat for the 3-0 defeat by France in Paris in October 1989, and as Celtic's fortunes began to decline, the big man, who was known as 'The Bear' and had stated that he wanted to end his playing days at Parkhead, sought a transfer! He was a fiery player at times, once sent off in a Scottish Cup Final, and by the time he left Celtic, he had become something of a victimised player in his own country.

He had appeared in 667 first team games for Celtic, when in January 1990 he joined Newcastle United for a fee of £500,000. He made a remarkable debut for the Magpies, leading them to a 5-4 victory over Leicester City after they had been 4-2 behind. His wholehearted displays almost took Newcastle to promotion in 1989-90, United failing in the play-offs. When Ossie Ardiles became Newcastle manager, he discarded Aitken when perhaps his vast experience was just what the Magpies needed.

He became player-coach at St Mirren, but after one season at Love Street, he joined Aberdeen as the Pittodrie club's player-manager. Three years later he hung up his boots to concentrate on management.

DAVIE COOPER
Winger

Born: David Cooper, Hamilton, 25 February 1956
Died: 23 March 1995
Height: 5ft 8in
Weight: 12st 5lb
Clubs: Hamilton Avondale; Clydebank; Glasgow Rangers; Motherwell; Clydebank
Scotland caps: 22
Scotland goals: 6
1980 v Peru (drew 1-1), v Austria (drew 1-1)
1984 v Wales (won 2-1) 1 goal, v England (drew 1-1)
1985 v Yugoslavia (won 6-1) 1 goal, v Iceland (won 3-0), v Spain (won 3-1), v Spain (lost 0-1), v Wales (lost 0-1)
1986 v Wales (drew 1-1) 1 goal, v East Germany (drew 0-0), v Australia (won 2-0) 1 goal, v Australia (drew 0-0), v Holland (drew 0-0), v West Germany (lost 1-2), v Uruguay (drew 0-0)
1987 v Bulgaria (drew 0-0), v Luxembourg (won 3-0) 2 goals, v Republic of Ireland (lost 0-1), v Brazil (lost 0-2)
1990 v Norway (drew 1-1), v Egypt (lost 1-3)

Davie Cooper was to convert one of the most famous penalties in Scottish history when his late spot-kick, after coming on as a substitute, earned a draw against Wales in a World Cup qualifier, which, to all intents and purposes, took the Tartan Army to the 1986 finals in Mexico. Typically, he showed amazing poise and nerve to fire the ball past Neville Southall as an entire nation watched with bated breath. Sadly, the night was not to prove one of celebration, as the high stakes and tension proved too much for boss Jock Stein, who died from a heart attack after the game.

There were very few in the long history of Scottish soccer who could match the ability of 'Coop'. It was at Clydebank where he first came to notice, as a young and exciting winger with a truly amazing left foot. He quickly came to the notice of the bigger clubs, and in June 1977 he joined Jock Wallace's Rangers.

He was an instant success. After a season of anti-climax in 1976-77, following the treble of the year before, Rangers got back on the rails with another triple crown in Cooper's first campaign. With Jock Wallace stepping down after those glorious nine months, the Ibrox club was to embark on an era which would see them miss out on the League title until 1986-87. It was harsh on Cooper, who would probably have been at the peak of his powers at this stage.

By 1980, he had come to the attention of the Scottish selectors, and he made his debut against Peru. Though it took until 1984 for his international career to begin in earnest, his total of 22 caps is far lower than it should have been—a result prompted by his own indifference to performing on that particular stage.

His Rangers career spanned 12 years, and brought a rich array of domestic honours—three League Championship medals, three Scottish Cup winners' medals and seven League Cup winners' medals. Ironically, his career with Rangers, which had been so glorious, ended on a sad note, as he played the last of his 643 first team games in the rather lacklustre defeat at the hands of Celtic in the Scottish Cup Final.

In August 1989 he joined Motherwell for only £50,000. While at Fir Park, he resurrected his international career and helped the Steelmen, who had not lifted a trophy for 39 years, win the Scottish Cup, overcoming hot favourites Dundee United 4-3 in the final. By 1993 his appearances were becoming more infrequent, and he rejoined his first club Clydebank.

The tragic and premature cutting down of one of the last great entertainers north of the border, due to a brain haemorrhage, sparked unprecedented mourning throughout the whole of Scotland.

DAVIE PROVAN
Winger/ Midfield

Born: David Alexander Provan, Gourock, 8 May 1956
Height: 5ft 8in
Weight: 10st 3lb
Clubs: Port Glasgow; Kilmarnock; Glasgow Celtic
Scotland caps: 10
Scotland goals: 1
1980 v Belgium (lost 0-2), v Belgium (lost 1-3), v Portugal (won 4-1), v N Ireland (lost 0-1)
1981 v Israel (won 3-1) 1 goal, v Wales (lost 0-2), v England (won 1-0)
1982 v Sweden (won 2-0), v Portugal (lost 1-2), v N Ireland (drew 1-1)

Davie Provan won his first Scottish cap as a substitute for Joe Jordan in a 2-0 defeat against Belgium in Brussels in November 1979. In fact, Provan's first four appearances for the national side were from the bench, but when he did start his first game against Israel in April 1981, he found the net in a 3-1 win.

Later that season he was a member of the Scotland side that beat England 1-0 at Wembley.

A former Paisley shipping clerk, he began his career with Kilmarnock, where his displays of thrilling wing play persuaded Celtic manager Billy McNeill to pay £100,000 for his services. Teasing the life out of opposition defences, he was an attacking revelation during the Scottish Cup Final as Celtic beat Rangers 1-0.

He was a member of the Celtic League Championship-winning sides of 1980-81 and 1981-82, and though he didn't score too many goals—42 in 302 League and Cup games—he led the Celtic fightback in the Scottish Cup Final of May 1985, when one of his free-kicks in the 75th minute twisted high past Hamish McAlpine in the Dundee United goal and into the top corner, in Celtic's 2-1 win.

The viral complaint that led to Davie Provan's retirement first manifested itself during the 3-0 defeat against Rangers at Ibrox in November 1985. As the second half got under way, he felt totally listless and drained. It was over a year later when Davie Provan was diagnosed as having Myalgic Encephalomyelitis (ME).

In November 1987 a testimonial dinner was held in Glasgow to honour Davie Provan—one of the greatest Celtic wingers of all time.

EAMONN BANNON
Midfield

Born: Eamonn John Bannon, Edinburgh, 18 April 1958
Height: 5ft 9in
Weight: 11st 11lb
Clubs: Link BC; Heart of Midlothian; Chelsea; Dundee United; Heart of Midlothian
Scotland caps: 11
Scotland goals: 1
1980 v Belgium (lost 1-3)
1983 v N Ireland (drew 0-0), v Wales (won 2-0), v England (lost 0-2), v Canada (won 2-0)
1984 v East Germany (lost 1-2) 1 goal
1986 v Israel (won 1-0), v Romania (won 3-0), v England (lost 1-2), v Denmark (lost 0-1),
     v West Germany (lost 1-2)

Midfielder Eamonn Bannon, who began and ended his playing career with Hearts, made his debut for the Tynecastle club in a 4-0 home win over Kilmarnock in February 1977. In his first full season with the club, he scored 12 goals in 39 games as they finished the campaign runners-up in the First Division to Morton, who won the Championship on goal difference. Midway through the following season, he left Hearts to play for Chelsea, but he failed to settle at Stamford Bridge, and in October 1979 he signed for Dundee United for a fee of £165,000.

In his first full season at Tannadice, he was a member of the United side that won the League Cup, beating Dundee 3-0 in the final. That same season,

United reached the final of the Scottish Cup but went down 4-1 to Rangers after the first meeting had ended goalless. Bannon was on the losing side in four Cup Finals, the last, in 1988, being his last appearance in a United shirt. His greatest triumph came in 1982-83, when he helped the Terrors win the League Championship, finishing a point ahead of both Celtic and Aberdeen.

While with United, Bannon won 11 full caps for Scotland, his only goal coming in the 2-1 defeat by East Germany in 1984. He went on to score 72 goals in 280 league games in nine years at Tannadice, before, in July 1988, he signed for Hearts for £225,000.

He spent a further five seasons with Hearts, helping them finish runners-up in the Premier Division in 1991-92.

On hanging up his boots, he became manager of Falkirk, only to lose his job after a disagreement with the club chairman six months later. Falkirk had been fined £25,000 for playing a trialist, John Clark, in a First Division match against St Mirren.

STEVE ARCHIBALD
Forward

Born: Steven Archibald, Glasgow, 27 September 1956
Height: 5ft 11in
Weight: 11st 1lb
Clubs: Crofoot United; Fernhill Athletic; Clyde; Aberdeen; Tottenham Hotspur; Barcelona (Spain); Blackburn Rovers; Hibernian; Espanol (Spain); St Mirren; East Fife; Benfica (Portugal)
Scotland caps: 27
Scotland goals: 4

1980 v Portugal (won 4-1) 1 goal, v N Ireland (lost 0-1), v Poland (lost 0-1), v Hungary (lost 1-3) 1 goal

1981 v Sweden (won 1-0), v Israel (won 1-0), v N Ireland (drew 1-1), v Israel (won 3-1), v N Ireland (won 2-0) 1 goal, v England (won 1-0)

1982 v N Ireland (drew 0-0), v Portugal (lost 1-2), v Spain (lost 0-3), v Holland (won 2-1), v New Zealand (won 5-2) 1 goal, v Brazil (lost 1-4), v USSR (drew 2-2)

1983 v East Germany (won 2-0), v Switzerland (lost 0-2), v Belgium (lost 2-3)

1984 v East Germany (lost 1-2), v England (drew 1-1), v France (lost 0-2)

1985 v Spain (lost 0-1), v England (won 1-0), v Iceland (won 1-0)

1986 v West Germany (lost 1-2)

Having started his career with junior clubs Crofoot United and Fernhill Athletic, Steve Archibald, who was to score on his full international debut as a substitute against Portugal, joined Clyde as a part-timer, though he had played one match for East Stirling.

A member of Clyde's 1978 Second Division winning team, Archibald continued his training as a Rolls-Royce mechanic, and it was only when he joined Aberdeen for £25,000 in January 1978 that he became a full-time professional. He helped the Dons to the Scottish League Cup Finals of 1979 and 1980 and the Scottish League title in 1980 before his goalscoring exploits tempted Spurs

Steve Archibald playing for Tottenham Hotspur

into parting with £800,000 for his signature in May 1980.

His skilful, strong running and unquenchable thirst for goals made him a great favourite of Spurs' fans, and, with Garth Crooks the perfect foil, he led the attack in both the 1981 and 1982 FA Cup Final successes, scoring Spurs' goal in the 1982 League Cup Final against Liverpool. Archibald later fell out with Spurs' manager Keith Burkinshaw, and having helped the club lift the UEFA Cup in 1984, he signed for Terry Venables' Barcelona for £1.25 million.

In his first season in Spain, he added the Spanish title to a growing list of honours, and led Barcelona's attack in the 1986 European Champions Final. Following the signings of Mark Hughes and Gary Lineker, it was clear that Archibald's services would only be needed in an emergency, and midway through the 1987-88 season he was allowed to join Blackburn Rovers on loan.

In August 1988 his contract with Barcelona was paid up, and he returned to Scottish football with Hibernian, where he continued to score regularly. But in his second season, he was unable to get into the team and went back to Spain to play for Espanol. Ten months later he returned to Scotland to join St Mirren. Released in 1991, he had spells with Clyde and East Fife, where he was player-coach. A fall-out with the powers-that-be at Bayview Park saw him resign and join the staff of Portuguese giants Benfica.

ALEX McLEISH

Central defender

Born: Alexander McLeish, Glasgow, 21 January 1959
Height: 6ft 1in
Weight: 12st 4lb
Clubs: Glasgow United; Aberdeen; Motherwell
Scotland caps: 77

1980 v Portugal (won 4-1), v N Ireland (lost 0-1), v Wales (won 1-0), v England (lost 0-2),
v Poland (lost 0-1), v Hungary (lost 1-3)

1981 v Sweden (won 1-0), v Israel (won 1-0), v N Ireland (drew 1-1), v Israel (won 3-1),
v N Ireland (won 2-0), v England (won 1-0)

1982 v Sweden (won 2-0), v Spain (lost 0-3), v N Ireland (drew 1-1), v Brazil (lost 1-4)

1983 v Belgium (lost 2-3), v Switzerland (drew 2-2), v Wales (won 2-0), v England (lost 0-2),
v Canada (won 2-0), v Canada (won 3-0), v Canada (won 2-0)

1984 v Uruguay (won 2-0), v Belgium (drew 1-1), v East Germany (lost 1-2),
v N Ireland (lost 0-2), v Wales (won 2-1), v England (drew 1-1), v France (lost 0-2)

1985 v Yugoslavia (won 6-1), v Iceland (won 3-0), v Spain (won 3-1), v Spain (lost 0-1),
v Wales (lost 0-1), v England (won 1-0), v Iceland (won 1-0)

1986 v Wales (drew 1-1), v East Germany (drew 0-0), v Australia (won 2-0),
v Australia (drew 0-0), v England (lost 1-2), v Holland (drew 0-0), v Denmark (lost 0-1)

1987 v Belgium (lost 1-4), v England (drew 0-0), v Brazil (lost 0-2)

1988 v Belgium (won 2-0), v Bulgaria (won 1-0), v Luxembourg (drew 0-0),
v Saudi Arabia (drew 2-2), v Malta (drew 1-1), v Spain (drew 0-0),
v Colombia (drew 0-0), v England (lost 0-1)

1989 v Norway (won 2-1), v Yugoslavia (drew 1-1), v Italy (lost 0-2), v Cyprus (won 3-2),
v France (won 2-0), v Cyprus (won 2-1), v England (lost 0-2), v Chile (won 2-0)

1990 v Yugoslavia (lost 1-3), v France (lost 0-3), v Norway (drew 1-1), v Argentina (won 1-0),
v East Germany (lost 0-1), v Egypt (lost 1-3), v Costa Rica (lost 0-1),
v Sweden (won 2-1), v Brazil (lost 0-1)

Capped 77 times by Scotland, Alex McLeish was just 18 years old when he made his Aberdeen debut against Dundee United in January 1978. During his early days with the Pittodrie club, he often lined up in midfield before settling at centre-half for the remainder of his long and distinguished playing career.

In 1980, McLeish won a League Championship winners' medal as the Dons finished one point ahead of runners-up Celtic. It was also the year he won his first international cap playing in a 4-1 defeat of Portugal at Hampden Park. There then followed that halcyon period in which the Dons won honour after honour. Much of that success of course was down to the partnership at the heart of the Aberdeen defence of Alex McLeish and Willie Miller. For most of his time at Pittodrie, McLeish was used to deputising as team captain for Miller when the Aberdeen skipper was injured, and when Miller retired in 1990 it was McLeish who took over the skipper's armband.

At the end of his first season as captain, McLeish chipped a bone in his ankle, an injury that caused him to miss most of the 1991-92 campaign. A hamstring problem meant that he was again missing at the start of the following season, an injury that also kept him out of the Skol Cup Final defeat at the hands of Rangers. However, he had recovered in time for the club's run to the Tennants Scottish Cup Final, where the Dons lost 2-1 to, who else but Rangers. He stayed at Pittodrie for a further two seasons, but in the summer of 1994, after playing in 458 league games, he was surprisingly allowed to join Motherwell as player-manager.

He remained at Fir Park until 1997-98 when he left to become Hibs' manager. In his first season in charge at Easter Road, he led the club to the First Division Championship, 23 points ahead of runners-up Falkirk. Rangers later made a move for him, and in his first season at Ibrox, they won both domestic Cup Finals and finished runners-up in the Premier League. In 2002-03, Rangers won the League Championship as well as the two domestic cup competitions, and after a season without any honours, won the title and League Cup in 2004-05. McLeish led Ranger's assault on Europe in 2005-06, but before the campaign was over, it was announced that he would be parting company with the club in the summer.

GORDON STRACHAN
Midfield

Born: Gordon David Strachan, Edinburgh, 9 February 1957
Height: 5ft 6in
Weight: 10st 3lb
Clubs: Dundee; Aberdeen; Manchester United; Leeds United; Coventry City
Scotland caps: 50
Scotland goals: 5
1980 v N Ireland (lost 0-1), v Wales (won 1-0), v England (lost 0-2), v Poland (lost 0-1),

v Hungary (lost 1-3)

1981 v Sweden (won 1-0) 1 goal v Portugal (drew 0-0)

1982 v N Ireland (drew 0-0), v Portugal (lost 1-2), v Spain (lost 0-3), v Holland (won 2-1),
v New Zealand (won 5-2), v Brazil (lost 1-4), v USSR (drew 2-2)

1983 v East Germany (won 2-0), v Switzerland (lost 0-2), v Belgium (lost 2-3),
v Switzerland (drew 2-2), v N Ireland (drew 0-0), v Wales (won 2-0),
v England (lost 0-2), v Canada (won 2-0) 1 goal, v Canada (won 3-0),
v Canada (won 2-0)

1984 v East Germany (lost 1-2), v N Ireland (lost 0-2), v England (drew 1-1),
v France (lost 0-2)

1985 v Spain (lost 0-1), v England (won 1-0), v Iceland (won 1-0)

1986 v Wales (drew 1-1), v Australia won 2-0), v Romania (won 3-0) 1 goal,
v Denmark (lost 0-1), v West Germany (lost 1-2) 1 goal, v Uruguay (drew 0-0)

1987 v Bulgaria (drew 0-0), v Republic of Ireland (drew 0-0), v Republic of Ireland (lost 0-1)

1988 v Hungary (won 2-0)

1989 v France (won 2-0)

1990 v France (lost 0-3)

1991 v USSR (lost 0-1), v Bulgaria (drew 1-1), v San Marino (won 2-1) 1 goal

1992 v Switzerland (drew 2-2), v Romania (lost 0-1), v N Ireland (won 1-0),
v Finland (drew 1-1)

Gordon Strachan represented Scotland in two World Cups, his own personal highlight being a memorable celebration with the advertising boards against West Germany in Mexico '86. He retired from international football in 1992 having earned his 50th and final cap against Finland.

He started his illustrious career with Dundee, but after 60 appearances for the Dens Park club he moved to Aberdeen for £50,000 in November 1977, and it was at Pittodrie, during a purple spell, that he would eventually win just about every honour possible—two Premier Division Championship medals in 1979–80 and 1983-84, a hat-trick of Scottish Cup winners' medals between 1982 and 1984, and a European Cup Winners' Cup medal in 1983. His form was such that, at the end of that first successful season with the Dons, he won his first full Scottish cap, when selected to play against Northern Ireland.

Pittodrie was stunned in May 1984, when, after scoring 55 goals in 183 games, he left the club to join his former boss, Alex Ferguson, at Manchester United. By the end of his first season at Old Trafford, he had won an FA Cup winners' medal following a 1-0 extra-time win over Everton. In nearly five years with United he had been an automatic choice, injuries apart, so it came as something of a surprise when he was sold to Leeds United before the transfer deadline in 1989.

Showing renewed vigour on being appointed captain, he immediately led Leeds to the Second Division Championship, and, as an ever-present and the club's top scorer with 16 league goals, he was honoured as the 'Footballer of the Year' for 1991. Two years later, at the age of 35, he led Leeds to the League Championship. He went on to play for the Elland Road club until March 1995, when he announced that the end of his marvellous career had arrived.

Somewhat out of the blue, he joined Coventry City as Ron Atkinson's assistant,

Gordon Strachan

but then extended his playing career to aid a side struggling in the Premiership danger zone. A year later he succeeded Big Ron as the Sky Blues' manager, a position he held until 2001. In October of that year he took over as manager of Southampton, leading the Saints to the 2003 FA Cup Final before resigning his post. After a spell out of the game, he replaced Martin O'Neill as manager of Celtic, and in 2005-06, led the Bhoys to the League Championship.

BILLY THOMSON
Goalkeeper

Born: William Thomson, Linwood, 10 February 1958
Height: 6ft 3in
Weight: 12st 3lb
Clubs: Glasgow United; Partick Thistle; St Mirren; Dundee United; Motherwell; Glasgow Rangers; Dundee;
Scotland caps: 7
1980 v N Ireland (lost 0-1)
1981 v N Ireland (drew 1-1), v N Ireland (won 2-0)
1982 v Portugal (lost 1-2)
1983 v N Ireland (drew 0-0), v Canada (won 2-0)
1984 v East Germany (lost 1-2)

A 6ft 3in goalkeeper, Billy Thomson was without doubt one of the best of his era. His formative years were centred on Linwood, after which he played his early football for Glasgow United. His impressive displays between the posts led to Partick Thistle offering him terms in 1975. His opportunities at Firhill were limited by the Scottish international keeper Alan Rough, and though he never made a first team outing for the Jags, he did win two Under-21 caps for Scotland.

In the summer of 1978, a £40,000 fee took him to St Mirren, and after representing Scotland at Under-23 level and playing for the Scottish League, he won the first of his seven full international caps in May 1980 when he played against Northern Ireland. In fact, Thomson's first three appearances for his country were to be against Northern Ireland. Thomson went on to play in over 200 games for the Paisley club, before in June 1984 he left Love Street for Dundee United for a reported fee of £75,000.

He made two Scottish Cup Final appearances for the Tannadice club, but was on the losing side each time as Celtic won 2-1 in 1985 and his former club St Mirren 1-0 after extra-time in 1987. Thomson was an automatic choice for the Terrors for seven years, until losing his place to Alan Main in 1991 when he joined Motherwell.

For three years he vied for the No.1 jersey with Sieb Dykstra, and though he was more flamboyant, Billy Thomson was highly dependable and more experienced.

If proof were needed of Billy Thomson's ability, it came in 1994 when Rangers signed him as cover for Andy Goram. His first-class career ended at Dundee, where he ultimately coached one of Scotland's current international keepers, Rob Douglas.

PETER WEIR
Winger

Born: Peter Russell Weir, Johnstone, 18 January 1958
Height: 6ft 0in

Weight: 11st 9lb
Clubs: Neilston Juniors; St Mirren; Aberdeen; Leicester City; St Mirren; Ayr United;
Scotland caps: 6
1980 v N Ireland (lost 0-1), v Wales (won 1-0), v Poland (lost 0-1), v Hungary (lost 1-3)
1983 v Switzerland (drew 2-2)
1984 v N Ireland (lost 0-2)

A tall, deceptively pacy left-flank forward with notable dead-ball skills and crossing acumen, Peter Weir won the first four of his Scottish caps while dazzling the Love Street faithful. He was soon involved in a part-exchange deal which valued him at £300,000 and set a new transfer record between two Scottish clubs, as he left St Mirren for Aberdeen in May 1981.

He made a quiet start for the Dons, but two goals against UEFA Cup holders Ipswich Town seemed to signal the start of Weir's Aberdeen career, and he quickly showed the form that had prompted Alex Ferguson to sign him. A blistering performance in the European Cup Winners' Cup Final against Real Madrid in Gothenburg, when he played such a crucial part in the goal by John Hewitt, will forever be remembered by Dons fans. He shared in most of the glories of Aberdeen's 1980s renaissance, earning medals from two Premier Division Championship campaigns and three Scottish Cup wins to go with that European Cup Winners' Cup triumph.

Following the departure of Eric Black to Metz, a player with whom Weir had struck up a good understanding, the winger's form began to suffer. He had become a marked man, and the crunching challenges took their toll.

In 1987 he joined Leicester City, linking elegantly with Gary McAllister and occasionally delighting those nostalgic for the intricacies of the touchline dribbling art. With his family unable to settle, he returned to Scotland to play with his first professional club, St Mirren. He retired in 1992 with an ankle injury, after performing player-coach duties at Ayr United.

ALAN BRAZIL
Forward
Born: Alan Bernard Brazil, Glasgow, 15 June 1959
Height: 6ft 0in
Weight: 12st 4lb
Clubs: Ipswich Town; Tottenham Hotspur; Manchester United; Coventry City; Queen's Park Rangers
Scotland caps: 13
Scotland goals: 1
1980 v Poland (lost 0-1), v Hungary (lost 1-3)
1982 v Spain (lost 0-3), v Holland (won 2-1), v N Ireland (drew 1-1), v Wales (won 1-0), v England (lost 0-1), v New Zealand (won 5-2), v USSR (drew 2-2)
1983 v East Germany (won 2-0), v Switzerland (lost 0-2), v Wales (won 2-0) 1 goal, v England (lost 0-2)

Although the famous Celtic Boys Club was not officially linked with the Glasgow

Alan Brazil playing for Ipswich Town

giants, the Parkhead side were usually quick to spot any available talent, but they overlooked Alan Brazil who joined Ipswich Town.

A Scottish youth international, he made his league debut in a 2-1 defeat at Manchester United in January 1978. He was a member of the entertaining and highly successful side built by Bobby Robson, that challenged for major honours and won the UEFA Cup in 1981. Having played for the Scotland Under-21 team, Brazil made his full international debut against Poland in May 1980, and during his stay at Portman Road, won eight Under-21 caps and 11 full caps.

A consistent goalscorer, his best season was 1981-82 when he scored 28 goals in 44 League and Cup games. On 16 February 1982, Southampton visited Portman Road as the League leaders, and had suffered only one defeat in their last 13 matches. Brazil scored a hat-trick within the space of five minutes in the first-half, and went on to net all five goals in Town's 5-2 win.

He had scored 80 goals in 210 first team games, when in March 1983 he joined Tottenham Hotspur for a fee of £450,000. Finding that his style of play did not really fit in with that of Spurs, he was allowed to move on for £750,000 to Manchester United, who had been keen to sign him before he left East Anglia. Again Brazil was unable to recapture his outstanding form of Portman Road or adapt to the pattern of his club, and after an unhappy time at Old Trafford, he joined Coventry City. At Highfield Road he began to rediscover his old touch, but after five months, he returned to London, this time signing for Queen's Park Rangers. However, he played in only four league games for the Loftus Road club before suffering a serious back injury that forced him to retire from League football.

He continued to play in non-League circles for a number of clubs before becoming mine host at the Black Adder Inn in Ipswich. Brazil is now a radio presenter with Talk Sport.

ALLY DAWSON
Full-back

Born: Alistair Dawson, Johnstone, 25 February 1958
Height: 5ft 10in
Weight: 11st 10lb
Clubs: Glasgow Rangers; Blackburn Rovers; Airdrieonians
Scotland caps: 5
1980 v Poland (lost 0-1), v Hungary (lost 1-3)
1983 v N Ireland (drew 0-0), v Canada (won 2-0), v Canada (won 2-0)

Ally Dawson joined Rangers as a 17-year-old schoolboy in the summer of 1975, and was promptly taken on a world tour by the Ibrox club's manager Jock Wallace. Though at school he had been a forward, he was soon converted into a full-back, able to play on either flank.

Over the next couple of seasons, he developed into a skilful and cultured defender, who liked nothing better than to get forward in support of his attack. In 1978-79 he was a member of the Rangers sides that won the Scottish Cup and League Cup Finals, and though he was appointed club captain, he never quite became the wholly exceptional player everyone expected him to be, because of a serious injury he sustained on a club tour of Canada in 1980, when he fractured his skull.

He recovered, of course, and went on to represent Scotland five times in full internationals, as well as picking up another Cup winners' and three further League Cup winners' medals. By the time he won the last of his four League Cup medals in 1986-87, he had moved into the centre of the Rangers defence, going on to appear in 316 games for the Ibrox club, before a £25,000 move to Blackburn Rovers in the close season.

He spent two seasons at Ewood Park, but much of his time with the Lancashire club was spent in the treatment room as he suffered a spate of niggling injuries. Unable to hold down a regular first team spot, he returned to Scotland and joined Airdrie, but once again injuries hampered his progress and he was forced into premature retirement.

RAY STEWART
Full-back/Midfield

Born: Raymond Strean McDonald Stewart, Stanley, 7 September 1959
Height: 5ft 11in
Weight: 12st 0lb

Clubs: Errol Rovers; Dundee United; West Ham United
Scotland caps: 10
Scotland goals: 1
1981 v Wales (lost 0-2), v N Ireland (won 2-0) 1 goal, v England (won 1-0)
1982 v N Ireland (drew 0-0), v Portugal (lost 1-2), v Wales (won 1-0)
1984 v France (lost 0-2)
1987 v Republic of Ireland (drew 0-0), v Luxembourg (won 3-0), v Republic of Ireland (lost 0-1)

Ray Stewart

When West Ham United manager John Lyall signed Ray Stewart from Dundee United for a fee of £430,000 in August 1979, he became the most expensive teenager in British football. Though he was uncapped when he arrived at Upton Park, within two years he made his full international debut for Scotland, this meaning that he had represented his country at all levels. In that two-year period, he also won an FA Cup winners' medal and scored in the League Cup Final.

He made his debut for West Ham alongside Billy Bonds at the heart of the Hammers' defence in a 2-0 League Cup win at Burnley, but played in midfield for his home debut against Sunderland, which West Ham won by the same score. His strong tackling and ferocious shooting had much to do with the Hammers winning the FA Cup in 1980; in fact he was the club's top scorer in that successful run. One of the most successful spot-kick specialists in the country, he returned to Wembley in 1981 as the Hammers faced Liverpool in the League Cup Final. He showed great composure as he placed his right-foot shot past Ray Clemence for the last-minute penalty equaliser in front of a 100,000 crowd, but, unfortunately for the Hammers, Liverpool won the replay.

Stewart thrived on responsibility, and when Alvin Martin was absent, he took over the captaincy. In 1981-82, he scored 10 league goals, and a further three in Cup competitions in the club's first season back in the top flight. He continued to score some important goals, including six in 1985-86, the club's best-ever First Division campaign when they finished third, but then injuries, including one to the main anterior cruciate ligament, hampered his later years with the club.

In May 1991 he played the last of his 431 games for West Ham against Charlton Athletic. Given a free transfer by the Hammers, he returned north of the Border to join St Johnstone, first as coach, then as community officer at McDiarmid Park.

PAUL STURROCK

Forward

Born: Paul Whitehead Sturrock, Elton, 10 October 1956
Height: 5ft 9in
Weight: 10st 4lb
Clubs: Bankfoot Juniors; Dundee United
Scotland caps: 20
Scotland goals: 3

1981 v Wales (lost 0-2), v N Ireland (won 2-0), v England (won 1-0)
1982 v Portugal (lost 1-2) 1 goal, v N Ireland (drew 1-1), v Wales (won 1-0),
     v England (lost 0-1)
1983 v East Germany (won 2-0) 1 goal, v Switzerland (lost 0-2), v Belgium (lost 2-3),
     v Canada (won 2-0), v Canada (won 3-0), v Canada (won 2-0)
1984 v Wales (won 2-1)
1985 v Yugoslavia (won 6-1) 1 goal
1986 v Israel (won 1-0), v Holland (drew 0-0), v Denmark (lost 0-1), v Uruguay (drew 0-0)
1987 v Belgium (lost 1-4)

An all-time Dundee United great, Paul Sturrock was signed for the Tannadice club by manager Jim McLean when he was a 17-year-old player for Bankfoot Juniors. He made his first team debut in the European Cup Winners' Cup against Jiul Petroseni in September 1974, United winning 3-2 on aggregate, although his first goals for the club didn't come until the following April, when he netted both United's goals in a 2-2 draw with Rangers.

During his 15 seasons with United, Sturrock scored 109 goals in 385 league games, with his best season being 1981-82, when he netted 15 goals in 31 games. An important member of the United side that won the League Championship in 1982-83, he also helped the Tannadice club win the League Cup in 1980-81, beating Dundee 3-0 in the final.

Winning the first of his 20 Scottish caps against Wales in 1981, Sturrock was unlucky not to win more international honours.

In June 1989 he was appointed Dundee United's first team coach, but four years later, he left Tannadice to take over the manager's job at St Johnstone from John McClelland. He succeeded in taking the club from the Scottish First Division to the Premier League in 1996-97. Following an approach from Hibs, he signed a contract with St Johnstone that would have kept him at McDiarmid Park until 2002. All that changed in September 1998, when he returned to his beloved Tannadice as Dundee United's manager.

In October 2000 he went to manage Plymouth Argyle, and in 2001-02 led them to the Third Division Championship. The Pilgrims were heading the Second Division table, when in March 2004 he left Home Park to take over the reins of Premiership Southampton. His stay at St Mary's was brief, and in September 2004 he was appointed boss of Sheffield Wednesday.

TOMMY BURNS
Midfield

Born: Thomas Burns, Glasgow, 16 December 1956
Height: 5ft 11in
Weight: 11st 6lb
Clubs: Maryhill Juniors; Glasgow Celtic; Blackpool; Kilmarnock
Scotland caps: 8
1981 v N Ireland (won 2-0)
1982 v Holland (won 2-1), v Wales (won 1-0)
1983 v Belgium (lost 2-3), v N Ireland (drew 0-0), v Canada (won 2-0), v Canada (won 2-0)
1988 v England (lost 0-1)

Tommy Burn's best season for Celtic was 1981-82, and, as Scotland were short of real class for the 1982 World Cup, it seemed logical that he would be selected. He was named in Jock Stein's initial 40 from which the squad would be picked, but despite a good game against Wales at the end of May, he was ultimately not selected for the final party of 22.

Having made his Celtic debut as a substitute against Dundee in April 1975, Tommy Burns soon established himself as a first team regular at Parkhead and won his first League Championship medal in 1976-77. He won another Championship medal in 1978-79 and his first Scottish Cup badge against Rangers in 1980. The architect behind the club's League Championship victories of 1980-81 and 1981-82, he won the first of eight caps against Northern Ireland in May 1981. Though he was a regular in the Scottish side for the next couple of seasons, he had to wait until 1988 for his first crack at the English. Scotland lost 1-0, and it was Burns' last appearance for the national side.

Winning another Scottish Cup medal in 1985 as Celtic beat Dundee United 2-1, and another Championship badge in 1985-86, he played the last of his 500 games, in which he scored 81 goals, in December 1989, before leaving to play for Kilmarnock.

At Rugby Park, the fans chanted his name from beginning to end of the game against Hamilton Academicals, demanding that he be made manager. He duly took Killie into the Premier Division the following season, before leaving to take charge at his beloved Celtic. He led the Parkhead club to victory over Airdrie in the 1995 Scottish Cup Final before parting company. He later had a spell managing Reading, but is now back at Parkhead as Celtic's Youth Development Manager.

JIM BETT
Midfield

Born: James Bett, Hamilton, 25 November 1959
Height: 5ft 11in
Weight: 12st 3lb
Clubs: Dundee; Airdrieonians; Valur FC (Iceland); SK Lokeren (Belgium); Glasgow Rangers; SK
  Lokeren (Belgium); Aberdeen; Heart of Midlothian; Dundee United

Scotland caps: 25
Scotland goals: 1
1982 v Holland (won 2-1)
1983 v Belgium (lost 2-3)
1984 v Belgium (drew 1-1), v Wales (won 2-1), v England (drew 1-1), v France (lost 0-2)
1985 v Yugoslavia (won 6-1), v Iceland (won 3-0), v Spain (won 3-1), v Spain (lost 0-1),
v Wales (lost 0-1), v England (won 1-0), v Iceland (won 1-0) 1 goal
1986 v Wales (drew 1-1), v Australia (won 2-0), v Israel (won 1-0), v Holland (drew 0-0)
1987 v Belgium (lost 1-4)
1988 v Hungary (won 2-0)
1989 v Yugoslavia (drew 1-1)
1990 v France (lost 0-3), v Norway (drew 1-1), v Argentina (won 1-0), v Egypt (lost 1-3),
v Malta (won 2-1)

Signed on an 'S' form by Dundee, then allowed to move to Airdrie and then Valur of Iceland, midfielder Jim Bett looked destined to be given the tag of 'journeyman player'.

However, a move to Belgian side SK Lokeren in the summer of 1979 proved to be the catalyst for a significant upturn in the Hamilton-born player's fortunes, and within a year he had attracted the attention of Rangers, to whom he was transferred for a fee of £180,000 in May 1980.

Jim Bett spent three seasons at Ibrox, winning a Scottish Cup Final medal in 1981 and a League Cup winners' medal the following year. Also in 1982, his performances earned him the first of 25 full international caps against Holland.

In May 1983, Bett returned to Lokeren where he spent a further two years before Aberdeen paid £300,000 for his services. Sadly, the early months of his Pittodrie career saw him hampered by injury, though his artistry and vision in the middle of the park soon made him a huge favourite with the Dons' fans. In his first season, Aberdeen won the Scottish Cup, beating Hearts 3-0 in the final. He remained a first team regular for the next few seasons, and in 1990-91 when the Dons pushed Rangers right to the wire for the League Championship, Bett was the club's only ever-present.

He continued to play for Aberdeen for a further three seasons, but by the end of the 1993-94 campaign, his appearances were becoming restricted through injury and a number of up-and-coming youngsters. On leaving Pittodrie, he joined Hearts, but after a season at Tynecastle, he moved to Dundee United, helping them win promotion from the First Division before retiring from playing.

ALLAN EVANS
Defender
Born: Allan Evans, Dunfermline, 12 October 1956
Height: 6ft 1in
Weight: 13st 2lb
Clubs: Dunfermline United; Dunfermline Athletic; Aston Villa; Leicester City; Victoria Vistas
(Canada); Brisbane United (Australia); Darlington

1982 v Holland (won 2-1), v N Ireland (drew 1-1), v England (lost 0-1),
v New Zealand (won 5-2)

Allan Evans in Aston Villa colours

Allan Evans' football career started in a uniquely unsettling manner in 1973-74, when, as a 16-year-old amateur, he broke his leg during his debut for Dunfermline Athletic against Rangers. He bounced back, however, to star for the Pars as both a central defender and an out-and-out striker.

On leaving East End Park, he joined Aston Villa in the summer of 1977, spending much of his first season in the club's reserve side. Continuing to play up front, he netted six goals in a match against Sheffield United, and this earned him his first team debut. After a handful of games leading the attack, he was moved into the pivotal defensive berth, though he still continued to score his fair share of goals.

Evans was instrumental in Villa's success of the early eighties, inspiring them to win both the League Championship in 1981 and the European Cup the following year.

Picking up four Scottish caps—the last in a World Cup qualifier against New Zealand in 1982—he later assumed Villa's captaincy, before experiencing successive relegation and promotion seasons during his 469 games tenure at Villa Park.

On leaving the Villans he joined Leicester City, but despite his vast experience, he proved every bit as prone to costly errors as his more junior defensive colleagues while the team plummeted to the depths of Division Two.

He then had what looked like a playing swansong in Canada and Australia before returning to the Football League, albeit for four minutes of competitive action with Darlington. When former Villa colleague Brian Little became Leicester City manager, Allan Evans was his first recruit to the coaching staff, and when Little took over the reins at Aston Villa, Evans followed him to his beloved former club.

ARTHUR ALBISTON
Left-back
Born: Arthur Richard Albiston, Edinburgh, 14 July 1957
Height: 5ft 7in

Weight: 11st 5lb
Clubs: Manchester United; West Bromwich Albion; Dundee; Chesterfield; Chester City
Scotland caps: 14
1982 v N Ireland (drew 1-1)
1984 v Uruguay (won 2-0), v Belgium (drew 1-1), v East Germany (lost 1-2),
      v Wales (won 2-1), v England (drew 1-1)
1985 v Yugoslavia (won 6-1), v Iceland (won 3-0), v Spain (won 3-1), v Spain (lost 0-1),
      v Wales (lost 0-1)
1986 v East Germany (drew 0-0), v Holland (drew 0-0), v Uruguay (drew 0-0)

Arthur Albiston has the unique distinction of having made his FA Cup debut in a Wembley Final, when, as a 19-year-old, he was called up against Liverpool for the 1977 Final. Ninety minutes later, after just one Cup game, he was the proud owner of an FA Cup winners' medal.

The big occasion never over-awed Albiston, who had made his senior debut for Manchester United in front of a 55,000 crowd as the Reds faced Manchester City in a 1974 League Cup game.

A strong, thoughtful defender, Albiston took a couple of seasons to establish himself, but after his surprise Cup Final appearance, became a first team regular. Subsequent FA Cup Final appearances followed in 1979—Arsenal (lost 2-3), 1983—Brighton and Hove Albion (won 4-0 after a 2-2 draw) and 1985—Everton (won 1-0), and he was also in United's 1983 Milk Cup Final team. Following United's defeat of Everton, Albiston became the first United player ever to win three FA Cup winners' medals.

Capped by Scotland as a schoolboy, he went on to make his full Scottish debut in 1982 against Northern Ireland. By the mid-1980s, he had established himself in the heart of the Scottish defence and went on to collect a total of 14 caps, including a trip to Mexico for the 1986 World Cup Finals.

The Edinburgh-born defender had appeared in 482 League and Cup games for Manchester United when, in 1988, he left Old Trafford to join West Bromwich Albion. After just one season at the Hawthorns, he moved on to Dundee on a free transfer, later playing for Chesterfield and Chester City before hanging up his boots.

JIM LEIGHTON
Goalkeeper
Born: James Leighton, Johnstone, 24 July 1958
Height: 6ft 1in
Weight: 12st 9lb
Clubs: Dalry Thistle; Aberdeen; Manchester United; Reading; Dundee; Hibernian; Aberdeen
Scotland caps: 91
1983 v East Germany (won 2-0), v Switzerland (lost 0-2), v Belgium (lost 2-3),
      v Switzerland (drew 2-2), v Wales (won 2-0), v England (lost 0-2), v Canada (won 3-0),
      v Canada (won 2-0)
1984 v Uruguay (won 2-0), v Belgium (drew 1-1), v N Ireland (lost 0-2), v Wales (won 2-1),
      v England (drew 1-1), v France (lost 0-2)

1985 v Yugoslavia (won 6-1), v Iceland (won 3-0), v Spain (won 3-1), v Spain (lost 0-1), v Wales (lost 0-1), v England (won 1-0), v Iceland (won 1-0)

1986 v Wales (drew 1-1), v East Germany (drew 0-0), v Australia (won 2-0), v Australia (drew 0-0), v Israel (won 1-0), v Denmark (lost 0-1), v West Germany (lost 1-2), v Uruguay (drew 0-0)

1987 v Bulgaria (drew 0-0), v Republic of Ireland (drew 0-0), v Luxembourg (won 3-0), v Republic of Ireland (lost 0-1), v Belgium (lost 1-4), v England (drew 0-0)

1988 v Hungary (won 2-0), v Belgium (won 2-0), v Bulgaria (won 1-0), v Luxembourg (drew 0-0), v Saudi Arabia (drew 2-2), v Malta (drew 1-1), v Spain (drew 0-0), v Colombia (drew 0-0), v England (lost 0-1)

1989 v Norway (won 2-1), v Cyprus (won 3-2), v France (won 2-0), v Cyprus (won 2-1), v England (lost 0-2), v Chile (won 2-0)

1990 v Yugoslavia (lost 1-3), v France (lost 0-3), v Norway (drew 1-1), v Argentina (won 1-0), v Malta (won 2-1), v Costa Rica (lost 0-1), v Sweden (won 2-1), v Brazil (lost 0-1)

1994 v Malta (won 2-0), v Austria (won 2-1), v Holland (lost 1-3)

1995 v Greece (lost 0-1), v Russia (drew 0-0), v San Marino (won 2-0), v Japan (drew 0-0), v Ecuador (won 2-1), v Faroe Islands (won 2-0)

1996 v Greece (won 1-0), v Finland (won 1-0), v Sweden (lost 0-2), v San Marino (won 5-0), v Australia (won 1-0), v Denmark (lost 0-2), v United States (lost 1-2)

1997 v Sweden (won 1-0), v Estonia (won 2-0), v Austria (won 2-0), v Sweden (lost 1-2), v Wales (lost 0-1), v Malta (won 3-2), v Belarus (won 1-0)

1998 v Belarus (won 4-1), v Latvia (won 2-0), v Denmark (lost 0-1), v Finland (drew 1-1), v United States (drew 0-0), v Brazil (lost 1-2), v Norway (drew 1-1), v Morocco (lost 0-3)

1999 v Lithuania (drew 0-0), v Estonia (won 3-2)

Jim Leighton

The most capped goalkeeper in Scottish international history, Jim Leighton played the last of his 91 games against Estonia in October 1998 at the age of 40.

He made his debut for Aberdeen in a 4-1 win at Hearts on the opening day of the 1978-79 season, but he had to spend another four years at Pittodrie before taking over from Bobby Clark as Aberdeen's first-choice keeper. His outstanding performances for the Dons saw Jock Stein take him to the 1982 World Cup Finals as third choice goalkeeper, and soon afterwards he selected him to succeed Alan Rough against East Germany in October 1982.

After conceding nine goals in his first six internationals, Leighton conceded only 15 in his next 26 appearances. He was one of only three players to appear in all eight qualifying games for Scotland in the 1986 World Cup Finals—Alex McLeish and Willie Miller, who formed the backbone of Aberdeen's success in the eighties, were the others. Leighton's displays in Iceland and Australia ensured Scotland went the distance. In Mexico, his reputation was enhanced when, towards the end of the game with Uruguay, he produced a wonderful reflex save, while his energetic chasing of the ball to quicken the taking of goal-kicks was demonstrative of his overall spirit and inspiration.

At Pittodrie, Leighton won two League Championship medals and four Scottish Cup winners' medals. He also collected a European Cup Winners' Cup medal as the Dons beat Real Madrid in May 1983.

After beating off challenges from a number of overseas clubs for his signature, Manchester United manager Alex Ferguson paid a British record £750,000 for Leighton's services. He arrived at Old Trafford with a reputation as one of the world's leading keepers, and was seen as a key figure in the rebirth of the Red Devils as a major power. During the 1989-90 season, United reached the FA Cup Final, but Leighton's performances in the second half of the season meant that some United fans were turning on him. Though Ferguson kept faith with him, he was responsible for all three of Crystal Palace's goals in a 3-3 draw. For the replay, Ferguson opted for Les Sealey and the Cup went to Old Trafford. Sadly, in such traumatic circumstances, Leighton's Old Trafford career was finished.

After a loan spell with Reading, he joined Dundee for £150,000 in February 1992. Consumed with bitterness and his football world seemingly in tatters, Leighton then joined Hibernian, and his performances for the Easter Road club led to him winning a recall to the Scotland side. In the summer of 1997 he rejoined Aberdeen, and continued to play for the Dons for the next three seasons before deciding to retire.

RICHARD GOUGH
Central defender

Born: Charles Richard Gough, Stockholm, Sweden, 5 April 1962
Height: 6ft 0in
Weight: 11st 12lb
Clubs: Charlton Athletic; Dundee United; Tottenham Hotspur; Glasgow Rangers; San Jose Earthquakes (United States); Nottingham Forest; Everton; Northern Spirit (Australia)
Scotland caps: 61
Scotland goals: 6

1983 v Switzerland (drew 2-2), v N Ireland (drew 0-0), v Wales (won 2-0),
      v England (lost 0-2), v Canada (won 2-0), v Canada (won 3-0) 1 goal,
      v Canada (won 2-0)
1984 v Uruguay (won 2-0), v Belgium (drew 1-1), v East Germany (lost 1-2),
      v N Ireland (lost 0-2), v Wales (won 2-1), v England (drew 1-1), v France (lost 0-2)
1985 v Spain (lost 0-1), v England (won 1-0) 1 goal, v Iceland (won 1-0)
1986 v Wales (drew 1-1), v East Germany (drew 0-0), v Australia (drew 0-0),
      v Israel (won 1-0), v Romania (won 3-0) 1 goal, v England (lost 1-2),
      v Denmark (lost 0-1), v West Germany (lost 1-2), v Uruguay (drew 0-0)

1987   v Bulgaria (drew 0-0), v Republic of Ireland (drew 0-0), v Luxembourg (won 3-0),
        v Republic of Ireland (lost 0-1), v Belgium (lost 1-4), v England (drew 0-0),
        v Brazil (lost 0-2)

1988   v Hungary (won 2-0), v Saudi Arabia (drew 2-2), v Spain (drew 0-0),
        v Colombia (drew 0-0), v England lost 0-1)

1989   v Yugoslavia (drew 1-1), v Italy (lost 0-2), v Cyprus (won 3-2) 2 goals,
        v France (won 2-0), v Cyprus (won 2-1)

1990   v France (lost 0-3), v Argentina (won 1-0), v East Germany (lost 0-1), v Egypt (lost 1-3),
        v Poland (drew 1-1), v Malta (won 2-1), v Costa Rica (lost 0-1)

1991   v USSR (lost 0-1), v Bulgaria (drew 1-1)

1992   v San Marino (won 4-0) 1 goal, v N Ireland (won 1-0), v Canada (won 3-1),
        v Norway (drew 0-0), v Holland (lost 0-1), v Germany (lost 0-2), v USSR (won 3-0)

1993   v Switzerland (lost 1-3), v Portugal (lost 0-5)

The Swedish-born, South African-raised, Scottish international was one of the most durable and reliable men in the game, winning 61 caps for his country.

Disappointingly, one of the doubters was former national boss Andy Roxburgh, who expressed reservations about the legitimacy of Gough's injuries on international duty, an accusation which was to be one of many disputes between the pair, and caused Gough to retire from the Scotland scene after the disastrous 5-0 collapse in Portugal in 1993. It was all the more disturbing for the national side, as Gough had been inspirational in Scotland's European Championship Finals appearance in 1992, and named in the team of the tournament on its completion.

Gough spent seven months at Charlton as a 16-year-old, but returned to Johannesburg because of homesickness. However, the following year he decided to have another go of making a career in professional football and joined Dundee United. He succeeded in spectacular fashion, establishing himself as an outstanding defender, equally at home at full-back or central defence. He helped United win the 1983 Scottish League title and reach the finals of both the Scottish Cup and League Cup in 1985. Voted Scottish PFA 'Player of the Year' in 1986, he left Tannadice in August of that year, joining Spurs for a fee of £700,000.

Immediately appointed captain by manager David Pleat, he led Spurs to the 1987 FA Cup Final and played for the Football League against the Rest of the World in the League's Centenary match in August 1987. Unfortunately for Spurs, his family were unable to settle in London, and he was allowed to move to Rangers for a fee of £1.5 million.

Alongside his former Spurs team-mate Graham Roberts, he helped Rangers lift the Skol Cup in his first season at Ibrox, and went on to add to his list of honours with nine League Championship medals, three Scottish Cup winners' medals and six League Cup winners' medals. Continuing to display the form that made him one of the most accomplished defenders in the British game, he was also voted 'Player of the Year' by the Scottish Football Writers' Association in 1989. He had scored 35 goals in 424 games for Rangers, when, in May 1998, he left Ibrox to join American side San Jose Earthquakes on a free transfer.

He returned to British football in March 1999, joining Nottingham Forest, and impressed so much that his former club Spurs tried to re-sign him on transfer deadline day. Unable to prevent Forest's relegation from the Premiership, he then joined Walter Smith's Everton. Despite his 37 years, he was one of the success stories of the 1999-2000 season, an inspirational figure both on and off the field. Sadly, his second season on Merseyside was blighted by injuries and he left to play in Australia for Northern Spirit.

CHARLIE NICHOLAS
Forward

Born: Charles Nicholas, Glasgow, 30 December 1961
Height: 5ft 10in
Weight: 11st 0lb
Clubs: Glasgow Celtic; Arsenal; Aberdeen; Glasgow Celtic; Clyde
Scotland caps: 20
Scotland goals: 5

1983 v Switzerland (drew 2-2) 1 goal, v N Ireland (drew 0-0), v England (lost 0-2),
v Canada (won 2-0), v Canada (won 3-0) 1 goal, v Canada (won 2-0)
1984 v Belgium (drew 1-1) 1 goal, v France (lost 0-2)
1985 v Yugoslavia (won 6-1) 1 goal, v Iceland (won 3-0) 1 goal, v Spain (lost 0-1),
v Wales (lost 0-1)
1986 v Israel (won 1-0), v Romania (won 3-0), v England (lost 1-2), v Denmark (lost 0-1),
v Uruguay (drew 0-0)
1987 v Bulgaria (drew 0-0), v England (drew 0-0)
1989 v Cyprus (won 2-0)

Charlie Nicholas, who scored a tremendous goal against Switzerland on his international debut, joined Celtic and made his league debut for the club against Kilmarnock in August 1980. Still not yet 20, he finished that season scoring 25 goals in 42 games when helping Celtic to the Scottish League Championship. In 1981-82, a series of injuries including a broken leg sidelined him for most of the season, although he did manage to play in enough games to help Celtic retain the League Championship. However, it was 1982-83 when he really hit the headlines, scoring over 50 competitive goals.

He finished as Scotland's leading scorer and was voted Scottish Footballer of the Year, won six Scottish caps and gained a Rothmans special award.

Arsenal beat off the challenge of Liverpool and Manchester United to secure his signature for £800,000 in June 1983. It was the most publicised transfer for a good number of years, as Nicholas became the instant idol of the North Bank. On his day there was no more skilful footballer than Charlie Nicholas, performing feats with the ball which most players would not even dream of. The beginning of his Arsenal career did not go to plan, for though he only missed one league game, he only scored 11 goals. His goalscoring performance did not improve in 1984-85, but by this time he had been moved back into a deeper midfield position. With new manager George Graham in charge, Nicholas spent long periods out of the side, with a definite rift between the two apparent.

Charlie Nicholas (www.snspix.com)

Nicholas was determined to have the last laugh, and appeared to have done so after scoring both goals in the 1987 Littlewoods Cup Final against Liverpool.

But, in January 1988, the 'King' of the North Bank was transferred to Aberdeen for £400,000. He spent three seasons at Pittodrie, before returning to Celtic for the 1990-91 season, and was an important member of their squad before joining Clyde, where he ended his career.

NEIL SIMPSON
Midfield

Born: Neil Simpson, London, 15 November 1961
Height: 5ft 11in
Weight: 10st 6lb
Clubs: Middlefield Wasps; Aberdeen; Newcastle United; Motherwell; Cove Rangers
Scotland caps: 5
1983 v N Ireland (drew 0-0)
1984 v Uruguay (won 2-0), v France (lost 0-2)
1987 v England (drew 0-0)
1988 v England (lost 0-1)

An Englishman by birth but brought up near Aberdeen, Neil Simpson is one of only a few players to have been capped by the Scots although born over the Border.

Simpson came to Pittodrie on an 'S' form, and made an early breakthrough into the Dons' first team in 1980 due to injuries to Gordon Strachan and John McMaster, making an instant impression in the heart of the Aberdeen midfield. Although remembered for his battling, powerhouse qualities, he also displayed a delightful touch on the ball.

During the season he first won international recognition, Aberdeen won the Scottish Cup and the European Cup Winners' Cup, and in the game against Bayern Munich at a packed Pittodrie, Simpson more than played his part by scoring the equaliser to get the Dons back in the game. He always seemed to weigh in with vital goals, including the opener in the 2-0 Super Cup victory over Hamburg in 1984. It was a history-making goal, bringing the Super Cup to Pittodrie, home of the only Scottish club to win two European trophies.

Simpson's career went from strength to strength, and though manager Alex Ferguson left to take charge of Manchester United, Simpson was determined to remain loyal to the Dons. Sadly, that determination was to prove his downfall. In October 1988, Rangers visited Pittodrie for a vital league match for both clubs. A tense and fraught game saw Simpson commit a bad foul on Rangers' Ian Durrant. The Scottish international was stretchered off the field and was out of the game for over two-and-a-half years.

There ensued a media witch-hunt—Simpson became public enemy number one—and Durrant revealed that he intended to sue the Aberdeen midfielder for the events of that fateful day. Simpson left Pittodrie to play for Newcastle United, but his stay on Tyneside was dogged by injury. He then returned to Scotland and Motherwell, but the Durrant incident could not be laid to rest and he returned to the north-east to play Highland League football for Cove Rangers. On hanging up his boots, he became the SFA Development Officer for Moray.

MARK McGHEE

Forward

Born: Mark Edward McGhee, Glasgow, 20 May 1957
Height: 5ft 10in
Weight: 12st 12lb
Clubs: Bristol City; Morton; Newcastle United; Aberdeen; SV Hamburg (Germany); Glasgow Celtic; Newcastle United; IK Braga (Sweden); Reading
Scotland caps: 4
Scotland goals: 2
1983 v Canada (won 2-0) 1 goal, v Canada (won 3-0)
1984 v N Ireland (lost 0-2), v England (drew 1-1) 1 goal

Mark McGhee, who scored on his international debut against Canada after coming on as a substitute for Charlie Nicholas, also netted on his last appearance for the national side in a 1-1 draw against England at Hampden Park in May 1984.

The burly striker joined Bristol City as a youngster, before returning to Scotland with Morton in 1975, where his performances attracted the attentions of several sides including Newcastle United, who signed him at the tail end of 1977 for £150,000. He never really settled at St James Park, and in March 1979 he was snapped up by Aberdeen for just over half of what Newcastle paid for him.

In his first season at Pittodrie, he helped the Dons win the League Championship as he developed into an unorthodox goalpoacher, able to hold the ball up, link well and finish with deadly accuracy from the tightest of chances. The highlight of McGhee's stay with the Dons came in 1982-83, when his cross was met by John Hewitt for the dramatic European Cup Winners' Cup winner. The following year, his last with Aberdeen, he helped the Dons defeat Hamburg to lift the Super Cup. Little did he know that he was playing against his next employers! A second League Champions' medal was added to his collection, before he scored the extra-time winner against Celtic to win the 1984 Scottish Cup for the Pittodrie club.

Having scored 100 goals in 263 first team outings, McGhee joined SV Hamburg for £285,000. He remained in Germany for a year-and-a-half before coming back to Scotland with Celtic for another major medal haul—champions in 1986 and 1988 and Cup winners in 1988 and 1989. He later had another spell with Newcastle and played in Sweden for IK Braga, before being appointed player-manager of Reading.

He took the Royals to the Second Division Championship in 1993-94, before being appointed manager of Leicester City. After just a year at Filbert Street, he defected to Wolves, citing a lack of ambition at the East Midlands club. Though he led Wolves to the play-offs in 1996-97, he eventually paid the price for the club's lack of success in November 1998. He later took charge of Millwall, and in 2000-01, his first season with the club, led them to the Second Division Championship. In the summer of 2003, he made way for Dennis Wise at the New Den, and in October of that year, he became manager of Championship side Brighton and Hove Albion, helping them win promotion in his first season on the south coast. Early in 2006-07, McGhee parted company with the Seagulls.

DAVIE DODDS
Forward

Born: David Dodds, Dundee, 23 September 1958
Height: 6ft 0in
Weight: 11st 11lb
Clubs: Dundee United; Neuchatel Xamax (Switzerland); Aberdeen; Glasgow Rangers
Scotland caps: 2
Scotland goals: 1
1984 v Uruguay (won 2-0) 1 goal, v N Ireland (lost 0-2)

Capped at schoolboy, youth and Under-21 levels, Davie Dodds made his full international debut for Scotland against Uruguay at Hampden Park in September

1983. Coming off the bench to replace Frank McGarvey, he netted Scotland's second goal in a 2-0 win.

Davie Dodds signed for Dundee United in May 1975, and was taken to Spain by the club during their summer tour. On his return to Tannadice he made his league debut aged just 18, in a game against Arbroath, scoring twice in a 3-1 win. Dodds was United's leading scorer in five out of the next seven seasons. Only McCoist and McGarvey scored more Premiership goals than Dodds, as he found the net 103 times in 249 games for the Terrors. While with United he helped them win the League Cup in 1980-81, beating Dundee 3-0, and the League Championship in 1982-83. In March 1986 he announced he was leaving the Tannadice club to join Swiss side Neuchatel Xamax for £180,000, but the move was unsuccessful, and in September of that year he returned to Scotland to play for Aberdeen who paid £215,000 for his services.

He spent three seasons with the Pittodrie club, and his last in 1988-89 saw the Dons finish runners-up in the Premier Division and the League Cup. A tall, rather awkward mover but clever in the air and adept at holding a forward line together, Dodds joined Rangers in September 1989.

Bought no doubt as cover for Ally McCoist and Mo Johnston, he forced his way into the Rangers side, and in his first season with the Ibrox club, won a Premier Division Championship medal. It was under Walter Smith's management that he took up a coaching position at Ibrox, before leaving the club in 1997.

PAUL McSTAY
Midfield

Born: Paul Michael Lyons McStay, Hamilton, 22 October 1964
Height: 5ft 10in
Weight: 10st 7lb
Clubs: Glasgow Celtic
Scotland caps: 76
Scotland goals: 9

1984 v Uruguay (won 2-0), v Belgium (drew 1-1), v East Germany (lost 1-2),
      v N Ireland (lost 0-2), v Wales (won 2-1), v England (drew 1-1)
1985 v Yugoslavia (won 6-1), v Iceland (won 3-0) 2 goals, v Spain (won 3-1), v Spain (lost 0-1),
      v Wales (lost 0-1)
1986 v East Germany (drew 0-0), v Australia (drew 0-0), v Israel (won 1-0) 1 goal,
      v Uruguay (drew 0-0)
1987 v Bulgaria (drew 0-0), v Republic of Ireland (drew 0-0), v Luxembourg (won 3-0),
      v Republic of Ireland (lost 0-1), v Belgium (lost 1-4) 1 goal, v England (drew 0-0),
      v Brazil (lost 0-2)
1988 v Hungary (won 2-0), v Belgium (won 2-0) 1 goal, v Bulgaria (won 1-0),
      v Luxembourg (drew 0-0), v Saudi Arabia (drew 2-2), v Spain (drew 0-0),
      v Colombia (drew 0-0), v England (lost 0-1)
1989 v Norway (won 2-1) 1 goal, v Yugoslavia (drew 1-1), v Italy (lost 0-2),
      v Cyprus (won 3-2), v France (won 2-0), v Cyprus (won 2-1), v England (lost 0-2),
      v Chile (won 2-0)

1990   v Yugoslavia (lost 1-3), v France (lost 0-3), v Norway (drew 1-1), v Argentina (won 1-0),
       v East Germany (lost 0-1), v Egypt (lost 1-3), v Poland (drew 1-1), v Malta (won 2-1),
       v Costa Rica (lost 0-1), v Sweden (won 2-1), v Brazil (lost 0-1)
1991   v Romania (won 2-1), v USSR (lost 0-1), v Bulgaria (drew 1-1)
1992   v San Marino (won 4-0) 1 goal, v Finland (drew 1-1) 1 goal, v United States (won 1-0),
       v Canada (won 3-1), v Norway (drew 0-0), v Holland (lost 0-1),
       v East Germany (lost 0-2), v USSR (won 3-0) 1 goal
1993   v Switzerland (lost 1-3), v Portugal (drew 0-0), v Italy (drew 0-0), v Malta (won 3-0),
       v Portugal (lost 0-5), v Estonia (won 3-0), v Estonia (won 3-1)
1994   v Italy (lost 1-3), v Holland (lost 0-1)
1995   v Finland (won 2-0), v Faroe Islands (won 5-1), v Russia (drew 0-0)
1996   v Australia (won 1-0)
1997   v Estonia (drew 0-0), v Estonia (won 2-0), v Austria (won 2-0)

Paul McStay, who became the third in his family to captain Celtic when he took over from Roy Aitken in January 1990, also succeeded big Roy as Scotland's skipper, until four years later he was dropped by Craig Brown. Surpassing Danny McGrain's Parkhead record of 62 Scottish caps, McStay went on to make 76 appearances for his country, his last against Austria at Celtic Park in April 1997.

A genuinely nice guy, when he scored two goals against Iceland at Hampden in October 1984 in a World Cup tie, he gave the credit to his dad! 'He kept on at me to have a go at goal before the game' said McStay. 'He told me I wasn't scoring nearly enough goals. He talked me into those two goals!' McStay, who was always looking to get forward, once played in seven consecutive international matches in which the opposition failed to score, and, remarkably, 13 of his 76 international appearances ended in goalless draws!

A former Scotland schoolboy, who scored twice at Wembley in a 5-4 win over England in June 1980, he made his Celtic debut in a 4-0 League Cup win over Queen of the South in January 1982, a season in which the Bhoys won the Championship. Later that year, he won a League Cup winners' medal as Celtic beat Rangers 2-1 in a final played in continuous heavy rain. McStay won his first Scottish Cup medal against Dundee United in May 1985, and then scored the fourth goal when Celtic stole the title at Love Street in 1986.

In 1987-88 he was outstanding as Celtic did the double, while in 1989, against Rangers in the Scottish Cup Final, he was head and shoulders above the rest in a 1-0 win. McStay's only other piece of silverware in his time at Parkhead came in 1995, when he was a member of the Celtic side that beat Airdrieonians 1-0 to lift the Scottish Cup. McStay, who was both a loyal and long servant of Celtic Football Club, played his last game in the green and white hoops against Raith Rovers in April 1997.

DOUG ROUGVIE

Full-back / Central defender

Born: Douglas Rougvie, Ballingry, 24 May 1956
Height: 6ft 2in

Weight: 13st 8lb
Clubs: Dunfermline United; Aberdeen; Chelsea; Brighton and Hove Albion; Shrewsbury Town;
Fulham; Dunfermline Athletic; Montrose; Huntly; Cove Rangers
Scotland caps: 1
1984 v N Ireland (lost 0-2)

In a long career, Doug Rougvie was capped once for his country against Northern Ireland in December 1983.

Signed by Aberdeen from junior outfit Dunfermline United, he spent most of his early time at Pittodrie farmed out to now-defunct junior side Rosemount, before being recalled. Though he was given an extended run in the first team at centre-half by Alex Ferguson, the form of the Miller-McLeish partnership meant that he spent much of his time playing at left-back.

He picked up a League Championship medal as the Dons stormed to the title in 1979-80, and was very much an integral part of the Aberdeen successes of the early 1980s. A Scottish Cup winners' medal followed in 1981-82, as the Dons beat Rangers 4-1 after extra time; and then the following season, after switching to right-back, he helped Aberdeen win the European Cup Winners' Cup, beating Real Madrid 2-1, again after extra time. Ten days later he was still at right-back as Aberdeen beat Rangers 1-0 to lift the Scottish Cup for a second successive year. Rougvie won a third Scottish Cup winners' medal in 1984 as Celtic were beaten 2-1.

Shortly after this success, the big defender left Pittodrie to join Chelsea for £150,000. Ferocious in the tackle and strong in the air, his rampaging style endeared him to the Stamford Bridge fans. Though always bringing passion and enthusiasm to his football, his three years with the Blues were disappointing. Unable to adapt to the demands of First Division football, it was clear that he had no part to play in John Hollins' long-term plans, and in the summer of 1987, he was transferred to Brighton and Hove Albion.

He later played for Shrewsbury, Fulham, Dunfermline Athletic and then Montrose as player-manager. Spells as a Highland League manager at Huntly and Cove Rangers followed, with Doug continuing to turn out as he approached his 40th birthday.

MO JOHNSTON
Forward

Born: Maurice Johnston, Glasgow, 13 April 1963
Height: 5ft 9in
Weight: 10st 7lb
Clubs: Partick Thistle; Watford; Glasgow Celtic; Nantes (France); Glasgow Rangers; Everton;
Heart of Midlothian; Falkirk; Kansas City (United States)
Scotland caps: 38
Scotland goals: 14
1984 v Wales (won 2-1) 1 goal, v England (drew 1-1), v France (lost 0-2)
1985 v Yugoslavia (won 6-1) 1 goal, v Iceland (won 3-0), v Spain (won 3-1) 2 goals,
v Spain (lost 0-1), v Wales (lost 0-1)

1986 v East Germany (drew 0-0)

1987 v Bulgaria (drew 0-0), v Republic of Ireland (drew 0-0), v Luxembourg (won 3-0) 1 goal, v Republic of Ireland (lost 0-1)

1988 v Hungary (won 2-0), v Belgium (won 2-0), v Luxembourg (drew 0-0), v Saudi Arabia (drew 2-2) 1 goal, v Spain (drew 0-0), v Colombia (drew 0-0), v England (lost 0-1)

1989 v Norway (won 2-1) 1 goal, v Yugoslavia (drew 1-1) 1 goal, v Italy (lost 0-2), v Cyprus (won 3-2) 1 goal, v France (won 2-0) 2 goals, v Cyprus (won 2-1) 1 goal, v England (lost 0-2), v Chile (won 2-0)

1990 v France (lost 0-3), v Norway (drew 1-1), v East Germany (lost 0-1), v Poland (drew 1-1) 1 goal, v Malta (won 2-1), v Costa Rica (lost 0-1), v Sweden (won 2-1), v Brazil (lost 0-1)

1992 v Switzerland (drew 2-2), v San Marino (won 4-0)

From 1985 to 1990, Mo Johnston was a regular selection for Scotland, and his six goals from eight games in the qualifying group were a major factor in Scotland reaching the 1990 World Cup Finals in Italy. Sadly, an embarrassing defeat by Costa Rica in the first game effectively put an end to any further progress, and some unfavourable post-match publicity prompted Johnston to announce his premature retirement from international football. However, after one year out he was persuaded to revoke his decision.

Snapped up by Partick Thistle in 1980, Johnston scored 41 goals from 85 games in just over three years at Firhill, before proving to be an inspired signing for Watford following the departure of Luther Blissett to AC Milan. In only his third game for the Hornets, he netted a hat-trick against Wolves at Molineux in only eight minutes, and at the end of the season he had scored 20 goals in 29 games. Johnston was also a member of the Watford side that reached that season's FA Cup Final, only to lose 2-0 to Everton. Unable to settle in the south, he asked for a transfer, and in November 1984 his wishes were granted when he returned to Scotland to play for Celtic.

He scored 52 goals in 99 games for the Bhoys, winning the Scottish Cup in 1985 and the Premier League in 1985–86 in three seasons at Parkhead, before signing for the French club Nantes. Returning to Britain two years later, he made headline news when becoming the first Catholic player to play for Rangers, after turning down a return to Celtic!

In two seasons at Ibrox he played in 65 league games, scoring 26 goals, and won two Scottish Cup medals and a Scottish Premier League Championship medal in 1989-90.

In another surprise twist to his career, he joined Everton in November 1991. It seemed like a shrewd move to boost the Toffees' declining fortunes, but he was unable to provide any spark to the team who finished in mid-table. Returning home to Scotland, he played for Hearts and Falkirk before crossing the Atlantic to end his playing days with Kansas City.

MAURICE MALPAS
Full-back/Midfield

Born: Maurice Malpas, Dunfermline, 3 August 1962
Height: 5ft 8in
Weight: 10st 11lb
Clubs: Leven Royals; Dundee United;
    Scotland caps: 55

1984 v France (lost 0-2)

1985 v England (won 1-0), v Iceland (won 1-0)

1986 v Wales (drew 1-1), v Australia (won 2-0), v Australia (drew 0-0), v Israel (won 1-0),
v Romania (won 3-0), v England (lost 1-2), v Holland (drew 0-0), v Denmark (lost 0-1),
v West Germany (lost 1-2)

1987 v Bulgaria (drew 0-0), v Republic of Ireland (lost 0-1), v Belgium (lost 1-4)

1988 v Belgium (won 2-0), v Bulgaria (won 1-0), v Luxembourg (drew 0-0),
v Saudi Arabia (drew 2-2), v Malta (drew 1-1)

1989 v Norway (won 2-1), v Yugoslavia (drew 1-1), v Italy (lost 0-2), v Cyprus (won 3-2),
v France (won 2-0), v Cyprus (won 2-1), v England (lost 0-2), v Chile (won 2-0)

1990 v Yugoslavia (lost 1-3), v France (lost 0-3), v Norway (drew 1-1), v Egypt (lost 1-3),
v Poland (drew 1-1), v Malta (won 2-1), v Costa Rica (lost 0-1), v Sweden (won 2-1),
v Brazil (lost 0-1)

1991 v Romania (won 2-1), v Bulgaria (drew 1-1), v USSR (lost 0-1), v Bulgaria (drew 1-1),
v San Marino (won 2-1)

1992 v Switzerland (drew 2-2), v Romania (lost 0-1), v San Marino (won 4-0),
v N Ireland (won 1-0), v Finland (won 1-0), v United States (won 1-0),
v Canada (won 3-1), v Norway (drew 0-0), v Holland (lost 0-1), v Germany (lost 0-2)

1993 v Switzerland (lost 1-3), v Portugal (drew 0-0), v Italy (drew 0-0)

Dundee United's most capped player, Maurice Malpas appeared 55 times for the national side after making his international debut against France in Marseilles in June 1984. A Scotland regular for almost ten years, he appeared in both the 1986 and 1990 World Cup Finals prior to making his last appearance against Italy at Ibrox in November 1992.

He joined the Tannadice club from Leven Royals in 1978, but had to wait until November 1981 before making his United debut in a 4-0 defeat of Airdrieonians. The following season, his first full campaign, he was a member of the side that won the League Championship, finishing a point ahead of runners-up Celtic. Over the next 18 seasons, Malpas missed very few games, picking up a UEFA Cup runners-up medal in 1987 as United lost 1-0 to Gothenburg.

Though he appeared in Cup Final defeats in 1985, 1987, 1988 and 1991, he was captain of the side that won the trophy for the first time in 1994, beating Rangers 1-0 in the final.

One of the few successes in Scotland's 1990 World Cup campaign, Malpas returned to Tannadice, and at the end of the following season, was voted the Scottish Football Writers' 'Player of the Year'. Also that summer he became United's player-coach in recognition of his experience. Malpas, who played the last of his 646 League and Cup games for the club at Celtic on the final day of the 1999-2000 season, is now Motherwell's coach.

Steve Nicol playing for Liverpool

STEVE NICOL

Full-back/Midfield

Born: Stephen Nicol, Irvine, 1 December 1961
Height: 5ft 10in
Weight: 12st 6lb
Clubs: Ayr United; Liverpool; Notts County; Sheffield Wednesday; West Bromwich Albion
Scotland caps: 27

1985   v Yugoslavia (won 6-1), v Iceland (won 3-0), v Spain (won 3-1), v Wales (lost 0-1)

1986   v Wales (drew 1-1), v East Germany (drew 0-0), v Australia (won 2-0),
        v England (lost 1-2), v Denmark (lost 0-1), v West Germany (lost 1-2),
        v Uruguay (drew 0-0)

1988   v Hungary (won 2-0), v Bulgaria (won 1-0), v Saudi Arabia (drew 2-2),
        v Spain (drew 0-0), v Colombia (drew 0-0), v England (lost 0-1)

1989   v Norway (won 2-1), v Yugoslavia (drew 1-1), v Cyprus (won 3-2), v France (won 2-0)

1990   v Yugoslavia (lost1-3), v France (lost 0-3)

1991   v Switzerland (won 2-1), v USSR (lost 0-1), v San Marino (won 2-1)

1992   v Switzerland (drew 2-2)

Steve Nicol made his international debut for Scotland against Yugoslavia in September 1984, a match the Scots won 6-1, and after playing in the 1986 World Cup Finals, he became a fairly regular selection for the next six years or so. He then became an innocent victim of the constant 'club versus country' tug-of-war between Liverpool and Scotland, and in September 1991 he made his 27th and final appearance against Switzerland.

Before going south to join Liverpool in October 1981, Steve Nicol had spent just over two seasons with Ayr United, having impressed at full-back after signing from a local boys' club.

It was 1983-84 before he won a regular place in the Liverpool side, but ended the campaign with League Championship and European Cup winners' medals. Nicol played on the right side of midfield before taking over the right-back position from Phil Neal in October 1985, but following the signing of Barry Venison, he alternated between full-back and midfield.

In September 1987, Nicol scored his first and only senior hat-trick as the Reds won 4-1 at Newcastle United. In 1988-89 he was switched to central defence after both Gary Gillespie and Alan Hansen were injured, and he performed so well in this emergency role that he was voted the Football Writers' Association 'Footballer of the Year' in 1989. Injuries hampered his progress over the next couple of seasons, but in 1991-92, Nicol was one of the few senior players at Anfield to escape long-term injury, and ended the campaign with his third FA Cup winners' medal.

Nicol played a full part in the Reds' almost unbroken run of success, winning four League Championship medals before being given a free transfer and joining Notts County. In November 1995, Nicol signed for Sheffield Wednesday and was a great calming influence on the younger players. He had a brief loan spell with West Bromwich Albion, before being released by the Owls in the summer of 1998.

MURDO MacLEOD
Midfield

Born: Murdo Davidson MacLeod, Glasgow, 24 September 1958
Height: 5ft 9in
Weight: 12st 4lb
Clubs: Partick Thistle; Glasgow Amateurs; Dumbarton; Glasgow Celtic; Borussia Dortmund (Germany); Hibernian
Scotland caps: 20
Scotland goals: 1
1985 v England (won 1-0)
1987 v Republic of Ireland (drew 0-0), v Luxembourg (won 3-0), v England (drew 0-0), v Brazil (lost 0-2)
1988 v Colombia (drew 0-0), v England (lost 0-1)
1989 v Italy (lost 0-2), v Chile (won 2-0) 1 goal
1990 v Yugoslavia (lost 1-3), v France (lost 0-3), v Norway (drew 1-1), v Argentina (won 1-0), v East Germany (lost 0-1), v Poland (drew 1-1), v Sweden (won 2-1), v Brazil (lost 0-1)
1991 v Romania (won 2-1), v Switzerland (won 2-1), v USSR (lost 0-1)

Murdo MacLeod won the first of his 20 caps when he came off the bench to replace Gordon Strachan in the 1-0 defeat of England at Hampden in May 1985.

He arrived at Parkhead from Dumbarton in November 1978 and was an instant hit. The hardworking MacLeod patrolled the midfield, winning tackles, dispatching telling passes and scoring with booming drives. No-one would have believed that a team that had misfired so badly the previous term could have won the League Championship in the space of 12 months, but that's exactly what Celtic achieved. In an exhausting finale, Celtic faced Rangers at Parkhead, knowing a victory would win the title from the defending holders. Despite being down to 10 men, Celtic came from behind to lead 3-2, before MacLeod added a fourth.

He was the driving force behind everything Celtic accomplished in the eighties, the two Scottish Cups of 1980 and 1985, the League Cup of 1982 and the three Championships of 1980-81, 1981-82 and 1985-86. He had scored 81 goals in 394 games for Celtic when, out of contract in the summer of 1987, he opted to join Borussia Dortmund.

MacLeod spent three seasons playing in the Bundesliga, before, in October 1990, returning to Scotland to join Hibs as their player-coach. Having helped the Easter Road club to a 2-0 win over Dunfermline Athletic in the 1991-92 League Cup Final, he went on to manage Dumbarton and Partick Thistle before becoming assistant-manager to Wim Jansen at Celtic during the 1997-98 season. The campaign ended with a League Championship, but also saw the two men leaving Celtic Park.

DAVID SPEEDIE
Forward

Born: David Robert Speedie, Glenrothes, 20 February 1960
Height: 5ft 7in
Weight: 11st 0lb
Clubs: Barnsley; Darlington; Chelsea; Coventry City; Liverpool; Blackburn Rovers; Southampton; Birmingham City; West Bromwich Albion; West Ham United; Leicester City
Scotland caps: 10
1985   v England (won 1-0)
1986   v Wales (drew 1-1), v East Germany (drew 0-0), v Australia (drew 0-0), v England (lost 1-2)
1989   v Yugoslavia (drew 1-1), v Italy (lost 0-2), v Cyprus (won 3-2), v Cyprus (won 2-1), v Chile (won 2-0)

David Speedie was an abrasive, argumentative player of rare inspiration. He had come up the hard way, earning his living at the bottom of a coal mine for almost a year before Barnsley offered him a contract.

Unable to hold down a regular place at Oakwell, he moved to Darlington, and it was from here that Chelsea manager John Neal paid £80,000 for his services in the summer of 1982. After scoring twice on his debut against Oldham Athletic, Speedie became a fixture in the Chelsea side, bringing some much needed zest to a Stamford Bridge side short on confidence. He was an influential member of the side that won the Second Division Championship in 1983-84 and went on to challenge for further honours over the next two years.

He netted a hat-trick in the 1986 Full Members Cup Final against Manchester

City, but in general his finishing lacked the ruthlessness expected of a top marksman. He was frequently dropped back into midfield to find space, and much of his best work was done there. He supplied Kerry Dixon with many of his openings and they came to be regarded as one of the most dangerous pairings in English football. Never one to keep his feelings to himself, his ceaseless aggression earned him a string of bookings, and as a consequence, he was regularly unavailable for selection.

He won the first of his 10 caps against England in May 1985, but the rich promise the Blues had shown since their return to the top flight was to remain unfulfilled, and as his form slumped, he was transferred to Coventry City for £750,000 in July 1987.

David Speedie playing for Chelsea

Speedie became a great favourite with the Highfield Road faithful, and as the Sky Blues finished seventh in 1988-89, he was the club's leading scorer with 14 goals, including a hat-trick against Middlesbrough.

He was subsequently transferred to Liverpool to add a little zip to the Anfield club's annual title challenge, before joining Blackburn Rovers where he scored 23 goals in 36 games. He then moved to Southampton, from where he had loan spells with Birmingham City, West Bromwich Albion and West Ham United, before joining Leicester City where he ended his first-class career.

GRAEME SHARP
Forward

Born: Graeme Marshall Sharp, Glasgow, 16 October 1960
Height: 6ft 1in
Weight: 11st 8lb
Clubs: Eastercraigs FC; Dumbarton; Everton; Oldham Athletic
Scotland caps: 12
Scotland goals: 1
1985 v Iceland (won 1-0)
1986 v Wales (drew 1-1), v Australia (won 2-0), v Australia (drew 0-0), v Israel (won 1-0), v Romania (won 3-0), v Uruguay (drew 0-0)
1987 v Republic of Ireland (drew 0-0)
1988 v Belgium (won 2-0), v Bulgaria (won 1-0), v Luxembourg (drew 0-0), v Malta (won 1-1) 1 goal

Graeme Sharp playing for Everton

342 *Scotland! Scotland!*—The 1980s

The pinnacle of Graeme Sharp's meteoric rise to stardom, following his transfer to Everton from Dumbarton for £120,000 in April 1980, came when Jock Stein gave him his first full Scottish outing in the World Cup qualifier against Iceland in May 1985. He went on to win 12 caps, and was never on the losing side, as Scotland in ten of his games didn't concede a goal. Sharp's only goal for the national side came on his final appearance in a 1-1 draw against Malta.

He was a virtual unknown when he arrived at Goodison Park, and became unsettled and was slow to break into a struggling team, so much so that he even considered moving on. However, following the appointment of Howard Kendall, his career began to blossom and he enjoyed a series of fruitful combinations, first with Adrian Heath, then Andy Gray, and finally, Gary Lineker.

It was Sharp who scored the Blues' opening goal in the 1984 FA Cup Final victory over Watford, while the following season he headed the equaliser against Bayern Munich in the European Cup Winners' Cup semi-final. In 1984-85, Sharp scored 30 goals in all competitions, the most spectacular and satisfying of all his strikes coming in the Merseyside derby at Anfield. As well as netting his own quota of goals, Graeme Sharp was an extremely unselfish provider, whose positional sense was remarkably acute. He was an aerial playmaker, who combined deftness and power with the ability to distribute as accurately with his head as most contemporaries could with their feet.

After injuries restricted his appearances towards the end of Everton's League Championship-winning season of 1986-87, Sharp's goal tally began to deteriorate. However, he still holds the record as the Blues' top post-war goalscorer.

He left Everton in the summer of 1991, joining Oldham Athletic for £150,000. When Oldham manager Joe Royle returned to Goodison Park, Sharp became the Latics' manager, but resigned his post in February 1997. The popular striker is now a pundit on local radio.

ANDY GORAM
Goalkeeper

Born: Andrew Lewis Goram, Bury, 13 April 1964
Height: 5ft 11in
Weight: 11st 6lb
Clubs: Oldham Athletic; Hibernian; Glasgow Rangers; Notts County; Sheffield United; Motherwell; Manchester United; Coventry City; Oldham Athletic
Scotland caps: 43

1986 v East Germany (drew 0-0), v Romania (won 3-0), v Holland (drew 0-0)
1987 v Brazil (lost 0-2)
1989 v Yugoslavia (drew 1-1), v Italy (lost 0-2)
1990 v East Germany (lost 0-1), v Poland (drew 1-1), v Malta (won 2-1)
1991 v Romania (won 2-1), v Switzerland (won 2-1), v Bulgaria (drew 1-1), v USSR (lost 0-1), v Bulgaria (drew 1-1), v San Marino (won 2-1)
1992 v Switzerland (drew 2-2), v Romania (lost 0-1), v San Marino (won 4-0), v Finland (drew 1-1), v Norway (drew 0-0), v Holland (lost 0-1), v Germany (lost 0-2), v USSR (won 3-0)

1993   v Switzerland (lost 1-3), v Portugal (drew 0-0), v Italy (drew 0-0), v Malta (won 3-0),
       v Portugal (lost 0-5)
1994   v Holland (lost 0-1)
1995   v Finland (won 2-0), v Faroe Islands (won 5-1), v Russia (drew 1-1), v Greece (lost 0-1)
1996   v Sweden (lost 0-2), v Denmark (lost 0-2), v Colombia (lost 0-1), v Holland (lost 0-0),
       v England (lost 0-2), v Switzerland (won 1-0)
1997   v Austria (drew 0-0), v Latvia (won 2-0), v Estonia (drew 0-0)
1998   v Denmark (lost 0-1)

Andy Goram began his career with Oldham Athletic, spending seven seasons at Boundary Park and winning the first of his 43 caps against East Germany in October 1985, when the Tartan Army sang 'You're not English any more'. Goram qualified to play for Scotland by parentage, after being a member of the England Under-21 squad without playing. He was the Latics' first World Cup player when called into Scotland's 22-man squad for the 1986 Finals in Mexico.

Agile and safe, Goram was a worthy successor to Athletic's international goalkeepers of yesteryear, namely Bert Gray (Wales) and Jack Hacking (England). He had made 192 League and Cup appearances for Oldham when Hibernian used the £200,000—and much more besides—which they had just been awarded by a transfer tribunal in respect of Michael Weir's move to Luton Town.

On his arrival at Easter Road, Goram set about his campaign to win a regular international place. That arrived, but there were still no honours at club level, and so in June 1991, Goram travelled along the M8 from Edinburgh to Glasgow to join Rangers for a fee of £1 million. Whilst with Hibs, Goram scored a goal in a 3-1 win over Morton on the final day of the 1987-88 season.

A double international, being a fine enough cricketer to have represented Scotland in the summer game, things did not go smoothly for him on his arrival at Ibrox. After suffering some unlikely league defeats, a Goram error caused a League Cup semi-final loss to his previous club Hibernian at Hampden Park. He then had to watch his former team-mates beat Dunfermline in the final and get their hands on the silverware that he craved.

Success was not long in coming for this fine keeper, for in his first season with the club, he helped Rangers win the League Championship and the Scottish Cup. In 1992-93 he was a key figure in Rangers' treble-winning line-up, but it was his displays in Europe which really caught the eye, particularly away from home, where he was in inspirational form in the matches against Leeds United and Marseilles. Player and Footballer of the Year honours followed, but in 1993-94 he was troubled by injuries, and only appeared in eight games. In the summer of 1994, Rangers manager Walter Smith placed Goram on the transfer list, having finally lost patience with the keeper's cavalier attitude towards training and his more thorough approach towards socialising!

However, Goram decided to try and save his career, and his performances in 1994-95 as Rangers again won the League Championship were outstanding. Rated one of the best goalkeepers in Europe, Goram went on to help Rangers win two more League titles and Scottish Cup and League Cup honours, before, following brief spells with Notts County and Sheffield United, he joined Motherwell.

Andy Goram (www.snspix.com)

He had appeared in 69 games for the Steelmen, when a goalkeeping crisis at Manchester United prompted Sir Alex Ferguson to sign him as a stop-gap. He appeared in two Premier League games for the Reds before joining Coventry City. Following a knee injury that required keyhole surgery, he ended his career where he had started, with Oldham Athletic, making his debut in the 7-1 home defeat by Cardiff City!

FRANK McAVENNIE
Forward

Born: Francis McAvennie, Glasgow, 22 November 1959
Height: 5ft 10in
Weight: 11st 0lb
Clubs: Johnstone Burgh; St Mirren; West Ham United; Glasgow Celtic; West Ham United; Aston Villa; Glasgow Celtic; Swindon Town; Airdrieonians; Falkirk; St Mirren
Scotland caps: 5
Scotland goals: 1
1986 v Australia (won 2-0) 1 goal, v Australia (drew 0-0), v Denmark (lost 0-1), v West Germany (lost 1-2)
1988 v Saudi Arabia (drew 2-2)

Frank McAvennie playing for West Ham

Making his international debut against Australia, it was Frank McAvennie's goal that helped the Scots clinch their place in the 1986 World Cup Finals in Mexico.

One of the game's most popular strikers, Frank McAvennie began his career with St Mirren in 1980, and went on to score 50 goals in 135 games before joining West Ham United for a fee of £340,000 in the summer of 1985.

A relatively unknown player when he arrived at Upton Park, no one could have anticipated the impact he made on the English First Division. He had won five Scotland Under-21 caps at Love Street, but it was his performances for the Hammers which brought him full international recognition. In 1985-86, McAvennie topped the club's goalscoring charts with 26 league goals, a figure only bettered by Gary Lineker. He had an indifferent season in 1986-87, and when, after only eight games of the following campaign, Celtic came in with a £750,000 offer, neither player nor club could refuse.

In his first season at Parkhead, he rediscovered his goalscoring touch, helping Celtic to the Scottish League and Cup double. However, before the end of the next season, he was back at Upton Park, trying to save the Hammers from relegation. John Lyall paid £1.25 million to bring McAvennie back to West Ham, but an old injury limited his appearances to eight and the club dropped into the Second Division. Worse was to come, for on the opening day of the 1989-90 season, McAvennie broke his leg in the match at Stoke. He was back in the frame the following season, scoring 10 goals in 24 starts as the Hammers won promotion to the top flight. In 1991-92 he had scored only three goals in 15 starts in the First Division, but doubled his tally with a superb hat-trick against Nottingham Forest in what turned out to be his farewell game.

After a brief spell with Aston Villa, he rejoined Celtic and took his tally of goals for the Bhoys to 49 in 105 games before, following a loan spell with Swindon Town, he had a series of trials with Airdrie, Falkirk and St Mirren before deciding to retire.

PAT NEVIN
Outside-right

Born: Patrick Kevin Francis Michael Nevin, Glasgow, 6 September 1943
Height: 5ft 6in
Weight: 11st 9lb
Clubs: Gartcosh United; Clyde; Chelsea; Everton; Tranmere Rovers; Kilmarnock
Scotland caps: 28
Scotland goals: 5

1986 v Romania (won 3-0), v England (lost 1-2)
1987 v Luxembourg (won 3-0), v Republic of Ireland (lost 0-1), v Belgium (lost 1-4)
1988 v Luxembourg (drew 0-0)
1989 v Cyprus (won 2-1), v England (lost 0-2)
1991 v Romania (won 2-1), v Bulgaria (drew 1-1), v San Marino (won 2-1)
1992 v United States (won 1-0) 1 goal, v Germany (lost 0-2), v USSR (won 3-0)
1993 v Malta (won 3-0) 1 goal, v Portugal (lost 0-5), v Estonia (won 3-1) 2 goals
1994 v Switzerland (drew 1-1), v Malta (won 2-0), v Holland (lost 0-1), v Austria (won 2-1), v Holland (lost 1-3)
1995 v Faroe Islands (won 5-1), v Russia (drew 1-1), v San Marino (won 2-0)
1996 v Sweden (lost 0-2), v San Marino (won 5-0) 1 goal, v Australia (won 1-0)

One of the few players of modern times who could justifiably claim to have natural balance and grace of movement, Pat Nevin won 28 caps for Scotland over a 10-year period, the first against Romania in March 1986.

Pat Nevin played his early football for Clyde before joining Chelsea in May 1983 for a fee of £95,000. In his first season at Stamford Bridge, he helped the London club win the Second Division Championship, contributing 14 vital goals. Nevin maintained his high standards in the top flight the following season, his looping curling crosses providing Kerry Dixon and David Speedie with a steady stream of chances. However, as Chelsea lost their way, he saw less of the ball and was usually closely marked by two or three men. Following defeats at the hands of Middlesbrough in the play-offs in May 1988, Nevin exercised his right to move on and joined Everton, a transfer tribunal setting the fee at £925,000 after bitter wrangling.

The thoughtful winger, a devotee of obscure rock bands and Russian literature, soon demonstrated his ability to leave defenders trailing in his wake, and this ensured that he was quickly accepted by the more discerning Everton supporters. Perhaps Nevin's finest moment in an Everton shirt came in the FA

Pat Nevin during his time at Everton

Cup semi-final in 1989 when he scored the goal to beat Norwich City. Sadly his joy was totally overshadowed by the tragic events which had unfolded in the other semi-final at Hillsborough that same afternoon.

His form was so persuasive in 1990-91 that he not only won a recall to the Scotland side, but after the return of Howard Kendall had failed to bring about a change of fortune, he moved across the Mersey to play for Tranmere Rovers.

He missed very few games in five seasons with the Prenton Park club, and though no longer in the top flight, he continued to be selected for Scotland. As PFA Chairman, Pat Nevin was a great ambassador for the game of football, later ending his playing career with Kilmarnock, whom he helped to fourth place in the Premier League in 1997-98. He has maintained his interest in the game by working in the media.

ROBERT CONNOR
Midfield

Born: Robert Connor, Kilmarnock, 4 August 1960
Height: 5ft 11in
Weight: 11st 4lb
Clubs: Ayr United; Dundee; Aberdeen; Kilmarnock; Partick Thistle; Queen of the South
Scotland caps: 4
1986 v Holland (drew 0-0)
1988 v Saudi Arabia (drew 2-2)
1989 v England (lost 0-2)
1991 v Romania (won 2-1)

Midfielder Robert Connor began his career with Ayr United, making his debut for the Somerset Park club against Partick Thistle midway through the 1977-78 season, but despite some outstanding displays, he failed to prevent their relegation from the Premier Division.

Connor missed very few games in seven seasons with the Honest Men, going on to score 28 goals in 223 league games before joining Dundee in 1984.

At Dens Park, Connor came into prominence—his determination and silky skills in the middle of the park helping him win his first full cap as a replacement for Eamonn Bannon in a goalless draw against Holland in Eindhoven. Connor, who had previously made a couple of appearances for Scotland at Under-21 level, was soon the target for the leading clubs of the day, and in August 1986, Aberdeen paid £350,000 to take him to Pittodrie.

Not only did he win three further caps for Scotland, but he helped the Dons finish runners-up in the Premier Division in seasons 1988-89, 1989-90 and 1993-94. Connor was also in the Aberdeen side that won the Scottish Cup and League Cup in 1990, beating Celtic (9-8 on penalties after a goalless draw) and Rangers 2-1 respectively. Connor stayed at Pittodrie until the summer of 1994, when he left to join his home-town team Kilmarnock.

After two seasons at Rugby Park, Connor had a brief spell with Partick Thistle before ending his first-class career with Queen of the South.

ALLY McCOIST
Forward

Born: Alistair Murdoch McCoist, Bellshill, 24 September 1962
Height: 5ft 10in
Weight: 12st 0lb
Clubs: St Johnstone; Sunderland; Glasgow Rangers; Kilmarnock
Scotland caps: 61
Scotland goals: 19

1986 v Holland (drew 0-0)

1987 v Luxembourg (won 3-0), v Republic of Ireland (lost 0-1), v Belgium (lost 1-4),
v England (drew 0-0), v Brazil (lost 0-2)

1988 v Hungary (won 2-0) 2 goals, v Belgium (won 2-0) 1 goal, v Malta (drew 1-1),
v Spain (drew 0-0), v Colombia (drew 0-0), v England (lost 0-1)

1989 v Yugoslavia (drew 1-1), v France (won 2-0), v Cyprus (won 2-1) 1 goal,
v England (lost 0-2)

1990 v Yugoslavia (lost 1-3), v France (lost 0-3), v Norway (drew 1-1) 1 goal,
v East Germany (lost 0-1), v Egypt (lost 1-3) 1 goal, v Poland (drew 1-1),
v Malta (won 2-1), v Costa Rica (lost 0-1), v Sweden (won 2-1), v Brazil (lost 0-1)

1991 v Romania (won 2-1) 1 goal, v Switzerland (won 2-1), v Bulgaria (drew 1-1) 1 goal,
v USSR (lost 0-1), v Bulgaria (drew 1-1)

1992 v Switzerland (drew 2-2) 1 goal, v San Marino (won 4-0) 1 goal,
v N Ireland (won 1-0) 1 goal, v Finland (drew 1-1), v United States (won 1-0),
v Canada (won 3-1) 1 goal, v Norway (drew 0-0), v Holland lost 0-1),
v Germany (lost 0-2), v USSR (won 3-0)

1993 v Switzerland (lost 1-3) 1 goal, v Portugal (drew 0-0), v Italy (drew 0-0),
v Malta (won 3-0) 2 goals, v Portugal (lost 0-5)

1996 v Greece (won 1-0) 1 goal, v Finland (won 1-0), v San Marino (won 5-0) 1 goal,
v Australia (won 1-0) 1 goal, v Denmark (lost 0-2), v Colombia (lost 0-1),
v England (lost 0-2), v Switzerland (won 1-0) 1 goal

1997 v Austria (drew 0-0), v Sweden (won 1-0), v Estonia (drew 0-0), v Austria (won 2-0)

1998 v Belarus (won 4-1)

1999 v Lithuania (drew 0-0), v Estonia (won 3-2)

Rangers' all-time leading goalscorer, extrovert and crowd favourite, Ally McCoist actually needed three invitations to join the Ibrox club before making the move in 1983.

As a schoolboy he said no to a John Greig approach and signed for St Johnstone instead. He was aged just 16 when he made his first team debut for them in April 1979, and then, in season 1980–81, he snapped up 23 goals for the Saints, this prompting a number of clubs to chase his signature. The story goes that McCoist and a St Johnstone director were at Ibrox discussing a possible transfer when the St Johnstone director received a call from Sunderland offering £100,000 more. So McCoist, still only 18 years old, went to the Wearsiders for a fee of £400,000.

His time at Roker Park, in a team that was always struggling, was not a success, and in June 1983 he at last signed for Rangers for £185,000. He was not welcomed rapturously by the Rangers fans, who were well aware of his history

Ally McCoist playing for Sunderland

and questioned his commitment to the Ibrox club. His first couple of seasons with Rangers were difficult, but McCoist was determined to succeed, and his eventual success at club level was rewarded with the first of 61 caps when he played against Holland in April 1986. In fact, McCoist has been the national side's most reliable striker of recent times, although his record of 19 goals does not come close to his club statistics.

He has twice lifted the 'Golden Boot', awarded to European football's top marksman in his domestic league—those honours arrived in 1991-92 and 1992-93 when he was truly on fire, scoring 68 times in 72 games. After breaking his leg when playing for Scotland in their 5-0 defeat in Portugal in 1993, McCoist bounced back to score a sensational overhead winner in the 1993-94 League Cup Final against Hibs, after coming on as a substitute.

At the tail end of 1994, his contribution to Scottish football and Rangers was recognised as he picked up an MBE at Buckingham Palace. His scoring feats alone—he netted 355 goals for Rangers—dictate that he will be remembered as one of Scotland's greatest-ever marksmen. He had won nine League Championship medals, nine League Cup and two Scottish Cup medals when, in the summer of 1998, he left to continue his career with Kilmarnock.

His first full start for Killie saw him score a hat-trick in a 3-0 win over Hearts. In the Rugby Park crowd that day was Scotland manager Craig Brown, who, having left him out of the '98 World Cup party for France, asked him to play for Scotland again! His last first-class game was on 20 May 2001, when he helped Kilmarnock beat Celtic 1-0, after which he has become a most accomplished television personality.

BRIAN McCLAIR
Forward/ Midfield

Born: Brian John McClair, Bellshill, 8 December 1963
Height: 5ft 9in
Weight: 12st 2lb
Clubs: Motherwell; Glasgow Celtic; Manchester United; Motherwell
Scotland caps: 30
Scotland goals: 2

1987   v Luxembourg (won 3-0), v Republic of Ireland (lost 0-1), v England (drew 0-0),
      v Brazil (lost 0-2)

1988   v Bulgaria (won 1-0), v Malta (drew 1-1), v Spain (drew 0-0)

1989   v Norway (won 2-1), v Yugoslavia (drew 1-1), v Italy (lost 0-2), v Cyprus (won 3-2),
      v France (won 2-0)

1990   v Norway (drew 1-1), v Argentina (won 1-0)

1991   v Bulgaria (drew 1-1), v Bulgaria (drew 1-1), v San Marino (won 2-1)

1992   v Switzerland (drew 2-2), v Romania (lost 0-1), v N Ireland (won 1-0),
      v United States (won 1-0), v Canada (won 3-1), v Norway (drew 0-0),
      v Holland (lost 0-1), v Germany (lost 0-2), v USSR (won 3-0) 1 goal

1993   v Switzerland (lost 1-3), v Portugal (drew 0-0), v Estonia (won 3-0),
      v Estonia (won 3-1) 1 goal

A regular member of the Scottish national team for six years following his debut in 1987, Brian McClair was included in the squad for the 1992 European Championship Finals in Sweden, and after failing to score for Scotland in 25 games, he broke his duck with a goal in the 3-0 win over the USSR. Unfortunately, despite that win, Scotland went out of the tournament after earlier losing to Holland and Germany.

Brian McClair went south to sign as an apprentice with Aston Villa in July 1980, but was not offered a professional contract and returned to Scotland to join his local club, Motherwell. After his goals helped the Steelmen win promotion, Billy McNeill signed him for Celtic in the summer of 1983. His first season at Parkhead saw him find the net 23 times in 35 league games, and in a total of 175 games for the club, he scored 121 goals. He also won a Scottish Cup medal in 1985 and a Premier Division Championship medal in 1985-86.

Desperate to re-establish themselves at the forefront of English soccer and to replace Mark Hughes, Manchester United signed him during the close season for a fee of £850,000. In his first season at Old Trafford he became the first player since George Best in 1967-68 to notch up more than 20 Football League goals in a season, with 24 strikes, including a hat-trick against Derby County. Following the return of Hughes, the two of them formed a formidable partnership, culminating in United beating Crystal Place in the 1990 FA Cup Final. The following year the Reds beat Barcelona 2-1 to win the European Cup Winners Cup, and in 1992, McClair scored the winner in the League Cup Final against Nottingham Forest. In 1992-93 he played for most of United's Championship-winning season in midfield, and over the next couple of seasons he continued in that position, where his canny skills and remarkable vision gave the side that extra dimension.

A great clubman, he went on to earn a deserved testimonial in 1996-97, a season which ended with him winning his fourth Championship medal. The following season, McClair, who was by then United's senior professional, spent most of the campaign on the bench, and in the close season of 1998, after scoring 128 goals in 474 games, signed for Motherwell, the club he started out with.

He never quite re-established his old reputation, and when Blackburn Rovers asked him to be their assistant-manager, he returned to Lancashire.

JIM McINALLY
Left-back/Midfield

Born: James Edward McInally, Glasgow, 19 February 1964
Height: 5ft 7in
Weight: 10st 4lb
Clubs: Glasgow Celtic; Dundee; Nottingham Forest; Coventry City; Dundee United; Raith Rovers; Dundee
Scotland caps: 10
1987 v Belgium (lost 1-4), v Brazil (lost 0-2)
1988 v Malta (drew 1-1)
1991 v Bulgaria (drew 1-1), v Bulgaria (drew 1-1)
1992 v United States (won 1-0), v Norway (drew 0-0), v USSR (won 3-0)
1993 v Germany (lost 0-1), v Portugal (lost 0-5)

A tireless and versatile player, Jim McInally, who was capped 10 times by Scotland, began his career with Celtic. Following the appointment of Davie Hay as manager, he found himself the club's fourth-choice left-back, and went out on loan to Dundee. While at Dens Park he scored the goal that kept Dundee in the Premier Division in 1984. Though Hay offered him a contract, McInally thought his chances might be better off elsewhere, and he joined Nottingham Forest for a nominal fee.

Signed primarily as cover for Viv Anderson and Kenny Swain, Forest eventually sold him to Coventry City, but his stay at Highfield Road was short-lived, and five months after joining the Sky Blues he returned to Scotland to play for Dundee United.

At Tannadice he was switched to midfield, his form prompting Andy Roxburgh to give him his first cap against Belgium in April 1987. An integral part of United's defence-midfield system, he later walked out on the club after they had turned down his written transfer request. Eventually the differences were resolved and he continued to play for the Terrors for a further seven seasons. In 1987 he was a member of the United side that lost 1-0 to Gothenburg in the UEFA Cup Final, but after being a losing finalist in the Scottish Cup in 1987, 1988 and 1991, he was part of Ivan Golac's 1994 Tannadice team that took the Cup from Rangers at Hampden with a 1-0 victory, depriving the Ibrox club of a back-to-back treble. He had made 302 league appearances for United, when in 1995 he moved to Raith Rovers for £150,000.

Later appointed player-coach at Stark's Park, he then became Jimmy Thomson's assistant before Tommy McLean took him back to Dundee United. Within a year he was on the move again, this time joining Dundee, and in April 1998 he won a First Division medal after they were promoted to the Premier Division.

IAN WILSON
Midfield

Born: Ian William Wilson, Aberdeen, 27 March 1958
Height: 5ft 8in
Weight: 10st 7lb
Clubs: Aberdeen; Dundee; Elgin City; Leicester City; Everton; Besiktas (Turkey); Derby County; Bury; Wigan Athletic; Peterhead
Scotland caps: 5
1987 v England (drew 0-0), v Brazil (lost 0-2)
1988 v Belgium (won 2-0), v Bulgaria (won 1-0), v Luxembourg (drew 0-0)

Belated but deserved international recognition came Ian Wilson's way at the age of 29, when he followed his call-up at 'B' level in April 1987 with his full international debut against England a month later.

After playing junior football for Aberdeen and Dundee, his career began in earnest with then Highland League club Elgin City. Blending constructive and combative play in the middle of the park, he caught Leicester City manager Jock Wallace's eye and arrived at Filbert Street for a £30,000 fee.

A key member of both Wallace's and Gordon Milne's promotion sides, Wilson impressed most in the latter, adopting an advanced role which saw him coming in late behind Gary Lineker and Alan Smith and claiming his fair share of goals. Unfortunately for him, he fell victim to the Leicester habit of selecting midfielders in full-back positions, and though he re-emerged as a mature motivator and anchorman, City were relegated and he moved on to Everton for a fee of £300,000.

At Goodison he picked up an FA Cup runners-up medal as a substitute for Everton in 1989, then rejoined Gordon Milne in Turkey, where he qualified for both League and Cup medals as Besiktas achieved the domestic 'double' for the first time ever in 1990.

On his return to England he failed to turn round the fortunes of both Derby County and Bury, both of whom proved relegation-bound within months. After a brief non-contract spell with Wigan Athletic, his career turned full circle as he became manager of Highland League side Peterhead.

Ian Wilson

He later received another call from Gordon Milne to become his assistant at Nagoya Grampus Eight in Japan.

ERIC BLACK
Forward

Born: Eric Black, Bellshill, 1 October 1963
Height: 5ft 10in
Weight: 11st 3lb
Clubs: Aberdeen; Metz FC (France)
Scotland caps: 2
1988   v Hungary (won 2-0), v Luxembourg (drew 0-0)

Eric Black was still a teenager when he made his debut for Aberdeen in a 1-1 Pittodrie draw with 'New Firm' rivals Dundee United in October 1981, taking just nine minutes to open the scoring when he headed home a Gordon Strachan corner.

Towards the end of his debut season, he came on as a substitute in the 4-1 extra-time Scottish Cup Final triumph over Rangers. He also scored on his European debut in a 3-2 UEFA Cup third round first leg win over SV Hamburg.

The following season of 1982-83 was without doubt Eric Black's most successful campaign with the Pittodrie club. In May 1983, in Gothenburg, it was Eric Black's shot that opened the scoring to send Aberdeen on their way to a 2-1 victory over Real Madrid in the European Cup Winners' Cup Final. Ten days later, he fired the only goal of the Scottish Cup Final as the Dons beat Rangers. Early the following season, a back injury turned out to be more serious than at first thought, but by the turn of the year he was back in the Dons side and scored in the 2-1 Scottish Cup Final defeat of Celtic.

More success followed for Black in 1984-85, as Aberdeen won the Scottish Premier League title, and then, in the Skol Cup Final of 1985-86, he netted twice in a 3-0 Aberdeen win over Hibernian. In May 1986, Don's manager, Alex Ferguson dramatically dropped Black from the side to face Hearts, because he had publicly stated he would be leaving Pittodrie to join Metz when his contract expired. Aberdeen won the Cup and Black moved to France.

He enjoyed a highly successful spell with Metz, winning two full international caps for Scotland before injury brought his career to a premature end.

After a spell working as an SFA Community Coach, he joined the coaching staff at Celtic. He later worked as assistant-manager to Gary McAllister at Coventry City, but replaced him as manager when McAllister resigned for personal reasons. Black's tenure was short-lived, and he was replaced by Peter Reid.

STEVE CLARKE
Right-back
Born: Stephen Clarke, Saltcoats, 29 August 1963
Height: 5ft 9in
Weight: 11st 10lb
Clubs: Beith; St Mirren; Chelsea
Scotland caps: 6
1988 v Hungary (won 2-0), v Belgium (won 2-0), v Bulgaria (won 1-0),
        v Saudi Arabia (drew 2-2), v Malta (drew 1-1)
1994 v Holland (lost 1-3)

Full-back Steve Clarke began in Scottish junior football with Beith, before signing for St Mirren and making his debut against Hibernian in September 1982. Transferring south of the border to Chelsea, he had appeared in 187 League and Cup games for the Love Street club.

In his first full season at Stamford Bridge, Clarke won five full caps for Scotland, the first against Hungary at Hampden Park in September 1987. During his early days with Chelsea, he found himself sharing the right-back duties with Welsh international Gareth Hall, but eventually he established himself as the club's first-choice No.2. Though he was often beset by injuries, he was the club's 'Player of the Year' for 1993-94, and had many of Chelsea's older supporters claiming him to be one of the best right-backs at Stamford Bridge since the war.

However, when Chelsea signed Romanian international Dan Petrescu from Sheffield Wednesday, Clarke's days at Stamford Bridge looked numbered, but Chelsea's then longest-serving player showed his adaptability by moving across to occupy the left-hand position in the Blues' three-man central defensive formation.

Elevated to club captain in 1996-97, he just seemed to get better as he got older, and was awarded a testimonial against PSV Eindhoven in recognition of his ten years at the Bridge. Over the course of the season, his unflappability and positional sense made him an integral part of the Blues' side, and he ended the campaign as the proud possessor of an FA Cup winners' medal after Chelsea had beaten Middlesbrough. The following season he won League Cup and European Cup Winners' Cup medals and later became only the eighth player in the club's history to make over 400 appearances—this under seven different managers!

Now one of Chelsea's two assistant-managers under Jose Mourinho, he helped Chelsea to the Premier League Championship in 2004-05, and at the time of writing has just repeated the achievement in 2005-06.

IAN DURRANT
Midfield
Born: Ian Durrant, Glasgow, 29 September 1966
Height: 5ft 8in
Weight: 9st 7lb
Clubs: Glasgow United; Glasgow Rangers; Everton; Kilmarnock
Scotland caps: 20
1988 v Hungary (won 2-0), v Belgium (won 2-0), v Malta (drew 1-1), v Spain (drew 0-0)
1989 v Norway (won 2-1)
1993 v Switzerland (lost 1-3), v Portugal (drew 0-0), v Italy (drew 0-0), v Portugal (lost 0-5)
1994 v Italy (lost 1-3), v Malta (won 2-0)
1999 v Estonia (won 3-2), v Faroe Islands (won 2-1), v Germany (won 1-0),
v Faroe Islands (drew 1-1), v Czech Republic (lost 2-3)
2000 v Bosnia (won 2-1), v Estonia (drew 0-0), v Holland (drew 0-0),
v Republic of Ireland (won 2-1)

As a youngster, Ian Durrant was quite brilliant and displayed the sort of passing ability that most players can only dream of. But one afternoon in 1988 forever changed Ian Durrant's career, and football fans will never know just what levels the popular Glaswegian may have reached.

The wild tackle by Aberdeen's Neil Simpson that shattered the midfielder's knee and the two-year lay-off it caused have been well-documented. The fact that an out-of-court settlement was reached for compensation was proof enough of its recklessness. Durrant was aged just 21, and had already made 122 appearances for the Ibrox club.

On his return to action, his imagination and vision helped power the club's 44-game unbeaten run of 1992-93, before he forced his way back into the Scotland set-up. He went on to win six League Championship medals, three League Cup medals—including scoring in the 1993-94 Final against Hibs—and two Scottish Cup winners medals, not to mention playing a significant role in the club's best European campaign for over 20 years, when he collected significant goals against Lyngby and Marseilles. Shortly after these successes, questions were being asked about Durrant's fitness, and he was loaned out to Everton. He impressed during his stay at Goodison Park, but returned to Scotland after the Ibrox club were reluctant to release him. Yet it seemed that he did not have the fitness required to play football week-in, week-out. Also his misfortune was compounded in that he was being asked to play in an alien way to his natural style, because the Scottish League could not be tailored to his skilful talents.

Durrant left Rangers in July 1998 to join Kilmarnock, where his form led to him winning another recall to Scotland's colours. He was a regular throughout his first two seasons at Rugby Park, but an injury in the CIS Cup Final against Celtic in March 2001, which Killie lost 3-0, kept him out of action for 14 months. He then came off the bench as a late substitute against Dundee United in May 2002, basically to say farewell to the fans.

GARY GILLESPIE
Central defender

Born: Gary Thomson Gillespie, Bonnybridge, 5 July 1960
Height: 6ft 3in
Weight: 13st 0lb
Clubs: Grangemouth BC; Falkirk; Coventry City; Liverpool; Glasgow Celtic; Coventry City
Scotland caps: 13
1988 v Belgium (won 2-0), v Bulgaria (won 1-0), v Spain (drew 0-0)
1989 v Norway (won 2-1), v France (won 2-0), v Chile (won 2-0)
1990 v Yugoslavia (lost 1-3), v East Germany (lost 0-1), v Egypt (lost 1-3), v Poland (drew 1-1), v Malta (won 2-1), v Brazil (lost 0-1)
1991 v Bulgaria (drew 1-1)

Gary Gillespie as a Liverpool player

Gary Gillespie was captain of Falkirk when Coventry City manager Gordon Milne paid £75,000 to take him to Highfield Road in the summer of 1977. He missed very few games over the next five seasons, being ever-present in 1982-83, his last season with the club. During his time with the Sky Blues, he made eight appearances for Scotland at Under-21 level. He left Coventry City for Liverpool in July 1983 after the Merseysiders had paid £325,000 for his services.

During his years at Liverpool, Gillespie won a couple of Championship medals and numerous runners-up medals. A tall, elegant figure at the heart of Liverpool's defence, he formed a formidable partnership with Alan Hansen. Unfortunately he was always susceptible to injury, and seemed no sooner to have returned to the team than he would be back on the treatment table. Had he been less injury-prone, he would without doubt have played many more games and matured into an outstanding central defender. As it was, he spent over seven years at Anfield and only appeared in 211 League and Cup games, before joining Celtic for a fee of £925,000 in August 1991.

Though he scored on his Celtic debut in a 4-1 defeat of his first club Falkirk, Gillespie struggled to hold down a regular spot in his early days with the Bhoys, and was eventually allowed to rejoin Coventry to ease the club's wage bill.

Injuries restricted his appearances on his return to Highfield Road, and he was then controversially sent off at Hillsborough. He subsequently became the Sky Blues' player-coach, before injury finally put paid to his playing days.

DEREK WHYTE
Central defender
Born: Derek Whyte, Glasgow, 31 August 1968
Height: 5ft 11in
Weight: 12st 12lb
Clubs: Glasgow Celtic; Middlesbrough; Aberdeen; Partick Thistle
Scotland caps: 12
1988 v Belgium (won 2-0), v Luxembourg (drew 0-0)
1989 v Chile (won 2-0)
1992 v United States (won 1-0)
1993 v Portugal (drew 0-0), v Italy (drew 0-0)
1995 v Japan (drew 0-0), v Ecuador (won 2-1)
1996 v United States (lost 1-2)
1997 v Latvia (won 2-0)
1998 v Finland (drew 1-1)
1999 v Germany (won 1-0)

Derek Whyte, who was only on the losing side once in his 12 international appearances for Scotland, was also part of a Scotland defence that didn't concede a goal in nine of those games, including his first seven appearances for the national side.

His impact as a defender for Celtic was immediate, and he seemed destined for a future as the Bhoys captain. He made his debut in a 1-1 draw against League title favourites Hearts in February 1986 as Celtic surged up the table to take the Championship at the last gasp. He won another Championship medal in 1988, plus Scottish Cup medals in 1988 and 1989. In the latter of these finals, he cleared a Mark Walters shot off the line just after Joe Miller had scored for Celtic against Rangers. He went on to appear in 276 games for Celtic before, following a disagreement over terms, he left Parkhead to join Middlesbrough.

Whyte, who was a virtual ever-present in the Boro side for his first few seasons with the Teeside club, helped them win the First Division Championship in 1994-95, and after some sterling displays the following season as the club returned to the top flight, won selection for Scotland's 1996 European Championship squad. In 1996-97 he played a major role in the club's two cup runs, and though Boro lost their Premiership status, it wasn't for the want of trying on Derek Whyte's part—his strong running out of defence and good distribution being the main features of his play. He had played in 195 games for Boro, when in December 1997 he was transferred to Aberdeen.

Though he was selected for Craig Brown's Scotland World Cup squad in France, he failed to make an appearance as the Scots crashed out of the tournament at the group stage. He continued to be a regular at the heart of the Dons' defence for the next four seasons, before leaving Pittodrie to continue his career with Partick Thistle.

GORDON DURIE
Forward
Born: Gordon Scott Durie, Paisley, 6 December 1965
Height: 5ft 10in
Weight: 13st 0lb
Clubs: Hill O'Beath; East Fife; Hibernian; Chelsea; Tottenham Hotspur; Glasgow Rangers
Scotland caps: 43
Scotland goals: 7
1988   v Bulgaria (won 1-0)
1989   v Italy (lost 0-2), v Cyprus (won 2-1)
1990   v Yugoslavia (lost 1-3) 1 goal v East Germany (lost 0-1), v Egypt (lost 1-3),
          v Sweden (won 2-1)
1991   v Switzerland (won 2-1), v Bulgaria (drew 1-1), v USSR (lost 0-1), v Bulgaria (drew 1-1),
          v San Marino (won 2-1) 1 goal
1992   v Switzerland (drew 2-2) 1 goal, v Romania (lost 0-1), v San Marino (won 4-0) 1 goal,
          v N Ireland (won 1-0), v Finland (drew 1-1), v Canada (won 3-1), v Norway (drew 0-0),
          v Holland (lost 0-1), v Germany (lost 0-2)
1993   v Switzerland (lost 1-3), v Italy (drew 0-0)
1994   v Switzerland (drew 1-1), v Italy (lost 1-3), v Holland (lost 0-1), v Holland (lost 1-3)
1996   v United States (lost 1-2) 1 goal, v Holland (drew 0-0), v England (lost 0-2),
          v Switzerland (won 1-0)
1997   v Austria (drew 0-0), v Sweden (lost 1-2), v Malta (won 3-2), v Belarus (won 1-0)
1998   v Belarus (won 4-1), v Latvia (won 2-0) 1 goal, v France (lost 1-2) 1 goal,
          v Finland (drew 1-1), v Colombia (drew 2-2), v Brazil (lost 1-2), v Norway (drew 1-1),
          v Morocco (lost 0-3)

Though Durie's performances for the national team have been enough to earn a silver medal from the SFA in their Hall of Fame scheme, they do not tell the entire story. Amongst his seven goals were vital strikes against San Marino and Switzerland in Scotland's unlikely qualification for the 1992 European Championship, but there have also been disasters—a horror performance against Egypt in 1990 and a ludicrous penalty conceded against Romania in that same European campaign.

Durie first came to prominence at East Fife, where his strong running as much as his goal prowess persuaded Hibs to swoop for him. It was at Easter Road that he really made his mark on the Scottish game, although, save for a

League Cup runner-up medal against Aberdeen in the 1985-86 season, he had nothing tangible to show for his successful spell there.

After attracting attention from scouts south of the Border, Durie joined Chelsea, who paid £380,000 for his services in April 1986. Initially he found it difficult to hold down a first team place, but after David Speedie had joined Coventry, he became a regular up front alongside Kerry Dixon. Although continually dogged by injuries, he went on to score 62 goals in 152 games, including five in a 7-0 win at Walsall as the Blues ran away with the 1988-89 Second Division Championship.

On the eve of the 1991-92 season he was transferred to Tottenham Hotspur for £2.2 million, and though his goalscoring touch initially deserted

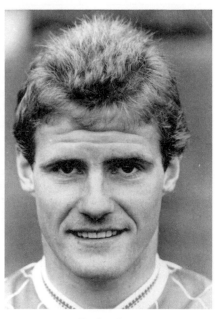

Gordon Durie

him, he bounced back with a hat-trick against Coventry City. Even so, his time at White Hart Lane was not as successful, with a 'cheating' charge, although it was eventually dismissed, hanging over him. He also had a very public bust-up with manager Ossie Ardiles over a substitution he did not agree with.

Joining Rangers in the run-in to the 1993-94 season, he proved a worthwhile acquisition, scoring 12 goals from only 23 starts as the Light Blues won the League Championship. His greatest performance in a Rangers' shirt came in the 1996 Scottish Cup Final, when he scored the first Cup Final hat-trick since Dixie Deans managed the feat against Hibs in 1972, as Rangers beat Hearts 5-1. Also that season, he netted four goals in a 7-0 defeat of Hibs, but after that, injuries began to take their toll and he appeared less and less, until hanging up his boots towards the end of the decade.

GARY MACKAY
Midfield

Born: Gary Mackay, Edinburgh, 23 January 1964
Height: 5ft 9in
Weight: 10st 5lb
Clubs: Salvesen BC; Heart of Midlothian
Scotland caps: 4
Scotland goals: 1
1988 v Bulgaria (won 1-0) 1 goal, v Luxembourg (drew 0-0), v Saudi Arabia (drew 2-2),
v Malta (drew 1-1)

Andy Roxburgh, who had been in charge of the Scotland youth team when Gary Mackay was a member, gave him his first full cap in a European qualifier against Bulgaria in Sofia in November 1987. Scotland were already out of contention, but Mackay came on as a substitute for Paul McStay and scored the only goal of the game in the closing moments—this denied Bulgaria a place in the 1988 European Finals. Their place went to the Republic of Ireland, and, for his efforts, Mackay received a crate of Irish whiskey, and the SFA, a crate of champagne, from their Irish counterparts!

He made his debut for Hearts as a 16-year-old in a League Cup tie at Somerset Park and went on to play in a club-record 515 league games for the Tynecastle club. His first season for the club ended with them being relegated from the Premier League—the third time in five seasons.

Mackay was soon a fixture in the Hearts side. Building up an almost telepathic understanding with John Robertson, his ability to break from midfield, run at defenders and play accurate passes at pace, were the main features of Mackay's game. He also had an eye for goalscoring and was the scorer of some spectacular goals.

In 1986, Mackay's incisive and perceptive play helped Hearts come within a whisker of lifting the League Championship, especially after he had scored from long range to settle the home game against Clydebank. But defeats against Dundee and then Aberdeen in the Cup Final thwarted their attempts for silverware.

Though he played four times for Scotland, honours at club level eluded him. He appeared in a further two Cup Finals—but Hearts lost 5-1 to Rangers in 1996 and 4-3 to the same opponents the following season.

He went on to score 88 goals in 737 games, before, having worked in the Commercial Department, he severed his links with Hearts in March 1997 to become Alex Macdonald's assistant at Airdrie, and then later manager there, before himself being replaced by Ian McCall.

JOHN COLLINS
Midfield

Born: John Angus Paul Collins, Galashiels, 31 January 1968
Height: 5ft 7in
Weight: 10st 10lb
Clubs: Hutchison Vale BC; Hibernian; Glasgow Celtic; AS Monaco (France); Everton; Fulham
Scotland caps: 58
Scotland goals: 12
1988   v Saudi Arabia (drew 2-2) 1 goal
1990   v East Germany lost 0-1), v Poland (drew 1-1), v Malta (won 2-1)
1991   v Switzerland (won 2-1), v Bulgaria (drew 1-1) 1 goal
1992   v N Ireland (won 1-0), v Finland (drew 1-1)
1993   v Portugal (drew 0-0), v Malta (won 3-0), v Germany (lost 0-1), v Portugal (lost 0-5), v Estonia (won 3-0) 1 goal, v Estonia (won 3-1)
1994   v Switzerland (drew 1-1) 1 goal, v Holland (lost 0-1), v Austria (won 2-1),

v Holland (lost1-3)

1995 v Finland (won 2-0) 1 goal, v Faroe Islands (won 5-1) 2 goals, v Russia (drew 1-1),
v Greece (lost 0-1), v Russia (drew 0-0), v San Marino (won 2-0) 1 goal,
v Faroe Islands (won 2-0)

1996 v Greece (won 1-0), v Finland (won 1-0), v Sweden (lost 0-2), v San Marino (won 5-0),
v Australia (won 1-0), v Denmark (lost 0-2), v United States (lost 1-2),
v Colombia (lost 0-1), v Holland (drew 0-0), v England (lost 0-2),
v Switzerland (won 1-0)

1997 v Austria (drew 0-0), v Latvia (won 2-0) 1 goal, v Sweden (won 1-0),
v Estonia (drew 0-0), v Austria (won 2-0), v Sweden (lost 1-2), v Malta (won 3-2)

1998 v Belarus (won 4-1), v Latvia (won 2-0), v France (lost 1-2), v Finland (drew 1-1),
v Colombia (drew 2-2) 1 goal, v United States (drew 0-0), v Brazil (lost 1-2) 1 goal,
v Norway (drew 1-1), v Morocco (lost 0-3)

1999 v Lithuania (drew 0-0)

2000 v Bosnia (won 2-1), v Estonia (drew 0-0), v Bosnia (won 1-0) 1 goal, v England (lost 0-2),
v England (won 1-0)

A hardworking, left-sided midfield player with a venomous shot, John Collins had a proud and distinguished international career. The holder of 58 caps, he scored on his debut in a 2-2 draw with Saudi Arabia in 1988, and was on the winning side against England in the last of his appearances.

There are few players considered more professional than John Collins—on the field he just gets on with the game without resorting to dissent, feigning injury or ill-temper, while off the field, he is equally modest and gentlemanly.

He made his Hibs debut against Aberdeen in August 1985, and, after making an immediate impact, became hugely popular with the Easter Road faithful. Celtic were poised to sign him in 1988, when to everyone's surprise, Collins contracted himself to Hibernian for another two years. He went on to make the last of his 194 League and Cup appearances for Hibs, in which he scored 21 goals, in May 1990, and later that summer he did sign for Celtic for £1 million.

One of his most memorable displays for the Bhoys in his early days at Parkhead came against Cologne in the UEFA Cup first round second leg. Celtic started 2-0 down, but Collins ran amok, and Celtic took the tie 3-2 on aggregate. Following Paul McStay's example of the previous summer, he committed himself to a further three years with the club, before damaging knee ligaments in the UEFA Cup game against Young Boys of Berne. Taking over the captaincy from McStay, he led Celtic to victory in the Scottish Cup Final of 1995 as they beat Airdrie 1-0. He went on to score 53 goals in 260 games, before leaving to join French club AS Monaco on a free transfer in the summer of 1996.

After two years in France, in which he remained a regular in the Scotland side, he signed for Everton for a fee of £2.5 million. He recovered from the shock of seeing a penalty-kick saved on his Everton home debut—Mark Bosnich saved the effort after watching Collins score an identically struck effort against Brazil in the World Cup—to enjoy a solid start to his Premiership career. Sadly, he suffered the first serious injury of his senior career, and midway through the season had to undergo surgery. He returned better than ever in readiness for the

1999-2000 campaign, going on to win more tackles over the course of the season than any other Premiership player.

Somewhat surprisingly, in the summer of 2000, Collins became Jean Tigana's first signing for Fulham. It was an inspired choice, as he led the Cottagers to the First Division Championship. Predictions that he would find it difficult to last the pace in the top flight proved unfounded, before a series of niggling injuries took their toll and he retired.

JOHN COLQUHOUN
Winger
Born: John Mark Colquhoun, Stirling, 14 July 1963
Height: 5ft 7in
Weight: 10st 0lb
Clubs: Stirling Albion; Glasgow Celtic; Heart of Midlothian; Millwall; Sunderland; Heart of Midlothian; St Johnstone
Scotland caps: 2
1988   v Saudi Arabia (drew 2-2), v Malta (drew 1-1)

John Colquhoun had scored 51 goals in 102 appearances for his home-town team Stirling Albion when Celtic manager David Hay brought him to Parkhead as cover for Davie Provan. The day he signed for Celtic, he had been scratching about for a UEFA Cup ticket to Nottingham Forest's game against Celtic, and was hoping to go down to the game on a Stirling CSC bus—instead he travelled with the team!

Unable to make much headway with the Bhoys, he joined Heart of Midlothian for a fee of £50,000 in May 1985. A winger of genuine pace and great close-control, his speed caused most defenders problems, and, after scoring on his debut in a 1-1 draw against his former club Celtic, he went on to play a great part in the Tynecastle club coming so close to a League and Cup double in 1985-86. He also had a knack of scoring important goals, and the following season scored the only goal of the Scottish Cup semi-final against Dundee United, which sent Hearts into their first Scottish Cup Final for ten years.

Able to steer clear of injuries, he missed very few matches for Hearts over the next few seasons, but at the end of the 1990-91 campaign, in which he had been Hearts' only ever-present, he was allowed to join Millwall in a £400,000 deal. After a season at the Den, he then spent a year with Sunderland before Sandy Clark brought him back to Hearts in readiness for the 1993-94 season, as part of the £500,000 transfer that took Derek Ferguson to Roker Park.

He continued to find the net on a regular basis until featuring less under new manager Tommy McLean who succeeded Clark. When Jim Jefferies took over the reins, Colquhoun found himself back in favour, scoring Hearts' goals in a 5-1 Scottish Cup Final defeat by Rangers at Hampden Park. He then found himself a victim of Jefferies' continued rebuilding, and towards the end of the 1996-97 season, after scoring 101 goals in 496 games for Hearts, he joined St Johnstone on a free transfer.

After just a handful of appearances he decided to hang up his boots at the age of 34, to pursue a career as a media pundit.

HENRY SMITH
Goalkeeper
Born: Henry Smith, Lanark, 10 March 1956
Height: 6ft 2in
Weight: 12st 0lb
Clubs: Leeds United; Heart of Midlothian; Ayr United
Scotland caps: 3
1988 v Saudi Arabia (drew 2-2)
1992 v N Ireland (won 1-0), v Canada (won 3-1)

Though he was born in Lanarkshire, Henry Smith was brought up in Yorkshire and worked as a miner before being taken on by his local club, Leeds United. At Elland Road he kept some impressive company, for he was at the club at the same time as Scottish international keepers David Harvey and David Stewart, plus the up-and-coming David Seaman and John Lukic. It was little wonder that Smith failed to force his way into the Leeds first team!

Hearts manager Tony Ford paid just £2,000 to bring Smith to Tynecastle in 1981, and though few had heard of him, he was to make a considerable mark. He spent 15 years at Tynecastle and set a new club shut-out record in the League, with 171 clean sheets, and went on to play for Scotland on three occasions.

At the time of his arrival at Tynecastle, Hearts were in the First Division, but with Smith playing in every one of the 39 league games (and conceding just 39 goals), Hearts were back in the Premier Division for the start of the 1983-84 season. Such was Henry Smith's consistency that he played in 195 consecutive league games for Hearts between March 1982 and April 1987. Even when he did miss a game, Smith then embarked on another unbroken run of 180 matches that lasted until February 1991.

Though he then lost his place to Nicky Walker, he soon regained it, and in 1991-92 he was again ever-present as Hearts finished runners-up to Rangers in the League. Having already won two full caps, his consistency was rewarded at the end of the campaign when he won his third Scottish cap against Canada.

Over the next four seasons, following regular changes of managers, Smith found himself in and out of the Hearts' side, and after Jim Jefferies signed French international keeper Gilles Rousset, Smith, who was approaching 40 and had played in 701 games for the club, left to end his career with Ayr United.

DEREK FERGUSON
Midfield
Born: Derek Ferguson, Glasgow, 31 July 1967
Height: 5ft 8in
Weight: 10st 11lb
Clubs: Gartcosh United; Glasgow Rangers; Dundee; Heart of Midlothian; Sunderland; Falkirk

Scotland caps: 2
1988 v Malta (drew 1-1), v Colombia (drew 0-0)

Midfield player Derek Ferguson represented Scotland at youth, Under-21 and senior international level, and was seen by many to have as good a future in the game as Celtic's Paul McStay. However, after joining Rangers from Gartcosh United in the summer of 1983, injuries, misdemeanours and other problems off the field hindered his early days with the Ibrox club.

Eventually he began to produce the form that he had showed in junior football, and helped Rangers win the League Championship and League Cup in 1986-87, followed by a further League Cup success in 1987-88 and another League Championship triumph in 1988-89. That season, Ferguson's form was such that he won two full caps for Scotland, playing in the drawn games against Malta and Colombia.

He then struggled with a spate of niggling injuries, and was able to contribute little to the Rangers side in 1989-90; and in the midwinter, when the possibility of a transfer arose, it was clear that the Rangers management had lost patience with the player. Ferguson, who had scored nine goals in 145 games, was loaned out to Dundee early in 1990, before being transferred to Hearts the following summer.

A virtual ever-present in the Tynecastle club's side, the midfielder had three seasons with Hearts before trying his luck south of the border with Sunderland— the Wearsiders paying £750,000 for his services. His undoubted passing ability won him many fans at Roker Park, although he would have liked to have scored more than the one goal he did in 64 league appearances. On leaving Sunderland, Ferguson returned to Scotland to play for Falkirk, but after an impressive first season, he was hampered by injuries and forced to hang up his boots.

KEVIN GALLACHER
Forward

Born: Kevin William Gallacher, Clydebank, 23 November 1966
Height: 5ft 8in
Weight: 11st 6lb
Clubs: Duntocher BC; Dundee United; Coventry City; Blackburn Rovers; Newcastle United; Preston North End; Sheffield Wednesday; Huddersfield Town
Scotland caps: 53
Scotland goals: 9
1988 v Colombia (drew 0-0), v England (lost 0-1)
1989 v Norway (won 2-1), v Italy (lost 0-2)
1991 v San Marino (won 2-1)
1992 v Romania (lost 0-1), v San Marino (won 4-0), v N Ireland (won 1-0),
    v Norway (drew 0-0), v Holland (lost 0-1), v Germany (lost 0-2), v USSR (won 3-0)
1993 v Switzerland (lost 1-3), v Portugal (drew 0-0), v Portugal (lost 0-5),
    v Estonia (won 3-0) 1 goal, v Estonia (won 3-1)
1994 v Italy (lost 1-3) 1 goal, v Malta (won 2-0)
1996 v Australia (won 1-0), v Denmark (lost 0-2), v Colombia (lost 0-1), v Holland (lost 0-0)

1997 v Sweden (won 1-0), v Estonia (drew 0-0), v Estonia (won 2-0),
v Austria (won 2-0) 2 goals, v Sweden (lost 1-2) 1 goal, v Wales (lost 0-1),
v Malta (won 3-2), v Belarus (won 1-0)

1998 v Belarus (won 4-1) 2 goals, v Latvia (won 2-0) 1 goal, v France (lost 1-2),
v Finland (drew 1-1), v United States (drew 0-0), v Brazil (lost 1-2),
v Norway (drew 1-1), v Morocco (lost 0-3)

1999 v Lithuania (drew 0-0), v Estonia (won 3-2), v Faroe Islands (drew 1-1),
v Czech Republic (lost 2-3)

2000 v Bosnia (won 2-1), v Bosnia (won 1-0), v Lithuania (won 3-0), v England (lost 0-2),
v France (lost 0-2), v Republic of Ireland (won 2-1)

2001 v San Marino (won 2-0), v Croatia (drew 1-1) 1 goal, v Belgium (drew 2-2),
v San Marino (won 4-0)

Kevin Gallacher, who played in all three of his country's World Cup games in 1998, won his 50th cap for Scotland in the World Cup qualifier against San Marino in October 2000, being honoured with the captaincy of the side to mark the occasion.

A member of a footballing family, being the grandson of the legendary Patsy Gallacher, who played for Celtic between 1911 and 1925, Kevin Gallacher began his career with Dundee United. He appeared in two Scottish Cup Finals and the UEFA Cup Final of 1987 for the Tannadice club before going south of the Border to join Coventry City for £900,000 in January 1990.

He was hampered by injuries during his time at Highfield Road,

Kevin Gallacher playing for Blackburn

but it didn't deter Blackburn Rovers' manager Kenny Dalglish from paying £1.5 million for his services in March 1993.

However, the versatile front runner suffered a horrendous triple fracture of a leg in a match against Arsenal at Highbury in February 1994. He reappeared in the Rovers' side midway through the following season, but after scoring the winning goal against Crystal Palace, ended the day with his leg back in plaster after it was broken in the same spot! Tough, he fought his way back to full fitness, but it was 1996-97 before he won a regular place in the Blackburn side, netting his first hat-trick for the club in a 3-1 defeat of Wimbledon. In 1997-98, Gallacher had his best-ever season for the club, scoring 20 goals in all competitions, including a hat-trick in the Premier League defeat of Aston Villa. He had scored 52 goals in 161 games for Blackburn, when in 1999 he became Newcastle United manager Bobby Robson's first signing.

Though seen as a short-term buy, his performances clearly impressed his new manager, and enabled him to retain his place in the Scotland side. Injuries, including a torn right hamstring, kept him out of the Newcastle side for the first part of the 2000-01 season, and he was later released on a free transfer. After brief loan spells with Preston North End and Sheffield Wednesday, his last port of call was Huddersfield Town, for whom he also had a spell on loan.

ANDY WALKER
Forward

Born: Andrew Francis Walker, Glasgow, 6 April 1965
Height: 5ft 8in
Weight: 10st 7lb
Clubs: Baillieston Juniors; Motherwell; Glasgow Celtic; Newcastle United; Bolton Wanderers; Glasgow Celtic; Sheffield United; Hibernian; Raith Rovers; Ayr United; Carlisle United; Partick Thistle; Isernia (Italy); Alloa Athletic
Scotland caps: 3
1988 v Colombia (drew 0-0)
1995 v Finland (won 2-0), v Faroe Islands (won 5-1)

A striker of lightning quick reflexes, Andy Walker began his career with Motherwell, scoring the goal against Brechin City which clinched promotion in May 1985. They would have suffered relegation twelve months later but for a League re-organisation, although he managed to score against both the Glasgow giants. He was Motherwell's leading scorer in 1986-87, but he kicked off the following season with Celtic after a £350,000 move.

He had a magnificent first season, scoring 31 goals as the Bhoys went on to win the League and Cup double. He also won three Under-21 caps and the first of his three international caps. He missed the 1989 Cup Final because of a horrendous injury at Aberdeen, when Brian Irvine smacked the ball into his face and almost detached a retina. Unfortunately he didn't hit the same vein of form in subsequent seasons with Celtic as they began to struggle at league level.

In September 1991 he had his first taste of the English game when he played two Second Division games while on loan with Newcastle United. In January 1992 he joined Bolton Wanderers on loan, before making a permanent transfer the following month for a fee of £160,000. Walker, who found the net in nine of his first 12 League and Cup games, ended the season as the club's 'Player of the Year'. In 1992-93, Walker, who scored the opening goal of the campaign after just 47 seconds against Huddersfield Town, netted 26 goals in 32 league games as the Wanderers won promotion to the First Division. His season's total of 33 equalled a post-war club record set by Nat Lofthouse twice during the 1950s. He was also selected for the PFA Second Division side, but his season came to an abrupt end when he sustained a ligament injury against Swansea City. Though he returned to first team action, scoring a memorable goal in the FA Cup win against Arsenal, Celtic paid £550,000 to take him back to Parkhead.

Unable to find the net with the consistency he had done at Burnden Park, he joined Sheffield United before his travels took him on to Hibs, Raith Rovers, Ayr United, Carlisle United, Partick Thistle, Italian club Isernia and, finally, Alloa Athletic as they chased and ultimately won promotion from the Second Division.

He then retired to become a football agent and continue writing his very witty and perceptive Sunday newspaper column.

IAN FERGUSON
Midfield
Born: Ian Ferguson, Glasgow, 15 March 1967
Height: 5ft 10in
Weight: 10st 2lb
Clubs: Clyde; St Mirren; Glasgow Rangers
Scotland caps: 9
1989 v Italy (lost 0-2), v Cyprus (won 3-2), v France (won 2-0)
1993 v Malta (won 3-0), v Estonia (won 3-1)
1994 v Malta (won 2-0), v Austria (won 2-1), v Holland (lost 1-3)
1997 v Estonia (drew 0-0)

A major blight on Ian Ferguson's career was his lamentable international record, which frustrated successive managers Andy Roxburgh and Craig Brown. A debut against Italy in December 1988 was only the prelude to a string of squad withdrawals for a variety of injuries.

When he first burst onto the scene with Clyde in 1985-86, he was already earmarked as a star in the making, and Alex Smith at St Mirren was impressed enough to take the budding starlet to Paisley in 1986. It was a move the Buddies were to be grateful for many times over, when, at the tail end of the 1986-87 season, it seemed that the whole of Renfrewshire was at Hampden to see them beat Dundee United 1-0 in the Cup Final. After a dull ninety minutes, it was Ferguson, then only 20, who crashed home the winner for the Buddies' first major silverware in 37 years. Only months later, Rangers handed over £1 million to secure his signature—the first seven-figure fee agreed by two Scottish clubs.

Many critics saw him as potentially one of the great players of the Scottish game, others felt a certain bitter element in his character might prevent that. He was very successful in 1988-89, scoring in the 3-2 League Cup Final win over Aberdeen, but then missed a huge number of matches over the next few seasons due to a combination of illness and injury, but returned to score the vital winner against CSKA Moscow during Rangers' spectacular 1992-93 European Champions' League run. The following season he held the midfield together, at a time when the Ibrox club was in the grip of an injury crisis, playing more matches than anyone else.

Yet for all his success—nine League Championship medals, six League Cup and four Cup winners' medals, in a Rangers career that saw him forced to retire through injury—there have been low points, most notably in 1993-94, when the temperamental Ferguson was red-carded for spitting on Dundee United's

Gordon Petric. Despite the fact that the Yugoslavian had clearly elbowed Ferguson, the furore was massive and there were calls for him to be kicked out of Ibrox, but Walter Smith's common-sense prevailed, and the punishment was kept within the walls of the club—although the SFA hammered the errant midfielder with a lengthy match ban.

ALAN McINALLY
Forward
Born: Alan Bruce McInally, Ayr, 10 February 1963
Height: 6ft 2in
Weight: 11st 8lb
Clubs: Ayr United; Glasgow Celtic; Aston Villa; Bayern Munich (Germany); Glasgow Celtic; Ayr
    United; Kilmarnock
Scotland caps: 8
Scotland goals: 3
1989 v Cyprus (won 3-2), v Chile (won 2-0) 1 goal
1990 v Yugoslavia (lost 1-3), v France (lost 0-3), v Argentina (won 1-0), v Poland (drew 1-1),
    v Malta (won 2-1) 2 goals, v Costa Rica (lost 0-1)

Alan 'Rambo' McInally, the son of the great Jackie of Kilmarnock in the 1960s, began his career with his home-town team Ayr United in 1980. His goalscoring feats for the Honest Men led to a number of top flight Scottish clubs showing an interest in him, and it came as no surprise when he left Somerset Park to join Celtic in the summer of 1984.

McInally was rarely seen in his first two seasons at Parkhead as a result of a mysterious back injury sustained during the warm-up in a game against St Mirren at Love Street in September 1984. Even when this had cleared up, his form was so patchy that he didn't get an extended run in the team until 1985-86. It was then that he showed glimpses of the form that had taken him to Parkhead in the first place, but even so, at the end of the campaign, he was allowed to join Aston Villa.

Again his early form with Villa was poor, and there came a time when it looked like he would return north of the Border to play for St Mirren. However, Villa manager Graham Taylor gave him another chance, and he responded by taking the First Division by storm, scoring 19 goals before Boxing Day 1988. He was a constant threat to the top flight defences, his form winning him the first of eight full caps for Scotland as a substitute against Cyprus. Then, on his full debut, he scored the opening goal in a 2-0 win over Chile.

Allowed to join Bayern Munich in the summer of 1990, he was a martyr to the knee trouble that was eventually to force his early retirement two years later.

He returned to Parkhead to work with Celtic physiotherapist Brian Scott in the hope of making a comeback. Loaned out to Ayr United, he played in a friendly against Kenny Dalglish's Blackburn Rovers, before being given a chance by Tommy Burns at Kilmarnock. Sadly it didn't work out, and he was forced to retire for good.

DAVE McPHERSON
Defender

Born: David McPherson, Paisley, 28 January 1964
Height: 6ft 3in
Weight: 11st 12lb
Clubs: Glasgow Rangers; Heart of Midlothian; Glasgow Rangers; Heart of Midlothian; Carlton (Australia)
Scotland caps: 27
1989 v Cyprus (won 2-1), v England (lost 0-2)
1990 v Norway (drew 1-1), v Malta (won 2-1), v Costa Rica (lost 0-1), v Sweden (won 2-1), v Brazil (lost 0-1)
1991 v Switzerland (won 2-1), v Bulgaria (drew 1-1), v USSR (lost 0-1), v Bulgaria (drew 1-1), v San Marino (won 2-1)
1992 v Switzerland (drew 2-2), v Romania (lost 0-1), v San Marino (won 4-0), v N Ireland (won 1-0), v Finland (drew 1-1), v United States (won 1-0), v Canada (won 3-1), v Norway (drew 0-0), v Holland (lost 0-1), v Germany (lost 0-2), v USSR (won 3-0)
1993 v Switzerland (lost 1-3), v Italy (drew 0-0), v Malta (won 3-0), v Portugal (lost 0-5)

Dave McPherson, who went on to win 27 full caps for Scotland, played in the 1990 World Cup Finals in Italy and the 1992 European Championships in Sweden.

He first broke through into the Rangers side as a teenager in 1982-83, and was immediately tipped as a great prospect for the future. Good in the air and comfortable on the ground, he looked set to be a fixture in the Rangers team for years. He was also good value for goals from the back, or in his occasional performances in midfield too, and notched no less than four in one UEFA Cup tie in an 8-0 win over Valetta of Malta.

Forming an impressive backbone to the defence with Terry Butcher, he helped Rangers win their first League Championship for nine years in 1986-87, but after manager Graeme Souness blamed him for the humiliating defeat at the hands of Hamilton, he was allowed to join Hearts.

His partnership with Craig Levein in 1987-88 was the cornerstone on which Hearts built their title challenge, and it helped the team finish runners-up to Celtic. Manager Alex Macdonald appointed him captain of the team, and in 1989-90 they finished third behind Aberdeen on goal difference. Under Joe Jordan, McPherson was one of only two ever-presents as the Hearts side embarked on a memorable 15-match unbeaten run. However, the new Hearts manager was intent on building his own team, and so McPherson went back to Ibrox in June 1992 for a fee of £1.3 million.

Two seasons of honours followed, including a key role in Rangers' glorious European run of 1992-93 when the club came within a whisker of a place in the Championship Final. But despite a treble in his first season back, he was made the scapegoat the following campaign as Rangers were denied a second consecutive treble.

His second departure from Ibrox was under less pleasing circumstances than the first. Rejoining Hearts, he went on to score 37 goals in 416 games in his two spells at Tynecastle, before leaving the club in the summer of 1999 to take up the option of playing in Australia with Carlton.

PETER GRANT
Midfield

Born: Peter Grant, Bellshill, 30 August 1965
Height: 5ft 9in
Weight: 11st 9lb
Clubs: Glasgow Celtic; Norwich City; Reading; Bournemouth
Scotland caps: 2
1989 v England (lost 0-2), v Chile (won 2-0)

A tigerish competitor, noted for his ball-winning ability and great appetite for the game, Grant's proudest moment during his early days with Celtic must have come during the game against Dundee at Parkhead in April 1988. The Bhoys had just clinched the League title, but Grant, who had broken his foot at St Mirren a few weeks before the game, was not playing. A packed house chanted his name until he came out on crutches and joined the team!

On his return to full fitness, his form led to him winning full international honours, first as a substitute against England on 27 May 1989, and then from the start against Chile three days later.

He helped Celtic win the Scottish Cup that season as the Bhoys beat Rangers 1-0 in the final. Again he was hampered by injuries—torn knee ligaments in the game against Aberdeen on 15 January 1994, a game that was eventually abandoned due to fog—restricted his appearances. But again he bounced back, going on to score 21 goals in 473 League and Cup games, before a £200,000 transfer took him to Norwich City in the summer of 1997.

He impressed everyone at Carrow Road with his thoroughly professional approach, and over the next two seasons his boundless enthusiasm and consistency were the main features of his play. Allowed to join Reading in the close season of 1999, he spent less than a year at the Madejski Stadium before moving to Bournemouth as the Dean Court club's player-coach. After playing in the majority of the club's opening games of the 2000-01 season, Grant hung up his boots to become the club's head coach.

STUART McKIMMIE
Defender

Born: Stuart McKimmie, Aberdeen, 27 October 1962
Height: 5ft 8in
Weight: 10st 7lb
Clubs: Banks O'Dee; Dundee; Aberdeen; Dundee United
Scotland caps: 40
Scotland goals: 1
1989 v England (lost 0-2), v Chile (won 2-0)
1990 v Argentina (won 1-0) 1 goal, v Egypt (lost 1-3), v Costa Rica (lost 0-1),

v Brazil (lost 0-1)

1991 v Romania (won 2-1), v Switzerland (won 2-1), v Bulgaria (drew 1-1),
v San Marino (won 2-1)

1992 v Switzerland (drew 2-2), v Romania (lost 0-1), v N Ireland (won 1-0),
v Finland (drew 1-1), v United States (won 1-0), v Canada (won 3-1),
v Norway (drew 0-0), v Holland (lost 0-1), v Germany (lost 0-2), v USSR (won 3-0)

1993 v Portugal (lost 0-5), v Estonia (won 3-1)

1994 v Switzerland (drew 1-1), v Italy (lost 1-3), v Holland (lost 0-1), v Austria (won 2-1),
v Holland (lost 1-3)

1995 v Finland (won 2-0), v Faroe Islands (won 5-1), v Russia (drew 1-1), v Greece (lost 0-1),
v Russia (drew 0-0), v Faroe Islands (won 2-0)

1996 v Greece (won 1-0), v Finland (won 1-0), v Sweden (lost 0-2), v Denmark (lost 0-2),
v Colombia (lost 0-1), v Holland (drew 0-0), v England (lost 0-2)

Though he began his career with Dundee, whom he joined from Banks O'Dee in 1980, the Aberdeen-born full-back left Dens Park in December 1983, after making 80 appearances, to join his home-town club.

Less than a month after joining the Dons, he had picked up a European Super Cup winners medal after Aberdeen had beaten Hamburg over two legs. By the end of that 1983-84 season, McKimmie had added League Championship and Cup winners' medals to his collection. In his early years at Pittodrie, McKimmie became well used to picking up honours, with another League title, the Scottish Cup and the Skol Cup over a period of two seasons.

After this, the Dons experienced a lean time of things. The Skol Cup Final of 1987-88 saw Rangers beat Aberdeen on penalty-kicks, while twelve months later, the Ibrox side retained the trophy, winning 3-2 inside normal playing time. Aberdeen's double cup-winning season of 1989-90, when Celtic were beaten 9-8 on penalties after a goalless draw in the Cup Final and Rangers 2-1 in the League Cup Final, McKimmie won what was the first of 40 full international caps.

Another appearance in the Scottish Cup Final followed, before in 1994-95 he was made team captain in place of the now departed Alex McLeish. However, it turned out to be a memorable campaign for all the wrong reasons. After defeats to Skonto Riga in the UEFA Cup and Stenhousemuir in the Tennents Scottish Cup, the club just avoided relegation via the newly introduced play-off system. Yet six months later, McKimmie was back at Hampden, lifting the now renamed Coca Cola Cup after a 2-0 final win over Dundee.

Towards the end of the following season, McKimmie was told his services were no longer required, and he left Pittodrie to spend a season with Dundee United. On leaving Tannadice he became heavily involved in the media as a television and radio pundit.

THE 1990s

Throughout the 1990 World Cup campaign, Scotland lived on their nerves, and a feeble 3-0 defeat by France had left them needing a point at Hampden against Norway if they were to edge out France. Ally McCoist brilliantly scored the goal they needed to give them a cushion when he flicked the ball over Erik Thorsvedt. And they needed the cushion. With a minute left, Scottish goalkeeping blunders returned to haunt them as Jim Leighton misjudged a speculative long-range shot and the Norwegians equalised.

Sadly, Scotland maintained their usual record; for the seventh time they failed to get past the first phase: they experienced yet another embarrassing defeat, 1-0 to Costa Rica; but a stirring display against Brazil almost got them into the second round until a late goal put them on the plane home.

Though Scotland lost 2-0 to Germany in the 1992 European Championships, they completely outplayed them and did them a huge favour by beating CIS 3-0.

Scotland's 5-0 defeat in Portugal in April 1993 severely damaged their chances of qualifying for the 1994 World Cup Finals, and with England, Northern Ireland and Wales also failing to qualify, this was the first time since the Home Countries had entered the World Cup in 1950 that all four were absent.

In Euro '96 the Scots had done remarkably well in their first match, holding Holland 0-0, but the game against England was the big one. With 12 minutes to go and 1-0 down, Scotland were awarded a penalty. A brilliant save by David Seaman from Gary McAllister not only dashed their hopes, but within seconds, Paul Gascoigne had scored a virtuoso goal to complete Scotland's misery. Though an Ally McCoist goal was enough to beat Switzerland in their final group match, the late goal that England conceded in their 4-1 defeat of Holland meant that the Scots were edged out of the quarter-finals by the Dutch. This preserved their perfect record of never having qualified for the second phase of the finals of any major tournament they have reached!

In 1998 Craig Brown led Scotland to the World Cup Finals in France. After a courageous and rather unlucky defeat in the opening match against Brazil, the Scots fought a fine draw against the strong Norwegians before crashing to a disappointing defeat by Morocco. So the World Cup adventure was over, but the impact on the tournament by the colourful and noisy Tartan Army will long be remembered.

ROBERT FLECK
Forward

Born: Robert William Fleck, Glasgow, 11 August 1965
Height: 5ft 8in
Weight: 11st 9lb
Clubs: Possil YM; Glasgow Rangers; Partick Thistle; Norwich City; Chelsea; Bolton Wanderers; Bristol City; Norwich City; Reading
Scotland caps: 4
1990 v Argentina (won 1-0), v Sweden (won 2-1), v Brazil (lost 0-1)
1991 v USSR (lost 0-1)

Initially unable to make the grade with Rangers, Robert Fleck joined Partick Thistle on loan and scored on his full debut at Ayr United. On his return to Ibrox, he played his first game for the Glasgow giants against Hearts in April 1984 but didn't win any honours there until 1987.

Then he earned a Scottish Premier League Championship medal with 19 goals including the winner against St Mirren in the final game of the season. He also won a Scottish League Cup winners' medal with a substitute appearance in the final against Celtic. He won another Scottish League Cup winners' medal the following season, scoring in the final against Aberdeen which ended 3-3, Rangers winning on penalties.

In December 1987 he joined Norwich City for a fee of £580,000 and quickly got into his stride at Carrow Road. During 1988-89 he was the Canaries' leading scorer, and helped the club reach the semi-finals of the FA Cup and finish fourth in Division One. After scoring 40 goals in 143 games for Norwich, he left to join Chelsea in August 1992, the Stamford Bridge club paying £2.1 million for his services.

He never found his best form with the London club, and in the latter part of 1993 joined Bolton Wanderers on loan as the Lancashire club looked to consolidate their top-flight status. Substituted in the final game of his loan spell, he then joined Bristol City in a similar capacity before rejoining Norwich City for a £650,000 fee.

He went on to score 84 goals for the Carrow Road club to take him into third place in the Canaries all-time scoring charts, before joining Reading in March 1998.

He scored in the club's first-ever match at the Madejski Stadium, but a serious back problem forced his retirement from playing and a return to Norwich. He remained in football by coaching Gorleston, a team in the Eastern Counties League.

CRAIG LEVEIN
Central defender

Born: Craig Levein, Dunfermline, 22 October 1964
Height: 6ft 1in
Weight: 12st 4lb
Clubs: Cowdenbeath; Heart of Midlothian

Scotland caps: 16

1990 v Argentina (won 1-0), v East Germany (lost 0-1), v Egypt (lost 1-3), v Poland (drew 1-1),
v Malta (won 2-1), v Sweden (won 2-1)
1992 v Romania (lost 0-1), v San Marino (won 4-0)
1993 v Portugal (drew 0-0), v Germany (lost 0-1), v Portugal (lost 0-5)
1994 v Switzerland (drew 1-1), v Holland (lost 0-1)
1995 v Finland (won 2-0), v Faroe Islands (won 5-0), v Russia (drew 1-1)

Craig Levein went on to make 16 full international appearances for Scotland after making his debut in a 1-0 win over Argentina in March 1990. He was outstanding in the 2-1 defeat of Sweden in the 1990 World Cup in Italy, but a thigh injury sustained in that match meant that he missed the final group game against Brazil. In March 1993 he became the first Hearts player since Dave Mackay, some 35 years earlier, to captain Scotland when he led the side in a friendly at Ibrox against Germany.

One of the most accomplished central defenders of his generation, Craig Levein began his career with Cowdenbeath, and after just a handful of appearances he became a target for a number of Premier Division clubs. After impressing against Hearts in the League Cup at the start of the 1983-84 season, the Tynecastle club's manager Alex Macdonald paid £35,000 for his services.

It didn't take long for Levein to win a regular place in the team, and he went on to score 21 goals in 462 games in an outstanding Tynecastle career. This total would have been many more but for two serious knee injuries—the first, cruciate ligament damage in a reserve game against Hibs at Easter Road, and the second in January 1988 when his knee gave way in the match against Rangers. On each occasion he was out of action for over a year, and on each occasion was told to consider hanging up his boots.

Both times he came back courageously, and though he was unfortunate not to be part of the Hearts team that eventually ended their long spell without silverware in 1998, he came close to it. Levein missed the title decider with Dundee in 1986 after suffering a virus on the eve of the match. There are many Hearts supporters who believe that if he had taken his place in the centre of defence that day at Dens Park, the club would not have conceded the late goals that so cruelly cost them the League Championship.

After a short spell as coach with Livingston, he accepted an offer to manage his first club Cowdenbeath, before returning to his beloved Tynecastle as Hearts' boss. Later replaced by John Robertson, he took over the managerial reins at Leicester City in November 2004 but later parted company with the Foxes. He is now back in football management after taking over at Raith Rovers on a non-contract basis.

STUART McCALL

Midfield

Born: Andrew Stuart Murray McCall, Leeds, 10 June 1964
Height: 5ft 7in

Weight: 12st 0lb
Clubs: Bradford City; Everton; Glasgow Rangers; Bradford City; Sheffield United
Scotland caps: 40
Scotland goals: 1
1990 v Argentina (won 1-0), v East Germany (lost 0-1), v Egypt (lost 1-3),
v Poland (drew 1-1), v Malta (won 2-1), v Costa Rica (lost 0-1),
v Sweden (won 2-1) 1 goal v Brazil (lost 0-1)
1991 v Switzerland (won 2-1), v USSR (lost 0-1), v San Marino (won 2-1)
1992 v Switzerland (drew 2-2), v Romania (lost 0-1), v San Marino (won 4-0),
v United States (won 1-0), v Canada (won 3-1), v Norway (drew 0-0),
v Holland (lost 0-1), v Germany (lost 0-2), v USSR (won 3-0)
1993 v Switzerland (lost 1-3), v Portugal (drew 0-0), v Portugal (lost 0-5)
1994 v Italy (lost 1-3), v Holland (lost 0-1), v Austria (won 2-1), v Holland (lost 1-3)
1995 v Finland (won 2-0), v Russia (drew 1-1), v Greece (lost 0-1)
1996 v Greece (won 1-0), v Denmark (lost 0-2), v United States (lost 1-2),
v Colombia (lost 0-1), v Holland (drew 0-0), v England (lost 0-2),
v Switzerland (won 1-0)
1997 v Austria (drew 0-0), v Latvia (won 2-0)
1998 v Denmark (lost 0-1)

Stuart McCall, by virtue of his Scottish heritage, became a valued member of the national side and will be long-remembered for a crucial goal against Sweden in the 1990 World Cup Finals.

The red-haired midfielder began his career with Bradford City, and it didn't take long for him to become a big star there. It was at Valley Parade that he received his first international recognition—for England Under-21s. Thankfully he did not play for the young English, although he was perilously close as an unused substitute. It was also at Bradford that he endured his worst memory in football—the fire disaster which plunged British football into mourning in 1985. McCall played in the fateful game against Bristol City. A move to a bigger club seemed inevitable, and in the summer of 1988 he moved to Everton for £850,000.

Surprisingly, McCall failed really to establish himself at Goodison Park, and his finest moment with the Toffees came as a substitute when he came on in the 1989 FA Cup Final and scored both Everton's goals in a 3-2 defeat by Liverpool.

In August 1991, McCall left Merseyside and he moved to Scotland to play for Rangers, the Ibrox club paying £1.2 million for his signature. He quickly established himself in the Rangers' side, proving himself the perfect workhorse in midfield as well as an accomplished wide midfielder. His willingness to play anywhere led to him wearing every outfield shirt at Ibrox bar No.11. Though his career highlights with Rangers were many and varied, his goal against Aberdeen in the 1992-93 Skol Cup Final was a crucial one and paved the way for an eventual 2-1 success. In his time at Ibrox, McCall won five Premier League Championships, two Cup Finals and three League Cup Finals before returning to Valley Parade in the 1998 close season.

Given a three-year contract and appointed club captain, he won all of the club's Player of the Year awards in 1998-99 and continued to lead by example, belying his age. In the summer of 2000 he was appointed assistant to City manager Chris Hutchings, and when Hutchings was sacked, he took over as caretaker manager for a fortnight until Jim Jefferies arrived. One of Bradford City's all-time greats, he went on to score 55 goals in 454 games before being given a free transfer.

Joining Sheffield United as player-coach, he was a key member of the Blades' side, his energetic displays bringing out the best in the younger midfielders around him. McCall is still at Bramall Lane as assistant-manager to Neil Warnock.

GARY McALLISTER
Midfield

Born: Gary McAllister, Motherwell, 25 December 1964
Height: 6ft 1in
Weight: 11st1 2lb
Clubs: Fir Park BC; Motherwell; Leicester City; Leeds United; Coventry City; Liverpool
Scotland caps: 57
Scotland goals: 5

1990 v East Germany (lost 0-1), v Poland (drew 1-1), v Malta (won 2-1)
1991 v Romania (won 2-1), v Switzerland (won 2-1) 1 goal, v Bulgaria (drew 1-1),
   v USSR (lost 0-1), v San Marino (won 2-1)
1992 v Switzerland (drew 2-2), v San Marino (won 4-0), v N Ireland (won 1-0),
   v Finland (drew 1-1), v United States (won 1-0), v Canada (won 3-1) 2 goals,
   v Norway (drew 0-0), v Holland (lost 0-1), v Germany (lost 0-2),
   v USSR (won 3-0) 1 goal
1993 v Switzerland (lost 1-3), v Portugal (drew 0-0), v Italy (drew 0-0), v Malta (won 3-0)
1994 v Switzerland (drew 1-1), v Italy (lost 1-3), v Malta (won 2-0), v Holland (lost 0-1),
   v Austria (won 2-1), v Holland (lost1-3)
1995 v Finland (won 2-0), v Russia (drew 1-1), v Greece (lost 0-1), v Russia (drew 0-0),
   v San Marino (won 2-0)
1996 v Greece (won 1-0), v Finland (won 1-0), v Sweden (lost 0-2), v San Marino (won 5-0),
   v Australia (won 1-0), v Denmark (lost 0-2), v United States (lost 1-2),
   v Colombia (lost 0-1), v Holland (drew 0-0), v England (lost 0-2),
   v Switzerland (won 1-0)
1997 v Austria (drew 0-0), v Latvia (won 2-0), v Estonia (drew 0-0), v Estonia (won 2-0),
   v Austria (won 2-0), v Sweden (lost 1-2), v Wales (lost 0-1), v Malta (won 3-2),
   v Belarus (won 1-0) 1 goal
1998 v Belarus (won 4-1), v Latvia (won 2-0), v France (lost 1-2)
1999 v Czech Republic (lost 1-2)

A vital member of the Scottish national side for almost a decade, Gary McAllister captained his country in the 1996 European Championships, but after being barracked by the fans on his return to the side against the Czech Republic, he announced his retirement after winning 57 caps.

He started out with his home-town side Motherwell, and was an integral part of the side that won the First Division Championship under the astute leadership of Tommy McLean. However, in the summer of 1985 he joined Leicester City, and though the Foxes dropped into the Second Division, over the next three seasons he was the club's leading scorer. His brilliant form was eventually recognised at full international level when he was capped against East Germany in April 1990. It was inevitable that a bigger club would make a move for him, and the following summer, Leeds United on their return to the top flight paid £1 million to take him to Elland Road.

Gary McAllister

He made an immediate impact and was ever-present as the Yorkshire club finished fourth in Division One. He then played a major role in Leeds' League Championship triumph of 1991-92. The following season saw him break an arm and end the campaign with his foot in plaster owing to a hairline fracture. Returning to action as the club's captain, he was the driving force behind most of Leeds' attacking moves, using great all-round vision and specialising in long diagonal passes to switch the play and wrong-foot defenders.

An outstanding professional, he contributed a number of vital goals including netting a hat-trick against Coventry City during the 1995-96 season. He had an excellent Euro '96, but will mainly be remembered for his penalty miss against England! Shortly afterwards, McAllister, who had scored 46 goals in 295 games, was sensationally transferred to Coventry City for £3 million.

After looking tired in his first season at Highfield Road, he collapsed during the early part of the 1997-98 season with a torn cruciate ligament. It wasn't operated on immediately in the hope that he could still make France '98, but after resting up, he collapsed again in a reserve game and underwent the operation. Eventually returning to full fitness, he had an outstanding 1999-2000 season, a campaign which prompted his move to Liverpool in the close season.

Signed on a 'Bosman' free transfer, neither manager nor player could have foreseen the impact he was going to make on the Reds' team at the end of his first season at Anfield as they closed in on their triple targets of FA Cup, UEFA Cup and Champions' League qualification. In the 5-4 UEFA Cup Final defeat of Deportivo Alaves, he had a hand in four of Liverpool's goals and scored a spot-kick himself. It was inevitable that his next season with the club would be an anti-climax, and the following summer he was appointed the new manager of his former club, Coventry City.

Sadly, due to personal problems, he decided to resign his post midway through his second season in charge at Highfield Road. Always the professional both on and off the field, all football supporters will hope that one day he will return to the game he graced for over 20 years.

BRYAN GUNN
Goalkeeper
Born: Bryan James Gunn, Thurso, 22 December 1963
Height: 6ft 2in
Weight: 13st 13lb
Clubs: Invergordon BC; Aberdeen; Norwich City; Hibernian
Scotland caps: 6
1990 v Egypt (lost 1-3)
1993 v Estonia (won 3-0), v Estonia (won 3-1)
1994 v Switzerland (drew 1-1), v Italy (lost 1-3), v Holland (lost 1-3)

Bryan Gunn's consistency in the Norwich City goal was rewarded at international level when Scotland picked him for the match against Egypt in May 1990. Although he made errors which resulted in two goals in a disappointing 3-1 defeat, he returned to the side in 1993, going on to win six full caps.

He began his first-class career with Aberdeen, but much of his time at Pittodrie was spent as understudy to Jim Leighton, and in October 1986 he joined Norwich City for a fee of £150,000. Gunn's performances in his first season at Carrow Road ensured the Canaries of fifth place in the First Division.

An ever-present when City finished third in the Premier League in 1992-93, Gunn made a number of outstanding saves, with the one from Tony Cottee's bicycle-kick in the match against Everton being particularly memorable. That season he was voted Norwich's Player of the Year, but it wasn't all roses. Sadly, his two-year-old daughter died of leukaemia, but he showed remarkable courage when immediately coming back to first team duty. After missing the second-half of the 1994-95 campaign with a broken ankle when his experience and organisational qualities were sorely missed, he returned the following season to miss just a few games. That campaign also saw him save three penalties in the Coca Cola Cup tie shoot-out at Bolton.

He had a very successful testimonial year in 1996-97, but after coming under threat from the emerging Andy Marshall, he took on a dual role that allowed him to keep playing and have an involvement on the commercial side. Fourth in the all-time list of appearances for the Canaries with 477, he signed for Hibernian on a short-term contract after the initial request for a three-month loan fell foul of the Scottish FA's regulations.

Following Mike Walker's resignation as manager of Norwich City, Bryan Gunn submitted an application for the vacant post at Carrow Road, but he was unsuccessful in his bid to enter the management side of the game.

TOMMY BOYD
Full-back

Born: Thomas Boyd, Glasgow, 24 November 1965
Height: 5ft 11in
Weight: 12st 8lb
Clubs: Motherwell; Chelsea; Glasgow Celtic
Scotland caps: 72
Scotland goals: 1

1991 v Romania (won 2-1), v Switzerland (won 2-1), v Bulgaria (drew 1-1), v USSR (lost 0-1)

1992 v Switzerland (drew 2-2), v Romania (lost 0-1), v Finland (drew 1-1),
v Canada (won 3-1), v Norway (drew 0-0), v USSR (won 3-0)

1993 v Switzerland (lost 1-3), v Portugal (drew 0-0), v Italy (drew 0-0), v Malta (won 3-0),
v Germany (lost 0-1), v Estonia (won 3-0), v Estonia (won 3-1)

1994 v Italy (lost 1-3), v Malta (won 2-0), v Holland (lost 0-1), v Austria (won 2-1)

1995 v Finland (won 2-0), v Faroe Islands (won 5-1), v Russia (drew 1-1), v Greece (lost 0-1),
v Russia (drew 0-0), v San Marino (won 2-0)

1996 v Greece (won 1-0), v Finland (won 1-0), v Sweden (lost 0-2), v San Marino (won 5-0),
v Australia (won 1-0), v Denmark (lost 0-2), v United States (lost 1-2),
v Colombia (lost 0-1), v Holland (drew 0-0), v England (lost 0-2),
v Switzerland (won 1-0)

1997 v Austria (drew 0-0), v Latvia (won 2-0), v Sweden (won 1-0), v Estonia (drew 0-0),
v Estonia (won 2-0) 1 goal, v Austria (won 2-0), v Sweden (lost 1-2), v Wales (lost 0-1),
v Malta (won 3-2), v Belarus (won 1-0)

1998 v Belarus (won 4-1), v Latvia (won 2-0), v France (lost 1-2), v Denmark (lost 0-1),
v Finland (drew 1-1), v Colombia (drew 2-2), v United States (drew 0-0),
v Brazil (lost 1-2), v Norway (drew 1-1), v Morocco (lost 0-3)

1999 v Lithuania (drew 0-0), v Estonia (won 3-2), v Faroe Islands (won 2-1),
v Czech Republic (lost 1-2), v Germany (won 1-0), v Faroe Islands (drew 1-1),
v Czech Republic (lost 2-3)

2001 v Latvia (won 1-0), v Croatia (drew 1-1), v Australia (lost 0-2), v Belgium (drew 2-2),
v San Marino (won 4-0), v Poland (drew 1-1)

2002 v Belgium (lost 0-2)

One of the game's finest full-backs, Tommy Boyd's international career brought him membership of the SFA's Hall of Fame, reserved for those with over 50 national caps. He won the first of his 72 caps as a substitute at Hampden Park against Romania in September 1990, during a European Championship tie, and started a Scotland match for the first time a few weeks later against Switzerland.

A speedy, direct and quick-tackling player, he was the classic overlapping full-back, who could play equally well in midfield.

Boyd joined Motherwell in 1983 as a YTS signing and made rapid progress until he became one of the youngest club captains in the Premier Division. His incisive play and shrewd thinking won him many admirers and he won international recognition for Scotland at 'B' level against Yugoslavia at Fir Park in March 1990, by which time he had already won five Under-21 caps. There is no doubt that Tommy Boyd made his reputation with Motherwell, linking superbly with Davie

Cooper, and it was fitting that he should leave Fir Park holding the 1991 Scottish Cup aloft after a 4-3 extra-time defeat of Dundee United.

He joined Chelsea for a fee of £800,000 shortly after the final, but failed to settle in London, and returned to Scotland with Celtic in a swap deal which took Tony Cascarino to Stamford Bridge.

Ironically, during his first season with Celtic, Boyd made his first return to Fir Park, where he conceded a penalty and was sent-off for fouling Motherwell's Dougie Arnott. Boyd went on to have a long and successful career with the Bhoys, playing in 405 games, many as captain, in his nine seasons with the club. He won three League Championship medals, two Scottish Cup winners medals and three League Cup winners medals, including helping Celtic win the treble in 2000-01. On hanging up his boots, he joined the club's backroom staff.

BRIAN IRVINE
Defender

Born: Brian Irvine, Bellshill, 24 May 1965
Height: 6ft 2in
Weight: 13st 0lb
Clubs: Falkirk; Aberdeen; Dundee; Ross County
Scotland caps: 9
1991 v Romania (won 2-1)
1993 v Germany (lost 0-1), v Estonia (won 3-0), v Estonia (won 3-1)
1994 v Switzerland (drew 1-1), v Italy (lost 1-3), v Malta (won 2-0), v Austria (won 2-1),
  v Holland (lost 1-3)

Brian Irvine won all of his nine international caps with Aberdeen whom he joined from Falkirk in 1985, making his debut for the Dons in a 6-0 win at bottom of the table Clydebank on the final day of the 1985-86 season.

Over the next couple of seasons he found himself in and out of the Aberdeen side, which was hardly surprising since established internationals Alex McLeish and Willie Miller formed the heart of the Dons' defence. It was 1988-89 before he became involved on a more regular basis—a campaign in which the Dons finished runners-up to Rangers in the League and lost 3-2 to the Ibrox club in the Skol Cup Final.

However, the Dons made amends the following year with Irvine outstanding in a 2-1 defeat of Rangers after extra time. In May 1990, Aberdeen and Celtic met in the Scottish Cup Final, but even after extra time neither team could find the net. The destination of the trophy was down to the outcome of a penalty shoot-out. With the scores tied at 8-8, Brian Irvine blasted the ball past Pat Bonner to win the cup for Aberdeen.

In the early nineties, Irvine gave the Dons excellent service, missing very few games—his form leading to full international recognition as he won the first of nine caps.

Then in the summer of 1995 his world fell apart when he was told he was suffering from the debilitating disease multiple sclerosis. Many would have given in to such devastating news, but Brian Irvine fought back to full fitness. However, just under two years later, he was told he could leave the club and joined Dundee.

He helped the Dens Park side return to the Premier Division but later refused the offer of a new contract to team up with newly promoted Ross County, for whom he was a regular until hanging up his boots at the end of the 2002–03 season.

JOHN ROBERTSON
Forward

Born: John Robertson, Edinburgh, 2 October 1964
Height: 5ft 6in
Weight: 10st 3lb
Clubs: Edina Hibs; Heart of Midlothian; Newcastle United; Heart of Midlothian; Livingston
Scotland caps: 16
Scotland goals: 3
1991 v Romania (won 2-1) 1 goal, v Switzerland (won 2-1) 1 goal, v Bulgaria (drew 1-1), v San Marino (won 2-1)
1992 v San Marino (won 4-0), v N Ireland (won 1-0), v Finland (drew 1-1)
1993 v Italy (drew 0-0), v Malta (won 3-0), v Germany (lost 0-1), v Estonia (won 3-0)
1995 v Japan drew 0-0), v Ecuador (won 2-1) 1 goal, v Faroe Islands (won 2-0)
1996 v Greece (won 1-0), v Sweden (lost 0-2)

There has been no greater modern–day goalscorer for Hearts than John Robertson, who went on to score a league record 214 goals in the Jam Tarts' colours, thus surpassing the feats of Alfie Conn, Willie Bauld and then Jimmy Wardhaugh.

Robertson made his debut for Hearts when he came on as a substitute in a match against Queen of the South in February 1982, a match the Tynecastle club won 4-1. In the Hearts side that day was his brother Chris, and the two played together for the final 17 minutes. It was the only time they did, because Chris departed at the end of the season and John did not play another competitive game until the following season.

Over the ensuing seasons, Robertson scored goals for fun. Good with both feet, he also scored more than his fair share with his head, and when Hearts returned to the Premier Division in 1983, he scored two in a thrilling 3-2 win over Hibs to take his season's total to 20. His 20 goals in 1985-86 took Hearts to within touching distance of the League title, while in 1987-88, his 31 goals attracted the attention of a host of clubs, including Arsenal, Nottingham Forest, Leeds United and Newcastle.

The Magpies paid out a club record fee of £750,000 to take Robertson to St James Park, but he was never played in a free role up front by Newcastle manager Willie McFaul. Many followers of the club were totally perplexed as to why such a quality player only managed seven full outings in a black and white shirt before rejoining Hearts.

The change of managers at Tynecastle in the 1990s did not blunt Robertson's sharpness, and he scored a valuable Scottish Cup semi-final goal in 1996 which helped Hearts into the final for the first time in 10 years. The following season he scored against Celtic in extra time in the League Cup quarter-final and he found the net in the final against Rangers, Hearts going down 4-3. Though his playing days at Tynecastle were coming to an end, he was on the bench for the 1998 Scottish Cup Final against Rangers, when he finally secured a winners' medal for his unrivalled service to the club over a period of 16 years.

After 720 matches for Hearts, he left to join Livingston as player-coach, helping the West Lothian club win promotion to the First Division at the end of the 1998-99 season. He had hung up his boots to become the club's first team coach when Livingston won the First Division Championship in 2000-01. After parting company with the club following the appointment of Marcio Maximo Barcellos as head coach, he had a spell in charge of Hearts, but has recently replaced Paul Lambert as manager of Livingston.

MIKE GALLOWAY
Midfield
Born: Michael Galloway, Oswestry, 30 May 1965
Height: 6ft 0in
Weight: 13st 0lb
Clubs: Berwick Rangers; Mansfield Town; Halifax Town; Heart of Midlothian; Glasgow Celtic; Leicester City
Scotland caps: 1
1992 v Romania (lost 0-1)

Turned down by Leicester City as a 16-year-old prospect on the grounds of size, Mike Galloway joined Berwick Rangers. Primarily regarded as a defensive midfielder, his performances led to him joining Mansfield Town where he also played at full-back and as a striker. Halifax Town manager Mick Jones was so impressed with Galloway that he made sponsored walks to raise the transfer fee to take Galloway to The Shay.

At Halifax, he was watched by Rangers' boss Graeme Souness, but Hearts astonished Scottish football by securing Galloway's services for the bargain fee of £60,000. He played as a striker for Hearts in Europe in 1988-89 with such success that when Celtic came in for him, it took £500,000 to prise him away from Tynecastle.

His early form at Parkhead was outstanding and led to him winning a couple of Scottish Under-21 caps—as an over-age player, qualified as the son of a Scottish soldier, during 1989-90. He was elevated to senior status in October 1991 when Scotland faced Romania in Bucharest, while at club level he featured as a substitute in Celtic's 1990 Cup Final defeat (on penalties) by Aberdeen and in the starting line-up for the 1994-95 League Cup Final against Raith Rovers, again lost on penalties.

After various fines for breaches of club discipline, Galloway joined Leicester City on loan in January 1995. However, he injured a hamstring during his first training session and the loan was postponed pending his fitness. Impressing with his strength and energetic commitment, he again suffered injury, but despite a further loan spell, the Foxes didn't want a permanent deal and Galloway returned to Celtic.

DAVID ROBERTSON
Left-back
Born: David Robertson, Aberdeen, 17 October 1968
Height: 5ft 11in
Weight: 11st 0lb
Clubs: Deeside BC; Aberdeen; Glasgow Rangers; Leeds United
Scotland caps: 3
1992 v N Ireland (won 1-0)
1994 v Switzerland (drew 1-1), v Holland (lost 0-1)

Despite his outstanding displays at left-back for Aberdeen and Rangers, both at home and in Europe, David Robertson suffered at international level, making just three appearances, because of the link-up between Celtic's Tommy Boyd and John Collins.

Robertson began his career with his home-town club Aberdeen, making the first of 135 league appearances for the Dons against Hamilton in August 1986. He made 34 appearances in the Premier League that season, establishing himself as the Pittodrie club's regular No.3. In 1989-90, Aberdeen, under the guidance of Alex Smith, beat Rangers in the club's third successive League Cup Final showdown. More glory was to come at Hampden as Aberdeen also lifted the Scottish Cup after a thrilling penalty shoot-out with Celtic which saw Brian Irvine fire the winner in a 9-8 success. At the end of the following season, Robertson decided to leave Pittodrie, and Walter Smith, eager to start accumulating Scots because of the Euro restrictions, signed him for a fee which the League tribunals set at £930,000.

After arriving at Ibrox, he ended his first season with a League Championship and League Cup winners' medal. The following season, 1992-93, was Rangers' treble-winning season, and emphasised Robertson's increasing importance through his sterling displays at home and in the club's glorious Champions League run. Having made seven appearances for Scotland at Under-21 level, he eventually made his full international debut in 1992 prior to the European Championship finals in a warm-up game against Northern Ireland. Robertson went on to win six League Championships with Rangers, and had success in three Cup and League Cup finals. Having appeared in 246 games for the Ibrox club, he left to join Leeds United for a fee of £500,000 in May 1997.

George Graham, who had been tracking Robertson ever since he took over the reins at Elland Road, feared the Rangers defender might move abroad for free as his contract was due to expire. He took a little while to adjust to the game in the Premiership, and was just finding his form when he tore a cartilage in training which later forced him to part company with the club.

KEITH WRIGHT
Forward
Born: Keith Wright, Edinburgh, 17 May 1965
Height: 5ft 11in
Weight: 11st 0lb
Clubs: Melbourne Thistle; Raith Rovers; Dundee; Hibernian; Raith Rovers; Morton;
Cowdenbeath
Scotland caps: 1
1992 v N Ireland (won 1-0)

A squad player for three European Championship games, Wright finally got the call to play for his country on 19 February 1992 in a friendly against Northern Ireland. Though it proved to be Keith Wright's only cap, he still had his moments at club level.

A boyhood supporter of Hibs, it seemed his dream of playing for the Easter Road club would not be realised when he started his career with Raith Rovers in 1983. From Starks Park, he joined Dundee, where he formed an impressive strike partnership with Tommy Coyne. During his time at Dens Park, the goals flowed regularly and eventually he joined Hibs in 1991—the fee of £450,000 partly coming from the sale of Paul Wright to St Johnstone.

In 1991-92 when Hibs won the Skol Cup, Keith Wright scored in every round of the competition, including the final which Hibs won 2-0 against Dunfermline Athletic. Not surprisingly, he ended his first season at Easter Road as Hibs' leading scorer with 17 goals, and it was this feat that led to him winning international recognition. He continued to find the net on a regular basis, finishing the 1993-94 season as Hibs top scorer with 19 goals. Injuries blighted his career towards the end of his stay at Easter Road, and in 1997 he rejoined his first Scottish club, Raith Rovers.

From Raith he moved to Morton, playing for the Cappielow Park club until 2000. He then became Gary Kirk's assistant-manager at Cowdenbeath before later taking over the reins of the Central Park club. He was in charge until being replaced by David Baikkie, and is now Midlothian's football development officer.

DAVE BOWMAN
Midfield
Born: David Bowman, Tunbridge Wells, 10 March 1960
Height: 5ft 10in
Weight: 11st 2lb
Clubs: Salvesen BC; Heart of Midlothian; Coventry City; Dundee United; Raith Rovers
Scotland caps: 6
1992 v Finland (drew 1-1), v United States (won 1-0)
1993 v Germany (lost 0-1), v Estonia (won 3-0)
1994 v Switzerland (drew 1-1), v Italy (lost 1-3)

Though he was born in Tunbridge Wells, midfielder Dave Bowman began his career with Hearts, making his debut for the Tynecastle club against Airdrieonians in August 1980. Bowman was a regular in the Hearts side for almost five seasons, with his best term being 1982-83 when he scored five goals in 39 games as the Jam Tarts finished the season as First Division runners-up, one point behind champions St Johnstone. Having appeared in 16 games for Hearts, Bowman left the Tynecastle club midway through the 1984-85 season to try his luck south of the Border with Coventry City.

His stay at Highfield Road was brief, and in the summer of 1986 he returned to Scotland to play for Dundee United.

Nicknamed 'Psycho' for his hard style of play, he soon made his name at Tannadice for his aggressive tackling. He helped the Terrors reach the Scottish Cup Final in seasons 1987-88, 1990-91 and 1993-94, with their only success coming in the last of these finals when they beat Rangers 1-0. In 1995-96, Bowman helped United win promotion to the Premier Division as runners-up in the First Division to Dunfermline Athletic.

Bowman, who won six full caps for Scotland while with Dundee United, the first against Finland in March 1992, was an important member of the Tannadice club's side for almost 12 seasons. During the course of the 1995-96 season, the United board offered him a testimonial in recognition of his fine skills and loyalty. Bowman left Tannadice at the end of the 1997-98 season to join Raith Rovers where he later ended his playing career.

Bowman is now back with his beloved Dundee United as the Tannadice club's coach.

DUNCAN FERGUSON
Forward

Born: Duncan Ferguson, Stirling, 27 December 1971
Height: 6ft 4in
Weight: 14st 6lb
Clubs: Carse Thistle; Dundee United; Glasgow Rangers; Everton; Newcastle United; Everton
Scotland caps: 7
1992 v United States (won 1-0), v Canada (won 3-1), v Holland (lost 0-1)
1993 v Germany (lost 0-1)
1995 v Greece (lost 0-1)
1997 v Austria (drew 0-0), v Estonia (drew 0-0)

Big Dunc soon showed that he was one of the hottest young talents in Britain when he began his career with Dundee United. He was a rarity in the domestic game, a highly skilled big forward, good on the ground and in the air. Under the oppressive reign of Jim McLean, he found it hard to feel comfortable and had various brushes with the Tannadice taskmaster, including walk-outs and public slanging matches.

In the summer of 1993, Ferguson became the most expensive footballer in Britain

Duncan Ferguson playing for Everton

as Rangers shelled out £3.75 million for his services. After an injury-blighted season, his first goal for the club was quickly forgotten as he earned a police charge and a record 12-game ban from the SFA for a headbutting offence on Raith's John McStay. He was subsequently sentenced to three months in gaol.

When the Rangers manager Walter Smith let him go on loan to Everton for three months, his form, though solid enough, suggested that both sides would be happy to stick to that agreement too. But after he netted in the Merseyside derby, Everton paid £4.3 million, and over the next few months he proved a key element in the club's rise from the foot of the table. He won an FA Cup winners medal as a second-half substitute against Manchester United, before injuries began to hamper his progress at Goodison. On his return he scored a number of spectacular goals and returned to international duty for Scotland, winning caps against Austria and Estonia in World Cup qualifying matches.

Everton manager Howard Kendall pulled a masterstroke of psychology midway through the 1997-98 season when he named Ferguson as captain, and in his first match as skipper, he netted a hat-trick against Bolton Wanderers. However, Ferguson later informed the Scottish FA that he no longer wished to be considered for selection for the national side.

In November 1998, Ferguson joined Newcastle United for £7 million, but much of his time on Tyneside was injury-ridden and he later returned to Goodison for a second spell. Though he has continued to suffer from a spate of cruel injuries, he had one of his best seasons at the club in 2004-05 when he proved a major influence both on and off the pitch. David Moyes got the best out of him by employing him as a substitute, and he could usually be relied upon to make things happen when entering the fray. Released by Everton in the summer of 2006, he remains a free agent.

ALAN McLAREN
Defender
Born: Alan McLaren, Edinburgh, 4 January 1971
Height: 5ft 11in
Weight: 11st 6lb
Clubs: Cavalry Bank; Heart of Midlothian; Glasgow Rangers
Scotland caps: 24
1992 v United States (won 1-0), v Canada (won 3-1), v Norway (drew 0-0)
1993 v Italy (drew 0-0), v Malta (won 3-0), v Germany (lost 0-1), v Estonia (won 3-0), v Estonia (won 3-1)
1994 v Italy (lost 1-3), v Malta (won 2-0), v Holland (lost 0-1), v Austria (won 2-1)
1995 v Finland (won 2-0), v Faroe Islands (won 5-1), v Russia (drew 1-1), v Greece (lost 0-1), v Russia (drew 0-0), v San Marino (won 2-0), v Japan (drew 0-0), v Ecuador (won 2-1), v Faroe Islands (won 2-0)
1996 v Finland (won 1-0), v Sweden (lost 0-2), v San Marino (won 5-0)

Alan McLaren was still in his teens when he captained Hearts, and then had boss Alex Macdonald proclaiming 'He'll be the captain of Scotland.' That prediction certainly looked possible at the time, and after winning 24 caps, he undoubtedly would have done so if a serious knee injury had not forced him to retire in May 1998.

During his time with Hearts, McLaren helped the Tynecastle cub finish runners-up in the Premier Division in 1991-92. During 249 games for Hearts, he had played in four European campaigns and it was against the mighty Bayern Munich that he convinced Scottish football followers that he was going to the very top in the game.

McLaren joined Rangers in October 1994 after a protracted and confusing transfer deal. The eventual agreement saw Hearts take Dave McPherson back and a large sum of money, believed to be about £1.2 million, in exchange for McLaren.

Having developed into a dominant centre-back, right-back or midfield marker, McLaren helped Rangers to win the League Championship in his first season at Ibrox. In fact, he was almost the complete defender as he fitted into the side with ease after his move, with potentially torrid matches against Celtic and Hearts in his first three matches.

Sadly, this blossoming talent, who was indispensable to the national team, suffered a serious knee injury, and though he tried a number of comebacks, he was finally forced into premature retirement.

GORDON MARSHALL
Goalkeeper

Born: Gordon George Banks Marshall, Edinburgh, 19 April 1964
Height: 6ft 2in
Weight: 13st 0lb
Clubs: Glasgow Rangers; East Stirling; East Fife; Falkirk; Glasgow Celtic; Stoke City; St Mirren; Kilmarnock; Motherwell
Scotland caps: 1
1992 v United States (won 1-0)

Beginning his career with Rangers, Gordon Marshall was just 15 when he broke his leg playing for the club's reserve side. On recovering he went on loan to East Stirling when Charlie Kelly was injured, before, being unable to make the grade at Ibrox, he signed for East Fife.

At Bayview, he developed into a class goalkeeper, the best East Fife had had for many years, but after making 138 appearances, he moved on to Falkirk. A virtual ever-present, he helped the Bairns win the First Division Championship in 1990-91, his form alerting Glasgow's two big clubs. Rangers wanted him back as understudy to Andy Goram, but he opted to join Celtic.

After Packy Bonner's form took a dip, Marshall made his debut in a 3-0 win at Airdrie and went on to hold down a regular place in the side. His form was such that Andy Roxburgh gave him his Scottish cap against the United States in the Mile High Stadium in Denver, where he kept another clean sheet in a difficult game. Though Bonner eventually regained his first team spot, Marshall, who had loan spells with Stoke City and St Mirren, remained at Parkhead until

January 1998, when after making exactly 100 league appearances, he signed for Kilmarnock for a fee of £150,000.

The experienced keeper missed very few games in his stay at Rugby Park and in 2000-01 helped the club to the League Cup Final where they went down 3-0 to his former club, Celtic. Marshall then moved on to Motherwell where his form was outstanding, until, at the age of 41, he lost his place to Graeme Smith. The popular Marshall is now on the coaching staff at Hibernian.

EOIN JESS
Forward

Born: Eoin Jess, Aberdeen, 13 December 1970
Height: 5ft 9in
Weight: 11st 10lb
Clubs: Glasgow Rangers; Aberdeen; Coventry City; Aberdeen; Bradford City; Nottingham Forest; Northampton Town
Scotland caps: 18
Scotland goals: 2
1993 v Italy (drew 0-0), v Malta (won 3-0)
1994 v Switzerland (drew 1-1), v Italy (lost 1-3), v Holland (lost 0-1), v Austria (won 2-1), v Holland (lost 1-3)
1995 v Finland (won 2-0)
1996 v Sweden (lost 0-2), v San Marino (won 5-0) 1 goal, v United States (lost 1-2), v Colombia (lost 0-1), v England (lost 0-2)
1998 v Denmark (lost 0-1)
1999 v Czech Republic (lost 1-2) 1 goal, v Germany (won 1-0), v Faroe Islands (drew 1-1), v Czech Republic (lost 2-3)

Once on the books of Rangers as a schoolboy, Eoin Jess later joined Aberdeen and made his debut for the Dons in a goalless home draw against Motherwell in May 1989. Less than six months later, Jess was gracing Hampden Park as Aberdeen won the Skol Cup after a 2-1 extra-time success over Rangers.

During the course of the 1990-91 season, Jess netted two hat-tricks as Aberdeen won 3-2 at Tannadice against Dundee United, and the second even more spectacular, as he scored all four goals in a 4-1 defeat of Dunfermline Athletic. He remained a regular in the Aberdeen side over the next few seasons, inspiring the club to two domestic finals and runners-up spot in the Premier Division in 1992-93. In November 1995 he helped Aberdeen lift the then renamed Coca-Cola Cup with a 2-0 win over Dundee, and it wasn't long after this that he announced his intention of trying his luck in the Premiership—in February 1996 he was transferred to Coventry City for £1.7 million.

He took some time to adapt to the English game, so much so that he lost his place in the national squad, but played for the 'B' team in Denmark. A slight player with superb ball skills, an excellent first touch and a good turn of speed, he later returned to Pittodrie. After another three seasons with the Dons in which he took his tally of goals to 94 in 374 games, he was loaned out to Bradford City, later joining the Valley Parade club on a permanent basis.

In 2001-02 he was the Bantams' leading scorer with 14 goals. Playing in the centre of midfield, he had an outstanding season, playing in more first team games than anyone else. His form prompted Nottingham Forest to lure him to the City Ground, but it was a disappointing campaign for Jess who made many of his appearances from the substitute's bench. Though he began to appear on a more regular basis, much of his time at Forest saw him hampered by injuries, and in the summer of 2005 he moved on to Northampton Town where his strike against Notts County was a contender for Goal of the Season.

SCOTT BOOTH
Forward

Born: Scott Booth, Aberdeen, 16 December 1971
Height: 5ft 9in
Weight: 11st 10lb
Clubs: Deeside BC; Aberdeen; Borussia Dortmund (Germany); Utrecht (Holland); FC Twente (Holland); Aberdeen
Scotland caps: 21
Scotland goals: 6
1993 v Germany (lost 0-1), v Estonia (won 3-0) I goal, v Estonia (won 3-1)
1994 v Switzerland (drew 1-1), v Malta (won 2-0)
1995 v Faroe Islands (won 5-1) I goal, v Russia (drew 1-1) I goal
1996 v Finland (won 1-0) I goal, v San Marino (won 5-0) I goal, v Australia (won 1-0), v United States (lost 1-2), v Holland (drew 0-0), v Switzerland (won 1-0)
1998 v Denmark (lost 0-1), v Finland (drew 1-1), v Colombia (drew 2-2), v Morocco (lost 0-3)
2001 v Poland (drew 1-1) I goal
2002 v Croatia (drew 0-0), v Belgium (lost 0-2), v Latvia (won 2-1)

Scott Booth ended his playing days with his home-town club Aberdeen after playing for three foreign clubs. Booth also started his career with the Dons after joining them from Deeside Boys Club in 1988.

He established himself as a regular member of the Aberdeen side in 1990-91, helping the club finish the campaign as runners-up to Rangers. In fact, Aberdeen, who had been runners-up to the Ibrox club the two previous seasons, finished in second place in 1992-93 and 1993-94 again both times to Rangers. In 1992-93, Booth was a member of the Aberdeen side that lost 2-1 to Rangers in the League Cup Final, and then by the same scoreline against the same opposition in the Cup Final.

He was compensated somewhat by winning the first of 21 international caps when he came off the bench against Germany. Booth's first international goal came on his next appearance when, replacing Hearts' John Robertson against Estonia, he scored within minutes of coming on.

When Aberdeen won the League Cup in 1995-96, beating Dundee 2-0, Booth was an important member of the Dons' side. However, overall his partnership with Eoin Jess never quite fulfilled its undoubted potential, either at club or national level, and the classy striker moved under freedom of contract in the summer of 1997 to German giants Borussia Dortmund.

After a mediocre first season, he helped Dortmund to fourth place in the Bundesliga, though Bayern Munich were runaway champions. After a loan spell with Dutch club Utrecht, Booth remained in Holland playing for FC Twente, and in 2000-01 helped them win the Dutch Cup, beating PSV Eindhoven on penalties. After two seasons of mid-table placings, Booth returned to Scotland for a second spell with Aberdeen, taking his tally of goals to 57 in 194 matches before retiring at the end of the 2003-04 season.

NICKY WALKER
Goalkeeper
Born: Joseph Nicol Walker, Aberdeen, 29 September 1962
Height: 6ft 2in
Weight: 12st 10lb
Clubs: Elgin City; Keith; Inverness Caledonian; Leicester City; Motherwell; Glasgow Rangers; Falkirk; Dunfermline Athletic; Heart of Midlothian; Burnley; Partick Thistle; Ross County
Scotland caps: 2
1993 v Germany (lost 0-1)
1996 v United States (lost 1-2)

After playing in the Highland League for Elgin City, Keith and Inverness Caledonian, Nicky Walker, scion of the Walker shortbread family, joined Jock Wallace's Leicester City in the summer of 1980. He was soon winning Scottish youth caps, and after a series of impressive displays in the Foxes' reserve side, he stepped up for Second Division action after Mark Wallington's record-breaking run came to an end through injury. Walker impressed with his confidence and clean handling after a shaky start at Stamford Bridge.

He left Filbert Street in January 1983 to play for Motherwell before again joining Jock Wallace at Rangers. Here he developed into an Ibrox regular until displaced by England international Chris Woods in 1986. However, he replaced the suspended Woods in the 1988 League Cup Final as Rangers beat Aberdeen 5-3 on penalties, after the game had ended all-square at 3-3. Though he had loan spells with both Falkirk and Dunfermline Athletic, he played a number of games in Rangers' Scottish Premier League Championship success of 1988-89.

At the end of that season, he left Rangers to join Hearts for a fee of £125,000, competing for the No.1 jersey with the evergreen Henry Smith. In February 1992 he joined Burnley on loan, and after a number of outstanding displays, Clarets' manager Jimmy Mullen tried to sign him permanently as they prepared for life in the 'new' Division Two.

It was not to be, however, and he remained at Tynecastle, where, in March 1993, at the age of 30, he received a surprise call-up into the Scottish side for the home encounter with Germany.

In December 1994 he joined Partick Thistle where he won a second cap against the United States. He was in Scotland's squad for Euro '96, but had to watch from the sidelines as Andy Goram played in all three matches for the Scots.

STEVE WRIGHT

Right-back

Born: Stephen Wright, Bellshill, 27 August 1971
Height: 5ft 10in
Weight: 12st 2lb
Clubs: Eastercraigs FC; Aberdeen; Glasgow Rangers; Wolverhampton Wanderers; Bradford City; Dundee United; Scunthorpe United
Scotland caps: 2
1993 v Germany (lost 0-1), v Estonia (won 3-0)

Beginning his career with Aberdeen, right-back Steve Wright had made 145 league appearances for the Pittodrie club when in June 1995 he left the Granite City club to join Rangers. Aberdeen had asked for a somewhat unrealistic £2.5 million, while Rangers were offering £800,000. A war of words broke out in Aberdeen before an independent tribunal set the fee at just under £1 million.

During his time at Pittodrie, Wright had made 14 appearances for the Scotland Under-21 side and made his full international debut against Germany. At Ibrox, Wright suffered a spate of injuries that prevented him from winning a regular place in the Rangers side, and in March 1998 he had a brief loan spell with Wolverhampton Wanderers. Still unable to force his way into the Rangers side, having made just 12 League and Cup appearances in three seasons, he signed for Bradford City on a free transfer.

He hadn't been at Valley Parade long when a knock on his knee forced him to have an operation for a slight tear to his medial ligament. On recovering, he returned to the Bantams' side, but as a player who refused to shirk a tackle, he suffered a number of ankle injuries which restricted his number of first team appearances. In August 2000, Wright returned to Scotland to play for Dundee United, but again he was hampered by injuries.

During the 2002-03 season, Wright answered emergency calls on two occasions from Scunthorpe United, but with the club unable to offer him a longer deal, he subsequently returned to a coaching post north of the border.

COLIN HENDRY

Central defender

Born: Edward Colin James Hendry, Keith, 7 December 1965
Height: 6ft 1in
Weight: 12st 7lb
Clubs: Islavale; Dundee; Blackburn Rovers; Manchester City; Glasgow Rangers; Coventry City; Bolton Wanderers; Preston North End; Blackpool
Scotland caps: 51
Scotland goals: 3
1993 v Estonia (won 3-0), v Estonia (won 3-1)
1994 v Malta (won 2-0) 1 goal, v Holland (lost 0-1), v Austria (won 2-1), v Holland (lost 1-3)
1995 v Finland (won 2-0), v Faroe Islands (won 5-1), v Greece (lost 0-1), v Russia (drew 0-0), v San Marino (won 2-0)

Colin Hendry playing for Blackburn

1996 v Finland (won 1-0), v Sweden (lost 0-2), v San Marino (won 5-0), v Australia (won 1-0),
v Denmark (lost 0-2), v United States (lost 1-2), v Colombia (lost 0-1),
v Holland (drew 0-0), v England (lost 0-2), v Switzerland (won 1-0)

1997 v Austria (drew 0-0), v Sweden (won 1-0), v Estonia (drew 0-0), v Estonia
(won 2-0), v Austria (won 2-0), v Sweden (lost 1-2)

1998 v Latvia (won 2-0), v Denmark (lost 0-1), v Finland (drew 1-1), v Colombia (drew 2-2),
v United States (drew 0-0), v Brazil (lost 1-2), v Norway (drew 1-1),
v Morocco (lost 0-3)

1999 v Lithuania (drew 0-0), v Estonia (won 3-2), v Faroe Islands (won 2-1),
v Germany (drew 1-1)

2000 v Bosnia (won 2-1), v Estonia (drew 0-0), v Bosnia (won 1-0), v England (lost 0-2),
v England (won 1-0), v France (lost 0-2)

2001 v Latvia (won 1-0), v San Marino (won 2-0), v Croatia (drew 1-1), v Australia (lost 0-2),
v Belgium (drew 2-2), v San Marino (won 4-0) 2 goals

Scoring twice on his 51st and final international appearance, Colin Hendry captained Scotland during the 1998 World Cup Finals in France.

He was playing for Dundee when Blackburn Rovers' manager Don Mackay took him to Ewood Park for a fee of £30,000 in March 1987. The Scottish club had a few reservations about letting Hendry go south of the border, and insisted that they receive half of any subsequent transfer fees.

He made his Rovers debut as a replacement for Glenn Keeley in the Full Members Cup match against Ipswich Town, and when Keeley was restored to the side, he was moved to lead the attack. It was in this position that he endeared himself to Rovers' fans when he scored the only goal of the Full Members Cup Final win over Charlton Athletic. When Keeley left Ewood Park, Hendry was given the No.5 shirt. His performances led to a number of top clubs following his progress, and in November 1989, after having been left out of the team following a contractual dispute, he left to join Manchester City for £700,000.

A great favourite at Maine Road, he was the club's first choice centre-half until the arrival of Keith Curle, when he left to return to Ewood Park. Under the guidance of Blackburn's new manager Kenny Dalglish, Hendry became a much more polished defender than he had been during his first spell with the club. Hendry was outstanding during Rovers' Premier League Championship winning season of 1994-95, scoring crucial goals at Aston Villa and Leeds United. Not surprisingly, he was selected for the PFA Premier League team of the year. Hendry continued to display the last-ditch tackles and brave headers at Ewood Park until 1998, when after scoring 34 goals in 384 League and Cup games in his two spells with the club, he left to play for Rangers.

After an unhappy time at Ibrox, he returned to Premier League action with Coventry City in February 1999. The fee was not disclosed, though it was believed to be on a 'pay as you play' basis, but he soon fell out of favour, and in December 2000, joined Bolton Wanderers. He was outstanding in his early games for the Wanderers, establishing a formidable partnership in the Bolton defence with Gudni Bergsson. He also chipped in with some useful goals, but despite being a valued member of the Bolton squad, he was loaned out to both Preston North End and Blackpool. Replacing Steve McMahon as manager of

Blackpool in the summer of 2004, Hendry himself has since parted company with the Seasiders, and joined Boston United as their coach.

PHIL O'DONNELL
Midfield
Born: Philip O'Donnell, Bellshill, 25 March 1972
Height: 5ft 10in
Weight: 11st 0lb
Clubs: Motherwell; Glasgow Celtic; Sheffield Wednesday; Motherwell
Scotland caps: 1
1994 v Switzerland (drew 1-1)

Phil O'Donnell, whose one cap for Scotland was as a substitute in a 1-1 draw against Switzerland at Pittodrie in September 1993, began his career with Motherwell, for whom his distribution and use of the ball were excellent from the very beginning. However, as he matured he became stronger, and some of his surging runs brightened up the dullest of afternoons.

Having made his Motherwell debut in November 1990, it was with a fitting sense of timing that he saved his first Steelmen goal for the 1991 Scottish Cup Final triumph over Dundee United, a match the Fir Park club won 4-3 after extra time. Already a Scottish youth international, by 1993 he had added eight Under-21 caps to his collection, his performances eventually leading to him winning that full international cap. In January 1994, Motherwell beat Celtic 2-1, with O'Donnell scoring both goals. It was probably the best game he had in Motherwell's colours, and shortly afterwards, Celtic manager Tommy Burns lured him to Parkhead, paying the Steelmen a £1.75 million fee.

Replacing the suspended Paul McStay, he made an instant and startling impact, with both Celtic goals on his debut as the Bhoys beat Partick Thistle 2-1. At the end of his first season at Parkhead he won another Scottish Cup winners medal as Celtic beat Airdrieonians 1-0. He also won a Premier League Championship medal in 1997-98, but much of his time with Celtic was spent on the treatment table. In five seasons with the club, he managed just 121 first team appearances, before in July 1999, along with team-mate Simon Donnelly, being allowed to join Sheffield Wednesday on a free transfer.

He endured a most frustrating first season at Hillsborough, making just one appearance as substitute before undergoing surgery on his troublesome knee. It was a similar story over the next couple of campaigns, and after three seasons with the Yorkshire club in which he made just 13 league starts, he parted company. Now back at Fir Park, the veteran midfielder is an important member of the Motherwell squad.

BILLY McKINLAY
Midfield

Born: William McKinlay, Glasgow, 22 April 1969
Height: 5ft 9in
Weight: 11st 6lb
Clubs: Hamilton Thistle; Dundee United; Blackburn Rovers; Leicester City; Bradford City; Preston North End; Clydebank; Leicester City; Fulham
Scotland caps: 29
Scotland goals: 4

1994 v Malta (won 2-0) 1 goal, v Holland (lost 0-1), v Austria (won 2-1) 1 goal, v Holland (lost 1-3)

1995 v Faroe Islands (won 5-1) 1 goal, v Russia (drew 1-1), v Greece (lost 0-1), v Russia (drew 0-0), v San Marino (won 2-0), v Japan (drew 0-0), v Ecuador (won 2-1), v Faroe Islands (won 2-0) 1 goal

1996 v Finland (won 1-0), v Sweden (lost 0-2), v San Marino (won 5-0), v Australia (won 1-0), v Denmark (lost 0-2), v Holland (drew 0-0)

1997 v Sweden (won 1-0), v Estonia (won 2-0)

1998 v Latvia (won 2-0), v France (lost 1-2), v Denmark (lost 0-1), v Finland (drew 1-1), v Colombia (drew 2-2), v United States (drew 0-0), v Brazil (lost 1-2)

1999 v Estonia (won 3-2), v Faroe Islands (won 2-1)

A grafting central midfielder, who scored on his international debut in a 2-0 defeat of Malta, he began his career with Dundee United whom he joined from Hamilton Thistle in the summer of 1985.

In just over 10 years on the staff at Tannadice, McKinlay, who had won Scottish schoolboy and youth honours, added Under-21 and 'B' international level honours to his collection before making his full debut for the national side. Though he failed to win any domestic honours with Dundee United, he had scored 31 goals in 284 League and Cup games for the Terrors before Blackburn Rovers paid £1.75 million for him in October 1995.

He had to wait for several weeks to receive his debut, but then he was told by manager Ray Harford that he had little future at Ewood Park! He was only given a regular place in the Rovers' side after Tony Parkes took over as caretaker manager in 1996-97. Patrolling the area in front of the defence, he was a huge success with his tigerish tackling, key interceptions and coolness on the ball. Although suspensions and injuries did not help to establish him in the Scotland team, he was named in the 22-strong party for the 1998 World Cup Finals in France, though he was used just once as a substitute against Brazil. A hernia operation early the following season and the re-occurrence of the problems which hospitalised him again the following February restricted his fist team appearances.

In fact, injury kept him out for the entire 1999-2000 season, and after recovering from the long-term groin injury, had loan spells with Leicester City and Bradford City. McKinlay, who had a spell with Clydebank in early 2001-02, later attracted national media attention when he agreed to play for nothing at Leicester to try and win a contract. He was rewarded with a one-month deal which was subsequently extended until the end of the 2002-03 season, a campaign in which he helped the

Foxes win promotion to the Premiership. After being offered a new contract, he continued to make a valuable contribution to Leicester's midfield, but with age catching up with him, he was released in the close season. He joined Fulham with the brief to assist the development of the reserve team players, although he did make the occasional first team appearance.

ROBERT McKINNON
Left-back
Born: Robert McKinnon, Glasgow, 31 July 1966
Height: 5ft 11in
Weight: 11st 4lb
Clubs: Rutherglen Glencairn; Newcastle United; Hartlepool United; Motherwell; Twente Enschede (Holland); Heart of Midlothian; Clydebank; Raith Rovers
Scotland caps: 3
1994 v Malta (won 2-0)
1995 v Japan (drew 0-0), v Faroe Islands (won 2-0)

In his only outing for Newcastle United, youngster Robert McKinnon stood in for Kenny Wharton in a tough away fixture at White Hart Lane. He suffered along with the rest of the defence as Spurs inflicted a heavy 5-1 defeat. McKinnon didn't last the 90 minutes and never reached the first team again, being transferred to Hartlepool United.

However, the ginger-haired left-back developed enormously at the Victoria Ground, and in January 1992 returned to Scotland with Motherwell who paid £125,000 for his services. Proving to be one of Tommy McLean's most astute signings, he became one of the best players in the Motherwell side. Possessing a flair for getting forward in what was the era of the overlapping full-back, he was one of the first Bosman problems to hit the Fir Park club. Having just represented Scotland at full international level, he was lured away to Twente Enschede of Holland in the summer of 1996, with Motherwell receiving no money whatsoever. He didn't do as well in Dutch football, and in July 1998 he signed for Hearts.

Though injuries hampered his first season at Tynecastle, he remained with Hearts until the summer of 2000, though his first team opportunities were limited. Joining Clydebank, McKinnon was a virtual ever-present in his first season with the Bankies, though the following season he was moved from left-back to the centre of the Clydebank defence.

The club were then replaced by Airdrie United and McKinnon moved on to play for Raith Rovers, whom he helped win the First Division Championship in 2002-03.

JOHN McGINLAY
Forward
Born: John McGinlay, Inverness, 8 April 1964
Height: 5ft 9in
Weight: 11st 6lb

Clubs: Nairn County; Hanimex (New Zealand); Yeovil Town; Elgin City; Shrewsbury Town; Bury; Millwall; Bolton Wanderers; Bradford City; Oldham Athletic

Scotland caps: 13

Scotland goals: 4

1994 v Austria (won 2-1) 1 goal, v Holland (lost 1-3)

1995 v Faroe Islands (won 5-1) 1 goal, v Russia (drew 1-1), v Greece (lost 0-1), v Russia (drew 0-0), v San Marino (won 2-0), v Faroe Islands (won 2-0) 1 goal

1996 v Sweden (lost 0-2)

1997 v Sweden (won 1-0) 1 goal, v Estonia (drew 0-0), v Estonia (won 2-0), v Austria (won 2-0)

John McGinlay

John McGinlay played his early football in the Highland League with Nairn County before spending a season in New Zealand playing for Hanimex. On his return he was signed by then Gola League club Yeovil Town, and after spending three and a half seasons with the Somerset club, joined Elgin City. In his first season with them he netted 33 goals, and this led to Shrewsbury Town manager Ian McNeill paying £25,000 for his services in February 1989.

Having scored 31 goals in 68 games for Shrewsbury, he joined Bury for a fee of £175,000. In a brief stay at Gigg Lane, McGinlay netted a hat-trick against Bolton Wanderers, the team he was to make his name with before Bruce Rioch paid £80,000 to take him to Millwall. The London club reached the play-offs in 1990-91, but in September 1992, Rioch, who was by now the Bolton boss, splashed out £125,000 for the prolific marksman.

He ended his first season at Burnden Park with 22 goals, which included scoring in both FA Cup ties against Liverpool and the all-important penalty goal that won promotion against Preston on the final day of the season. In 1993-94, McGinlay grabbed 33 goals to equal a post-war club record held by Nat Lofthouse and Andy Walker for total goals in a season. In 1994 he earned his first full Scottish international cap, scoring in a 2-1 win in Austria, going on to net four goals in 13 matches.

He hit his 100th league goal of his career in March 1995, ironically to earn the points for Bolton against his former club Millwall at the New Den. His 100th goal for the Wanderers came against Crystal Palace in November 1996 and in the same month he hit a hat-trick against Spurs in the Coca-Cola Cup to help

Bolton to a 6-1 win. It was entirely fitting that he should strike the final goal at Burnden Park in a 4-1 win over Charlton Athletic, and he went on to score 118 goals in 245 games for the Wanderers before a £625,000 fee took him to Bradford City. He later ended his career with Oldham Athletic before spending a brief spell coaching in America.

DUNCAN SHEARER
Forward

Born: Duncan Nichol Shearer, Fort William, 28 August 1962
Height: 5ft 10in
Weight: 10st 9lb
Clubs: Inverness Clachnacuddin; Chelsea; Huddersfield Town; Swindon Town; Blackburn
    Rovers; Aberdeen; Inverness Caledonian Thistle
Scotland caps: 7
Scotland goals: 2
1994 v Austria (won 2-1), v Holland (lost 1-3) 1 goal
1995 v Finland (won 2-0) 1 goal, v Russia (drew 0-0), v San Marino (won 2-0), v Faroe Islands
    (won 2-0)
1996 v Greece (won 1-0)

Having played his early football for Chelsea and Huddersfield Town, Duncan Shearer made his name under Glenn Hoddle and Ossie Ardiles at Swindon Town. He was the leading scorer at the County Ground for two seasons, going on to net 78 goals in 159 league games before in March 1992 being transferred to Blackburn Rovers for a fee of £800,000.

Shearer, who won selection for that season's PFA award-winning Second Division team, helped Rovers win promotion to the Premiership via the play-offs. However, he didn't figure in Blackburn's plans for the top flight and was allowed to join Aberdeen.

At Pittodrie, Shearer rediscovered his shooting boots, netting twice on his debut and ended the season with 28 goals as the Dons finished runners-up to Rangers on all fronts. The following season Aberdeen again fell short in the League, with Shearer a shining light once more with 26 goals. Billy Dodds arrived from St Johnstone in readiness for the following season, and though he was seen as the perfect foil to Shearer, it didn't work out and the Dons slipped to the foot of the table with just three games left. New manager Roy Aitken steered the Dons back to within touching distance of Dundee United, who were due to visit Pittodrie. If the Dons had lost this game, they would have been relegated for the first time in their history. Aberdeen won 2-1 with Shearer and Dodds scoring a goal apiece, and went on to win their remaining games including the two-legged play-off against Dunfermline Athletic.

Shearer's form was rewarded with long overdue international recognition, and he went on to score twice in his first three appearances. He also found the net in that season's Coca-Cola Cup Final before he started to find himself on the bench. In 1997 he joined Inverness Caledonian Thistle, later becoming their assistant-manager. Shearer is now back at his beloved Pittodrie as assistant-manager to Dons' boss Steve Paterson.

JOHN SPENCER
Forward

Born: John Spencer, Glasgow, 11 September 1970
Height: 5ft 7in
Weight: 9st 10lb
Clubs: Glasgow Rangers; Morton; Lai Sun (Hong Kong); Chelsea; Queen's Park Rangers; Everton; Motherwell; Colorado Rapids (United States)
Scotland caps: 14
1995 v Russia (drew 1-1), v Greece (lost 0-1), v San Marino (won 2-0), v Japan (drew 0-0)
1996 v Finland (won 1-0), v Australia (won 1-0), v Denmark (lost 0-2),
  v United States (lost 1-2), v Colombia (lost 0-1), v Holland (drew 0-0),
  v England (lost 0-2), v Switzerland (won 1-0)
1997 v Latvia (won 2-0), v Wales (lost 0-1)

Small for a striker, John Spencer had strength and a shrewd footballing brain which served him well. He was confined for long spells to the Rangers reserve side and had a loan spell with Morton, before a move to Lai Sun in Hong Kong sparked his career into life.

Moving to Chelsea in the summer of 1992 as cover for their striking partnership of Robert Fleck and Mick Harford, he soon ousted the Scottish international and, after a couple of seasons, his impressive displays earned him his first full cap for the game against Russia in November 1994. During this spell he scored one of the best goals ever scored by a Chelsea player, as the Blues visited Austria Vienna in the Cup Winners' Cup. Running from his own penalty area, he rounded the goalkeeper to give Chelsea the tie on away goals. In 1995-96, Spencer was Chelsea's leading scorer, forcing his way into the Scotland squad for Euro '96, which sadly ended at the group stage. He had scored 43 goals in 137 games for Chelsea, when in November 1996 he was surprisingly allowed to join Queen's Park Rangers for £2.5 million.

He made a stunning start with the Loftus Road club, scoring nine goals in his first 12 games, including his first-ever hat-trick in a 3-1 home win over Barnsley. Unfortunately, in 1997-98, injury and behind-the-scenes disruption affected his form, and he was allowed to go on loan to Everton. He made such an impression that Toffees' manager Howard Kendall felt obliged to make the move permanent, and following a scare over a heart scan, the player was eventually given the all-clear to complete the move.

However, he failed to find the net in a first team game and returned to Scotland to play for Motherwell, initially on loan. Having made a big impact at Fir Park, Motherwell fans were delighted when he joined them permanently. He went on to score 18 goals in 49 games, before injury forced his retirement from the Scottish game.

Spencer then made a comeback in the United States Major League with

Colorado Rapids, and having spent four seasons playing across the Atlantic, now hopes to set up a coaching school in the States.

COLIN CALDERWOOD
Central defender

Born: Colin Calderwood, Stranraer, 20 January 1965
Height: 6ft 0in
Weight: 12st 11b
Clubs: Mansfield Town; Swindon Town; Tottenham Hotspur; Aston Villa; Nottingham Forest; Notts County
Scotland caps: 36
Scotland goals: 1

1995 v Russia (drew 0-0), v San Marino (won 2-0) 1 goal, v Japan (drew 0-0), v Ecuador (won 2-1), v Faroe Islands (won 2-0)

1996 v Greece (won 1-0), v Finland (won 1-0), v Sweden (lost 0-2), v San Marino (won 5-0), v United States (lost 1-2), v Colombia (lost 0-1), v Holland (drew 0-0), v England (lost 0-2), v Switzerland (won 1-0)

1997 v Austria (drew 0-0), v Latvia (won 2-0), v Sweden (won 1-0), v Estonia (drew 0-0), v Estonia (won 2-0), v Austria (won 2-0), v Sweden (lost 1-2)

1998 v Belarus (won 4-1), v Latvia (won 2-0), v France (lost 1-2), v Denmark (lost 0-1), v Finland (drew 1-1), v Colombia (drew 2-2), v United States (drew 0-0), v Brazil (lost 1-2), v Norway (drew 1-1)

1999 v Lithuania (drew 0-0), v Estonia (won 3-2), v Faroe Islands (drew 1-1), v Czech Republic (lost 2-3)

2000 v Bosnia (won 2-1), v Bosnia (won 1-0)

Colin Calderwood made his Football League debut for Mansfield Town in the most unusual circumstances, just 52 days after his 17th birthday at Crewe Alexandra in March 1981. Unfortunately his registration forms did not reach the Football League in time, and the club had two points deducted for playing an unregistered player! He went on to play in 117 games for Mansfield before Swindon Town paid a tribunal fixed fee of £30,000 for his services in the summer of 1985.

On his arrival at the County Ground he was appointed club captain by manager Lou Macari, and the 20-year-old led the Robins to the Fourth Division Championship in his first season. Calderwood, who went on to play in 121 consecutive league games from his debut, led Swindon to their second successive promotion in 1986-87 via the play-offs after finishing third in Division Three. In 1989-90 he skippered Swindon to the Second Division play-offs and victory over Sunderland, only for the Football League to deny the Robins the promotion they had earned. He gained recognition for his outstanding displays in the Swindon defence when appearing for the Football League against the Italian Serie 'B' side on a couple of occasions. Captaining Swindon to success in the play-off final against Leicester City, he missed out on leading the Robins in the top flight when Spurs' manager Ossie Ardiles signed him for £1.25 million—the fee, fixed by an independent tribunal, was three times the figure Spurs offered Swindon.

His form alongside Sol Campbell at the heart of the Spurs defence led to him winning the first of 36 full caps for Scotland when he played against Russia. An important member of the national side for the next five years, playing in Euro '96 and the 1998 World Cup, in almost half the games in which he appeared, Scotland kept a clean sheet!

At White Hart Lane he was occasionally played out of position in midfield, and this cost him his place in the Scotland set-up. Calderwood, who had appeared in 199 games in almost six years with the North London club, jumped at the opportunity of joining Aston Villa for £225,000 in March 1999.

Immediately striking up a good understanding in defence with Gareth Southgate, he was unlucky to lose his place in Villa's three-man defence to the up and coming youngster Gareth Barry. This caused him to leave Villa Park after just a year to sign for Nottingham Forest, but after just a handful of games for the City Ground club, he suffered a dislocated ankle and broken fibula against Birmingham City. On recovering he had a loan spell with Notts County before announcing his retirement at the end of the 2000-01 season. In October 2003, Calderwood was appointed manager of Northampton Town.

DARREN JACKSON
Forward

Born: Darren Jackson, Edinburgh, 25 July 1966
Height: 5ft 7in
Weight: 11st 2lb
Clubs: Broxburn Amateurs; Meadowbank Thistle; Newcastle United; Dundee United; Hibernian; Glasgow Celtic; Coventry City; Heart of Midlothian; Livingston
Scotland caps: 28
Scotland goals: 4

1995 v Russia (drew 0-0), v San Marino (won 2-0), v Japan (drew 0-0), v Ecuador (won 2-1), v Faroe Islands (won 2-0)

1996 v Greece (won 1-0), v Finland (won 1-0), v Sweden (lost 0-2), v San Marino (won 5-0), v Australia (won 1-0), v Denmark (lost 0-2), v United States (lost 1-2)

1997 v Latvia (won 2-0) 1 goal, v Sweden (won 1-0), v Estonia (won 2-0), v Austria (won 2-0), v Sweden (lost 1-2), v Wales (lost 0-1), v Malta (won 3-2) 2 goals, v Belarus (won 1-0)

1998 v Denmark (lost 0-1), v Finland (drew 1-1) 1 goal, v Colombia (drew 2-2), v United States (lost 0-1), v Brazil (lost 1-2), v Norway (drew 1-1)

1999 v Lithuania (drew 0-0), v Estonia (won 3-2)

Darren Jackson could not have scored a more spectacular first goal for Scotland. It happened in the World Cup qualifier in Latvia with Scotland already 1-0 up and a little over ten minutes left to play. He intercepted a pass in the centre-circle, eluded two Latvian defenders to find himself with a 40-yard open run on goal. From just outside the box, he drilled an impressive shot into the bottom left-hand corner of the goal. In fact, throughout the World Cup build-up, Jackson, who formed a profitable partnership with Kevin Gallacher, began to endear himself to the Scottish fans.

He was given a chance by Newcastle United after scoring 19 goals as a part-time professional in his first season with Meadowbank Thistle, but he was moved around from position to position at St James Park and reluctantly agreed to a move back to Scotland with Dundee United, who paid £200,000 for him. His displays for the Tannadice club earned him a call-up to the Scotland Under-21 side, but in 1992 after four years with the Terrors he moved to Hibernian for a fee of £400,000.

Jackson's initial problem at Easter Road was dissent, and though he sounded off a little too often for referees and opposition fans, it was only because he disliked losing or letting himself down. Jackson had scored 50 goals in 173 league games for Hibs when he left Easter Road to sign for Celtic.

A few months after putting pen to paper, his life was endangered by fluid on the brain. Happily, the surgery he had to undergo was a success, but he was still unable to hold down a regular first team place. He spent a couple of months on loan to Coventry City and rejected a possible move to China. In the end he joined Hearts, where his arrival at Tynecastle refreshed not only his own career but also that of his new club. On parting company with Hearts, he moved to Livingston where he ended his career. Darren Jackson is now a football agent and, after gaining his licence in 2004, advises a number of Scottish Internationals.

PAUL BERNARD
Midfield

Born: Paul Robert Bernard, Edinburgh, 30 December 1972
Height: 5ft 9in
Weight: 11st 8lb
Clubs: Oldham Athletic; Aberdeen; Plymouth Argyle; St Johnstone; Northwich Victoria
Scotland caps: 2
1995 v Japan (drew 0-0), v Ecuador (won 2-1)

Paul Bernard turned professional with Oldham Athletic in the summer of 1991, making his Football League debut in the penultimate match of the season in a 2-0 win at home to Middlesbrough in May of that year, while still a trainee. He retained his place for the final match of the season against Sheffield Wednesday, remarkably scoring the equaliser after Oldham had trailed 2-0, and when Neil Redfearn converted a penalty in injury-time, the club were promoted as Second Division champions.

During Oldham's first season in the top flight for 68 years, he didn't win a regular place in the side until the turn of the year, when he scored goals in four consecutive matches. Called into the Scotland Under-21 side, he had another good season in 1992-93, but was unfortunate to suffer a shin fracture while on international duty.

After that he seemed to suffer more than his fair share of injuries, but at the end of the 1994-95 season he was selected for the Scottish tour of Japan in May, where he gained his first full international cap.

Early the following season, having scored 21 goals in 137 games, the highly rated midfielder joined Aberdeen for a fee of £1 million.

A player with great attitude, Bernard suffered with a terrible spate of injuries in his first four seasons at Pittodrie, but was a regular member of the Aberdeen side in 1999-2000 when he helped the Dons to both the Scottish Cup and League Cup Finals, only to lose 4-0 to Rangers and 2-0 to Celtic respectively. After playing in just a handful of games in 2000-01, he spent a long time on the sidelines with a career-threatening Achilles injury before, in December 2002, joining Plymouth Argyle on a free transfer.

But after just one season at Home Park, he was released by the Pilgrims and joined St Johnstone. Bernard appeared on a regular basis for the Saints until losing his place in the side during the early stages of the 2004-05 season. He then left to play non-League football for Northwich Victoria

CRAIG BURLEY
Midfield

Born: Craig William Burley, Irvine, 24 September 1971
Height: 6ft 1in
Weight: 11st 7lb
Clubs: Chelsea; Glasgow Celtic; Derby County; Dundee; Preston North End; Walsall
Scotland caps: 46
Scotland goals: 3

1995 v Japan (drew 0-0), v Ecuador (won 2-1), v Faroe Islands (won 2-0), v Greece (won 1-0)
1996 v Sweden (lost 0-2), v Australia (won 1-0), v Denmark (lost 0-2),
v United States (lost 1-2), v Colombia (lost 0-1), v Holland (drew 0-0),
v England (lost 0-2), v Switzerland (won 1-0)
1997 v Austria (drew 0-0), v Latvia (won 2-0), v Sweden (won 1-0), v Estonia (won 2-0),
v Austria (won 2-0), v Sweden (lost 1-2), v Malta (won 3-2), v Belarus (won 1-0)
1998 v Belarus (won 4-1), v Latvia (won 2-0), v France (lost 1-2),
v Colombia (drew 2-2) 1 goal, v United States (drew 0-0), v Brazil (lost 1-2),
v Norway (drew 1-1) 1 goal, v Morocco (lost 0-3)
1999 v Faroe Islands (won 2-1) 1 goal, v Czech Republic (lost 1-2)
2000 v Bosnia (won 2-1), v Estonia (drew 0-0), v Bosnia (won 1-0), v Lithuania (won 3-0),
v England (lost 0-2), v England (won 1-0), v Holland (drew 0-0),
v Republic of Ireland (won 2-1)
2001 v Croatia (drew 1-1), v Australia (lost 0-2), v Belgium (drew 2-2),
v San Marino (won 4-0)
2002 v Croatia (drew 0-0), v Belgium (lost 0-2), v Latvia (won 2-1)
2003 v Austria (lost 0-2)

A nephew of George Burley, the former Ipswich star and currently manager of Southampton, he was rewarded for his good displays in 1994-95 with the first of 46 full caps for Scotland in the match against Japan, thus being capped at every level.

He joined Chelsea in December 1987. Within a week of making his full Football League debut for the Stamford Bridge club, he was selected for the Scotland Under-21 team for the match against Denmark. A midfielder with great vision and long-range shooting ability, he suffered his fair share of injuries with the London club but still managed to impress Craig Brown, being an integral part of the Scottish squad for Euro '96. He featured in the bizarre World Cup qualifier in Tallinn in October 1996, when Estonia failed to appear and the match was abandoned after three seconds! He went on to play in 137 games for Chelsea before a £2.5 million move to Celtic in the summer of 1997.

In a little over two years at Parkhead, Burley helped Celtic win the Premier Division title in 1997-98 and the League Cup in the same season with a 3-0 win over Dundee United. After an unhappy start to the 1999-2000 season, Burley arrived at Pride Park after Derby County manager Jim Smith paid £3 million for his services.

His impact was immediate, and he and Kinkladze were instrumental in the Rams maintaining their Premiership status. Despite County's poor form the following season, Burley remained a regular for Scotland and was appointed club captain. He then suffered a number of serious injuries, including a cartilage operation and an Achilles tendon problem, and so missed much of Derby's relegation season. On regaining full fitness, he announced his retirement from international football, and after just six games under his uncle, the Rams released him.

He returned north of the Border to join Dundee, but his stay was only brief, as it was with his next two clubs, Preston North End and Walsall. After hanging up his boots, Burley became a TV pundit with the media company Setanta.

SCOT GEMMILL
Midfield

Born: Scot Gemmill, Paisley, 2 January 1971
Height: 5ft 11in
Weight: 11st 6lb
Clubs: Nottingham Forest; Everton; Preston North End; Leicester City; Oxford United; New Zealand Knights
Scotland caps: 26
Scotland goals: 1

1995 v Japan (drew 0-0), v Ecuador (won 2-1), v Faroe Islands (won 2-0)
1996 v San Marino (won 5-0), v Denmark (lost 0-2), v United States (lost 1-2)
1997 v Estonia (won 2-0), v Sweden (lost 1-2), v Wales (lost 0-1), v Malta (won 3-2), v Belarus (won 1-0)
1998 v Denmark (lost 0-1), v Finland (drew 1-1)
1999 v Germany (won 1-0), v Faroe Islands (drew 1-1)
2001 v San Marino (won 4-0), v Poland (drew 1-1)
2002 v Croatia (drew 0-0), v France (lost 0-5), v Nigeria (lost 1-2), v South Korea (lost 1-4), v South Africa (lost 0-2), v Hong Kong (won 4-0) 1 goal
2003 v Canada (won 3-1), v Republic of Ireland (lost 0-2), v Austria (lost 0-2)

The son of former Nottingham Forest and Scotland favourite, Archie Gemmill, he followed in his father's footsteps in going to the City Ground. A good all-round midfield player with vision and stamina in abundance, he won the first of 26 caps when he played in the goalless draw against Japan in Hiroshima in 1995.

Despite his indifferent form during the early part of his Forest career, he retained his place in the Scotland side for their World Cup matches, and eventually his form for the national side rubbed off on him at club level. For in 1997-98, Gemmill was an important member of the Forest side that went back to the Premiership at the first time of asking, following their relegation the previous season. A member of Scotland's World Cup Final 22 for France '98, he was not called upon and could only look on as the team went out at the end of the first stage, despite drawing with Norway.

Having refused to sign a new contract following his return from the World Cup, Nottingham Forest put him on a weekly agreement for the 1998-99 season. Although playing in the majority of Forest's Premiership games, he left after scoring 29 goals in 311 games and joined Everton in transfer deadline week.

Instrumental in helping the Toffees escape the drop, he proved an inspired purchase, until midway through the following season he suffered a succession of injuries that meant that his season petered out on a disappointing note. He returned to the side in 2000-01 and enjoyed his most consistent campaign after replacing Paul Gascoigne. He continued in a similar vein the following season as Scotland's new manager Berti Vogts gave him greater opportunities to show his talent on a regular basis at international level. Following another consistent season for the Goodison club, he joined Preston North End on loan in March 2004, prior to a permanent move to Leicester City in the close season.

He never quite grabbed a starting spot in the Foxes' line-up, and though he was a great help to the younger members of the club's midfield, he was released in the close season. After unsuccessful trials with Motherwell and Sheffield Wednesday, he linked up with Oxford United as player–coach but later left to join New Zealand Knights.

PAUL LAMBERT
Midfield

Born: Paul Lambert, Glasgow, 7 August 1969
Height: 5ft 11in
Weight: 9st 10lb
Clubs: St Mirren; Motherwell; Borussia Dortmund (Germany); Glasgow Celtic; Livingston
Scotland caps: 40
Scotland goals: 1

1995   v Japan (drew 0-0), v Ecuador (won 2-1)
1997   v Latvia (won 2-0), v Sweden (won 1-0), v Austria (won 2-0), v Sweden (lost 1-2),
            v Belarus (won 1-0)
1998   v Belarus (won 4-1), v Latvia (won 2-0), v Finland (drew 1-1), v Colombia (drew 2-2),
            v United States (drew 0-0), v Brazil (lost 1-2), v Norway (drew 1-1),
            v Morocco (lost 0-3)
1999   v Lithuania (drew 0-0), v Czech Republic (lost 1-2), v Germany (won 1-0),

Affectionately nicknamed 'the Kaiser' as a result of his incredibly successful time in Germany with Borussia Dortmund, Paul Lambert began his career with St Mirren.

He had won 11 Scotland Under-21 caps and had captained the Scotland Under-18 side while at Paisley. When Motherwell captured his signature in September 1993 for £125,000, it heralded the beginning of a few seasons in which the Fir Park club had a wonderful midfield. Both elegant and economical, Lambert won the first of his 40 full international caps against Japan while with Motherwell, but he left Fir Park under the Bosman ruling in the summer of 1996. The move was hard for Motherwell to bear, because Lambert at that time was probably worth in excess of £1 million.

Borussia Dortmund were able to prise him away for nothing, and

Paul Lambert in Celtic colours

during his spell in Germany he won a European Cup medal with them as they beat Juventus 3-1—the first British player to do so with a foreign club.

In 1997 he returned to Scotland, but in the colours of Celtic, and during his time with the Bhoys, he helped them to win four Premier Division titles, three League Cups and the Scottish Cup in 2001 when they beat Hibs 3-0.

Paul Lambert was Celtic's captain and a steadying influence both on and off the field. After claiming the Football Writers' Association Player of the Year award, he occasionally found himself left out by Martin O'Neill when the Celtic boss accommodated Chris Sutton in midfield. There is little doubt that after joining the Parkhead club, Paul Lambert was one of its most influential players. Famous for his composed nature, he played a great part in helping Celtic reach the 2003 UEFA Cup Final in Seville.

Lambert's contribution and the determination he brought to the Celtic side were undisputed, and the Parkhead club's fans will forever be appreciative for the success of the club, made ever more special by this talented, down-to-earth, inspiring player.

On parting company with the Bhoys, he was appointed team manager of Livingston, but after leading his team to the CIS Cup semi-final, he resigned after a defeat by relegation rivals Dunfermline, to be replaced by John Robertson.

BRIAN MARTIN
Defender
Born: Brian Martin, Bellshill, 24 February 1963
Height: 6ft 0in
Weight: 13st 0lb
Clubs: Albion Rovers; Shotts Bon Accord; Stenhousemuir; Falkirk; Hamilton Academicals; St Mirren; Motherwell; Stirling Albion; Partick Thistle
Scotland caps: 2
1995 v Japan (drew 0-0), v Ecuador (won 2-1)

At his peak, Brian Martin, who won two full caps during his time with Motherwell, was one of the Scottish League's best defenders. Though he wasn't particularly quick, his game was built around exceptional 'reading' of events and a wonderful sense of commitment.

His career had started at Albion Rovers before brief stints with Shotts Bon Accord and Stenhousemuir led to him signing for Falkirk, whom he helped finish First Division runners-up in 1985-86. After one season playing Premier League football he joined Hamilton Academicals, but was signed too late to prevent their relegation from the top flight. Just over a year later, he was on the move again, this time to St Mirren who had just won the Scottish Cup.

He left Love Street in November 1991 as Motherwell manager Tommy McLean paid £175,000 to take him to Fir Park. The potential he displayed at his previous clubs came to fruition at Motherwell, as he went on to play in 237 league games for the Steelmen. His displays led to him being selected for Scotland on two occasions, and he was a key member of the Motherwell side that finished runners-up in the Premier League in 1994-95. Martin ultimately left Motherwell under a cloud, having criticised the Fir Park club in the national press.

He then moved to Stirling Albion where his long-time defensive partner John Philliben was manager. From Stirling he eventually moved on to John Lambie's Partick Thistle, where he ended his playing days.

STEVIE CRAWFORD
Forward
Born: Stephen Crawford, Dunfermline, 9 January 1974
Height: 5ft 10in
Weight: 10st 7lb
Clubs: Rosyth Rec; Raith Rovers; Millwall; Hibernian; Dunfermline Athletic; Plymouth Argyle; Dundee United; Aberdeen; Dunfermline Athletic

Scotland caps: 25
Scotland goals: 4
1995   v Ecuador (won 2-1) 1 goal
2001   v Poland (drew 1-1)
2002   v France (lost 0-5)
2003   v Faroe Islands (drew 2-2), v Iceland (won 2-0), v Canada (won 3-1) 2 goals,
         v Portugal (lost 0-2), v Republic of Ireland (lost 0-2), v Iceland (won 2-1),
         v Lithuania (lost 0-1), v Austria (lost 0-2), v New Zealand (drew 1-1) 1 goal,
         v Germany (drew 1-1)
2004   v Norway (drew 0-0), v Faroe Islands (won 3-1), v Lithuania (won 1-0),
         v Holland (lost 0-6), v Romania (lost 1-2), v Estonia (won 1-0),
         v Trinidad and Tobago (won 4-1)
2005   v Hungary (lost 0-3), v Spain (drew 1-1), v Slovenia (drew 0-0), v Moldova (drew 1-1),
         v Sweden (lost 1-4)

The young Stevie Crawford signed 'S' forms for his home-town club Dunfermline Athletic, but Jimmy Nicholl took him to Raith Rovers when he was manager there.

Crawford played a major role with the Kirkcaldy club, helping them win the Coca-Cola Cup by beating Celtic 6-5 on penalties after the teams had drawn 2-2 after extra time, and promotion to the Premier League. He had scored 28 goals in 138 games for the Stark's Park club before leaving in the summer of 1996 to sign for Millwall.

Proving himself a pacy and skilful forward, he ended his first season at the New Den as the Lions' top scorer with 15 goals in all competitions, although he ended the campaign playing in midfield. After just one season with Millwall, he returned to Scotland to sign for Hibernian.

He had two very successful seasons with the Easter Road club, and in 1998-99 he was Hibs' leading scorer with 14 goals in 35 games as they won promotion to the Premier League as First Division Champions. Surprisingly finding himself out of favour, he was then re-united with his old boss Jimmy Nicholl when he moved to Dunfermline on loan in October 1999. He was a huge hit, ending the campaign as the Pars' top scorer with 16 goals, a feat which won him the First Division Player of the Year award.

He opted to stay with the Pars when his Hibs contract expired in the summer of 2000. Forming a great partnership with Craig Brewster after he was signed for the 2002-03 season, the two complemented each other well to produce quite a lot of goals. Crawford's share was 19, including a hat-trick in a 4-2 win at Dundee—an SPL goalscoring record for the Pars—and he was recalled to Berti Vogts' national squad.

Crawford, who scored the winning goal against Ecuador on his international debut while with Raith in 1995, also re-established his international career during his time with Dunfermline. He had scored 73 goals in 194 games for the Pars when in the summer of 2004 he joined Plymouth Argyle. Failing to settle in the West Country, he joined Dundee United and featured in their line-up for the Scottish Cup Final defeat by Celtic. There is no doubt that his signing added an extra dimension to United's play and strengthened the team. After a spell with Aberdeen he returned to Dunfermline for a second spell.

TOSH McKINLAY

Left-back

Born: Thomas Valley McKinlay, Glasgow, 3 December 1964
Height: 5ft 7in
Weight: 11st 10lb
Clubs: Dundee; Heart of Midlothian; Glasgow Celtic; Stoke City; Kilmarnock
Scotland caps: 22

1996 v Greece (won 1-0), v Finland (won 1-0), v Denmark (lost 0-2); v Colombia (lost 0-1),
v England (lost 0-2), v Switzerland (won 1-0)

1997 v Austria (drew 0-0), v Latvia (won 2-0), v Sweden (won 1-0), v Estonia (drew 0-0),
v Estonia (won 2-0), v Austria (won 2-0), v Sweden (lost 1-2), v Wales (lost 0-1),
v Malta (won 3-2), v Belarus (won 1-0)

1998 v Belarus (won 4-1), v Latvia (won 2-0), v France (lost 1-2), v United States (drew 0-0),
v Brazil (lost 1-2), v Morocco (lost 0-3)

Left-back Tosh McKinlay twice came off the bench for Scotland in first round games before the side were eliminated from the 1998 World Cup at that stage— the second occasion against Morocco in St Etienne proved to be the last of his 22 full international appearances.

As a boy, Tosh McKinlay was a huge Celtic fan, but it was with Dundee that he started his first-class career, signing for the Dens Park club in the summer of 1981. McKinlay was a virtual ever-present in the Dundee side, and though they failed to win any domestic honours in his six-and-a-half seasons with the Dark Blues, he had appeared in 204 League and Cup games when he was transferred to Hearts just before Christmas 1988.

He was one of the Tynecastle club's most consistent performers over the next few seasons, few wingers getting the better of him. In 1991-92 he helped Hearts finish runners-up to Rangers in the Premier League. His displays for Hearts led to interest from a number of clubs south of the Border, but when he did leave Tynecastle after appearing in 241 games, it was Celtic boss Tommy Burns who splashed out £350,000 to take him to Parkhead.

An enthusiastic player, McKinlay helped Celtic win the Scottish Cup, beating Airdrie 1-0 in the final. His displays around this time earned McKinlay, who had played for Scotland at Under-21 and 'B' level, the first of 22 full caps, when in August 1995, he helped Scotland beat Greece 1-0. Sadly injuries hampered his progress at Parkhead, and though he was an important member of the side, helping them finish runners-up in the Premier League in 1996-97, he was allowed to join Stoke City on loan.

Sent-off on his Potters debut, he was suspended for three games. But just as his suspension was starting, he was recalled to the Celtic squad prior to leaving Parkhead in the summer of 1999 to see out his career with a season playing for Kilmarnock. McKinlay is now a football agent.

BRIAN O'NEIL
Defender/ Midfield

Born: Brian O'Neil, Paisley, 6 September 1972
Height: 6ft 1in
Weight: 12st 4lb
Clubs: Glasgow Celtic; Porirua Viard (New Zealand); Nottingham Forest; Aberdeen; Wolfsburg (Germany); Derby County; Preston North End
Scotland caps: 7
1996 v Australia (won 1-0)
1999 v Germany (won 1-0)
2000 v Lithuania (won 3-0), v Holland (drew 0-0), v Republic of Ireland (won 2-1)
2001 v Australia (lost 0-2)
2006 v Austria (drew 2-2)

Brian O'Neil represented Scotland in the World Youth Cup in 1989 and scored the goal against Portugal that put Young Scotland into the final. On the big day itself, he had a penalty saved by the Saudi keeper in normal time, and then missed another in the shoot-out!

After joining Celtic and despite talent in abundance, he showed a tendency to play off the pace of the game, and in his early days at Parkhead, he was largely a fringe player. After a loan spell in New Zealand with Porirua Viard, he rejoined the Bhoys, and though his displays earned him selection for the Scotland Under-21 side, domestic honours eluded him. In March 1997 he was loaned to Nottingham Forest before leaving Celtic to join Aberdeen on a free transfer in the close season.

He spent just one season at Pittodrie before trying his luck in German football with Wolfsburg. He enjoyed two fairly successful seasons on the continent before, in the summer of 2000, he joined Derby County in the exchange deal that saw Stefan Schnoor return to Germany. Unfortunately, just two minutes into his County debut against Manchester United, he suffered a serious knee injury that led to a long lay-off. Injuries again hampered his progress the following season, and in November 2002, his contract was terminated.

After a trial period with Preston North End, he secured a long-term contract, demonstrating a simple but effective passing game that improved the play of many of those around him, most notably Nigerian Dickson Etuhu. Showing little sign that the passing years were taking their toll, his excellent form led to a surprise recall to the national side for the friendly against Austria.

BILLY DODDS
Forward

Born: William Dodds, New Cumnock, 5 February 1969
Height: 5ft 8in
Weight: 11st 2lb
Clubs: Chelsea; Partick Thistle; Dundee; St Johnstone; Aberdeen; Dundee United; Glasgow Rangers; Dundee United; Partick Thistle

Scotland caps: 26
Scotland goals: 7
1997 v Latvia (won 2-0), v Wales (lost 0-1), v Belarus (won 1-0)
1998 v Belarus (won 4-1)
1999 v Estonia (won 3-2) 2 goals, v Faroe Islands (won 2-1) 1 goal, v Germany (won 1-0),
     v Faroe Islands (drew 1-1), v Czech Republic (lost 2-3)
2000 v Bosnia (won 2-1) 1 goal, v Estonia (drew 0-0), v Bosnia (won 1-0), v Lithuania (won
     3-0), v England (lost 0-2), v England (won 1-0), v France (lost 0-2), v Holland (drew 0-0),
     v Republic of Ireland (won 2-1)
2001 v Latvia (won 1-0), v San Marino (won 2-0), v Australia (lost 0-2),
     v Belgium (drew 2-2) 2 goals, v San Marino (won 4-0) 1 goal, v Poland (drew 1-1)
2002 v Croatia (drew 0-0), v Belgium (lost 0-2)

Beginning his career south of the border with Chelsea, Billy Dodds made his league debut in the London derby against Arsenal in March 1987, but on being unable to make much headway at Stamford Bridge, he joined Partick Thistle on loan.

After a good season at Firhill, he joined Dundee and became an instant hit at Dens Park. Dodds, who was the club's leading scorer in the majority of his seasons with the club, helped them win the First Division Championship in 1991-92 when he topped the scoring charts with 19 goals. In 1994 he left Dens Park when St Johnstone paid out a club record fee of £300,000 to secure his services. However, his stay at McDiarmid Park was brief, and later that year, Aberdeen broke their outgoing transfer record when paying £800,000 for Dodds' scoring abilities.

While at Pittodrie, Dodds won the first of his 26 international caps, scoring his first goals for his country in the 3-2 win over Estonia. In 1995-96 he helped the Dons win the League Cup, beating his former club Dundee 2-0 in the final. Dodds became Dundee United manager Paul Sturrock's first signing when he was exchanged for Robbie Winters.

His Tannadice career got off to a whirlwind start with a hat-trick on his first start, the opposition being former club St Johnstone. He more than played his part in helping United secure their Premier status in 1998-99, with 16 league goals, and continued his outstanding form to become Scotland's first choice striker. In December 1999 he was transferred to Rangers and spent three years at Ibrox. He scored 10 goals in 16 games to help them win the Premier Division Championship in his first season with the club, and netted in the 4-0 Cup Final win over Aberdeen.

Dodds returned to Tannadice in January 2003, and though most of his time with the club in his second spell was spent on the bench, he remained an important member of the United squad until joining Partick Thistle until the end of the 2005-06 season. He is now continuing his work in football as an analyst/commentator on BBC Radio Scotland.

JACKIE McNAMARA
Midfield

Born: Jackie McNamara, Glasgow, 24 October 1973
Height: 5ft 8in
Weight: 9st 7lb
Clubs: Dunfermline Athletic; Glasgow Celtic; Wolverhampton Wanderers
Scotland caps: 33

1997 v Latvia (won 2-0), v Sweden (won 1-0), v Estonia (drew 0-0), v Wales (lost 0-1)
1998 v Denmark (lost 0-1), v Colombia (drew 2-2), v United States (drew 0-0),
v Norway (drew 1-1), v Morocco (lost 0-3)
2000 v Holland (drew 0-0)
2001 v San Marino (won 2-0)
2002 v Belgium (lost 0-2), v France (lost 0-5)
2003 v Iceland (won 2-0), v Iceland (won 2-1), v Lithuania (lost 0-1),
v New Zealand (drew 1-1), v Germany (drew 1-1)
2004 v Faroe Islands (won 3-1), v Germany (lost 1-2), v Lithuania (won 1-0),
v Holland (won 1-0), v Holland (lost 0-6), v Wales (lost 0-4),
v Trinidad and Tobago (won 4-1)
2005 v Spain (drew 1-1), v Slovenia (drew 0-0), v Sweden (lost 1-4), v Italy (lost 0-2),
v Moldova (won 2-0)
2006 v Austria (drew 2-2), v Italy (drew 1-1), v Norway (won 2-1)

The son of Celtic and Hibs player Jackie McNamara senior, Jackie began his career with Dunfermline Athletic, whom he helped reach the League Cup Final of 1991-92. The Pars lost 2-0 to Hibs, but a couple of seasons later, he helped them finish runners-up in the First Division, a feat they repeated the following season before winning the title in 1995-96.

By that time, McNamara had left East End Park to join Celtic for a fee of £600,000, making his debut against Falkirk in October 1995. He began his Celtic career as an orthodox right full-back, before what were seen as apparent defensive limitations saw him converted to the role of right-sided midfielder. He regularly won Player of the Year awards during his first few seasons at Parkhead, and was prominent in the club's title winning season of 1997-98, a campaign when they also won the League Cup, beating Dundee United 3-0 in the final.

Jackie McNamara when playing for Celtic

Having won the first of his 33 caps against Latvia in October 1996, McNamara was part of Scotland's squad for the '98 World Cup in France. On his return to Celtic, he suffered a long run of niggly injuries which triggered off an ongoing struggle to command a regular place. He also struggled until recently to obtain regular inclusion in the various Scotland squads.

McNamara was the longest-serving player at Parkhead, and in his latter days with the club, it was only when Martin O'Neill used him intelligently and less sparingly that he got back to his best form. The scorer of some vital goals during the club's successful Cup campaigns of recent seasons, McNamara captained Celtic in both legs of the UEFA Cup quarter-final defeat of Barcelona. His last competitive game for the Glasgow giants was in the 2004-05 Scottish Cup Final, when he led the Bhoys to victory over Dundee United. Having played in 347 games for Celtic, he was awarded a testimonial in May 2005 when 53,000 supporters turned out to see Celtic play the Republic of Ireland.

Wolves manager Glenn Hoddle persuaded McNamara to join the Molineux club, this in spite of the Hoops making a last ditch attempt to keep their skipper. He slotted straight into the Wolves side at right-back, but after three appearances for Scotland, he suffered a cruciate knee ligament injury that will see him sidelined for most of the season.

CHRISTIAN DAILLY
Defender
Born: Christian Edward Dailly, Dundee, 23 October 1973
Height: 6ft 0in
Weight: 12st 0lb
Clubs: Dundee United; Derby County; Blackburn Rovers; West Ham United
Scotland caps: 64
Scotland goals: 6
1997 v Wales (lost 0-1), v Malta (won 3-2) 1 goal, v Belarus (won 1-0)
1998 v Belarus (won 4-1), v Latvia (won 2-0), v France (lost 1-2), v Denmark (lost 0-1), v Finland (drew 1-1), v Colombia (drew 2-2), v United States (drew 0-0), v Brazil (lost 1-2), v Norway (drew 1-1), v Morocco (lost 0-3)
1999 v Lithuania (drew 0-0)
2000 v Bosnia (won 2-1), v Estonia (drew 0-0), v Bosnia (won 1-0), v Lithuania (won 3-0), v England (lost 0-2), v England (won 1-0), v France (lost 0-2), v Holland (drew 0-0), v Republic of Ireland (won 2-1)
2001 v Latvia (won 1-0), v San Marino (won 2-0), v Australia (lost 0-2), v Poland (drew 1-1)
2002 v Croatia (drew 0-0), v Belgium (lost 0-2), v Latvia (won 2-1), v France (lost 0-5), v Nigeria (lost 1-2) 1 goal, v South Korea (lost 1-4), v South Africa (lost 0-2), v Hong Kong (won 4-0) 1 goal
2003 v Denmark (lost 0-1), v Faroe Islands (drew 2-2), v Iceland (won 2-0) 1 goal, v Canada (won 3-1), v Portugal (lost 0-2), v Republic of Ireland (lost 0-2), v Iceland (won 2-1), v Lithuania (lost 0-1), v Austria (lost 0-2), v New Zealand (drew 1-1), v Germany (drew 1-1)
2004 v Norway (drew 0-0), v Germany (lost 1-2), v Lithuania (won 1-0), v Holland (won 1-0), v Wales (lost 0-4), v Romania (lost 1-2), v Denmark (lost 0-1)
2005 v Moldova (won 2-0) 1 goal, v Belarus (drew 0-0)
2006 v Austria (drew 2-2), v Italy (drew 1-1), v Belarus (lost 0-1), v Slovenia (won 3-0),

Christian Dailly has been a regular in the Scotland side for the last few seasons, playing in all the group games in the 1998 World Cup Finals as well as skippering the team on a number of occasions; he scored a vital goal in the Euro 2004 qualifier in Iceland.

The holder of the record number of Scottish Under-21 caps with 34, Christian Dailly began his career with his home-town team Dundee United, playing in 173 League and Cup games for the Tannadice club. He moved from a central attacking position through midfield and into central defence, starring in the 1-0 1994 Scottish Cup Final win over Rangers. After helping the Terrors finish the 1995-96 season as runners-up in the First Division, it looked as if he would be moving to play on the continent. But this fell through and he joined Derby County for £1 million.

Though he began his Rams' career playing in a defensive midfield role, he was soon switched to the back following an injury to Igor Stimac. Dailly spent two seasons playing for Derby County before, in the summer of 1998, Blackburn Rovers paid £5.3 million for his services.

A player in the mould of the top Europeans, he struggled in his early days at Ewood Park as he was played out of position at right-back. It was only after being switched to play alongside Craig Short at the heart of the Rovers' defence that he became the linchpin of the club's back four. Sadly, this didn't last, and

Christian Dailly (www.snspix.com)

it came as no surprise when he left Ewood Park in January 2001, joining West Ham United for £1.75 million.

He played brilliantly in the FA Cup victories at Manchester United and Sunderland, but then suffered a broken foot in the quarter-final against Spurs. He was restored to full fitness in 2001-02, and was the Hammers' only ever-present as his partnership with Tomas Repka flourished at the heart of the West ham defence. However, due to the constant changes in the West Ham back line the following season, Dailly only appeared in just half of the club's Premiership games as they lost their top flight status. Appointed the club's captain, he led them to the play-offs in 2003-04 and then again the following season, when he was beset with knee ligament problems. Now with the Hammers back in the Premiership, Dailly remains an important member of the Scotland squad and has appeared in 63 internationals.

SIMON DONNELLY
Forward

Born: Simon Thomas Donnelly, Glasgow, 1 December 1974
Height: 5ft 9in
Weight: 11st 0lb
Clubs: Glasgow Celtic; Sheffield Wednesday; St Johnstone; Dunfermline Athletic; Partick Thistle
Scotland caps: 10
1997 v Wales (lost 0-1), v Malta (won 3-2)
1998 v Latvia (won 2-0), v France (lost 1-2), v Denmark (lost 0-1), v Finland (drew 1-1),
     v Colombia (drew 2-2), v United States (drew 0-0)
1999 v Estonia (won 3-2), v Faroe Islands (won 2-1)

Striker Simon Donnelly's first nine appearances for his country involved him coming off the bench, and it was only on his last appearance against the Faroe Islands in October 1998 that he started the game.

The son of Tom Donnelly, who played for Rangers and Motherwell, he made his Celtic debut as a substitute in the goalless draw at Hibernian in March 1994. He was an integral member of the Celtic side for the next four seasons, and during that time he helped the Parkhead club win the Scottish Cup in 1995, when they beat Airdrie 1-0 in the final, and the 1997-98 Premier Division title when they pipped Rangers by two points. It was his best campaign for the Bhoys as he netted 10 goals from 21 starts, forming a formidable strike force with Henrik Larsson. Donnelly had scored 42 goals in 196 first team outings for Celtic when, in the summer of 1999, he joined Sheffield Wednesday along with Celtic colleague Phil O'Donnell.

Although he made the starting line-up for the opening game of the 1999-2000 season against Liverpool, he had a very frustrating campaign thanks to a string of injury problems. He then missed almost all of the following season with persistent hamstring trouble, though he did return for the last couple of games when he scored a cracking winner in the Yorkshire derby against Barnsley. Injury once again blighted Donnelly's Hillsborough career in season's 2001-02 and 2002-03, and though he then played as a schemer rather than a striker, he only appeared in 62 games in four seasons with the Owls.

On leaving the Yorkshire club, he returned to Scotland and in 2003-04, scored 11 goals in 43 games for St Johnstone before signing for Dunfermline Athletic. One of those goals knocked the Pars out of the CIS Insurance Cup! After an impressive first season at East End Park, Donnelly remained an important member of the Pars' squad, until he joined Partick Thistle prior to the start of the 2006-07 season.

BRIAN McALLISTER

Central defender

Born: Brian McAllister, Glasgow, 30 November 1970
Height: 5ft 11in
Weight: 12st 5lb
Clubs: Wimbledon; Plymouth Argyle; Crewe Alexandra
Scotland caps: 3
1997 v Wales (lost 0-1), v Malta (won 3-2), v Belarus (won 1-0)

Shortly after making his Football League debut for Wimbledon, Brian McAllister was loaned out to Plymouth Argyle for a short spell. He broke into the Wimbledon side during the 1992-93 season, replacing Gary Elkins at left-back, but sendings-off at Crystal Palace and Tottenham Hotspur brought him a suspension that forced him to miss much of the latter half of the campaign.

In fact, McAllister like so many others at Wimbledon, found it difficult to break into the first team during the next few seasons, and in March 1996 he spent a three-month loan period at Crewe Alexandra. In 1996-97, the versatile and reliable defender, who started the season as a first team regular, suffered a bad leg injury and lost out to Chris Perry and Dean Blackwell, who formed a good solid partnership at the heart of the Dons' defence. Despite this, McAllister, who started his Wimbledon career when they were at Plough Lane, won the first of three Scottish caps when he was selected to play against Wales.

Sadly, injuries hampered his progress the following season, though when he did turn out, he never let the side down. Known amongst the Dons fans as the 'Scottish Womble', McAllister held the ball up well and was strong in the air, especially when dealing with the top strikers. Also possessing a good left foot, he was more than capable of hitting wonderful long passes behind the opposing full-backs.

The Achilles heel injury he suffered during the 1997-98 season kept recurring, and in the summer of 2000, McAllister, who had appeared in only 104 games during a decade with the club, was forced to hang up his boots.

NEIL SULLIVAN

Goalkeeper

Born: Neil Sullivan, Sutton, 24 February 1970
Height: 6ft 0in
Weight: 12st 11lb

Clubs: Wimbledon; Crystal Palace; Tottenham Hotspur; Chelsea; Leeds United
Scotland caps: 28
1997 v Wales (lost 0-1)
1998 v France (lost 1-2), v Colombia (drew 2-2)
1999 v Faroe Islands (won 2-1), v Czech Republic (lost 1-2), v Germany (won 1-0),
v Faroe Islands (drew 1-1), v Czech Republic (lost 2-3)
2000 v Bosnia (won 2-1), v Estonia (drew 0-0), v Bosnia (won 1-0), v England (lost 0-2),
v England (won 1-0), v France (lost 0-2), v Holland (drew 0-0), v Republic of Ireland
(won 2-1)
2001 v Latvia (won 1-0), v San Marino (won 2-0), v Croatia (drew 1-1), v Belgium (drew 2-2),
v San Marino (won 4-0), v Poland (drew 1-1)
2002 v Croatia (drew 0-0), v Belgium (Lost 0-2), v Latvia (won 2-1), v France (lost 0-5),
v South Korea (Lost 1-4)
2003 v Republic of Ireland (lost 0-2)

Neil Sullivan

Despite playing twice for Scotland in 1997-98, Sullivan was out of luck in the World Cup Finals in France and could only sit and watch as Jim Leighton saw out all three games. He later gained a lot of personal satisfaction from his clean sheet in Scotland's 1-0 victory over Germany, and gave two good performances against England in the European Championship qualification play-off matches.

Beginning his career with Wimbledon, he found his appearances limited in his early days with the club due to the wonderfully consistent Hans Segers missing just one game in three years. Sullivan continued to wait patiently in the wings, making his second appearance for the Dons exactly a year after his debut. He then joined Crystal Palace on loan before returning to Wimbledon as Seger's understudy for a further couple of seasons. Replacing the Dutchman for the final few games of the 1994-95 season, he had the misfortune to be carried off with a broken leg following a collision with Nottingham Forest's Jason Lee.

On regaining full fitness, he returned to first team action midway through the 1995-96 season, proving himself to be one of the Premiership's top keepers. Confounding his critics with a call-up to the Scotland side, he gave some wonderful displays for the Dons over the next few seasons—including a superb save in an FA Cup victory over Manchester United, and saving a Michael Owen penalty. A good organiser of the defence, his inspirational form was observed by some of the bigger clubs, and in June 2000, after making 224 appearances for Wimbledon, he joined Tottenham Hotspur.

He had an outstanding first two seasons at White Hart Lane, although he suffered a bad injury and lost his place to Kasey Keller. He then moved to Chelsea as understudy to Carlo Cudicini, and 21 months after his last game for Spurs, he made his Chelsea debut in a Carling Cup match against Reading.

He joined Leeds United in the summer of 2004, and the following season in which he saved four penalties, and was voted the Yorkshire club's Player of the Year, he was the only player at Elland Road to appear in every competitive game. Many Leeds fans thought he was worthy of an international recall, but the nearest he came to it was a workout with the Scottish training camp ahead of the game against Italy in March 2005.

DAVIE WEIR
Central defender

Born: David Gillespie Weir, Falkirk, 10 May 1970
Height: 6ft 2in
Weight: 13st 7lb
Clubs: Falkirk; Heart of Midlothian; Everton
Scotland caps: 52
Scotland goals: 1

1997 v Wales (lost 0-1), v Malta (won 3-2)

1998 v France (lost 1-2), v Denmark (lost 0-1), v Finland (drew 1-1), v Norway (drew 1-1), v Morocco (lost 0-3)

1999 v Estonia (won 3-2), v Faroe Islands (won 2-1), v Czech Republic (lost 1-2), v Germany (won 1-0), v Faroe Islands (drew 1-1), v Czech Republic (lost 2-3)

2000 v Bosnia (won 2-1), v Estonia (drew 0-0), v Bosnia (won 1-0), v Lithuania (won 3-0), v England (lost 0-2), v England (won 1-0), v Holland (drew 0-0)

2001 v Latvia (won 1-0), v San Marino (won 2-0), v Croatia (drew 1-1), v Australia (lost 0-2), v Belgium (drew 2-2), v San Marino (won 4-0), v Poland (drew 1-1)

2002 v Croatia (drew 0-0), v Belgium (lost 0-2), v Latvia (won 2-1) 1 goal, v France (lost 0-5), v Nigeria (lost 1-2), v South Korea (lost 1-4), v South Africa (lost 0-2), v Hong Kong (won 4-0)

2003 v Denmark (lost 0-1), v Faroe Islands (drew 2-2)

2005 v Italy (lost 0-2), v Moldova (won 2-0), v Belarus (drew 0-0)

2006 v Italy (drew 1-1), v Norway (won 2-1), v Belarus (lost 0-1), v Slovenia (won 3-0), v United States (drew 1-1), v Switzerland (lost 1-3), v Bulgaria (won 5-1), v Japan (drew 0-0), v Faroe Islands (won 6-0), v Lithuania (won 2-1), v France (won 1-0), v Ukraine (lost 0-2)

First capped in 1997, Davie Weir has gone from strength to strength, winning 46 caps for Scotland, including playing in the 1998 World Cup Finals in France.

He played his early football for Celtic Boys Club before accepting a soccer scholarship in the United Stares at the University of Indiana. When he returned home, he joined Falkirk in August 1992 and had four great seasons with his home-town club, helping the Bairns to win the First Division Championship in 1993-94 and also the League Challenge Cup.

In July 1996, Hearts secured his quality and consistency when paying £300,000 for his services, and shortly after his arrival at Tynecastle, he scored in the League Cup Final as Hearts lost 4-3 to Rangers. The Ibrox giants were again Hearts' opponents in the 1998 Cup Final, but with Weir outstanding at the heart of the Tynecastle club's defence, they gained revenge with a 2-1 win. A composed and classy defender, he led Hearts into Europe before, in February 1999, he joined Everton for a fee of £250,000.

On his arrival on Merseyside, he used his skills to good effect in the Blues' successful fight against relegation from the Premiership. In 1999-2000, Weir had an outstanding season, though his quiet and reserved demeanour meant that he did not receive the headlines his play deserved at times. Boasting an astonishing level of consistency, a rib injury kept him out of action for two games towards the end of the season, the first time he had missed two successive matches through injury in the last seven years! Following the continued absence of Richard Gough through injury, Weir was made captain, and in 2001-02 he was named Everton's Player of the Season. He was even linked with a summer move to Manchester United, such was his consistency. Injuries, though, did catch up with him in 2003-04, though the following season he won a recall to the national team under new manager Walter Smith, and since has continued to feature on a regular basis for both Everton and Scotland.

DAVID HOPKIN
Midfield

Born: David Hopkin, Greenock, 21 August 1970
Height: 5ft 1in
Weight: 11st 0lb
Clubs: Port Glasgow Rangers; Morton; Chelsea; Crystal Palace; Leeds United; Bradford City; Crystal Palace; Morton
Scotland caps: 7
Scotland goals: 2
1997 v Malta (won 3-2), v Belarus (won 1-0)
1998 v Belarus (won 4-1) 2 goals, v France (lost 1-2)
1999 v Czech Republic (lost 1-2)
2000 v Bosnia (won 2-1), v Bosnia (won 1-0)

Despite coming on as a substitute and scoring twice in a 4-1 win over Belarus, David Hopkin, who was a regular member of Craig Brown's squad, was not included among the final 22 when the Scotland manager named his squad for France '98.

David Hopkin began his career with his home-town club Morton, and spent three seasons at Cappielow Park after joining them from local junior side Port Glasgow Rangers. Signed by Chelsea for a fee of £300,000 in September 1992, his appearances from the bench outweighed his starts during his first couple of seasons at Stamford Bridge, and in the summer of 1995 he moved to Crystal Palace for £850,000.

He soon proved to be a big hit with the Palace fans, playing in all but one game in the 1995-96 season and scoring 12 goals. Hard-running and direct, and a good tackler, he was a member of the Palace squad that disappointingly lost out in the Wembley play-off final. The following season he scored 17 goals and put himself in line for a call up to the Scottish squad and, at the same time, powered Palace into the Premiership via the play-off victory over Sheffield United at Wembley—his wonderfully curled 25-yarder in the closing minutes winning it for the Londoners.

Arguably the best midfielder in the Nationwide League, Hopkin left Selhurst Park during the close season, signing for Leeds United who paid £3.25 million for him. George Graham made him club captain, but thereafter he failed to live up to expectations due to a variety of reasons—injury, illness and family bereavements. Eventually finding his true form, he was surprisingly allowed to leave Elland Road in the summer of 2000, becoming Bradford City's record signing when they paid £2.5 million to take him to Valley Parade.

After suffering damage to his ankle ligaments during the early part of the 2000-01 season, he struggled to win back his place, and the following March rejoined Crystal Palace for a cut price £1.5 million, adding his battling qualities to the Eagles' successful fight against relegation. Finding himself spending long periods in the treatment room, he then rejoined his home-town club Morton, whom he helped win the Third Division Championship.

MATT ELLIOTT
Central defender

Born: Matthew Stephen Elliott, Wandsworth, 1 November 1968
Height: 6ft 3in
Weight: 14st 10lb
Clubs: Epsom and Ewell; Charlton Athletic; Torquay United; Scunthorpe United; Oxford United; Leicester City; Ipswich Town
Scotland caps: 18
Scotland goals: 1

1998 v France (lost 1-2), v Denmark (lost 0-1), v Finland (drew 1-1)
1999 v Lithuania (drew 0-0), v Faroe Islands (won 2-1), v Czech Republic (lost 1-2), v Faroe Islands (drew 1-1)
2000 v Holland (drew 0-0), v Republic of Ireland (won 2-1)
2001 v Latvia (won 1-0), v San Marino (won 2-0) 1 goal, v Croatia (drew 1-1), v Australia (lost 0-2), v Belgium (drew 2-2), v San Marino (won 4-0)
2002 v Croatia (drew 0-0), v Belgium (lost 0-2), v Latvia (won 2-1)

Called up for Scotland, through his grandmother's nationality, a selection that saw him eventually form a formidable partnership with Colin Hendry, he was selected in the final 22 for the World Cup Finals in France. Despite being on the bench throughout Scotland's three games in Group A, he did not come on to the field of play and could only watch as the side were eliminated at the earliest stage.

A commanding centre-back, he appeared in just one game for Charlton

Athletic, before playing lower league football for Torquay United, Scunthorpe United and Oxford United. It was while at the Manor Ground, where he was appointed club captain, that he began to dominate in the air and prove his worth at set pieces. He helped Oxford win promotion to the First Division in 1995-96, when he was also voted the club's Player of the Year. Having scored 24 goals in 175 League and Cup games for Oxford, he became Leicester City's record signing when he joined the Foxes in January 1997 for a fee of £1.6 million.

In his first full campaign at Filbert Street, Elliott acted as club captain when Steve Walsh was out injured and he scored a number of vital goals. Over the next couple of seasons, he was always solid and formidable at the back, adding spot-kick responsibility to his duties—he was also employed as an emergency striker at various points of the campaigns. In 1999-2000, Matt Elliott's coolly placed header against Aston Villa sent Leicester to Wembley for the seventh time in nine seasons. Leading the Foxes out beneath the Twin Towers, he headed a goal in each half against Tranmere Rovers to secure the Worthington Cup for his team and the Man-of-the-Match trophy for himself. The following season the goals seemed to dry up at club level, but he actually notched his first international goal against San Marino in October 2000, and also managed to hit the woodwork in the return fixture at Hampden in March 2001. A red card in the match against West Ham United the following season seemed to knock his confidence, and he was eventually omitted from Berti Vogts' younger-looking international squad.

He was back to his best in 2002-03, leading the Foxes to promotion to the Premiership as his wealth of experience clearly made up for any lack of pace, and his astute reading of the game led to masterly defensive performances throughout the campaign. After a loan spell with Ipswich Town as they pushed for promotion play-off spot, Elliott returned to the Walker Stadium, but having played in 290 games for Leicester, injury brought an end to his distinguished playing career.

CALLUM DAVIDSON
Full-back/Wing-back

Born: Callum Iain Davidson, Stirling, 25 June 1976
Height: 5ft 10in
Weight: 11st 8lb
Clubs: St Johnstone; Blackburn Rovers; Leicester City; Preston North End
Scotland caps: 17
1999 v Lithuania (drew 0-0), v Estonia (won 3-2), v Faroe Islands (won 2-1),
  v Czech Republic (lost 1-2), v Germany (won 1-0), v Faroe Islands (drew 1-1),
  v Czech Republic (lost 2-3)
2000 v Estonia (drew 0-0), v Bosnia (won 1-0), v Lithuania (won 3-0), v England (won 1-0),
  v France (lost 0-2)
2001 v Latvia (won 1-0), v Poland (drew 1-1)
2002 v Latvia (won 2-1)
2003 v Iceland (won 2-0), v Canada (won 3-1)

Callum Davidson began his career with St Johnstone, where his displays led to a number of top clubs north and south of the border showing an interest in his future.

Signed by Blackburn Rovers for a fee of £1.75 million in February 1998, he arrived at Ewood Park with hamstring trouble, then developed a septic toe; and when given his Football League debut against Arsenal after eight weeks, promptly pulled a muscle after an hour and didn't play again for the rest of the season!

In 1998-99 his quick tackling, enthusiastic forward running and fine positional covering saw him drafted into the Scottish team, but it was while representing the national team that he became a victim of foul play, forcing him to miss games for Blackburn because of recurring headaches. After that his form at club level never matched his form for Scotland, especially in the 1-0 win over England at Wembley, and Rovers' fans never saw him play to his true potential.

In July 2002, Davidson joined Leicester City for £1.7 million, replacing Steve Guppy as left wing-back. His presence provided the Foxes' defence with a more solid look, before intermittent injury problems kept him out of contention for a place at both club and international level. Though he was back in the side in 2001-02, he failed to live up to his reputation, perhaps his best outing coming when he was asked to operate in an unfamiliar central midfield role!

Davidson made the headlines in the summer of 2002 when suffering a broken jaw in a much publicised incident, but received a hero's welcome when returning to first team action with the Foxes. Moved into midfield on a permanent basis, he was a revelation, adding extra impetus to the Leicester promotion drive despite being dogged by a troublesome groin injury throughout the campaign. This form prompted Berti Vogts to recall him to the national squad. Injuries then hampered his form, and after 114 appearances he moved to Preston North End.

Though he is an important member of the Deepdale club's side, his catalogue of injuries since returning to the north-west would have taxed the staunchest of resolves.

BARRY FERGUSON
Midfield

Born: Barry Ferguson, Glasgow, 2 February 1978
Height: 5ft 11in
Weight: 11st 7lb
Clubs: Glasgow Rangers; Blackburn Rovers; Glasgow Rangers
Scotland caps: 34
Scotland goals: 2

1999 v Lithuania (drew 0-0)
2000 v Bosnia (won 2-1), v Estonia (drew 0-0), v England (lost 0-2), v England (won 1-0), v France (lost 0-2), v Republic of Ireland (won 2-1) 1 goal
2001 v Latvia (won 1-0), v Australia (lost 0-2), v Belgium (drew 2-2)
2003 v Denmark (lost 0-1), v Faroe Islands (drew 2-2) 1 goal, v Iceland (won 2-0), v Republic of Ireland (lost 0-2), v Iceland (won 2-1)

2004 v Norway (drew 0-0), v Faroe Islands (won 3-1), v Germany (lost 1-2),
v Lithuania (won 1-0), v Holland (won 1-0), v Holland (lost 0-6)

2005 v Hungary (lost 0-3), v Spain (drew 1-1), v Slovenia (drew 0-0), v Norway (lost 0-1),
v Moldova (drew 1-1), v Italy (lost 0-2), v Moldova (won 2-0), v Belarus (drew 0-0)

2006 v Italy (drew 1-1), v Norway (won 2-1), v Belarus (lost 0-1), v Switzerland (lost 1-3),
v France (won 1-0), v Ukraine (lost 0-2)

When Rangers completed the treble in 2002–03, skipper Barry Ferguson played through a painful pelvic problem and at times dragged his team-mates through games they could well have lost or drawn. Though he has always had undoubted ability, he added goals to his armoury during that campaign, and the 18 he provided—including eight from the penalty-spot—were critical to the team's success. Ferguson deservedly won the Players and Football Writers' Player of the Year awards.

Barry Ferguson (www.snspix.com)

Ferguson made his Rangers debut as a substitute for Gattuso in a 1-0 win over Hibs in December 1997, and went on to be a first team regular for the next five seasons. During that time he helped Rangers win two Premier League titles, three Scottish Cups and two League Cups. Having scored 24 goals in 149 Scottish Premier League games, he left Ibrox in August 2003 to sign for Graeme Souness' Blackburn Rovers for a reported fee of £7.5 million.

Ferguson, who made his international debut against Lithuania in a European Championship qualifier in October 1998 and has been a regular ever since, has now represented the national side on 32 occasions.

After making his Rovers debut in a 3-1 home defeat at the hands of Liverpool, the Anfield club were also Blackburn's opponents when Ferguson netted his first goal for the Lancashire side, but the Reds won that League Cup tie 4-3. He was a regular in the Blackburn side, but shortly after netting his first Premiership goal against Birmingham City in a 4-0 win at St Andrew's, he suffered a broken knee cap and was forced to miss the rest of the season. Souness appointed him club captain, but the appointment of new manager Mark Hughes made him reconsider his future.

With only an hour left in the transfer window, a £4.5 million deal was struck and Ferguson left Ewood Park to move back to Rangers. His return to Ibrox was a good move. Once back he helped his team to a 7-1 League Cup drubbing of Dundee United. Continuing to captain Scotland, he also assisted the Ibrox club to a surprise last-gasp success in winning the SPL title, but then he suffered an injury which kept him out of the game for over six months. His return to the national side in October 2006 was in the famous victory over France at Hampden in the qualifier for the 2008 European Championship.

NEIL McCANN
Forward

Born: Neil McCann, Greenock, 11 August 1974
Height: 5ft 9in
Weight: 11st 4lb
Clubs: Dundee; Heart of Midlothian; Glasgow Rangers; Southampton; Heart of Midlothian
Scotland caps: 26
Scotland goals: 3
1999   v Lithuania (drew 0-0), v Czech Republic (lost 2-3)
2000   v Bosnia (won 2-1), v Estonia (drew 0-0), v England (won 1-0), v France (lost 0-2), v Holland (drew 0-0), v Republic of Ireland (won 2-1)
2001   v Latvia (won 1-0) 1 goal, v San Marino (won 2-0), v Australia (lost 0-2)
2002   v Croatia (drew 0-0), v Latvia (won 2-1), v France (lost 0-5), v Nigeria (lost 1-2)
2003   v Republic of Ireland (lost 0-2)
2004   v Faroe Islands (won 3-1) 1 goal, v Germany (lost 1-2) 1 goal, v Holland (won 1-0), v Holland (lost 0-6), v Romania (lost 1-2), v Denmark (lost 0-1)
2005   v Italy (lost 0-2)
2006   v Italy (drew 1-1), v Norway (won 2-1), v United States (drew 1-1)

Greenock-born forward Neil McCann, who has won 26 caps for Scotland since making his international debut as a substitute for Ally McCoist in a goalless draw against Lithuania in October 1998, began his career with Dundee. Unable to make the grade with the Dens Park club, he joined Hearts in the summer of 1996 and soon established himself with the Tynecastle club.

He ended his first season with an appearance in the League Cup Final, but Hearts lost 4-3 to Rangers in a seven-goal thriller. The following season, McCann had his best-ever campaign in terms of goals scored, netting 10 in 35 games and helping Hearts win the Scottish Cup Final, beating Rangers 2-1. In fact, he had impressed the Ibrox club's management team so much that in December 1998 they paid £2 million for his services.

McCann was to spend four and a half seasons with Rangers, helping them win three League Championships, four Scottish Cups and three League Cups. In the only season Rangers failed to lift the title, 2001-02, McCann netted his only hat-trick for the club in a 5-0 defeat of Kilmarnock. Although almost half of his 138 first team appearances were as a substitute, McCann was an important member of the Rangers squad, and it came as a great surprise when Alex McLeish allowed him to join Southampton in a £1.5 million deal.

The positive aspect of his move to the south coast club was that it brought an instant recall to the Scotland side, for whom he scored in a 3-1 win over the Faroe Islands—the negative aspect was that he failed to impress the St Mary's regulars. The unsettled managerial situation at the club didn't help, and more than half of his appearances, as at Ibrox, have come off the bench. McCann later returned north of the border for a second spell with Hearts.

ALLAN JOHNSTON
Winger

Born: Allan Johnston, Glasgow, 14 December 1973
Height: 5ft 9in
Weight: 11st 0lb
Clubs: Tynecastle BC; Heart of Midlothian; Rennes (France); Sunderland; Birmingham City; Bolton Wanderers; Glasgow Rangers; Middlesbrough; Sheffield Wednesday; Kilmarnock
Scotland caps: 18
Scotland goals: 2
1999 v Estonia (won 3-2), v Faroe Islands (won 2-1), v Czech Republic (lost 1-2),
v Germany (won 1-0), v Faroe Islands (drew 1-1) 1 goal,
v Czech Republic (lost 2-3) 1 goal
2000 v Estonia (drew 0-0), v France (lost 0-2), v Republic of Ireland (won 2-1)
2001 v San Marino (won 2-0), v Croatia (drew 1-1), v San Marino (won 4-0)
2002 v Nigeria (lost 1-2), v South Korea (lost 1-4), v South Africa (lost 0-2),
v Hong Kong (won 4-0), v Denmark (lost 0-1), v Faroe Islands (drew 2-2)

After beginning his career with Hearts, Johnston's early performances earned him selection for the Scotland Under-21 side, and though almost half of his total appearances for the Tynecastle club were as a substitute, he did enough to persuade French club Rennes to sign him in the summer of 1996.

His stay on the continent was brief, and in March 1997, 'Magic' joined Sunderland for a fee of £550,000. Impressing the Black Cats fans with his wing play, he also operated in midfield, and his first goal for the club against Everton will go down in Roker folklore, as the last at the famous old ground. Unable to prevent the Wearsiders' relegation, he was one of the club's key players in their promotion push the following season. He netted a hat-trick at Huddersfield and won selection for Scotland at 'B' level. In 1998-99 he helped Sunderland win the First Division Championship and won the first of 18 full caps against Estonia. Not surprisingly he won selection for the PFA First Division award-winning side.

Offered a new contract, he refused to sign, and so manager Peter Reid excluded him from his future plans. He went on loan to Birmingham City and later Bolton Wanderers, helping the Lancashire club reach the First Division play-offs. In the close season he joined Rangers, but failed to establish himself in the Ibrox side. Just a little over a year later he returned south of the border to sign for Middlesbrough for a fee of £1 million.

After some good early performances for the Riverside club, he found himself restricted to just Worthington Cup appearances in 2002-03. He eventually went out on loan to Sheffield Wednesday in search of first team football, but after breaking a toe in a training collision, he returned to the Riverside to recuperate.

Johnston joined Kilmarnock prior to the start of the 2004-05 season, and since arriving at Rugby Park has been a regular in the Killie side.

STEPHEN GLASS
Midfield
Born: Stephen Glass, Dundee, 23 May 1976
Height: 5ft 9in
Weight: 11st 0lb
Clubs: Crombie Sports; Aberdeen; Newcastle United; Watford
     Hibernian
Scotland caps: 1
1999 v Faroe Islands (won 2-1)

Stephen Glass began his career with Aberdeen, helping the Dons beat Dundee 2-0 in the 1996 Scottish League Cup Final. A regular first teamer at Pittodrie for three-and-a-half seasons, the nimble winger, who supplements a high work-rate with the ability to control the ball at speed, appeared in 128 games for the Dons before, in the summer of 1998, Newcastle United paid £650,000 for his services.

After making his Football League debut as a substitute against Liverpool, his subsequent performances earned him a regular place in the Magpies' side. Providing the service sought by Alan Shearer, his all-round game blossomed as the 1998-99 season progressed. After suffering a bad knee injury at Coventry in February 1999, he underwent an operation that was thought would end his season. But he came back towards the end of the campaign and made an appearance as a substitute in that season's FA Cup Final.

Earlier chosen as a substitute for Scotland against Estonia, though he did not play, he made his full debut, from the bench, against the Faroe Islands in October 1998 at his former ground of Pittodrie.

In 1999-2000, the knee injury flared up again and he was restricted to just a handful of substitute appearances. Disappointed at not being able to hold down a regular first team place, he asked for a transfer. Though he later came off the list, resolved to fight for his place in the Magpies' first team, he was used mostly as a squad player, and in the summer of 2001, he joined Watford on a free transfer.

Though an injury delayed his debut for the Hornets, this archetypal left-winger, with fine ball-playing skills and an accurate cross, had an outstanding second season at Vicarage Road when he also turned out at left-back. Ironically, after scoring Watford's 'Goal of the Season' in the FA Cup quarter-final against Burnley, he was told he would be released at the end of the season—a victim of the club's needs to cut costs.

He joined Hibernian, and though he appeared regularly in the first-half of the 2003-04 season, he then lost his place. He was a virtual ever-present the following season, helping the Easter Road club to third place in the Scottish Premier Division, and since then he has continued to be an important member of the Hibs' side.

DON HUTCHISON
Midfield

Born: Donald Hutchison, Gateshead, 9 May 1971
Height: 6ft 1in
Weight: 11st 8lb
Clubs: Hartlepool United; Liverpool; West Ham United; Sheffield United; Everton; Sunderland; West Ham United; Millwall; Coventry City
Scotland caps: 26
Scotland goals: 6

1999 v Czech Republic (lost 1-2), v Germany (won 1-0) 1 goal
2000 v Bosnia (won 2-1) 1 goal, v Estonia (drew 0-0), v Lithuania (won 3-0) 1 goal, v England (lost 0-2), v England (won 1-0) 1 goal, v France (lost 0-2), v Holland (drew 0-0), v Republic of Ireland (won 2-1) 1 goal
2001 v Latvia (won 1-0), v San Marino (won 2-0) 1 goal, v Croatia (drew 1-1), v Australia (lost 0-2), v Belgium (drew 2-2), v San Marino (won 4-0)
2002 v Croatia (drew 0-0), v Belgium (lost 0-2), v Latvia (won 2-1)
2003 v Republic of Ireland (lost 0-2), v Iceland (won 2-1), v Lithuania (lost 0-1), v Austria (lost 0-2)
2004 v Norway (drew 0-0), v Lithuania (won 1-0), v Holland (won 1-0)

Don Hutchison celebrated his first full international start with the winning goal against the European Champions, Germany, on German soil! He also scored the winner in the second leg of the Euro 2000 play-off against England at Wembley.

He turned professional with Hartlepool United, but seven months later the north-east club, desperate for cash, sold him to Liverpool for £175,000, after videos showing his abilities had been sent to all the leading clubs. A regular member of the first team squad at Anfield, he went on to appear in 56 League and Cup games, before, in August 1994, he joined West Ham United for £1.5 million.

Survival in the Premiership in 1994-95 was only secured after an excellent 3-0 win over Liverpool, with former Red Hutchison scoring twice. However, following the arrival of Iain Dowie, Hutchison was rarely selected, and in January 1996, he was transferred to Sheffield United for £1.2 million, becoming the Blades' record signing. He had played in 91 games for the Yorkshire club when Everton signed him for £1 million in February 1998.

He had his best Premiership season at Goodison and was voted 'Player of the Year' by the club's supporters. He was also recognised in the game, as manager Walter Smith named him first team captain and Craig Brown rewarded him with a call-up to the Scotland squad for the match against the Czech Republic. He continued to shine for Everton in 1999-2000, but contract talks broke down towards the end of the campaign with such bitterness that he was stripped of the captaincy and placed on the transfer list. In the summer of 2000, he became one of Peter Reid's 'steals' when he joined Sunderland for £2.5 million.

Although he took a little time to settle, he soon came into his own, and his superb contribution to Sunderland's campaign was recognised when he was voted the Supporters Association's 'Player of the Year'. Amazingly, the right-sided midfielder was allowed to leave the Stadium of Light early the following season, rejoining West Ham United for a fee of £5 million.

He soon settled back into life at Upton Park, but then had the misfortune to suffer a torn cruciate ligament against Middlesbrough in February 2002, and this ruled him out for the rest of the season. On his return to fitness he continued to represent Scotland, winning caps against the Republic of Ireland, Lithuania and Austria, but was unable to regain a place in the Hammers' starting line-up. Though he was dogged by injuries, he helped West Ham reach the play-offs in 2003-04. Persistent knee problems flared up during the club's promotion-winning season of 2004-05, and after appearing in 110 games in his two spells with the club, he joined Millwall prior to a move to Coventry City on loan. Hutchison scored on his debut, and in doing so helped City halt a run of four successive defeats.

COLIN CAMERON
Midfield

Born: Colin Cameron, Kirkcaldy, 23 October 1972
Height: 5ft 6in
Weight: 10st 6lb
Clubs: Lochore Welfare; Raith Rovers; Heart of Midlothian; Wolverhampton Wanderers; Millwall (loan); Coventry City
Scotland caps: 28
Scotland goals: 1

1999 v Germany (won 1-0), v Faroe Islands (drew 1-1)

2000 v Lithuania (won 3-0) 1 goal, v France (lost 0-2), v Republic of Ireland (won 2-1)

2001 v Latvia (won 1-0), v San Marino (won 2-0), v Croatia (drew 1-1), v Australia (lost 0-2), v San Marino (won 4-0), v Poland (drew 1-1)

2002 v Croatia (drew 0-0), v Belgium (lost 0-2), v Latvia (won 2-1), v France (lost 0-5)

2003 v Republic of Ireland (lost 0-2), v Lithuania (lost 0-1), v Austria (lost 0-2), v Germany (drew 1-1)

2004 v Norway (drew 0-0), v Faroe Islands (won 3-1), v Germany (lost 1-2), v Lithuania (won 1-0), v Wales (lost 0-4), v Romania (lost 1-2), v Denmark (lost 0-1)

2005 v Spain (drew 1-1), v Moldova (drew 1-1)

Colin Cameron started his career at Raith Rovers, and after being farmed out to Sligo Rovers to complete his apprenticeship, he returned to Jimmy Nicholl's side to win two First Division title in 1992-93 and 1994-95—sandwiched in between was a notable League Cup Final win after a thrilling penalty shoot-out with Celtic. While with Raith, Cameron, an industrious and intelligent midfield player, earned rave reviews, and there was genuine interest from Aberdeen before Jim Jefferies moved swiftly to take him to Hearts in 1996. The £400,000 deal saw John Millar move to Raith in part exchange.

After helping Hearts beat Rangers 2-0, he returned to Stark's Park to help his new club beat Raith 3-1. Bizarrely, he collected a trophy that day, having been voted Raith's 'Player of the Year'! After missing the Cup Final against Rangers because he was cup-tied, he appeared in the League Cup Final in 1997, but Hearts lost narrowly 4-3 to Rangers. That season he had the distinction of being the only Scottish Premier League player to appear in every match for his club. In 1998 he scored from the penalty-spot after 90 seconds of the Cup Final against Rangers, as the Tynecastle club went on to win 2-1 to collect their first silverware for 36 years. Despite missing most of the 1998-99 season through injury, he was called up to make his full international debut against Germany. Having scored 61 goals in 197 games for Hearts, Cameron left Tynecastle in August 2001 to sign for Wolverhampton Wanderers for a fee of £1.75 million.

The hard-working midfielder helped to inspire the Molineux club to five successive wins, getting in some telling tackles and interceptions. In 2002-03 he scored twice in the club's first home match against local rivals Walsall, but was injured in his next outing. On his return to fitness he featured regularly, and seemed to cover every blade of grass for the Wolves' cause. As well as helping Wolves win promotion to the Premiership, he won his 19th cap for Scotland when playing in the 1-1 draw with Germany. Injuries hampered his progress in the top flight and he was powerless to stop the club's immediate return to the First Division. Capped 28 times by Scotland, Colin Cameron, following a loan spell with Millwall, left Molineux to join Coventry City.

PAUL RITCHIE

Central defender

Born: Paul Simon Ritchie, Kikrkcaldy, 21 August 1975

Height: 5ft 11in

Weight: 12st 0lb
Clubs: Links United; Heart of Midlothian; Bolton Wanderers; Glasgow Rangers; Manchester City; Portsmouth; Derby County; Walsall; Dundee United
Scotland caps: 7
Scotland goals: 1
1999 v Germany (won 1-0), v Czech Republic (lost 2-3) 1 goal
2000 v Lithuania (won 3-0), v England (lost 0-2), v France (lost 0-2), v Holland (drew 0-0)
2004 v Wales (lost 0-4)

A hugely influential central defender, Paul Ritchie made his mark at international level when he headed a fine goal in a European Championship qualifier against the Czech Republic in Prague in June 1999, going on to win seven caps.

As a schoolboy, he gained a reputation as being a dependable and solid defender, with a first-class attitude to the game that was evident from an early age. Ritchie made his Hearts debut against Celtic in September 1995. Though not the tallest of central defenders, he makes his presence felt in the air, and the timing of his jump ensures that he wins more than his fair share of headers. Ritchie played alongside a number of central defenders in his time at Tynecastle, adapting accordingly. After playing in a 5-1 defeat against Rangers in the 1996 Cup Final, he gave an outstanding display two years later at Celtic Park when Hearts finally managed to get their hands on some silverware with a 2-1 win over the Ibrox club.

Having appeared in 161 games for Hearts, he joined Bolton Wanderers on loan for three months in December 1999, primarily to cover for Mark Fish's absence on international duty. With rumours flying around that he would be signing for Rangers in the summer, he was signed on a short-term contract until the end of the season. He made a crucial contribution to the Wanderers' late run which took them to the play-offs, but the Bolton fans were disappointed when, in the close season, he completed his expected move to Rangers.

After failing to secure a first team place at Ibrox, he returned south of the Border to join Manchester City for a fee of £500,000. His first season at Maine Road saw him hampered by both pelvic and groin injuries. In fact, it was only after a visit to a specialist that he was able to resume training. Even when fit he found himself out of the first team reckoning at City, and had brief loan spells with both Portsmouth and Derby County prior to joining Walsall.

During his time at the Bescot Stadium, he won a recall to the national side for the game against Wales, and was voted the Saddlers' 'Player of the Year'. On leaving Walsall, Ritchie joined Dundee United, but after a good first season at Tannadice, he suffered a catalogue of injuries, and was recently released.

ROBBIE WINTERS
Midfield/ Forward
Born: Robert Winters, East Kilbride, 4 November 1974
Height: 5ft 10in
Weight: 11st 12lb
Clubs: Muirhead Amateurs; Dundee United; Aberdeen; Luton Town; Brann Bergen (Norway)

Robbie Winters, who won his one and only full international cap when he came on as a substitute for Ian Durrant in the memorable 1-0 win over Germany in Bremen in April 1999, began his career with Dundee United.

He was a virtual ever-present in the six seasons he was at Tannadice, and though he was part of the side that suffered relegation from the Scottish Premier Division in 1994–95 after the club had finished bottom, five points adrift of Aberdeen, he was instrumental in them returning to the top flight the following season as runners-up to Dunfermline Athletic. Winters remained with Dundee United until the summer of 1998, when, after scoring 41 goals in 147 games, he was transferred to Aberdeen for a fee of £700,000.

In his first season at Pittodrie, he struck up a good understanding up front with Eoin Jess, his total of 12 league goals including a hat-trick in a 3-1 defeat of Dunfermline Athletic. He netted another treble the following season as the Dons won a remarkable game against Motherwell at Fir Park 6-5. His third hat-trick for Aberdeen came during the early part of the 2000-01 season as the Dons beat Dundee United 5-3. The following season, the only campaign in which he didn't net a hat-trick, he was the club's leading scorer! He had found the net 45 times in 152 first team outings when he left to join Luton Town on a non-contract basis.

He made just one appearance for the Hatters, and after being substituted at half-time, he left soon afterwards and subsequently signed a long-term deal with Norwegian club Brann Bergen, for whom he continues to impress.

2000 and Beyond

After a valiant but unsuccessful attempt to lead Scotland into the 2002 World Cup Finals, Craig Brown decided to call it a day. He had done extremely well, making the most of the limited talent available, and of course it didn't help that some players who might well have made telling contributions in the international side were not even given games in their club teams. The new Scotland manager was former German international Berti Vogts.

Sadly, the national team moved quickly from one disappointment to another, although rays of light did occasionally penetrate the gloom. Things gradually began to improve and we saw teams in which many home-based Scots were selected. At one stage, it looked as if Scotland would qualify automatically for the 2004 European Championship Finals in Portugal, and a draw against Germany at Hampden Park was distinctly encouraging. However, a 2-1 defeat in the return in Germany meant that Scotland finished as runners-up and met Holland in a two-legged play-off. Hopes were high following a 1-0 win over the Dutch at Hampden, but Scotland were completely outplayed in the second leg, crashing to a 6-0 defeat. Vogts resigned his post in November 2004, and the following month the SFA appointed Walter Smith as his successor.

Despite a brief revival of fortunes under the new manager, Scotland's hopes of reaching the 2006 World Cup Finals in Germany were ended after a defeat to Belarus at Hampden Park. Since then, Scotland have started the 2008 Euro Championship with a bang and at the time of writing had won the first three of their qualifying matches, including a wonderful 1-0 victory over France at Hampden.

MARK BURCHILL
Forward

Born: Mark James Burchill, Broxburn, 18 August 1980
Height: 5ft 8in
Weight: 10st 2lb
Clubs: Glasgow Celtic; Birmingham City; Ipswich Town; Portsmouth; Dundee; Wigan Athletic; Sheffield Wednesday; Rotherham United; Heart of Midlothian; Dunfermline Athletic
Scotland caps: 6
2000 v Bosnia (won 1-0), v Lithuania (won 3-0), v England (lost 0-2), v England (won 1-0), v France (lost 0-2), v Holland (drew 0-0)

A member of Celtic's Premier League Championship winning side of 1999-2000, he got off to an explosive start at Parkhead the following term, netting a hat-trick within four minutes in the 7-0 thrashing of Luxembourg's Jeunesse Esch in a UEFA Cup qualifying round tie. However, he failed to win a regular place in Martin O'Neill's team, and was soon on his way to Birmingham City in a loan deal.

Burchill was an effective striker blessed with blinding pace, the ability to kick with either foot and the knack of being in the right place at the right time. He did well at St Andrew's, netting five goals from seven starts and becoming a huge crowd favourite, to the extent that fans raised a petition to pressure the club into signing him permanently. However, the transfer fell through and he joined Ipswich Town on loan for the remainder of the season. Not as successful at Portman Road, he returned to Parkhead once the season had ended.

Towards the end of the 2001 close season, he joined Portsmouth for a fee of £600,000 and scored twice on his debut in a 4-2 defeat of Grimsby Town. He had netted four goals in five matches when a freak training ground accident resulted in damage to a cruciate ligament, and he was sidelined for the remainder of the season. Despite making a full recovery, he seemed to be out of favour at Fratton Park, and at the turn of the year, the striker, who has won six caps for Scotland, returned north of the Border to spend the second-half of the campaign on loan at Dundee.

Returning to the south coast club, he had further spells on loan with Wigan Athletic, Sheffield Wednesday and Rotherham United, before returning to Scotland to sign for Hearts on a permanent basis. He enjoyed better fortunes at Tynecastle, scoring four times from seven starts, but now, having left the Jam Tarts, he is playing for Dunfermline Athletic.

GARY McSWEGAN
Forward

Born: Gary John McSwegan, Glasgow, 24 September 1970
Height: 5ft 8in
Weight: 11st 2lb
Clubs: Glasgow Rangers; Notts County; Dundee United; Heart of Midlothian; Barnsley; Luton Town; Kilmarnock; Ross County; Inverness Caledonian Thistle
Scotland caps: 2
Scotland goals: 1
2000 v Bosnia (won 1-0), v Lithuania (won 3-0) 1 goal

Bustling striker Gary McSwegan, who scored Scotland's third goal in the 3-0 European Championship qualifier against Lithuania on his second appearance for the national side, began his career with Rangers. He received a dreadful blow when, in a reserve game with Celtic, his leg was badly broken by a dreadful tackle from the Celtic goalkeeper Ian Andrews, who was ordered off.

After making a full recovery, he endeared himself to Rangers fans by scoring a memorable Champions League goal against Marseilles, and he also scored the goal at Airdrie which won the League Championship for Rangers in 1992-93. At the end of that season, he left Ibrox to join Notts County for a fee of £400,000.

His early days at Meadow Lane were hampered by hamstring problems, and though he returned to score 26 goals in 80 games (including 17 as substitute) his ability to shoot on sight would have netted him many more had it not been for injuries. After just four games at the beginning of the 1995-96 season, McSwegan was discarded by County manager Colin Murphy, who sold him to Dundee United for £375,000.

In his first season at Tannadice, he scored 17 goals and ultimately helped United back into the Premier League after a season of First Division football. One of the highlights of his stay with Dundee United must have been when he came off the bench to score against his former club Rangers at Ibrox. He went on to score 47 goals for United in 116 games before in October 1998, leaving to join Hearts.

His form at Tynecastle led to him winning two full caps for Scotland as he rediscovered his shooting boots, but then injuries again affected his progress, and after recovering, he spent loan spells south of the border with Barnsley and Luton Town. He then rejoined Hearts before leaving to continue his career with Kilmarnock. After a season at Rugby Park, McSwegan moved on to play for Ross County, but following his release in the summer of 2006, he signed for Inverness Caldeonian Thistle.

JONATHAN GOULD
Goalkeeper
Born: Jonathan Alan Gould, Paddington, 18 July 1968
Height: 6ft 1in
Weight: 13st 7lb
Clubs: Clevedon Town; Halifax Town; West Bromwich Albion; Coventry City; Bradford City; Gillingham; Glasgow Celtic; Preston North End; Hereford United; Bristol City; Hawke's Bay United (New Zealand)
Scotland caps: 2
2000 v Lithuania (won 3-0)
2001 v Australia (lost 0-2)

The son of Bobby Gould, he played his early football for Western League club Clevedon Town prior to signing for Halifax Town in 1990. A long-term back injury to the Yorkshire club's regular keeper David Brown meant that he didn't have to wait too long for his Football League debut in a 5-3 defeat of Blackpool. After later losing his place to Lee Bracey, he was released and signed by his father for West Bromwich Albion, but was not called upon for first team action.

After being dismissed by the Albion, Bobby Gould took over the reins at Coventry City, and one of his first signings was his son to provide cover for Steve Ogrizovic. He made a spectacular debut for the Sky Blues, producing a number of fine saves in a 5-1 defeat of Liverpool. Rumoured to be on the verge of the Scotland squad, it all went wrong for him in the game against Wolves at Molineux. He came on as a substitute after Ogrizovic had been sent off, and conceded two goals in his first two minutes on the pitch!

Shortly afterwards he joined Bradford City, but a horrific injury at Molineux—not his luckiest ground—where he received 18 stitches in a face wound plus two sendings-off later in the 1996-97 season, restricted his number of appearances.

He joined Celtic in the summer of 1997, missing just the opening game of the 1997-98 season as the Bhoys won the League Championship. Keeping 17 clean sheets in 35 games, he was the club's first-choice keeper for the next few seasons, winning another League Championship in 2000-01 and the League Cup in 1997-98, 1999-2000 and 2000-01. His form was such that he won his first full cap for Scotland in the European Championship qualifier against Lithuania which the Scots won 3-0.

After losing out to Rob Douglas, he followed Craig Brown to Preston North End, where his displays made him one of the best keepers outside of the Premier League. In fact, his performances between the posts led to him being recalled to the Scotland squad for the Euro 2004 play-offs. After losing his place through injury, he found himself well down the pecking order and moved to Bristol City, prior to trying his luck in New Zealand with National League side, Hawke's Bay United.

STEVEN PRESSLEY
Central defender

Born: Steven Pressley, Elgin, 11 October 1973
Height: 6ft 0in
Weight: 11st 1lb
Clubs: Inverkeithing BC; Glasgow Rangers; Coventry City; Dundee United; Heart of Midlothian
Scotland caps: 32

2000 v France (lost 0-2), v Republic of Ireland (won 2-1)

2003 v Iceland (won 2-0), v Canada (won 3-1), v Portugal lost 0-2), v Iceland (won 2-1), v Lithuania (lost 0-1), v Austria (lost 0-2), v New Zealand (drew 1-1), v Germany (drew 1-1)

2004 v Norway (drew 0-0), v Germany (lost 1-2), v Lithuania (won 1-0), v Holland (won 1-0), v Holland (lost 0-6), v Romania (lost 1-2), v Denmark (lost 0-1), v Estonia (won 1-0), v Trinidad and Tobago (won 4-1)

2005 v Hungary (lost 0-3), v Italy (lost 0-2), v Moldova (won 2-0), v Belarus (drew 0-0)

2006 v Austria (drew 2-2), v Norway (won 2-1), v Belarus (lost 0-1), v Slovenia (won 3-0), v United States (drew 1-1), v Faroe Islands (won 6-0), v Lithuania (won 2-1), v France (won 1-0), v Ukraine (lost 0-2)

Big 'Elvis', as he is affectionately known by the Gorgie faithful, is a tough-tackling and dominating central defender, whose career began when Rangers called him up from Inverkeithing Boys Club in the summer of 1990. He made his debut for the Ibrox club in 1992 and went on to appear in eight games during the course of the 1992-93 season as Rangers lifted another title. He appeared in another 23 games the following season as Rangers retained the title, but in the early part of the 1994-95 campaign, the rugged defender joined Coventry City for a fee of £630,000.

Described as 'the new Richard Gough', Pressley, who captained the Scotland Under-21 side, for whom he played 27 times, looked an excellent prospect for the future, his strong points being his speed and aerial power. However, he failed to settle at Highfield Road, and after just one season, he returned north of the border to sign for Dundee United in a £750,000 transfer deal.

He was a key player in United's successful campaign of 1996-97, which saw them finish third in the Premier Division, and the following season helped the Terrors reach the League Cup Final, where they went down 3-0 to Celtic. In the summer of 1998, after he was offered a lucrative contract by United, Pressley, who was by then out of contract, chose to sign for Hearts.

Though he took some time to settle at Tynecastle after being required to operate in a number of positions in an ever-changing defensive structure, he was ever-present in seasons 1999-2000 and 2000-01 and has missed very few games in his time with the club. Continually producing solid, competitive and confident displays at the heart of the club's defence, he leads by example, having been appointed club captain following Colin Cameron's departure to Wolves in September 2001. He has subsequently helped Hearts to finish third in the League on three occasions, to reach the Scottish Cup and League Cup semi-finals, and to win the Scottish Cup in 2006. Immense in defence and a driving force of the team, Pressley, who has played in over 300 games for the Jambos, has the mental strength for crucial penalties and regularly scores from the spot.

PAUL TELFER
Midfield
Born: Paul Norman Telfer, Edinburgh, 21 October 1971
Height: 5ft 9in
Weight: 11st 6lb
Clubs: Luton Town; Coventry City; Southampton; Glasgow Celtic
Scotland caps: 1
2000   v France (lost 0-2)

Right-sided midfield player Paul Telfer began his Football League career with Luton Town, making his first team debut as a substitute in the penultimate game of the 1990-91 season at Everton. He established himself as a first team regular midway through the club's relegation season of 1991-92, and over the next four seasons missed very few matches. Not a prolific scorer, he had found the net 22 times in 165 games for the Hatters, when in July 1995 he joined Coventry City for a fee of £1.5 million.

During his first season with the Sky Blues, he was called up for the Scotland 'B' team and tipped for full international honours, but injuries and a loss of form ruled him out of the last few games of the 1995-96 season and he was overlooked. An aggressive ball-winner, he had a much improved season in 1996-97 and an even better one the following term, when he was again selected for Scotland at 'B' international level.

Though not a dirty player, his poor disciplinary record caused him to be called up in front of the FA during the course of the 1998-99 season. In 1999-2000 his consistent form was rewarded with a full Scottish cap against World Champions France, when manager Craig Brown was full of praise for his performance. Sadly, the Coventry utility player broke a leg in the game against Aston Villa towards the end of the Sky Blues' relegation season of 2000-01.

On recovering from this setback, he followed his manager Gordon Strachan on a 'Bosman' free transfer to Southampton. He played his early games for the Saints in midfield before filling in for the injured skipper Jason Dodd on the right-side of the back four. Telfer ended the campaign as a member of the Southampton side that were beaten by Arsenal in the FA Cup Final at the Millennium Stadium. Telfer found himself playing under three different managers at St Mary's, none of whom could do without him in their team, but having played in 149 games, he followed former boss Gordon Strachan to Parkhead, where he ended the campaign with a League Championship medal.

GARY NAYSMITH

Full-back

Born: Gary Andrew Naysmith, Edinburgh, 16 November 1979
Height: 5ft 7in
Weight: 11st 8lb
Clubs: Whitehill Welfare; Heart of Midlothian; Everton
Scotland caps: 32
Scotland goals: 1

2000 v Republic of Ireland (won 2-1)
2001 v Latvia (won 1-0), v San Marino (won 2-0), v Croatia (drew 1-1)
2002 v Croatia (drew 0-0), v Belgium (lost 0-2)
2003 v Denmark (lost 0-1), v Iceland (won 2-0) 1 goal, v Portugal (lost 0-2),
        v Republic of Ireland (lost 0-2), v Iceland (won 2-1), v Lithuania (lost 0-1),
        v Austria (lost 0-2), v New Zealand (drew 1-1), v Germany (drew 1-1)
2004 v Norway (drew 0-0), v Faroe Islands (won 3-1), v Germany (lost 1-2),
        v Lithuania (won 1-0), v Holland (won 1-0), v Holland (lost 0-6), v Wales (lost 0-4)
2005 v Hungary (lost 0-3), v Spain (drew 1-1), v Slovenia (drew 0-0), v Norway (lost 0-1),
        v Moldova (drew 1-1), v Italy (lost 0-2)
2006 v Bulgaria (won 5-1), v Japan (drew 0-0), v Faroe Islands (won 6-0),
        v Lithuania (won 2-1)

Gary Naysmith played his early football for Whitehill Welfare prior to joining Heart of Midlothian in the summer of 1996. Over the next four seasons, the tough-tackling full-back was a virtual ever-present in the Tynecastle club's side, helping them win the Scottish Cup in 1998 with a 2-1 defeat of Rangers. Capped by Scotland against the Republic of Ireland, he had played in 119 games for Hearts before Everton won a tug-of-war with Coventry City for his services in October 2000.

Everton fans were well satisfied with their capture from Hearts, especially after he marked his debut against Newcastle United with a dream pass for Kevin Campbell to hit the winning goal. Sadly, an appalling gash in his knee which required 37 stitches effectively cut short his first season in English football. The

2001-02 season wasn't much different, for after some gutsy performances which saw him establish himself as a full Scottish international, his season was again curtailed by a painful ankle injury that required surgery.

A committed and ever-willing full-back, who loves to get forward and attack, he has proved himself one of Everton's most potent goal creators from the left flank, but strangely doesn't get on the scoresheet as much as he would like. In 2002-03 he was employed on the left-hand side of midfield, when he was also one of only a few players to emerge with any credit from Scotland's performances at international level, scoring his first goal in a 2-1 defeat of Iceland.

He also found the net in successive matches for Everton as he showed typical tenacity and pace in a Blues side that finished seventh in the Premiership. Injuries, notably a hernia operation, limited his appearances in 2003-04, while it was the good form of others that kept him out of the side for much of the following season. Despite fearing that his football career might be over during the early stages of the 2005-06 season, Naysmith has just signed a deal that will keep him at Goodison Park until 2008.

GARY HOLT
Midfield

Born: Gary James Holt, Irvine, 9 March 1973
Height: 6ft 0in
Weight: 12st 11lb
Clubs: Glasgow Celtic; Stoke City; Kilmarnock; Norwich City; Nottingham Forest
Scotland caps: 10
Scotland goals: 1
2001 v Latvia (won 1-0), v Croatia (drew 1-1)
2002 v France (lost 0-5)
2004 v Denmark (lost 0-1), v Estonia (won 1-0), v Trinidad and Tobago (won 4-1) 1 goal
2005 v Hungary (lost 0-3), v Slovenia (drew 0-0), v Norway (lost 0-1), v Moldova (drew 1-1)

Gary Holt was in the army when he was spotted playing and recommended to Celtic manager Lou Macari. Unable to break into the Parkhead club's first team, he joined Stoke City, but again failed to make the grade.

A life-long Kilmarnock fan, he joined the Rugby Park club in the summer of 1995 and made his first team debut as a substitute in a 3-0 defeat at Motherwell. It was Killie's Cup-winning season of 1996-97 before he became a first team regular, his presence in the side helping Kilmarnock to stave off relegation.

While with Kilmarnock, Gary Holt won two full caps for Scotland, and in both matches he came on as an injury-time substitute—firstly for Billy Dodds in a 1-0 away win in Latvia, and the other for Paul Dickov in a 1-1 draw in Croatia. His other caps came following his transfer to Norwich City, and in his time at Carrow Road, he took his total of international appearances to 10.

Gary Holt, who has a tattoo of the Kilmarnock club crest on his leg, was actually married at Rugby Park. He had scored nine goals in 184 games for Killie when in March 2001 he joined Norwich City for a fee of £100,000.

The Canaries beat off several rivals for his signature in a pre-deadline day swoop. Holt, who is a hardworking, combative midfield player, had an outstanding season in 2001-02 when he was voted the Carrow Road club's 'Player of the Year'. Nicknamed 'Three Lungs' by the Norwich faithful due to his amazing stamina and running power, he enjoyed another good season in 2002-03 before the following term helping the East Anglian club win promotion to the Premiership. His form in that campaign was such that he won a recall to Berti Vogts' Scotland squad, whilst he was an ever-present in Nigel Worthington's side. He continued to add to his tally of Scotland caps in 2004-05, but he was later laid low by a serious illness which saw him hospitalised. He later returned to action, but after 182 appearances for the Canaries, he parted company with the club.

Holt was transferred to Nottingham Forest in the summer of 2005 in a swap deal with Matthieu Lois Jean, and has since proved to be one of the City Ground club's better players.

PAUL DICKOV
Forward

Born: Paul Dickov, Livingston, 1 November 1972
Height: 5ft 6in
Weight: 11st 9lb
Clubs: Arsenal; Luton Town; Brighton and Hove Albion; Manchester City; Leicester City; Blackburn Rovers; Manchester City
Scotland caps: 10
Scotland goals: 1
2001 v San Marino (won 2-0), v Croatia (drew 1-1), v Australia (lost 0-2)
2003 v Faroe Islands (drew 2-2)
2004 v Faroe Islands (won 3-1) 1 goal, v Holland (won 1-0), v Holland (lost 0-6), v Wales (lost 0-4)
2005 v Slovenia (drew 0-0), v Norway (lost 0-1)

Paul Dickov joined Arsenal in the summer of 1989 after starring for the Scottish youth team, whom he helped to the final of the Mini-World Cup. In 1991-92 he won the first of his four Scottish Under-21 caps against Yugoslavia, before making his Premier League debut at Southampton in March 1993. Later that season he helped Scotland to the semi-finals of the Toulon Under-21 Tournament.

Following loan spells with Luton and Brighton, the small striker won a European Cup Winners' Cup medal when being named in Arsenal's 16-man squad against Parma in 1994. He continued to spend most of his time at Highbury on the bench, until in the summer of 1996, Manchester City manager Alan Ball paid the Gunners £1 million to secure Dickov's services.

He had a good run in the City side under four different managers, and he was one of the club's few successes in what was generally a disappointing time for the Blues. Under Joe Royle he was given an extended run in the side and rewarded the manager's faith by scoring a brilliant hat-trick in the space of 14 minutes in a 4-0 defeat of Lincoln City. After helping City win promotion to the Premiership, his performances in the top flight led to him winning his first full cap for Scotland in the 2-0 defeat of San Marino in October 2001.

A prolonged Achilles injury restricted his appearances the following season, and after scoring 41 goals in 181 games he joined Leicester City. In 2002-03, as the Foxes won promotion to the Premiership, he became the first Leicester player to net 20 goals in a season for seven years. Voted the club's 'Player of the Year', he was also selected for the PFA Division One team of the season. Though he eventually managed to overcome the problems that arose from the club's trip to La Manga, he was unable to prevent the Foxes from losing their top flight status. It was a campaign in which he continued to find the net in the Premiership and netted his first international goal, before suffering with his colleagues at the hands of Holland in the Euro 2004 play-offs.

In the summer of 2004, Dickov joined Blackburn Rovers for £150,000, and in his first season with the club was the top scorer. Isolated up front, he ran non-stop, always seeking to make himself available and close down defenders throughout the game. Dickov left Rovers to rejoin Manchester City in the summer of 2006.

DOMINIC MATTEO
Defender
Born: Dominic Matteo, Dumfries, 24 April 1974
Height: 6ft 1in
Weight: 11st 12lb
Clubs: Liverpool; Sunderland; Leeds United; Blackburn Rovers
Scotland caps: 6
2001 v Australia (lost 0-2), v Belgium (drew 2-2), v San Marino (won 4-0)
2002 v Croatia (drew 0-0), v Belgium (lost 0-2), v France (lost 0-5)

Having started his career with Liverpool, Dominic Matteo was called up by the England party to be on World Youth Cup standby, before joining Sunderland on loan in an effort to gain more experience.

However, with four experienced central defenders ahead of him at Liverpool, he had few opportunities to advance his career in his early days at Anfield. Eventually established in the Reds' side since 1996-97, he earned a call-up for Glenn Hoddle's England, playing for the Under-21 side after he had given the club an added dimension and enabled them to maintain a strong position near the top of the Premiership. In 1997-98 he played for the England 'B' side against Chile, but failed to have an extended run in the Liverpool side in which to fulfil his rich promise as a central defender. Over the following season, Matteo was reduced to something of a bit-part player at Liverpool, but in 1999-2000 he was a virtual ever-present, learning to adjust to the mental demands of the role.

Despite rumours that he was going to be sold to Celtic, Gerard Houllier kept faith with him, and Matteo repaid his manager's faith by turning in some fine performances. Yet surprisingly, in the close season, having made 155 appearances for the Reds, he was sold to Leeds United for £4.75 million.

He began the following season on the sidelines with a knee injury, and he had to wait until the Champions League match against AC Milan before making his Leeds debut. The highlight of his first season at Elland Road was undoubtedly his near-post header in the return game against the Italian giants in the San Siro Stadium, the 1-1 draw confirming Leeds' qualification for the second stage.

A player with great vision, skill and athleticism, he won his first full cap for Scotland when he played in the friendly against Australia. Consistently producing good performances for the Yorkshire club, his versatility enabled him to fill a variety of positions, before in 2002-03, as the club's new skipper, he settled into the centre of the Leeds defence. His campaign was interrupted by a number of injuries, and ironically he stepped down from international duty with Scotland in the hope that he might stay clear of the treatment room! It wasn't to be, and he missed a number of games in 2003-04 as Leeds lost their Premiership status.

Matteo remained in the top flight by joining Mark Hughes' Blackburn Rovers, where, despite opportunities at centre-back, he settled into the side at left-back. Sadly, injuries have taken their toll on the Rovers defender since then.

STEVE CALDWELL
Central defender

Born: Stephen Caldwell, Stirling, 12 September 1980
Height: 6ft 0in
Weight: 11st5lb
Clubs: Newcastle United; Blackpool; Bradford City; Leeds United; Sunderland
Scotland caps: 10
2001 v Poland (drew 1-1)
2003 v Republic of Ireland (lost 0-2)
2004 v Wales (lost 0-4), v Trinidad and Tobago (won 4-1)
2005 v Moldova (won 2-0), v Belarus (drew 0-0)
2006 v Austria (drew 2-2), v Slovenia (won 3-0), v United States (drew 1-1),
         v Switzerland (lost 1-3)

A product of the Newcastle United youth system, Steve Caldwell broke into the Magpies' first team squad during the 2000-01 season. After coming off the substitute's bench at Manchester City, he scored on his full debut in the Worthington Cup against Bradford City.

A regular during the season for the Scotland Under-21 side, he was joined by his younger brother Gary, who was also on Newcastle's books but yet to appear in the first team. Also, towards the end of that campaign, the young central defender made his full international debut in the friendly against Poland.

Though he started the pre-2001-02 season in the Newcastle line-up, Andy O'Brien's return to fitness saw him displaced, and he did not make the first team again all season. A strong tackler who reads the game well, he was loaned out to Blackpool, and later Bradford City, in an attempt to further his experience of senior football. During the course of these loan spells he featured at both right-back and centre-half, and became a big favourite with both sets of supporters after some fine displays.

He still couldn't force his way into the Newcastle line-up at the start of the 2002-03 season, and it was early November before injuries gave him his first game of the season against Middlesbrough. Caldwell capped a fine display at the heart of the Magpies defence by netting his first Premiership goal in a 2-0 win. Thereafter he remained an important member of the first team squad, his performances leading to him winning further honours for the national side.

Competent, self-assured and comfortable on the ball, he never let the side down whenever called upon, but in February 2004 he joined Leeds United on loan. Once the Elland Road club's relegation was confirmed, he returned to St James Park before joining rivals Sunderland under the freedom of contract.

He went on to form an excellent central defensive partnership with Black Cats' skipper Gary Breen, and scored five goals from his position at the back. One of these—a typically powerful header against Leicester City—clinched promotion for the Wearsiders. With Sunderland securing the Championship title, he collected a well-deserved winners' medal in his first season with the club. However, Sunderland propped up the Premiership for most of the 2005-06 season, and at the end of it made an immediate return to the Championship.

ANDY McLAREN
Midfield/ Forward
Born: Andrew McLaren, Glasgow, 5 June 1973
Height: 5ft 10in
Weight: 11st 8lb
Clubs: Rangers BC; Dundee United; Reading; Livingston; Kilmarnock; Hibernian; Falkirk; Dundee United; Morton; Dundee
Scotland caps: 1
2001 v Poland (drew 1-1)

Andy McLaren started out with Dundee United, having joined the Tannadice club in 1989. He spent ten years with the Terrors, helping them win the Scottish Cup in 1994 and finish runners-up in the First Division in 1995-96. He had scored 18 goals in 206 League and Cup games for United when, in March 1999, he left to play for Reading, the Royals paying £100,000 for his services.

The Under-21 international showed only glimpses of his ability to take on players and get forward which had characterised his career in Scottish football, and early the following season he had a three-month spell with Livingston but failed to make his mark. He returned to the Madejski Stadium before, in the summer of 2000, returning north of the Border to play for Kilmarnock, after a drink and drugs scandal saw him sacked by the Berkshire club.

He had a tremendous first season with Killie, proving all the doubters wrong. Towards the end of that campaign, Craig Brown used him as a second-half substitute for Colin Cameron in a 1-1 away draw with Poland—his only cap for Scotland.

He remained with Kilmarnock for a further two seasons, taking his tally of appearances in which he scored 17 goals to 99, before deciding not to take up the offer of a further two-year contract.

He went on trial with Hibs at the start of the 2003-04 season, hoping to get a contract from his ex-Kilmarnock manager Bobby Williamson, who was then in charge at Easter Road. The Hibs board would not let Williamson sign him, and after trial games with Falkirk, he rejoined his first club Dundee United. Following a good first season with the Tannadice club, McLaren left United early the following campaign to join Morton. He served the Cappielow Park club well until leaving on a free transfer to play for Dundee.

CHARLIE MILLER
Midfield
Born: Charles Miller, Glasgow, 18 March 1976
Height: 5ft 8in
Weight: 12st 2lb
Clubs: Glasgow Rangers; Leicester City; Watford; Dundee United; Brann (Norway)
Scotland caps: 1
2001 v Poland (drew 1-1)

A scheming midfield player, capable of delivering defence-splitting passes, Miller first came to the public's notice in 1993. At 16 he was playing in the star-studded Rangers reserve team, and by the age of 17, he had been selected for the Ibrox club's first team, making his debut against Aberdeen.

By Christmas 1994, Miller had played a dozen matches in the Rangers first team, and influential figures in the game were raving about the teenager. By the end of that season, a full call-up was on the cards, but suspension and injury took their toll, and he had to be content with a League Championship medal. In fact, Miller had to wait until he had left Ibrox before winning full international honours.

He went on to win further League Championship medals in 1995-96 and 1996-97, and a Scottish League Cup winners' medal that last season as Rangers beat Hearts 4-3. After that injuries began to take their toll, and in October 1999, after losing his place to Paul Gascoigne and a loan spell with Leicester City, Charlie Miller, who had scored 15 goals in 117 games for Rangers, joined Watford for a fee of £350,000.

He soon demonstrated his talent for the telling pass at Vicarage Road before his lack of match fitness cost him a regular place in the starting line-up. Unable to break back into the side, he had a trial with Wigan Athletic before returning to Scotland to play for Dundee United.

Miller was the inspirational figure and key player behind United's resurgent run to Premier League safety in the second-half of the 2000-01 season. Such was Charlie Miller's impact—five goals in 24 games—that he won his first-ever

Scotland cap against Poland in April 2001 and was United's 'Player of the Year'. Though not as impressive since then, he has reaffirmed his propensity to score spectacular and important goals which maintained the club's Premier Division status. He later left Tannadice to try his luck in Norwegian football with Brann.

KENNY MILLER
Forward

Born: Kenneth Miller, Edinburgh, 23 December 1979
Height: 5ft 8in
Weight: 11st 3lb
Clubs: Hutchison Vale; Hibernian; Stenhousemuir; Glasgow Rangers; Wolverhampton Wanderers; Glasgow Celtic
Scotland caps: 28
Scotland goals: 8

2001 v Poland (drew 1-1)

2003 v Iceland (won 2-1), v Lithuania (lost 0-1), v Austria (lost 0-2), v Germany (drew 1-1) 1 goal

2004 v Lithuania (won 1-0), v Holland (won 1-0), v Holland (lost 0-6), v Wales (lost 0-4), v Romania (lost 1-2), v Estonia (won 1-0), v Trinidad and Tobago (won 4-1)

2005 v Hungary (lost 0-3), v Spain (drew 1-1), v Norway (lost 0-1), v Moldova (drew 1-1), v Sweden (lost 1-4), v Italy (lost 0-2), v Moldova (won 2-0), v Belarus (drew 0-0)

2006 v Austria (drew 2-2) 1 goal, v Italy (drew 1-1) 1 goal, v Norway (won 2-1) 2 goals, v Belarus (lost 0-1), v Slovenia (won 3-0), v Switzerland (lost 1-3) 1 goal, v Faroe Islands (won 6-0), v Lithuania (won 2-1)

A rangy striker, Kenny Miller began his career with Hibernian and made his Scottish League debut for the Easter Road club as a substitute in the 1-1 draw against Motherwell in November 1997. Unable to win a regular place in the Hibs side, he was loaned out to Stenhousemuir the following November, and after scoring eight goals for them, he returned to Hibs.

After coming off the bench in the first few games of the 1999-2000 season, he won a place in the starting line-up and went on to end the season as Hibs' leading scorer with 11 league goals—two of these coming in a 2-2 draw with Rangers, a display that prompted the Ibrox club to pay £2 million for his services at the end of that season.

Though more than half his first team appearances in 2000-01 were as a substitute, Kenny Miller still managed to score five goals—four in the first half— as Rangers demolished St Mirren 7-1. He had made a handful of appearances at the beginning of the following season before being loaned out to Wolverhampton Wanderers in September 2001.

He made a big impression at Molineux, but then dislocated a shoulder. He had not fully recovered when his three-month loan period ended, but was signed permanently for a fee of £3 million just before the turn of the year. Ironically, he could not get into the Wolves side at first, such was the form of Dean Sturridge and Nathan Blake. He won a regular place in 2002-03, but still

Kenny Miller (www.snspix.com)

struggled to find the net early on. Then, following the club's FA Cup victory over Newcastle United, his confidence soared and he scored in seven successive matches to equal a post-war club record. Following a goalless draw against

Watford, he netted his first hat-trick against Crystal Palace to make it 12 goals in nine games. He continued to find the net regularly thereafter, scoring a total of 24 in all competitions, including a vital strike in the play-off final victory against Sheffield United at the Millennium Stadium, as Wolves won through to play in the Premiership.

Though he continued to be a regular in the Wolves side, he could do nothing to halt their immediate return to the First Division. He was the club's top scorer in 2004-05 with 20 goals and continued to represent Scotland, for whom he has scored five goals in six games, including both goals in the 2-1 World Cup qualifying win over Norway. Having scored 63 goals in 191 games for Wolves, he left to join Celtic in the summer of 2006 and has continued to shine for the national team.

BARRY NICHOLSON
Midfield

Born: Barry Nicholson, Dumfries, 24 August 1978
Height: 5ft 10in
Weight: 10st 6lb
Clubs: Glasgow Rangers; Dunfermline Athletic; Aberdeen
Scotland caps: 3
2001 v Poland (drew 1-1)
2002 v Latvia (won 2-1)
2005 v Sweden (lost 1-4)

Midfielder Barry Nicholson was an 'S' form signing for Rangers in the summer of 1995, but the Dumfries-born player struggled to make much impact with the Ibrox club, and though he made six appearances during the club's League Championship-winning season of 1998-99, he had only made a dozen appearances by the time he signed for Dunfermline Athletic in a £200,000 deal in July 2000.

A cool and skilful playmaker, he made a difficult choice in leaving the Glasgow giants to play at Dunfermline, but following the progress he made at East End Park, he definitely made the correct decision. Following his debut for the Pars in August 2000, Nicholson was a virtual ever-present, and this helped him progress from the Scottish Under-21 team to the full national side, making the first of three appearances in the 1-1 draw with Poland.

On the opening day of the 2001-02 season, Nicholson scored two of Dunfermline's goals in a 5-2 defeat of Motherwell, going on to end the campaign as the Pars' leading scorer with seven goals! He continued to find the net the following season when he didn't miss a single game. In 2003-04, Nicholson, who won a recall to the national side, was outstanding as the Pars finished fourth in the Premier Division and reached the Scottish Cup Final. In that game, which the Pars lost 3-1 to Celtic, Nicholson captained the side in the absence of Scott Thomson.

Having scored 30 goals in 208 appearances for Dunfermline, Nicholson left the East End club to sign for Aberdeen in the summer of 2005, for a fee of £250,000 and has since proved to be a revelation with the Pittodrie club.

JOHN O'NEIL
Midfield

Born: John O'Neil, Bellshill, 7 June 1971
Height: 5ft 8in
Weight: 11st 7lb
Clubs: Dundee United; St Johnstone; Hibernian; Falkirk; Gretna
Scotland caps: 1
2001   v Poland (drew 1-1)

Midfielder John O'Neil began his career with Dundee United, though he wasn't in the side in 1994 when the Tannadice club won the Scottish Cup, beating Rangers 1-0 in the final. Shortly after that success, O'Neil left United to play for St Johnstone, helping the McDiarmid Park club win the First Division Championship in 1996-97. He was also a member of the St Johnstone side that lost 2-1 to Rangers in the 1998 League Cup Final. A virtual ever-present for the six seasons he was with the Saints, he left the Perth club in the summer of 2000 to join Hibs.

During his first season at Easter Road, John O'Neil was capped by Scotland against Poland, a match that ended all-square at 1-1.

Appointed Hibs' captain, O'Neil's tough tackling and accurate passing skills were a feature of the Easter Road club's play for the next three seasons. Also in his first campaign with the club, he helped them reach the Scottish Cup Final, and though he had a good game, Hibs lost 3-0 to Celtic.

Hibs' manager Bobby Williamson was asked to make cuts to the wage bill, and John O'Neil, one of the Easter Road club's biggest earners, was handed a free transfer, having scored nine goals in 86 league games for Hibs.

He joined Falkirk in August 2003, and in his first season at Ochilview Park, he was a virtual ever-present as the club finished fourth in the First Division. The following season, the Bairns won the First Division Championship, finishing 15 points clear of second-placed St Mirren. O'Neil remained a regular in the Falkirk side during their 2005-06 Premier Division campaign, but has since moved on to play for Gretna.

GAVIN RAE
Defender/Midfield

Born: Gavin Rae, Aberdeen, 28 November 1977
Height: 5ft 11in
Weight: 10st 4lb
Clubs: Dundee; Glasgow Rangers
Scotland caps: 9
2001   v Poland (drew 1-1)
2002   v Latvia (won 2-1)

2003 v Germany (drew 1-1)
2004 v Norway (drew 0-0), v Faroe Islands (won 3-1), v Germany (lost 1-2),
v Lithuania (won 1-0), v Holland (lost 0-6), v Romania (lost 1-2)
2006 v Bulgaria (won 5-1), v Japan (drew 0-0)

Able to play in midfield or defence, Gavin Rae began his career with Dundee, whom he joined in the summer of 1996. Making his debut as a substitute in a 1-0 home defeat at the hands of Airdrieonians in September of that year, he found himself a regular member of the club's first team squad in 1997-98, making six starts as Dundee won the First Division Championship.

In his early days with the club, Rae played mainly in midfield, where his running at the opposition defences had the crowd on its feet. Packing a powerful shot in either foot, as some of his early goals demonstrated, one of his most popular strikes came in the 2-2 draw at Tannadice against neighbours and rivals Dundee United.

In March 2001, his performances were duly noted when he won the first of nine full international caps in a 1-1 draw with Poland.

Missing very few matches for Dundee, his game continued to improve under the careful guardianship of manager Ivano Bonetti, and he was often linked with moves to 'bigger' clubs. A member of the Dundee side that lost 1-0 to Rangers in the 2003 Scottish Cup Final, Rae had scored 25 goals in 217 games for the Dens Park club when, in January 2004, Rangers paid £250,000 for his services.

Though now playing as a defender, it didn't take him long to get on the scoresheet, netting in a 4-0 win over former club, Dundee. A regular in the Scotland side, his 2004-05 campaign was destroyed by injury problems, as one suffered in an SPL match against Dundee United in April 2004 kept him out of action for almost six months. Just as he was looking to return to action, he suffered tendonitis of the quadriceps muscle in his right leg and he missed the whole of the 2004-05 season. Rae is now looking for an injury-free campaign, but recapturing his old form may be tough after such a long-term absence.

DOUGIE FREEDMAN
Forward

Born: Douglas Alan Freedman, Glasgow, 21 January 1974
Height: 5ft 10in
Weight: 11st 2lb
Clubs: Queen's Park Rangers; Barnet; Crystal Palace; Wolverhampton Wanderers; Nottingham Forest; Crystal Palace
Scotland caps: 2
Scotland goals: 1
2002 v Latvia (won 2-1) 1 goal v France (lost 0-5)

Unable to make the grade with Queen's Park Rangers, Dougie Freedman finished the 1994-95 season as both Barnet's and the Third Division's highest scorer. Quick, with good touch and vision, he earned a Scottish Under-21 call-up as the goals flew in from every angle and with either foot. One of the finds of the season, with many big clubs casting envious eyes in his direction, he was elected by his fellow professionals to the PFA award-winning Third Division side.

It came as no surprise when, in September 1995, Crystal Palace paid £800,000 to take him to Selhurst Park. After a slow start, he netted a hat-trick against Wolves, a feat he repeated, inside 12 minutes, later in the season against Grimsby Town, to end the campaign with 20 goals as Palace went from the foot of Division One to the play-offs. He started the 1996-97 season as he ended the previous campaign, reaching double figures by the end of November; however, a loss of form saw him spend much of the second-half of the season on the bench. Though he knew he was suspended for the play-off final, he came off the bench in the play-off semi-final first leg and scored two goals in the 89th and 90th minutes to give Palace a 3-1 aggregate lead. This was ultimately good enough to take them to Wembley and then regain their Premiership status.

Allowed to join Wolves for £800,000, he ended his first season at Molineux as the club's top scorer, and though he experienced a brief outing for Scotland 'B', he was surprisingly omitted from the squad for the FA Cup semi-final. That season was his only one with Wolves, as he left to play for Nottingham Forest after their manager Dave Bassett paid £950,000 for him.

Despite not having a regular partner all season, he did well, though Forest lost their place in the Premiership. An intelligent striker, good at turning defenders, he then lost form and found himself in and out of the Forest side. Subsequently he returned to Crystal Palace, where he formed a productive partnership with Clinton Morrison. His form was recognised when he was awarded his first full cap—scoring against Latvia at Hampden Park—and won a place in the PFA's First Division team. A hernia operation disrupted his 2002-03 season, but he returned to action, netting a hat-trick on the opening day of the 2003-04 season to help fire Iain Dowie's side into the Premiership via the play-offs. Though he struggled to make much of an impact in the Premiership and Palace were relegated, in November 2005, in a match against Brighton and Hove Albion, Dougie Freedman became only the seventh man to score 100 or more goals for the club.

SCOTT SEVERIN
Midfield

Born: Scott Severin, Stirling, 15 February 1979
Height: 5ft 10in
Weight: 11st 2lb
Clubs: Gairdoch United; Heart of Midlothian; Aberdeen
Scotland caps: 15

2002   v Latvia (won 2-1), v South Korea (lost 1-4), v South Africa (lost 0-2),
         v Hong Kong (won 4-0)
2003   v Denmark (lost 0-1), v Iceland (won 2-0), v Canada (won 3-1), v Portugal (lost 0-2)
2005   v Hungary (lost 0-3), v Sweden (Lost 1-4)
2006   v Austria (drew 2-2), v Bulgaria (won 5-1), v Japan (drew 0-0)
2007   v Faroe Islands (won 6-0), v Lithuania (won 2-1)

A tough-tackling and dynamic midfielder, Scott Severin played his early football for Alva Academy and Gairdoch United, from whom he joined Hearts in the summer of 1992. In his early days at Tynecastle, he helped Hearts win the 1993 BP Youth Cup Final, and then had a spell in the juniors with Musselburgh Athletic. After making excellent progress in the club's reserve side, his contract was renewed in May 1998, and towards the end of the following season, he made his first team breakthrough in the aftermath of those who departed following the Scottish Cup win, playing in a 3-1 win at Dundee United, in what was a difficult end to that campaign.

Severin's energy and ball-winning ability were vital to the balance of the Hearts midfield, and this helped establish his position in the squad. He helped Hearts finish third in the 1999-2000 Premier Division, and from then on he missed very few games.

A regular member of the Scotland Under-21 team, he also had a spell as captain, but then on becoming an over-age player, he was selected for the full national squad, making his debut in a 2-1 win over Latvia. With Berti Vogts looking towards younger players, he continued to represent Scotland, but having helped the Jambos to again finish third in the Premier Division in 2003-04, he left Tynecastle to join Aberdeen.

A regular in the Dons' midfield, he helped them finish fourth in the Premier Division in his first season at Pittodrie, and at the start of the 2005-06 campaign, his form had won him a recall to the national side for the friendly against Austria, after which he has held his place in the side.

GARY CALDWELL
Defender
Born: Gary Caldwell, Stirling, 12 April 1982
Height: 5ft 11in
Weight: 12st 0lb
Clubs: Newcastle United; Darlington; Hibernian; Coventry City; Derby County; Hibernian
Scotland caps: 21
Scotland goals: 2
2002 v France (lost 0-5), v Nigeria (lost 1-2), v South Korea (lost 1-4), v South Africa (lost 0-2)
2004 v Romania (lost 1-2), v Denmark (lost 0-1), v Estonia (won 1-0),
v Trinidad and Tobago (won 4-1) 1 goal
2005 v Hungary (lost 0-3), v Spain (drew 1-1), v Slovenia (drew 0-0), v Norway (lost 0-1),
v Moldova (drew 1-1), v Italy (lost 0-2)
2006 v Slovenia (won 3-0), v United States (drew 1-1), v Switzerland (lost 1-3),
v Bulgaria (won 5-1), v Japan (drew 0-0), v France (won 1-0) 1 goal, v Ukraine (lost 0-2)

The younger brother of Steve Caldwell, this classy defender had yet to make his first team debut for Newcastle United when he joined Darlington on loan in November 2001. Injuries had ruled out all but one of the Quakers' central defenders, and Caldwell, who was drafted into the side for his league debut against Rochdale, immediately formed a formidable partnership at the heart of the Darlington defence with David Brightwell.

Gary Caldwell celebrates the winning goal against France in October 2006
(www.snspix.com)

Caldwell's quickness of thought and accurate distribution of the ball stood out in the Third Division, but after just four games he was recalled to St James Park. Within a matter of weeks he went on loan again, this time in the Scottish Premier Division with Hibernian.

His performances for the Easter Road club led to him winning his first full cap against France, and though the Scots lost 5-0, he kept his place for the tour of Africa and Asia, where he added further caps to his collection.

During the summer of 2002, Gary Caldwell joined Coventry City on a 12-month loan deal, but on his arrival at Highfield Road, he was hampered by a knee injury that he had picked up in pre-season training. As well as playing in defence, he also had a spell in central midfield and impressed the management and fans alike with his very positive attitude to First Division football. At the start of the 2003-04 season, Caldwell joined Derby County, also on loan, but after returning to Newcastle, he joined Hibernian in the January transfer window and featured regularly for the Easter Road club in the second-half of the season.

Accomplished in defence or in the midfield holding role, Caldwell is an important member of the Hibs' side, missing just one game in 2004-05 as the club finished third in the Scottish Premier Division, and fourth the following season, whilst continuing to represent the national side. The bad memories of his debut were banished when he scored the winning goal against France and sent the whole of Scotland into euphoria during the national team's spectacular victory at Hampden in the 2006 European Championship qualifiers.

STEPHEN CRAINEY
Defender

Born: Stephen Crainey, Glasgow, 22 June 1981
Height: 5ft 9in
Weight: 9st 11lb
Clubs: Glasgow Celtic; Southampton; Leeds United
Scotland caps: 6
2002 v France (lost 0-5), v Nigeria (lost 1-2)
2003 v Denmark (lost 0-1), v Faroe Islands (drew 2-2)
2004 v Romania (lost 1-2), v Denmark (lost 0-1)

Beginning his career with Celtic, full-back Stephen Crainey would have loved nothing more than to shake off the tag as 'one for the future', for after six years in the Parkhead club's senior squad, it was becoming a little tiresome!

Crainey made his Celtic debut as a substitute for Jackie McNamara in a 4-1 home win over St Johnstone in March 2000, prior to making his first start the following month in a 4-0 defeat of Motherwell. Though he would have hoped the following season to have played on a more regular basis, he made just two league appearances. However, in 2001-02, Crainey not only made 15 appearances for the Bhoys as they won the Premier Division Championship, but won the first of six full international caps when he played for Scotland against France in a match the Scots lost 5-0.

Stephen Crainey

Finding it difficult to establish himself in Martin O'Neill's favoured 3-5-2 formation, he only really appeared when the Celtic boss began to experiment with a four-man defensive formation. After just six games of the 2003-04 season, Crainey was allowed to leave Parkhead and join Southampton for a fee of £500,000—the Saints at that time being managed by Gordon Strachan.

He made an encouraging debut against Arsenal, but then his opportunities to impress were limited by a combination of Danny Higginbotham's outstanding form at left-back, a brief return from Graeme Le Saux, and the shifts in the Saints' management, but towards the end of the season he looked particularly effective when playing behind Anders Svensson down the left flank. Even so, he was allowed to leave St Mary's, joining Leeds United, initially on loan.

He became the Yorkshire club's first cash signing when moving permanently for a fee of £200,000, and after settling in at left-back, showed an increasing willingness to get forward and shoot. Just as he was finding his best form, he sustained knee ligament damage that forced him to miss over half the season. He returned to action the following season, but missed the play-off final after being sent off in the semi-final win over Preston North End.

STEVEN THOMPSON
Forward

Born: Steven Thompson, Paisley, 14 October 1978
Height: 6ft 2in
Weight: 12st 5lb
Clubs: Dundee United; Glasgow Rangers; Cardiff City
Scotland caps: 16
Scotland goals: 3
2002 v France (lost 0-5), v Nigeria (lost 1-2), v Hong Kong (won 4-0) 1 goal
2003 v Denmark (lost 0-1), v Faroe Islands (drew 2-2), v Iceland (won 2-0),
      v Canada (won 3-1) 1 goal, v Republic of Ireland (lost 0-2), v Austria (lost 0-2),
      v Germany (drew 1-1)
2004 v Faroe Islands (won 3-1), v Germany (lost 1-2), v Romania (lost 1-2)
2005 v Hungary (lost 0-3), v Norway (lost 0-1), v Moldova (drew 1-1) 1 goal

Paisley-born forward Steven Thompson began his career with Dundee United, making his debut as a substitute for Robbie Winters in a 1-0 defeat of Hearts. Over the next couple of seasons, Thompson found himself in and out of the United side, and it was 1999-2000 before he won a regular place in the team.

It was during the course of that season that Thompson netted his first senior goal for the club in a 2-0 win over local rivals Dundee at Dens Park. Though not a prolific scorer for the Terrors, he had taken his tally to 18 in 133 league matches, including six in the opening 20 games of the 2002-03 season when Rangers manager Alex McLeish signed him for the Ibrox club.

Thompson, who had made his full international debut as a substitute in the 5-0 defeat by France in 2002, scored two vital goals in the closing stages of the campaign to help Rangers win the Premier Division title. In 2003-04 he had his best season in terms of goals scored when he netted eight—his two in the 3-3 draw at former club Dundee United in April 2004 bringing him particular pleasure. The following season he made the majority of his 24 appearances from the bench as Rangers won the League title, while in early 2005-06 he found his international appearances limited due to his lack of first team opportunities with Rangers.

Thompson parted company with the Ibrox club in January 2006, joining Cardiff City for a fee of £250,000, and made an explosive start to his Ninian Park career by scoring twice in the space of three minutes on his debut as Cardiff beat Burnley 3-0. He is currently starring for the Bluebirds as they lead the Championship.

ROB DOUGLAS
Goalkeeper

Born: Robert Douglas, Lanark, 24 April 1972
Height: 6ft 3in
Weight: 14st 12lb
Clubs: Livingston; Dundee; Glasgow Celtic; Leicester City
Scotland caps: 19

2002 v Nigeria (lost 1-2), v South Africa (lost 0-2), v Hong Kong (won 4-0)
2003 v Denmark (lost 0-1), v Faroe Islands (drew 2-2), v Iceland (won 2-0),
v Portugal (lost 0-2), v Iceland (won 2-1), v New Zealand (drew 1-1),
v Germany (drew 1-1)
2004 v Norway (drew 0-0), v Faroe Islands (won 3-1), v Germany (lost 1-2),
v Lithuania (won 1-0), v Holland (won 1-0), v Holland (lost 0-6), v Wales (lost 0-4)
2005 v Italy (lost 0-2)
2006 v Austria (drew 2-2)

Former brickie Rob Douglas played his early football for Livingston, where his performances led to him joining Dundee in the summer of 1997.

An ever-present in his first season at Dens Park, he helped the Dark Blues win the First Division Championship, keeping 17 clean sheets in 36 league games. In fact, he had played 348 minutes football for Dundee before he conceded his first goal. Over the next few seasons, his displays led to him being included in the Scotland squad, but it wasn't until after his move to Celtic for a fee of £1.2 million in October 2000 that he won selection at full international level.

Martin O'Neill beat off competition from Rangers' boss Dick Advocaat to sign the impressively-built keeper, though it took a while for him to become accustomed to the

Rob Douglas

pressures of playing football for a club of Celtic's stature. Following an Old Firm debut disaster on 26 November 2000 when Rangers beat Celtic 5-1 at Ibrox, he took a while to win over many Celtic fans, though he did help the Bhoys win the treble. However, in 2001-02, he confounded those critics with some exceptional performances, especially in the Champions League qualifiers against Ajax.

Though there were occasions when he lacked authority—especially on crosses—and he occasionally caused pulses to race in terms of overall command of his penalty-box—Rob Douglas' shot-stopping ability was second to none. One of the best Celtic keepers since young Packie Bonner, Douglas seemed set for a lengthy Parkhead career, but in 2003-04 when Celtic won the League Championship, he found himself sharing the goalkeeping duties with David Marshall. It was a similar story the following season, and in the summer of 2005, he opted for a move down south to join Leicester City, where his displays in the Championship have been outstanding.

KEVIN McNAUGHTON
Defender
Born: Kevin McNaughton, Dundee, 28 August 1982
Height: 5ft 10in
Weight: 10st 6lb
Clubs: Aberdeen; Cardiff City
Scotland caps: 3
2002 v Nigeria (lost 1-2)
2003 v Denmark (lost 0-1)
2005 v Sweden (lost 1-4)

Kevin McNaughton made his first team debut for Aberdeen in a 2-1 win over St Mirren in August 2000. Aged only 17, he went on to appear in the majority of games for the Dons that season. At the end of the campaign, McNaughton, who was still eligible for the club's youth side, was a member of the Aberdeen team that lifted the trophy.

A virtual ever-present in 2001-02, he was outstanding both at left-back and occasionally in central defence as the Dons ended the campaign in fourth place. Not surprisingly, he was named as the Scottish Premier League's 'Young Player of the Season'. Injuries hampered his progress the following season, but he did manage to get on the scoresheet for the first time when he scored the winner in a 2-1 defeat of Livingston.

McNaughton's form for the Dons led to him winning the first of three caps, against Nigeria, in April 2002. Playing on his own ground of Pittodrie, in a midfield role, he was upstaged by the mercurial Jay Jay Okocha, but was back in the side for the game against Denmark four months later. Replaced by Stephen Crainey at half-time, McNaughton won a recall to the national side in November 2004, but the Scots were well beaten 4-1 by Sweden.

McNaughton left Pittodrie to join Cardiff City where his displays in the back four have helped the Welsh club to the top of the Championship.

GRAHAM ALEXANDER
Right-back

Born: Graham Alexander, Coventry, 10 October 1971
Height: 5ft 10in
Weight: 12st 7lb
Clubs: Scunthorpe United; Luton Town; Preston North End
Scotland caps: 26

2002 v Nigeria (lost 1-2), v South Korea (lost 1-4), v South Africa (lost 0-2),
v Hong Kong (won 4-0)
2003 v Denmark (lost 0-1), v Faroe Islands (drew 2-2), v Canada (won 3-1),
v Portugal (lost 0-2), v Republic of Ireland (lost 0-2), v Iceland (won 2-1),
v Lithuania (lost 0-1), v New Zealand (drew 1-1)
2004 v Lithuania (won 1-0), v Romania (lost 1-2)
2005 v Moldova (won 2-0), v Belarus (drew 0-0)
2006 v Austria (drew 2-2), v Italy (drew 1-1), v Norway (won 2-1), v Belarus (lost 0-1),
v Slovenia (won 3-0), v United States (drew 1-1), v Switzerland (lost 1-3),
v Lithuania (won 2-1), v France (won 1-0), v Ukraine (lost 0-2)

In April 2002, Graham Alexander became Preston North End's first full Scottish international for over 40 years when he came on as a second-half substitute against Nigeria.

He began his career as a right-sided midfield player with Scunthorpe United, possessing a good turn of speed and packing an explosive shot in both feet. In the summer of 1995 he left the Irons to join Luton Town, and over the course of his first season at Kenilworth Road he showed he could operate in both defence and midfield. His best campaign for the Hatters was 1997-98, when despite being asked to play at full-back to cover for injuries, he had his best season in terms of goals scored. He had found the net 17 times in 182 games for Luton, when in March 1999 he joined Preston North End.

Soon after his arrival at Deepdale, he was switched to right-back on a permanent basis. He was ever-present during the club's Second Division Championship-winning season of 1999-2000, and was well worth his place in the PFA award-winning Second Division side. Over the course of the following season, Alexander coped admirably with the higher grade of football, and though he suffered a punctured lung, his positive overlapping, powerful free-kicks and sound defensive play were a feature of the club's run-in to the play-offs. In the season when he won full international honours, Alexander was also selected for the PFA Division One team.

He continued to show consistency for North End, and in 2003-04 when he also regained his place in the national side, he made his 600th senior appearance against his home-town club Coventry City and scored from the penalty-spot in his 200th game for Preston. His form under current Preston manager Billy Davies saw him again win selection for the PFA Championship team of the 2004-05 season, and he continues to be an important member of the Deepdale club's side, as well as currently the first-choice right-back for the national team.

GARRY O'CONNOR
Forward

Born: Garry O'Connor, Edinburgh, 7 May 1983
Height: 6ft 1in
Weight: 12st 9lb
Clubs: Salvesen BC; Hibernian; Lokomotiv Moscow
Scotland caps: 9
Scotland goals: 2
2002 v Nigeria (lost 1-2), v South Korea (lost 1-4), v Hong Kong (won 4-0)
2005 v Italy (lost 0-2)
2006 v Austria (drew 2-2) 1 goal v Slovenia (won 3-0), v United States (drew 1-1),
v Faroe Islands (won 6-0) 1 goal, v France (won 1-0)

Sensational young striker Garry O'Connor was still a teenager, and hadn't even made an appearance for the Scotland Under-21 team, when he replaced Steven Thompson after 74 minutes of Scotland's match against Nigeria at Pittodrie in April 2002.

After playing his early football for Salvesen Boys Club, O'Connor signed for Hibernian in May 1999, impressing all around him with his determined displays for the Easter Road club's reserve side. He was 17 when he was given his first team debut in April 2001, coming off the bench to replace Libbra in a 2-0 win over Dundee at Dens Park.

In 2001-02 he burst onto the scene with 10 league goals in the space of just 13 games towards the end of the campaign, after earlier making a number of substitute appearances. Ending the season as Hibs' leading scorer, he wasn't quite as prolific in 2002-03, though he did manage to score a most spectacular counter goal in a 3-0 win over Partick Thistle at Firhill.

There followed some difficult times for Garry O'Connor, but in 2004-05 he was back to something like his best. He started the season off in sensational style by grabbing a last minute winner in the local derby against Hearts. Showing a steely determination he netted 19 goals in all competitions as Hibs finished the season in third place in the Premier Division. His consistency throughout the campaign led to a recall to the Scotland squad, and in August 2005 he netted his first goal at international level in a 2-2 draw with Austria. In March 2006 he left Hibs to join Lokomotiv Moscow for £1.6 million to become the first British player in the Russian Premier League.

MICHAEL STEWART
Midfield

Born: Michael James Stewart, Edinburgh, 26 February 1981
Height: 5ft 11in
Weight: 11st 11lb
Clubs: Manchester United; Royal Antwerp (Belgium); Nottingham Forest; Heart of Midlothian; Hibernian
Scotland caps: 3

Midfielder Michael Stewart was one of a number of young Manchester United players to make his mark in the first team during the course of the 2000-01 season. He made a couple of appearances in the Worthington Cup before making his Premiership bow against Middlesbrough towards the end of the campaign.

The combative central midfielder was a regular for Scotland at Under-21 level, going on to win seven caps. In 2001-02 he showed some excellent touches when coming off the bench at Sunderland in October—a match the Reds went on to win 3-1. Stewart went on to feature in a handful of first team games, including the end-of-season matches against Ipswich Town and Charlton Athletic.

He made his first full international debut against Nigeria in April 2002 and also featured in the summer tour to the Far East.

Combining midfield aggression and technique in equal measure, Michael Stewart had to play the waiting game at Old Trafford. In 2003-04 Stewart had loan spells with Belgian club Royal Antwerp and Nottingham Forest, before rejoining the Reds in the new year. In the four seasons he was involved in the United first team set-up he made just 14 appearances, and so the following season opted for a move to the Scottish Premier Division with Hearts.

After a season at Tynecastle, Stewart left to join the Jambos' rivals, Hibernian, in the summer of 2005 on a one-year deal. No doubt he will be hoping to kick-start his career again under Tony Mowbray at Easter Road.

ROBBIE STOCKDALE
Right-back
Born: Robert Keith Stockdale, Redcar, 30 November 1979
Height: 5ft 11in
Weight: 11st 3lb
Clubs: Middlesbrough; Sheffield Wednesday; West Ham United; Rotherham United; Hull City; Darlington (loan); Tranmere Rovers
Scotland caps: 5
2002 v Nigeria (lost 1-2), v South Korea lost 1-4), v South Africa (lost 0-2), v Hong Kong (won 4-0)
2003 v Denmark (lost 0-1)

One of a number of exciting youngsters at Middlesbrough, full-back Robbie Stockdale, whose tackles are decisive and pace on the ball breathtaking, made the transition from obscurity to Premiership during the 1998-99 season, when injuries to senior squad members left the door open to him, and over the next couple of seasons, he appeared fairly regularly.

Unable to make much headway during the 2000-01 season, he went on loan to Sheffield Wednesday where he covered for injuries at full-back. On his return to the Riverside, he continued his development in the club's reserve team. He won an England Under-21 cap when he came off the substitute's bench for the final twenty minutes of the 6-1 friendly win over Georgia.

The following season his fortunes underwent amazing changes, for not only did he win a regular place in the Middlesbrough side, appearing in 28 Premiership games, but he also made his full international debut for Scotland in the friendly against Nigeria, this in spite of him having previously appeared for England at Under-21 level.

Stockdale, who qualified for Scotland because his grandparents were born there, was given a new lease of life following the appointment of Steve McLaren as the Boro manager. Though injuries hampered his progress, midway through the 2002-03 season, he found himself when fully fit competing for the right-back spot with England Under-21 international Stuart Parnaby. Finding himself out of favour following the arrival at the Riverside of Danny Mills, he had loan spells with West Ham United and Rotherham, where his cultured performances for the Yorkshire club proved invaluable in the battle to avoid relegation.

He later joined the Millers on a permanent basis, before, in the January 2005 transfer window, he moved to Hull City, helping them finish as runners-up to Luton Town and so win promotion to the Championship. Unable to hold down a place in the higher grade of football he went on loan to Darlington prior to signing for Tranmere.

GARETH WILLIAMS
Midfield

Born: Gareth John Williams, Glasgow, 16 December 1981
Height: 5ft 11in
Weight: 11st 10lb
Clubs: Nottingham Forest; Leicester City
Scotland caps: 5
2002 v Nigeria (Lost 1-2), v South Korea (lost 1-4), v South Africa (lost 0-2),
v Hong Kong (won 4-0)
2003 v Portugal (lost 0-2)

A hardworking and skilful midfielder, Gareth Williams was one of a number of talented Nottingham Forest youngsters to make their Football League debut during the course of the 1999-2000 season, when he came off the bench at Blackburn Rovers on Boxing Day. However, he then spent most of the following season continuing his development in the club's reserve side, although he did enjoy a decent run of senior action in the weeks leading up to the turn of the year.

The talented youngster captained the Nottingham Forest side on many occasions during the 2001-02 season, when he was a virtual ever-present in the City Ground club's first team. So impressive were his displays that towards the end of the campaign, he made his full international debut in the Pittodrie friendly against Nigeria.

The following season, Williams added another dimension to his play as his tackling improved immensely. Also, he scored his first senior goal for the club in a 1-1 home draw against Coventry City, and showed great courage by appearing in the play-offs against Sheffield United with a badly damaged shoulder.

Having won his fifth cap against Portugal, he continued to represent Scotland at Under-21 level. Following a change of management at Forest, Williams was encouraged to play in a more attacking role, and scored five goals in the closing stages, including a double against Crystal Palace. In the summer of 2004, Williams, who had made 154 appearances for Forest, left the City Ground and joined rivals Leicester City for a fee of £500,000.

Though he took a while to settle into his new surroundings, he soon found his ability to get into scoring positions from midfield an asset that endeared him to the Foxes' fans. Since then he has looked more and more indispensable as his time at the Walker Stadium has progressed.

SCOTT DOBIE
Forward
Born: Robert Scott Dobie, Workington, 10 October 1978
Height: 6ft 1in
Weight: 12st 8lb
Clubs: Carlisle United; Clydebank; West Bromwich Albion; Millwall; Nottingham Forest
Scotland caps: 6
Scotland goals: 1
2002 v South Korea (lost 1-4) 1 goal, v South Africa (lost 0-2), v Hong Kong (won 4-0)
2003 v Denmark (lost 0-1), v Faroe Islands (drew 2-2), v Portugal (lost 0-2)

A tall, well-built player, Dobie began his career with Carlisle United, where, after a loan spell with Clydebank, he turned in some influential performances.

With his height and natural aggression he showed signs of becoming an effective target man, his aerial power bringing him a number of goals. Perhaps his most important strike in a Carlisle shirt was the injury-time winner against Chester at the Deva Stadium in April 2000—a goal that for drama and execution almost matched that by the legendary Jimmy Glass the previous May. Dobie's best season for the Cumbrian club was 2000-01, when his excellent form and 12 goals attracted interest from higher-level clubs.

He eventually joined West Bromwich Albion—a snip of a signing at £125,000—and took over from the departed Lee Hughes, who had joined Coventry City. Dobie scored nine goals in his first 12 matches. Though the goals then began to dry up, he rediscovered his scoring touch in the final few games as Albion surged on towards promotion to the Premiership—Dobie ending the campaign as the club's leading scorer with 12 goals.

During the course of the season, he was capped by Scotland, making a goalscoring debut in a 4-1 defeat by South Korea.

In 2002-03, the pacy striker made more substitute appearances than any other West Bromwich Albion player. Despite his enthusiasm, he failed to hold down a regular place in the side, with injuries to groin and thigh not helping. Though the club lost their top-flight status, Dobie was an important member of the Albion side that returned to the Premiership at the first time of asking. However, with Kanu and Geoff Horsfield beginning the 2004-05 season as the main strike force, he moved on to Millwall in search of first team football.

At the New Den he was generally used on the right-hand side of midfield rather than up front, but even so, it came as a great surprise when just three months later he opted to join his former boss Gary Megson at Nottingham Forest, where he has since suffered with a serious hip injury.

KEVIN KYLE
Forward

Born: Kevin Alastair Kyle, Stranraer, 7 June 1981
Height: 6ft 3in
Weight: 13st 7lb
Clubs: Ayr Boswell; Sunderland; Huddersfield Town; Darlington; Rochdale; Coventry City
Scotland caps: 9
Scotland goals: 1
2002 v South Korea (lost 1-4), v South Africa (lost 0-2), v Hong Kong (won 4-0) 1 goal
2003 v Denmark (lost 0-1), v Faroe Islands (drew 2-2), v Canada (won 3-1),
        v Portugal (lost 0-2), v New Zealand (drew 1-1)
2004 v Denmark (lost 0-1)

Some impressive displays in Sunderland's reserve and youth teams earned Kevin Kyle the first of eight Scottish Under-21 caps when he played against Latvia in September 2000.

Unable to force his way into the Sunderland side, he spent most of the 2000-01 campaign out on loan to gain valuable first team experience. On joining Huddersfield Town, he made his league debut as a substitute against Bolton Wanderers, and then it was on to Darlington where he netted twice in eight appearances. His final loan spell was with Rochdale, before he returned to the Stadium of Light and made a handful of appearances from the substitute's bench.

Seen by many in the north-east as a possible successor to Niall Quinn, the 6ft 3in striker is certainly not afraid to compete in the physical stakes, and though in 2001-02 he again only appeared for the first team off the bench, he made his first full international appearance for Scotland against South Korea. He also netted his first goal in the 4-0 defeat of Hong Kong, a game in which caps were awarded by Scotland but one that was not considered a full international by FIFA.

He finally made the breakthrough into the Sunderland side the following season, scoring his first goal in the red and white of the Wearsiders in a 3-2 Worthington Cup win at Arsenal. Although still learning his trade—he has now won nine full caps for Scotland—his aerial power has already earmarked him down as a star of the future. He almost wrote himself into Wearside folklore towards the end of that campaign, but his last-minute headed equaliser against rivals Newcastle United was, very harshly, disallowed!

Kyle was instrumental in the Black Cats reaching the First Division play-offs and FA Cup semi-finals, scoring 16 goals along the way. An old-fashioned style centre-forward, he endured a torrid time in 2004-05, being reduced to only a handful of starts as a persistent hip injury forced him to watch from the sidelines. Sunderland swept to promotion to the Premiership, but even with a now fit Kevin Kyle back in their ranks, they unfortunately made an immediate return to the Championship. Since then, Kyle has left the Black Cats to play for Coventry City.

MAURICE ROSS
Defender
Born: Maurice Ross, Dundee, 3 February 1981
Height: 5ft 11in
Weight: 11st 11lb
Clubs: Glasgow Rangers; Sheffield Wednesdsay ; Wolverhampton Wanderers; Millwall
Scotland caps: 13
2002 v South Korea (lost 1-4), v South Africa (lost 0-2), v Hong Kong (won 4-0)
2003 v Denmark (lost 0-1), v Faroe Islands (drew 2-2), v Iceland (won 2-0),
v Canada (won 3-1), v Portugal (lost 0-2), v New Zealand (drew 1-1),
v Germany (drew 1-1)
2004 v Norway (drew 0-0), v Germany (lost 1-2), v Holland (lost 0-6)

Defender Maurice Ross, who won the first of his 13 full caps for Scotland against South Korea in 2002, looks to have a long international career ahead of him, that is providing he can stay free from injuries.

He made his Rangers debut during the course of the 1999-2000 season, coming on for Claudio Reyna in a 7-1 win over his home-town club Dundee at Dens Park, but then returned to the club's reserve side before making another appearance as a substitute the following season. He was a star in the youth teams and captained the Rangers Under-21s to win the Championship during the 2000-01 campaign. In 2001-02, Ross established himself in the Rangers back four, helping the club win both cup competitions.

The following season, Ross, who scored his first goal for the club in a 2-0 defeat of Livingston, was a member of the Rangers squad that succeeded in completing the treble, winning the title on goal difference from Celtic and beating Dundee 1-0 in the Scottish Cup Final and Celtic 2-1 in the League Cup Final.

Scotland manager Berti Vogts took a chance on the Rangers player and handed him an international call-up when he'd only made a few appearances for the Gers. Ross made his debut for Scotland against South Korea in May 2002, and went on to feature prominently in the team as they tried and failed to secure a place in Euro 2004.

Injuries have since hampered his progress at Ibrox, but he did help Rangers win the Premier Division title in 2004-05. Despite the influx of overseas players and a change of manager at the club, Maurice Ross hoped to play on a much more regular basis, but he was allowed to leave Ibrox, and after two brief spells at Sheffield Wednesday and Wolves, signed for Millwall.

JAMES McFADDEN
Forward

Born: James McFadden, Glasgow, 14 April 1983
Height: 5ft 10in
Weight: 11st 1lb
Clubs: Motherwell; Everton
Scotland caps: 31
Scotland goals: 9
2002 v South Africa (lost 0-2)
2003 v Canada (won 3-1), v Austria (lost 0-2), v New Zealand (drew 1-1)
2004 v Faroe Islands (won 3-1) 1 goal, v Germany (lost 1-2), v Lithuania (won 1-0),
     v Holland (won 1-0) 1 goal, v Holland (lost 0-6), v Wales (lost 0-4),
     v Romania (lost 1-2) 1 goal, v Denmark (lost 0-1), v Estonia (won 1-0) 1 goal,
     v Trinidad and Tobago (won 4-1)
2005 v Hungary (lost 0-3), v Spain (drew 1-1), v Slovenia (drew 0-0), v Norway (lost 0-1),
     v Sweden (lost 1-4) 1 goal, v Moldova (won 2-0) 1 goal, v Belarus (drew 0-0)
2006 v Norway (won 2-1), v Slovenia (won 3-0) 1 goal, v United States (drew 1-1),
     v Switzerland (lost 1-3), v Bulgaria (won 5-1) 1 goal, v Japan (drew 0-0),
     v Faroe Islands (won 6-0) 1 goal, v Lithuania (won 2-1), v France (won 1-0),
     v Ukraine (lost 0-2)

Though still only 23, Everton's James McFadden is a regular in Walter Smith's national squad, having scored seven goals in his 25 appearances at full international level, including the only goal of the game to beat Holland in the 2004 European Championships play-off first leg.

Beginning his career with Motherwell, he made his debut for the Fir Park club as a substitute for Greg Strong in a 3-0 home defeat at the hands of Dundee in December 2000, prior to making his first start against Rangers three months later.

In 2001-02, McFadden's first full season in the Motherwell side, he was the club's joint-top scorer with 10 goals in 24 games, including a spell of five in four consecutive games. Though the Steelmen finished bottom of the Premier Division in 2002-03, McFadden topped the Fir Park club's scoring charts with 13 goals, and on the last day of the season netted his first hat-trick in the space of 11 minutes, as Motherwell beat Livingston 6-2. It was sweet revenge, for Livingston had beaten them each time in the three previous league meetings that season. McFadden played in the opening three games of the 2003-04 season, netting both goals in a 2-2 draw with Partick Thistle, his final game for Motherwell, before joining Everton for a fee of £1.25 million.

One of the most sought-after talents from north of the Border, his signing was a major boost for Everton fans in what was a generally disappointing season. McFadden is a mesemerising dribbler who is difficult to dispossess, and he also has fine two-footed crossing and finishing ability. He scored his first goal for the Blues at Spurs in 2004-05, and after difficulties breaking into the Everton side on a regular basis, has now after a good run of first team football regained his confidence, to confirm his reputation as one of the finest young talents produced by Scotland in recent years.

LEE WILKIE
Central defender
Born: Lee Wilkie, Dundee, 20 April 1980
Height: 6ft 4in
Weight: 13st 4lb
Clubs: Downfield Juniors; Dundee; Plymouth Argyle; Notts County; Falkirk
Scotland caps: 11
Scotland goals: 1
2002 v South Africa (lost 0-2), v Hong Kong (won 4-0)
2003 v Iceland (won 2-0), v Canada (won 3-1), v Portugal (lost 0-2),
v Iceland (won 2-1) 1 goal, v Lithuania (lost 0-1), v Austria (lost 0-2),
v Holland (won 1-0), v Holland (lost 0-6)
2004 v Faroe Islands (won 3-1)

A tall, strong centre-half, Lee Wilkie began his career with home-town club Dundee, establishing himself in the Dark Blues side during the course of the 1999-2000 season. Injuries and a loss of form meant that his first team opportunities were limited, and midway through the following season, he went on loan to Plymouth Argyle.

He played in two away games for the Pilgrims before returning north of the Border, but his only subsequent appearance in the Dundee starting line-up came in the last game of the season against Hearts. Though he was tracked by several top English clubs, and appeared for Dundee in the Inter Toto Cup, he went on loan to Notts County. Though he continued to dominate in the air, he received few opportunities at Meadow Lane before returning to Dens Park. He subsequently spent a further three months on loan at Falkirk before rejoining Dundee where he won a regular first team spot.

Lee Wilkie's season ended on a very positive note when he made his bow for Scotland at full international level, featuring in the games against South Africa and a Hong Kong XI.

In 2002-03, Wilkie was a virtual ever-present and scored his first goals for the Dens Park club at set pieces in the games against Kilmarnock and Aberdeen. He also continued to figure for the national side and scored his first goal for his country in a 2-0 defeat of Iceland.

In January 2004, Wilkie damaged cruciate knee ligaments in the local derby against Dundee United, and was out of the game for a year. He returned to first team action in January 2005, and had figured in just 12 league games when, in the game against Dunfermline Athletic, he ruptured the cruciate ligaments in his knee for a second time. Wilkie was stretchered off after catching his studs in the turf in a seemingly innocuous challenge on Dunfermline's Iain Campbell. It looks as though he could face being out of the game for a further 18 months.

WARREN CUMMINGS
Left-back
Born: Warren Cummings, Aberdeen, 15 October 1980

Height: 5ft 9in
Weight: 11st 8lb
Clubs: Chelsea; Bournemouth; West Bromwich Albion; Dundee United; Bournemouth
Scotland caps: 1
2002 v Hong Kong (won 4-0)

A strong left-back with good pace, Warren Cummings is a product of the Chelsea youth system. Unable to make the grade at Stamford Bridge, he joined Second Division Bournemouth on loan in October 2000 and made his Football League debut in a 5-2 win at Bury. He made an excellent contribution in his three-month stay at Dean Court, and helped the Cherries turn their season around to become challengers for a place in the play-offs.

He returned to Stamford Bridge for a while before joining West Bromwich Albion on loan in March 2001, as Gary Megson, the Baggies' boss, sought extra options on the left-side of defence. Appearing regularly for the Scotland Under-21 side, he returned to the Hawthorns on loan the following season, though he only got the occasional outings in the senior side, being mainly used as a substitute.

After spending the first-half of the 2002-03 season on loan at Dundee United, Cummings joined Bournemouth on loan from Chelsea in the new year. The left-back produced solid performances in virtually every game he played, impressing with his great vision and passing ability. Everyone at the club was delighted when the deal was made permanent, and Cummings, who had made nine appearances for Scotland at Under-21 level, was rewarded with his first full international cap in the 4-0 defeat of Hong Kong.

An ever-present in the Bournemouth side in 2003-04, he contributed two excellent goals against Wrexham and Wycombe Wanderers as his all-round game improved. He also performed in a left-midfield role when the Cherries reverted to three at the back. The following season he was named in the PFA League One team of the year, though he missed the run-in with a broken ankle. Now back to his best, the Bournemouth defender remains the south coast club's most consistent performer.

PAUL GALLACHER

Goalkeeper

Born: Paul Gallacher, Glasgow, 16 August 1979
Height: 6ft 0in
Weight: 10st 12lb
Clubs: Dundee United; Airdrieonians; Norwich City; Gillingham; Sheffield Wednesday
Scotland caps: 8
2002 v Hong Kong (won 4-0)
2003 v Canada (won 3-1), v Republic of Ireland (lost 0-2), v Lithuania (lost 0-1), v Austria (lost 0-2)
2004 v Romania (lost 1-2), v Denmark (lost 0-1), v Estonia (won 1-0)

An outstanding goalkeeper, who is hoping to emulate his father Jim's distinguished career in Scottish football with Clydebank and latterly Arbroath, Paul Gallacher was capped by Scotland at Under-21 level at the end of the 1998-99 season.

During the course of the following campaign, he had a three-month loan spell with Airdrieonians before returning to Tannadice to make his Dundee United first team debut against St Johnstone. Also that season he made numerous appearances on the substitute's bench, to make the campaign one of advancement for him. The suspension of the club's regular keeper Alan Combe in January 2001 gave Gallacher his big breakthrough, and he retained the No.1 shirt for the remainder of the 2000-01 season, with a series of impressive displays between the posts. He continued to be the club's first-choice goalkeeper in 2001-02, when he was ever-present in the United side. His displays that campaign led to him earning inclusion in the full Scotland squad.

Gallacher earned his first cap in a match against Hong Kong in the Reunification Cup in May 2002, when he came off the bench to replace Celtic's Rob Douglas. Five months later he made his first full international start in a friendly against Canada, and has since gone on to win eight caps.

Gallacher left Tannadice in the summer of 2004 to join Norwich City as cover for Robert Green following their return to the Premiership. An unfortunate pre-season injury saw him slip to third choice, and his only first team experience in the 2004-05 season came on loan spells at Gillingham and Sheffield Wednesday. Unable to oust England international Robert Green, Gallacher was linked with a return to Scotland, but after Green joined West Ham Utd, Gallacher opted to remain at Carrow Road.

DEREK McINNES
Midfield
Born: Derek John McInnes, Paisley, 5 July 1971
Height: 5ft 8in
Weight: 12st 0lb
Clubs: Gleniffer Thistle; Morton; Glasgow Rangers; Stockport County; Toulouse (France); West Bromwich Albion; Dundee United; Millwall
Scotland caps: 2
2003 v Denmark (lost 0-1), v Portugal (lost 0-2)

The hard-tackling midfield player began his career with Morton, whom he joined from Gleniffer Thistle in the summer of 1988. His displays for the Cappielow Park club, for whom he made 255 League and Cup appearances and helped win the Scottish Second Division Championship in 1994-95, attracted the attention of a number of the game's top clubs, and in November 1995, Rangers paid £250,000 to take him to Ibrox.

Though never an automatic choice for the Glasgow giants, he was a member of the Rangers side that won the Premier Division title in 1996-97 before injuries began to take their toll. In November 1998 he joined Stockport County on a three-month loan spell, his intention being to get back to match fitness and return to Scotland. This he ultimately did, but not before Stockport had tried to secure him on a permanent basis following a series of highly impressive displays. On returning to Ibrox he had a season being in and out of the Rangers side before moving to France to play for Toulouse.

His spell with the French club was short, and in the summer of 2000 he crossed the Channel to sign for West Bromwich Albion for a fee of £450,000. On his arrival at the Hawthorns, he linked up again with boss Gary Megson, who had previously signed him on loan at Stockport. After proving effective as a midfield anchorman, he suffered cruciate ligament damage to his right knee. Corrective surgery and a long rehabilitation period followed, and it was the 2001-02 season before he was fully fit. After helping the club win promotion to the Premiership, McInnes had an unfortunate start to life in the top flight when he was red carded in the opening game at Old Trafford, and then suffered a knee injury in training while suspended!

International recognition came late to Derek McInnes, as he made his Scotland debut in August 2002, coming on for the last ten minutes against Denmark in a friendly. Three months later, against Portugal, he was substitute again, coming on midway through the first half.

In July 2003, McInnes left the Hawthorns and joined Dundee United, where he was immediately installed as team captain. He brought a high level of professionalism to the side, and his dependable performances helped the club to a fifth place finish in his first season with the club. Playing at the heart of the club's midfield, McInnes remained an important member of the Dundee United side until linking up with Millwall in the 2006 close season.

RUSSELL ANDERSON
Defender

Born: Russell Anderson, Aberdeen, 25 October 1978
Height: 5ft 11in
Weight: 10st 9lb
Clubs: Dyce Juniors; Aberdeen
Scotland caps: 9
2003 v Iceland (won 2-0), v Canada (won 3-1), v Portugal (lost 0-2),
  v Republic of Ireland (lost 0-2)
2005 v Norway (lost 0-1), v Sweden (lost 1-4)
2006 v Austria (drew 2-2), v Bulgaria (won 5-1), v Japan (drew 0-0)

Aberdeen's Russell Anderson made his international debut in the European Championship qualifying game against Iceland when, with just seconds remaining, he came off the bench to replace Gary Naysmith in the 2-0 win. He then started the game against Canada, and has now appeared in seven games for the national side.

He played his early football for Dyce Juniors, before joining his home-town team. He made his debut for the Dons in a 2-0 home defeat at the hands of Dunfermline Athletic in January 1997, going on to play in the last 14 games of that season. Since then, with the exception of 2000-01, when injury forced him to miss the entire season, he has been a regular in the Aberdeen side, playing at both right-back and in the centre of defence.

He was a member of the Dons' side that lost 2-0 to Celtic in the League Cup Final of 2000, and one that lost 4-0 to Rangers in that season's Cup Final, this in spite of the club finishing bottom of the Premier Division. With the reorganisation of the top flight now incorporating 12 teams, Aberdeen were fortunate to avoid relegation.

Following his season off through injury, he bounced back the following term to help Aberdeen to fourth place in the Premier Division, their best finish for years—a position they achieved again in 2004-05. Though not a prolific scorer, he did score one of the club's quickest goals when he netted in a matter of seconds in a 2-1 defeat of Livingston in September 2002. Since then, Anderson, who is the Dons' team captain, has appeared in over 250 games for the Pittodrie club.

PAUL DEVLIN
Midfield

Born: Paul John Devlin, Birmingham, 14 April 1972
Height: 5ft 9in
Weight: 11st 5lb
Clubs: Stafford Rangers; Notts County; Birmingham City; Sheffield United; Notts County; Birmingham City; Watford; Walsall; Tamworth
Scotland caps: 10
2003   v Canada (won 3-1), v Portugal (lost 0-2), v Republic of Ireland (lost 0-2),
v Iceland (won 2-1), v Lithuania (lost 0-1), v Austria (lost 0-2),
v New Zealand (drew 1-1), v Germany (drew 1-1)
2004   v Norway (drew 0-0), v Faroe Islands (won 3-1)

A £40,000 signing from Stafford Rangers, Paul Devlin began his Football League career with Notts County, helping the Meadow Lane club win the Autowindscreen Shield at Wembley in 1995. Playing on either flank or right down the middle, he had scored 33 goals in 180 games for County when his home-town club Birmingham City paid £200,000 to take him to St Andrew's.

A life-long City fan, his arrival solved an acute problem—he could score from the penalty-spot! He ended his first full season as the club's leading scorer and was voted the Blues' 'Player of the Year'; and though his brave and aggressive play made him popular with the fans, it did result in the occasional red card! After falling out of favour with manager Trevor Francis, Devlin signed for Sheffield United on transfer deadline day in March 1998.

Unable to hold down a regular place in his early days at Bramall Lane, he joined Notts County on loan before returning to become a key figure in the Blades' revival under Neil Warnock. Never a player to shirk a challenge, he managed to curb his tendency to over-react and ended the 1999-2000 season as the Blades' 'Player of the Year'. Despite often being marked by two opposition defenders, he still managed to create many chances with his foraging down the right-hand side. After becoming unsettled he rejoined Birmingham City on loan with a view to a permanent transfer.

He was instrumental in the Blues winning promotion to the top flight via the play-offs, and then scored the club's first-ever Premiership goal against Leeds United at St Andrew's that set up the team's opening win. He made his international debut in a 3-1 win over Canada, and featured regularly in the national squad thereafter, winning, in total, 10 caps.

He moved to Watford for a fee of £150,000 in September 2003 and made more starts and played in more matches than anyone at Vicarage Road—in fact, his only absence was due to a short suspension! A hamstring injury and an ongoing toe problem, which eventually necessitated an operation, restricted his appearances the following season, and in January 2006 he joined Walsall.

Devlin was injured on his Walsall debut, and then on his return to first team action, the fiery midfielder was sent-off! He later fell out with the club and left to play non-League football for Tamworth.

IAN MURRAY
Midfield
Born: Ian Murray, Edinburgh, 20 March 1981
Height: 6ft 0in
Weight: 11st 5lb
Clubs: Hutchison Vale; Dundee United; Hibernian; Alloa Athletic; Glasgow Rangers
Scotland caps: 6
2003 v Canada (won 3-1)
2005 v Moldova (drew 1-1), v Sweden (lost 1-4)
2006 v Belarus (lost 0-1), v Bulgaria (won 5-1), Japan (drew 0-0)

Left-sided midfielder Ian Murray, who captained Scotland at Under-21 level, won his first full international cap against Canada in October 2002 when, with a quarter-of-an-hour to go, he came off the bench to replace Dundee's Lee Wilkie in a 3-1 win for the Scots.

Having played his early football for Hutchison Vale Boys Club, Murray was on the books of Dundee United when Hibs secured his signature in the summer of 1999. After impressing in the Easter Road club's reserve side, he made his first team debut against his former club in January 2000, in a match that ended goalless. The following season he had a brief loan spell with Alloa, but returned to help Hibs to third place in the Premier League, and in the course of doing so, netted his first league goal for the club in a 1-1 draw at champions elect Celtic at Parkhead. Also that season, he helped Hibs to reach their first Scottish Cup Final for 22 years, but they went down 3-0 to Celtic.

Murray, who was a member of the Scottish Under-21 side, was also a virtual ever-present in the Hibs side. Able to play anywhere, he has a tremendous natural fitness which carries him all over the field during the course of a game, and, in 2002-03, Murray, who scored eight times from midfield, was voted the club's 'Player of the Year'. Injuries hampered his progress the following season, and he was forced to miss the whole of the second half of the campaign. In 2004-05, he proved his worth as captain, helping Hibs to finish third. His only goal that season was the winner in a tight league game against Motherwell.

After returning from international duty against Belarus, Murray completed his free transfer switch from Hibs to Rangers, signing for the Ibrox club on a three-year deal. The versatile player will undoubtedly prove an indispensable asset to the Glasgow side.

JAMIE SMITH
Winger

Born: Jamie Smith, Alexandria, 20 November 1980
Height: 5ft 7in
Weight: 11st 0lb
Clubs: Glasgow Celtic; Den Haag (Holland); Aberdeen
Scotland caps: 2
2003 v Republic of Ireland (lost 0-2), v Austria (lost 0-2)

A product of Celtic's youth system, Jamie Smith progressed through the ranks at Parkhead where he developed physically and mentally to become a very useful member of Martin O'Neill's first team squad.

He made his Premier Division debut as a substitute for Didier Agathe in a 6-0 rout of Aberdeen, and in a match in which Henrik Larsson netted a hat-trick, Smith completed the scoring two minutes from time. He went on to appear in seven games as Celtic won the League Championship. He also made an appearance from the bench as the Bhoys beat Kilmarnock 3-0 in the League Cup Final, with Larsson netting another treble. He played in a similar number of matches in 2001-02 as Celtic retained the title.

Quick, skilful and extremely fit, Smith is also versatile—capable of shining on either wing or even in a

Jamie Smith

striking role. After enjoying an excellent spell in the Celtic side, Smith made an unexpected full international debut when he replaced Neil McCann against the Republic of Ireland. He also made another appearance off the bench in Scotland's next international game against Austria.

Towards the end of that season, he was involved in some of Celtic's scintillating

UEFA Cup adventures, when he was handed a part in games against Liverpool and Boavista.

Injuries hampered his progress in 2003-04, and after coming out of contract at the end of that season, he joined Dutch club Den Haag for a season. In the summer of 2005 he returned to Scotland to play for Aberdeen, where he has impressed both in midfield and attack, scoring a number of vital goals. His form led to him being recalled to the national squad for the friendly against Switzerland in March 2006, but unfortunately, due to hamstring problems, he withdrew on the day that the squad was announced! Now back to his best, he will be hoping for a recall to the national squad soon.

ANDY GRAY
Defender/ Midfield

Born: Andrew David Gray, Harrogate, 15 November 1977
Height: 6ft 1in
Weight: 13st 0lb
Clubs: Leeds United; Bury; Nottingham Forest; Preston North End; Oldham Athletic; Bradford City; Sheffield United: Sunderland; Burnley
Scotland caps: 2
2003 v Lithuania (lost 0-1), v New Zealand (drew 1-1)

The son of Frankie Gray, he began his career with Leeds United, making his debut as an 18-year-old winger-cum-striker against West Ham United in January 1996.

Very quick, skilful and a superb crosser of the ball, he was selected for the Scotland Under-21 squad on three occasions, before having to withdraw each time because of injury. However, he managed to make a full recovery and force himself into the Leeds team towards the end of the 1996-97 season.

Loaned out to Bury, he netted his first league goal after appearing as a substitute at Reading, but on his return to Elland Road he suffered a frustrating time, being unable to win a recall to first team action.

Transferred to Nottingham Forest for a fee of £175,000, he found himself a member of a side struggling to come to terms with life in the Premiership. On losing his place, he had loan spells with Preston North End and Oldham Athletic before returning to the City Ground. He then showed his versatility by appearing as a right wing-back as well as playing wide on the right or left of midfield. Over the next couple of seasons he struggled to make an impact in the Forest side, and in the summer of 2002, having made just 76 League and Cup appearances in four seasons, he was allowed to join Bradford City on a free.

He enjoyed a terrific first season with the Bantams, ending the campaign as the club's leading scorer with 15 goals and winning the 'Player of the Year' award. A virtual ever-present, he was rewarded for his great performances with his first full cap for Scotland in the 1-0 defeat by Lithuania. Despite another season of consistent performances, he was unable to prevent the Bantams' relegation to Division Two.

In February 2004, he moved to rivals Sheffield United where, used as a striker and linking up well with his former team-mate Ashley Ward, he scored in each of his first three games. Gray ended the 2004-05 season as the Blades' top scorer, his form leading to him winning a recall to the Scotland international squad. He remained an important member of the United side as they push for promotion to the Premiership, but in the summer of 2005, joined Sunderland. Unable to make much impression at the Stadium of Light, he went on loan to Burnley where he scored in each of his first three home games.

ANDY WEBSTER
Defender
Born: Andrew Webster, Dundee, 23 April 1982
Height: 5ft 11in
Weight: 11st 4lb
Clubs: Arbroath; Heart of Midlothian; Wigan Athletic
Scotland caps: 22
Scotland goals: 1
2003 v Austria (lost 0-2), v New Zealand (drew 1-1), v Germany (drew 1-1)
2004 v Norway (drew 0-0), v Faroe Islands (won 3-1), v Wales (lost 0-4), v Estonia (won 1-0), v Trinidad and Tobago (won 4-1)
2005 v Hungary (lost 0-3), v Spain (drew 1-1), v Slovenia (drew 0-0), v Norway (lost 0-1), v Moldova (drew 1-1), v Sweden (lost 1-4), v Moldova (won 2-0), v Belarus (drew 0-0)
2006 v Austria (drew 2-2), v Italy (drew 1-1), v Norway (won 2-1), v Slovenia (won 3-0), v United States (drew 1-1) 1 goal, v Switzerland (lost 1-3)

This solid defender played youth football for his local club before accepting a Skill Seeker Contract in September 1999 rather than going on to study sports science at University. He made his debut for Arbroath in the Challenge Cup against Stirling Albion in 2000. Webster also featured in matches against Ross County and in the Scottish Cup tie against Motherwell at Fir Park, before making his first team breakthrough at Gayfield Park at the beginning of the 2000-01 season in a 3-0 defeat of Stenhousemuir.

Playing in his best position in the centre of the defence, Webster helped Arbroath win promotion to the First Division in 2001-02, his performances raising interest from a host of clubs in Scotland and England. Trials at Tynecastle and with Charlton Athletic followed, and his profile was raised still further when Hearts made their first bid, with the initial offer rejected by Arbroath. However, after the player himself rejected a move to Dundee United, Hearts stepped in again to sign Webster on a five-year deal.

With power in the air and strength in the tackle, Webster formed a splendid defensive partnership with Steven Pressley, and this has played an important part in Hearts finishing third in the League for a couple of seasons and playing regularly in the UEFA Cup. It was in this latter competition that Webster scored a number of vital goals against SC Braga and NK Zeljeznicar—in fact, his goal against Braga was the first ever at the Murrayfield Stadium.

The tough centre-back appeared in the League Cup semi-final in February 2003, and later that year he scored the goal against Hibs that won the inaugural Festival Cup. In addition, during 2002-03, he started to receive international recognition, winning the first of 22 caps against Austria. A regular in the Hearts side until the end of the 2005-06 season, he has recently signed for Wigan Athletic.

BRIAN KERR
Midfield
Born: Brian Kerr, Motherwell, 12 October 1981
Height: 5ft 8in
Weight: 11st 2lb
Clubs: Newcastle United; Coventry City; Livingston; Motherwell
Scotland caps: 3
2003 v New Zealand (drew 1-1)
2004 v Estonia (won 1-0), v Trinidad and Tobago (won 4-1)

A product of Newcastle United's academy scheme, he impressed so much in the youth and reserve teams that, at the age of 18, he was called up to the senior squad, making his debut as a late substitute at Coventry City in September 2000. Shortly afterwards he dislocated a shoulder in training, and then on returning to action, suffered a repeat of the same injury!

Still recovering from the dislocated shoulder, he missed the start of the 2001-02 season, but on his return to full fitness, he was awarded the captaincy of the Magpies' reserve side. After leading the team to the top of the table, he was given a couple of brief substitute appearances in that season's FA Cup competition, but failed to add to his solitary league appearance.

During the 2002 close season, Kerr made his debut for the Scotland Under-21 side against Denmark. Loaned out to Coventry City where he featured on the right-side of midfield, he returned to St James Park to make his Premiership start in the 1-0 home win over Liverpool on New Year's Day 2003. The rest of the season saw him make occasional appearances for the Magpies' first team in a defensive central midfield role.

His performances led to him making his full international debut for Scotland against New Zealand in May 2003, in a match that ended with honours even at 1-1.

He spent most of the 2003-04 season out on loan. He was a regular for SPL side Livingston in the early part of the campaign, only to suffer a broken right leg towards the end of November. Once fit, he spent the last six weeks of the season on loan at Coventry, but was then released by Newcastle and joined his home-town club Motherwell, passing up a trial with one time European champions, Borussia Dortmund.

Unfortunately, injury problems struck Kerr early in his Motherwell career, meaning that his first team debut was delayed until April 2005, where he helped the Steelmen to a 3-1 win over Aberdeen at Pittodrie. The season ended all too quickly for the midfielder, who, after improving considerably with each passing game, is now a regular in the Motherwell side.

DARREN FLETCHER
Midfield

Born: Darren Barr Fletcher, Edinburgh, 1 February 1984
Height: 6ft 0in
Weight: 13st 4lb
Clubs: Manchester United
Scotland caps: 27
Scotland goals: 4

2004 v Norway (drew 0-0), v Lithuania (won 1-0) 1 goal, v Holland (won 1-0),
v Holland (lost 0-6), v Wales (lost 0-4), v Denmark (lost 0-1), v Estonia (won 1-0),
v Trinidad and Tobago (won 4-1) 1 goal

2005 v Hungary (lost 0-3), v Spain (drew 1-1), v Slovenia (drew 0-0), v Norway (lost 0-1),
v Moldova (drew 1-1), v Moldova (won 2-0), v Belarus (drew 0-0)

2006 v Italy (drew 1-1), v Norway (won 2-1), v Belarus (lost 0-1), v Slovenia (won 3-0) 1 goal,
v United States (drew 1-1), v Switzerland (lost 1-3), v Bulgaria (won 5-1),
v Japan (drew 0-0), v Faroe Islands (won 6-0) 1 goal, v Lithuania (won 2-1),
v France (won 1-0), v Ukraine (lost 0-2)

An upright and elegant midfielder, who possesses good touch and passing skills, he was, in his early days with Manchester United, being touted as the latest big prospect down at Old Trafford. All these attributes were soon put to the test against Basel and Deportivo in the Champions' League, when he rose to the occasion in commanding fashion. Around this time, Fletcher showed that he was susceptible to injuries, breaking the same toe five times and having a permanent pin inserted!

With Scotland boss Berti Vogts tracking him, he continued to shine with a clutch of first team appearances in all competitions during the 2003-04 season. On the international front, having made his debut against Norway, he helped Scotland to the European Championships play-offs before falling to Holland.

With expectations high, and comparisons being made with former Red David Beckham, he continued to show promise in 2004-05, despite his somewhat limited first team opportunities for Manchester United. Even so, he appeared in 30 games in all competitions, and one statistic that might well have gone unnoticed by United and Scotland supporters is that he was on the losing side only twice—against Chelsea in the last home Premiership game and against Arsenal in the FA Cup Final. In 2005-06 he played a significant role in all of the Reds' Cup campaigns, his only goal coming in the Premiership victory over eventual champions, Chelsea.

STEPHEN PEARSON
Forward/ Midfield

Born: Stephen Pearson, Lanark, 2 October 1982
Height: 6ft 1in

Weight: 11st 6lb
Clubs: Motherwell; Glasgow Celtic
Scotland caps: 6
2004 v Holland (won 1-0), v Wales (lost 0-4)
2005 v Hungary (lost 0-3), v Spain (drew 1-1), v Norway (lost 0-1), v Sweden (lost 1-4)

Stephen Pearson began his career with Motherwell—a product of the Fir Park club's successful youth policy. He made his league debut for the Steelmen as a substitute in a 1-1 draw at Hibernian in March 2001. Pearson was a regular in the Motherwell side, making over 70 appearances until his £350,000 transfer to Celtic in the 2004 January transfer window.

A life-long Celtic fan, many observers predicted that he would spend as much time on the bench as he would on the park in the months that were to follow, but with his direct running and willingness to break beyond the strikers adding an extra dimension to Celtic's play, he looked a veritable bargain! It was an injury to Welsh international John Hartson that enabled Pearson to hold down a regular place in the team for the rest of the 2003-04 season. He was voted the Scottish 'Young Player of the Year', helping the Hoops win the Scottish League and Cup double.

Lifting a weight of attacking responsibility from the shoulders of Stilian Petrov, he continued the fine form at the end of the 2003-04 season into the 2004-05 one, and though he only played in nine games at the start of the campaign, he remains an exciting prospect for the future.

Widely regarded as one of the most talented young players in Scotland, he won the first of six full international caps for the national side when coming on as a substitute in the 2004 European Championship play-off with Holland, which the Scots won 1-0.

There were rumours that Pearson might part company with the Bhoys in the 2006 January transfer window, with Preston North End the frontrunners for his signature, but with Pearson having forced his way back into the first team, manager Gordon Strachan stated that the Scottish international would not be leaving Parkhead.

PAUL GALLAGHER
Forward
Born: Paul Gallagher, Glasgow, 9 August 1984
Height: 6ft 1in
Weight: 12th 0lb
Clubs: Blackburn Rovers; Stoke City (loan)
Scotland caps: 1
2004 v Wales (lost 0-4)

A tall, lean striker, Paul Gallagher scored regularly at reserve and youth team level for Blackburn Rovers in 2002-03, including a hat-trick against Aston Villa to help the Lancashire club clinch the FA Academy Under-19s title. Left-footed, with pace and a natural eye for goal, he made his Premiership debut when coming off the bench in a game against Arsenal in March 2003.

He proved to be the surprise packet at Ewood Park the following season, demonstrating a maturity beyond his years and an eye for an opportunity. Always willing to try the unexpected, he received fewer chances in the first team than other more experienced players because of the gravity of the club's situation, but even so, he won his first full international cap for Scotland when he played in the 4-0 defeat by Wales.

The young striker never really made the progress expected of him in 2004-05. He managed even fewer starts and most of his appearances came from the bench. When he did come on, he was often forced to come on in emergencies and assume a variety of roles. His goal against Fulham was striking at its best, but his work-rate was not as impressive as it should have been, and Rovers fans will be hoping he can really progress at Ewood Park in the not too distant future.

However, with Craig Bellamy and Morten Gamst Pedersen occupying the strikers' berths, and fellow Scottish international Paul Dickov on the books at that time, Gallagher opted for a season's long loan with Stoke City, scoring 11 goals in 37 games before returning to Ewood Park.

GRAEME MURTY
Full-back

Born: Graeme Stuart Murty, Saltburn, 13 November 1974
Height: 5ft 10in
Weight: 11st 10lb
Clubs: York City; Reading
Scotland caps: 3
2004 v Wales (lost 0-4)
2006 v Bulgaria (won 5-1), Japan (drew 0-0)

Graeme Murty began his career with York City, making 141 appearances for the Minstermen, including an appearance in their legendary win over Manchester United in the Coca-Cola Cup, while he also scored the winner in a 3-2 victory over Everton in the same competition.

Reading manager Tommy Burns paid £700,000 for his services in the summer of 1998, but his first year at the Madejski Stadium was plagued by injury as he only made eight appearances for the Royals. In fact, he suffered a number of injuries over the next couple of seasons, and it was the home game against Millwall in January 2001 that proved to be something of a turning point as he made his comeback with a very impressive substitute's performance. He went on to help Reading reach the Division Two play-off final, and he scored what has proved to be his only goal of his Royals career so far with an excellent drive from outside the box in the game against Bristol City.

Murty had an outstanding 2001-02 season. He was virtually ever-present at right-back, and his precision in the tackle, plus immaculate passing and countless brave last-ditch clearances in front of goal earned him deserved recognition with selection for the PFA Division two team. He was also nominated as the supporters' 'Player of the Season' as the Royals won promotion to the First Division, a feat which activated another £50,000 payment to his former club York.

He continued to be a model of consistency in the higher grade of football, and in 2003-04 was again named as the supporters' 'Player of the Season'. International recognition came his way when selected by Berti Vogts for the Scotland Future team against Turkey, and later Murty made his full international debut as a substitute in the friendly against Wales later in the campaign. The club's longest-serving player, he took over as the club captain following the departure of Adrian Williams to Coventry City.

Often described as the best full-back outside the Premiership, this no longer is the case as the Royals led the Championship by a long way at the end of the 2005-06 season, and they are playing top flight football in 2006-07.

JOHN KENNEDY
Central defender
Born: John Kennedy, Bellshill, 18 August 1983
Height: 6ft 2in
Weight: 13st 7lb
Clubs: Glasgow Celtic
Scotland caps: 1
2004 v Romania (lost 1-2)

A tall and commanding central defender, John Kennedy first represented Celtic at the tender age of just 16, when manager Kenny Dalglish rewarded him for the promise he had been showing at youth level with a senior call-up for the game against Motherwell in April 2000, a match the Bhoys won 4-0. He had made four appearances off the bench before starting his first game on the final day of the season in a 2-0 home win over Dundee United.

The arrival of Martin O'Neill saw the big central defender return to the club's youth ranks, but after three years during which his patience was tested to its limits, Kennedy returned to first team action during the 2003-04 season, and he was among the stars of the Parkhead club's show of defensive heroism against Barcelona in the Nou Camp.

An impressive showing in the Old Firm derby against Rangers came next, followed quickly by a Scotland call-up for the match against Romania. Just as the young defender's star seemed to be in the ascendancy, he suffered a devastating knee injury on his full international appearance as a result of a horrific tackle from Romania's Vio Ganea.

Kennedy has since travelled to America to undergo a career-saving knee reconstruction at the hands of the world-renowned surgeon Dr Richard Steadman.

PETER CANERO
Defender
Born: Peter Canero, Glasgow, 18 January 1981
Height: 5ft 10in
Weight: 11st 4lb
Clubs: Kilmarnock; Leicester City; Dundee United
Scotland caps: 1
2004 v Denmark (lost 0-1)

Peter Canero began his career as a youth player at Rugby Park, making his first team debut for Kilmarnock in their match against Aberdeen at the start of the 1999-2000 season. During the course of his time with Kilmarnock, Canero helped the club reach the 2001 League Cup Final, where they went down 3-0 to Celtic and scored 11 goals in 130 games.

With Canero out of contract in the summer of 2004, Kilmarnock wisely decided to sell him to Leicester City during the January transfer window for a fee of £250,000. A series of impressive performances for the Foxes, when he was asked to operate on the right side of midfield, led to him being called up to the senior Scotland squad in April 2004. Canero was called into action after just quarter of an hour of the 1-0 defeat by Denmark, but a hip injury brought his season to a premature close, so denying him the opportunity to add to his international caps at the end of May.

His 2004-05 season was dogged by injury, and while he looked to have claimed the right-back position as his own following the appointment of Craig Levein as manager, he was again laid low by injury. Having made just 13 outings in twelve months at the Walker Stadium, he was released in the summer.

Canero became Dundee United manager Gordon Chisholm's fifth signing after he took over the reins at Tannadice and all Terrors fans will be hoping he can steer clear of injuries and help the club go forward.

MALKY MACKAY
Central defender
Born: Malcolm George Mackay, Bellshill, 19 February 1972
Height: 6ft 1in
Weight: 11st 7lb
Clubs: Queen's Park; Glasgow Celtic; Norwich City; West Ham United; Watford
Scotland caps: 5
2004 v Denmark (lost 0-1), v Estonia (won 1-0), v Trinidad and Tobago (won 4-1)
2005 v Spain (drew 1-1), v Slovenia (drew 0-0)

Almost a throwback to the days of the traditional stopper-style centre-half, Malky Mackay began his career with Queen's Park, making 77 appearances before leaving to join Celtic in the summer of 1993. In five seasons at Parkhead, Mackay made just 52 appearances in all competitions, and in August 1998 he joined Norwich City for a fee of £350,000.

He showed himself to be particularly strong in the air, both defensively and as an attacking threat at set-play situations, when he was so unlucky with the number of headers which were kept out by the woodwork. A natural leader on the pitch, always encouraging his team-mates, willing them on to greater efforts, he was a great favourite of the Carrow Road faithful.

In 2001-02, he formed an outstanding central defensive partnership with Craig Fleming, and thoroughly enjoyed the confrontation playing against a big centre-forward brings. He skippered the side in Iwan Roberts' absence and proved himself an excellent leader. Injuries prevented him from holding down a regular place the following season, but in 2003-04 he was back to his best, enjoying another fantastic season for the Canaries.

His place in Canary folklore was further cemented by his two-goal display against local rivals Ipswich Town at Carrow Road in March 2004 in what was his 200th league appearance for the East Anglian club. The following month he was so proud to receive his first full Scotland cap in the friendly against Denmark. His contribution to the Norwich cause was further recognised when he was voted into the PFA Division One team of the season.

After leading Norwich to promotion, he was surprisingly allowed to join West Ham United for a fee of £300,000 in the close season. The central defender provided strong leadership on and off the pitch, and his experience was of great value to the Hammers' cause. With West Ham winning the play-off final, they swapped places with his former club!

Following a number of new signings by West Ham manager Alan Pardew, Mackay left Upton Park and joined Watford. It certainly seems that he has what it takes to get out of the Championship, having achieved promotion with each of his last two clubs in the last couple of seasons, and making it three as the Vicarage Road club successfully secured a place in the top flight in 2006.

RICHARD HUGHES
Midfield

Born: Richard Daniel Hughes, Glasgow, 25 June 1979
Height: 5ft 9in
Weight: 9st 12lb
Clubs: Atalanta (Italy); Arsenal; Bournemouth; Portsmouth; Grimsby Town
Scotland caps: 5
2004 v Estonia (won 1-0), v Trinidad and Tobago (won 4-1)
2005 v Norway (lost 0-1), v Sweden (lost 1-4)
2006 v Austria (drew 2-2)

Being of Scottish birth, Richard Hughes was a surprise Arsenal signing from Atalanta in August 1997, but unable to make the breakthrough at Highbury, he moved to Bournemouth prior to the start of the 1998-99 season.

He made his Football League debut on the opening day of the season against Lincoln, and quickly established himself as an integral part of the Cherries' midfield. Despite not being blessed with great pace, he proved himself an excellent dribbler of the ball, and his form that season led to him making four appearances for the Scotland Under-21 side. Injuries disrupted his progress the following season, but he was back to his best in 2000-01 as the Cherries just missed out in the end-of-season play-offs. Hughes continued to feature regularly for the Under-21 side, and in June 2002, Portsmouth paid £100,000 for his services.

Having caught the eye with his early season displays, his progress was halted by complications in a hamstring strain, before he lost the tip of a finger after trapping it in a training-room door! On recovery he went out on loan to Grimsby Town, where he created an immediate impact by setting up a goal for player-manager Paul Groves within a minute of his debut! Though he was a great favourite at Blundell Park, he returned to the south coast club to continue his career.

It was towards the end of the 2003-04 season before he won a regular place in the side, and his first goal for the club was the winner against Liverpool in an FA Cup replay at Fratton Park. The combative midfielder, who always gives 100% effort in the cause of the team, remains an important member of the Portsmouth side as they struggled to maintain their Premiership status. However, at the time of writing the south coast club have had a successful run. and had a spell at the top of the Premiership!

DAVID McNAMEE
Full-back

Born: David McNamee, Glasgow, 10 October 1980
Height: 5ft 11in
Weight: 11st 2lb
Clubs: St Mirren; Blackburn Rovers; Livingston; Coventry City
Scotland caps: 4
2004 v Estonia (won 1-0), v Trinidad and Tobago (won 4-1)
2006 v Bulgaria (won 5-1), v Japan (drew 0-0)

Tough-tackling full-back David McNamee played his early football in the Scottish First Division with St Mirren, making his debut for the Buddies in a 1-0 win at Stranraer on the opening day of the 1998-99 season. He went on to miss very few games in what was his only season for the club, helping them finish in fifth place. His performances had attracted interest from clubs north and south of the Border, but it was to Blackburn Rovers that McNamee moved in the close season.

Despite his consistency in Rovers' reserve team, McNamee couldn't force his way into the Blackburn first team, and along with his former St Mirren team-mate Burton O'Brien, he left Ewood Park to return to Scotland to play for Livingston.

Making his debut for Livingston as a substitute at Dundee in September 2002, he made his first start the following week against Rangers, and soon earned himself a reputation as one of Scotland's most attacking full-backs. McNamee, who can play right or left back, was a member of the Livingston side that won the CIS Cup in 2004, beating Hibernian 2-0 in the final.

Twice capped by Scotland, playing the full 90 minutes of his debut against Estonia and as a late substitute against Trinidad and Tobago, he was always in the Livingston starting line-up when available. However, his robust style of play has saw him suspended on a number of occasions, and this has forced him out of crucial games for Livingston.

After snapping his Achilles tendon in a 2-0 defeat at Kilmarnock in May 2005, McNamee was an important member of the Livingston side, and he made appearances for the Almondvale Stadium club, before signing for Coventry City in July 2006.

NIGEL QUASHIE
Midfield

Born: Nigel Francis Quashie, Peckham, 20 July 1978
Height: 6ft 0in
Weight: 12st 4lb
Clubs: Queen's Park Rangers; Nottingham Forest; Portsmouth; Southampton; West Bromwich Albion
Scotland caps: 14
Scotland goals: 1
2004 v Estonia (won 1-0), v Trinidad and Tobago (won 4-1) 1 goal
2005 v Hungary (lost 0-3), v Spain (drew 1-1), v Slovenia (drew 0-0), v Sweden (lost 1-4), v Italy (lost 0-2)
2006 v Austria (drew 2-2), v Italy (drew 1-1), v Slovenia (won 3-0), v United States (drew 1-1), v Switzerland (lost 1-3), v Faroe Islands (won 6-0), v Lithuania (won 2-1)

Nigel Quashie started out with Queen's Park Rangers where his form for the Loftus Road club led to him winning England Under-21 honours. Strong on the ball, with good touch and a willingness to get into areas where he can test the goalkeeper, Quashie suffered with both illness and injury during his time with the London club, but throughout his stay he continued to be included in both the England Under-21 and 'B' squads.

Prior to the start of the 1998-99 season, Nottingham Forest paid £2.5 million for Quashie's services. After taking time to settle at his new club, he broke his foot, but even on his return to full fitness, he found himself in and out of the Forest side.

Transferred to Portsmouth for a cut-price £200,000, he impressed in his first season at Fratton Park, netting a number of spectacular goals, the best coming against Norwich when he ran with the ball from the halfway line before unleashing a tremendous 40-yard shot into the top corner of the net. He continued to demonstrate his midfield talents with Pompey, and was instrumental in them winning the First Division title in 2002-03, when he contributed a number of valuable goals. A troublesome knee injury hampered his efforts as he tried his best among the Premiership's elite, but even so, he was rewarded with the first of 12 full international caps against Estonia.

Quashie had scored 14 goals in 163 games for Portsmouth when he made the controversial decision to transfer to neighbours Southampton for £2.1 million in January 2005. At instant hit with the Saints' fans, he appeared to be everywhere at once, but even he couldn't prevent Southampton from losing their top flight status.

Nigel Quashie has since left St Mary's and went on in 2005-06 to display his energy and passion with splendid guile back in the Premiership with West Bromwich Albion. Unfortunately the Baggies lost their top flight status, and Nigel Quashie is now playing his football in the Championship.

CRAIG GORDON
Goalkeeper

Born: Craig Gordon, Edinburgh, 31 December 1982
Height: 6ft 4in
Weight: 12st 2lb
Clubs: Heart of Midlothian
Scotland caps: 19
2004 v Trinidad and Tobago (won 4-1)
2005 v Spain (drew 1-1), v Slovenia (drew 0-0), v Norway (lost 0-1), v Moldova (drew 1-1), v Italy (lost 0-2), v Moldova (won 2-0), v Belarus (drew 0-0)
2006 v Austria (drew 2-2), v Italy (drew 1-1), v Norway (won 2-1), v Belarus (lost 0-1), v Slovenia (won 3-0), v United States (drew 1-1), v Switzerland (lost 1-3), v Faroe Islands (won 6-0), v Lithuania (won 2-1), v France (won 1-0), v Ukraine (lost 0-2)

Goalkeeper Craig Gordon has been associated with Hearts since the age of 12, playing for the Tynecastle Boys' Club and Hearts Boys' Club. He signed a full professional contract in 1999, and soon became a star in the club's youth and Under-21 sides. In May 2000 he played his part in the Youth Cup Final victory over Rangers with a number of outstanding saves, and the following season, he was a member of the side that won the Youth League Championship.

The tall shot-stopper was loaned out to Cowdenbeath in September 2001, but three months later he was recalled to Tynecastle after an injury to Finnish international keeper Antti Niemi. Gordon made his competitive debut for Hearts in October 2002 in a 1-1 draw at Livingston, and was then on the bench for the remainder of the season.

Tepi Moilanen, another Finnish international keeper, joined the club from Preston North End, but in October 2003, Gordon took over from him and became a worthy winner of the Bank of Scotland 'Young Player of the Season' award after helping Hearts to claim third place in the Premier League. On becoming Hearts' first-choice keeper, he produced several match-winning performances, including a stunning display in the UEFA Cup tie at Bordeaux.

In May 2004, Gordon earned his first international cap, playing for Scotland against Trinidad and Tobago. Now having been capped 15 times for the national side, he has also appeared for the youth, Under-21 and 'B' teams.

Having gained further European and international experience over the past couple of seasons, his sure handling and commanding displays, particularly in the World Cup matches, should confirm his place as a Scotland regular. Although he will always be a target for other clubs, he recently signed a contract that will keep him at Tynecastle until 2007.

JAMIE McALLISTER
Defender
Born: Jamie McAllister, Edinburgh, 26 April 1978
Height: 5ft 10in
Weight: 11st 0lb
Clubs: Queen of the South; Aberdeen; Livingston; Heart of Midlothian; Bristol City
Scotland caps: 1
2004 v Trinidad and Tobago (won 4-1)

A quick and skilful defender who likes to get forward and rarely wastes a pass, Jamie McAllister played for Bellshill Boys Club before being recruited by Queen of the South in the summer of 1996. He quickly became one of the most promising players in the lower divisions, and helped the Dumfries club to reach the Challenge Cup Final in November 1997. His style and consistency had attracted the attention of a number of clubs, and in May 1999, his services were secured by Aberdeen for a fee of £100,000.

The industrious defender played in almost 150 competitive games for the Dons, and as well as seeing European action, appeared in the League Cup Final for the Pittodrie club in March 2000 and in the Scottish Cup Final two months later—unfortunately for him, he was on the losing side on both occasions.

In June 2003, he left Aberdeen to join Livingston, where as well as being very comfortable in the left wing-back position, he also felt at home in midfield. His attacking instincts were certainly evident when Livingston reached the 2004 League Cup Final, as he scored one of his side's goals in a 2-0 win over Hibernian. His performance in that final was outstanding and led to him winning his first cap for Scotland in the friendly against Trinidad and Tobago in May 2004.

With some uncertainty about his future at Livingston and his contract having expired, Hearts were able to move in to secure McAllister's transfer on a two-year deal. Since his arrival at Tynecastle, he has settled into the squad and has also been on standby for the national team. With Hearts having led the Premier Division for much of the 2005-06 season, opponents had to beware of his free-kicks. McAllister has since left Tynecastle to join Bristol City.

DAVID MARSHALL
Goalkeeper
Born: David Marshall, Glasgow, 5 March 1985
Height: 6ft 3in
Weight: 13st 0lb
Clubs: Glasgow Celtic

Scotland caps: 2
2005   v Hungary (lost 0-3), v Sweden (lost 1-4)

Having risen through the ranks at Parkhead, goalkeeper David Marshall made his senior debut for the Hoops during the course of the 2002-03 season in the 3-0 Scottish Cup victory over St Johnstone. He really made a breakthrough the following season, taking over the reins from Rob Douglas following his sending-off in the UEFA Cup clash with Barcelona and then Douglas's injury.

Though he had been tipped for greatness, no-one could have predicted that David Marshall's rise to fame and prominence would be so quite meteoric. A magnificent heroic performance in the Nou Camp—followed swiftly by another starring role at Ibrox—ensured, however, that the teenage goalkeeper became a favourite of the Celtic supporters almost overnight!

Such is his promise that he signed a four-year deal with the Bhoys in March 2004, and his performances thereafter have merely reaffirmed that he will be a massive asset for years to come. He went on to justify that contract in 2004-05 as he made 24 appearances for the Hoops, keeping seven clean sheets. Marshall also made his full international debut for Scotland against Hungary, and later added a second cap against Sweden—but conceded seven goals over the two matches!

Under Gordon Strachan, Marshall is no longer the club's first-choice keeper, and it may be that he needs a season-long loan spell to gain further experience.

LEE McCULLOCH
Forward/ Midfield
Born: Lee Henry McCulloch, Bellshill, 14 May 1978
Height: 6ft 5in
Weight: 13st 6lb
Clubs: Cumbernauld United; Motherwell; Wigan Athletic
Scotland caps: 8
2005   v Moldova (drew 1-1), v Italy (lost 0-2), v Moldova (won 2-0), v Belarus (drew 0-0)
2006   v Belarus (lost 0-1), v Bulgaria (won 5-1), v Japan (drew 0-0), v France (won 1-0),

Lee McCulloch made his debut as a substitute for Motherwell in a 3-0 win at Raith Rovers in August 1996, going on to appear in 15 games that season, all but one from the bench. Though he failed to find the net during that spell, he opened his account with two goals in a 6-2 defeat of Hibs midway through the following season. His performances in attack for Motherwell led to him winning 14 caps at Under-21 level for Scotland, his first against Latvia in 1997. In 1999-2000, McCulloch's 12 goals helped the Steelmen finish fourth in the Premier Division and attracted the scouts to Fir Park.

In March 2001, he was part of a double swoop by Wigan Athletic manager Bruce Rioch, who took McCulloch and Steve McMillan to the JJB Stadium. Having scored his first goal for the club with an acrobatic overhead kick in a 3-2 win over Oxford United, great things were expected of McCulloch in 2001-02. He started the campaign well, scoring in his first two games, but as the season wore on he found himself spending most of his time on the bench. The following season he was converted from striker to midfield—one of the success stories of Wigan's season—although he later reverted to the front line following injuries to Andy Liddell and Nathan Ellington.

McCulloch, whose physical presence enables him to hold the ball up well, played on the left-side of midfield for much of the 2003-04 season, scoring a number of vital goals. The following season, as the Latics won promotion to the Premiership, McCulloch scored 14 goals and was named as the Players' 'Player of the Season'. His performances led to him collecting his first Scotland cap in the World Cup qualifier against Moldova in October 2004 from the bench, and he made his full debut in Walter Smith's first game in charge against Italy.

Rewarded for his efforts with an extension to his contract, he has been a revelation in the top flight as the Latics began the season by taking the Premiership by storm.

STEVEN HAMMELL
Defender
Born: Steven Hammell, Glasgow, 18 February 1982
Height: 5ft 9in
Weight: 11st 11lb
Clubs: Bearsden BC; Motherwell; Southend United
Scotland caps: 1
2005 v Sweden (lost 1-4)

When Steve McMillan was suspended towards the end of the 1999-2000 season, 18-year-old Steven Hammell filled in for him at left-back, making his debut in a 2-1 defeat against Aberdeen at Pittodrie. When McMillan left for Wigan in March 2001, Hammell became the Steelmen's first-choice left-back and since then has missed very few games.

His talents up and down Motherwell's left flank have not gone unnoticed, and he has regularly been involved with the national side at various levels. After numerous appearances for Rainer Bonhof's Scotland Under-21 side, Hammell finally graduated to the senior side when he came off the bench as a substitute in the friendly against Sweden at Easter Road in November 2004—a match the Scots lost 4-1.

Further recognition would undoubtedly have followed in the 'B' international against Germany the following month, had the Motherwell defender not been injured in the warm-up and forced to withdraw from the side.

Hammell, who made his 200th League and Cup appearance for Motherwell during the course of the 2004-05 season—not bad for a player who was just 23 at the time—has been the subject of constant transfer speculation. But each time the transfer windows have opened, he has handled each bout of rumours with dignity, never once letting it affect his performances for the Fir Park club.

Hammell had appeared in games for Motherwell, when in the summer of 2006 he came south of the Border to play for Southend United.

PAUL HARTLEY
Forward/ Midfield

Born: Paul Hartley Glasgow, 19 October 1976
Height: 5ft 9in
Weight: 10st 4lb
Clubs: Mill BC; Hamilton Academicals; Millwall; Raith Rovers; Hibernian; St Johnstone; Heart of Midlothian
Scotland caps: 11
Scotland goals: 1
2005 v Italy (lost 0-2), v Moldova (won 2-0)
2006 v Italy (drew 1-1), v Norway (won 2-1), v Belarus (lost 0-1), v Slovenia (won 3-0) 1 goal, v United States (drew 1-1), v Faroe Islands (won 6-0), v Lithuania (won 2-1), v France (won 1-0), v Ukraine (lost 0-2)

An exciting and direct attacker or a central midfield player, Paul Hartley has the pace and skill to turn matches, and his crossing and shooting skills are a huge asset to his side.

Starting out with Hamilton Academicals, he soon became one of the most dangerous frontmen in the First Division, but even so, the Accies were relegated. The Lanarkshire club then accepted Millwall's offer of £400,000, and 'JR', as he was known to his team-mates, became a great favourite at The Den. While in London he was unlucky not to have had more goals to his credit, but he did win international honours for Scotland at Under-21 level.

In August 1997, he decided to return to Scotland and joined Raith Rovers for a fee of £150,000. He helped Rovers to third place in the First Division in 1997-98, but midway through the following season he was lured to Hibernian. He helped Hibs win the First Division Championship, and in 1999-2000 he was a regular in the side that took Hibs to sixth place in the Premier League and to the Scottish Cup semi-finals. Even so, he could not settle at Easter Road and he was recruited by St Johnstone.

Unfortunately, the Saints were relegated in 2001-02, but the following season, Hartley's creative ability and goals assisted the Perth club to third place in the First Division.

Then, with his contract expired, Hearts were able to secure his services, and in his first season at Tynecastle, the Jambos finished third in the Premier League. In December 2004 he represented Scotland at 'B' international level against Germany, and then, in March 2005, made his full international debut against Italy. He was instrumental in Hearts' Cup-winning 2005-06 season, and while he was possibly disappointed not to move to Celtic in the 2006 January transfer window, he has not let this affect his game or commitment to the Hearts cause.

DEREK RIORDAN
Forward

Born: Derek Riordan, Edinburgh, 16 January 1983
Height: 5ft 11in

Weight: 11st 12lb
Clubs: Hibernian; Cowdenbeath; Glasgow Celtic
Scotland caps: 1
2006 v Austria (drew 2-2)

After making his debut in the Edinburgh derby against Hearts in December 2001, a match that ended all-square at 1-1, Derek Riordan made fleeting appearances in the Hibs side under manager Frank Sauzee, before joining Cowdenbeath on loan. He made just two appearances for the Central Park club in January 2003 but on his second and final appearance, he netted a hat-trick in a most remarkable game as Cowdenbeath won 7-5 at Brechin City!

He returned to Easter Road and made the breakthrough towards the end of that 2002-03 season, scoring twice in a 3-1 defeat of Aberdeen.

He then underlined his claims as one of the most exciting young talents in the Scottish game during the following campaign, when only injury prevented him from reaching 20 goals for the season. This was all the more remarkable considering he played most of the season in a wide midfield position.

He missed the start of the 2004-05 season through injury, but on his return he more than made up for lost time, quickly establishing himself in Tony Mowbray's side—Riordan was again the club's leading scorer—his total of 23 goals in 43 League and Cup games including a hat-trick in a 3-0 defeat of Kilmarnock.

Having been called up to the Scotland squad at the end of the 2004-05 season, Riordan, who scored his 50th goal for Hibs in October 2005, won his first full international cap for Scotland when he replaced Kenny Miller at half-time in the friendly against Austria, which ended all-square at 2-2. Having scored 64 goals in 146 games for Hibs, Riordan joined Celtic in June 2006.

CRAIG BEATTIE
— Forward
Born: Craig Beattie, Glasgow, 16 January 1984
Height: 6ft 0in
Weight: 11st 7lb
Clubs: Glasgow Celtic
Scotland caps: 2
2006 v Italy (drew 1-1), v Norway (won 2-1)

Although this pacy and direct striker started out as a schoolboy with Rangers, Craig Beattie rose through the ranks at Parkhead to make his official debut for the Bhoys in the European Champions League clash with FBK Zalgiris Kaunas in August 2003, a match the Hoops won 1-0.

Beattie had announced his arrival on the first team stage during Celtic's pre-season tour of Sweden in the summer of 2003, and impressed sufficiently to earn a three-year contract with the Parkhead club. Having previously caught the eye at youth and Under-21 level, Beattie featured in numerous high-profile matches—most notably against Barcelona in the UEFA Cup.

He went on to make 17 appearances during 2003-04, and scored his first senior goal for the club in a 2-0 win over Partick Thistle and his first league goal in the 1-1 draw with Motherwell. However, in 2004-05 he struggled to continue his breakthrough, and all of his 11 league appearances were made from the bench—however, he did score four goals, including one in the 6-0 win against Dunfermline Athletic.

Remaining an important prospect for the future, Beattie has been given more of a run in the Celtic side in 2005-06 and his performances have led to him winning two full international caps for Scotland in the World Cup qualifiers against Italy and Norway.

SHAUN MALONEY
Forward

Born: Shaun Maloney, Mirri, Malaysia, 24 January 1983
Height: 5ft 6in
Weight: 11st 0lb
Clubs: Glasgow Celtic
Scotland caps: 2
2006 v Belarus (lost 0-1), v United States (drew 1-1)

Shaun Maloney is a genuinely exciting talent, quick, inventive, skilful and more than capable of serving up the spectacular! The Malaysian-born player is a product of the Celtic youth system, and made his senior debut for the Hoops in the Old Firm derby at Ibrox in April 2001, shortly after joining the club. For the record, Celtic won 3-0.

Nevertheless, after that, Maloney struggled to convince Martin O'Neill that he was worthy of a regular place in the side, either in attack or, as many believe is his best position, in the hole behind the strikers.

The 2003-04 season was widely tipped to see Maloney make his big breakthrough, but disaster struck on 23 February 2004 when Maloney suffered ligament damage in an Under-21 match against Partick Thistle. Not only did it rule him out for the rest of that campaign, but he was expected to be out of action for at least nine months. The diminutive striker travelled to the United States to be operated on by Dr Richard Steadman—the man also charged with rescuing John Kennedy's career—and thankfully he has since returned to action and is a regular in Gordon Strachan's team.

However, in 2004-05 he could never really shake off the injury from the previous season and only played in three games—two of which were from the substitute's bench. A player with great stamina and a great eye for goal, Maloney has Malaysian, Irish and Scottish ties, but opted to play for the Scots. Having been a regular in the Under-21 side, he made his first full international start in the World Cup qualifier against Belarus.

SCOTT BROWN

Midfield

Born: Scott Brown, Dunfermline, 25 April 1985
Height: 5ft 5in
Weight: 10st 0lb
Clubs: Hibernian
Scotland caps: 1
2006 v United States (drew 1-1)

The youth production line at Hibernian's Easter Road ground has never been more in focus than in recent years, and Scott Brown is yet another fine example of why that is so.

Making his first team debut for Hibs as a substitute in a 3-1 home win over Aberdeen in May 2003, Brown then started the remaining three games of the campaign, scoring three goals including two in a 2-1 defeat of Livingston. The natural skills shown by Brown seemed to increase with every first team appearance—former manager Bobby Williamson admitted that he was surprised by the impact that the player had on the Hibs first team.

He missed just a couple of games in 2003-04, and though he proved that he can score goals with either foot, it is in creating openings from nothing that his true talent is revealed. This, coupled with his trickery and uncompromising attitude, rarely to the liking of Premier League opponents, led to him winning honours for Scotland at Under-21 level.

An injury in the early stages of the 2004-05 season did nothing to dampen his enthusiasm, but it did restrict him to just two goals in 24 League and Cup appearances in that campaign. Brown was back to his best in 2005-06, and his form led to him winning his first cap for Scotland in the friendly against the United States, when he came off the bench to replace Nigel Quashie.

NEIL ALEXANDER

Goalkeeper

Born: Neil Alexander, Edinburgh, 10 March 1978
Height: 6ft 1in
Weight: 11st 0lb
Clubs: Edina Hibs; Stenhousemuir; Livingston; Cardiff City
Scotland caps: 3
2006 v Switzerland (lost 1-3), v Bulgaria (won 5-1), v Japan (drew 0-0)

After playing junior football for Edina Hibs, goalkeeper Neil Alexander signed for Stenhousemuir, where his performances alerted Livingston, whom he joined in the summer of 1998. In his first season at Livingston, he helped the Livi Lions win the Second Division Championship, and then in 2000-01, he helped the club win promotion to the Premier League.

In the close season he joined Cardiff City, the Bluebirds paying £200,000 for his services, and he went on to be the club's only ever-present in the 2001-02 season. His displays between the posts for City led to him being called up by Scotland manager Berti Vogts for the tour to the Far East, where he sat on the bench in all three matches.

The agile keeper grew in confidence the following season, and finished on a high with three successive clean sheets for the Bluebirds in the Second Division play-offs. He still earned a regular place in Berti Vogts' Scotland squad, but was left frustrated as he was still waiting for a first cap by the end of the season. The 2003-04 campaign proved to be a disappointing one for Neil Alexander, for, midway through the season, he lost his place to Martyn Margetson and spent the remainder of the campaign on the bench.

In fact, when the 2004-05 season got underway, Neil Alexander was the Welsh club's third choice keeper, but then a dip in form by Tony Warner and an injury to Martyn Margetson meant that he was thrust back in the starting line-up. His performances thereafter were massively significant in Cardiff's ultimate survival, and in 2005-06, he was not only the club's first choice keeper as they pushed for a place in the play-offs, but his form also led to him winning his first cap in the friendly against Switzerland, and appearance in the Kirin Cup games against Bulgaria and Japan.

GARY TEALE
Midfield

Born: Gary Teale, Glasgow, 21 July 1978
Height: 6ft 0in
Weight: 11st 6lb
Clubs: Clydebank; Ayr United; Wigan Athletic
Scotland caps: 5
2006 v Switzerland (lost 1-3), v Bulgaria (won 5-1), v Japan (drew 0-0),
v Faroe Islands (won 6-0), v France (won 1-0)

A right-sided midfield player, Gary Teale began his career with Clydebank in 1996. In just over two seasons at Burnbrae, he made 77 appearances before joining Ayr United for a fee of £70,000 in October 1998. His impressive displays when he caused defenders all sorts of problems with his blistering pace and mazy runs down both flanks, attracted the attention of a number of clubs. He impressed Wigan Athletic manager Paul Jewell in a pre-season friendly, but returned to Somerset Park to take his tally of goals to 18 in 121 matches, before eventually joining the Latics for a fee of £200,000 in December 2001.

Gary Teale is certainly at his best when running at opposition defences, and though he came close to scoring on a number of occasions, his only goal of the 2001-02 season came in a 3-1 win at Notts County. During the close season it was hoped that he would benefit from a course of body building exercises with Wigan Warriors Rugby League club, but he made an indifferent start to the 2002-03 campaign. Eventually, though, he made the right-wing position his own and seemed to get better with each game, scoring a stunning goal in the 3-1 home victory over Chesterfield.

Midway through the following season, Teale broke into the Scotland squad, but after scoring two stunning goals in the away wins at Preston and Ipswich, he broke his collarbone in the game against Stoke City. In 2004-05 he didn't really establish himself in the side until midway through the campaign, and he went on to play his part in helping the Latics win promotion to the Premiership.

During the Latics' great start to life in the top flight, he proved that he could still leave any defender in his wake, and his performances saw him make his first full appearance for the national side in the 3-1 friendly defeat by Switzerland at Hampden Park, prior to appearances in the Kirin Cup and the 2008 European Championship qualifiers.

KRIS BOYD
Striker

Born: Irvine, 18 March 1983
Height: 5ft 11in
Weight: 11st 9lb
Clubs: Kilmarnock; Glasgow Rangers
Scotland caps: 5
Scotland goals: 4
2006   v Bulgaria (won 5-1) 2 goals, v Japan (drew 0-0), v Faroe Islands (won 6-0) 2 goals, v Lithuania (won 2-1), v Ukraine (lost 0-2)

Prolific goalscorer Kris Boyd began his career with Kilmarnock, making his debut as a substitute against Celtic on the last day of the 2000-01 season. Midway through the following season, the departures of the mercurial Ally McCoist and Christopher Cocard gave Boyd more of an opportunity at first team level, while in 2002-03 he netted 12 goals and won the club's 'Young Player of the Year' award. His form that season also led to him being a regular in the Scotland Under-21 side. The 2003-04 campaign was even better for the Kilmarnock striker, as he found the net 15 times and spent a period on trial south of the Border with Wolverhampton Wanderers. Though a move to Molyneux didn't materialise, it did give the young Boyd a taste of the big time!

Goals kept flowing, and in the following campaign, he netted all Killie's goals in a 5-2 defeat of Dundee United. In fact, Boyd did have the ball in the net six times, but one was harshly ruled out as the referee blew up for an infringement. His goalscoring prowess for the Rugby Park club saw Cardiff City make an offer of £500,000 for his services, but Boyd turned down the chance to move into the Championship.

In December 2005, it was announced that Boyd would sign for Rangers in the January transfer window. In an unprecedented move, Boyd waived half of his £40,000 signing-on fee which Kilmarnock were due to pay him under the terms of his contract, to help fund the youth set-up from which he benefited during his early days at the club.

Boyd made his Rangers debut in a Scottish Cup third round tie against Peterhead, scoring a hat-trick in a 5-0 win! During the course of the second half of the 2005-06 season, Boyd scored 20 goals in 17 starts for the Ibrox club, and in doing so, he became the first player to finish top scorer at two clubs in one season, having scored 17 goals for Kilmarnock before his move to Rangers.

Boyd made his full international debut for Scotland against Bulgaria in the Kirin Cup, scoring twice in a 5-1 win. The prolific marksman also added another brace at international level as Scotland beat the Faroe Islands 6-0 in a 2008 Euro Championship qualifier, yet he still has to convince Rangers boss Paul Le Guen that he deserves a place in the Rangers starting line-up!

CHRIS BURKE
Midfield

Born: Glasgow, 2 December 1983
Height: 5ft 9in
Weight: 11st 2lb
Clubs: Glasgow Rangers
Scotland caps: 2
Scotland goals: 2
2006 v Bulgaria (won 5-1) 2 goals, v Japan (drew 0-0)

Having started out with Celtic Boys Club, midfielder Chris Burke joined Rangers where he was a product of the Ibrox club's youth academy. He broke into the Rangers SPL side in March 2002, scoring the last goal in a 5-0 rout of Kilmarnock.

A pacy midfielder, Burke widely became recognised as one of the Ibrox club's best young talents. Although occasionally struggling with consistency, he began to show exceptional ability, and won a regular place in Alex McLeish's side during the 2003-04 season. During the opening game of the 2004-05 season against Aberdeen, Burke fainted on the pitch, and was out of the side for a good number of weeks with a mysterious virus.

Thankfully, since then he has come back strongly, and after becoming a regular member of the Scotland Under-21 side, also represented Rangers in the UEFA Champions League games against Internazionale, Porto and Villareal.

On 11 May 2006, Burke won his first full cap for Scotland, coming off the bench in the Kirin Cup game against Bulgaria and scoring twice in a 5-1 victory. He kept his place in the squad for the game against Japan which ended goalless, but after some impressive displays for the Ibrox club, will be hoping to cement a regular place in the national side for the forthcoming Euro 2008 Championship games.

LEE MILLER
Striker

Born: Lee Adamson Miller, Lanark, 18 May 1983
Height: 6ft 2in
Weight: 11st 7lb

Clubs: Falkirk; Bristol City; Heart of Midlothian (loan); Dundee United; Aberdeen
Scotland caps: I
2006 v Japan (drew 0-0)

Striker Lee Miller began his professional career with Falkirk, where after working his way up through the ranks, he formed a prolific partnership up front with Owen Coyle in 2002-03. He went on to score 20 goals as the club won the Scottish First Division Championship. His form that season had attracted the attention of a number of English sides, and in the close season he joined Bristol City, who paid £300,000 to secure his services.

However, despite flashes of good play, he struggled to find his best form at Ashton Gate and was allowed to go on loan to Hearts. At Tynecastle, he rediscovered his scoring touch, netting 11 times from 22 starts. His form won him a call up to the full Scotland squad, and prompted Bristol City to raise their asking price for Miller. Though Aberdeen and Hearts had offers accepted, Miller eventually opted for a move to Dundee United—the Tannadice club paying £225,000.

He managed to keep this form going throughout the 2005-06 season, and was rewarded with his first full international appearance in the Kirin Cup game against Japan. With the game goalless, Miller came off the bench, but try as he might he couldn't get the breakthrough.

He made a disappointing start to the 2006-07 season, failing to find the net in the four games he played, and so Craig Brewster decided to start rebuilding for the future, and let Miller join Jimmy Calderwood's Aberdeen on a free transfer.

ROB NEILSON
Right-back
Born: Glasgow, 19 June 1980
Height: 5ft 11in
Weight: 11st 0lb
Clubs: Heart of Midlothian
Scotland caps: I
2006 v Ukraine (lost 2-0)

Rob Neilson is currently Hearts' longest-serving player, having joined the Jambos from Rangers Boys Club in 1996. During his early years at Tynecastle he won Scottish youth honours, and in May 1998 helped Hearts beat Dundee United in the final of the Scottish Youth Cup. Two years later he won Scottish Under-21 honours, this despite not having turned out for the club's first team. In 1999-2000 he turned out for the Hearts side that won the Premier Reserve League. Midway through that season he had a spell on loan at Cowdenbeath before establishing himself in the Hearts' side. At the start of the 2002-03 season he had another spell on loan, this time at Queen of the South, whom he helped to beat Brechin City in the Challenge Cup Final. After returning to Tynecastle, he won a regular place in the Hearts side, occasionally turning out at centre-half and in midfield, as well as his usual right-back position. Possessing an amazing long throw, he played his part in the club finishing third in the Premier League in 2002-03 and 2003-04 and with it a place in the UEFA Cup. His first goal for the club proved to be the winner against Swiss side Basel. Neilson won the first of what could be a good number of Scottish caps when he played in the qualifier for the 2008 European Championship against Ukraine.

STEPHEN McMANUS
Defender
Born: Lanark, 10 September 1982
Height: 6ft 2in
Weight: 13st 0lb
Clubs: Glasgow Celtic
Scotland caps: 1
2006 v Ukraine (lost 2-0)

A product of Celtic's youth academy, Stephen McManus made his first start for the Bhoys under manager Martin O'Neill during the 2003-04 season. A left-sided defender, he played regularly for the Scottish Under-18 side and appeared more frequently for the Celtic first team in 2004-05. That season saw him score his first goal for the club in an 8-1 League Cup mauling of Falkirk. It was during the 2005-06 season that McManus cemented his place in the Parkhead club's side, appearing in 42 games and scoring eight goals for Gordon Strachan's side. However, he does need to work at his disciplinary record, as he picked up 10 yellow cards during the course of the campaign. Able to play in a variety of defensive positions, he made his first full international debut as a substitute for fellow new cap Rob Neilson in the 2-0 defeat by Ukraine in October 2006.

STATISTICS

MOST CAPPED PLAYERS SINCE 1946

1	Kenny Dalglish	102	11	John Collins	58
2	Jim Leighton	91	12=	Roy Aitken	57
3	Alex McLeish	77		Gary McAllister	57
4	Paul McStay	76	14=	Denis Law	55
5	Tommy Boyd	72		Maurice Malpas	55
6	Willie Miller	65	16=	Billy Bremner	54
7	Christian Dailly	64		Graeme Souness	54
8	Danny McGrain	62	18=	Kevin Gallacher	53
9=	Richard Gough	61		Alan Rough	53
	Ally McCoist	61		George Young	53

TOP GOALSCORERS SINCE 1946

1=	Kenny Dalglish	30	12=	Kevin Gallacher	9
	Denis Law	30		Bobby Johnstone	9
3	Lawrie Reilly	22		Paul McStay	9
4	Ally McCoist	19		James McFadden	9
5	Mo Johnston	14		Jackie Mudie	9
6=	John Collins	12		John Robertson	9
	Alan Gilzean	12		Ian St John	9
	Billy Steel	12		Davie Wilson	9
9	Joe Jordan	11	20=	Ralph Brand	8
10=	Bobby Collins	10		Archie Gemmill	8
	Colin Stein	10		Graham Leggatt	8

INDEX OF PLAYERS

Fernie, Willie 79
Flavell, Bobby 25
Fleck, Robert 375
Fleming, Charlie 68
Fletcher, Darren 477
Forbes, Alex 21
Ford, Donald 251
Forrest, Jim 103
Forrest, Jim 171
Forsyth, Alex 237
Forsyth, Campbell 149
Forsyth, Tom 216
Fraser, Doug 187
Fraser, Willie 80
Freedman, Dougie 451

Gabriel, Jimmy 125
Gallacher, Kevin 366
Gallacher, Paul 468
Gallagher, Paul 478
Galloway, Mike 384
Gardiner, Ian 100
Gemmell, Tommy 172
Gemmell, Tommy 87
Gemmill, Archie 209
Gemmill, Scot 407
Gibson, Davie 141
Gillespie, Gary 358
Gilzean, Alan 147
Glass, Stephen 429
Glavin, Ronnie 283
Glen, Archie 89
Goram, Andy 343
Gordon, Craig 485
Gough, Richard 327
Gould, Jonathan 437
Govan, Jock 28
Graham, Arthur 286
Graham, George 222
Grant, John 106,
Grant, Peter 372
Gray, Andy 271
Gray, Andy 474
Gray, Eddie 195
Gray, Frank 275
Green, Tony 210
Greig, John 150
Gunn, Bryan 380

Haddock, Harry 81

Haffey, Frank 121
Hamilton, Alex 137
Hamilton, George 17
Hamilton, Willie 164
Hammell, Steven 488
Hansen, Alan 296
Hansen, John 228
Harper, Joe 238
Hartford, Asa 230
Hartley, Paul 489
Harvey, David 238
Haughney, Mike 70
Hay, David 206
Hegarty, Paul 298
Henderson, Jackie 66
Henderson, Willie 140
Hendry, Colin 394
Herd, David 107
Herd, George 101
Herriott, Jim 191
Hewie, John 89
Holt, Davie 142
Holt, Gary 441
Holton, Jim 240
Hope, Bobby 188
Hopkin, David 422
Houliston, Billy 40
Houston, Stewart 270
Howie, Hugh 35
Hughes, Billy 260
Hughes, John 162
Hughes, Richard 482
Humphries, Wilson 61
Hunter, Ally 233
Hunter, Willie 123
Husband, Jackie 7
Hutchison, Don 430
Hutchison, Tommy 248

Imlach, Stewart 104
Irvine, Brian 382
Jackson, Colin 261
Jackson, Darren 404
Jardine, Sandy 208
Jarvie, Drew 213
Jess, Eoin 391
Johnston, Allan 428
Johnston, Leslie 31
Johnston, Mo 335
Johnston, Willie 165

Johnstone, Bobby 54
Johnstone, Derek 241
Johnstone, Jimmy 155
Jordan, Joe 245

Kelly, Hugh 60
Kelly, Johnny 40
Kennedy, Jim 148
Kennedy, John 480
Kennedy, Stewart 262
Kennedy, Stuart 290
Kerr, Andy 87
Kerr, Brian 476
Kyle, Kevin 464

Lambert, Paul 408
Law, Denis 108
Lawrence, Tommy 146
Leggatt, Graham 90
Leighton, Jim 325
Lennox, Bobby 180
Leslie, Lawrie 124
Levein, Craig 375
Liddell, Billy 11
Linwood, Alex 46
Little, Johnny 65
Logie, Jimmy 64
Long, Hugh 15
Lorimer, Peter 202

Macari, Lou 234
Macaulay, Archie 19
MacDonald, Alex 277
MacDougall, Ted 263
MacFarlane, Willie 26
Mackay, Dave 98
MacKay, Dunky 111
Mackay, Gary 361
Mackay, Malky 481
MacLeod, Johnny 135
MacLeod, Murdo 339
Maloney, Shaun 491
Malpas, Maurice 337
Marshall, David 486
Marshall, Gordon 390
Martin, Brian 410
Martin, Fred 72
Martin, Neil 163
Martis, John 126
Mason, Jimmy 38

Masson, Don 281
Mathers, Dave 78
Matteo, Dominic 443
McAllister, Brian 419
McAllister, Gary 378
Mcallister, Jamie 486
McAvennie, Frank 346
McBride, Joe 180
McCall, Stuart 376
McCalliog, Jim 181
McCann, Bert 112
McCann, Neil 427
McClair, Brian 352
McCloy, Peter 242
McCoist, Ally 350
McColl, Ian 47
McCreadie, Eddie 160
McCulloch, Lee 487
McDonald, Joe 88
McFadden, James 466
McGarr, Ernie 199
McGarvey, Frank 301
McGhee, Mark 331
McGinlay, John 399
McGrain, Danny 242
McGrory, Jack 158
McInally, Alan 370
McInally, Jim 353
McInnes, Derek 469
McKean, Bobby 278
McKenzie, Johnny 69
McKimmie, Stuart 372
McKinlay, Billy 398
McKinlay, Tosh 412
McKinnon, Robert 399
McKinnon, Ron 167
McLaren, Alan 389
McLaren, Andy 22
McLaren, Andy 445
McLean, George 188
McLean, Tommy 192
McLeish, Alex 312
McLintock, Frank 145
McManus, Stephen 497
McMillan, Ian 59
McNamara, Jackie 415
McNamee, David 483
McNaught, Willie 52
McNaughton, Kevin 458
McNeill, Billy 133

McPhail, John 45
McPherson, Dave 371
McQueen, Gordon 255
McStay, Paul 333
McSwegan, Gary 436
Millar, Jimmy 143
Miller, Charlie 446
Miller, Kenny 447
Miller, Lee 495
Miller, Willie 2
Miller, Willie 268
Mitchell, Bobby 56
Mochan, Neil 76
Moir, Willie 48
Moncur, Bobby 189
Morgan, Willie 183
Morris, Henry 45
Mudie, Jackie 94
Mulhall, George 120
Munro, Frank 214
Munro, Iain 303
Murdoch, Bobby 166
Murray, Ian 472
Murray, Jimmy 102
Murray, Steve 228
Murty, Graeme 479

Narey, David 284
Naysmith, Gary 440
Neilson, Rob 496
Nevin, Pat 347
Nicholas, Charlie 329
Nicholson, Barry 449
Nicol, Steve 338

O'Connor, Garry 460
O'Donnell, Phil 397
O'Hare, John 207
O'Neil, Brian 413
O'Neil, John 450
Ormond, Willie 71
Orr, Tommy 57

Parker, Alex 85
Parlane, Derek 244
Paton, Andy 60
Pearson, Stephen 477
Pearson, Tommy 24
Penman, Andy 173
Pettigrew, Willie 278

Plendereith, Jackie 128
Pressley, Steven 438
Provan, David 147
Provan, Davie 308

Quashie, Nigel 484
Quinn, Pat 136

Rae, Gavin 450
Redpath, Willie 37
Reilly, Lawrie 38
Ring, Tommy 67
Rioch, Bruce 265,
Riordan, Derek 489
Ritchie, Billy 140
Ritchie, Paul 432
Robb, Dave 214
Robertson, Archie 86
Robertson, David 385
Robertson, Hugh 139
Robertson, Jimmy 157
Robertson, John 292
Robertson, John 383
Robinson, Bobby 252
Ross, Maurice 465
Rough, Alan 279
Rougvie, Doug 334
Rutherford, Eddie 33

Schaedler, Erich 254
Scott, Alex 95
Scott, Jim 174
Scott, Jocky 217
Scoular, Jimmy 55
Severin, Scott 452
Sharp, Graeme 341
Shaw, Dave 4
Shaw, Jock 18
Shearer, Bobby 132
Shearer, Duncan 401
Simpson, Neil 330
Simpson, Ronnie 182
Sinclair, Jackie 177
Smith, Dave 175
Smith, Eric 116
Smith, Gordon 16
Smith, Henry 365
Smith, Jamie 473
Smith, Jimmy 190
Souness, Graeme 257